Lecture Notes in Computer Science 1629

Edited by G. Goos, J. Hartmanis and J. van Leeuwen

Springer
Berlin
Heidelberg
New York
Barcelona
Hong Kong
London
Milan
Paris
Singapore
Tokyo

Helmut Leopold   Narciso García (Eds.)

Multimedia Applications, Services and Techniques – ECMAST'99

4th European Conference
Madrid, Spain, May 26-28, 1999
Proceedings

Springer

Series Editors

Gerhard Goos, Karlsruhe University, Germany
Juris Hartmanis, Cornell University, NY, USA
Jan van Leeuwen, Utrecht University, The Netherlands

Volume Editors

Helmut Leopold
Telekom Austria Headquarters
Postgasse 8, A-1011 Vienna, Austria
E-mail: helmut.leopold@telekom.at

Narciso García
Universidad Politécnica de Madrid
Escuela Técnica Superior de Ingenieros de Telecommunicación
Grupo de Tratamiento de Imágenes (GTI)
Ciudad Universitaria s/n, E-28040 Madrid, Spain
E-mail: narciso@gti.upm.es

Cataloging-in-Publication data applied for

Die Deutsche Bibliothek - CIP-Einheitsaufnahme

Multimedia applications, services and techniques : 4th European
conference ; proceedings / ECMAST '99, Madrid, Spain, May 26 -
28, 1999. Helmut Leopold ; Narciso García (ed.). - Berlin ;
Heidelberg ; New York ; Barcelona ; Hong Kong ; London ; Milan ;
Paris ; Singapore ; Tokyo : Springer, 1999
    (Lecture notes in computer science ; Vol. 1629)
    ISBN 3-540-66082-8

CR Subject Classification (1998): H.5.1, H.4, H.5, H.3, H.2, C.2

ISSN 0302-9743
ISBN 3-540-66082-8 Springer-Verlag Berlin Heidelberg New York

© Springer-Verlag Berlin Heidelberg 1999
Printed in Germany

Typesetting: Camera-ready by author
SPIN: 10703325   06/3142 – 5 4 3 2 1 0   Printed on acid-free paper

Preface

The liberalisation in the telecommunication market and thus the advent of competition has had a tremendous impact on business in this area. New operators have started to offer telecommunication services in competition with the classical national network operators. This in turn will have an impact on the market share, the tariff structure, the Quality of Service (QoS) and the services offered to the end customers.

A way to maintain or increase revenue for network operators is to additionally offer new services to the customers. The final target is a so-called "Full Service Network (FSN)", which is capable of offering all types of bi-directional multimedia services.

The provisioning of new telecommunication services in general and new multimedia services in particular is made possible by the availability of several new technologies as well as through advances in standardisation. R&D policies world-wide but especially in Europe have forced the development of new networking technologies such as ATM, xDSL and HFC as well as new video technologies as defined by DVB and DAVIC.

At the application level, recent developments include Internet telephony, Web-TV and the growing use of images and video components in Internet and Intranet environments. The major questions that remain include the nature of the convergence, i.e. the multimedia applications and services based on the new enabling technologies; and the pace of convergence, i.e. the speed with which a new generation of integrated networks will emerge, resulting in new networking infrastructures on which the new multimedia applications and services bring new possibilities to the end customers. ECMAST'99, organised by ACTS and COST 264, is focusing on exactly these issues.

The European Commission ACTS Programme and the new COST 264 Action are initiatives that promote research and development activities on multimedia applications, services and techniques. The ECMAST conference is a recurrent event promoted by the European Commission (Directorate General XIII B) aimed at disseminating the results of research and development projects on multimedia communication and related activities being carried out in Europe and elsewhere.

ECMAST'99 is the first world-wide forum on the new multimedia era of technologies, services and applications which presents the global results of the Fourth Framework Programme of European Research. It is also a starting point for the new Information Society Technologies (IST) Programme of the European Commission under its Fifth Framework Programme.

The ECMAST'99 call for papers resulted in 87 submissions. Following a stringent reviewing process, the programme committee selected 37 technical papers to be presented at the conference. In addition, several authors have accepted the invitation to present their project results at a poster/demo session. These technical presentations in combination with the keynote talks (Narciso García, UPM, ES and Georg Lütteke, PHILIPS EACEM, D) provide an insight into the current state of the art in multimedia applications, services and techniques.

The keynote speech of Bill St Arnaud of CANARIE, entitled "The future of the Internet is not multimedia", and the panel session chaired by Bob Foster of BT to discuss the question "Is there a multimedia business for network and service operators?" will couple research work with the business potential in this area. Three tutorials to be held before the start of the conference complete the programme of ECMAST'99.

On behalf of the programme committee we would like to thank all the authors for their contributions which were of course the prerequisite for the high technical level of the conference. Equally, we would like to thank the reviewers for their excellent and hard work and for meeting the tight time schedule. Special thanks are due to the members of the steering committee, the members of the programme committee and of course also the members of the organising committee, amongst whom an extra special vote of thanks goes to José Antonio Guerra (HISPASAT) who made a tremendous contribution to the organisation of this conference.

We thank the European Commission, where the ACTS projects and the COST 264 community have formed the basis for much technical content as well as the organisational aspects of the conference. The secretary of the steering committee, Leon Van Noorden of EC DG XIII B, deserves special mention because of his invaluable contribution to the successful establishment of this conference. We also wish to acknowledge the financial support of the European Commission, which is an important stimulus for such an event.

April 1999   Helmut Leopold and Narciso García

Steering Committee

Chairmen
A. Danthine   University of Liège, B
D. Wood   EBU, CH

Members:
L. Chiariglione   CSELT, I
N. García   UPM, ES
S. Fdida   LIP6-University Paris 6, F
M. Morganti   Italtel Spa, I
R. Nicol   BT, UK
R. Schäfer   Heinrich-Hertz-Inst., D
C. Schwarz   CCETT, F
D. Hutchison   Lancaster University, UK
S. Gil   HISPASAT, ES

Ass. Member
A. de Albuquerque   EC-DG-XIII, B

Secretary
L. van Noorden   EC-DG-XIII, B

Programme Committee

Chairmen
H. Leopold   Telekom Austria, A
N. García   UPM, ES

Vice Chairmen
A. Vicente   TELEFONICA, ES
G. Ventre   Univ. Napoli, I

Secretary:
L. Van Noorden   EC-DG-XIII, B

Members
E. Badiqué   EC-DG-XIII, B
D. Beaumont   BT, UK
C. Bertin   CNET, F
T. Braun   University of Bern, CH
A. Casaca   IST/NESC, P
T. Chen   Carnegie Mellon University, USA
P. Christ   RUS Stuttgart, D
G. Coulson   Lancaster University, UK

Organising Committee

Chairman
F. Rueda   HISPASAT, ES

Members
A. Fumarola   HISPASAT, ES
D. López   HISPASAT, ES
A. Molina   HISPASAT, ES
J.A. Guerra   HISPASAT, ES

ECMAST'99 is organised by HISPASAT.

Contact   HISPASAT, S.A.
                            Apdo. 95000
                            28080 MADRID (SPAIN)
                            E-Mail: ecmast99@hispasat.es
                            Tel.: +34-91-7102540
                            Fax.: +34-91-3728941
                            URL: http://www.hispasat.com/ECMAST99/

The conference is sponsored and supported by:

Commission of the European Union (DG XIII B)
EUREL

Table of Contents

Invited Paper 3

Distributed Objects

Invited Paper 4

The SICMA Teleteaching Trial on ADSL and Itranet Networks*

F. Cortes[2], V. Darlayiannis[1], M. Herreo[2], G. Kyriakaki[1], R. Lüling[2], Y. Maragoudakis[1], Y. Mavraganis[1], K. Meyer[2], N. Pappas[1]

[1] Laboratory of Distributed Multimedia Information Systems and Applications
Technical University of Crete, Greece
[2] Department of Mathematics and Computer Science
University of Paderborn, Germany

Abstract. The provision of interactive multimedia services, such as video-on-demand, teleshoping and distance learning, to a large number of users, still remains a challenging issue in the multimedia area. Despite of recent technological advances in all levels of the distributed multimedia infrastructure (storage, network, compression, standardization etc..), there is a strong need for feedback from public trials. Trial descriptions and evaluations, by revealing potential system limitations and measuring end user reactions, will provide valuable input towards the large-scale deployment of such services. In this paper, we present the teleteaching trial that was held at the end of 1998, at Limburg University (Belgium), in the context of ACTS SICMA project. We describe in detail the overall architecture and present results/implementation experiences for the parts of the system, putting the main emphasis on the server. We present technical integration issues between DAVIC and Internet server protocols (RTSP, DSM-CC etc..), and discuss the overall trial results.

1 Introduction

The SICMA project (Scaleable Interactive Continuous Media Servers - Design and Application) is part of the program on "Advanced Communication Technologies and Services (ACTS)" of the European Union. The general aim of SICMA is to design a scaleable media server for the delivery of continuous multimedia information, over high speed networks, to a large number of clients. Server's efficiency, interoperable and scaleable architecture are demonstrated with the help of relevant applications, in the context of two public trials. In first SICMA trial, the server was used to support the "Virtual Endeavour" application at Natural History Museum, London, in summer 1997. This year, the server was integrated in a teleteaching application at Limburg University, Belgium, where it provides video on demand services for the students.

The SICMA server complies to the DAVIC standard [3]. The DAVIC Services are built on top of the KYDONIA system [2], a multimedia object-based

---

* This work was supported by the EU project SICMA, AC071 in the framework of the program "ACTS - Advanced Communication Technologies and Services"

management system, that has been developed by MUSIC/TUC in previous European projects and is expanded within SICMA for providing full multimedia support. The main features of the system are: storage management for multimedia objects, real-time data pumps towards multiple clients over ATM, multimedia object modeling, text and video access methods, browsing and content addressability techniques.

While supporting the DAVIC standard, we decided to expand the SICMA media server to support the IETF standards for delivery of continuous media formats (RTSP/RTP/RTCP). In this way, the server is able to provide services in environments that comply to both standards. Media content is stored once on the server but can be made available using both protocol families.

The final aim of SICMA is to build a parallel multimedia server because parallel systems are able to deal with a very large disk array. Compared to sequential systems, they are able to store a larger number of media streams and to serve the requests of a larger number of users at the same time. While parallel systems are hard to use for certain problems, they seem to be well suited for the delivery of continuous media. This is because users usually access streams stored on the server independently from each other. Thus, a natural parallelism is given and can be exploited most efficiently by a parallel system. In this paper, we present an evaluation of the server system within the teleteaching application that was integrated as the second SICMA trial at the end of 1998. This application demonstrates the performance of the SICMA server for the delivery of continuous media information, within a local Intranet that is build up by ATM and standard Ethernet, as well as by using an ADSL network.

The paper is structured as follows: In next section the teleteaching trial is described in detail. After this, the SICMA media server is presented. Results-experiences from the trial finish the paper.

2 Teleteaching trial overview

The aim of this trial was to demonstrate the performance of the SICMA media server technology by integrating it into an available teleteaching environment. The main requirement was the delivery of MPEG encoded data to client systems, being connected to the server via the Intranet of the University as well as via ADSL lines. In the following subsections we describe the teleteaching system being developed and used for the SICMA project and afterwards the integration of the SICMA media server in this environment.

2.1 The teleteaching system at Limburg University

The teleteaching system developed at Limburg University Center (LUC) is a generic system for the creation and delivery of multimedia teleteaching content, stored on a server system, to a large number of clients (PC systems). The system is based on standard Internet technologies, e.g. HTML pages, CGI scripts, JAVA applets, standard database integration and related systems. The overall system is based on three types of server systems:

- Web servers (storing conventional web information, pictures, texts, ...)
- Database servers (hosting a relational database allowing to perform search operations on the overall content)
- Media servers (storing media assets, e.g. audio and video streams that are streamed from the server to the client)

The student, as a user of the teleteaching system does not recognize the three systems, but has access to the overall content via a standard web interface that integrates all information sources in a seamless way. The standard way to access the teleteaching application is via a search menu that allows to search for items stored on the web server and on the media server. Using the results of a search operation, the user gets a list of all items that fall into his interest. These can be single lectures, pointers to external resources on the Internet, single items like slides, animations, video streams and many other monomedia items. Using suitable plug-ins these items can be displayed and animated for the user.

To develop a teleteaching application, interested professors get access to a number of tools that allow an easy integration of their content in a full teleteaching application. The tools provide a number of frameworks for the integration and indexing of texts, graphics, video clips and other monomedia components. In this way, an interested professor can easily integrate his content into a teleteaching application without knowing the technical details of the underlying software models and server systems.

2.2 Integration of the SICMA server into the teleteaching application

The second trial phase of the SICMA project, presented in this paper, aims at demonstrating the scalability of the SICMA media server system. In the first SICMA trial [7], only a small number of user clients were used to demonstrate the functionality of the server system. In the second trial phase a larger number of clients are connected to the server system. It was foreseen to allow the integration of at least 70 clients accessing the server in parallel.

The SICMA server system was integrated into a teleteaching application that is already available at Limburg University Center. This teleteaching application is fully integrated into some of the lessons held at the University. The idea of this application is, that some lessons, as well as supporting material for the overall course, are only available in electronic form, so that students have no other choice than using the server to get all material for their exams. The existing system contains a database for searching, a sequential HTTP server that stores conventional material (text, pictures, etc...) and a sequential video server that presents some videos to the students. This sequential video server is proved to be the bottleneck was replaced by the SICMA parallel video server system. The role of the SICMA server is better shown in Figure 1 , that describes the overall chain of the trial. Thus, the SICMA server is fully integrated into a real-world application that is used by students of different faculties at LUC. The current implementation of the teleteaching application is used by students from within the University. For the SICMA trial phase, a number of external student homes are connected to this teleteaching service using ADSL modem technology.

For the SICMA trial phase multimedia material from the Medical Faculty, the Applied Economics Faculty and the Science Faculty consisting of different media types like video, pictures and text are used. The following amount of video information is selected:

- Medical Faculty: about 10 hours of video material
- Applied Economics Faculty: 20 tapes of 0.5 to 1 hour of video material
- Science Faculty: about 3 hours of video material

The groups of students, involved in the second trial are:

- Applied Economics Faculty: More than 100 students were selected to participate in the trial. The course targeted was the language teaching course.
- Medicine Faculty: A group of about 15 to 20 students. The course is a "Capita Selecta" course, in which the professor has "closer control" on the students involved.
- Science Faculty: A group of about 20 students were targeted.
- Some of the students living in the students home were chosen for a residential trial, the other ones have to use computers on the campus.

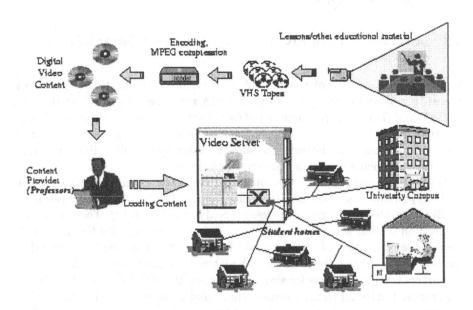

Fig. 1. VoD teleteaching architecture

The SICMA media server is based on the Parsytec CC parallel computer system. This general-purpose distributed memory parallel computer architecture is configured to be used as a media server with a number of disks and external communication devices (ATM cards, Ethernet cards) as presented in Figure 2.

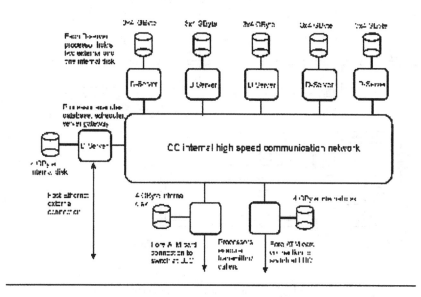

Fig. 2. Server Component architecture

The architecture allows to store about 70 GByte of media content and deliver this via two ATM (155 Mbit/sec) cards to the external communication network. The server can be accessed (for controlling the delivery of media streams) via a Fast Ethernet interface. Figure 3 presents the integration of the SICMA media server based on the CC system in the overall structure of the network that was used for the second trial phase of SICMA. The SICMA server is connected to a Ethernet switch at LUC that leads to the class rooms as well as to a SDH networks that connects to the ADSL central office switches.

3 The SICMA media server

3.1 General

From June to September of 1997, the SICMA server was used in the context of the first SICMA trial, at the Natural History Museum of London [7]. The server was delivering, over an ATM network, multimedia material (videos, images) to two PC clients that were located in a museums exhibition room. The main goal concerning the server, was to test the applicability of the DAVIC protocols (DSM-CC, CORBA IIOP, MPEG2 TS over AAL5 etc..) in an open public

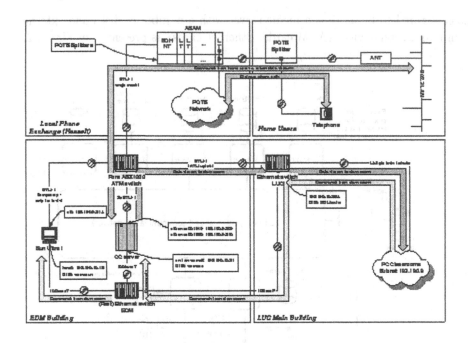

Fig. 3. Trial Network Architecture

trial, as far as there were not any previous DAVIC implementations and public experiments.

The second SICMA trial put requirements on the server system that had to do more with performance than interoperability aspects. The server had to support a large number of concurrent clients (at least 70), manage a big amount of video content (70 GBytes) and prove its ability to scale up and down. Moreover, we decided to develop, integrate and test in this trial, the server-related video streaming protocols that were starting to appear from the Internet community (RTSP, RTP etc..). The server was successfully integrated into the teleteaching application environment and provided a video-on-demand service for the students of the University. In this chapter, we describe the core architectural components of the server, together with results and experiences on critical points, gained from system development and testing in the teleteaching trial.

3.2 System Architecture

The server software architecture is comprised of several modules which enable the provision of interactive multimedia services, in a way compliant to state-of-the art standards (DAVIC, RTSP). Moreover, the design follows a scaleable approach without any performance bottlenecks. In this way, server throughput can be increased by the addition of extra resources (processors, network cards etc..). Figure 4 describes a general view of the core system components.

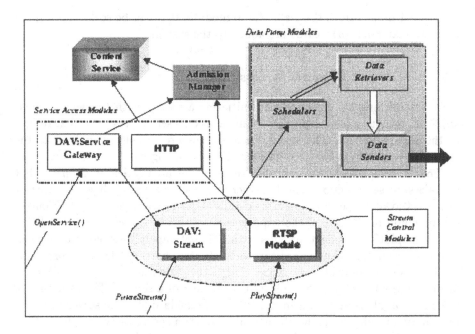

Fig. 4. Server Architecture

The server architecture, shown in the above picture, enables the provision of full video-on-demand functionality: insertion/deletion of video titles, playing/browsing on video streams. The server components can be divided in the following groups:

- The Service Access group that provides functionality for opening stream services and is comprised of the DAVIC Service Gateway element for the DAVIC clients and the HTTP server for the Internet clients.
- The Stream Control modules, that are responsible for controlling the advance of media streams (Stream Element for DAVIC and RTSP for Internet).
- The Content Service that implements the physical data model of the server, maintains descriptors, indexes etc.. It is used for as a storage manager for inserting/deleting video content.
- The Admission Control component that maintains system load and "decides" for the acceptance of new client requests.
- The Data Pump modules (Schedulers, Data Retrievers/Senders) that retrieve multimedia data from disks and send it over the network.

The modules that affect servers interoperability with the external world (clients, networks) are the Service Access modules, the Stream Control modules as well as the Data Senders. These components implement protocols identified in DAVIC and Internet standards and inter-operate with other systems in a predefined way (certain interfaces and protocols stacks). The scalability of the server is achieved mainly from the Data Pump modules that can be scaled up if more processors and networks cards are added to the system.

3.3   Service and Resource Access Modules

After establishing a connection and initiating a session with the server, client applications issue a command for opening a specific service/resource that resides in the server domain. The server finds the resource, opens it and sends the necessary information back to the client for interacting with the resource.

For this role, DAVIC has identified the Service Gateway Service Element that organizes the service domain of the server and enables external clients to discover and select available services [3]. More details about the Service Gateway Element can be found in [7]. One of the requirements of this trial was to support different client platforms, client systems with different capabilities. For this reason, a profile describing client's hardware and software characteristics (e.g protocols stacks, modem bandwidth, presence of MPEG-2 demultiplexers, network interface), is passed to the server, during the opening of a service. The structure of the client profile is described in the DSM-CC standard [5]. The server uses this information to identify if the client is able to use a specific service. The Service Gateway element is unique for the server system, and thus must have a very good performance for handling all client requests. The implementation is based on threads.

For the integration in Internet environments and the use of RTSP/RTP protocols, the Service Gateway module is implemented in form of a HTTP server that offers access to web pages that host the services offered by the media server. Using this open approach, that allows to access media streams stored on the server via URLs (the RTSP standard takes up the URL format of web servers using an own protocol, e.g. rtsp://.... to access media streams) it is possible to integrate non-realtime media data, e.g. standard web information and realtime data in a seamless way.

3.4   Stream Control Modules

The SICMA server provides functionality for manipulating continuous media streams. This is done through the interfaces of DAVIC Stream Service Element and RTSP module that enable VCR-like operations on video streams (stop, pause, fast-forward etc..). The interface of Stream Service Element is defined by the DSM-CC standard [5]. It employs a state machine to keep information about the current status of the stream. It also simulates an internal clock for predicting the position on the timeline of the media stream. The implementation has to be lightweight thread-based with not much CPU overhead- because for each client there exists a separate Stream Service Object. Another important point is the ability of Stream Service objects to discover abnormal client termination, by including a mechanism to check the validity of the command channel connection. In this way a Stream object does not wait for the next request, but when it encounters a broken connection, releases all the reserved resources (memory, threads, bandwidth).

Using the RTSP protocol for manipulating the delivery of continuous media streams from the server to a client, it is possible to control this delivery in different ways. As an example it is possible to give an exact timing when the delivery of a media stream should start. Thus, media delivery can be scheduled according to a play-list. This feature can be used in broadcast delivery of media streams, e.g. for Business TV applications or teleteaching. Another interesting feature is to start the delivery of parts of the streams identified by timing indexes. This allows collecting interesting topics from a larger media stream within one web page where each link points to different parts of the media stream. In this way, interesting indexing mechanisms for media streams can be implemented.

3.5 Content Service

The content service element for the SICMA media server gives information for the internal organization of the media storage and delivery to the other modules of the server. The content service element provides information about the data placement to identify the storage devices where parts of the media stream can be found. In this way, it also provides information for a random access to the media stream that is necessary to implement functionality as described above for controlling the delivery of the media streams. The content service element is also responsible to perform insertion and deletion operation for media streams. Thus, it provides a suitable user interface that allows for the administrator to manage the overall media server content. For the SICMA media server, it is possible to manage the content via a web interface that allows performing a remote content managing.

The implementation of VCR functionality, e.g. Fast-Forward and Fast-Reverse is also managed by the content service element. We implement these functions by storing separate media streams for fast forwarding in both directions. This is the most general way of implementing this function. It also provides best performance results as the visual quality is better using this approach like others delivering only some parts of the stored media stream (I-frames). We have also implemented an index for MPEG-1 System streams for random positioning within the stream.

3.6 Admission Manager

The admission control module is responsible for handling user requests for accessing the media server and starting the delivery of a media stream. Because of the inherent realtime properties of continuous media as video and audio and because of the large requirements in terms of processor and disk performance it is necessary to perform an accurate bookkeeping of resources that are already used by some users for the delivery of media streams. The admission manager needs two kind of information. The first is a detailed performance model of the media server, e.g. bandwidth of the storage devices, external communication interfaces, processors. For a distributed memory parallel computer system that is used in the SICMA project another important factor is the bandwidth of the internal communication network connecting storage devices and external communication interfaces. The second information needed to decide about the acceptance of a user request is the performance that is needed to deliver a specific media stream in terms of disk bandwidth, communication bandwidth and other measures.

Whereas the information about the media server is a function of the concrete machine and maintained by the admission manager, the information about the resources that have to be allocated for the delivery of a stream are hosted by the Content Service.

On request of a user to deliver an identified media stream, this stream is delivered if the available resources are large enough to satisfy the resources necessary for the delivery of this stream. In this way, the admission manager decides about the acceptance of a user request on the basis of the available and requested resources.

3.7 Scheduler

The scheduler is one of the central components of the media server as it is responsible for the actual delivery of media information from the server to the clients. In SICMA we use a scheduling scheme based on earliest deadline first scheduling. Thus, the scheduler maintains a timeline identifying the time for the delivery of a data packet from the server to the client for each of the stream. Whenever this time has expired, the scheduler triggers the data retrievers to send the requested media packet to the data senders which deliver this to the external communication device.

3.8 Data Retrievers / Data Senders

The increased demands of this trial, in terms of high data bandwidth and large number of concurrent clients, lead to redesigning the Delivery System (DS) of the SICMA server. The architecture of the new Delivery System follows the design criteria of the proxy at server architecture that is recommended in the literature for large scale parallel video- on- demand servers [6], [8]. According to this architecture, the DS runs in a multiprocessor environment with a number of delivery nodes that communicate and receive appropriate data blocks, via high speed (server internal) network, from a set of storage nodes/processors (Data Retrievers or DAMS) and route them to the customers. The term proxy refers to the functionality of the delivery nodes to resequence and merge the data units, that receive from multiple storage nodes, into a coherent video stream before it will be delivered to a client. Based on these special buffer management techniques the DS is capable to serve/transmit video streams that have been stripped on the storage nodes of the server. Furthermore, the scalable design of the system enables its expansion to as many as available nodes equipped with network transmission cards. In this way (parallel/ distributed scalable architecture) a grate number of parallel video streams is efficiently supported by the server.

The DS, as part of a DAVIC compliant server like the SICMA-server, followed the DAVIC 1.0 specification [3] and adopted the S1 data flow. DAVIC 1.0 defines the S1 flow as a uni-directional flow from the Server to the clients carrying encoded MPEG-1, MPEG-2 video/audio content using MPEG-2 transport protocol (MPEG-2 TS over ATM/AAL5). The actual implementation of the S1 followed by the DS, considers a generic (abstract) transmission module able to support not only MPEG-2 Transport Stream over ATM/AAL5, but a variety of communication protocols. So far, apart from the mapping of MPEG-2 TS over ATM/AAL5, also UDP/IP and TCP/IP over ATM as well as RTP protocol libraries have been implemented and embodied in the transmission module. In the trial, RTP and UDP/IP protocols were employed for the delivery of video streams from the server to the clients during the trial phase. The software architecture of the DS, that is also referred as Video Pump Subsystem (VPS), is pictured in the following figure and consists of three main submodules named Load Scheduler Module (LSM), Video Pump Generator (VPG) and Video Pump Objects (VPOs).

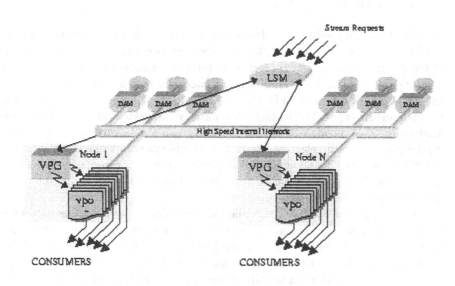

Fig. 5. Delivery System Architecture

The LSM receives requests from the Stream Control modules, to serve the delivery of new video streams and, based on load balancing scheduling techniques, distributes the requests to the less weighted delivery node. The selection of the appropriate delivery node is based on statistics that show the number of video streams served in each node, as well as on their encoding rates. The VPG is located on each delivery node and its responsibility is to fire new VPOs when it is triggered by the LSM to do so. It is also responsible for the estimation of the delivery load in the node that is located as well as to inform the LSM about the status of this load.

The Video Pump Objects constitute the heart of the delivery system since they encapsu- late primary functions like intelligent buffer management, rate control, packetization and delivery operations. For every requested video, the VPG fires one VPO to serve the delivery of the corresponding stream to the consumer. Each VPO consists of 2 threads, the Receiver and the Transmitter which are sharing a common buffer. The Receiver fills the buffers with the stripped data units of the video stream that receives from the Data Retriever (DAM) modules. It is also responsible for merging the stripped data units in order to reconstruct the video blocks (proxy functionality). The Transmitter at the same time reads the full parts of the buffer and transmits the data to the client according to the encoding bit rate of the stream. The synchronization between the Receiver and Transmitter threads of each VPO is coordinated via inter-process communication (semaphores).

4 The Client Application

The client system used in the teleteaching trial at Limburg University is a standard PC (with a minimum of 166 Mhz, Pentium processor). This PC runs one of the standard web browsers (Microsoft Internet explorer or Netscape communicator) and accesses the overall server system via a web interface. The access to standard web information is done us- ing suitable plug-ins that are available for these media types. The audio/video material integrated into the teleteaching application was encoded in MPEG-1 quality using a bitrate of 1.5 Mbit/sec. To decode this media element the Active Movie system available on Windows 95/98/NT is used. To allow an online streaming from the media server to the user client a client software has been developed that establishes a communication lines between client and server.

For the use of the DAVIC compliant server a Corba interface was used here. This is implemented by setting up a permanent process on the client that communicates with the browser on the one hand and the server on the other hand allowing a flexible and elegant Corba interface in this way. To use the RTSP interface, the communication primitives were directly integrated into the plug-in. Both plug-ins allow an easy navigation and VCR like functionality of the media stream.

5 Trial Results and Experiences

The second SICMA trial focussed on the delivery of a complete teleteaching application to a number of about 40 clients installed within the University of Limburg, as well as to about 40 clients installed at student homes and connected to the University network via ADSL. The trial was set up in the last semester of 1998 at the University and supported the lectures in different faculties over this semester. Concerning the innovation of this trial, only very few experiences had been made before in connecting student apartments with ADSL lines to the University backbone. A similar trial is currently held at the University of Muenster, Germany where lecture information is delivered to student homes via ADSL. During this trial phase, a large number of students accessed the server system using the DAVIC compliant interface as well as the RTSP/RTP interface. It was observed that after the trial integration and initial tests the SICMA media server was stable and supported the envisioned application well. System architecture fulfilled interoperability, scalability and performance requirements. The server was able to support approximately 70 concurrent clients, retrieving MPEG-1 video streams at 1.5 Mbits/sec. This throughput limitation was mainly due to CPU overhead on Data Sender processors. Response time between subsequent requests was tolerable. Scalability was achieved by increasing the number of Data Retrievers and Data Senders. One scheduler was able to support 70 concurrent clients, so it was not necessary to fire more schedulers for the trial needs. As it concerns server functionality, the full range of video on demand operations was supported: insert/delete videos, play, stop, pause, fast-forward, fast backward. An important issue is the ability to install video content, at the same time when the server is serving consumer clients. This feature was not supported, so the system was not accessible from students, during content insertion. We are working on this, and especially to a more advanced feature, the ability to store video content in real time, while being able to deliver other videos at the same time.

Trial tests shown that a critical point, concerning server stability, is the proper release of resources (e.g socket connections, buffers), in case when clients terminate abnormally, without closing their sessions. The server has to discover such situations and all modules related to the provision of the service should be informed to release reserved resources. The current integration between DAVIC and Internet protocols in the server can be con- sidered as an initial step towards building a multi-protocol server. We are currently investigating a server architecture that will allow for dynamic switching between different protocol families, in way transparent to the client application.

Since the PC clients of the trial were not equipped nor with MPEG-2 TS demultiplexers, neither with ATM network cards (due to cost reasons), it wasnt possible to investigate the performance of the server under the situation of having to transmit small size packets (376 bytes), as it is specified by DAVIC (mapping of 2 MPEG-2 TS packets to one AAL-5 packet or 8 ATM cells [4]). Recently, FORE released an ATM API for Windows, so we have the chance, together with an MPEG-2 TS demultiplexer card from Optibase to investigate performance issues for the S1 data flow of DAVIC (MPEG-2 TS/AAL5). Another major topic was the absence of an appropriate protocol/system to reserve network resources. This could be done if there existed a DAVIC compliant ATM based- delivery system or the RSVP protocol for IP environments was supported in the trial network infrastructure.

Reactions of students and teachers at Limburg University indicate that an increased support of teaching with audio/visual elements is of large interest. This is because the videos, giving detailed description of certain topics that could not be covered by conventional material, eased the learning and understanding of some topics considerably. But as this depends always on the available material, more attention has to be put on the selection and indexing of material. In current phase, we run a detailed evaluation of the trial. Users are interviewed how the technical system as well as the integration of content supported their learning process.

6 Summary - Future Work

We presented a teleteaching trial, held in Limburg University (Belgium), in the context of ACTS SICMA project. The video on demand needs of the teleteaching application were supported by the SICMA system, which was responsible for managing and delivering MPEG video streams over the local university Intranet, composed of ATM and standard Ethernet, as well as over ADSL lines to student homes. The server supports DAVIC and IETF protocols and follows a scaleable architecture. Results and implementation experiences from the trial were presented. Future work on the server includes full DAVIC and IETF compatibility, real time storage functionality and deployment of a distributed server hierarchy. The main conclusion is that there are not any major technical problems for the provision of interactive distributed multimedia services, in large scale.

References

1. S. Christodoulakis and Peter Triantafillou: Research and Development Issues for Large-Scale Multimedia Information Systems. *ACM Computing Surveys - Special Issue on Multimedia Information Systems*, December 1995.
2. S. Christodoulakis, N. Pappas, G. Kyriakaki, Y. Maragoudakis, Y. Mavraganis, ganis, C. Tsinaraki: The KYDONIA Multimedia Information Server, *Proceedings of Second European Conference on Multimedia Services Applications and Techniques*, ECMAST 97, Milan
3. Digital Audio-Visual Council, Service Provider System Architecture and Interfaces, DAVIC 1.0 Specification Part 03, 1995.
4. Digital Audio-Visual Council, High and Mid Layer Protocols, DAVIC 1.0 Specification Part 07, 1995.
5. Digital Storage Media Command and Control International Standard, ISO/IEC JTC/SC29/WG11 N1300 p1 MPEG 96/. (Tampere).
6. Jack Y.B Lee: Parallel Video Servers: a tutorial, *IEEE Multimedia, April, June 1998, pp 20-28.*
7. C. Brandt, G. Kyriakaki, W. Lamotte, R. Lüling, Y. Maragoudakis, Y. Mavraganis, K. Meyer, N. Pappas: The SICMA Multimedia Server and Virtual Museum Application, *Proceedings of Third European Conference on Multimedia Services Applications and Techniques, ECMAST 98, Berlin.*
8. A.L. Narasimha Reddy, R. Haskin: Video Servers, in *The Communications Handbook*, CRC Press, Oct. 1996.

Usability Assessment of Collaborative Shared-Space Telepresence Shopping Services

James Anderson, Rachael Vincent, and Mervyn A. Jack

{jad, rachael, maj}@ccir.ed.ac.uk
Centre for Communication Interface Research
University of Edinburgh
80 South Bridge, Edinburgh, EH1 1HN
Tel: +44 131 650 2784   Fax: +44 131 650 2784

Abstract. This paper describes the methodology and procedure of usability trials undertaken as part of the ACTS Teleshoppe project; it also details and analyses the results of the trials. The aim of the trials was to assess user attitudes to a collaborative shared-space shopping service. Usability data were obtained using a series of Likert-style questionnaires and through a 'focus group' discussion performed with a representative subset of the trial participants. The paper presents this data and draws conclusions relevant to the future direction of research and implementation for such shopping services. In particular, the results of the trials indicate a generally positive attitude towards the collaborative shopping service used. Furthermore, those aspects of the service viewed negatively by the users are for the most part aspects which can be easily rectified and not due to technological limitations.

1 Introduction

The Teleshoppe project [1] is concerned with the application of advanced multimedia and virtual reality technologies in order to simulate the 'touch and feel' of physical shopping, thus enhancing the usability of the user interface for a telepresence shopping experience. The purpose of the user trials described in this paper was to investigate the usability of a virtual reality and multimedia-based multiuser (shared-space) teleshopping service when experienced by a number of participant groups (with three collaborating shoppers per group). In addition to the assessment of general usability, particular emphasis was placed on the effectiveness of collaboration of participants within each group and their resultant ability to complete set tasks satisfactorily. The trials also investigated user attitudes to a 'real human' shopping assistant who appeared in different forms to the participants. The well-established 'Likert' style of usability questionnaires was used throughout to facilitate quantitative measurement of usability issues [2,3] and the 'focus group' method for obtaining broad usability data was also employed [4,5].

2 Methodology

The experiment consisted of a set of three tasks to be performed by each participant group in a shopping scenario within a three-dimensional virtual environment. Each group consisted of three people who described themselves as 'friends' prior to the trial. The three participants within each group cohabited the mall simultaneously but in separate locations, being able to see one another as 'avatar' representations within the virtual environment and communicating via real-time audio multicasting software. Each group completed the three tasks in a random order.

During one of the shopping sessions, the collaborating shoppers had access to a 'Personal Shopping Advisor' who appeared as a fourth avatar within the virtual environment. The purpose of the Advisor was to provide advice on where departments or products might be found and on whether cheaper or better value products were available elsewhere within the store.

During another of the three shopping sessions, the collaborating shoppers had access to a 'Customer Service Assistant' who could be called by means of a button on the computer screen and would appear within a video window in the top left corner of the screen (via real-time network audio-video software). The purpose of the Assistant was to provide further information on products and to offer special discounts on items of interest. Participants were specifically asked to negotiate with the Assistant to obtain discount vouchers.

The order in which the Personal Shopping Advisor and the Customer Service Assistant were available for two of three sessions was randomised for each group.

After completing each task (or after using the store for 20 minutes in any one session) each participant was asked to complete a usability questionnaire assessing their experience of using the shopping service, the perceived ease with which they were able to complete the task, and general attitudes towards the collaborative element of the service. Additional questions were included for those sessions in which the Personal Shopping Advisor or the Customer Service Assistant was available.

After completing all three shopping sessions, each participant was asked to complete a final questionnaire which invited comparisons between the sessions in which the Personal Shopping Advisor or the Customer Service Assistant was available.

In addition to the usability questionnaires, one person from each participating group was asked to return the following week to take part in a focus group. The focus group allowed open discussion of the merits and weaknesses of the shopping service, concentrating particularly on significant issues raised by an analysis of the questionnaire results.

3 Scenario

The scenario presented to the trial participants was that of a 'virtual reality department store' where three-dimensional graphics and spatial audio were used to give the consumer a feeling of presence within the virtual environment—an environment which would also be simultaneously inhabited by other consumers. The participants were asked to complete tasks which necessarily involved co-operation with the other members of the group. The three tasks were:

- to buy a home computer system with a total budget of £2000
- to buy a home entertainment system with a total budget of £1500
- to buy a set of sports equipment for a local school with a total budget of £800

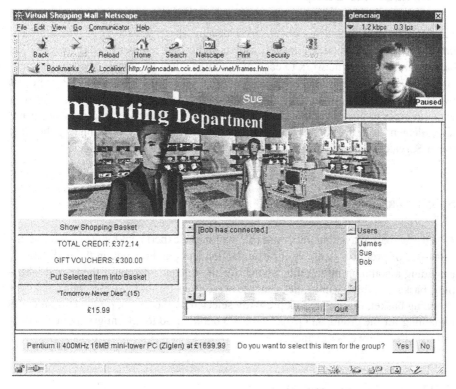

Fig. 1. Screen shot of shopping interface including video link to Customer Service Assistant (located in top-left of screen during experiment)

The shopping interface (Fig. 1) for each participant included:

- a 3D view of the mall (including, when in view, the other group members)
- a shared 'shopping basket' to display the items which have been purchased by the group and their remaining credit
- a panel to display the names of the other people present within the store
- a panel to display further information and pricing for products selected in the store

By clicking on products within the various shops in the mall, the participants were able to gain further information about a product and then had the option to 'select' that product on behalf of the group. Once a product had been selected for the group, any member of the group then had the opportunity to place the item into the shared shopping basket. Clearly, a substantial amount of communication, co-operation and co-ordination was required between the participants in order to complete the task to the satisfaction of the group.

4 Client/Server Design

The usability trial followed a client/server design whereby a server provided the entire experience (3D models, images, video, audio and multiuser data) over a local bandwidth-adjustable network to each of the three client machines. The service emulated a live web-based Internet teleshopping service using mainly HTTP protocols over a TCP/IP network. Both the client and server platforms were running *Vnet* software[1] in order to implement the shared-space aspect of the service and *iVisit* software[2] to implement both the audio communication element and the video link for the Customer Service Assistant.

5 Database-Driven Design

A SQL database played an important role within the experiment by *(1)* containing the catalogue of products available for examination and purchase within the mall and *(2)* providing a common information source for the implementation of the shared 'shopping basket'. Tables within the database were used to hold *(a)* the contents of the shopping basket, *(b)* the product presently selected by the group, *(c)* the current credit remaining for the group, and *(d)* a 'refresh' counter used to inform group members of events initiated by other members.

6 Hardware Configuration

The trial server was a fast PC platform running MS Internet Information Server 3.0, MS SQL Server 6.5, a multiuser shared-space server of some description, and with a fast PCI-bus network card. The trial clients were to be fast PC platforms running a suitable web-browser (with Java and VRML capability) and corresponding multiuser shared-space client software. The following server and client configurations were adopted for the trials:

---

[1] http://ariadne.iz.net/~jeffs/vnet/
[2] http://www.ivisit.com

SERVER CONFIGURATION	CLIENT CONFIGURATION
- Intel Pentium II 350MHz - 2GB SCSI hard disk - PCI network card - 128MB RAM memory - Microsoft Windows NT 4.0 Server - Installed with: *Microsoft Internet Information Server 3.0, Microsoft SQL Server 6.5, Vnet* software (including Java classes for both server and client) and *iVisit* video conferencing software	- Intel Pentium II 350MHz - 1GB SCSI hard disk - PCI network card - 128MB RAM memory - 128-bit graphics card with >2MB video memory and 3D hardware acceleration - Microsoft Windows NT 4.0 Server - Installed with: *Netscape Communicator 4.05, CosmoPlayer 2.1* VRML browser plug-in and *iVisit* video conferencing software

7 Experiment Implementation

The shopping interface for the trial consisted primarily of a VRML shopping mall being displayed by, and under the control of, the *Vnet* multiuser Java-based software. The shared 'shopping basket' was implemented by means of a Java applet. The basic interface consisted of an HTML page with frames containing:

1. the view of the virtual shopping mall
2. the *Vnet* client control panel (displaying the names of other people within the shared space)
3. the 'shopping basket' applet
4. temporary dialogue options (for such events as confirming selection of a product on behalf of the group)
5. detailed product information for items in the store selected by participants

Communication with the SQL database was performed via JDBC drivers within the Java applets.

8 Questionnaire Results

The trial was run with twelve groups of three participants: 36 participants in total with varying demographics (sex, age and social backgrounds).

Fig. 2 shows in graphical form the results of the usability questionnaires for those sixteen questions which were common to the three session questionnaires. The vertical axis indicates the average user attitude to the usability aspect in question from 1 (most negative) through 4 (neutral) to 7 (most positive).

Fig. 3 shows in graphical form the results of the usability questionnaire for the session involving the Customer Service Assistant for those questions unique to that session. The vertical axis is the same as for Fig. 2.

Fig. 4 shows in graphical form the results of the usability questionnaire for the session involving the Personal Shopping Advisor for those questions unique to that session. The vertical axis is the same as for Fig. 2.

Fig. 5 shows in graphical form the results of the final questionnaire completed after all three experiment sessions. The vertical axis indicates the level of agreement with the statement in question, from 1 (strongly disagree) through 4 (neutral) to 7 (strongly agree).

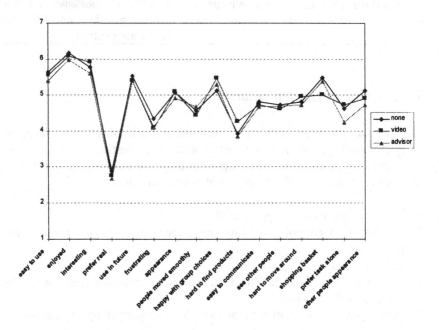

Fig. 2. Results of usability questionnaires for all sessions

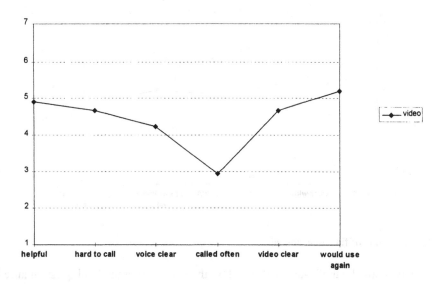

Fig. 3. Results of usability questionnaire for Customer Service Assistant session

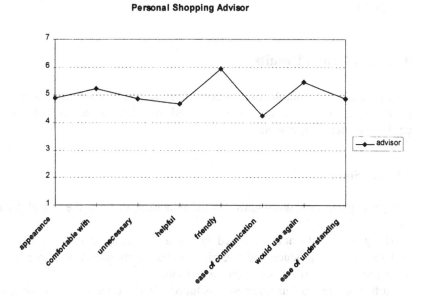

Fig. 4. Results of usability questionnaire for Personal Shopping Advisor session

Final Questionnaire

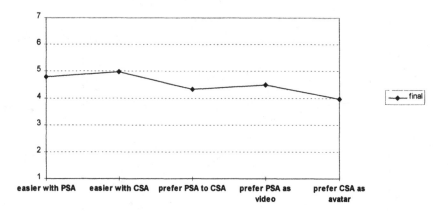

Fig. 5. Results of final questionnaire

A two-tailed paired *t*-test performed on the results from the final questionnaire indicated a significance of less than 0.01 for the first two statements: the users considered the task easier when the Personal Shopping Assistant was present (p=0.001134) and when the Customer Service Assistant was available (p=0.0000048). The responses to the other three statements on the final questionnaire showed no comparable significance.

9 Focus Group Results

Seven participants from the trial agreed to take part in a group discussion to discuss their experience further. They were selected to reflect the demographic spread of participants in the experiment.

9.1 The Store

The participants were unanimous in their enjoyment of using the virtual department store.

The group would have preferred the prices of items to have appeared on the shelves below the products and sale offers to be clearly shown on screen rather than having to seek the information from an assistant.

Further suggested improvements included *(1)* a greater choice of products; *(2)* more goods on each of the shelves; *(3)* the ability to buy every item, even the ones which did not come in boxes; *(4)* a less regimented layout which is more friendly and personal; *(5)* a 'pay' button instead of the cash tills (which were difficult to find); and

(6) confirmation of the contents of their basket to decrease the possibility of buying goods by mistake.

9.2 Group Interaction

"One of the best things was being able to chat with your friends."

The participants agreed that being able to talk enhanced the shopping experience and this mode of communication was unanimously preferred above that of communicating through typing text. According to one participant, it was " easier to talk than figure out what was going on at the screen." The microphone-headset did not cause any problems.

Virtually shopping with a group was considered to be fun and preferable to shopping on one's own.

The time delay (~0.5s) present in the network-based audio link "caused you to be at cross purposes a lot," and led to individuals repeating themselves. On occasions, duplicate instances of products were put into the shopping basket by group members, but this was not considered to be a problem since returning goods to the store was a straightforward procedure. The break-up of sound when all the avatars were moving was considered slightly annoying. However, the audio link was considered to be a satisfactory way of communicating.

9.3 The Avatars, Advisor and Assistant

According to the focus group, the avatars did not need improvement, although the ability to gesture would have been beneficial. Having the names suspended over the figures made it easy to recognise friends. The group speculated about whether one needed to be visually represented, but ultimately agreed that seeing where friends were standing helped to clarify which goods were in the different areas. The presence of other shoppers in the store was considered acceptable, provided that they did not block the user's view and that the option to "turn them off" was available.

The group was divided between a preference for the Personal Shopping Advisor and the Customer Service Assistant.

The primary benefit of the Customer Service Assistant was that seeing a real person provided a more personal and human touch and assured the group that they weren't dealing with a computer. However, it was considered to take too long to get a response when after calling the Assistant, and communication seemed to be more problematic than with the Personal Shopping Advisor. One reason given for this was the need to explain your enquiry to the Assistant, whereas the Advisor was perceived to be always listening and so could offer help at any time. (In fact, the Customer Service Assistant had continuous audio contact with the group members during the trial sessions.) Another possible reason could be the sound/lips mismatch which seemed unnatural and combined with a 'blocky' image made it difficult to communicate. The image in the corner of the screen was considered to be the right size (160x120 pixels) although the group would have liked to see "more of the face and less of the shoulders."

According to the group, the "immediacy" of the Personal Shopping Advisor and his/her ability to listen into the shopping groups' conversations (and thus provide help straight away) made the service provided an improvement over that of the Customer Service Assistant. The Advisor was also able 'physically' to show groups round the shop and to take them to the relevant departments.

9.4 The Shopping Basket

There was some confusion about how to work out the total credit remaining for the shopping group, mainly due to the 'gift vouchers' method of discounting used in the trial. Displaying one overall total and noting the discount gained on each item next to its description in the shopping basket was suggested as an alternative.

The group agreed that they would be quite willing use the virtual department store to buy items which are not 'variable', *e.g.* goods from supermarkets, videos and CDs. The group noted that selling items at competitive rates would encourage people to shop 'virtually'.

The virtual department store was felt to be an improvement on catalogue shopping, however real shopping was still considered preferable. The primary benefits were cited as *(1)* the ability to shop with friends in a different location to you and *(2)* the flexibility of shopping from home.

10 Conclusions

The following conclusions may be drawn from the results of the four usability questionnaires completed by the trial participants:

* there was a generally positive attitude towards the overall shopping experience;
* there was a generally positive attitude towards both the Customer Service Assistant (CSA) and the Personal Shopping Advisor (PSA) features;
* the shopping task was significantly facilitated both by the presence of the Personal Shopping Assistant and by the availability of the Customer Service Assistant;
* the presence of the CSA or the PSA did not significantly affect user attitudes towards the common features and aspects of the shopping service;
* the network-based audio connection allowed satisfactory communication between both the participants within each group and the participants and the CSA or the PSA;
* there was no significant desire to change the visual representation of either the CSA to an avatar format or the PSA to a video format;

- despite a generally positive attitude toward the service, participants would still prefer to use a real department store to the virtual department store used in the trial.

The results of the focus group discussion confirmed the above conclusions and emphasised the users' positive attitudes towards the collaborative element of the service. In addition, it should be noted that the main criticisms levelled at the virtual store used in the trial for the most part concern aspects which can very easily be rectified, *e.g.* the paucity of the product database, the lack of information provided for items, the awkward implementation of the shopping basket, *etc.*, and do not reflect technological limitations or barriers. The primary exception is that of the audio link. The time delay and degradation caused by the decrease in available CPU power when rendering the virtual store (during periods of user movement) caused difficulties in communicating and thus adversely affected usability. A useful line of future research would investigate the extents to which varying network bandwidth and latency with respect to the networked audio communication influence the service usability.

Acknowledgments

This work was funded as part of the Teleshoppe project, supported as part of the European Commission's ACTS Programme (Project AC099).

References

1. I. McKay, M. Jack, L. Parker, J. Andrews, O. Villemaud, J-P. Lefevre, *"Teleshoppe - Usable Teleshopping with Multimedia and Virtual Reality"*, Proceedings of the European Conference on Multimedia Applications, Services and Techniques (ECMAST'96), May 1996.
2. R. A. Likert, *A Technique for the Measurement of Attitudes*, Archives of Psychology, vol. 140, 1932.
3. H. Coolican, *Research Methods and Statistics in Psychology*, Hodder & Stoughton, 1994.
4. D. W. Stewart, P. N. Shamdasani, *Focus Groups: Theory and Practice*, Sage Publications, 1990.
5. R. A. Krueger, *Focus Groups: A Practical Guide for Applied Research*, Sage Publications, 1994.

Risk Methodology for
Multimedia Projects Assessments

Kjell Stordahl*, Nils Kristian Elnesgaard#, Leif Aarthun Ims§, Borgar Tørre Olsen§

*Telenor Nett, PO Box 6701 St Olavs Plass, 0130 Oslo, Norway
E-mail: kjell.stordahl@telenor.com
#TeleDanmark, Research and Development, Telegade 2, 2630 Tåstrup, Denmark
§Telenor, Research and Development, PO Box 83, 2007 Kjeller, Norway

Abstract. The paper describes a methodology for performing quantitative risk analysis of multimedia projects, as developed in the ACTS projects OPTIMUM and TERA. A framework for risk analysis is presented, encompassing key elements such as choice of probability density functions, correlation between important variables, simulation performance, methodology for cost predictions, demand forecasts, tariff predictions and associated uncertainties. The TERA tool for techno-economic evaluation is presented and the important steps in network evaluation identified. The paper examines how much the most critical factors contribute to the overall risk profile of telecommunications operator projects and studies the dependencies between variables.

1   Introduction

This paper describes a methodology for performing risk analysis of multimedia projects. The main criteria for evaluation of a network deployment or implementation of a new network structure are net present value (NPV), payback period and internal rate of return (IRR). Two important questions are: What is the deviation from the calculated values if some of the assumed values are changing and what is the distribution of the calculated values if some of the assumed conditions are uncertain? To be able to draw right decisions, it is of crucial importance both to have knowledge about how much the calculated values of net present value, payback period, internal rate of return etc are changing when the assumptions are changing, and in addition the related probability for these events.

Application of risk methodology to a large extent answers these questions. The critical variables like penetrations forecasts, tariff evolution, market share, evolution of component costs and operations and maintenance costs are described not only by the their expected value, but also by a probability density describing the probable deviation from the expected value. The risk analysis is carried out in performing a large number of simulations based on these probability densities.

2 Demand for multimedia applications

In 1994 an international postal Delphi survey among experts in 10 European countries was carried out to predict the future demand for multimedia applications [13]. To update the forecasts a comprehensive two rounds on site Delphi survey was carried out during the OPTIMUM workshop «Techno-economics of Multimedia Networks» in Aveiro, Portugal 20-22/10 1997 [15].

A *Delphi survey* is a method by which the opinions of experts are canvassed, in order to achieve consensus on a particular issue. The methodology involves asking a set of questions, analysing the results and resubmitting the questions to the experts, together with a summary of the first round results. The experts then resubmit their opinions, which may have changed following consideration of results from the previous round. The procedure can be repeated a number of times, and usually it leads to a reduction in the variance of the answers received.

The following main groups of multimedia applications were covered in the study:

1 Tele-entertainment

- Multimedia telegame
- Virtual reality
- Video on demand
- Audio/music on demand

2 Information services

- Information retrieval
- Electronic magazines
- Information retrieval by intelligent agents
- Electronic newspapers

3 Teleshopping

- Teleshopping
- Advertising

4 Private communication services

- Videophone
- Teleconferencing

5 Teleworking

- Videophone
- Joint editing/publishing
- Teleconferencing
- Teleparticipation
- Information retrieval
- Multimedia applications

6 Telelearning

- Video on demand
- Videophone
- Virtual reality

7 Telecommunity

- Telesurveillance
- Videphone
- Telediagnostics

The main results from the Delphi study are:

- Ranking of the application groups
- Demand curves for application groups (Usage versus price)
- Forecasts for 2Mb/s, 8Mb/s and 26Mb/s accesses
- Demand curves for the accesses (Demand versus tariff)
- Tariff predictions for the accesses (Tariff as a function of time)

In section 3.7 – 3.10 the broadband forecasts for 2 – 26Mb/s to transport the described multimedia applications are shown together with the tariff predictions. The forecasts and the tariff predictions are necessary input for calculating the costs and revenues for upgrading the network to carry multimedia services.

3   Risk calculations

The risk framework presented is developed in order to analyse the risk with an effective and uniform methodology. The important elements are:

- Choice of probability density functions
- Potential establishment of correlation between important variables
- Simulation performance
- Methodology for cost predictions and uncertainties
- Methodology for demand forecasts and uncertainties
- Methodology for tariff predictions and uncertainties.

The calculation of the project values has to be performed many times with the input elements selected randomly from a set of distributions on each of the input elements. The input elements are market penetration, market shares of the different services, cost elements and engineering parameters etc. From the distribution of the output values the risk criteria are derived.

3.1 Choice of probability functions

When risk analysis is performed the uncertainties in the assumptions have to be quantified with respect to probability functions and limits of the uncertain variables Since, it is meaningless to operate with negative costs, tariffs or forecasts, the Beta distribution is introduced to solve the problem of negative values. The Normal distribution may be used, but in cases where there are significant probabilities for generating negative values, the Beta function is recommended.

An example of probability functions for tariffs is illustrated in figure 1. Suppose that we know the exact tariff for a broadband connection in 1999. In year 2000 the tariff will decrease, but still our estimate of the expected tariff is rather good. Hence the probability distribution describing the tariff variation has a small standard deviation. *The uncertainty in the tariff estimate will increase as a function of time. At the same time the expected value of the tariff is decreasing as a function of time.*

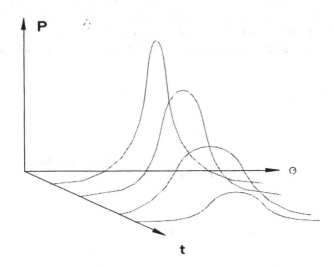

Figure 1. The probability distribution as a function of time

3.2 Correlation between important variables

In some situations, especially when risk analysis is performed in order to examine the effect of uncertainty in cost predictions on various components, there is a need for introduction of correlation between input variables. The TERA[1]/OPTIMUM[2] tool uses Crystal Ball© as a simulation program package. The simulation package includes options for establishing models with correlated variables. In the input sheet the estimate of the correlation between each variable has to be defined.

---

[1] *TERA: Techno-economic results from ACTS*

[2] *OPTIMUM: Optimised Multimedia Network Architectures*

3.3 Simulation performance

When performing sensitivity and risk analysis, the uncertain parameters are described by suitable probability density functions. The techno-economic scenario is then calculated a certain number of times using Monte Carlo or Latin Hypercube simulation; each time a random number is picked from each distribution. In general, it is difficult to give an advice of number of simulations, since this depends on the complexity of the case under study. The best way to control the problem, is to perform test-simulation series and calculate the uncertainty in the output distributions. Based on experience so far, the sufficient number of simulations might be between 500 and 10,000.

3.4 Risk simulations

Figure 2 illustrates how the risk assessment is performed. One probability density is defined for each variable studied. The important variables are: Component costs, penetrations for the services studied, market shares for the services, tariffs for the services etc. The normal distribution is often used to describe the fluctuations of a variable. The normal distribution is uniquely defined when the expected value and the

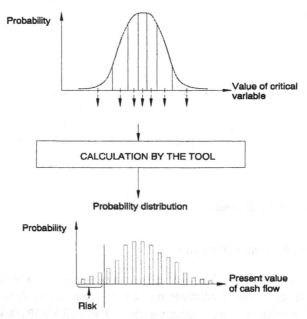

Figure 2. Risk simulations

standard deviation are known. If there is a significant probability for generation of negative values, the Beta function is used instead of the normal distribution. The Beta function is defined when the expected value and the standard deviation are given together with the realization interval for the variable.

The expected value is for each year the estimated component cost, penetration, market share, tariff etc. In the following paragraphs a methodology for estimating the standard deviations is described.

Since there is a strong correlation between consecutive observations from one year to the next, it is not possible to perform independent simulations for the whole time series. Independent simulations may cause that the demand fluctuates up and down instead of a more smooth increase. One possibility is to introduce correlation between the observations, another possibility is to make one simulation for the time series. Then all observations in the time series will either be larger than the expected trend or smaller. Since the number of simulations is rather high, the described simulation procedure is acceptable.

3.5 The extended learning curve model

The extended learning curve for prediction of component costs has been developed in the RACE 20087/TITAN project and further developed in the ACTS 226/OPTIMUM and ACTS 364/TERA projects. Wright and Crawford's learning curve models [1-3] for cost predictions as a function of the production volume were examined. In the TITAN project the models for cost predictions were extended not only to estimate the costs as a function of number of produced units, but also as a function of time [4]. The cost prediction curve is dependent of a set of parameters: Reference cost at a reference time, learning curve coefficient which reflect the type of component, penetration at the starting time and penetration growth in the market of the component. The cost data base contains estimates on these parameters for all components and generates cost predictions based on the extended learning curve. The methodology takes into account the variation in uncertainty for different technologies. For example, the uncertainty in the cost of civil works is smaller than the uncertainty in the cost of electronics. In addition, a time component which increases the relative uncertainty is implemented in the model.

The cost prediction of each network component is described by expansion of the learning curve given as function of the parameters:

$f(0)$: The predicted costs at time 0
$n(0)$: The relative proportion of produced components at time 0
Δt : The time interval between 10% and 90% penetration
K : The relative decrease in the cost by the double production

The extended learning curve function is given by:

$$f(t) = f(f(0), n(0), \Delta t, K, t) \qquad 1$$

$$= f(0) \, [n(0)^{-1} \, (1 \, + \, \exp[\, \ln(1/n(0) - 1) \, - \, 2 \, t \, \ln9/\Delta t] \,)^{-1} \,]^{\log_2 K} \qquad 2$$

3.6 Uncertainty estimates of cost predictions

The methodology described, suggests to estimate the uncertainty proportional to the time and to the cost predictions by the extended learning curve model. The uncertainty estimates are expressed by standard deviations.

It is reasonable to assume that the uncertainty in the cost predictions is *proportional* to:

    t :   the time
    f(t) : the cost predictions

Suppose that the relative uncertainty in the costs increases with a given percentage each year. Then the relative uncertainty can be expressed as a linear function:

$$u(t) = 1 + a\,t \qquad\qquad 3$$

where a is the yearly increase.

The relative uncertainty related to the learning curve is given by the expression:

$$f(t)/f(0) \qquad\qquad 4$$

Then the uncertainty of the cost predictions expressed by the standard deviation is given by:

$$s(t) = const\ u(t)\ f(t)/f(0 \qquad\qquad 5$$

When t=0, we get s(0) = const. Hence we get the following expression for the standard deviation:

$$s(t) = s(0)\ u(t)\ f(t)/f(0) \qquad\qquad 6$$

The standard deviation function is dependent of the standard deviation at time 0 and the parameter a and of course of the relative change in the learning curve. A reasonable estimate for the standard deviation at time 0, s(0), should be proportional to the cost, f(0), at time 0. Hence

$$s(0) = const\ f(0) = b\ f(0) \qquad\qquad 7$$

Now, if b = 0.15, then the standard deviation, s(0), is equal to 15% of the cost estimate at time 0. We decide to estimate the standard deviation by using the last expression. When the risk analysis is carried out, a set of different values of b will be used for each technical solution.

Substitution of the last equation into the previous one, gives:

$$s(t) = b\ u(t)\ f(t) \qquad\qquad 8$$

or

$$s(t) = b\ (1 + a\,t)\ f(t) \qquad\qquad 9$$

In some situations the concept relative standard deviation is used in statistical analysis. The relative standard deviation is given by s/f. Putting $t = 0$ in the equation, we get:

$$s(0)/f(0) = b \qquad\qquad 10$$

Hence b is the relative standard deviation at time 0. When t is different from 0, we get the following expression for the relative standard deviation:

$$s(t)/f(t) = b(1 + a\,t) \qquad\qquad 11$$

Hence the relative standard deviation is a function of the parameters a and b. Table 1 illustrates how the relative uncertainty changes as a function of a and b.

Table 1. Relative standard deviations

$t \rightarrow$		0			5			10		
$a \downarrow$	$b \rightarrow$	0.10	0.15	0.20	0.10	0.15	0.20	0.10	0.15	0.20
0.01		0.10	0.15	0.20	0.11	0.16	0.21	0.11	0.17	0.22
0.05		0.10	0.15	0.20	0.13	0.19	0.25	0.15	0.23	0.30
0.10		0.10	0.15	0.20	0.15	0.23	0.30	0.20	0.30	0.40
0.20		0.10	0.15	0.20	0.20	0.30	0.40	0.30	0.45	0.60

The table shows that the relative standard deviations increases as a function of time (because a>0). If the relative standard deviation exceeds 0.30 or 30%, it is necessary to use a truncated distribution not to negative simulation values. Of course it is also possible to use other functions than the suggested linear function. It is also possible to use a set of fixed values representing the standard deviation for each year. The table is so far a guideline for selection of reasonable a and b values for estimating the standard deviation.

3.7 Cost prediction by the extended learning curve

The extended learning curve is defined in the first part of the section. The parameters in the learning curve are: $f(0)$, $n(0)$, Δt and K. In the OPTIMUM cost database, the following values are used for the various volume classes:

Table 2. Variation in $n(0)$ and Δt for each volume class

Volume class	$n(0)$	Δt
1	0.5	5
2	0.1	5
3	0.01	5
4	0.5	10
5	0.1	10
6	0.01	10
7	0.001	50

The K values are defined as shown in Table 3:

Table 3. K values

Component class	K
Civil work	1
Copper	1
Installation	1
Sites and enterprises	0.95
Fibre	0.9
Electronics	0.8
Advanced optical components	0.7

In the cost database all components are listed with a given n(0), Δt and K value in addition to the estimated cost f(0) at time 0. Then the extended learning curve is uniquely defined and the prediction of the costs is determined. Hence combinations of a, b, f(0), n(0), Δt and K gives the variation in the estimated standard deviations. In addition, each component is described by a confidence class which can be used as a guideline to determine a and b.

3.8 Demand forecast modelling

Analytical forecasting models have been developed, replacing conventional input tables in the TERA tool. The models are based on the results from the last Delphi survey performed at the last OPTIMUM workshop in Aveiro in October 1997 [15]. Different analytical forecasting models for fitting the Delphi data are tested. The extended Logistic model with three parameters gives a rather good fitting for 2 Mb/s, 8Mb/s and 26 Mb/s.

The model is defined by the following expression:

$$Y_t = M / (1 + \exp (\alpha + \beta t))^\gamma \qquad\qquad 12$$

where the variables are defined as follows:

Y_t : Demand forecast at time t
M : Saturation level
t : Time
α, β, γ : Parameters

The parameters α, β, γ can not be estimated simultaneously by ordinary least square regression since the model is unlinear in the parameters. Instead, a stepwise procedure is used to find the optimal parameter estimates.

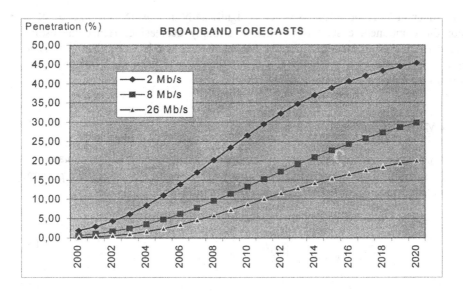

Figure 3 Broadband penetration forecasts

In addition specific forecasting models for symmetric and asymmetric demand penetration are constructed. The models and also the forecasts for symmetric and asymmetric accesses described in [15].

3.9 Uncertainty estimates for the demand forecasts

Demand forecasts are of course rather uncertain. Since we have used a stepwise estimation procedure to estimate the parameters in the model, we can not use the traditional procedures to find the confidence interval of the forecasts. A relevant alternative is to use the same methodology as for the costs. The relative standard deviation $s(t)/Y_t$ is equal to:

$$s(t)/Y_t = b(1 + a\,t) \qquad\qquad 13$$

where

    Y_t: is the forecast at time t
    $s(t)$: is the standard deviation of the forecasts at time t
    b: is the relative standard deviation at time 0
    a: is the increase in the linear increase in the relative uncertainty per year

Table 1 is used to see the changes in the relative uncertainty for different values of a and b. The equation for the estimated standard deviation is given by:

$$s(t) = Y_t\,b(1 + a\,t) \qquad\qquad 14$$

The function Y_t is the forecasts which is significantly increasing as a function of time. For the component costs this function is strongly decreasing. Hence the estimated standard deviation for the forecasts are increasing much more than the standard deviation for the cost predictions. The last equation defines the estimated standard deviations for given values of a and b.

3.10 Model for tariff predictions

The tariffs are given as functions of the penetration according to the demand curves extracted from the OPTIMUM Delphi survey [15]. The tariffs are service penetration dependant, which is needed in a reasonable risk model.

The suggested demand model based on three parameters was:

$$y = e^{(\alpha + \beta p)^{\gamma}} \qquad\qquad 15$$

where

y :	Demand
p :	Price
α, β, γ:	Parameters in the model

The parameter estimates are found by OLS regression on the Delphi demand data for given γ values. The estimation gave a fairly good fitting. A variant of this model is based on the assumption that the demand is 100% when the price is 0. Evaluation of the results showed that the fitting was not satisfactory. Therefore, the demand model is not based on this assumption.

An alternative demand model uses the above three parameter equation together with two restrictions:

- The tariff is fixed the starting year
- The tariff is fixed in the long run.

The restrictions are included because it is important to utilise "near future knowledge" in the model. In addition a hypothesis is made that the long term broadband costs will converge towards today's telephone costs. The tariff predictions are found by inserting the demand forecast into the above equation and solving the equation with respect to the tariff pt:

$$p_t = [\, (\ln y_t)^{1/\gamma} - \alpha \,] \,/\, \beta \qquad\qquad 16$$

When the forecasts y_t are inserted into the model for different t values, we get tariff prediction as a function of time. A more detailed description of demand model is given in [15]. Figure 4 illustrates the tariff evolution for 2Mb/s, 8Mb/s and 26 Mb/s asymmetric and symmetric access. *The tariff includes both annual subscription costs and annual traffic costs for expected use of the service.*

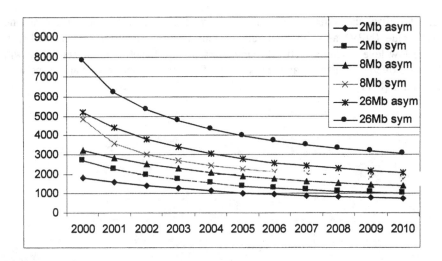

Figure 4. Expected annual tariff evolution(EURO) in the residential market for *2Mb/s, 8Mb/s and 26 Mb/s asymmetric and symmetric access. The annual tariff consists of subscription and traffic costs.*

3.11 Uncertainty estimates for tariff predictions

The tariffs are of course rather uncertain. It is suggested to use the same methodology as for the costs to estimate tariff uncertainty. The relative standard deviation $s(t)/p_t$ is equal to:

$$s(t)/p_t = b(1 + a\,t) \qquad\qquad 17$$

where

p_t: is the tariff prediction at time t
$s(t)$: is the standard deviation of the tariff prediction at time t
b: is the relative standard deviation at time 0
a: is the increase in the linear increase in the relative uncertainty per year
Table 1 shows the changes in the relative uncertainty for different values of a and b. The equation for the estimated standard deviation is given by:

$$s(t) = p_t\, b(1 + a\,t) \qquad\qquad 18$$

The last equation defines the standard deviation function for given values of a and b.

4   The TERA tool for techno-economic evaluations

Within the European programs RACE and ACTS the projects RACE 2087/TITAN and AC 226/OPTIMUM and AC364/TERA have developed a methodology and a tool for calculation of the overall financial budget of any access architecture [5-7]. The tool handles the discount system costs, operations, maintenance costs, life cycle costs, net present value (NPV) and internal rate of return (IRR).The tool has the ability to combine low level, detailed network parameters of significant strategic relevance with high level, overall strategic parameters for performing evaluation of various network architectures [8-11].

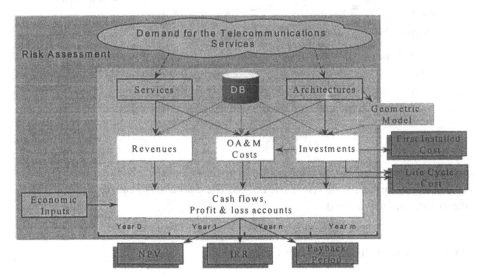

Figure 5. Model for techno-economic evaluations

5   Steps in network evaluation

The following steps are needed in the techno-economic evaluations of the network solutions:

– The services to be provided must be specified. The market penetration of these services over the study period will be defined. The services have associated tariffs i.e. the part of the tariff that is attributed to the network under study. From the combination of yearly market penetration and yearly tariff information OPTIMUM calculates the revenues for each year for the selected service set.

– Next, the architecture scenarios to provide the selected service set must be defined. This needs network planning expertise and is mostly outside of the framework of OPTIMUM methodology. However, OPTIMUM includes several geometric models, that will facilitate the network planning by automatically calculating lengths for cables and ducting. These geometric models are optional parts of the methodology and OPTIMUM can be used without them. The result of a architecture scenario definition is so called shopping list. This list indicate the volumes of all network cost elements (equipment, cables, cabinets, ducting, installation etc.) for each year of the study period and the location of these network components in different flexibility points and link levels.

- The costs of the network components are calculated using an integrated cost database developed within the OPTIMUM project, containing data gathered from many European sources. Architecture scenarios together with the cost database give investments for each year.

- The OA&M costs are divided into three separate components. Conceptually the three components are defined as follows:

- M1 - Represents the cost of repair parts. This component is included automatically in the models and is driven by the investments, i.e. the same approach as was used in TITAN for all OA&M costs.

- M2 - Represents the cost of repair work. This is also automatically included in the models. Detailed description of M2 component is given below.

- O&A - This component represents Operation and Administration costs and it has to be included manually when building models. Typically it would be driven by services, say by number of customers, or by number of critical network elements.

- Investment costs together with the OA&M costs give the life-cycle cost for the selected architecture scenario.

- Finally by combining service revenues, investments, operating costs and general economic inputs (e.g. discount rate, tax rate) OPTIMUM gives cash flows and other economic results (NPV, IRR, Payback period etc).

6 Analysis

A specific case study is presented for evaluating the risk effect of critical factors and the effect of modeling the dependencies between important variables. The defined case study is a downtown area where broadband services are offered during the period 2000 – 2009. The relevant services are 2 Mbit/s asymmetric, 2 Mbit/s symmetric and 8 Mbit/s asymmetric access. The penetration demand for the services and the tariff evolution is described earlier in the paper. The architecture deployed is fibre to the local exchange (FTTLex) including implementation of ADSL and HDSL technology. Figure 6 shows the architecture.

The costs of the network components are found in the TERA cost data base together with the related operations and maintenance cost for the described architecture. The geographical modelling of a downtown area has already been implemented as one of four main area types: downtown, urban, suburban and rural [16].

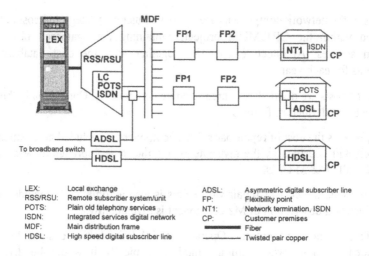

LEX:	Local exchange		ADSL:	Asymmetric digital subscriber line
RSS/RSU:	Remote subscriber system/unit		FP:	Flexibility point
POTS:	Plain old telephony services		NT1:	Network termination, ISDN
ISDN:	Integrated services digital network		CP:	Customer premises
MDF:	Main distribution frame			Fiber
HDSL:	High speed digital subscriber line			Twisted pair copper

Figure 6. The enhanced copper upgrade with ADSL for 2 Mbit/s asymmetric demand and HDSL for 2 Mbit/s symmetric demand.

6.1 How does the most critical factors contribute to the risk?

One key issue is how the most critical factors contribute to the risk. The critical factors evaluated are:

- broadband forecasts
- lost market share
- tariff predictions
- cost predictions.

A set of different risk assessments has been carried out for the broadband forecasts and the tariffs using the described TERA tool. For each assessment a specific uncertainty is generated for the critical variable. The uncertainty is defined as the relative standard deviation which is the standard deviation multiplied with 100 % and divided by the expected value. The values used for the relative standard deviation are 10 %, 20 %, 30 % and 40 %. The results are shown in figure 7.

The calculated net present value is 632,000 EURO. The net present value is defined as the discounted sum of all costs (investments cost , maintenance costs etc.) and the revenues for the project period. The potential number of subscribers in the area is 4,000.

When the relative standard deviation for the penetration is 10 %, then the standard deviation of the net present value is 16,100 EURO, or a relative standard deviation of 2.5 %. A 10 % relative uncertainty in the tariffs causes a standard deviation of the net

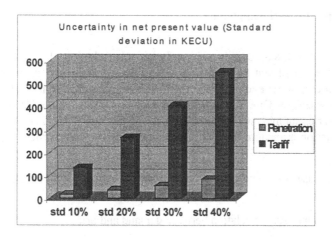

Figure 7. Uncertainty in net present value when the uncertainty in penetration and tariff prediction is increasing

present value of 134,000 EURO, or a relative standard deviation of 21.2 %. The uncertainty in the net present value increases significantly when the relative uncertainty in both the tariff and the penetration are increasing from 10 % to 40 %.

Experience from risk analysis shows that the net present value distribution generated from the repeated simulations is rather close to a normal distribution. The probability for an observation to deviate more than one times the standard deviation from the expected value is about 34 %. The figure above shows that this is the case when the relative standard deviation of the tariff a little bit more than 40 %. Figure 7 also shows that uncertainty in the tariffs causes much more uncertainty in the net present value than the same degree of uncertainty in the penetrations. The reason is that the uncertainty in the tariffs influences the net present value directly in one direction. The uncertainty in the penetration influences both the cost side and the revenue side, because reduced penetration reduces the investment and at the same time reduces the revenue and vice versa.

The same arguments can be used on lost market shares because of competition. If some percentage of the customers is lost to another competitor, the potential revenue is lost, but at the same time also the investments can be tuned down. Hence, the effect of lost market shares is not so critical as a reduction of the tariffs in the same degree. The competition generates both changes in market shares and obviously also changes in tariff level.

Some calculations have been carried out to evaluate the risk based on uncertainties in the costs. Prediction of the cost evolution is rather complicated because there are a lot of different components which have different cost evolution trend. The prediction of civil work and e.g. electronic components has quite different cost evolutions. The assessments showed that uncertainties in the costs, when the relative standard deviation to the weighted sum of the component costs was about 15 %, gave a standard deviation of the net present value of 111,100 EURO.

6.2 Dependencies in the modelling

Usually independent simulations are performed. In addition the behaviour of the variables in the model can be generated independently. However, there are important time dependencies in the evolution and there are also important relations between some of the critical variables. One way to fit these conditions is to simultaneously generate the whole time series taking into account the time dependency. Another possibility is to apply a correlation procedure for each simulation. The correlation procedure can also be applied:

− in order to use the same type of cost trend for similar components in the same architecture

− on demand curve for the relation between demand and price

− for penetration forecasts for different access capacities.

The following tables show the effect of the correlation modelling and the uncertainty in the net present value. The calculations are based on correlation between the offered broadband demand for 2 Mbit/s asymmetric, 2 Mbit/s symmetric and 8 Mbit/s asymmetric access, and on correlation within group of components in the same architecture. In addition the demand curve is used for the dependency between the demand and the tariff.

Table 4. Risk (%) of negative net present value as a function of uncertainties and correlation

Standard dev. Correlation	10%	20%	30%	40%
0%	0	0	10.5	16.9
25%	0	2.9	10.5	21.0
50%	0	4.3	12.0	22.6
75%	0	5.0	14.8	24.9
100%	0	6.6	16.4	25.4

Table 4 shows that the correlation only to a limited degree effects the risk of getting a negative net present value. The risk for a negative net present value is increasing with about 7 − 8% when the correlation is increasing from 0 to 100 %.

Even for rather high uncertainties of 10 − 30 %, there is not a very large risk for a negative net present value in the case of the FTTLex upgrade. However, the criteria of having a positive net present value is not a sufficient criteria for a broadband upgrade. There will be requirements for a significant return on the investments. The expected net present value for FTTLex architecture is calculated to 622,000 EURO. Table 5 shows the risks for having a deviation from the expected value of more than 200,000 EURO.

Table 5. Risk of a reduction of net present value > 200,000 EURO as a function of uncertainties and correlation

Standard dev. Correlation	10%	20%	30%	40%
0%	17.1	30.8	40.0	45.6
25%	20.4	31.9	41.5	47.1
50%	23.8	33.9	42.9	49.6
75%	26.4	36.7	43.3	47.6
100%	24.5	34.2	41.9	47.2

Table 5 confirms that the correlation modelling only to a limited degree effects the risks. The uncertainties, however, effect the risk extensively. When the relative uncertainty is 20 %, the risk for a drop in the net present value of minimum 200,000 EURO is rather significant: 30 – 35 %.

7   Conclusions

The major contribution of the work carried out is a methodology and a tool for carrying out quantitative risk assessment of multimedia projects. The methodology and tool developed in the ACTS projects OPTIMUM and TERA specifies a framework for risk analysis, which includes key elements such as choice of probability density functions, correlation between important variables, simulation performance, methodology for cost predictions, demand forecasts, tariff predictions and associated uncertainties. The contribution from themost critical factors to the overall risk profile of the telecommunications operator projects under study have been examined and the dependencies between variables analysed.

The following concluding remarks can be drawn:

– The results show that uncertainty in the tariffs causes much more uncertainty in the net present value than the same degree of uncertainty in the penetrations. The reason is that the uncertainty in the tariffs influences the net present value directly in one direction. The uncertainty in the penetration influences both the cost side and the revenue side, because reduced penetration reduces the investment and at the same time reduces the revenue and vice versa.

– Similarly, the results shows that uncertainty in the lost market shares due to competition causes much more uncertainty in the net present value than the same degree of uncertainty in the penetrations. If some percentage of the customers is lost to another competitor, the potential revenue is lost, but at the same time also the investments can be tuned down. Hence, the effect of lost market shares is not so critical as a reduction of the tariffs in the same degree. The competition generates both changes in market shares and obviously also changes in tariff level.

- The analysis illustrates that the correlation between critical variables only to a limited degree effects the risk of getting negative net present value. The increase of the risk for a negative net present value is increasing with about 7 – 8 % when the correlation is increasing from 0 to 100 %.

- Several issues remain for further work:

- It is important to do further evaluations of the probabilty to have 20 % relative standard deviation in the project net present value.

- The effect of churn is not taken into account in the present study, and should be included to reflect a very important feature of today's competitive situation.

- When performing risk analysis the tariffs are functions of the penetrations. This is probably not accurate apart from the nominal case extracted from the Delphi survey. We can have situations where combinations of random numbers drawn in the Monte Carlo simulation results in 2 Mb/s ASB being more expensive than 8 Mb/s SSB late in the study period! If we use time series only, the risk contribution due to penetrations will be smaller.

- The time lag between the fibre introduction year and the actual point in time when the operator can offer the advanced services (delivered by VDSL) must be taken into account, i.e. reflecting the influence of the actual network roll-out time.

References

1. T. P. Wright «Factors affecting the cost of airplanes» Journal of Aeronautic Science 3(4) 122-128, 1936.
2. J. R. Crawford «Learning curve, ship curve, ratios, related data».Locheed Aircraft Corporation, 1944.
3. L. E. Yelle «The learning curve: Histrorical revew and comprehensive survey». Decision Science 10(2) 302-328, 1979.
4. K. Stordahl, B.T. Olsen, "Demand Elasticity and Forecasts of Wide and Broadband. Service in the Residential Market Based on Results from an International Delphi Survey," 1995 International Communications Forecasting Conference, Toronto, Canada, June 13-16, 1995.
5. B. T. Olsen, A. Zaganiaris, K. Stordahl, L.Aa. Ims, D. Myhre, T. Øverli, M. Tahkokorpi, I. Welling, M. Drieskens, J. Kraushaar, J. Mononen, M. Lähteenoja, S. Markatos, M. De Bortoli, U. Ferrero, M. Ravera, S. Balzaretti, F. Fleuren, N. Gieschen, M. De Oliveira Duarte, E. de Castro, "Techno-economic evaluation of narrowband and broadband access network alternatives and evolution scenario assessment," IEEE Journal of Selected Areas in Communications, 14 (6), 1996, 1184-1203.
6. L. A. Ims, B. T Olsen, D. Myhre, J. Mononen, M. Lähteenoja, U. Ferrero, A. Zaganiaris, " Multiservice Access Network Upgrading in Europe: a Techno-economic Analysis," IEEE Communications Magazine, vol. 34, no. 12, Dec. 1996.
7. B. T. Olsen, L.A. Ims, T. Øverli, K. Stordahl, D. Myhre, M. Drieskens, J. Kraushaar, M. Tahkokorpi, M. Ravera, M. De Bortoli, A. Zaganiaris, S. Markatos, M. Lähteenoja, J. Mononen, F. Fleuren, "PNO and Cable Operator broadband upgrade technology alternatives: a techno-economic analysis," in Proc. Optical Fiber Conference 1996 (OFC '96), Feb. 25 - March 1, 1996, San Jose, USA.

8. B. T. Olsen, L.A. Ims, D. Myhre, K. Stordahl, R. Theivindrein: "Technoeconomic Evaluation of Optical Broadband Access Network Scenarios for the residential and business market," In Proc. 21st European Conference on Optical Communications 1995 (ECOC '95), Brussells, Belgium, September 14-17, 1995.

9. J. Saijonmaa, M. Tahkokorpi, I.Welling, "Cost of Investment and Revenue Modelling and Analysis of Various Networked Multimedia Services in PTO and Cable Operator Environments," in Proc. TELECOM '95, Technology Summit, vol. 2 pp 629-633, Oct, 3-11, 1995, Geneva, Switzerland.

10. K. Stordahl, L.A. Ims, B.T.Olsen, "Risk assessment and techno-economic analysis of competition between PNO and Cable operators," In Proc. Networks '96, 6th International Workshop on Optical Access Networks, Sydney, Australia, November 25-29, 1996.

11. Ims L A, K Stordahl, B T Olsen «Risk analysis of residential broadband upgrade in a competitive environment» IEEE Communications Magazine June 1997

12. P. Luck, "Broadband To The Home: Evolution Scenarios for Australia," In Proc. 13th Annual Conference European Fibre Optic Communications and Networks, EFOC&N '95, June 27-30, 1995, Brighton, UK.

13. Stordahl, K, Murphy, K "Methods for forecasting long term demand for wide and broadband services in the residential market," IEEE Communications magazine, 13, (2), 1995.

14. W. Pugh, G. Boyer, "Broadband Access: Comparing Alternatives," IEEE Communications Magazine 5, 1995.

15. Stordahl K, L Rand "Long term forecasts for broadband demand". Telektronikk no2, 1999

16. L. A. Ims, D. Myhre, B.T. Olsen, K. Stordahl, A. Ruiz-Cantera, B. Jacobs, B. Rose, M. C. Combes, J. Mononen, M. Lähteenoja, L. Budry, M. Salerno, U. Ferrero, V, Benedetto, D. Collins, "Economics of broadband access network upgrade strategies: the European perspective", In Proc. OHAN '98, Sydney, Australia, Nov 8-12, 1998.

Efficient End-Host Resource Management with Kernel Optimizations for Multimedia Applications

S. Lakshminarayanan[1] and Karthikeyan Mahesh[2]

[1] lakme@meena.iitm.ernet.in
Department of Computer Science and Eng.
Indian Institute of Technology-Madras
Chennai 600 036 India.
[2] karthik@cs.iitm.ernet.in
Department of Computer Science and Eng.
Indian Institute of Technology-Madras
Chennai 600 036 India.

Abstract

Multimedia applications have timing requirements that cannot be satisfied using time-sharing scheduling algorithms of general operating systems. Our approach is to provide for a resource reservation mechanism to cater to the real-time resource requirement[5] of multimedia applications. We propose the design of a *Resource Manager* which allocates and manages the end-host resources among the processes[7]. We identify three important resources at the end-host namely, the processor, memory and system bus cycles. A process reserves these resources by negotiating with the Resource manager.

The goals that we seek to achieve are: (a) real-time resource management using kernel supported reservation mechanisms, (b) optimal utilization of the various resources of the end-system and (c) kernel optimizations for reducing end-host communication overheads in distributed multimedia applications. We use a two-pronged approach to accomplish our goals. First, we adopt a reservation strategy coupled with priority process scheduling[13,14] to achieve real-time resource management. The reservation mechanism includes a processor and memory reserve abstraction which controls the allocation of processor cycles and memory space to the processes. The reservation scheme can allow applications to dynamically adapt in real-time based on system load and application requirements. Device requirements of a certain multimedia application is abstracted out as a kernel process for system bus reservation and device activation. Secondly, we adopt kernel optimizations to minimize end-host communication overhead in real-time multimedia applications. To improve the end-host performance in distributed multimedia applications, we unveil a new connectionless protocol, Reliable-UDP, in the kernel. We also present aggressive caching mechanism as a scheme for improving end-host performance. The performance of the Resource Manger was tested out with the generation of processes at random times and the results match the expected theoretical results. The connectionless protocol was tested out in a local distributed system and the results are also presented.

1 Introduction

Multimedia systems are computing systems that employ several types of media ranging from static ones, such as text and graphics, to dynamic ones such as audio and video. A multimedia system is often a distributed system in the sense that its components are located in different processing nodes of a local or wide area network. One of the important aspects of multimedia applications is real-time resource management. Many of the new multimedia applications like *Video-conferences* or *Distributed Video on Demand* share the resources of the distributed system. In order to provide efficient services to these applications, one must utilize these resources properly. Resource management policies dictate how resources are allocated, monitored optimized and released.

The resources of the distributed system are of two types: one being the resources at the end-host and the other being the network resources. The resources at the end-host include the processor, memory, the system bus and the peripherals and the network resources include the channels used for communication and the routers present in the network. In this paper we propose an efficient end-host resource management strategy. The resources that are in contention for such a system include CPU time, memory capacity and bus cycles. In many multimedia applications audio and video streams are transmitted and these streams have to be collected by the end-host and processed. A multimedia application, unlike normal applications has timing requirements that cannot be satisfied by normal operating systems. The schedulers in existing operating systems do no take care of the timing requirements of these applications into account. Due to this reason, the performance of the multimedia applications is often suboptimal.

In this paper we present a process scheduling strategy that takes into consideration the timing requirements of the multimedia application. We extend the idea of *processor capacity reserves*[4]—an abstraction of the Real Time Mach micro-kernel to our model to suit processor, memory and system bus requirements. The processor capacity reserves[3] allows application threads to specify their CPU requirements in terms of timing requirements. We extend the above concept to a model in which an application thread can request for a certain memory capacity to suit its applications. The capacity of memory allocated can be dynamically varied to suit the needs of the application. A multimedia application involving audio or video streams has to transfer data to the peripheral devices at periodic intervals of time. To support this mechanism, we provide bus reservation strategies as part of the *Resource manager* which controls the resource reservations of the various applications. The *Resource manager* is designed to allocate the minimum resource requirements to the multimedia application to achieve optimal performance.

In this paper, we have discussed the design of a connectionless and reliable protocol in the kernel called Reliable UDP. This is a high performance protocol over a local area network and the timeout algorithm of TCP has been modified to suit a LAN. We also discuss an aggressive caching mechanism where extra memory capacity reserve is allocated for bulk transfer in a distributed system. The performance of Reliable-UDP for small packets is substantially high when compared to that of TCP. The variation of timeouts has also been studied in this paper.

In section 2, we present our Working model followed by a discussion of the *Resource Manager* in section 3. In section 4, a description of Reliable UDP is given and the results of our simulations are presented in section 5. In section 6, we conclude giving directions for future work.

1.1 Related Work

In [3],[4] there is a discussion of operating systems support for Multimedia Applications. The approach towards solving this problem has been fundamentally different from the normal solutions for problems in Real Time systems. But the work has manly concentrated on processor capacity reserves[3] and not on other resources of an end-host system.

2 Working Model

A Distributed system is one in which various nodes are interconnected by the underlying network. The resources at the end-host can be abstracted using three parameters namely processing speed, memory capacity and peripherals. Let P_i, M_i, R_i represent the processing capability, memory capacity and device availability of the ith node in the multimedia system. A channel in the network offers a certain bandwidth B_j with a certain delay D_j where j is an index for the channel. Any distributed process running over the entire system uses both the network resources and the end-host resources. Any distributed process Q_k can be represented by its time varying resource requirements. Let $x_{ij}(t), y_{ij}(t), z_{ij}(t)$ represent the time-varying processor, memory and resource requirement of process i at node j. Let $b_{ij}(t)$ represent the bandwidth requirement of process i in the channel j at time t. Let K represent the total number of distributed processes. We have the following requirements from the system.

Node Requirements

$$\sum_{i=1}^{k} x_{ij}(t) \leq P_j$$

$$\sum_{i=1}^{k} y_{ij}(t) \leq M_j$$

$$\sum_{i=1}^{k} z_{ij}(t) \leq R_j$$

Channel Requirements

$$\sum_{i=1}^{k} b_{ij}(t) \leq B_j$$

Designing a distributed scheduling algorithm to service all the processes efficiently is the goal of the system. Many multimedia applications may have deadlines associated with it. The scheduling algorithm must include deadlines as an important parameter while scheduling the processes. A distributed multimedia application may involve various QoS requirements from the network[8]. In this paper, we concentrate on scheduling processes at the end-host based on their resource requirements. We assume that the network offers the required QoS for the various processes[9]. We obtain the resource abstraction of a distributed process at a single node and consider this abstraction to be the requirements of a local process at the node.

3 Resource manager

Every multimedia application has certain minimum resource requirements to be satisfied for optimum performance. These requirements can be specified by the processor time, memory buffer and I/O bandwidth required in a given time interval. For example, an MPEG video player which reads a file from disk and plays 30 frames of video per second, with say 10 ms processing time per frame, will need to be scheduled for 10 ms out of every 33 ms (1/30 s), buffer space in physical memory to hold one frame of video and enough bus cycles to read an MPEG frame from disk and write the decoded frame to the video framebuffer in the 33 ms. The OS must provide a way for the application to specify these requirements. In this case, the parameters specified are the processor time required in a given time interval, the size of the memory buffer, and the amount of data to be transferred through the bus in a given interval. In the rest of this section, we describe methods to specify and implement resource reservations for these three resources—processor time, I/O bandwidth and memory buffer resources.

3.1 Processor Time

To guarantee a certain amount of processor time to a process, the scheduler must take its reservations into account while scheduling it. The scheduling algorithm is typically priority based—using either fixed or dynamic priorities.

Fixed Priority Scheduling In a fixed priority scheduling scheme one must be able to assign priorities to processes such that each one is processed at its required rate. This can be done using the *rate monotonic* (RM) algorithm of Liu and Layland[13]. Here, the highest priority is assigned to the highest frequency task and the lowest priority is assigned to the lowest frequency task.

Let n be the number of tasks and let C_i and T_i be the computation time and period of task i. Liu and Layland[13] showed that all tasks will successfully meet their deadlines if

$$\sum_{i=1}^{n} \frac{C_i}{T_i} \leq n(2^{1/n} - 1)$$

When n is large, $n(2^{1/n} - 1) = \ln 2 = 0.69$. This means that as long as the total processor reservation is less than 69%, all tasks will meet their deadlines. This is a pessimistic bound. Here, a lot of computation time (31%), cannot be reserved. Lehoczky et.al[14] gave an average case analysis showing that tasks can be scheduled with upto 88% utilization.

Dynamic Priority Scheduling In contrast with fixed priority scheduling, the *earliest deadline*(ED) scheduling policy uses a dynamic priority scheme. The deadline of a task is defined as the end of the period during which the computation is to be finished. The task with the earliest deadline is scheduled to run. It can be shown that all tasks will successfully meet their deadlines under ED scheduling if

$$\sum_{i=1}^{n} \frac{C_i}{T_i} \leq 1$$

In ED scheduling the priority of a particular process is inversely proportional to the difference between the deadline and the present time. This however, does not require continuous updation of priority, but the scheduler needs to make updates at the end of every task.

We see that with ED scheduling, it is possible to reserve upto 100% of the CPU time and still meet all deadlines whereas with the rate monitoring method, deadlines are guaranteed only if the reservation is less than 69%.

3.2 Bus Resources

In section 3.1, we studied how the processing time of a CPU can be efficiently shared between processes. But processor time is not the only resource for which applications compete. Multimedia applications often need to transfer large amounts of data to a peripheral device in a given amount of time. In order to achieve this, applications must have guaranteed access to the bus.

The OS will provide system calls for bulk transfer of data between the memory and the device. Whenever a particular application requires the transfer of data from a resource to memory or vice versa before a particular deadline, then we adopt a policy of bus reservation. Note that direct control of bus resources is not an efficient methodology since it reduces the throughput considerably. to overcome this, we follow a policy of *preemption*, where the resource involved in the transfer requests for bus access in advance. With a small predictable delay, the application effectively gets access to the bus. Here again, priorities can be allocated to resources. Effectively the data transfer is accomplished within the required deadline with high probability.

3.3 Memory Buffer Resources

Multimedia applications typically use large memory buffers. For performance reasons, it is advantageous if the memory buffer is present in physical memory before it is accessed. If a buffer is not in memory when it is required, a page fault occurs, and the process sleeps until the page is fetched. This can cause a delay of the order of several ms—too large for a multimedia application. Memory buffers that are meant for holding data that is read from or to be written to a device should also be contiguous in physical memory so that they can be directly used for DMA transfers without a copy into kernel space. Support for reservation of memory buffers implies that the OS should provide a service by which the application can specify the size of the memory buffer (*memory capacity* of the application), the interval during which it should be present in physical memory and whether it needs to be contiguous.

In our method, the memory is logically split into 3 parts- A,B,C. A is used as a memory capacity reserve for multimedia applications. B is used as a common memory for all applications and C is used as a temporary memory for Distributed multimedia applications. The number of local and distributed multimedia applications dictate the logical split of memory between A, B and C. Whenever a process P requests a memory capacity M, then it is assigned a high proportion of M say pM in A and the rest of the capacity is adjusted in the common memory slot B. Memory capacity reservation is implemented by scheduling a transfer to bring the required pages into physical memory at a time before the time when the process wants to use the buffer. Processes that involve data transfer to a reserved memory buffer of an application are given high priority by the scheduler. The logical split is made dynamic with the help of memory location transfers between A, B and C. A change occurs in the logical split when memory of a particular finished task is allocated to another task.

3.4   Implementation of Resource Reservation in a Kernel

In this section, we propose a unified approach for managing all three resources— processor time, bus resources and memory buffer resources. The OS runs a *Resource Manager* process which keeps track of all existing reservations and performs admission control. All processes register their reservations with the *Resource Manager*. A particular registration of a process is a three tuple (a, b, c) denoting the reserves of the three resources. The *Resource Manager* verifies whether this reservation can be guaranteed at the current load (for example, if RM scheduling is used, the total reservation of processor time cannot exceed 69%) before admitting it. The *Scheduler* and the *Resource Manager* together implement the resource reservation service.

Reservations for processor time are handled directly. A reservation for a bus transfer of x bytes is handled with the help of *preemption*. An OS call is made to inform the device that data transfer of x bytes is accomplished within a particular deadline. A memory buffer reservation is always tied to a processor or a bus transfer reservation. It is required that the buffer be in physical memory *before* the task or the transfer is scheduled. The *Resource Manager* ensures that the buffer is in memory when it is required by the following method. It checks if the required space is present in the allocated space in A and if present , the transfer is immediately accomplished. If the buffer is not present, the memory is

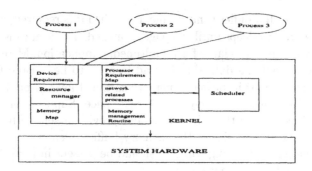

Fig. 1. Block Diagram of Implementation

allocated in B. This task is guaranteed enough time to evict an existing page and bring in the new page. Whenever the processor finds that the memory allocation in A for a particular processor is much below the expected value, a change in the logical split between A, B, C occurs.

The *Resource Manager* thus provides a unified interface to handle reservations for three classes of resources—CPU time, bus resources and memory buffer resources.

4 Kernel Optimizations for Distributed Multimedia Applications

Any Multimedia Application that runs over a distributed system communicates with the other systems present in the distributed domain. All these communications involve the use of the operating system at the end-hosts. Many multimedia applications like Videoconferencing or Video on Demand have real-time issues associated with them[11]. In order to effectively address these real time issues, one needs to minimize the overhead due to the data transfers between the end-host systems. In this section, we address issues relating to kernel optimizations at the end-hosts as part of providing efficient end-host support for communication.

4.1 A Connectionless and Reliable Transport Protocol — RUDP

We have implemented a transport protocol called Reliable UDP (RUDP) which is connectionless, reliable and provides timely delivery of packets in the kernel of our system to suit multimedia applications. This protocol supports efficient inter-process communication between two nodes in the distributed system without the overheads of connection oriented protocols like TCP.

Drawbacks of TCP TCP is poorly suited to frequent, short, request-response style traffic. Frequent connection setup and tear down costs burden servers with many connections in TIME_WAIT state. TCP's slow start algorithm for congestion avoidance interacts with short connections in a rather poor manner. The overhead involved in connection management severely limits the scalability and performance of our system. These mismatches between the needs of multimedia applications and the services of TCP have caused increased latency in real-time applications.

Implementation We have developed RUDP using the unreliable and connectionless UDP as a base protocol and have provided reliable and in-sequence delivery over it. We use sequence numbers and acknowledgements in order to achieve this.

Every packet sent from a node is assigned a sequence number which depends on the IP address of the receiving node and the destination port. A packet is uniquely identified by its sequence number, destination IP address and port number. A sequence number list is associated with every port in the node.

Acknowledgements are handled by allocating a standard port in each node as an acknowledgement port. A node sends acknowledgements to the acknowledgement port of the sender. When a node receives an acknowledgement, it updates the sequence number list of the corresponding port.

We have modified the TCP's congestion control mechanism to provide a timeout adjustment suitable to our application. Our timeout mechanism is well suited over a LAN set-up. Whenever a packet loss occurs the timeout is multiplied by a constant factor γ typically around 2. We have based our time-out algorithm to explicitly suit the sudden variations in RTT. Our time-out algorithm aims at keeping the time-out to within a constant factor of the RTT. Our algorithm ensures that following a congestion the timeout drops back to its initial value rapidly when compared to TCP.

4.2 Aggressive Caching Mechanism

Memory capacities are allocated to all multimedia applications. We propose the use of aggressive caching in multimedia applications which need to obtain streaming multimedia data from a remote source. This mechanism is especially very useful to the Distributed Video on Demand applications where one can perform bulk transfer between the two end nodes. Through this mechanism, a process that needs to obtain data from a remote node can fill its memory capacity alloted in partition C, by performing bulk transport of the data from the remote node. The presence of a large cache at the end-host improves the performance of the above operation. The message is broken into various packets and the RPC transport at the other end reassembles the fragments. A single acknowledgement is used for all the fragments. On the other hand a collective set of all selectively rejected packets and sequence numbers of unreceived packets is sent as a collective negative acknowledgement to the packets. The sending RPC transport retransmits these fragments alone. This process is used to ensure reliable data delivery.

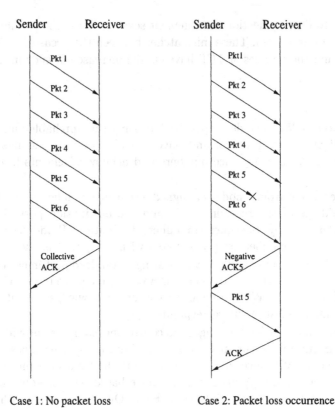

Case 1: No packet loss   Case 2: Packet loss occurrence

Fig. 2. Transfer mechanism used in Aggressive caching

5   Simulation Experiments

Experiments were performed to study the utility of operating system optimization on applications. Simulations were performed to analyse the effect of processor reservation support and communication optimizations on applications.

In the first experiment, we studied the impact of processor reservation strategies. We simulated a set of processes with different reservations and examined the long term behaviour of the system. In our experimental setup, we assumed three processes A,B,C with reservations of 40%, 30% and 20%, with the rest of the processor time given to processes without reservations. The processor utilization of each process vs time is shown in Figure 3.

From the above graph, we see that the processor time available to each process stabilizes around its reservation. This means that each process is guaranteed its reserved processor time.

The performance of RUDP was tested over a distributed cluster comprising of 3 nodes connected by a 10Mbps Ethernet link. The protocol was implemented on the Linux OS. Message passing of varying sizes were accomplished and the performance of our protocol in comparison to TCP was studied. The timeout variation of our protocol have also been measured.

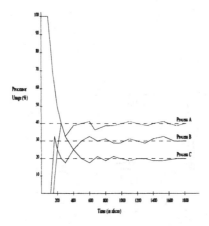

Fig. 3. Processor Time vs Time

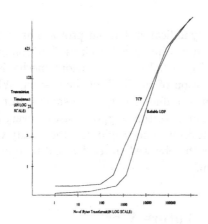

Fig. 4. Comparison of the Transmission time of our protocol with TCP

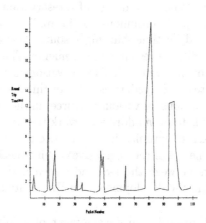

Fig. 5. Variation of RTT with time on a LAN

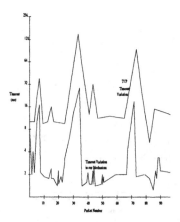

Fig. 6. Comparison of our Timeout mechanism with TCP

The results have clearly indicated that our protocol has a tremendous gain in performance for small and medium sized packets. The connection management overhead in our protocol is very less. The timeout mechanism of our protocol tries to model the fluctuation of the RTT of the system. When the network is relatively free the timeout is reduced to within a small factor of RTT to support multiple transmissions. Our algorithm supports fast recovery from congestion by ensuring that the timeout drops much rapidly to the steady value in comparison to TCP. This protocol is thereby well suited for real time applications running over a distributed system.

6 Conclusion and Future Work

In this paper, we have motivated the design of a reservation strategy of the resources of a system to support continuous media applications. The scheduling framework discussed, based on time -varying resource availability provides an effective way to specify real-time resource requirements. The Resource manager maintains the resources of the system. This reservation scheme can be directly extended to the distributed multimedia systems. In this reservation mechanism each reserve contain reservations for various resources in the distributed systems. In such a model, one needs to even address network resource reservation issues. We have also proposed kernel optimizations to reduce the communication overhead between systems. The use of the aggressive caching mechanism reduces the number of data transfers between the two end-systems. We plan to use these optimizations effectively in the development of a Distributed Video on Demand application.

We are also working towards the development of a full-fledged operating system sensitive to multimedia applications. This operating system will include the scheduling features and the optimizations provided over here.

References

1. John.K.Ousterhout et.al, The Sprite Network Operating System, *IEEE Computer*, Vol. 21(2): 23-36, 1988.
2. Michael N.Nelson, BrentB.Welch, John.K.Ousterhout, Caching in the Sprite Network File System, *ACM Transactions on Computer Systems*, Vol.6(1): 134-154, 1988.
3. Clifford W.Mercer, Stefan Savage and Hideyuki Tokuda, Processor Capacity Reserves: Operating Systems Support for Multimedia Applications, *In Proceedings of the IEEE International Conference on Multimedia Computing and Systems*, May 1994.
4. Chen Lee, Ragunathan Rajkumar and Cliff Mercer, Experiences with Processor Reservation and Dynamic QoS in Real-Time Mach, *In Proceedings of Multimedia Japan*, March 1996.
5. Hideyuki Tokuda, Tatsuo Nakajima and Prithvi Rao, Real-Time Mach: Towards a Predictable Real-Time System, *Proceedings of USENIX Mach Workshop*, October 1990.
6. M.Ott, G.Michelitsch and D.Reininger and G.Welling, An Architecture for Adaptive QoS and its Application to Multimedia Systems Design, *Special Issue of Computer Communications on Building Quality of Service into Distributed Systems*.
7. T.Abdelzaher and Kang G.Shin, End-host Architecture for QoS Adaptive Communication, *IEEE Real-Time Technology and Applications Symposium*, June 3-5, 1998.
8. A.Campbell, C.Aurrecoechea, L.Hauw, A review of QoS Architectures, *ACM Multimedia Systems Journal*, 1996.
9. A.Campbell, G.Coulson and D.Hutchison, A Quality of Service Architecture, *ACM Computer Communications Review*, April 1994.
10. A.Campbell, R.Liao, Y.Shobatake, Delivering Scalable Flows using QoS Controlled Handoff, *ATM Forum/97-0341*.
11. A.Vogel et al., Distributed Multimedia and QoS: A Survey, *IEEE Multimedia*, Summer 1995, pp 10-18.
12. A.Hafid and G.V.Bochmann, An Approach to Quality of Service Management for Distributed Multimedia Systems, *International Conference on Open Distributed Processing (ICODP-95)*, Australia, Feb 1995, pp 319-340.
13. C.L.Liu and J.W.Layland, Scheduling Algorithms for Multiprogramming in Hard Real Time Environment, *JACM*, 20(1): 46-61, 1973.
14. J.P.Lehoczky, L.Sha and Y.Ding, The Rate Monotonic Scheduling Algorithm: Exact Characterization and Average Case Behaviour, *In Proceedings of the 10th IEEE Real-Time Systems Symposium*, pp 166-171, Dec. 1989.

SOMMIT Project: Enabling New Serivces for the Next Generation of Digital TV Receivers

Roberto Becchini[1], Gianluca De Petris[2], Mario Guglielmo[2], Alain Morvan[3]

[1]SIA-Società Italiana Avionica SpA, Torino, Italy
Strada Antica di Collegno 253, 10146 Torino - Italy
Phone +39 011 7720 245 Fax +39 011 725679
URL: http://www.sia-av.it/ E-mail: becchini@sia-av.it
[2]CSELT-Centro Studi E Laboratori Telecomunicazioni, Torino, Italy
Via G. Reiss Romoli, 10148 Torino - Italy
Phone: + 39 011 228 6109 (De Petris)
Phone: + 39 011 228 6115 (Guglielmo)
Fax: + 39 011 228 6299
URL: http://www.cselt.it/
E-mail: gianluca.depetris@cselt.it
E-mail: mario.guglielmo@cselt.it
[3]CNET - Centre National d'Étude des Télécommunications
Direction des Interactions Humaines
4, rue du Clos Courtel
35512 Cesson-Sévigné Cedex - France
Phone: + 33 2 99 12 47 41 (Alain Morvan) Fax: + 33 2 9912 40 98
URL: http://www.ccett.fr/
E-mail: alan.morvan@cnet.francetelecom.fr

Keywords: MPEG-2, MPEG-4, AICI, Java

Abstract

The MPEG-2 standard has allowed Digital Television to become a reality at reasonable costs. The introduction of MPEG-4 will allow content and service providers to enrich MPEG-2 content with new 2D and 3D scenes capable of a high degree of interactivity even in broadcast environments. While ensuring compatibility with existing terminals, the user of the new terminal will be provided with other applications, such as Electronic Program Guides, Advanced Teletext, but also a new non-intrusive kind of advertisements. For these reasons, a scalable device opened both to the consolidated past (MPEG-2) and to the incoming future (MPEG-4) is considered a key issue for the delivery of new services. The presence of a Java Virtual Machine and a set of standard APIs is foreseen in the current terminal architecture, to give extended programmatic capabilities to content creators. This paper covers the application areas, the design and the implementation of a prototype for this terminal, which has been developed in the context of the ACTS SOMMIT project.

1. Introduction

The number of services and applications that the new digital revolution makes possible encourages the scientific and industrial world to make heavy investments in developing new technologies and tools. In this context the ISO/IEC MPEG (Moving Picture Expert Group) standardization group plays a key role in providing digital TV customers with more powerful tools in the area of multimedia communications.

After the MPEG-1 and MPEG-2 standards (that made Digital Television possible) the MPEG committee began the development of a new multimedia standard with wide industry participation: its name is MPEG-4 [14].

While MPEG-1 and MPEG-2 provided compression and synchronization tools to store or transmit moving pictures and associated audio, MPEG-4 adds the capability of composing various kinds of media (text, still images, 3D objects, moving pictures etc.) in the same complex scene, allowing the user to interact with it.

The market is focused towards the reuse of existing content and the integration of it with the new one. The new AIC (Advanced Interactive Content) Initiative was born under the hat of an IEC/ITA (Industrial Technical Agreement) in order to integrate the new technology (MPEG-4) with the existing ones (MPEG-2 and HTML), while ensuring compatibility of the integrated content with the old receivers. [16]

2. Applications

To understand the basic capabilities of the receiver the procedure of AICI, as in most Information Technology projects as MPEG, is to start with a description of the applications that the technology intends to address. This list is used as a reference to draft a set of requirements for the new technology. Each requirement is then detailed to such an extent that it can be used to issue a call for proposals or develop the needed specifications.

Here we are going to briefly describe some of the applications that are addressed by the AICI specifications [18]. One of these (the Electronic Program Guide, EPG) has already been prototyped by the Project and is described with more detail. This description is useful to understand the reasons behind the design and implementation of the SOMMIT[1] architecture, which will be addressed in detail in the next chapter.

2.1. AICI Applications

2.1.1.   Advanced Electronic Program Guide
Service providers utilizing various distribution media will offer a range of broadcast services within a "channel multiplex". Examples include the packages of services

---

[1] SOMMIT stands for Software Open MultiMedia Interactive Terminal

available on satellite systems such as DirecTV, and the set of digital services that a terrestrial TV broadcaster will offer within the 6/8MHz traditional analog TV "channel". When a receiver acquires a channel multiplex it will be desirable to provide a program guide or "home page" for the services. The presentation will include a text description (title) for each audio-visual program contained in the multiplex, perhaps with a visual thumbnail of the current video and an audio sound-clip, plus description of any data services associated specifically with this program. It will also contain a text and/or icon based index to the other data broadcast services in the multiplex. In addition, at the discretion of the service provider, the home page may also point to services outside this specific channel multiplex, such as MPEG-4 and HTML content on the World Wide Web if accessible.

2.1.2.   Buy-Me Button

When a commercial appears on TV, a "buy-me button" appears on top of the video. The user may select the button and advertising content appears. At the end of the commercial the button disappears. The "buy-me button" is synchronized with the broadcast content in the sense that it appears and disappears in a synchronized way.

Users may be afraid to miss what is happening on the screen if they interact with the "buy-me button", so optionally they may save the advertising content for later consumption. There may be several " buy-me buttons" and users choose the ones they want to interact with.

2.1.3.   Program Enhancement

Programs may be enhanced by presenting collateral information. This information may be in the form of text overlays, still images, spoken word (in different languages), graphics (with 2D or 3D data) or even audio/video. The user has the option to enable presentation of these data and perhaps arrange the layout of visual information on the screen. The presentation may include windowing techniques (picture-in-picture and picture-out-of picture), overlays and full screen compositions.

2.1.4.   Home Shopping

A retailer may publish an interactive catalog of their products. This catalog may be broadcast repeatedly over the broadcast network or on the Internet. Consumers may browse/navigate the catalog by product category, inspect products by manipulating videos and 3D models, and purchase products of interest, requesting delivery to the home. This may involve live discussion with a sales consultant. Over time, this application will develop to become increasingly sophisticated. Items such as furniture will be downloaded with a full range of finished material - the cloth swatches of today will be the graphic textures of tomorrow, and a couch for example will be viewable in every fabric and every color. Continuing this model to its ultimate conclusion, users will place the couch 3D model of their own living room and view it in situ under early morning sunlight conditions and late evening mood lighting conditions.

2.1.5.   Interactive Commercials

A commercial may provide detailed or additional information about a product upon a user's request. A user may electronically purchase a product being advertised. A discount coupon for a product may be delivered electronically to the user's retail outlet of choice. Commercials may be targeted and personalized to the user's needs, taste and profile. Rewards may be given to a user responding to a survey.

2.1.6. Demographic Programming

Multiple versions of programs, and in particular commercials, may be broadcast and directed to demographically distinct audiences. For example, while a commercial for baby food is being sent to young families, a commercial for sports cars might be sent to single people. Commercials might be tied in to discounts and special offers. Collection of user profiles and preferences might use the back-channel to collect the data.

2.2. The SOMMIT EPG Application

In this section we describe one of the applications developed by the SOMMIT Project. It is an application that implements an Electronic Program Guide (EPG) and runs on the terminal that has been prototyped by the Project.

This application extracts TV program information from an MPEG-2 Transport stream [17] and allows the selection of one of its programs.

The EPG GUI (Graphic User Interface) provides the user with one 3D tool for the navigation among the available TV programs and for the sorting of them according to the user preferences. For example, the user interacts with a 3D scene to select only the sport programs that are broadcast the same day. Then, the requested information is displayed in 2D format, along with a textual description of the event and a thumbnail picture associated to it. The picture can be either still or animated, according to the bandwidth of the channel.

The 3D tool offered to the user is not an immersive 3D world. This kind of metaphor was rejected for two reasons:
1. it may be difficult for a non accustomed person to use it with a simple remote control;
2. in terms of usability, the time spent to select a TV program could be felt too long and not really efficient.

Hence, another 3D metaphor has been selected: the Rubik Cube metaphor. The users can rotate the blocks in the 3D world in order that the faces in front of them display their choice.

Fig. 1. The Rubik Cube Metaphor

The selection of search criteria allows the user to find a set of real-time data coming from the MPEG-2 transport stream. These data comply with the DVB-SI (Digital Video Broadcast – Service Information) standard [15] and are composed of the following tables: NIT (Network Information Table), SDT (Service Description Table), BAT (Bouquet Association Table), EIT/PF, EIT/Schedule (Event Information Tables).

This information is displayed as a list of available programs. Then, the user can select one entry of the list and have further details, sometimes with a moving thumbnail of the program, and the possibility of switching to the program, if this is broadcast at the same moment (see figure 2).

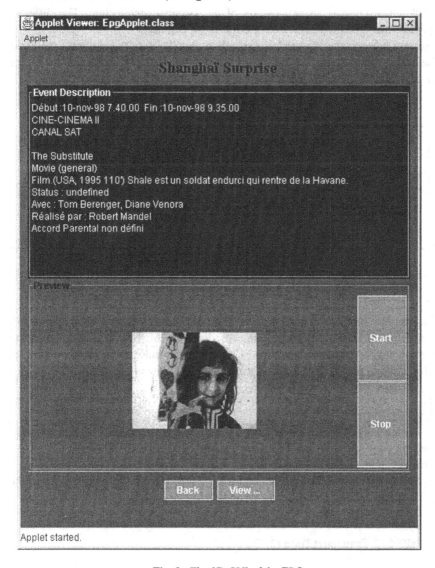

Fig. 2. The 2D GUI of the EPG

As we can see from the previous description, this application represents the first prototype of the AIC indications, which were anticipated by the Project.

The implementation of this application required a big effort also for the definition and implementation of the terminal on which it runs, in particular to ensure that the prototype was compliant to the recommendations of the standardization bodies.

In the following we are going to describe the terminal architecture and the contributions of the Project to the standardization bodies.

3. The Terminal Architecture

The following figure is an explanation of the terminal architecture. The different components are described in detail in the following paragraphs.

This section requires that the reader is somehow familiar with the concepts expressed in the standards that we point to. Where possible, simple explanations of the technology will be given.

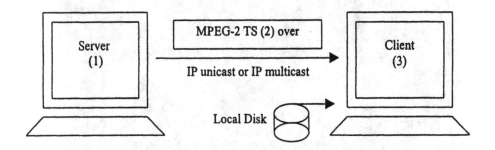

Fig. 3. The client-server architecture

The reference platform is composed of a Server, which streams MPEG-2 Transport data, and one or more Clients, capable of decoding MPEG data. The following description only takes into account the PC platform implementation, not the STB (Set Top Box) prototype. Refer to Figure 4 for a high level view of the platform.

3.1. Server (1)

The server runs on a simple PC with Pentium 133 MHz, Windows NT 4.0 or Windows 95, and a network card.

An application called IPump streams MPEG-2 TS over IP at constant bitrate. The setup has been tested so far with streams up to 8 Mbit/s.

3.2. MPEG-2 Transport Data (2)

To generate MPEG-2 TS data, we use a program that allows to multiplex MPEG-1 Audio, MPEG-2 Video, Private Data stream, part of Service Information (NIT, EIT, SDT).

To insert MPEG-4 information into an MPEG-2 TS stream, specifically in the Private Data stream before multiplexing, we generate PES (Packetized Elementary Stream) packets using another program written on purpose. PES packets contain in their payload other packets, whose format has been defined in the Project, and will be aligned with the specifications of the standard fora, when they are available. This payload, called MPEG-4 packet, is composed of a header (containing information for the client, such as name and size of the MPEG-4 application) and an MPEG-4 application.

3.3. Client (3)

The client is a PC with Windows 95 or NT, Pentium 400 MHz MMX (MMX is required for real-time MPEG-2 video decoding), and with a video card featuring YUV-RGB hardware conversion.

Integration between the A/V output of the MPEG-2 decoder and MPEG-4 player is done simply displaying into two different windows. A different approach may be needed in case of a STB not allowing multiwindowing. We are also implemented a version of the prototype which allows overlay of MPEG-4 on MPEG-2.

The following figure reports the details about the client platform.

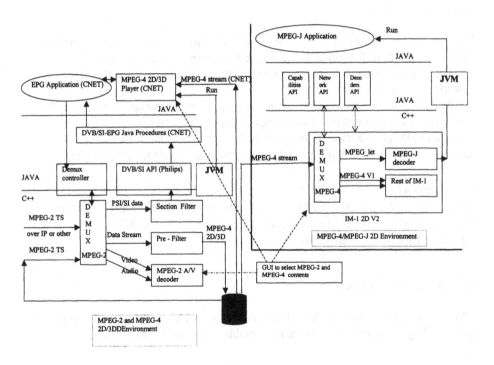

Fig. 4. Architecture of the Client

The terminal can be thought divided in two parts: an MPEG-2 related and an MPEG-4 related.

We are going to describe the way the application works. We suggest to follow the description on figure 4.

3.3.1 Demux MPEG-2

The demultiplexer receives MPEG-2 TS stream either over UDP (on any address and port) or from the hard disk. The user can choose through a suitable menu either way of receiving data.

MPEG-2 TS is separated into elementary streams and passed to an MPEG-2 MP@ML (Main Profile at Main Level) video decoder, an MPEG-1 Layer I and II Audio Decoder, a Pre-filter, and a Section Filter module.

3.3.2. Section Filter

The Section Filter module retrieves MPEG-2 PAT (Program Association Tables) and PMT (Program Map Tables) and chooses the first program in the stream. These tables in fact contain information on all the programs that can be retrieved in the stream, and how to tune in to one of them.

The Section Filter module moreover can be instructed by a Java application/applet to filter a particular PID and pass the corresponding SI/PSI (Service Information/Program Service Information) table to the Java application. This happens thanks to the DVB/SI API that also takes raw data and formats it for the application.

The DVB/SI API
This API is a DAVIC/DVB standard proposed by the Project and accepted by this body. Although we cannot give here a detailed description of this API, we shall explain its basic functionality later in this chapter.

3.3.3. MPEG-2 A/V Decoder

MPEG-2 A/V data is decoded in real-time and displayed by this module. To speed-up SW decoding, some parts are written in assembler using MMX instructions.

3.3.4 Pre-Filter

The Data Stream is passed to a pre-filter, which looks for MPEG-4 information, extracts the MPEG-4 application (a single file either of a 2D profile or a 3D profile) and saves it temporarily onto the disk.

A more recent version of the terminal prototype allows to stream the MPEG-4 data in real-time directly to the MPEG-4 player, without the need to cache it temporarily.

3.3.5 DVB/SI-EPG Java Procedures

The DVB/SI-EPG Java Procedures are helper classes written in Java on top of the DVB/SI API. They can ease the writing of an EPG.

3.3.6 Demux Control

A Java application, e.g. an EPG, can also control the Demultiplexer by forcing the PIDs (Program Identifiers) from which A/V/D information is retrieved and displayed.

3.3.7 MPEG-4 Application Selection

While the user is watching an MPEG-2 A/V stream, he/she can decide to launch one of the MPEG-4 applications that were downloaded. Depending on the profile this application is compliant to, either an MPEG-4 2D player or an MPEG-4 3D player is launched.
This player is outside the scope of the Project and is taken from the IM-1 group in the MPEG community. However, modification of this player to decode MPEG-J information is in the scope of the Project. We added the MPEG-J decoder which instantiates a Java Virtual Machine in the same address space of the 2D player. This allows the IM-1 2D player with MPEG-J functionality to be independent of the other applications calling it.
The MPEG-J 2D player implements most APIs (Network, Capabilities, Decoder) defined in the MPEG-J subgroup of MPEG, proposed by the Project and accepted, and allows to play both local Java applications and applications contained in the MPEG stream, called MPEG-let.
The MPEG-J 3D player implements also the EAI (External Authoring Interface) API also used in MPEG.

3.4. MPEG-J API

The idea to have a kind of "intelligence" associated with a basic or even complex multimedia application is not new. You can view over the Internet a lot of pages with video, audio, graphics and VRML scenes that can also perform "actions" even in a complex way. Mainly all these functionality are made possible by using a suitable program language to instruct the Web browser (or and independent execution engine). Two program languages are mainly used to associate to Web pages a sort of "intelligence": Java and ECMAScript (was JavaScript) [9] and [10].
In its unifying effort, MPEG-4 took this idea and these tools to describe a powerful framework for a multimedia system suitable both for the broadcast environment (service-driven) and for the Internet (application-driven environment).
To realize the Java based MPEG-4 framework, an Ad Hoc Group was created within MPEG-4 and its name is MPEG-J (MPEG-Java) AHG.

To allow the Java application/applet to interact with the MPEG-4 world, application program interfaces (API's) to the various components of an MPEG-4 terminal are defined. Furthermore, MPEG-J describes the delivery of application programs. Why Java? The choice of the Java language as a means of putting intelligence in MPEG-4 application was driven by a set of considerations that relates to the industrial usability of the MPEG-J system. Features of portability (platform independence) and object orientation have been carefully taken in consideration, but also the Java security model has been appreciated. Moreover, Java is a complete language, providing multithreading capabilities and interfaces to the native platform, a set of features that distinguish it from a basic scripting tool.

3.4.1. The Streaming of the Java Applications in the MPEG-4 Terminal

The byte code, compressed in a zip archive, is streamed as Access Units with time stamps. After the multiplexing of the components in an MPEG-4 stream, this can be delivered to the MPEG-4 terminal to be played. The basic steps for the execution of the MPEG-J Application are described in the following paragraph. The block called "MPEG-J decoder" in figure 4 executes these steps

If an application program is delivered as an MPEG-4 elementary stream, the MPEG-4 Player is notified by the reception of an MPEG-J stream Object Descriptor.

An MPEG-J session can thus be initiated as follow:

1. The MPEG-4 player starts an MPEG-J session. This will involve:
   - Instantiation of the Java Virtual Machine;
   - Instantiation of the Class Loader,
2. The MPEG-J decoder reassembles all the received packets containing MPEG-4 data in order to have the complete MPEG-J application ready to by executed.
3. The MPEG-J decoder loads the application/applet, and starts it. There can be more than one class with an entry point within one MPEG-J stream. Each time such a class containing an entry-point is received (a "run" method), execution will start there as a new thread.

This set of API specifications was submitted to the MPEG-J ad-hoc group on their request for the definition of a minimal set of APIs to control the terminal. Now these API are part of Version 2 of the MPEG-4 standard or the DAVIC/DVB specifications.

3.4.2. The Section Filter API

The objective of the Section Filter API is to provide a general mechanism allowing access to data held in MPEG-2 private sections. A mechanism is provided for inter-operable access to data, which is too specialized to be supported by -for instance- a high level Service Information API or which is not actually related to service information. The aim of the package is to provide a platform-neutral interface, which allows access to the MPEG-2 private sections present in an MPEG-2 Transport Stream. The package allows an application to create section filters, to connect section filters to a section source (Transport Stream) and to manage connecting and disconnecting of resources.

This interface is not displayed as a separate block in figure 4, but is contained in the DVB/SI block.

3.4.3. The Service Information API

The Service Information API allows retrieval and monitoring of SI data. It retrieves information on the network and on the available services from the resident network and service database module. Actually, the API should filter this information from the transport stream when requested, but the data is considered stable enough that using the resident database information is acceptable. The SI API does filter the other tables from the transport stream when requested, by using the PSI/SI database module. It should be mentioned that the Service Information API, the access to the Service Information database, is a specialization of the Section Filter. It can be considered as being implemented on top of the Section Filter. Performance considerations in systems that only require Service Information however might suggest implementing the Service Information directly on the MPEG-2 transport Stream. The Service Information API could on the one hand be considered as an example of a specialized interface to the private section and on the other hand as a recommendation for access to the Service information data when required.

This API is in the DVB/SI standard.

3.4.4. The Network API

The MPEG-J Network API allows simple control and statistical monitoring of the network component of the MPEG-4 player (Access Layer).

Through these APIs Java applications have the possibility of interacting with the Access Layer. This layer manages all the network resources and all the communication channels of the player toward the network (such a module uses the services provided by a particular subsystem of the MPEG-4 player called DMIF - Delivery Multimedia Integration Framework.) [1].

Because the level of abstraction provided by the MPEG-J Network APIs, the applications are unaware of the kind of connections that they are using (connections to LAN, WAN, Broadcast channels, local disks and so on) to access to a service.

The functionality provided by the architectural model that we proposed for the MPEG-J APIs can be split in two major groups:

- Network query: the ability to perform requests to the network module in order to get statistical information about the DMIF resources used by the MPEG-4 player has been recognized as an important feature.
- Channels control: a simple channel control mechanism is also provided. Using this feature an MPEG-J application can temporarily disable or enable existing Elementary Stream channel without any negative influence on the rest of the player. This feature fits with one of the general requirements of MPEG-J, that is, the capability to allow graceful degradation under limited or time varying resources [5].

3.4.5. The Terminal Capability & Profiles API

Program execution may be contingent upon the terminal configuration and its capabilities. An MPEG-J application may need to be aware of its environment, so that it can adapt its own execution and the execution of the various components, as they may be configured and running in the MPEG-4 terminal. The Terminal Capability API is responsible to provide access to dynamic and static terminal resources. A separation between static and dynamic terminal capabilities has been reflected in the API. As applications need to be notified when terminal capabilities change, an additional interface for that purpose has been defined (terminal capabilities could change dynamically when non MPEG-4 related applications run with the MPEG-4 terminal at the same time). Depending of the hosting machine it is possible that other running applications exist beyond the MPEG-4 one (for PC platform as an example but for Set Top Boxes this may not be true).

The purpose of the Profile API is to provide a facility that allows applications to find out what is the profile/level supported by the terminal where the application runs. Because profiles/levels are defined in the MPEG-4 standard and an application knows the terminal profile/level it can decide how to behave and what capabilities can operate in the terminal environment.4.   The Security in the Terminal

One of the key features in the terminal we are working on is the introduction of some security features. There are several aspects that must be considered here. From the service provider point of view, what matters when audiovisual information and applications are distributed in a digital format is to restrict the access to the legitimate users and to control the copying capabilities of the end-user device, e.g. the possibility to create copies perfectly identical to the received ones. For the Author is the knowledge of the use of its masterpieces that should be traced. From the users' perspective is the possibility of accessing several services of a plurality of providers by means of a unique device that is considered relevant. These aspects, and others too, are being considered by the Open Platform Initiative for Multimedia Access (OPIMA). The Open Platform Initiative for Multimedia Access (OPIMA) "has been set up to develop specifications enabling a consumer to obtain a receiver and begin to consume and pay for services, without having prior knowledge of which services would be consumed, in a simple way such as by operating a remote control device". Concerning the OPIMA platform it "is targeted at providing value-chain participants the ability to acquire, supply, process and consume multi-media services on a worldwide basis in accordance with the rights associated with these services. OPIMA specifically addresses intellectual property management and protection".

The solutions to the problems embedded in the scopes stated above are not trivial and may have a profound impact on the architecture of the terminal itself. The current opinion is that simply specifying the communication interfaces among the terminal modules or components cannot provide a suitable level of security, but the modules themselves must internally obey to certain rules. In addition the Operating System should provide some basic security functions as native services.

The SOMMIT partners have already forwarded proposals to OPIMA aimed at the definition of a service architecture capable of satisfying the related requirements.

The first contribution describes a solution to achieve the OPIMA goal of an open platform for multimedia access, based on an enhanced version of the DAVIC CA1 interface specification. The goal is reached by adding an open API to the security processing device (Smart Card), in such a way that any Service-Provider specific code could be downloaded into the Smart Card. The Java Card 2.0 API is proposed as the standard open interface to access the basic security functions of the smart card, in a card-independent way. The solution is backward compatible with the DAVIC CA1 and CA0 (DVB) interface specifications. Moreover, it is based on existing standards that can be easily adopted and integrated.

In the second proposal the Java VM is directly inserted in the terminal architecture. This change generates a major impact in terms of greater flexibility of the terminal that can directly execute different content management and protection systems at the cost of requiring a more powerful protection mechanism for the downloading and execution of the Java code.

SOMMIT, due to time and resources constraints, only wants to deal with those parts of the security related to the access to different services supplied by a plurality of providers with a unique device.

It is not in the SOMMIT workplan to modify the OS in such a way to support the four processes that are necessary to implement the OPIMA security. What will be done is to emulate those functions at the application layer. This can be used to check the whole security processes and verify the completeness and consistency of the OPIMA interface specifications.

4. Conclusions and Future Work

In this paper we have described a new approach to the multimedia communications based on the MPEG-4 and MPEG-2 standards and on Java technology. A complex EPG application has successfully validated the requirements for the architecture to implement new service scenarios.

The contribution made by the SOMMIT project to MPEG-4 and DAVIC/DVB, jointly with the efforts provided by all the others companies involved in the standardization groups, allowed the achievement of concrete results in multimedia standardization. In some cases the Project has anticipated the new standardization activities for integration of different technologies, such as the AIC Initiative, and has shown suitable applications to prove the concepts.

During this work we learnt that a lot of effort is still needed to reach a complete and more powerful multimedia framework. New tools and services could be developed and the old ones re-invented with a suitable standard that allows full interoperability among different environments (e.g.: broadcast vs. point-to-point) and products (developed by whatever industry).

Future developments of this work involve studies on applications and services that could benefit from the described terminal architecture. SOMMIT is currently developing other applications for its terminal, such as the "Buy me button" example, and is working further on the integration in a single environment of the HTML browser, MPEG-2 and MPEG-4.

Moreover, one of the key features in the terminal we are working on is the introduction of the security. As one of the SOMMIT aims is to build a terminal compliant to the standards, we aim at following the specifications of one of the most promising standardization fora, OPIMA, that allows the same terminal to be open to many service providers and services.

The present implementation is based on a PC platform that is indeed the most suitable environment for new developments: according to the SOMMIT workplan we have however started the porting of some of the new capabilities (namely MPEG-4) on a STB prototype. It is, in fact, the STB consumer equipment category that will ultimately provide the above applications to the users.

5. Acknowledgments

The authors would like to thank all the people that allowed the achievement of the results described in this document, namely all the partners of the SOMMIT Consortium: CSELT (Italy), Finsiel (Italy), SIA (Italy), Philips (Netherlands) and CCETT (France).

The Consortium acknowledges the European Commission DG XIII for having supported these research activities in the SOMMIT Project AC033, in the framework of the ACTS Programme.

6. References

1. ISO/IEC FCD 14496-6 Information technology- Generic coding of moving pictures and associated audio information- Part 6: Delivery Multimedia Integration Framework, 1998
2. ISO/IEC JTC1/SC29/WG11 N2358 MPEG-4 System Version 2 Overview July 1998
3. ISO/IEC JTC1/SC29/WG11 MPEG 98 Response to the request for APIs of the MPEG-J AHG May 1998
4. ISO/IEC JTC1/SC29/WG11 N2358p3 Text for WD3.0 System Version 2(MPEG-J) July 1998
5. ISO/IEC JTC1/SC29/WG11 N2456 MPEG-4 Requirements, version 10, December 1998
6. ISO/IEC, MPEG-4 Profile Requirements Version 5, ISO/IEC JTC1/SC29/WG11, MPEG97/1899, October 1997
7. Leonardo Chiariglione, MPEG and multimedia communications, CSELT, ICSE96, August 1996 (Internet public link: drogo.cselt.stet.it/ufv/leonardo/paper/isce96.htm)
8. Jean H.A. Gelissen, BALI, a broadcast application library interface, IBC98, September 1998

9. James Gosling, Bill Joy Guy Steele, The Java Language Specification, Addison-Wesley

10. Standard ECMA-262, ECMAScript Language Specification, 2nd Edition, August 98 (Internet public link: www.ecma.ch)

11. Rob Koenen, MPEG4 – Multimedia for our time, IEEE Spectrum, February 99 Vol.36 No.2

12. http://java.sun.com/docs/codeconv/html/CodeConventionsTOC.doc.html

13. ISO/IEC JTC1/SC29/WG11/N2614 MPEG-4 Intellectual Property Management & Protection (IPMP) Overview & Applications Document MPEG 98 December 1998

14. MPEG-4 official site: http://www.cselt.it/mpeg

15. ETSI standard ETS 300 468 "Service Information"

16. AICI Home Page in internet: http://toocan.philabs.research.philips.com/misc/aici

17. ISO/IEC IS 13818-1 Information technology- Generic coding of moving pictures and associated audio information- Part 1: Systems

18. http://toocan.philabs.research.philips.com:81/Get/File-70/AIC-I.Applications.Final.doc

Appendix: Acronyms

API: Application Programming Interface
AHG: Ad Hoc Group
AVO: Audio Visual Object
DMIF: Delivery Multimedia Integration Framework
FCD: Final Committee Draft
GUI: Graphical User Interface
MPEG: Moving Pictures Expert Group
MPEG-J: MPEG-4 Java based
QoS: Quality of Service
STB: Set Top Box
STU: Set Top Unit
URL: Unified Resource Locator
VRML: Virtual Reality Modeling Language

An Approach for Script-Based Broadcast Application Production

Andreas Kraft, Klaus Hofrichter

GMD FOKUS – Kaiserin Augusta Allee 31 – D-10589 Berlin – Germany
Kraft@fokus.gmd.de, Hofrichter@fokus.gmd.de

Abstract. Digital television services are now available in various countries in Europe and throughout the world featuring applications such as *Electronic Program Guide* and *Digital Teletext*. Future applications will combine television, real-time data broadcast and eventually Internet access to offer value-added services and Electronic Commerce applications for the residential use. This paper discusses possible approaches to implement and to manage applications for enhanced digital television services which exploit the broadcast technology by adding interactivity and multimedia. A production system is described, which provides means to address the specific characteristics of the broadcast environment. The ideas presented in this paper stem from the experience gained during the ACTS IMMP Project.

Introduction

The target audience for applications designed for the digital television are residential users – an audience which is entertainment oriented and not necessarily experienced with computer applications. The viewing environment is the living area, the client devices are consumer electronics: a television set, with a digital television decoder and a remote control for navigation within the television programs and the application. This environment introduces specific requirements for the application production.

It is necessary to consider that the digital television technology is designed in the first place to provide television services – plain television viewing is the most prominent usage. The applications which are additionally made available via the digital television technology have to keep this paradigm, which has an noteworthy impact on the design of digital television applications: The navigation within the application should allow to change to full-screen television at any time, and the user has most likely the expectation to "be entertained" instead of taking an active role while viewing television. This pattern may change in the long run as the services evolve, moving towards increased user involvement. But the pattern remains valid for the vast majority of applications in short and medium time-scale. The applications need also to provide a very simple user interface, which can be controlled via a remote control. The graphical user interface should be intuitive and should not rely on complex user interface elements such as scroll-bars or pop-up menus. Ideally, applications are as easy to use as a telephone.

A classical application for the digital television, the Electronic Program Guide (EPG), fits very well into the outlined environment. An EPG is supposed to support the navigation within a large number of television channels by presenting a listing of available television channels. A typical EPG application displays the current and upcoming events in the TV stations schedule. Depending on the design of the EPG the user may be able to filter the offer according to preferences such as "news" or "movies", to request additional information such as the headlines or a summary, or to tune to a selected television channel. The EPG information source depends on the systems design. The EPG may utilise DVB-Service Information, data broadcast, object carrousel, or on-line connections via modem to access the television schedule information.

Another common application is Digital Teletext. This application relies on the object carrousel to make the application data available on the client: the service provider inserts application data periodically in a carrousel-like transmission mechanism to the DVB data stream. The client has to wait for the requested application part until it is scheduled in the carrousel. This mechanism involves delays for the application presentation, but relieves the client from caching or complete application retrieval. It depends on the functionality of the client platform to which extend television viewing is integrated to Teletext applications: advanced platforms allow to control the video display as part of the application presentation.

The visual quality of the services offered by such applications depends on the technical capabilities of the client and the technology used for the application production itself. The functionality of the client is under discussion in various consortia and organisations such as DVB, ATSC, and AICI (see the reference list at the end of the paper). This paper concentrates on the production environment for the applications. The approach described here is not tightly related to a certain client technology. Instead, it aims to introduce an abstract application format which is mapped to the constraints of the concrete technology when needed.

The next section distinguishes between static, semi-static and dynamic applications. The authoring techniques and the suggested approach are described after this, together with a generic architecture for the application production. A conclusion and a list of references closes the paper.

Application and Page Types

From an authors and broadcasters point of view, there are at least three different types of applications. The difference here is how they are produced and stored on the server. A page-oriented application design is assumed for the following considerations.

- **Static pages** are produced once and stay unchanged for a long time on the server. Help pages, introduction pages, or product information pages are examples for this type. They are produced once and are only updated when some of the information on a page need to be changed.
- **Semi-static pages** consist of a static and a dynamic part. For most applications, the static part defines the framework and the layout of the pages, but leaves room for the dynamically generated content data. The previously mentioned EPG, the display of stock market information, or weather forecast are typical areas where this kind of page production is being used.
- **Dynamic pages** are produced every time when the information is requested. This might be necessary when the layout of the pages change depending on the content, or when the layout is determined dynamically during the production process. Examples for dynamic generated pages are personalised information pages like a shopping catalogue, or result pages of a search engine where additional related information are offered beside the actual search result.

Most of today's digital television applications consist of pages of at least one of the above types. A warehouse application is a good example where static pages are used for the product sheets to describe the offered goods, and dynamic pages are used to display information about the number of currently available pieces and prices.

The production of web-content and broadcast applications has certain commonalties. Though this paper concentrates on the specific aspects of the broadcast environment, it can be noted that some authoring techniques described later in this paper are also suitable for WWW applications.

There are various requirements for the authoring and production of an application which have to be addressed. Due to the limited bandwidth in a broadcast environment it is very important to produce bandwidth efficient applications. The smaller the applications are in size, the more applications can be inserted into a broadcast carousel. The general expectation is that the users should not wait more than 20 to 25 seconds for a page to be displayed after request in a Teletext-like application. The resulting bandwidth yields about 3 to 1.5 Mbyte available for applications, since the network operators in digital television environments assign typically between 1.000 and 500 Kbit per second for the object carrousel.

The bandwidth is used for application data and content data. Measurements have shown that the usage of rich multimedia content data has the most impact on the required bandwidth. The application data, which defines the functionality and navigation facilities of the application does not contribute significant to the application size. Due to that the number of pages available in the object carrousel depends much on the graphical design goals of the authoring process. Two typical design approaches are displayed below.

Background images and advertisement graphics

18.000 byte advertisement
60.000 byte text and background
850 byte application data

Yielding 37 pages in 3 Mbyte bandwidth

 Welcome to the Digital Television Group

Welcome to the DTG Information Application. The DTG represents over 70 companies working to bring digital television to the UK. Digital television will bring you more choice, both in free-to-air and new subscription services, higher quality sound and pictures, including more widescreen programming and exciting new interactive services.

Over the past 2 years, the DTG has been active setting the technical standards for digital terrestrial television. Now it is working to ensure that the new broadcasts conform to those standards and that new receivers work the way they should. It will also be providing marketing support for the retail trade.

Text-only content and small logo bitmap (shared across multiple pages)

400 byte text content (compressed)
400 byte application data
Yielding 3750 pages in 3 Mbyte bandwidth

Fig. 1. Two examples for different layouts and sizes of Teletext applications

Real-world applications will probably meet a compromise between these extreme designs. Please note that the application data volume does not change much for the displayed pages. The increased size of the application data for the left example is a result of more layout efforts and the clock and date display in the upper right corner.

The application data format does not have too much impact either. The use of formats such as MHEG, HTML/JavaScript or Java does not change the bandwidth utilisation. However, in case of the usage of Java it is important that the client system has the presentation class hierarchy pre-installed. Due to the bandwidth limitations and the fairly large Java library code, it is not advisable to distribute the complete application processing code. In the example above it is assumed that the Java byte-code for individual pages provides only instructions the layout and the behaviour specific for the separate pages. A declarative or scripted application format provides advantages, since the interpreter code is anyway residentially installed on the clients device.

There are many possibilities to optimise the bandwidth utilisation at authoring time: the usage of graphic elements for pages which concentrate on information presentation (e.g. stock market information) and not on the layout of the pages can be reduced. Usually, additional layout elements like coloured shapes or background and supporting graphics which add heavily to the size of an application are not vital. The idea for such applications is to utilise only a reduced set of layout procedures.

A table, for example, can be pre-formatted during the production. Instead of using texts for every part of the data in every column, only one string per row can be displayed. Another approach could be the transmission of a script which computes and produces a page on the client side. Careful measurements have to be made to determine the optimal transmission size.

However, sometimes an appealing layout of the pages is very important. Advertisements or similar application areas are very layout centric. Here, the application might not be complex from a computational point of view, but is still large in size because of the additional layout information and probably the graphical content. The careful placement in a carousel stream is important. It is, for example, perhaps possible to transmit those applications only every other round in the stream.

Another type of application utilises interactive pages. Here, scripts or other means must be implemented in the application in order to perform checking the users input and to react on it. This might increase the size of pages tremendously. It also might be very difficult to automatically create such a complex scene by using a template-like mechanism. However, it is possible to reuse building blocks to perform simple tasks, like, for example, validating the users input in an entry field.

Architecture

This section describes the embedding of the production environment on the left into the complete system architecture.

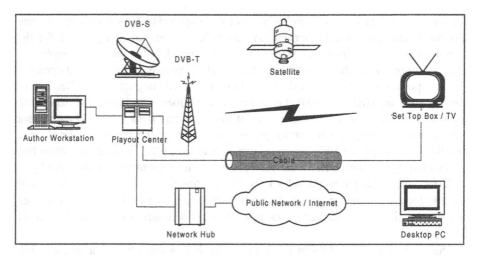

Fig. 2. Authoring for transmission methods and target platforms

Figure 2 illustrates the authoring station on the left, which delivers application data to the play-out centre. The data is transmitted to the clients via broadcast (DVB via satellite, cable, or terrestrial). The same application data is available via online networks such as Internet utilising ISDN or ATM/ADSL. The play-out centre converts the application to be suitable for the capabilities of the target system.

This approach allows to reuse the same content source for both on-line and broadcast environments. However, these environments require different application designs, which have an impact on the functionality as well: the authors have to consider substantial differences, in particular the bandwidth limitations for the broadcast, the missing back-channel, the different capabilities of the display client, and – perhaps most important – the distribution model: broadcast applications are always pushed to the client, and the client has to pick the actually requested information from the data-stream. On-line services such as the WWW are following a pull-model and can provide customized information, which results in a completely different service offer. The real-time capabilities of the broadcast environment (i.e. the application can be tightly synchronized with the TV program) provides functionality which is not available in the Web, and which has also an impact for the application design.

Please note that the application may be generated for different application domains utilising the same data source. The approach described below allows to define the applications functionality independent of the interchange method and interchange format. However, optimisation of the applications is required for each distribution channel individually.

Authoring Techniques

The different types of applications presented above requires different kind of application authoring techniques. It is required to differentiate between directly authoring of an application and publishing, and continuous application production, which is the usual method for template based applications.

Direct authoring is done manually by an application author page by page. Here, an authoring tool is used, which offers facilities to create multimedia objects and arrange them on the scene. Most tools also offer means to administrate the whole application, e.g. the transition between the different parts of an application. Those tools are, however, limited to a predefined set of functionality. An author can usually not perform special tasks with the tool, but has to program the application "by hand". This is not always possible, because the system may prevent direct access, and the author has to have specific knowledge about the system.

Another kind of authoring is to facilitate templates and building blocks, and to combine them in an authoring tool. The actual layout of an application is designed by an expert. Only predefined areas in the template can be filled with content for each page separately, or actions which are allowed by the template can be selected. An authoring tool supporting this approach can be fairly simple because is only has to support the application author filling in the gaps.

This authoring technique has the advantage of leading to stable and predictable applications, because an application author has no access to the underlying mechanisms of the applications. He provides the content data, and can change only some of the content attributes like, for example, the colour of a text.

An enhancement to this technique is to provide the same means for automated authoring. Here again, the framework is supplied by an expert who designs the templates. The places where the content data should be inserted later are marked by special elements. During the production process, the elements are replaced with the actual content data by a filter program which can produce the application.

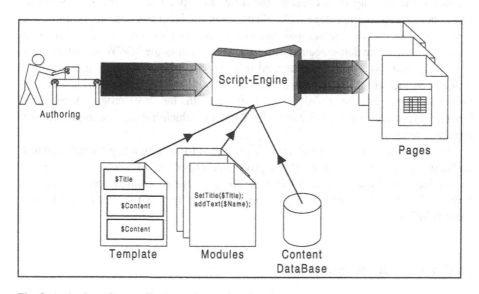

Fig. 3. Authoring of an application using various input sources

This way it is easily possible to build applications which have a mixture of static parts (like, for example, an introduction screen) as well as dynamically generated pages.

This method is well suited for applications which input data can be directly used without much calculations. Another refinement is to combine the template method with a scripting language. A template may define the general structure and layout of the application, but the content data is processed or created by scripts. This way, it is easy to perform conversions on content data before inserting it into the template. Using only the general template method, the data is most often pushed to the template process. Using scripts, the input data can not only be process, but additional input can be retrieved different sources.

Besides the mentioned advantages, this method, however, has also some disadvantages. The whole system must be managed very carefully, and a very high standard for quality assurance and testing must be set. Because of the scripting facility, programming and design errors can be harder detected in advance.

Authoring Environment with Script Support

This section describes a system which utilises a mixture between templates and scripting to produce interactive multimedia applications in various formats. The input for the application generator and the script interpreter consists of a number of scripts which contain procedures to assign content to pages. The layout of the pages is defined by a sequence of procedures. The following figure is an example for a simple script.

```
setTitle("Greetings");        % Set the page title
addText("Hello, World");      % Display greeting
for (i = 0; i < 5; i++)       % Append 5 empty lines
        addText("");
addText("Press Button to continue"); % Instructions

% Initialise the green button to jump to the next page
setButton(BT_Green, "Continue", nextScene);
```

Fig. 4. Script example

An expert designer has provided a set of procedures which can be used for the page design. The marked keywords in the box above are example of such procedures. The procedures assign data to a layout which is prepared by the expert. The *setTitle()* procedure, for example, sets the title for a page. How this is done and what the appearance of the page title actually is, is independent from the script. This way, an abstract authoring method can be used to describe the contents of scenes. How the pages are created is up to the script interpreter.

Procedures can also perform more complex tasks. The *setButton()* procedure in the example above is intended to provide some means to display the string *"Continue"* (with a Green background, if possible), and to create some kind of link which loads and starts the next scene.

An additional functionality of scripting is to provide an interface to external data to the production process. The following example shows a part of a script which creates a new page out of database entries. For this, pseudo-variables are used to refer to the fields of a data record.

```
addText("Name:      " + $name);    % Display the name
addText("Address:   " + $address); % the address
addText("Telephone: " + $telephone); % the phone number
addText("E-mail:    " + $email);   % the e-mail address
```

Fig. 5. Example of a template to display the fields of an address record

This script displays some address information taken from, for example, an address data base. The input data could be formatted in XML. The following figure shows an example for this:

```
<ADDRESS>
          <name>Lewis Carrol</name>
          <address>3, Wonderland</address>
          <telephone>555 2305</telephone>
          <email>lcarrol@alice.wl</email>
</ADDRESS>
```

Fig. 6. Sample input data

The advantage of this scripting approach is that it is highly flexible and configurable. By including other, predefined procedures, the demand for building blocks can be satisfied. This way it is possible to include procedures for forms, tables, or even simple games.

Conclusion

This paper comprises an introduction to the application types for digital television under consideration of the specific constrains of the broadcast environment. It turns out that the authoring process is of major influence for the performance of the application in terms of transmission speed. It is suggested to utilise scripted application production to include dynamic content to the application and to meet requirements of the target environment. Measurements done during example application design and trials provide valuable data to achieve optimal results during the authoring process.

Most of the work described in this paper is carried out within the framework of the ACTS IMMP project. One of the goals of the IMMP project to provide groundwork for future competitive authoring processes which exploit applications for digital television environments and broadcast networks as much as possible. It is possible to develop the outlined authoring system based on the results of the IMMP project.

Acknowledgements and References

This section comprises a list of references to important documents. A list of resources in the WWW with further information with relevance for the digital television closes the paper.

References

ISO/IEC IS 13522-5, Information technology — Coding of Multimedia and Hypermedia information — Part 5: MHEG Subset for Base Level Implementation.

ISO/IEC IS 13818-6, Information technology — Generic coding of moving pictures and associated audio information — Part 6: Extensions for Digital Storage Media Command and Control

Digital Terrestrial Television MHEG-5 Specification, version 1.04

EN 50221 Common Interface Specification for Conditional Access and other Digital Video Broadcasting Decoder Applications

ETS 300 706, Enhanced Teletext Specification

Resources

DVB: Digital Video Broadcast: *http://www.dvb.org*

ATSC: Advanced Television Standards Committee: *http://www.atsc.org*

AICI: Advanced Interactive Content Initiative:
http://toocan.philabs.research.philips.com/misc/aici

ATVEF: Advanced Television Enhancement Forum: *http://www.atvef.com*

DAVIC: Digital Audio-Visual Council: *http://www.davic.org*

W3C: World Wide Web consortium: http://www.w3.org/MarkUp/Activity.html

IMMP: Integrated Multimedia Project: *http://www-nrc.nokia.com/immp/*

IMMP: GMD FOKUS IMMP page: http://www.fokus.gmd.de/magic/projects/immp

MHEG-5 UG: MHEG-5 users Group: http://www.fokus.gmd.de/ovma/mug

The MHEG Centre: The MHEG Centre: http://www.fokus.gmd.de/magic/projects/ovma

GMD FOKUS – MAGIC: http://www.fokus.gmd.de/magic

The ATLANTIC Audio Demonstration System

A.J. Mason and N.J. Yeadon

BBC Research & Development
Kingswood Warren, Surrey
andrew.mason@rd.bbc.co.uk   nick.yeadon@rd.bbc.co.uk

Abstract. A broadcast programme production chain using compressed media is now feasible. The problem of quality degradation from successive decode/encode operations is well documented. The ATLANTIC project aims to use compressed data-streams as the standard encoding throughout the post-production and distribution chain without compromising technical quality. This paper describes a system that demonstrates how cascading can be avoided in the post-production and editing environment and, where cascading is unavoidable, how codec coding decisions can be hidden in a decoded PCM bit-stream and reused to minimise quality loss.

1   Introduction

The ATLANTIC project [1, 2] was started with the aim of developing the technologies required for the use of MPEG compressed signals throughout the programme production, distribution and emission chain. Underlying this are the themes of developing a network infrastructure based on ATM using standard TCP/IP communication protocols together with the means of handling MPEG coded signals without unnecessary deterioration in quality [3, 4].

Using standard IT protocols and networks allows the administrative and programme production technology to co-exist. The quality of service guarantees that are required by real-time applications associated with the replay or recording of audio or video signals can be made using ATM. This can be achieved if the facility to negotiate with the network management software can be made through the TCP/IP protocol stack. The work of INESC was directed at this problem.

Unnecessary programme technical quality deterioration is avoided by keeping the signals in their compressed form as much as is possible. Techniques have been developed to help maintain quality where decoding and re-encoding is unavoidable [5, 6]. This area has been investigated by the BBC and FhG.

This paper describes the results of the work in audio processing that were demonstrated at IBC in September 1998. Hardware and software from the ATLANTIC partners BBC, INESC, and Snell and Wilcox were successfully combined to produce a working demonstration.

There were two audio demonstration areas. One showed an editing system using a commercially available non-MPEG editing system connected to a computer network of servers and an off-line MPEG edit conformer. The other showed the "lossless" cascading of MPEG codecs used to route an MPEG audio signal through a conventional digital audio mixer. The first demonstration is a model of what might be used in a programme post-production area. The second is a model of a presentation, continuity or playout suite.

2   ATLANTIC Editing

The ATLANTIC editing or post-production model is made up of relatively cheap, standard desktop PC-based, audio editing systems connected to a number of file servers by a network. Also on the network is a dedicated "edit conformer". This is shown in Fig. 1.

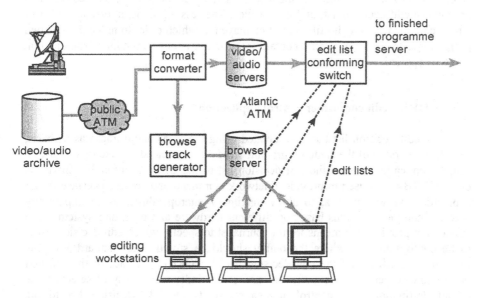

Fig. 1. ATLANTIC post-production model

The way in which a journalist, for example, would produce a programme is as follows. Editing is done on the desktop PC editing workstation, the "journalist's workstation", working with decoded MPEG audio tracks stored on the "browse server". The edit decision list is then sent to the edit conformer which makes an MPEG version of the same programme using the original MPEG coded material stored on the edit source server. Doing the conforming using the original MPEG source avoids re-encoding the decoded material that was used during the editing process. The finished programme as shown is stored on another server. (In the IBC demonstration, the finished programme was sent directly to a decoder for auditioning in real time).

3 User Interfaces

The journalist's workstation in our demonstration was a Pentium PC running Windows NT. It was a standard machine equipped with built-in audio interface and a 10baseT Ethernet interface.

3.1 Desktop PC editing system

The editing software was Cool Edit Pro from Syntrillium — a program commonly used within the BBC. The editing could be done using linear PCM audio files downloaded onto the local hard disc, or accessed over the Ethernet network. Using Cool Edit Pro in its multitrack mode causes it to do non-destructive editing and produce an edit decision list, or "session file". The session file is, in essence, a list of which parts of which audio files are to be played in which order to make the finished programme. In addition, it may contain information about amplitude variations that are to be applied.

3.2 CORBA edit conformer control application

Once the edit decision list has been created using the PCM audio tracks as its basis, the MPEG version of the same programme needs to be created. The journalist uses a simple application to send the edit decision list to the edit conformer for this to be done. CORBA was used to provide a network command and control interface for an application written in Java, to allow maximum interoperability and compatibility between computer systems based on different hardware and operating systems. The application provides the means for the journalist to specify which edit decision list is to be conformed, and where the output should be stored. The standard Java file dialogue is used to find the edit decision list. A CORBA interface to the finished programme server provides a network and server independent way of selecting the output destination. The control application sends the edit decision list to the conformer together with identifiers for the edit source server and finished programme servers. The edit conformer, the source and finished programme servers are all CORBA objects on the network. All can be chosen using the control application. A typical screen shot of Cool Edit Pro and the edit conformer control application is shown in Fig. 2.

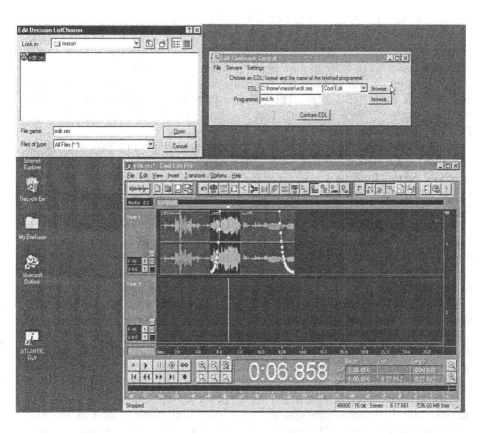

Fig. 2. Screen shot of 'Cool Edit Pro' and the conformer application

4 Networking

A mixed network connected the various pieces of IT equipment that were used. High speed links were made using an ATM network. Classical IP and AAL 5 were used on this. Lower speed links used conventional 10baseT Ethernet and TCP/IP.

For example, the file servers and edit conforming switch were connected by 155 Mbps ATM for the transfer of the MPEG source data, but the journalist's workstation needed only 10baseT for the transfer of the edit decision list and CORBA commands.

5 Audio edit conformer hardware system

The audio edit conformer is a signal processing box, connected to a MPEG file server by an ATM network, producing a real-time output of decoded MPEG audio. It responds to commands sent using CORBA, appearing as it does as a CORBA object to other machines on the network. The main service that it offers as a CORBA object is the conforming of MPEG audio data stored on the edit source server according to an edit decision list supplied as a parameter in the service request.

The structure of the conformer is shown in Fig. 3. The heart of the signal processing is the PCI/C44S card. This contains 4 TMS320C44 DSP chips to perform the manipulation of the MPEG data. This is mounted inside a PCI bus-based Pentium PC running under Linux.

The CORBA server is implemented by code written for the PC. This receives the edit decision list (in "native" format from the journalist's workstation), pre-processes it into an internal format and stores it on the local disc drive. Next it sends a command to the DSPs to conform the edit decision list. How this is achieved will be described later.

The DSP's require access to the MPEG audio files on the edit source server. This is made possible by a program, of a type usually referred to as a "host server", running on the PC. This provides a relay service for requests for data from files, output of characters to the screen, input of keystrokes from the keyboard, and so on. It provides to the DSP the services that are available to a program running on the host.

For use in a Linux environment some modifications were made to a commercially available host server programme. This also entailed the writing of a device driver to establish communication between the host server program and the DSP card. As is shown on the diagram, communication between host server and DSP takes place via an area of shared memory accessible on the PCI bus. Access to this memory area is established through calls to the device driver.

Both the host server program and the CORBA server program use the shared memory area to communicate with the DSP. Part of the area is used by the host server, and part by the CORBA server. A simple mailbox message exchange system is used.

The MPEG stream assembled from the various source files required, together with edits, fades etc. is transmitted out of an AES/EBU interface in IEC 61937 [7] format. For ease of demonstration, this AES/EBU stream is sent straight to a decoder. This decoder was implemented on another signal processing card, hosted by the same PC. In this case, the only facility provided by the PC is that of loading and starting the DSP code to do the decoding.

6 ATM interface

As was mentioned earlier, the edit source server is connected to an ATM network. One of the partners in the ATLANTIC project wrote a Linux device driver for a commercially available ATM card (a Fore Systems PCA200E). With this it is possible for the edit source server files to be accessed using a standard NFS protocol. The directory containing the MPEG audio files on the server can simply be mounted as part of the Linux PC's file system. However, using this mechanism there were no quality of service guarantees for data transfer. For this to be implemented properly would require a little more sophistication in the way that the DSP accessed the data from the server. For demonstration purposes, 0.25s of buffering was provided in the signal processing path to overcome anticipated network latencies.

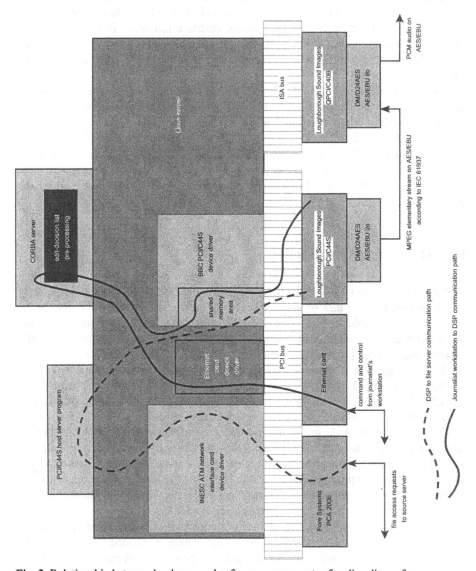

Fig. 3. Relationship between hardware and software components of audio edit conformer

7 Cascadable MPEG audio coding

A well known problem with low bit-rate coding systems is that repeated coding and decoding reduces the technical quality of the signal. Unfortunately there are times when this is unavoidable. An example of this is where a signal originating in MPEG form [8], to be transmitted in MPEG form, has to pass through an existing broadcast infrastructure which contains a conventional linear PCM mixing console.

The solution to this problem is "mole-assisted re-encoding". In anticipation of a downstream re-encoding, an MPEG decoder inserts information from the bitstream that it is decoding into its PCM output. This information, called a "mole", is then used by the downstream encoder to try to recreate an MPEG bitstream identical to the one given to the decoder.

The information that an MPEG audio encoder needs to recreate the original bitstream is, primarily, the bit-allocations and scale-factors. The subband sample values themselves are not required because these can be derived fairly accurately from the PCM signal.

As part of the ATLANTIC project, demonstration versions of a mole-generating decoder and a mole-assisted encoder have been developed. These show that the mole can be imperceptibly inserted into the PCM and can be recovered and used by the encoder.

8   Mole generating decoder

The extra task required of the decoder to generate and insert the mole is a relatively small overhead on the task of actually decoding the audio signal. All the data in the mole is readily available during the decoding process. Information from the MPEG header (for example number of channels and bit-rate), the bit-allocations and scale-factors have all been processed at some stage. The way in which this data is carried by the PCM signal is intended to reduce its audibility (relative to simpler schemes).

One bit of mole data is carried, in each sample of the PCM signal. The parity of each PCM sample used is modified so as to signal the value of a single bit of mole data. Odd parity indicates a "zero", even parity indicates a "one". The parity modification can be done in one of the lesser significant bits of the PCM sample depending on the resolution of the channel through which the signal has to go. Almost all digital audio equipment transmits at least 16 bits, some 20 bits and some 24 bits. Our demonstration equipment used the 16th bit — inaudible in most circumstances. It should be pointed out that the mole would only be present in a studio decoder output: a domestic decoder would have no need to insert the mole.

The exact mechanism by which the mole is carried is currently being reviewed as part of the international standardisation process. Other mechanisms, including the masking of the mole bit within dither are under investigation and may be found to be more suitable, less complex, or both.

The mole data consists of about 600 bits for each frame of MPEG data. Each MPEG frame is decoded to 1152 PCM samples (per channel) and these samples carry the mole data derived from the MPEG data. However, the delay through the synthesis filterbank in the decoder complicates the task of identifying exactly which 1152 PCM samples came from which MPEG frame. This has been done and the details are contained in the audio mole specification [9].

9 The decoder demonstration hardware system

The demonstration mole-generating decoder is based on TMS320C40 DSP chips on a proprietary signal processing board. This board is mounted in a PC to provide it with power and the means to have code loaded into it and run. It also allows the display of diagnostic messages during the development of the software.

A diagram of the decoder hardware is shown in Fig 4. The DSP card is connected to a number of peripheral cards. One of these is an RS-422 interface card on which the MPEG elementary stream is received. Another is an AES/EBU digital audio interface card on which the decoded audio output (including mole data) is transmitted. The third, the so-called "SSTC" receiver is associated with synchronisation which will be discussed in more detail later.

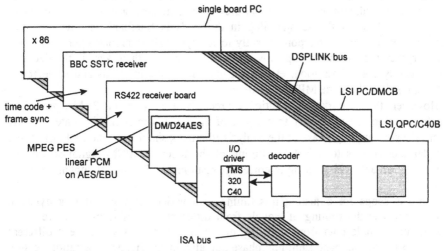

Fig. 4. Experimental ATLANTIC mole-generating audio decoder

There are two DSP's involved in the decoding operation. One of them simply handles the input and output of data (coded and decoded). The second performs the actual decoding operations.

In a commercial realisation of a decoder, all these processes would be performed by a single chip. However, it is easier during development to have the extra processing power available. In fact, it was the provision of reliable input and output that was the most difficult part of the construction. The PC's own RS-422 port could not be made to work reliably at the relatively high sustained data rate required (coupled with the need to transfer this data through the PC's operating system and a host server program to the DSP). The AES/EBU output also proved troublesome at higher sample resolutions.

The process of adding the mole to the output PCM signal amounted to about 24 instructions per sample — a small computational overhead compared to the rest of the decoding task.

The audibility of the mole (an issue in the studio environment only) was found to be acceptable except in extreme cases, even when put in the 16th bit.

10 Mole-assisted encoding

In the same way that an MPEG encoder is more complex and allows more flexibility in the design of the algorithms within it than a decoder, so the mole aspects of the encoder are more complex and allow more flexibility than those of the decoder.

The mole data should allow the mole-assisted encoder to generate the same MPEG bitstream from the PCM signal that was originally decoded by the mole-generating decoder. Simple things, such as having to encode at a lower bit-rate than the original MPEG stream, mean that the mole data has to be used selectively. Other, more subtle, problems require handling too.

Assuming that the mole data has been detected and extracted from the PCM signal, the next stage of processing is the analysis filterbank. This separates the signal into 32 subbands, and subsamples each band 32:1. The subband samples are not transmitted in the mole signal, so it is essential that they are regenerated properly from the PCM signal. The phase of the subsampling in the analysis filterbank is crucial in this respect. If it does not correspond exactly to the synthesis filterbank operation in the decoder, then the subband samples will not be the same as they were in the decoder. Consequently the quantisation, even using the same bit-allocations and scalefactors will not result in the same MPEG bitstream.

However, the mole data is positioned precisely in time in the PCM signal. The synchronisation preamble that forms part of the mole data frame indicates exactly where the subsampling phase of the analysis filterbank should be. The first task of the encoder therefore is to adjust the timing of the incoming PCM signal so that its analysis filterbank will subsample correctly, resulting in the correct subband sample values.

There is scope for adjusting this timing in a variety of ways. It is a dynamic process because the routing of signals from different sources is likely to result in discontinuous mole data from time to time. A new signal may require a different delay to bring the subband sampling phase into alignment. The demonstration version uses a simple linear interpolation mechanism to avoid clicks caused by simply dropping or repeating samples. More sophisticated, pitch-invariant, delay changing mechanisms could be used if necessary. There is a trade-off between the speed with which the encoder can adjust to a new phase of mole data and the perceptibility of the process of adjustment.

Once the subband samples are being produced correctly it should be possible to scale them using the scale-factors contained in the mole and then quantise them according to the bit-allocations in the mole. However, it has been found that small inaccuracies in the synthesis, truncation for output and analysis processes can lead to errors in the subband sample values. It is possible for these to go out of range of the quantiser when the relevant scale-factor has been applied. A check needs to be made to ensure that the scaled subband sample values are still valid and appropriate steps taken if they are not. "Appropriate" may simply mean limiting the values to ±1.0 at the extremes.

Quantising using the indicated bit-allocations should be straightforward, unless additional constraints have been placed on the encoder. As mentioned earlier, encoding at a lower bit-rate than the original MPEG stream presents a problem. For example, the requirement to find an extra 16 bits for a cyclic redundancy check in the output bitstream that might not have been present in the original stream almost certainly means that the bit-allocations will exceed the bit-rate desired. Some modification has to be made. Various strategies are possible, based, for example, on the bit-allocations indicated, or on a psycho-acoustic model of the mask to quantisation noise ratio derived from first principles from the PCM samples.

A more complex situation arises when two mono signals, each carrying its own mole data, are required to be coded into one bitstream. If the mole data in the two inputs is quite different there is scope for different approaches to its use.

11   The mole-assisted encoder demonstration hardware system

The hardware basis of the encoder is similar to the decoder. A proprietary DSP card with three TMS320C40 DSP chips is used. In this case, both the input and the output data are carried on AES/EBU interfaces. The "SSTC" synchronisation signal was not actually used in the demonstration version, but the requirement for it is described later. The various cards are contained in a PC which provides power to all the cards, and the facility to load and run the DSP code on the DSP card.

Three processors are used. One processes the input PCM to extract the mole signal and synchronise the audio to get the correct subsampling phase in the analysis filterbank. The second performs the filterbank and psycho-acoustic modelling, and the third performs the scaling and quantisation. The scaling and quantisation can be done either according to the mole data, if valid, or based on the psycho-acoustic model, if not.

The bitstream produced by the third processor is handed back to the first for transmission out of the AES/EBU interface in IEC 61937 format.

In practice, it is possible for the cascaded encode and decode operations to recreate identical bitstreams much of the time. Small differences do occasionally arise as a result of limitations in the accuracy of arithmetic representations of numbers. This might occur during the truncation of the output of the decoder's synthesis filterbank for output as PCM, or due to the finite resolution with which the filterbank coefficients themselves are specified. Usually, the differences are very small — of the order of 1 least significant bit in the decoded audio signal.

12   Two or more decoders: the requirement for a common timing reference

The requirement for encoders' incoming PCM to have the same phase alignment in successive analysis filterbanks was stated earlier. The position of the mole signal within the PCM enables the encoder to determine precisely the correct alignment of the subband-samples, making gradual adjustments, if necessary, to bring the sampling into phase. While this alignment is being adjusted (the adjustment is generally slow to avoid audible effects) an encoder must make its own coding decisions, with the potential risk of degraded quality. Once a stream is frame aligned correctly it will remain aligned until an interruption (e.g. pause, mute, stop, etc) or a switch to a different stream occurs.

In order to eliminate the need for re-alignment of the stream all decoders synchronise their output, including mole generation, to a 24ms (1152 sample) frame pulse derived from a studio-wide Studio System Time Clock (SSTC). The SSTC enables decoders to maintain alignment during normal operation and mute/demute, stop/start periods. The encoder can also receive the SSTC, allowing it to keep track of the mole alignment during crossfades, and immediately determine the position of the mole in the new stream. The encoder does, of course, still check the mole preamble is in the correct position, and search for it if is not. This ensures that encoders will continue to detect and process mole information even in the event of erroneous delays in the system or loss of SSTC frame pulse.

The SSTC receiver in each item of equipment produces a 48kHz audio sample clock to which each AES/EBU i/o card locks. This maintains sample clock alignment eliminates problems of sample rate drift between clocks.

Another essential function of the SSTC signal is to provide a studio-wide time reference for the MPEG decoders. This enables the encoded data-stream to be decoded to the Presentation Time Stamp references contained within the stream, of which a primary reason is to maintain lip-sync with an audio stream's associated video. The need to maintain frame alignment implies that the actual playout time may vary by up to ±12ms for each stream decode. Any timing changes that are made are encoded into the generated mole datastream, in an "introduced time offset" field, allowing downstream encoders and decoders to take this into account.

13   Cascaded MPEG coding demonstration system

A complete demonstration of the ATLANTIC techniques, including non-linear editing and continuity suites, was recently exhibited at the International Broadcasting Convention. The audio aspects of the exhibit comprised a pair of mole generating MPEG layer 2 decoders, connected through a digital mixer to a mole enabled MPEG encoder. A key feature of the demonstration was an indicator connected to the encoder showing when the encoder had detected a mole-signal buried in the incoming PCM bitstream. The ability to seamlessly cut between bitstreams with the minimum (one 24ms frame) of mole signal loss was proof of the continuous mole alignment provided by the SSTC clock. The two audio decoders were fed by a pair of MPEG-2 video & audio decoders (manufactured by Snell and Wilcox) acting, in this instance, as Transport Stream demultiplexers. Each Snell and Wilcox decoder had been modified to deliver the demultiplexed audio Packetised Elementary Stream to an RS422 i/o port on its backpanel; as opposed to its own internal audio decoder. The encoded bitstream can then be transmitted to the mole generating decoder via its RS422 receiver board.

This is shown schematically in Fig. 5.

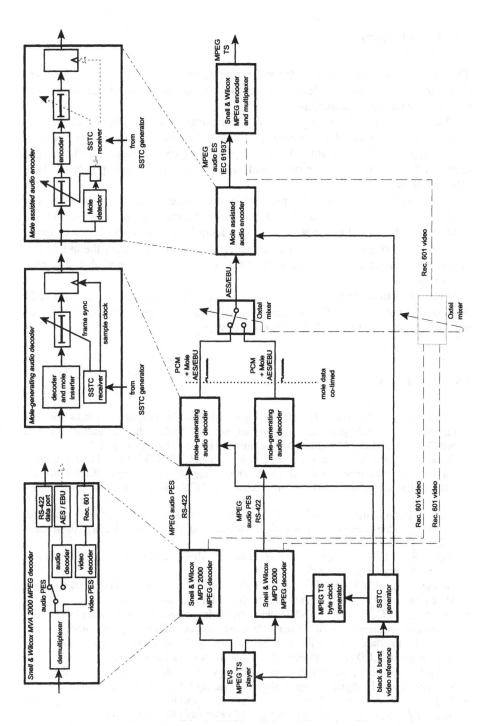

Fig. 5. Schematic diagram of cascaded MPEG coding demonstration

14 Conclusions

The unobtrusive way in which the mole signal can burrow "through" equipment means the introduction of mole assisted encoders and decoders would require minimal changes to existing infrastructure.

The complexity of the mole generation is quite negligible, requiring minor changes to a manufacturer's decoder firmware. The mole detection and extraction is relatively more complex, but this is still only a few percent of computational overhead. The demonstration of real-time decoders and encoders on moderately powerful DSPs affirms this fact.

Experiments have shown the perceptible difference in audio quality between multiple encode/decode cascades using mole technology and without mole technology. The virtual elimination of quality degradation that would be encountered in a cascaded programme chain using compressed data now facilities the use of this data in a professional environment with all the cost savings in bandwidth and storage this brings.

With the further development of the post-production facilities to conform edit decisions entirely in the MPEG domain this will enable the preservation of quality of our audio signals, or work at lower bit-rates, or both.

15 References

1. Wells, N.D., 1996. The ATLANTIC project: Models for programme production and distribution. Proceedings of the European Conference on Multimedia Applications Services and Techniques (ECMAST, 28-30 May, Louvaine-la-Neuve, Belgium) pp. 243-253.
2. Storey, R., Alves, A., Ruela, J., Teixeira, L. and Andrade, T., 1997. The ATLANTIC news studio: Reference model and field trial. Proceedings of the European Conference on Multimedia Applications Services and Techniques (ECMAST, 21-23 May, Milan, Italy) pp. 67-78.
3. Wells, N.D. and Gilchrist, N.H.C., 1998. ATLANTIC: Preserving video and audio quality in an MPEG-coded environment. International Broadcasting Convention (IBC98), Amsterdam, 11-15 September, 1998.
4. Wells, N.D. 1998. Transparent concatenation of MPEG compression. EBU Technical Review, Spring 1998, Vol. 275.
5. Fletcher, J.A., 1998. ISO/MPEG Layer 2 — Optimum re-encoding of decoded audio using a Mole signal. AES 104th Convention, Amsterdam, AES Preprint No. 4706.
6. Gilchrist, N.H.C., 1998. ATLANTIC audio: Preserving technical quality during low bit rate coding and decoding. AES 104th Connvention, Amsterdam, AES Preprint No. 4694.
7. IEC61937 Interface for non-linear PCM encoded audio bitstreams applying IEC60958. (Current status: CCDV — draft circulated as Committee Draft with Vote).
8. ISO/IEC 11172-3, 1993. Information technology — Coding of moving pictures and associated audio for digital storage media at up to about 1.5 Mbit/s. **Part 3: Audio**
9. Audio   Mole   specification   —
   http://www.bbc.co.uk/atlantic/169audio/169cont.htm

Object-Based Motion Parameterization Using Shape Adaptive Bilinear Warping

Ebroul Izquierdo, Fernando Lopes, and Mohammed Ghanbari

Department of Electronic Systems Engineering, University of Essex
Colchester, CO4 3SQ, United Kingdom
{ebroul, fjplop, ghan}@essex.ac.uk

Abstract. The estimation of parameters describing accurately the motion of arbitrarily shaped image areas is the basis of the next generation of video coding standards and multimedia techniques. In this paper we describe techniques for object segmentation and use this object information to carry out a generalized scheme for shape adaptive block-matching in the context of content based coding. Object segmentation is performed by applying different approaches tailored to the addressed application. These approaches range from very-low complexity techniques for real-time segmentation to object segmentation in very complex images. Once masks of objects in the scene are available each foreground object is considered independently for motion estimation. A regular wire-grid is defined on the whole image and the wire-grid nodes are classified according to their position with respect to the contour of the considered object. The mesh is deformed from frame to frame by applying a bilinear warping while the motion parameters are chosen to minimize the local block-distortion. The presented technique has been evaluated in the context of object-based video coding.

1 Introduction

Future telecommunication systems have to be based on efficient manipulation and representation of multimedia documents and have to provide new functionalities to the user. Clearly, such goals can only be achieved if the concerned information is treated by content instead by the meaning of a discrete signal as in the conventional approach. In this context, emerging video communication applications have to cope with different image processing tasks from which object segmentation and content-based motion estimation are core elements.

In this paper we present a technique for shape adaptive estimation of motion parameters based on previously extracted image segments. The presented approach can be divided into two main parts. The first is concerned with the segmentation of the relevant video objects while the second is related to the estimation of the associated motion parameters for coding. To cope with the first task an advanced segmentation toolbox comprising techniques with different levels of trade-off between complexity and degrees of freedom is used [4]. The toolbox consists of four segmentation schemes tailored for diverse applications. The first one consists of very-low complexity techniques for image segmentation addressing real-time applications under specific assumptions, e.g., head-and-shoulder video images from usual videoconferencing situations, and background/foreground separation in images with almost uniform background. In the second scheme a multi-resolution technique is presented in which segmentation with different levels of detail, according to the user needs, is targeted. For arbitrary natural scenes a one-parameter family of images is first generated by means of non-linear anisotropic diffusion and segmentation with the desired level of detail is obtained from the underlying scale space. The last two schemes address the most general object segmentation task of extracting masks of physical objects present in the scene. This task is carried out taking into account additional information about the 3D structure or the dynamic of single objects in the scene. The first of these two schemes comprises techniques for automatic object segmentation in images with moderate degree of complexity. The last scheme requires user interaction and has been designed to cope with the object segmentation task in very complex images. This is a semi-automatic approach addressing studio applications with the aim of reducing the cost of manual made object segmentation.

In the context of motion parameters estimation for coding, several approaches have been proposed in the past. An important class deals with mesh based techniques without regarding image content [5], [7]. The technique for motion compensation introduced in this paper belongs to this class, but in contrast to the techniques introduced in [5] and [7], our method exploit available segment information. The estimation of motion parameters is based on the deformation of small regular blocks according to a bilinear motion parameterization. Thus, a regular wire-grid is generated on the object of concern, then a bilinear warping of each block of the continuous mesh is performed using the object mask. Each block is classified as background, foreground or hybrid according to its position with respect to the object contour. The main strategy behind the applied warping approach is to improve iteratively and locally the estimated motion parameters exploiting this block classification and the segment information in an efficient way. For this aim each foreground object is considered independently and the background is faded out. The displacement of each grid node is estimated locally following a hierarchical strategy derived directly from the block classification. The final motion parameters are chosen to minimize the local block-distortion according to a minimum square error criterion. The paper is organized as follows: In section 2 the different elements of the used segmentation toolbox are described briefly. Section 3 deals with the estimation of the motion parameters. Selected results of computer simulations are presented in section 4 and the paper closes with a summary and further work in section 5.

2 Segmentation

Accurate masks of objects present in the scene are extracted by using an advanced segmentation toolbox introduced in [4]. For the sake of completeness we give in this section a glimpse of its most important elements. For a detailed description of all techniques comprised in this toolbox as well as an assessment of its performance we refer to [4]. The whole segmentation framework comprises four different schemes in which techniques with different levels of trade-off between complexity and degrees of freedom are available. These techniques are described briefly in the following.

2.1 Very-Low Complexity Segmentation for Real-Time Applications

The techniques implemented in this scheme are basically derived from simple interest operators for recognition of uniform image areas, and well-known thresholding approaches. We aim to address real-time segmentation for specific applications, e.g., head-and-shoulder video images from usual videoconferencing situations, and background/foreground separation in images with almost uniform background. The methods are based on the assumption that foreground and background can be distinguished by their gray level values, or that the background is almost uniform. Although this first scheme seems to be simplistic, it is very important and fundamental in real-time applications in which only techniques with very low degree of complexity can be implemented. Thresholding is perhaps the most common technique for elementary image segmentation. The determination of suitable thresholds involves the analysis of some function of the image intensity values. From a computational point of view, techniques based on the analysis of the histogram present a high degree of efficiency. Moreover, the distribution of the intensity values contains essential information about the position of optimal thresholds. To detect them in an easy but efficient manner, a peak detection function *pdf* similar to that introduced in [2] is generated via a simple averaging operation. The goal of this procedure is to estimate modes and local extrema in the histogram. Zeros of the curvature of the *pdf* determine the thresholds as well as the intensity value to be assigned to each class. Once the *pdf* has been defined, local extrema are estimated by detecting its zero-crossings. After histogram extrema have been detected, quantization of the image is carried out by assigning the histogram *mode* to all values between the start and the end of the respective peak. Using the quantized image a post-processing step is performed by assigning the binary value "1" to foreground points and "0" to the remaining points. Then, connected uniform areas are labelled using an efficient labelling procedure. Sequential numbers are assigned to different connected regions and they are stored as a field whose elements contain these numbers. At the same time, the number of pixels contained in each region is counted. All regions whose areas do not exceed a given threshold are declared non-homogeneous i.e., the binary value "1" is assigned to these regions. Finally, the obtained mask is smoothed using a max/min median filter.

2.2 Image Segmentation in Scale-Space

The second scheme is concerned with multiscale image simplification by anisotropic diffusion and subsequent image segmentation of the resulting smoothed images. The mathematical model supporting the implemented algorithms bases on the numerical solution of a system of nonlinear partial differential equations introduced by Perona and Malik [6] and later extended by several other authors [1], [3]. The idea at the heart of this approach is to smooth the image in direction parallel to the object boundaries, inhibiting diffusion across the edges. The goal of this processing step is to enhance edges keeping their correct position, reducing noise and smoothing regions with small intensity variations. Theoretically, the solution of this nonlinear partial differential equation with the original image as initial value tends to a piece-wise constant surface when the time (scale) tends to infinity. To speed up the convergence of the diffusion process a quantization technique is applied after each smoothing step. The stopping time of the diffusion process and the quantization degree determines the level of detail expressed in the segmented image.

2.3 Object Segmentation

Object segmentation in computer vision consists on the extraction of the shape of physical objects projected onto the image plane, ignoring edges due to texture inside the object borders. The objective of this extremely difficult image processing task is to recognize the shapes of complete physical objects present in the scene. It is intuitively clear that this more general segmentation cannot be carried out without additional information about the structure or motion of the object in the scene. The techniques for object segmentation presented in this paper can take into account disparity or motion fields as additional information. The first scheme for object segmentation comprises two different strategies: edge extraction and enhancement in scale-space followed by edge matching in two different views of the same scene, and accurate object segmentation by applying the watershed transform on previously extracted coarse object masks. The principal idea behind the first strategy is to extract edges at the location where the second derivative of the anisotropic-diffused image crosses zero (zero-crossings of the Laplacian). Small gaps in the resulting contours are then closed by linking them with straight lines. To simplify the contour matching procedure, in a subsequent processing step edges are approximated by polygonal lines. The problem of finding the best fit between image edges in two consecutive frames is finally solved by measuring their similarity via a suitable metric defined on the polygonal lines and the shape of the one-dimensional intensity function along the contour. Using the fact that different objects can be completely described by relevant edges and their dynamic, object masks are extracted by merging image areas undergoing similar motion in connected regions enclosed by a contour. The second strategy aims to extract very accurate masks of foreground objects assuming that coarse masks have been previously extracted from dense disparity or motion fields. The refinement of coarse object masks is carried out by applying the watershed transform. The implemented watershed transformation corresponds to a morphological segmentation technique that depend on the accuracy of the coarse object masks. Although these full automatic segmentation techniques produce impressive results in several cases, they are not always successful when the scene represented in the image has a high degree of complexity. Considering this fact we developed an interactive segmentation scheme consisting of two different tools. The first one is a graphical interface with which a coarse object mask can be delineated by the user. The second is the same morphological refinement tool used in the previously described segmentation scheme.

3 Shape Adaptive Estimation of Motion Parameters

The proposed motion estimation technique is based on a partitioned bilinear warping of a regular continuous mesh. Each segmented object is considered separately and the background is faded out. Then, a regular wire-grid composed of equal sized square blocks is defined on the resulting image with one foreground object and absolutely uniform background. The intersection of four block sides is associated with each grid node. Moreover, depending on its position, each block is classified as background, foreground or hybrid. Hybrid blocks (those blocks intersecting the object contour) with very small background or foreground area are classified as foreground or background respectively. An iterative procedure is used to move the nodes from their original positions in the regular grid in order to find the warped block that best fit with the corresponding image area in the previous frame. The generated distorted wire-grid is then superimposed on the previous frame to obtain a warped image that will be used as prediction for the current frame. A distortion measure between the warped previous frame and the current frame is used to optimize the displaced node positions. The motion vectors associated with the wire-frame nodes that influence foreground object areas constitute the motion information to be coded. Using the *Minimum Square Error* (MSE) as distortion measure the optimization process can be formulated as finding the displacement field $D = \{(d_x, d_y)\}$, for all $P = (x, y) \in Obj\}$ that minimizes the cost function:

$$F(d_x, d_y) = \sum_{P \in Obj} \left(I_t(x, y) - I_{t-1}(x - d_x, y - d_y)\right)^2, \qquad (1)$$

where $I_t(x, y)$ and $I_{t-1}(x, y)$ are the intensity values at the position (x, y) in frames t and $t - 1$ respectively and Obj is the foreground object domain in frame t. The individual motion of each node influences the prediction on a four block image area as illustrated in Fig. 1. Consequently, a causal sequence to move the nodes does not exist. Nodes which area of influence is only background are fixed and will not be displaced during the motion estimation process. Nodes that influence foreground areas are sorted in descending order according to the size of the image area defined by the intersection of the four adjacent blocks and the foreground object mask. After that, nodes are analyzed sequentially in the previously defined order. In the motion detection procedure each node is displaced in a 7×7 search window. For each one of the resulting test positions, four bilinear forward mappings associated with the four influenced quadrilaterals

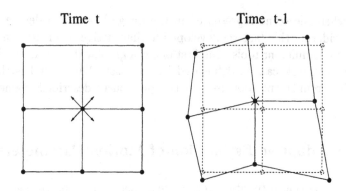

Fig. 1. The four blocks influenced by one grid node

are computed by using the following quadratic transformation (see Fig. 2).

$$\begin{bmatrix} x_{t-1} \\ y_{t-1} \end{bmatrix} = M \begin{bmatrix} 1 \\ x_t \\ y_t \\ x_t y_t \end{bmatrix},$$ (2)

where $\begin{bmatrix} x_t \\ y_t \end{bmatrix}$, $\begin{bmatrix} x_{t-1} \\ y_{t-1} \end{bmatrix}$ and $M = \begin{bmatrix} a_0 & a_1 & a_2 & a_3 \\ b_0 & b_1 & b_2 & b_3 \end{bmatrix}$ are the pixel coordinates in the

current frame (integer precision), the transformed coordinates for the same pixel in the previous frame (fractional precision) and the matrix of the transformation coefficients, respectively. Note that from a computational point of view, the map-

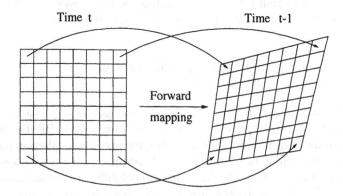

Fig. 2. Bilinear transformation acting on a specific block

ping (2) represents a very efficient compromise between the simple affine model (six parameter model) and the general conic transformation (twelve parameter model). Moreover, deforming a quadrilateral in the plane means that its four vertices should be moved. This fact conduces to a straightforward computation of the eight parameters involved in (2), because exactly four sampling positions are necessary to calculate them. Thus, on the one hand the model used in our approach is suitable to describe most cases of motion in natural scenes, what is not the case of the affine model, and in the other hand the computational complexity of (2) is very low and robust against numerical errors, what is not the case of the twelve parameter model. Nodes in the foreground of the current frame are constrained to be displaced within the foreground object mask in the previous frame. Furthermore, mesh integrity is guaranteed by constraining quadrilaterals to be convex and with area between half and double of its original (non-deformed) value. Using these transformations, the area inside the four influenced blocks is interpolated from the previous frame. Due to the continuous nature of the used transformation, the warped positions in the image plane, in general, do not coincide with the integer sampling positions of the image lattice. Pixels at non-integer positions are obtained by bilinear interpolation. The warped area is then compared with the corresponding image area in the current frame by using the distortion measure (1). In order to find the mesh warping associated with the minimum distortion in the sense given by (1), an iterative process is applied. In this process all nodes of the wire-grid are flagged with the label "1" (to be moved in the next iteration) or "0" (to keep fixed in the next iteration). The process is initialized by assigning the label "1" (to be moved) to all nodes of the wire-grid. The motion search is performed for each node according to the order previously defined. A motion vector is associated with the current node when the distortion measure for the new position is smaller than the minimum distortion value obtained during the preceding iteration. In this case the displaced node and its eight neighbouring nodes are labelled with "1". If a displacement showing a smaller distortion is not found in the current iteration the node is labelled with "0". After each iteration nodes are reordered and the whole process is repeated until all nodes have the label "0" (are fixed) or a specified number of iterations has been completed.

4   Computer Experiments

The performance of the presented technique has been assessed by several computer experiments. Some selected results obtained by processing the sequences CLAUDE and VOIT are presented in this section. The first sequence represents a typical videoconference situation (a person speaking on the front of textured background), the second one is a natural scene showing a car rotating in front of a static background. In both cases foreground masks have been obtained by using the segmentation toolbox described in section 2. Fig. 3 shows the considered foreground object in frame one (left) and two (right) for the sequence CLAUDE. Analogous segmented objects for the first (left) and second (right) frames of VOIT are shown in Fig. 4. In these representations the original intensity values are set inside of the foreground masks and the background has been faded out. A regular mesh with 16×16 pixels quadrilaterals was superimposed on the fore-

Fig. 3. Original foreground object in frame one (left) and two (right) of sequence CLAUDE. The background has been replaced by a constant intensity value

Fig. 4. Original foreground object in frame one (left) and two (right) of sequence VOIT. The background has been replaced by a constant intensity value

ground area of frame two. This mesh is shown in the left images of figures 5 and 6. The proposed motion estimation method has been applied using five iterations and a maximum search range of 10 pixels. A 7×7 search window has been used in each iteration. The images at the right of figures 5 and 6 show the warped wire-grids superimposed on frame one. These meshes represent the best matching quadrilaterals obtained after motion estimation. Finally, the reconstructed predicted foreground objects corresponding to frame two of CLAUDE (left) and VOIT (right) are shown in Fig. 7. This image synthesis has been carried out

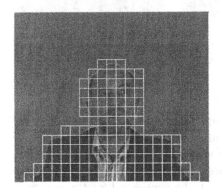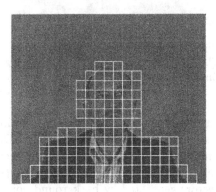

Fig. 5. Initial regular wire-grid (left) and warped wire-grid after motion estimation (right) in CLAUDE

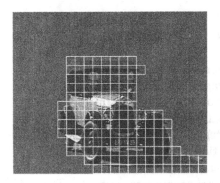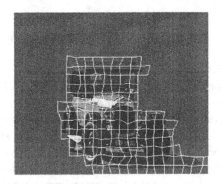

Fig. 6. Initial regular wire-grid (left) and warped wire-grid after motion estimation (right) in VOIT

by using the intensity values of the foreground object corresponding to frame one and the estimated motion parameters. To assess the performance of the introduced method, the *Peak Signal to Noise Ratio* (PSNR) has been measured

Fig. 7. Reconstructed foreground objects corresponding to frame two of sequence CLAUDE (left) and VOIT (right), using original intensity of frame one and the estimated motion parameters

for the foreground area of the prediction frame. The observed results of this assessment have been 32 dB for CLAUDE and 23 dB for VOIT. These values are similar to those obtained with the technique proposed in [7] when considering only the foreground area. However, in the presented method, no non-zero motion vectors generated by background noise need to be considered for transmission. In this way, up to 60% motion information reduction can be obtained keeping the relevant foreground objects quality. Furthermore, since nodes near object contours are not subject to random background displacements, more accurate prediction is achieved along these object boundaries where warping artifacts are also minimized. Since the mesh is continuous, the reconstructed images are free of block artifacts.

5   Summary and Further Work

A technique for estimation of motion parameters describing accurately the deformation in time of arbitrarily shaped image areas has been presented. Using an advanced segmentation toolbox masks of objects present in the scene are first extracted. This information is exploited efficiently in the introduced shape adaptive warping approach. The main strategy behind the method consists on a recursive improvement of the estimated motion parameters using the knowledge about the object shape. The final motion parameters are chosen to minimize the local block-distortion according to a minimum square error criterion. The used model represent a very efficient compromise between the simple affine model and the general second order polynomial models. A possible extension of the algorithm is the consideration of irregular quadrilaterals along the object contour in the warping mesh. This strategy could increase the performance of the method maintaining the stability and relative low computational complexity of the algorithm. Moreover, an extension of the method in this direction is straightforward. Further studies include an objective assessment of the performance by considering estimation of motion parameters over long periods of time and comparing the quality of reconstructed images and the compression rate with results supplied by other conventional methods.

Acknowledgements

The first and third authors are indebted to the Virtual Centre of Excellence in Digital Broadcasting and Multimedia Technology Ltd., U.K. for supporting the research leading to this paper. The second author would like to acknowledge the support of Instituto Superior de Engenharia de Coimbra and JNICT, Portugal.

References

1. Alvarez, L., Lions, P.L., Morel, J.M.: Image Selective Smoothing and Edge Detection by Nonlinear Diffusion. II, SIAM J. Numer. Anal., Vol. 29, No. 3, (1992) 845-866
2. Boukharouba, S., Rebordao, J.M., Wendel, P.L.: An Amplitude Segmentation Method Based on the Distribution Function of an Image. Computer Vision, Graphics, and Image Processing, vol. 29, (1985) 47-59
3. Catt, F., Dibos, F., Koeppler, G.: A Morphological Scheme for Mean Curvature Motion and Applications to Anisotropic Diffusion and Motion of Level Sets. SIAM J. Numer. Anal., Vol. 32, No. 6, (1995) 1895-1909
4. Izquierdo, E., Ghanbari, M.: Key Components for an Advanced Segmentation Toolbox. Submitted to IEEE Transactions on Circuits and Systems for Video Technology, Special issue on Content-Based Video Coding
5. Nakaya, Y., Harashima, H.: Motion Compensation Based on Spatial Transformations. IEEE Transactions on Circuits and Systems for Video Technology, vol. 4, no. 3, (1994) 339-356
6. Perona, P., Malik, J.: Scale Space and Edge Detection Using Anisotropic Diffusion. Proc. IEEE Comput. Soc. Workshop on Comput. Vision, (1987) 16-22
7. Sullivan, G.J., Baker, R.L.:Motion Compensation for Video Compression Using Control Grid Interpolation. International Conference on Acoustics, Speech and Signal Processing, (1991) 2713-2720

MPEG-4 PC –
Authoring and Playing of MPEG-4 Content for Local and Broadcast Applications

The MPEG-4 PC Consortium

P. Gerken, St. Schultz, G. Knabe; Q-Team Dr. Knabe Gesellschaft für Informations-
und Qualifikationssysteme mbH, Brauereistr. 11, D-41325 Korschenbroich, Germany
info@q-team.de, http://www.q-team.de

F. Casalino, G. Di Cagno, M. Quaglia; CSELT, Torino, Italy

J.-C. Dufourd, S. Boughoufalah, F. Bouilhaguet; ENST, Paris, France

M. Stepping, Th. Bonse; FernUni Hagen/FTK, Hagen/Dortmund, Germany

U. Mayer, J. Deicke, M. Glesner; TU Darmstadt, Darmstadt, Germany

Abstract. Goals and objectives of the European project "MPEG-4 PC – MPEG-4 System Implementation and Tools for Personal Computers" (ESPRIT #23191) are presented. An overview of the project's developments for authoring and playing, from local and remote sources, of content that conforms to the new multimedia standard ISO/IEC:14496, nicknamed MPEG-4, is given. Example applications for proving the functionalities and the powerfulness of the MPEG-4 standard, that is expected to become of great importance in the media world, are presented. A demonstration, including broadcast features, is planned during the ECMAST'99 Conference.

1   Introduction

A new standard, ISO/IEC:14496, nicknamed MPEG-4, [1] for the representation of audio-visual information in multimedia applications is being developed by the International Organisation for Standardisation, ISO, and the International Electrotechnical Committee, IEC. It considers the growing-together of the three market areas TV, computer and telecommunication and will support e.g. future ways of interactive TV. Benefits and the impact of the new standard are reported e.g. in [2]. MPEG-4 specifies essentially:

1. the coded representation of audio-visual information as visual and audio objects rather than as rectangular image frames and mixed sound signals, respectively;
2. a binary format for scene descriptions (BIFS) in the kind of computer programs;
3. a network-transparent transport mechanism in the context of the so-called MPEG-4 Delivery Multimedia Integration Framework, DMIF;
4. an interface for intellectual properties management and protection (IPMP) tools;

With these specifications the end-user will have, in contrast to conventional TV applications, the possibility to interact with the content, to the extent enabled by the author. Not only the author but also the end-user can have access to the single audio and visual objects rather than to the scene at large. The objects can even be called from different, local and remote, sources. Visual objects, that can even have arbitrary shapes, are e.g. the 2-D projections of persons in the scene. Audio objects are e.g. the voice of a single person or the sound of a single instrument in an orchestra. The IPMP interface makes the new standard especially attractive for authors. This way a high acceptance of MPEG-4 can be expected not only for compression purposes but also, and particularly, in the production area. Thus, MPEG-4 will provide the means for a new generation of (interactive) content. Before MPEG-4, every new media standard "merely" provided a new technology, e.g. digital TV; there was no need but also no possibility to build up a novel kind of content. MPEG-4 however provides a new philosophy for content creation. The new functionalities give novel features for the author and the end-user to interact with the content. In order to exploit these features, novel tools for authoring and playing this new kind of content are needed.

The European project *MPEG-4 PC* (ESPRIT #23191, full notation: "MPEG-4 System Implementation and Tools for Personal Computers") [3] deals with the first implementation of such an MPEG-4 authoring/playing system on a PC. Goals of the project are:

- The development of an authoring system that supports the MPEG-4 functionalities, especially interactivity, access to and manipulation of audio-visual objects.
- The development of a playing station for the playback of 2-dimensional MPEG-4 content from both local and remote sources.
- The development of a DMIF server/client structure and an application server for broadcasting MPEG-4 content.
- The promotion of the MPEG-4 standard and of the project achievements. For this purpose, demonstrations of prototype MPEG-4 applications are developed.
- Contribution to and even shaping of the MPEG-4 standard.

In the following sections, details about the authoring system (Section 2), the playing station (Section 3), the modules for broadcasting (Section 4), and the demonstrator (Section 5) are reported. Short conclusions (Section 6) complete this paper.

2   The Authoring System

For reasons of conciseness, only principal elements are described here.

2.1 User Interface

Figure 1 shows a screenshot of the preliminary user interface that contains the Editor with:

- The Object List
  This is a hierarchical listing of the objects in a scene. By clicking on an object icon certain operations can be performed: changing properties of an object, copying of an object together with all objects on lower hierarchy levels into a library (see below), renaming, removing, or adding behaviour (mouse sensitivity, draggability, visibility, blinking, movement) to an object. All objects are listed in the Object List, but only selected objects are displayable.
- The Routes Editor
  This editor defines the relations between the objects in a scene and the so-called BIFS nodes according to the specification of the MPEG-4 scene description. With this editor, also various kinds of interactivity with an object can be defined.

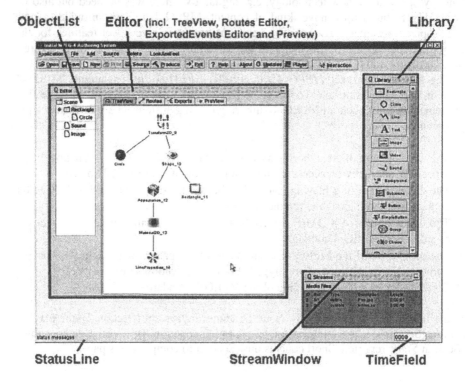

Fig. 1. Screenshot of the authoring system's preliminary user interface

- The Exported Events Editor
  This editor sets a list of input/output events for an object.
- The Tree View
  This is a visualisation of the scene construction in form of a tree. Note that the specification of an MPEG-4 scene description is hierarchical so that a scene can be well represented by a tree. Clicking on the tree nodes, i.e. the BIFS nodes, allows various types of manipulation. By shifting nodes or sub-trees the arrangement of the whole scene can be manipulated.
- The Preview

This window shows a snapshot of the created scene at the time set in the Time Field (see below). This gives the possibility of quick checks of (intermediate) authoring results.

Further elements of the preliminary user interface are:

- The Library
  The Library contains pre-defined objects, e.g. graphical primitives or buttons. The properties of each object can be set in a corresponding dialogue window. Author-defined objects can be stored in the Library for later re-use.
- The Stream Window
  Here all selected media streams are shown which the author may want to use during the authoring process. Setting of coding parameters is also done from within this window.
- The Status Line with the Time Field
  The Status Line shows system messages. In the Time Field, a time can be set for which the scene being created can be viewed in the Preview window.

2.2 The Authoring Process

In this sub-section, the very principal steps of authoring with the presented MPEG-4 authoring system are described.

1. Starting an application. Either a previously completed application must be opened if an application shall be re-edited, or a new application must be opened as null content.
2. Introduction of objects. Some objects require the selection of media streams.
3. The editing.
   - (3a) The spatial and temporal composition of the scene has to be defined.
   - (3b) Properties of objects and nodes, routes, event dependencies, behaviours, have to be set. In this step, the elements described in Sub-Section 2.1 are extensively used.
   - (3c) Interaction mode for setting interactivity among objects and the time dependent insertion/deletion of objects has to be activated, as appropriate.
   - (3d) Preview of intermediate results.
4. Setting of coding parameters.
5. Production of an MPEG-4 application file.
6. Calling of the MPEG-4 Playing Station and viewing of the application file.
7. Saving the application for later re-use.

3   The Playing Station

The MPEG-4 PC project contributes with its playing station to the so-called "Reference Software" of the Systems part of MPEG-4. The standard is divided into 6 parts: Systems, Visual, Audio, Conformance Testing, Reference Software, and DMIF.

The Reference Software is a reference implementation of the textual specifications in the other parts. The Reference Software for the Systems part consists of 3 elements: the playing station provided by the MPEG-4 PC project for 2-dimensional content, a playing station for 3-dimensional content, and a common core that includes e.g. a demultiplexer and the synchronisation layer.

Figure 2 shows the architecture of an MPEG-4 terminal. The main components are the DMIF layer (see below), the demultiplexer in the Systems layer, the BIFS and media decoders, the executive, and the presenter which includes the audio and visual renderers.

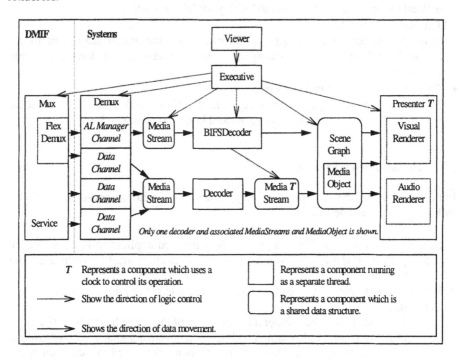

Fig. 2. Architecture of an MPEG-4 terminal

Whenever an application stream arrives at the terminal an executive is started. All steps of demultiplexing, decoding etc. to presenting the application are under the control of the executive. The demultiplexer decomposes the incoming application stream into its elementary streams and sends each of them to the appropriate decoding component. The executive is also responsible for creating the correct number and types of decoders, along with setting up the data paths between the components. As soon as the BIFS decoder finishes decoding the BIFS stream, the scene graph is constructed. The presenter reads the scene graph and calls the visual and audio renderers to display the scene.

The end-user can send events to the presenter in order to interact with the audio-visual objects or the scene composition.

The playing station supports JPEG, H.263, and MPEG-4 (including arbitrarily shaped objects) formats for video information, G.723 and AAC formats for audio information.

4 Delivery of Broadcast Information

MPEG-4 also defines a network-transparent transport mechanism (Delivery Multimedia Integration Framework, DMIF) for MPEG-4 data streams. Figure 3 shows the architectures of the different application scenarios.

The scenarios are:

- Local interactive – bidirectional data flow, all data stored locally
- Remote interactive – bidirectional data flow, network-transparent
- Broadcast – unidirectional data flow

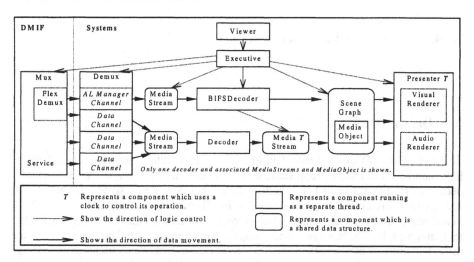

Fig. 3. The various delivery scenarios.
From top to bottom: broadcast, local interactive, remote interactive

The idea behind DMIF is that applications can always use the same interface, the so-called DMIF Application Interface DAI, no matter which delivery service is used. All services are transparent and the actual source of the MPEG-4 content doesn't need to be visible. The DAI cares for the correct adaptation to the particular network service.

Within the MPEG-4 PC project a prototype of a DMIF server/client delivery mechanism for broadcast scenarios is developed. It provides reliable, real-time, point-to-multipoint connections with a defined Quality of Service. Because of the lack of bi-directional data flow for signalling in unidirectional broadcast scenarios the project implements carrousel techniques in order provide the end-user the feature of a late tuning-in. Also part of the MPEG-4 PC project is the development of a broadcast application server that prepares MPEG-4 content for broadcast transmission. The set-up of the broadcast scenario is illustrated in Figure 4.

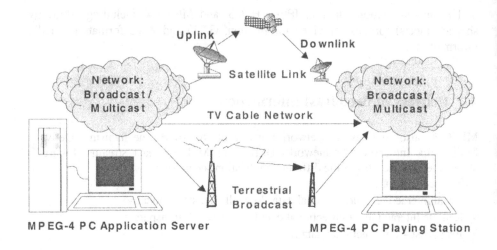

Fig. 4. Set-up for the broadcast scenario

5 Demonstrator

The aim of the MPEG-4 standard is to become THE future generic standard for a huge number of multimedia applications. For the design of prototype applications it is necessary to emphasise just the specific functionalities of this standard. One of its characteristics is to offer easy interactivity. In MPEG-4, the scenes consist of audio-visual objects, which may be natural or synthetic: videos, 2D and 3D images, sounds, text, graphics, human faces etc.. These objects can be manipulated by the end-user, to the extent allowed by the author: moving objects around, changing, deleting or adding objects, selection of different views, channels or of different languages for subtitles etc.. Functionalities of MPEG-4 and the project implementation which are intended to be verified by the developed demonstrations are specifically:

- Ability to manage multiple objects
- Interactivity
- Handling of multiple views/channels
- Support of arbitrarily shaped visual objects

The demonstrations under development within the Project MPEG-4 PC are restricted to applications with solely 2-dimensional content.

MPEG-4 is intended for a large panel of audiences of a broad social and professional variety. Several audiences have been identified as being of particular interest for the project demonstrations. We are analysing on the one side the general public and on the other side authors, art directors and engineers in order to send messages specific for each group with the demonstrations. In the following sub-sections, we give some comments about the audiences being analysed and present two example applications, the "Tour de France" and the "Election Night".

5.1 Audiences

- **General Public**

  The general public for MPEG-4 is formed in a large majority by TV viewers, but also by professionals at work. The objective of the demonstrator for this particular audience is to prove that MPEG-4 will allow them to be more (inter)active, to have more initiative and to customise the content and layout of the screen.

  - *the TV viewer at home*
    The viewer will have access to information that is not only national or regional, but also local. He/she will then access interactively localised weather forecasts, traffic information, election results or polls, or even all that but not for his/her town, but some other. He/she will not depend on the centralised choice of the channel managers, who need to present general information and cannot be too specific. He/she will also be able to retrieve information on many subjects.

  - *the professional at work*
    The demonstrator aims at proving that any professional at work can benefit from using MPEG-4, for instance, in the context of in-company training, technical documentation, communication, advertisement etc..

  As a conclusion of this analysis, our message to the general public is that, whether at home or at work, besides the richness of content, **MPEG-4 will give them the initiative and the choice of what to see and how to see it.**

- **Authors, Art Directors, and Engineers**

  This group should become convinced that MPEG-4 is THE technology of choice already in the near future, for both stored and (live) broadcast content. The objective of the demonstrator is therefore to show this group **the richness of new creative and technological features offered by MPEG-4 that will revolution their way of working.** For authors this means especially:

  - the interactivity that can be made available to the end-user,
  - the composition of many audio and visual objects in an integrated framework with accurate synchronisation,
  - the diversity of media types and the (possibly) large number of objects.

5.2 "Tour de France" Application

This application is mainly aimed at the general public at home. It shows conventional video and audio channels in an innovative, interactive set-up. It covers all variants of the public from "couch potatoes" to "techies". It is well-suited to demonstrate the relevance of MPEG-4 in the field of future-oriented interactive TV.

More content than what can be reasonably displayed is sent. The viewer is expected to make his/her choice among the different parts. The intent is to allow the user to compose his/her screen layout with a lot a freedom, choosing from a few audio, video and synthetic channels. The three synthetic channels are a map, describing the region of the race and the position of each racer with respect to the route, a rating of the racers, and a summary of important information.

The application consists of a main choice screen and four screen layouts with different levels of interactivity:

1. a regular MPEG-2-like TV screen with no interactivity,
2. a see-all screen for the race against the clock, where the screen is divided into quarter-sized parts for four channels and the viewer can zoom in on any,
3. a multiple-channels-in-one screen with a command bar and buttons, where e.g. by clicking on a group of racers in the command bar the view on that particular group can be selected and additional information such as geographical maps, altitude profiles, or information about a racer can be called.
4. an advanced screen with multiple channels where each can be chosen as the main channel while, in addition to layout #3, smaller versions of the other channels can be viewed in a bar on the right of the screen in order to be able to switch to the one which is most attractive for the end-user at a certain time.

Figure 5 gives screenshots of the choice screen and the layouts #2 through #4. The end-user can select among the different layouts and, within any layout except #1, among different views and can call additional information in a hypermedia fashion.

5.3 "Election Night" Application

The "Election Night" is also an application intended for TV-like broadcast, where the bandwidth required for a simple presentation of election or poll results as an animation is so small that a lot of additional information can be sent in the background. This information is then structured as accessible by the user through prearranged interactivity.

For example, a map of France will be displayed with national results, and it will stay on the screen unless the viewer uses a pointer to select a particular town. In this case, a map of the region around that town is displayed with more detailed information. Maps of all regions of France are sent with the map of France, but only displayed on demand. The user will also be able to configure his/her terminal to automatically switch to the detailed view around his/her town upon reception of localised information (election results, weather forecast, ...). The user will also be able to get a split screen with the map of France presented in one part, and the map of a specific region in the other.

Fig. 5. Screen layouts of the "Tour de France" application; top left: the main choice screen, bottom left: the see-all screen, top right: the multiple-channels-in-one screen with an increased level of interactivity (see the command bar and buttons), bottom right: the advanced screen with additional channels in small windows

The essential difference to the "Tour de France" application is in the complexity of the graphics content per voting site (face of candidates, image of site, bar charts) as well as the real-time updating of the figures.

6   Conclusions

Goals and objectives of the European project "MPEG-4 PC – MPEG-4 System Implementation and Tools for Personal Computers" have been presented. The software under development will allow the authoring and playing of content that conforms to the specification of the standard ISO/IEC:14496, called MPEG-4.

It is expected, e.g. by market analysts, media and technology experts, that MPEG-4 will have tremendous influence on the world of media, especially for content creators, art directors, and content providers and thus also for the consumers. The amount of money companies invest only in the specification of the standard is estimated at roughly 2 to 4 billion EURO, the highest amount ever paid for the specification of a multimedia standard. How much money companies have already invested in the development of MPEG-4 products and services is difficult to assess. Precise figures on that have not yet been published by market analysts; however a multiple of this sum, likely more than hundred times as much, can be expected. MPEG-4 covers many areas of multimedia, from hardware through software to services. Only for multimedia hardware and software, the revenue for the year 2000 is estimated by market analysts at more than 200 billion EURO with substantial increase in the following years. MPEG-4 products will occupy year by year more and more parts in the multimedia areas. This shows the importance of MPEG-4 also from a market point of view.

Application areas of MPEG-4 are e.g. (interactive) TV, infotainment, edutainment, computer-based training, advertisement, games, movies, streaming video over Internet/Intranet, collaborative scene visualisation, virtual meetings, real-time communications, surveillance, content-based storage and retrieval, digital AM broadcasting. For almost all of the mentioned applications, content needs to be created. MPEG-4 provides the means for the creation of a novel kind of content with which the end-user can interact. MPEG-4 authoring and playing systems will e that MPEG-4 will allow them to be more (inter)activre.

The development performed within the MPEG-4 PC project is the first combined implementation of an MPEG-4 authoring/playing systems, as known to the MPEG community. With this system it is possible to author and play the novel kind of (interactive) content on a regular PC; no specific hardware is needed. Thus, it is relatively easy to introduce it in the market, what shows the relevance of the project work. The project also contributes successfully to different parts of the standard, the Systems, the DMIF, the Reference Software, and the Conformance Testing specifications, as well as to the promotion of the new standard. The consortium has close contact and cooperation with other projects, companies, and institutions that either contribute with other elements to the standard, thus taking advantage e.g. by mutual use of software, or intend to develop MPEG-4 products or services.

At the end of the project duration there will be a prototype of the combined MPEG-4 authoring/playing system, that will provide basic functionalities for the creation and playback of 2-dimensional content from local and remote sources. It will then be usable in a number of applications of which examples are listed above, e.g. future-oriented TV where the end-user can interact with the scene or even with the audio-visual objects in the scene. The work will continue after the project by introducing further functionalities and increasing the performance so that the system will be able to also create and playback more complex content. 3-dimensional content will be also supported later, and the system will be built up in form of a modular scheme so that it will fit the needs of authors with different requirements and different budgets. Maintenance and continuing development of the authoring modules after completion of the project will be in the responsibility of Q-Team Dr. Knabe GmbH. Special releases will be developed for authors with very specific needs. Service for authors will be provided by training and by, partial or full, support in the design of content, the latter especially for casual authors.

Partial results of the project were demonstrated successfully to the press and the public during the first MPEG-4 (IP multicast) satellite transmission from the West

Coast of the US to Atlantic City, NJ, at the East Coast in October 1998. Since then, the development has progressed, and a demonstration with full, i.e. unidirectional, broadcast support is planned for the ECMAST'99 Conference.

Additional information about the MPEG-4 PC project and the MPEG-4 standard can be found in [3] and [4], respectively.

References

1. ISO/IEC, International Standard IS 14496 (1999)
2. Koenen, R.: MPEG-4 – Multimedia for our Time. IEEE Spectrum 36 (1999) 26-33
3. http://www.q-team.de/mpeg4/mpeg4pc.htm
4. http://cselt.it/mpeg

Single Frequency Networks for Digital Video Broadcasting

Jesús M. Fernández, J. Capdevila, R. García, S. Cabanillas, S. Mata, A. Mansilla and Jose M. Fernández

Engineering R&D
RETEVISION S.A., Spain
jefernand@retevision.es

Abstract. This paper introduces the Terrestrial Digital Video Broadcasting DVB-T, stating its innovative aspects and its major advantages for data broadcasting, particularly TV broadcasting. It also presents the experimental DVB-T network built up by Retevisión in the framework of the Spanish VIDITER project (Terrestrial Digital Video) and the European ACTS VALIDATE (Verification and launch of Integrated Digital Advanced Television in Europe) and ACTS MOTIVATE projects (Mobile Television and Innovative Receivers). The experience and some of the results of the different tests carried out by Retevisión are afterwards discussed.

Why digital TV Broadcasting?

Generally, the digital technology presents some major advantages in baseband efficiency, flexibility and RF performance that make its use very attractive to broadcasters.

Effectively, when addressing to TV broadcasting, the digital signals are more robust and the spectrum use is more efficient; more than one program may be broadcasted using the same bandwidth and having even better picture quality. Moreover those digital signals are easier to process and more computer friendly.

The only issue is how long will it take to completely change the technology considering the large number of analogue TV receivers worldwide. Some transition period will probably be started in which both technologies coexist (broadcasting the same TV contents in analogue and digital, often called SIMULCASTING, and some additional only-digital contents).

What is DVB?

The Digital Video Broadcasting Project (DVB) is a marked-led initiative to standardise digital broadcasting worldwide. It is formed of 240 members from more than 35 countries, in which there are representatives of broadcasters, manufacturers, network operators and regulatory bodies.

The DVB was formed in September 1993 and along these years has been producing several system specifications that have become standard in organisms as the ETSI (European Telecommunication Standard Institute) or CENELEC (European Committee for Electrotechnical Standardisation).

The DVB family of standards

The DVB has been producing different system specifications including satellite: DVB-S [EN 300421], cable: DVB-C [EN 300429], terrestrial: DVB-T [EN 300744], microwave: DVB-MVDS [EN 30048] and DVB-MMDS [EN 300749], community antenna: DVB-SMATV [EN 300743] and others.

The key word of the DVB standards is *interoperability*, all of them are part of a family of systems that make use of maximum commonality in order to enable the design of "synergetic" hard- and software.

The DVB transmission systems offer a "pipe" for data containers. They are transparent for SDTV (Standard Definition TV), EDTV (Enhanced Definition TV) and HDTV (High Definition TV), for audio at all quality levels and for all kinds of general data (multimedia data broadcasting).

All the specifications are based on the selection of the MPEG-2 (Moving Pictures Experts Group) for coding audio and video and for the system level.

DVB-T – Terrestrial digital video broadcasting

The DVB-T system for terrestrial broadcasting is probably the most complex DVB delivery system.

The key feature of the system is the use of COFDM (Coded Orthogonal Frequency Division Multiplexing). This is a very flexible wide-band multicarrier modulation system that uses different levels of forward error correction, time and frequency interleaving and two level hierarchical channel coding.

Basically, the information to be transmitted is split into a given number ("2k" 1705 or "8k" 6817) of modulated carriers with individual low bit rate, so that the corresponding symbol time becomes larger than the delay spread of the channel. A guard interval (1/4, 1/8, 1/16, 1/32 of the symbol time) is inserted between successive symbols to avoid intersymbol interference and to protect against echoes.

Depending on the channel characteristics, different parameters (sub carrier modulation – QPSK, 16QAM, 64QAM –, number of carriers – 2k, 8k –, code rate of inner protection, guard interval and modulation parameter - α) can be selected obtaining different *operation modes*. Every mode offers a trade-off between net bit rate and protection of the signal (against fading, echoes, etc.). Depending on the selected operation mode, 60 different net bit rates could be obtained ranging from 5 to 32 Mbps.

The selection of the COFDM modulation system presents two major advantages that make its use very interesting to terrestrial digital video broadcasting:

> COFDM improves the ruggedness of the system in the presence of artificial (long distance transmitters) or natural (multiple propagation) echoes. Actually, the echoes may benefit instead of interfere the signal if they fall inside the guard interval.

> On the one hand, COFDM provides a considerable degree of immunity to narrow-band interferers as maybe considered the analogue TV signals; and on the other hand it is seen by those analogue signals as white noise, therefore not interfering or having little effect upon them.

All these characteristics enable a more efficient use of the spectrum (possible use of the so-called *taboo* channels, which usually are the only available ones to start new DVB transmissions); and the introduction of Single Frequency Networks (SFN).

Moreover, portable and mobile reception of DVB-T signals is possible. One efficient way to achieve that is by using hierarchical transmissions, in which one of the modulated streams (so-called HP – High Priority stream), having higher protection against errors but reducing its net bit rate, is used for portable and mobile reception; while the other one (so-called LP – Low Priority stream), having lower protection and higher bit rate, is used for fixed reception.

The ACTS MOTIVATE project, in which Retevisión participates, is currently addressing such issues, demonstrating and assessing the mobile and portable reception of DVB-T and developing algorithms and models for new enhanced receivers optimised for such reception conditions.

Multimedia and Interactivity

Nowadays the importance for the broadcasters of offering new added value services, especially multimedia and interactivity, is out of question.

The number of applications is continuously growing and evolving. Among them: pay per view, NVoD, video on demand, home shopping, home banking, Internet access, etc.

Most of those interactive services are asymmetric; the user expects a great amount of information (several Kbps or even Mbps) but request this information through a low speed return channel (few Kbps).

DVB provides network independent protocols together with a full set of network dependent return channels (e.g. PSTN – ISDN, DECT, GSM, etc.).

The advantage of DVB transmissions is that they do not distinguish between data, video or audio (it may even be used to broadcast data which itself incorporates audio and video as some Internet pages do).

Besides, DVB-T provides the extra advantage of joining portable and mobile reception to the previously mentioned characteristics.

DVB data profiles

DVB foresees four ways of data broadcasting depending on the necessities:

♦ *Data piping*: asynchronous, non-synchronised, end to end data delivery.
♦ *Data streaming*: streaming oriented, end to end delivery of asynchronous, synchronous or synchronised data.
♦ *Multiprotocol encapsulation*: data services that require the transmissions of datagrams (as the ones of TCP-IP).
♦ *Data carousels*: data services that require periodic transmissions of data modules.

Single Frequency Networks

Traditionally, the analogue TV broadcasting had to face the problem of co-channel interferences by prohibiting the re-use of the same channel over considerable distances. This results in an extremely inefficient use of the spectrum. As shown in Figure 1, in conventional 9-frequency layouts, each channel is prohibited over approximately 89% of the land area.

Fig. 1. MFN frequency planing for Conventional Analogue TV

An alternative to those Multi Frequency Networks (MFN) is to use a set of transmitters spread throughout a given territory (a city, a region or even a country) temporally synchronised and transmitting at the same frequency. Such configuration is called Single Frequency Network (SFN).

The advantages are enormous in terms of spectrum efficiency. Whereas in analogue MFN a single SDTV program was transmitted over 9 RF channels, now more than one program could be broadcasted using a single RF channel. 9 Times less spectrum is used than in MFN! Or, 45 times more programs (assuming 5 SDTV programs per channel) can be broadcasted using the same spectrum!

Moreover, taking advantage of the beneficial effect of the echoes inside the guard interval, less power would be needed in locations on the verge of the coverage area of two neighbouring transmitters, signals coming from both would contribute to improve the overall carrier to noise ratio.

Shadowed areas can also be served by direct reamplification using a co-channel retransmitter often called "gap filler".

A drawback of SFNs is that the flexibility of dynamically replacing the contents of a program is lost. Effectively, all the transmitters of a SFN must broadcast the same contents in the same moment in time.

SFN Constraints

Following the main constraints that the SFN operation introduces into the network will be briefly assess:

Synchronisation constraints

All the signals broadcasted by the transmitters of a SFN must be synchronised in terms of frequency, time and bit.

The *frequency synchronisation* requires that a common reference oscillator shall drive all cascaded oscillators within each transmitter.

The *time synchronisation* requires that each transmitter shall broadcast the *nth* symbol at $Tn \pm 1\mu s$ (where Tn denotes the ideal instant for the *nth* symbol to be transmitted).

The *bit synchronisation* requires that the same symbol shall be transmitted at the same time. Therefore all carriers shall be identically modulated. Hence the same bits should modulate the same *kth* carrier.

In order to fulfil those requirements, DVB-T provides the MIP specification [TR101191]. By means of a *SFN adapter*, located at the output of the Transport Stream (TS) generation process, Megaframe Identification Packets (MIP) are inserted periodically into the TS. Modulators use those additional packets for the time and bit synchronisation.

The synchronisation mechanisms are based on the existence of two global external references: a frequency reference of 10 MHz and a time reference of 1 pps (pulse per second); and example of a global system providing such references is the GPS (Global Positioning System).

Transmitter requirements

A complete set of specific requirements for transmitters have been identified within the framework of the ACTS VALIDATE project.

- *Frequency stability.* Each carrier should be transmitted in a frequency within the interval $f_k \pm (\Delta f/100)$. The transmitter needs the external frequency reference for synchronisation in SFN (10 MHz).
- *Oscillators phase noise.* One of the most limiting factors found during the tests of transmitters and transposers was the phase noise of the oscillators. In some cases transmitters which are perfectly suitable for PAL transmissions appear to be of no use in the case of DVB-T because of phase noise.
- *Output back-off.* The maximum power that can be obtained by a given transmitter is limited by the non-linearity effect of the amplifiers, consequently affecting to

the quality of the reception. For each kind of transmitter used for DVB-T broadcasting there is a fixed output power value that maximises the coverage area. Transmitting below this value, the capabilities of the equipment are not fully used, and transmitting above, we obtain added system implementation losses, which are greater than the expected coverage gain. Typical back-off values are in the order of 6 dB or even more.

<u>Professional Gap fillers requirements</u>

Similar kinds of requirements stated for the transmitters are also applicable to professional gap-fillers or transposers. Though, in this case, the economic point of view should be taken into account. A transposer should be much cheaper than a transmitter, and consequently the overall requirements should not be so restrictive as for transmitters.

An additional requirement for the gap fillers is the maximum allowable gain in a given site. This gain is limited by the feedback loop gain, which is basically determined by the input/output antenna isolation. It has been proven in field tests that isolations above 100 dB, although difficult, can be feasible. The maximum gain of the transposer is then limited to the isolation value minus a security margin needed to avoid instability problems that cause strong additional implementation losses and can even produce the unavailability of the system in the area covered by the gap-filler. A typical security margin value can be around 20 dB.

Primary distribution network aspects

The primary distribution network addresses the transport of the TV signal in whatever format to the transmitter sites for its broadcasting.

The TV signal may be transported in digital format (i.e. using the MPEG-2 Transport Stream) or in analogue format (i.e. modulated according the DVB-T specification).

✓ *Decentralised generation of the DVB-T signal*

Addresses the transportation of the digital MPEG-2 Transport Stream through the primary distribution network and then modulating the signal inside each transmitter site.

The primary network may use fixed terrestrial (e.g. optical fibre, radio links) or satellite links. Various technologies or combination of them can be applied for such purpose (e.g. ATM, PDH, SDH, DVB-S, etc.).

Two major advantages arise from the use of this method:

➢ Flexibility: further levels of MPEG-2 multiplexing may be included, for example to provide regional programme variations, although in SFN this feature is not applicable.

➢ Signal quality: after the primary distribution the carrier to noise ratio is roughly preserved.

As drawbacks several DVB-T modulators are needed (one in each transmitter site) which increase the overall cost of the network and imply the need to synchronise them (see SFN Constraints). Another problem could be the jitter introduced by the multiplexing and remultiplexing processes.

✓ *Centralised generation of the DVB-T signal*

Addresses the modulation of the TV signal according the DVB-T specification at a central point and transporting through the primary distribution network the *analogue* COFDM signal.

The primary network may use fixed terrestrial (e.g. radio links) or satellite links.

The major advantage of using this method is that the number of DVB-T modulators in the network is reduced, being even possible one single modulator for the entire network. Most of the synchronisation problems of the SFN disappear, especially when using a satellite link in which not even static delays (as the ones introduced by terrestrial radio links) are introduced by the network.

Notwithstanding this method looses flexibility with respect to dynamically replace programs at the remultiplexer sites. Anyway this is not affecting in the case of SFN where no remultiplexing is allowed.

Another very important problem is that generally the final signal looses quality (i.e. the C/N is degraded in the primary distribution and this degradation can not be recovered) which translates into less coverage area.

Secondary distribution network aspects

The secondary distribution network addresses the broadcasting of the TV signal from the transmitter sites to the final user receiver.

As previously mentioned, the DVB-T provides several operation modes to adapt the signal to the radio channel characteristics. Every operation mode offers a trade-off between net bit rate that may be allocated to the TV programmes and protection of the signal against echoes, noise, fadings, etc.

Mode (FFT – GI)	Distance between neighbour transmitters
2k–1/32	2 Km
2k–1/4	17 Km
8k–1/32	9 Km
8k–1/4	68 Km

Table 1. Maximum transmitter site's separation depending on the operation mode for SFN (8 MHz channel)

An important issue for SFN is the use of *8k* modes (i.e. 6817 sub carriers), especially for wide area SFN (see Table 1), since this mode allow longer echoes (they have longer guard intervals) than the *2k* modes.

Spanish regulation

Following the Spanish Technical Regulation (issued the 16th of October 1998) on Digital Terrestrial Television will be briefly described:

Channel allocation

The following frequency bands are reserved for the DVB-T service:

a) 470 to 758 MHz (ch.: 21 to 56)

b) 758 to 830 MHz (ch.: 57 to 65) – Completely available from 31 October 1999.

c) 830 to 862 MHz (ch.: 66 to 69) – Completely available from 30 June 1999.

Service planning

Four SFN national coverage channels, carrying at least four services in each channel, will be set up in the 830-862 MHz band.

One channel with national coverage and regional re-multiplexing (regional SFN), carrying at least four services, will be set up in the 758-830 MHz band. Simulcast with the analogue TV.

One SFN regional coverage channel, carrying at least four services, will be set up in the 758-830 MHz band. Simulcast with the regional analogue TV.

N channels with local coverage will be set up in the 758-830 MHz band.

The 470-758 MHz band will be used for analogue TV transmissions, MFN and local broadcasting until the *analogue switch off*, the 1st of January 2013.

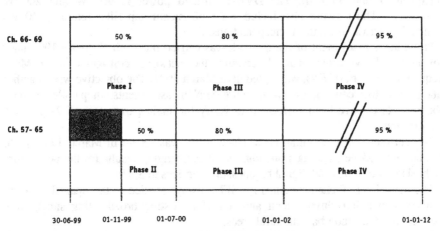

Fig. 2. Phases of the establishment of Terrestrial Digital TV in Spain

Time scale

The Figure 2 shows the four phases of the coverage plan.
The coverage is thought in terms of population, not territory.

> Phase I: SFN national channels, 50% coverage, 12 months duration from the 30th of June 1999.

> Phase II: National with regional re-multiplexing channel, 50%, 8 months duration from the 31st of October 1999.

> Phase III: all channels, 80% coverage, 18 months duration from the 30th of June 2000.

> Phase IV: all channels, 95% coverage, 10 years duration from the 31st December 2001.

Operational modes of DVB-T

The technical specifications of the Digital TV transmitters will follow the 8 MHz, 8k mode of the European Telecommunication standard EN 300 744.

The Retevisión experimental network

The experimental DVB-T network of Retevisión was built in the framework of the Spanish VIDITER project and the European ACTS VALIDATE project. It consists of two transmitters; one is located in Torrespaña (Madrid) and the other in Navacerrada (separated around 50 Km). The DVB-T emitted power is 900 W and 200 W respectively. The network also includes a professional gap filler (emitting 10 W) located 5 Km away from the Torrespaña transmitter.

Preliminary assessment of the network was carried out from February 1996 until November of the same year. Afterwards the network, configured as a Multi Frequency Network (MFN), was tested until March 1997. The objective was to gather data to establish comparisons with future SFN measurements. In parallel, several laboratory tests have been performed to verify the main parameters of the DVB-T specification.

The current SFN configuration, in channel 26, was set up in March 1998. Field tests are being done since then obtaining very encouraging results for the near future establishment of terrestrial digital broadcasting services in Spain.

The main DVB-T characteristics for SFN, always applied to the Spanish case (in terms of legislation, environment and reuse of existing broadcasting sites), were assessed in urban, suburban and rural areas.

In the framework of ACTS MOTIVATE project, the follow up of ACTS VALIDATE, more tests are foreseen during 1999 to assess portable and mobile reception.

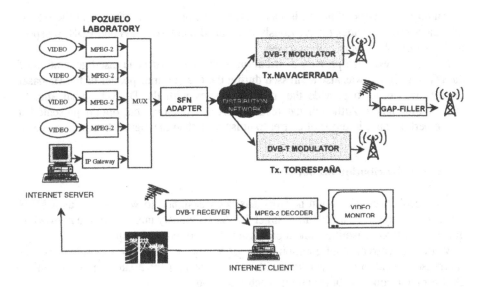

Fig. 3. Retevisión Experimental Digital Terrestrial TV network

NETWORK TOPOLOGY

Retevisión has installed a complete digital terrestrial TV chain, compliant with DVB-T, and made up of four parts:
- Production TV studio and master control room.
- Source coding, data insertion and programme multiplex.
- Primary distribution network (so-called gathering/transport network).
- Secondary distribution network (so-called broadcast network).

The production TV studio and the master control room are both located at the Retevisión's Laboratory premises, in Pozuelo de Alarcón (Madrid), and their role is to feed the experimental network with a programme bouquet (four programmes) embedded in a Transport Stream (TS). An additional data channel is also inserted into the TS in order to test data broadcasting services, like *Internet* access.

Primary distribution network

The primary distribution network has been designed to transport the signal from the Retevisión's Lab in Pozuelo up to the two transmitter sites: Torrespaña and Navacerrada.

The transport network was carrying the MPEG-2 TS from the Retevision's Lab to Torrespaña via an optical fibre link. From this point to the second transmitter site (Navacerrada), a digital radio link was used.

An important issue of the trials was related to the primary distribution of the signal, for that purpose, besides the previously mentioned methods, SDH and PDH transport of the MPEG-2 TS were both assessed.

Moreover, analogue primary distribution of the signal (decentralised generation of the DVB-T signal) was also addressed during the trials; a transponder of the Hispasat satellite was used to provide the transmitter sites with the DVB-T signal already OFDM modulated. Although the results were satisfactory this option presented a worse performance in terms of carrier to noise ratio than the digital distribution one.

Secondary distribution network

The secondary distribution network has been designed to work either as a MFN (dual frequency) or as a SFN in channel 26. As previously mentioned, the network is made out of two transmitters and a professional gap filler (or transposer).

With the current configuration, the generation of the DVB-T signal is not centralised, therefore at each transmitter site there is a modulator equipped with a GPS for the frequency, time and bit synchronisation.

The DVB-T modulators are able to reconfigure themselves using specific data sent within the MPEG-2 Transport Stream, following what has been established in the MIP specification for SFN (TR 101191).

Supporting laboratory tests

Hereafter some selected results of the most relevant laboratory tests carried out up to date are presented.

Reception in AWGN

Figure 4 represents the theoretical and measured *implementation losses* with the presence of Additive White Gaussian Noise (AWGN) for 8K, 64 QAM modes. It can be observed that the actual values are always lower than 3 dB respecting the theoretical ones.

Nevertheless the measured *noise factor* value for the professional equipment is greater than the expected value, this value (9 dB) has been taken as reference for the specific coverage studies, as recommended by the results obtained in the ACTS VALIDATE project.

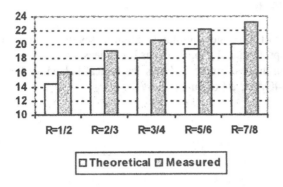

Fig. 4. C/N_{min} in AWGN

Protection ratios

The DVB-T signal presents ruggedness in front of high power PAL signals in both co-channel and adjacent channels.

The measured co-channel protection ratios (PR) against PAL signal for the mode 8K, sub-carrier modulation 64 QAM, code rate 2/3, guard interval 1/4 is about -2 dB. This means that the DVB-T signal could cope in the limit with co-channel PAL interferences if the peak sync power of the PAL signal is not more than 2 dB above the power of the DVB-T signal.

The PR measured values for adjacent channels (in the order of -24 dB) are more than 10 dB worst than the foreseen for commercial equipment.

With regard to interference from other DVB-T signals, the co-channel PR values are approximately the same ones as the C/N_{min} measured values for AWGN channel.

Multipath propagation

The performance of DVB-T against echoes has been broadly assessed and reported previously by different sources in the ACTS VALIDATE and MOTIVATE projects.

The implementation losses added ($\Delta C/N$) for 0 dB echoes within the guard interval were not greater than 8 dB in the operation mode previously mentioned (i.e. 8k, 64QAM, 2/3, 1/4).

The feasibility of receiving DVB-T signals in typical Rayleigh channels has been also tested. This issue is especially important in the case of portable and mobile reception.

Non-linearity effects

The behaviour of the system implementation losses due to non-linearity effects in transmitters and professional gap fillers has been measured in different equipment and DVB-T operation modes. Figure 5 shows the typical behaviour for 2/3, 3/4 and 5/6 code rates (8k, 64QAM, 1/4 of guard interval).

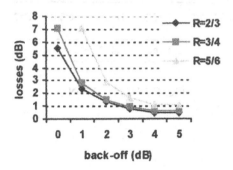

Fig. 5. Non-linearity effects in DVB-T

Feedback in SFN

When using professional gap fillers in a SFN (transposers) to cover shadowed areas, it is up to the network designer to select the gain of the different transposers in order to increase the coverage but avoiding the negative effect of a high gain due to the feedback limitations.

Figure 6 shows the behaviour of the implementation losses due to positive feedback measured in a typical transposer.

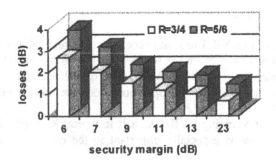

Fig. 6. Use of transposers in SFN

Effect of Phase Noise in Local Oscillators

Figure 7 shows the phase noise measured in the transposer local oscillator. It can be observed that the curve (the upper one in the figure) follows what was foreseen (the lower curve in the figure that has been issued by a signal generator). Therefore the spectral mask proposed by the ACTS VALIDATE project in ref. 9 has been verified.

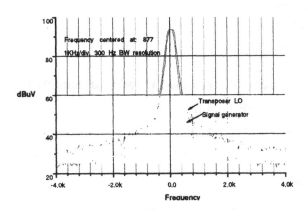

Fig. 7. Phase noise in Local Oscillators (LO)

Other measurements

Other laboratory measurements have been performed to assess the DVB-T specification in a real environment, some interesting aspects treated were: feasibility of distributing DVB-T signals through MATV installations (Master Antenna Television), technical feasibility of using *domestic gap-fillers* in SFN networks and an evaluation of the behaviour of the demodulators in presence of impulsive noise.

Laboratory tests of hierarchical modulation for portable and mobile reception have been recently started and will continue during 1999.

Field Tests

Hereafter some selected results of the most relevant field tests carried out up to date are presented.

The field trials were performed in the Retevisión DVB-T network settle in the area of Madrid. The network was configured as MFN and as SFN transmitting in channel 26 (514 MHz).

A mobile unit to obtain measurements in different areas (urban, suburban and rural) was equipped with the following elements:

- A telescopic directional antenna (10 m)
- An omnidirectional antenna (1,5 m)
- A GPS receiver
- DVB-T demodulator
- MPEG-2 decoder
- TV set
- BER meter
- Field strength meter
- Spectrum analyser
- Laptop PC

The following operation modes were mainly considered during the trials:

- 8k FFT, 64 QAM, 2/3 FEC, 1/4 GI
- 8k FFT, 64 QAM, 3/4 FEC, 1/4 GI

Received spectrum

The frequency spectrum of the received DVB-T signal was measured using an ESVB and scanning it with a resolution bandwidth of 120 KHz and a step of 50 KHz.

The standard deviation (σ) of the sampled values of the spectrum within the nominal bandwidth gives an indication of the type of transmission channel. Table 2 shows the assumed classification of channels according to its σ.

Sigma	Type of channel
$\sigma \leq 1$	Gaussian
$1 < \sigma < 3$	Ricean
$\sigma \geq 3$	Rayleigh

Table 2. Types of channel

Figures 8 and 9 show the spectrum received in Ricean (typical in rural and suburban environments) and Rayleigh channels (typical in urban areas).

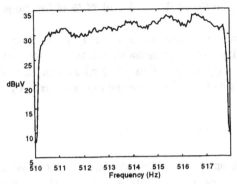

Fig. 8. DVB-T Frequency spectrum in Ricean channel (σ =2.04 dB)

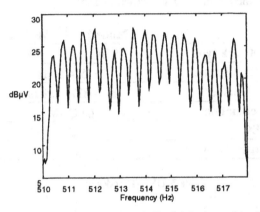

Fig. 9. DVB-T Frequency spectrum in Rayleigh channel (σ=3.48 dB)

Some areas of Madrid were presenting a strong PAL co-channel interference, however in some cases the DVB-T equipment was still able to decode and present the transmitted TV images. The received spectrum in those points looks as shown in figure 10.

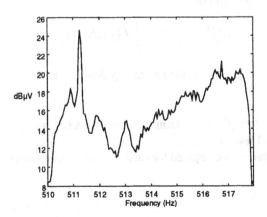

Fig. 10. PAL co-channel interference in the DVB-T spectrum

Correction factors for 70 %, 90 %, 95 % and 99 % of locations

In order to calculate the minimum field strength for planning purposes (fixed reception), the following field measurements related with the correction factors for locations in a small area (typically 100 m x 100 m) were done. It should be noted that these correction factors include effects that are not considered by propagation models (e.g. multipath).

Test procedure

Having the Yagi antenna placed at the top of a 10 meters mast, the mobile unit was following (at 5 Km/h uniform speed) a linear 100 m path. Meanwhile the measurement equipment was taking more than 1000 samples (one each 9.5 cm). The DVB-T modes examined in this test are shown in Table 3:

	Mode 1	Mode 2
Network type	SFN	MFN
UHF Channel	26 (514 MHz)	
FFT mode	8k (6817 carriers)	
Modulation	64 QAM	
FEC	2/3	
Guard Interval	1/4	

Table 3. DVB-T modes tested

Results

Figure 11 shows a field strength profile corresponding with a real data file. The X-axis represents the different points tested along the 100 m path and the Y-axis shows the measured voltage in dBµV. From this profile, it is possible to compute the median value ($V_{50\%}$) and additional signal levels ($V_{70\%}$ and $V_{95\%}$) where $V_{x\%}$ is defined according the following expression:

$$P(V > V_{x\%}) = \int_{V_{x\%}}^{\infty} f(v)\,dv = x\,\%$$

where $f(v)$ is the probability density function

The correction factors ($C_{x\%}$) are defined as the difference between the signal level at $V_{50\%}$ and the signal level at $V_{x\%}$.

The standard deviation is computed for each set of measurements (~1000 samples).

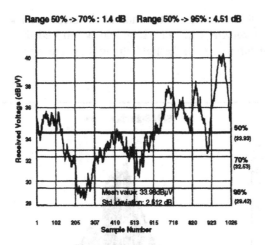

Fig. 11. 50%, 70% and 95% coverage levels

In MFN the estimation by means of the theoretical value (see ref. 10), i.e. assuming a log-normal distribution of the field strength for planning purposes, is on the measured values.

Figure 12 shows the field strength distribution of the values measured by the mobile unit in *suburban areas* subtracting the mean value corresponding to each route so as to emphasise the field strength dispersion.

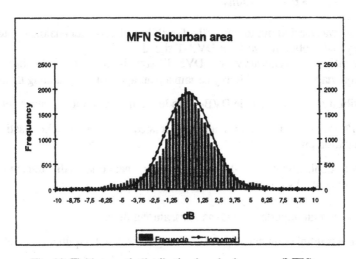

Fig. 12. Field strength distribution in suburban areas (MFN)

However in SFN the field strength can not be assumed to follow a log-normal distribution. For low coverage factors the estimation is already quite good but as coverage increases the difference between the measured and computed values enlarges, though, in principle, it depends on the network structure and the considered reception location.

Figure 13 shows the frequency distribution of the measured and computed values concerning to *suburban areas* in SFN. It should be noticed that the plotted values have been obtained subtracting to the field strength the mean value corresponding to the particular route.

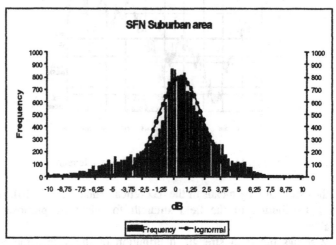

Fig. 13. Field strength distribution in suburban areas (SFN)

Analogue satellite transmissions

This test was carried out to verify the feasibility of using an analogue satellite link as primary distribution network for DVB-T signals.

The *centralised generation* of DVB-T signals and its following analogue distribution via satellite could imply certain advantages for SFN, among them:

- Possibility of using a single DVB-T modulation system for the entire network.

- Minimisation of the requirements associated with the synchronisation of the modulation process.

- Faster deployment of the broadcasting network. All transmitter sites straightforwardly covered.

But also certain important disadvantages, among them:

- Local remultiplexing not allowed. Although this is not required for SFN.

- Loss of C/N, which translates into a lower coverage area than in the digital case.

<u>Test procedure</u>

The transmission of the DVB-T signal was performed by means of the FM modulated system used in the analogue television and through the Fixed Satellite Services (FSS) of Hispasat.

The DVB-T signal FM modulated by a 70 MHz IF carrier was conveyed through a 36 MHz band-pass filter in order to bind the range frequency to the transponder's bandwidth.

Next, this signal was shifted to the transmission frequency by means of an up-converter so as to be boosted by a travelling wave amplification system (TWT).

The signal received from the satellite was then amplified using a low noise amplifier (LNA). Afterwards it was converted to an intermediate frequency (IF = 70 MHz) by a down-converter whose output was connected to a noise generator in order to change the C/N ratio at the FM demodulator input. In this way it was possible to check the noise margin reduction that the link was introducing.

To assess the effect of the satellite, two different tests were done; the first one, called *satellite loop*, was as explained above, the second, called *FM loop*, consisted in modulating and demodulating in FM the DVB-T signal without the transmission to the satellite.

The DVB-T modes tested were the following ones: 8k, 64 QAM, 1/4 GI and FEC 2/3 and 5/6.

<u>Results</u>

Figure 14 shows the behaviour of the link (BER vs. C/N) in the cases of FM loop and satellite loop.

It should be noticed that the satellite loop not only implies a degradation of the C/N ratio but also a change in the slope of the behaviour in comparisons with the FM loop.

Other characteristics stated were:

- The 25 MHz frequency deviation was admitted as the optimum value to achieve the best C/N ratio independently of the operating mode.

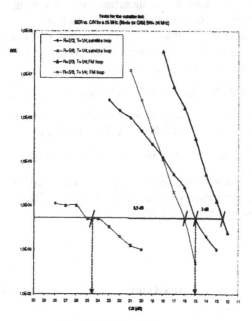

Fig. 14. BER vs. C/N

- The reduction of the noise margin due to the link was approximately 3 dB for the R=2/3 mode and 8 dB for the R=5/6 mode.

Minimum Carrier to Noise for reception

The minimum C/N for reception was also assessed during the field tests. For that more than 300 measurements were performed in portable and fixed reception with the help of the *mobile unit* previously described and using specially developed software. Figure 15 shows the fixed reception main screen, in which it is possible to visualise all the network parameters and the measurement results.

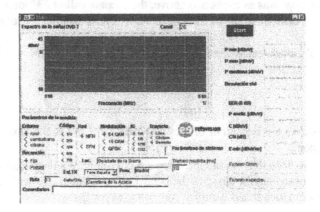

Fig. 15. Fixed reception measurement SW main screen

Hereafter the results obtained in a suburban environment, using the 8k, 64 QAM, 1/4 GI, 2/3 FEC DVB-T operational mode are represented.

All figures represent the obtained C/N_{min} in the different test points and compares those values with the theoretical ones (Ricean and Rayleigh channels). Two considerations should be taken into account:

1. 3 dB Implementation losses due to the receiver are included.

2. Theoretical values concerning SFN are under assessment. Therefore, the same estimated values are used for MFN and SFN indistinctly.

Figures 16 and 17 presents the results corresponding to the case of MFN and SFN.

In general, the received minimum carrier to noise ratio was as expected, the average value is well positioned between the theoretical Ricean and Rayleigh ones. The standard deviation is similar for MFN and SFN.

Future tests

Other field tests will be performed during 1999 to assess the DVB-T specification.

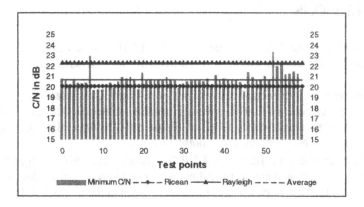

Fig. 16. MFN Fixed reception C/N$_{min}$ measurements

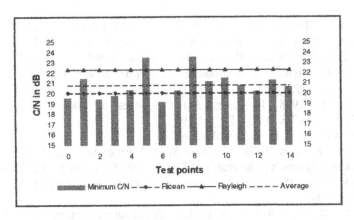

Fig. 17. SFN Fixed reception C/N$_{min}$ measurements

❑ **Multimedia and Interactivity**: Retevisión plans to start a new test campaign following the first experiences in which the feasibility of such features were demonstrated in the laboratory and experimental network, particularly with a FTP and Internet access applications.

❑ **Mobile Reception and Hierarchical Modulation**: *Mobile* TV reception is an important feature of the DVB-T specification that Retevisión intends to assess in depth, for that in the framework of the ACTS MOTIVATE project, a campaign of measurements will be started in short term period. The hierarchical modulation tests are going to follow the laboratory tests carried out recently to assess the usefulness for portable and mobile reception of such modulation scheme in a real environment.

CONCLUSIONS

The most important issues related to the DVB-T specification and Digital Terrestrial TV service planning have been assessed and demonstrated in a practical case.

The Retevision experimental network has been of great importance for evaluating different aspects such as initial coverage studies, multipath channel distortions, robustness against interferences (both of digital and analogue signals), transmitter non-linear distortions, oscillator phase noise, etc.

Moreover, an important feature of DVB-T networks, the SFN configuration, has been successfully implemented, providing very encouraging results for the future Digital Terrestrial TV regular service, foreseen in Spain in the summer of 1999.

BIBLIOGRAPHY

1. ETSI, 1997. Digital Video Broadcasting (DVB); Framing structure, channel coding and modulation for digital terrestrial television. EN 300 744
2. DVB, 1997. Specification of a Megaframe for SFN synchronisation. TS 101 191
3. ETSI, 1997. Digital Video Broadcasting (DVB); Measurement guidelines for DVB systems. ETR 290
4. VALIDATE, 1998. Implementation Guidelines to DVB-T. Del. D03 of ACTS/VALIDATE. DVB - TR 101 190
5. VALIDATE, 1998. Project Final Report.
6. Cañizares, P. et al, 1996. The first Spanish experience on digital terrestrial television broadcasting. International Broadcasting Convention. IEE No. 428
7. MOTIVATE, 1998. José M. Fernández et al. DVB-T tests in Spain. First results. Retevision/007
8. MOTIVATE, 1998. A. Mansilla et al. Analogue satellite transmission of a DVB-T signal. Retevision/006
9. VALIDATE, 1997. Transmitter Performance Specification. Del D14 of ACTS/VALIDATE
10. CEPT, 1997. The Chester 1997 Multilateral Coordination Agreement relating to Technical Criteria, Coordination Principles and Procedures for the introduction of DVB-T.

The Return Channel in Collective Installations

M. A. Panduro[1], A. M. Molina, D. Rodríguez.

[1] Department of Telecommunications
HISPASAT, S.A.
28023 Madrid, Spain
{mapanduro@hispasat.es, amolina@hispasat.es}

Abstract. This paper presents partial results of the technological ACTS project S3M[1] (AC313) which provides technological solutions to offer multimedia applications and interactive digital television services to users living in collective installations. These installations known as SMATV (Satellite Master Antenna Television Systems) are a combination of typical CATV networks and individual satellite installations. The main objective of the above project is to provide innovative solutions for the physical and medium access control layers for the interaction channel in these kind of collective installations. Additionally the S3M project is developing multimedia applications to be run on the mentioned infrastructures considering both scenarios of applications Small Office Home Office (SoHo) as well as Interactive Digital TV.

The S3M project have analysed the behaviour of the existing collective installations infrastructures (the new and the old installations) deriving the transfer functions of these networks and analysing the degradation suffered for the interaction channel signal when passing through the network and the installed devices. This paper presents the results obtained from simulations and measurements performed on these kind of networks when typical signals used in the return channel characteristics is passed through the network. Several type of installations (inductive, resistive, old and new) have been taken into account in the computer simulations and in the laboratory tests. The simulations and the measurements carried out have allowed to reassess the design parameters have been reassessed and has been derived that the solutions proposes by S3M project allows that the users living in collective installations can enjoy of the new emergent multimedia applications associated to the digital TV technology.

1 The Satellite Section for Collective Installations

During the last four years the DVB (Digital Video Broadcasting Group) was carrying out a strong activity for the definition of Interaction Channel solutions adapted to the different transmission media. In this sense, the DVB-RC Group (DVB Return Channel ad-hoc group) developed the specifications for the Interaction

---

[1] S3M ("Digital Interactive Satellite Terminals for Master Antenna Television Systems in the Third Millennium") is a R&D project of the ACTS Program partially founded by the European Commission. The following companies participate in the project: HISPASAT, AMPER DATOS, UNIVERSIDAD POLITECNICA DE MADRID, IKUSI, TELEFONICA VSAT, GCS, RAI RESEARCH CENTER, SIRE, GILAT, INDRA ESPACIO, VIA DIGITAL, EBU and PORTUGAL TELECOM.

Channel through PSTN and ISDN networks (approved as EN300 802), the Interaction Channel for Cable networks (EN 300 800), the Interaction Channel through LMDS and now the ad-hoc group is developing the Interaction Channel through Satellite. The Collective installations are also being considered by the DVB taking into account the results of the DIGISAT and S3M projects.

The return channel solution proposes by S3M uses the Broadcast Channel (DVB MPEG-2 Transport Stream) for the implementation of the Forward Interaction Path and uses a narrow-band Return Channel to communicate the user with the Interactive Service Provider (ISP). This return channel is made via the concatenation of two transmission media:

• Coaxial medium from the user to the SMATV head-end (the roof of the building).

• Satellite link to connect the SMATV head-end to the ISP.

The S3M project proposes an open architecture able to inter-operate with other alternative solutions. In this sense the satellite return channel can be used for individual users where the coaxial medium does not exist or on the other hand the connection between the building and the ISP can be implemented via a terrestrial link, a cable network, microwaves connection, etc. In Figure 1 the S3M system concept is depicted where the two sections are distinguished.

Figure 1: Satellite-Coaxial return channel solution for SMATV users

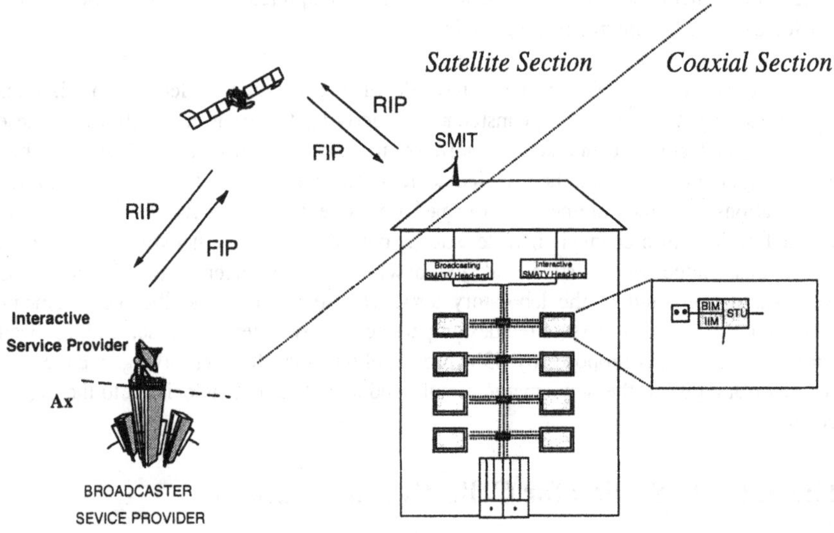

2. The Satellite Section of the Return Channel for SMATV

2.1 Description

The satellite solution under consideration in the project is based on existing satellite earth station technology adapted to the characteristics associated to multimedia applications traffic to be provided by the digital TV technology. The satellite terminal is connected to a SMATV grouping terminal that collects the return channel information from the users connected to the same collective installation. The user equipment at home communicates with the SMATV grouping terminal for sending the user data as well as for sending the synchronization, signalling and other control information. The Grouping terminal and the head-end collects all the information from the users and passed it to the Satellite interactive terminal. The satellite terminal is called Satellite Master Interactive Terminal (SMIT).

The Satellite Master Interactive Terminal (SMIT) is composed of the following elements (the block diagram of the SMIT is depicted in Figure 2):

- <u>Outdoor Unit (ODU)</u> which includes:

    - Up-converter and Solid State Power Amplifier (SSPA).
    - Feeder.
    - Parabolic Antenna.
    - Universal LNB providing the four simultaneous outputs (HH, HL, VH, VL).

- <u>Indoor Unit (IDU),</u> including:

    - Broadcast Interface Unit, following the ETS 300 473 specification.
    - DVB receiver/Outbound proprietary receiver to decode the signalling of the Satellite Section.
    - A satellite returns path interface unit which implements the adaptation function of the RC data to the satellite transmission media (modulation, coding, etc.).

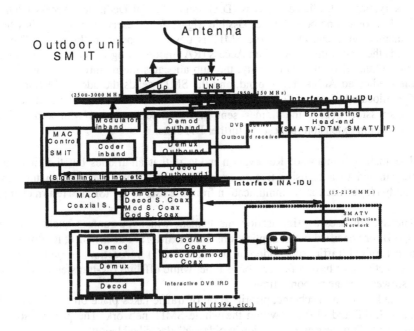

Fig.2: SMIT Block diagram

- The Access Control Module, which implements the Coaxial Section head-end, functions.

- The Network Interface Adapter, which implements the Coaxial Section head-end function management of the interactive, traffic in the SMATV network.

- User equipment composed of the IRD and the IIM to implement the return channel capabilities.

2.2 Access to the satellite

The access to the satellite is made using a new two-dimensional satellite access scheme (FTDMA) which combines the TDMA slotted Aloha and FDMA techniques based on a Reservation Scheme (this include priority, congestion and fairness techniques, allowing the network operator to offer Quality of Service to users) that greatly increases the efficiency in the bandwidth resources utilisation of the system. This allows the use of small size, low power and low cost SMITs.

Special attention has been paid to the handling of avalanche traffic defining the Medium Access Scheme. Using a FTDMA with reservations satellite access scheme, the SMIT network smoothes the peak avalanche traffic by distributing these packets in an efficient manner, over frequencies and time. This is accomplished by frequency-hopping bursts of packets, transmitted in Random Access and Dedicated Access bands.

Reservation is Dedicated Access (DA) and/or Partial Dedicated Access (PDA), on the fly, for a time period. One possible trigger for a reservation request is when the transmission queue at a remote SMIT is beyond a specified threshold. The SMIT sends the first frame in Random Access (RA) mode, along with a reservation request for additional frames. On the fly, the hub allocates the required amount of slots in the Dedicated Access (DA) band, and the SMIT sends the additional frames using the allocated slots. If, in the meantime, even more frames arrive at the SMIT transmission queue, the frames sent in DA mode are sent with a piggybacked reservation extension request for further DA slots.

The main advantage of Reservation mode is that all frames but the first one are transmitted in a collision-free manner. This has dramatic effects on the inbound bandwidth utilisation (communication from the user to the ISP, the return channel).

The system uses a prioritisation mechanism which guarantees quality of service (QoS) for specified ports, applications and/or SMITs. For instance, it allows on-line transactional traffic, such video-on-demand (VOD) transactions or on-line shopping transactions, to have a fast response time, while off-line file-transfer traffic is given a slower average response time.
In the Reservation scheme, prioritisation of traffic takes place on two levels: within each SMIT and globally within the whole SMIT network. The priority scheme is subject to "fairness and starvation avoidance," described below.

Prior to transmission, each SMIT, as well as the hub, attaches a priority level to each frame, using pre-configured priority levels for the various ports and applications. During transmission, frames are handled based on their priority level and according to the priority mechanisms.

In order to avoid capture of the reservation bandwidth by specific SMITs and "starvation" of ports, applications, low priority data or SMITs that have been assigned low priority levels, the network implements several fairness and starvation-avoidance mechanisms.

1. The network limits the bandwidth that can be assigned for Reservation/DA usage. In other words, the network reserves a specific amount of bandwidth for RA transmissions, so there will always be at least a minimum amount of RA slots available. RA slots are always fairly shared among all SMITs.

2. The amount of slots that can be reserved by a single reservation request is limited. In addition, new reservation requests have priority over piggybacked requests (for more DA slots). This prevents a single SMIT that is already transmitting in Reservation mode from hogging resources and ensures a fair allocation of reserved slots among all SMITs needing reserved slots.

3. Low priority traffic is not completely blocked. Rather, it is slowly allowed to be transmitted, unless the network is explicitly configured to completely block it. This avoids starvation of low priority data within a SMIT, as well as starvation of SMITs that only have low priority data.

These fairness and starvation-avoidance mechanisms ensure that the network performs as required, transmitting traffic from each and every SMIT, port and protocol, while optimising network throughput and resource utilisation.

The inbound /return channel- communication from the SMIT to the ISP), a resource shared and accessed by many SMITs, has a time-slot structure. The time-slot is of fixed length and is optimally configured for any given network in order to minimise inbound space-segment usage and total network cost.

However, inbound packets are of random length and are sometimes very short relative to the optimal time slot. In order to improve network efficiency, inbound transmission bursts may include several packets. Whenever a SMIT is transmitting a packet that is short enough to leave some room in the time-slot, the SMIT examines its transmission queue. If it finds a packet (or a few) that when combined with the first packet have a total length that still fits into the time-slot, the SMIT packs them together and transmits them in a single inbound burst.

This multiple packet burst feature improves inbound bandwidth efficiency, as well as increasing network performance and stability in the presence of traffic whose character changes randomly over time.

S3M project is developing the first SMIT prototypes which will be tested in the trials phase of the project.

3. The Coaxial Section of the Return Channel for SMATV

3.1 Introduction

The coaxial section supports the bi-directional communications between the User Terminal and the Interactive SMATV/MATV head-end, which is independent from the communication between the head-end and the service provider. This coaxial architecture is also opened to use alternative transmission media for the connection between the SMATV/MATV head-end and the service provider as for example: cable, satellite, terrestrial links, microwaves, etc. The Interactive Coaxial Head-End (also named Grouping Terminal) at the roof of the building provides the functionality required for signal transmission (modulation, demodulation, channel coding, network access, etc.) through its interface and channel adapter called Interactive Interface Module or SMATV modem. Different technical solutions have been identified by the DIGISAT and S3M projects matched to the technical and economical requirements of the collective installations. Three of them use the same SMATV/MATV coaxial network than the broadcast channel (using the lower frequency range, 15-35 MHz) and the other one uses a radio link between the user and the SMATV/MATV head-end.

There exist different technical solutions to establish the connection from the user with the SMATV Head-end. Two of them has been implemented and tested by the DIGISAT project (the one based on a subset of the En 300 800 and the one based on DECT technology) the third one is now been analysed and implemented by the S3M Project. This one is called Master Link Low rate TDMA. The following chapters describe this solution and present the first results obtained from computer simulations of the designed system.

3.2 Master Link Low Rate TDMA.

The system is based in a communication between the user modem (Interactive Interface Module-IIM) and the Grouping Terminal based on a Time Division Multiple Access (TDMA) on a single carrier. The downstream transmission (from the Grouping Terminal to the IIM) is used to provide synchronization and information to all IIM´s. This allows the IIM´s to adapt to the network and send synchronised information upstream. Upstream and downstream transmission is divided into time slots using the technique of Time Division Multiple Access (TDMA) on a carrier frequency. In order to control the multiple access of different IIM´s to the system, there is a need of a MAC address, that identifies a IIM connected to the system. This MAC address is assigned by the SMATV/MATV Head-end to a particular IIM as a consequence of the SIGN ON procedure, which is done after the initialisation of the IIM.

The system is based on GSM, using the GMSK modulation. This allows the use of standard and low cost GSM chipsets, concretely the GSM codec and I/Q Modulator/Demodulator for the RF part. The carrier gross bit rate is 271 Kbps. Both upstream/downstream transmissions use the same carrier. The system has been tested in the frame of the S3M Project demonstrating its performance in SMATV/MATV Systems.

3.3 Simulation

A computer simulation has been carried out in order to predict the behaviour of the design parameters working on different kind of SMATV installations. For the simulation purposes the following blocks were generated. See Figure 3.

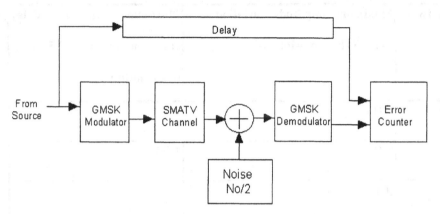

Figure 3: Simulation Block diagram

The GMSK signal without coding simulated is the one chosen for the return channel in the coaxial part of the system. The frequency band used in the simulations is from 15 to 35 MHz assigned to the return channel as recommended by DVB. The signal generated by he modulator is passed through a filter that represents the behaviour of typical SMATV installations.

The transmission chain adopted for the whole system was conformed of a uniform random bit generator, a GMSK modulator with BTxT equal to 0.3, a FIR filter of the coaxial channel, a White noise generator, a GMSK demodulator and a BER counter.

The modulator that was built is a FM modulator with a gaussian filter for pulse shaping and a deviation ratio h equal to 0.5 [1]. In the receiver the demodulator used is a coherent orthogonal I&Q (in-phase and quadrature) designed by Buda[2] with the same pre-detection optimum filter done by Murota[3], keeping in mind the characteristics of the real I&Q representation of a MSK signal [1].

This is an efficient and simple model to simulate GMSK, in a non-temporal fading environment as the coaxial channel is. This will only show the degradation due to the coaxial channel but not from the receiver performance, because of the exact phase and frequency synchronization at the receiver in the presence of white noise.
The binary rate used is 270.833 Kbit s/s. The transmission filter bandwidth is Btx=81.250 Khz to comply with BTxT = 0.3. The assigned bandwidth per carrier is 200 Khz.
The BER estimation method is based on Monte Carlo [4].

The SMATV channel is represented by its transfer function (amplitude and group delay) extracted from the characterization of the different networks used in the RACE DIGISMATV Project (RACE M1004). The simulated networks were of the two different types existing in the real installations (resistive and inductive). In

Table 1 appears the maximum amplitude and group delay variations of the different characterised networks in the frequency bands from 15 to 35 MHz in a 247.5 KHz of bandwidth.

Network	Maximum amplitude variation at a 247.5 KHz bandwidth (dB)	Maximum group delay variation at a 247.5 KHz bandwidth(ns)
A	0,09	2,32
B	0,07	1,71
C	0,17	3,61
D	0,09	2,96
E	0,77	38,68
F	0,21	7,76
G	7,34	539
H	0,06	2,48

Table 1. Maximum amplitude and group delay variations at a 247.5 bandwidth of network A to H [5].

From the table, its clear that the group delay distortion is not important for most of the simulated networks. It is because the bit period is around 1000 times higher than the maximum group delay variations.

In the case of network G, the group delay variation will be 436 ns in a 200 Khz bandwidth, which is around 12 % of the bit period. It means low degradation due to group delay distortion. The results obtained from the simulations have demonstrated that the degradation obtained by the group delay distortion is minimum when white noise is present.

The transfer functions of some of the resistive networks present an attenuation of 20 to 35 dB, while inductive networks have an attenuation from 20 to 52 dBs in the 15 to 35 MHz bandwidth.

One of the networks (network G) presents a notch that reaches 10 dB of amplitude variation and 600 ns group delay variation, when the neighbour outlet of the same floor is not correctly terminated in 75 Ω.

Because the GMSK signal is a narrow band signal, from table 1 the maximum amplitude variation on 247.5 Khz is 7.34 dB. This is a very high change in the amplitude that will of course cause degradation on the signal in the presence of white noise at the receiver. Network E presents high ripples of 5 dBs in the amplitude response, but in the GMSK bandwidth the amplitude variation goes not beyond 1 dB. The degradation obtained in the simulations was almost null in the presence of white noise.

3.4 Simulation Results

For simulation purposes the GMSK carrier was located in different places indicated with numbers 1,2 and 3 in Figure 4. Different tests points were identified in each network, for network G four critical points were identified A, B, C and D). Because the 4 critical points of network G are notch, the maximum degradation at the presence of white noise was expected at place 2. Place 3 is not the most dangerous for the signal because of its symmetry form.

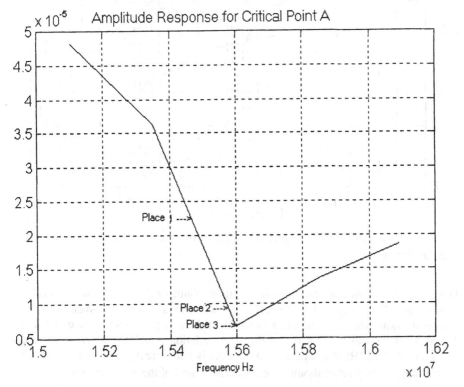

Figure 4. Critical point A of network G. Amplitude response vs frequency.

The highest degradation obtained in the presence of white noise was obtained using a carrier 20 KHz from the notch for critical points A, B and C.

The highest degradation for point D, was obtained with the carrier in place 1, because the carrier in place 3 does not see a notch.

The degradation obtained by the group delay distortion was minimum in the presence of white noise.

In the next figure the degradations of the Eb/No ratio of the GMSK signal in the presence of white noise due to the distortion of the amplitude response in the transfer function of the coaxial channel for the 4 critical points of network G is shown.

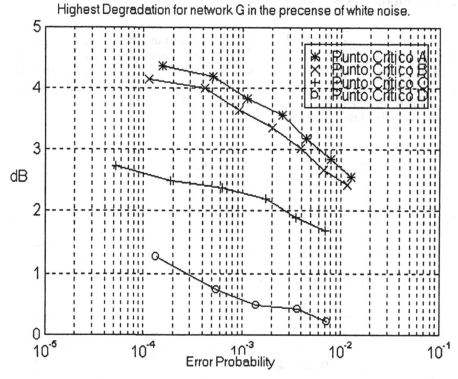

Figure 5. This is the highest degradation in the presence of white noise due to the coaxial channel.

The results of the simulations show the minimum value of degradation of the Eb/No ratio for the GMSK signal in the presence of white noise for the network G. If the communication system for network G works with error probabilities near but less than 0.05, there will be at least 2 dBs of degradation for GMSK carriers around 15.59 and 21.53 MHz if the neighbour 's outlet is not correctly terminated with 75 Ω. This degradation value should be considered as part of the noise sensibility of the receivers.

On the other hand, if the communication system for network G works with error probabilities much less than 0.05, there will be also degradations at frequencies 27.47 and 33.29 MHz.

A total amplitude attenuation of 20 dB to 52 dBs has been identified in all the networks. This should be taken into account in the implementation of the system.

4. Future work

This paper has presented the solution proposes by S3M project for the implementation of the return channel in collective installations. The results obtained up to now show the feasibility of the technical solutions adopted by the project.
During the next months the project will continue working and will complement the tests of the overall system (coaxial section plus satellite section). The project foresees to start the trials in May 99 and will finish at the end of this year.

5. Bibliography

1. Marvin K. Simon, Sami M. Hinedi,Willinam C. Linddsey," Digital Communications Techniques," Prentice Hall. New Jersey. 1994.
2. Rudi de Buda."Coherent Demodulation of Frequency-Shift Keying with Low Deviation Ratio," IEEE Trans. Commun., pp. 429-435, June 1972.
3. K. Murota, K. Kinishita, and K. Hirade, "GMSK modulation for digital mobile radio telephony, " IEEE Trans. Commun., vol. COM-29, pp. 1044-1050, July 1981.
4. Michel C. Jeruchin, Philip Balaban y K. Shanmugan, "Simulation of Communications Systems," Plenum, New York 1992.
5. TR 101 201: Interaction Channel for SMATV users, Guidelines for version based on satellite and coaxial sections.

Feasibility Model Implementation and Evaluation of an HFC S-CDMA Broadband Return Channel Concept

J. Enssle, H. Halbauer, J. Otterbach, G. Schwörer

Alcatel Corporate Research Center
Holderäckerstr. 35, 70499 Stuttgart, Germany
Tel.:+49 711 821-32213, Fax.: +49 711 821-32457
e-mail: {jenssle, hhalbau, jotterba, gschwoer}@rcs.sel.de

Abstract. Hybrid Fiber Coax (HFC) networks are considered a promising "last mile" infrastructure for interactive broadband multimedia services. The efficient utilization of the available return channel frequency spectrum and the specific ingress noise situation require an access network technology optimized for this environment. As an evolution of the current TDMA (time division multiple access) solutions (e.g. [1]), this paper proposes the S-CDMA (synchronous code division multiple access) technique for a reliable flexible broadband return channel implementation. Due to its spectral efficiency, robustness to narrowband and impulse distortions and flexibility to provide different bitrate and Quality of Service (QoS) to individual subscribers, it is very well suited for interactive multimedia services. This paper will give a description of the proposed S-CDMA system concept. The implementation of a feasibility model will be described and first measurements will be presented to demonstrate the feasibility and benefits of the basic system concept.

1 Introduction

To introduce future interactive multimedia services, the upgrade of todays point to multipoint distribution Cable Television (CATV) networks with reliable return channel communication mechanisms is mandatory. Current developments aim at the realization of full service broadband Hybrid Fiber Coax (HFC) networks carrying the full variety of distributive and interactive services i.e. analog and digital TV/video, audio services, telecommunication and multimedia services like tele-working, tele-shopping or internet/WWW-access and customized local services. The CATV coax access network is separated in coax cells that are fed by an overlay fiber network to limit the number of users per cell and increase the available capacity per user in upstream and downstream direction by frequency reuse (see Fig. 1).

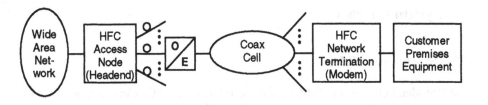

Fig. 1. Schematic HFC Network Architecture

The different multimedia services have heterogeneous upstream Quality of Service (QoS) requirements what makes the introduction of upstream communication capabilities with flexible bitrate allocation mechanisms necessary. In a first step it is planned to utilize the 5-30 MHz or 5-65 MHz band for upstream communications. However, this band suffers from massive ingress noise [9], [3] due to the operation of electrically powered devices and short wave radio broadcasting. Since the coax cable network is a tree and branch architecture the ingress is accumulated in the upstream direction. The available upstream frequency band is split in a number of return channels by frequency division multiplexing (FDM). Today, the time division multiple access (TDMA) technique is used to dynamically distribute the available capacity of such a channel over a given number of users.

On the other hand, using the CDMA technique, i.e. assigning individual code vectors to the users, the signal of every user covers the full available channel bandwidth and time resources but uses only part of the power spectral density. This way it equalizes the noise, that is fluctuating in intensity and frequency over time, and simultaneously offers a gain proportional to the bandwidth spreading factor. So, using CDMA additional flexibility is achieved by exploiting the possible capacity - robustness trade-off to provide optimum return channel capacity for the ingress noise situation given in a specific network environment. A multiple access control (MAC) mechanism is inherently comprised in a CDMA system applying a family of orthogonal code vectors that are shared dynamically among the users [10].

This paper will propose the use of the Synchronous Code Division Multiple Access (S-CDMA) technique in combination with Quadrature Phase Shift Keying (QPSK) modulation as an advanced solution for return channel communications in HFC networks. However, the application of S-CDMA is in no way restricted to the application of QPSK. If the return channel ingress noise situation allows (i.e. by proper plant maintenance), the system capacity and thus the spectral efficiency can be increased by the application of higher order modulation techniques due to the continuous type S-CDMA transmission scheme. A system concept implementing the proposed S-CDMA HFC return channel solution will be introduced in Section 2. The hardware implementation of the main physical layer building blocks in a so called feasibility (early prototype) demonstrator including a hardware HFC network testbed is described in Section 3. The measurements conducted to verify the system concept are presented in Section 4. Finally, conclusions will be given on the experience gained so far with the demonstrator and an outlook on further activities.

2   System Concept

2.1   Synchronous CDMA

The considerations for a CDMA system design for the HFC return channel have to take into account the unique situation of the HFC environment. In the downstream direction, the ingress situation is relaxed and high capacity transmission schemes as defined by DVB [4] or DAVIC [2] are applicable and will be used integrating the proposed S-CDMA return channel concept. The most important technical properties of a successful return channel solution are its robustness against ingress noise and its spectral efficiency [7].

Asynchronous CDMA systems are designed today for wireless applications (e.g. W-CDMA [8]). In such an environment, the design has to cope with multipath and fading channels, frequency instability due to the Doppler effect and power variations. All these impacts limit the achievable spectral efficiency of the system and a considerable spreading gain is necessary to achieve the desired robustness against interferers.

The main problem of asynchronous CDMA is the multiple access interference (MAI). Since the users of an asynchronous system are not aligned to each other, some degree of code orthogonality is lost creating a comparatively high level of system self induced noise (MAI). In other words, the noise floor is raised reducing the margin for external noise and thus reducing the available system capacity. It is impossible to find a set of codes for an asynchronous CDMA system that is orthogonal under all operating conditions, whereas for a CDMA system where all transmitters are synchronized so that their signals arrive symbol and chip (every symbol is transmitted as a sequence of so called chips that is given by the employed code) synchronous at the receiver may use orthogonal codes like (scrambled) Walsh Hadamard codes or preferentially phased Gold code variants resulting in no MAI, theoretically. Therefore, an S-CDMA system will provide the maximum capacity available comparable to the capacity of an ideal TDMA system.

Since in an HFC environment the transmitters are immobile, deviations of the main system parameters like the chip or carrier phase mainly result from the component tolerances and temperature effects. The expected deviations are thus quite small compared to a wireless environment. On the other side, the available upstream bandwidth is limited (notably in the designated low frequency band of approximately 5 to 30 MHz). Therefore it is advisable to make use of the system capacity advantage of a synchronous CDMA system by implementing slow synchronization control loops via the HFC downstream channel to guarantee the proper synchronization of all active transmitters.

The available capacity, i.e. the set of orthogonal codes, is shared dynamically among all active users. Codes can be assigned and de-assigned to a network termination (NT) dynamically. The information is transmitted in parallel using the set of assigned codes. In this way the transmission capacity is adapted to variable load situations and statistical multiplexing can be applied.

2.2 Basic System Architecture

The main building blocks of the proposed S-CDMA return channel communication system are depicted in Fig. 2. It is based on the direct sequence spread spectrum (DSSS) technique designed to implement a low delay transparent multipoint to point return channel. Mainly digital building blocks are used to allow the later cost-effective integration of the components.

After the serial/parallel conversion to use the currently assigned set of codes, the upstream data signal is spread over the designated upstream bandwidth to make its transmission resistant against spectrally confined noise independent of its frequency band. For synchronization purposes, all network termination chip clocks are phase synchronized to a headend (access node) reference broadcast via the downstream channel. The precise synchronization of the NTs is established by an acquisition protocol at power up and continuously controlled by individual tracking loops. Power level control is applied to assure that equal signal power from all modems is received at the headend. Since all signal and processing delays are fairly constant within the HFC network, slow control loops over the available downstream path are sufficient and do just represent very little overhead. Bitrate flexibility is obtained with a MAC layer protocol that dynamically assigns code vectors to the modems according to the bitrate demand of the used service. After Nyquist pulse shaping the spread signal is QPSK modulated and sent to the headend.

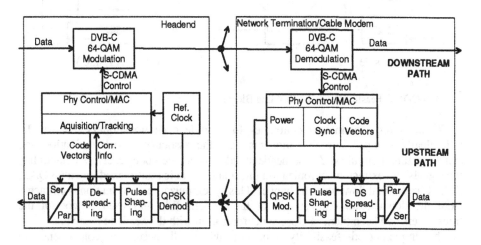

Fig. 2. S-CDMA Upstream Communication System

On the receiver side, after QPSK demodulation, the received signal is split to be processed separately for all active code vectors. The user data is extracted by despreading the individual signals with the proper code vector. Correlation information is extracted to measure the synchronization accuracy of the related modem. If necessary, the headend physical layer control adjusts the modem synchronization via the downstream control channel. Finally, the data of the modems using more than one code is parallel to serial converted.

3   Feasibility Model Implementation

3.1   Model Building Blocks

A block diagram of the headend, HFC testbed and modem feasibility model components implemented so far is depicted in Fig. 3.

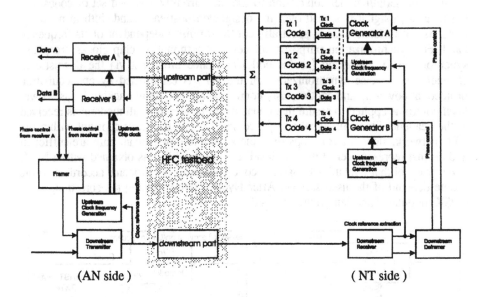

Fig. 3. S-CDMA Feasibility Model Building Blocks

For the return channel, it comprises four single code transmitters that can be individually grouped into two modems with the associated clock derivation and synchronization circuitry. At the headend side two single code receivers demodulate the signals and extract synchronization information that is multiplexed into a 64 QAM DVB-C compliant downstream channel. This synchronization information is extracted from the downstream data stream at the modem side and used to control the transmitters and keep them in close synchronization with the headend receivers.

The implemented feasibility model provides all necessary components to investigate the physical layer performance of the proposed S-CDMA return channel system concept. The realization and parameters of the individual components will be described in more detail in the next subsections.

3.2   System Parameters

The system parameters of the feasibility model implementation are summarized in Table 1 for the S-CDMA return channel and in Table 2 for the DVB-C downstream channel. The return channel provides a total capacity of 8.2 Mbit/s. At a code length of 128 chips every code represents a data rate of 64 kbit/s. The available capacity is shared dynamically among all active users, i.e. the individual user data rate is an integer multiple of 64 kbit/s and increments and decrements are possible during the duration of a connection. Thus, statistical multiplexing is supported for bursty traffic like e.g. Internet traffic. The forward channel provides a capacity of 41.4 Mbit/s using standard DVB-C equipment.

Table 1. Return channel system parameters

Spreading code family	Extended PPG codes of length 128
Spreading gain	21.07 dB
Data rate per code	64 kBit/s
Maximum number of codes	128
Total data rate per channel	(64 kBit/s * 128) = 8.2 Mbit/s
Modulation format	DQPSK
Chip rate per code	64 kBit/s * 128/2 = 4.096 Mchip/s
Roll-off factor	R = 0.4
Channel bandwidth	5.73 MHz
RF center frequency	20 MHz

Table 2. Downstream channel system parameters

Modulation format	64 QAM
Data rate	41.4 Mbit/s
MPEG-2 transport stream with FEC included	RS (204,188,16)
Symbol rate	6.9 Msymbols/s
Roll-off factor	R = 0.15
Channel bandwidth	8 MHz
RF center frequency	442 MHz / S38

3.3 Transmitter and Receiver

BER Tester

Headend Baseband
Processing

Headend
RF-BB downconversion
=======➔

=======➔
Modems
BB-RF modulation

S-CDMA
Baseband
Modems
Equipment

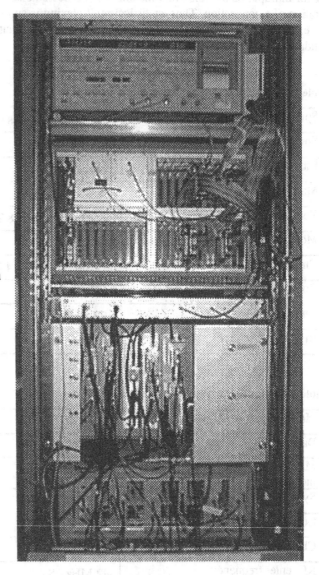

Fig. 4. S-CDMA transmitter and receiver components

The S-CDMA transmitters and receivers are implemented by CPLDs (complex programmable logic devices) and low cost DSPs (digital signal processors) in a rapid prototyping approach using commercially available evaluation boards where possible. Although the later integration of all components is kept in mind the prime goal of the feasibility model implementation is to provide the needed functionality and performance to demonstrate the capabilities of the S-CDMA return channel concept.

The use of CPLDs and DSPs provides the flexibility that is needed for the rapid introduction of system concept improvements that inevitably occur at an early design phase.

The rack holding the transmitter and receiver components is depicted in Fig. 4. At the bottom, 4 single code baseband QPSK transmitter boards and 2 pseudo random number generator boards compliant with the sequences used in BER (bit error rate) testing equipment (like the one seen on top of the stack) are installed. 4 independent baseband to RF converters are located above the baseband transmitters. On the right, RF outlets are provided to interface the S-CDMA equipment to the optical links and the passive coax network emulator or connect the transmitters directly to the receivers. The receiver RF to baseband converter is integrated in the thin box in the middle of the set-up. The baseband processing units of the receiver are located at the top. DSP boards are used for the final demodulation of the signals and provide the interface to the PCs that control the receiver operations and collect data for the graphical visualization equipment monitoring the receivers.

A snapshot of the visualization screens is provided in Fig. 5. Synchronization and tracking information as well as a constellation plot for the received data symbols can be analyzed independently in real time.

Fig. 5. Receiver visualization set-up

3.4   HFC Network Emulator

The HFC network emulator encompasses an active optical feeder representing an optical overlay network "to the last amplifier", a passive coaxial tree and branch network section and an inhouse network section. Altogether, the emulator set-up models very well the situation of a typical HFC network and is constructed using components as deployed in the field. A diagram of the emulator building blocks is given in Fig. 6.

Low attenuation fiber feeders implemented by two single mode fiber coils (4 km downstream and 5.1 km upstream) are used to transmit the bidirectional optical signals from the headend to the distribution equipment in the field. The optical transmission equipment is shown in Fig. 7. At the headend, a downstream transmitter and upstream receiver including E/O and O/E converters are integrated into a small subrack. At the BONT (Broadband Optical Network Termination) or ONU (Optical Networking Unit) side the O/E conversion for the downstream direction and the E/O conversion for upstream are integrated in an outdoor casing to be mounted in a street cabinet. Coils with different fiber types [5], [6] and lengths can be inserted in the emulator to vary the attenuation and dispersion of the signals.

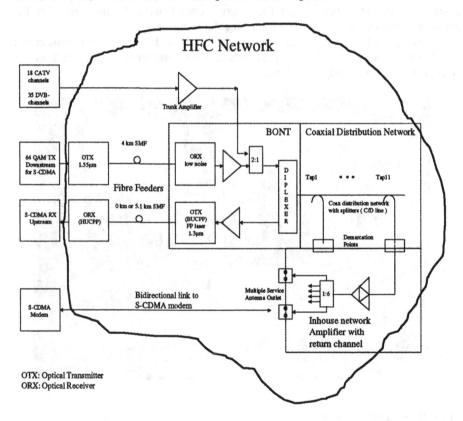

Fig. 6. HFC Network Emulator Block Diagram

The upstream transmitter is realized with a low cost Fabry Perot (FP) laser module. A diplexer separates the down- and upstream frequency bands. The useable upstream band was set to 5 - 30 MHz and the downstream occupies the spectrum from 47 – 862 MHz. A downstream background load of 18 analog PAL channels, FM stereo channels and 35 carriers for 64 QAM DVB-C digital TV is electrically combined in the BONT with the DVB-C channel (at 442 MHz) carrying the data for the modems.

Fig. 7. Headend and BONT Optical Components

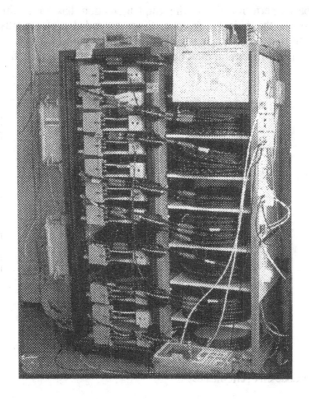

Fig. 8. Passive Coax Network Emulator

The BONT is connected to the coaxial distribution network (Fig. 8). The operator side of the coax network part is located on the left. The middle part (two racks) represents the network itself. On the right hand side, the private or customer premises part is situated. The two outdoor subracks on the left side contain trunk and distribution amplifiers in the field application normally installed inside the street cabinets. The two main racks contain the passive coax part of the network with trunk and distribution line cables and taps for the subscriber links as installed underground in typical German CATV networks. On the front of the left rack 11 demarcation points are installed, providing the separation between the network operator and private customer premises network sections. The customer premises network emulation on the right hand side is realized with low cost antenna cables, an inhouse amplifier and a number of wall outlets to connect the cable modems, TV sets, etc..., as well as different noise sources to contaminate the upstream band.

4   Measurement Results

4.1   Basic Feasibility Model Performance and Synchronization

First, the basic performance of the implementation has to be investigated and compared to the theoretical reference. Since extended preferentially phased Gold codes are used that are orthogonal pseudo random sequences it is important to verify that all codes perform similar although they differ slightly in their frequency domain properties.

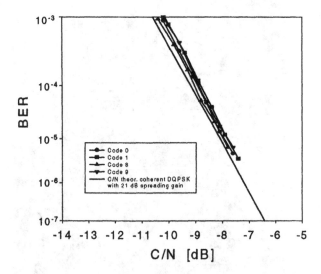

Fig. 9. Single Code C/N Performance

Fig. 9 shows exemplarily the bit error rate (BER) performance of 4 different optimally synchronized codes without the HFC testbed with respect to the theoretical limit. Optimum synchronization is established by providing the same external chip clock to the transmitter and receiver. The performance of all codes is very close and the implementation loss of the feasibility model is well below 1dB. Therefore, code 1 will be used for all further investigations of more realistic system operation scenarios.

Fig. 10 compares the following 6 set-ups:

A: Reference setup (Fig. 9): One active code, optimum synchronization

B: One active code, PLL chip clock derivation from DVB-C downstream byte clock

C: Four active codes, PLL chip clock derivation from downstream byte clock, all transmitters use the same clock (represent a single modem)

D: Four active codes, two transmitter groups, i.e. representing two modems with individual clock derivation from downstream

E: Same as D, HFC testbed with 0 km optical fiber included in upstream path

F: Same as E, in addition optical fibre (5.1 km) included in upstream path

Fig. 10 (a) shows that the derivation of the modem chip clock from the DVB-C downstream byte clock with a conventional PLL is suitable for the requirements of the S-CDMA system and no performance degradation is detectable in comparison with the optimum synchronization experiment. The results for the inclusion of the HFC testbed and the return fiber path are illustrated in Fig. 10 (b). The passive coax part provides just a tiny increase of the return channel noise level but the fiber path leads to a small additional degradation of about 0.5 dB due to return path amplifier and FP laser generated noise.

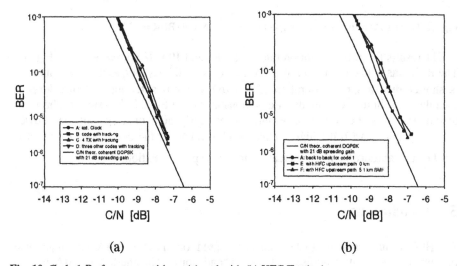

(a)   (b)

Fig. 10. Code 1 Performance without (a) and with (b) HFC Testbed

All in all, the implemented feasibility model performs well in the HFC environment. So, this setup is very suitable to investigate the impact of various noise sources on the S-CDMA system performance.

4.2 Impulse Noise Resistance

To evaluate the S-CDMA system performance when subject to impulse noise a "gated white Gaussian noise" setup was implemented to model the impulse noise typically measured in an HFC network. The noise model is characterized by the noise pulse duration, the pulse repetition frequency and the carrier to noise ratio C/N_{pulse} during the "on"-phase.

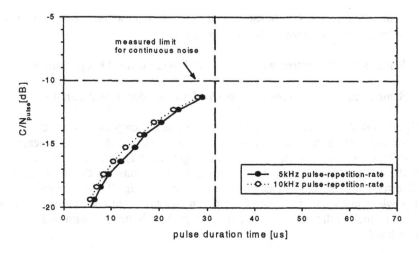

Fig. 11. Code 1 Performance with respect to Impulse Noise (BER = 10^{-3})

The results for pulse repetition rates of 5 kHz and 10 kHz are presented in Fig. 11. The BER was held constant for all measurements at 10^{-3}. As long as the noise duration is shorter than a symbol duration (31.25 µs) a significantly higher noise level is tolerable than in the continuous case demonstrating the S-CDMA system's robustness to impulse noise. For an impulse duration of nearly 30% of a symbol the allowed C/N_{pulse} is at least 6 dB higher than the C/N value for the continuous case that is reached asymptotically when increasing the noise pulse duration.

5   Conclusions

An HFC return channel system concept based on the S-CDMA technique was presented. Due to its impulse and narrowband noise robustness S-CDMA is well suited for this environment. It presents an evolution to todays TDMA systems increasing the overall available return channel capacity by operating in highly noise contaminated frequency bands or employing higher order modulation schemes. A rapid prototyping hardware experimentation platform was built encompassing the main S-CDMA transmitter and receiver building blocks as well as an HFC network testbed with low cost return channel laser modules. It was shown that the established platform performs close to the theoretical limit with little implementation loss and is thus well suited for further qualitative system performance analyses.

Further work will concentrate on the demonstration of the system concept's potential to provide flexible subscriber access by means of dynamic return channel bitrates and QoS. Suitable MAC layer solutions have to be investigated for packet or cell based communication at higher layers.

Finally, the evolution of todays DVB Standards, based on TDMA return channel solutions, to incorporate the proposed advanced S-CDMA modulation format and to provide for the coexistence of both return channel solutions in a frequency division manner is a key topic for further activities.

6 Acknowledgements

The work described in this paper was partly funded by the European Union through the project AC311 FLEXIMACS within the ACTS program.

7 Abbreviations

AN	Access Node
BER	Bit Error Rate
CATV	Cable TV
DAVIC	Digital Audio-Visual Council
DSSS	Direct Sequence Spread Spectrum
DVB	Digital Video Broadcasting
FDM	Frequency Division Multiplexing
HFC	Hybrid Fibre Coax
MAC	Multiple Access Control
MAI	Multiple Access Interference
NT	Network Termination
QAM	Quadrature Amplitude Modulation
QoS	Quality of Service
QPSK	Quadrature Phase Shift Keying
S-CDMA	Synchronous Code Division Multiple Access
TDMA	Time Division Multiple Access
W-CDMA	Wireless CDMA

References

1. D. Boettle et. al., ATM Applications over Hybrid Fibre Coax Trials, ISS '97, Toronto, September 21-26, 1997.
2. DAVIC1.3 Specification Part 8, Lower Layer Protocols and Physical Layer Interfaces, Rev. 6.3, 1997.
3. C. A. Eldering, N. Himayat, F. M. Gardner, CATV Return Path Characterization for Reliable Communications, IEEE Communications Magazine, August 1995, pp. 62-69.
4. ETSI, ETS 300 429, Digital broadcasting systems for television, sound and data services, December 1994.
5. ITU-T, Recommendation G.652: Transmission Systems and Media, Digital Systems and Networks, Characteristics of a single-mode optical fibre cable, April, 1997.
6. ITU-T, Recommendation G. 653: Transmission Systems and Media, Digital Systems and Networks, Characteristics of a dispersion-shifted single-mode optical fibre cable, April, 1997.
7. Y. L. C. de Jong, R. P. C. Wolters, H. P. A. van den Boom, A CDMA Based Bidirectional Communication System for Hybrid Fiber-Coax CATV Networks, IEEE Transactions of Broadcasting, Vol. 43, No. 2, June 1997, pp. 127-135
8. TIA/EIA/IS-95-A, Mobile Station-Base Station Compatibility Standard for Dual-Mode Wideband Spread Spectrum Cellular System, TIA/EIA Interim Standard, Telecommunications Industry Association, May 1995.
9. R. P. C. Wolters, Characteristics of Upstream Channel Noise in CATV-networks, IEEE Transactions on Broadcasting, Vol. 42, No. 4, December 1996, pp. 328-332.
10. R. P. C. Wolters, Bi-directional Transmission in Hybrid Fibre-Coax CATV-networks; A Framework, Eindhoven University of Technology, 1995, ISBN 90-5282-547-5

Analysis of a Multiple Service MAC Layer for Two-Way Two-Layer LMDS Networks

T. Martin, J. You, A. Marshall

The Queen's University of Belfast,
Department of Electrical and Electronic Engineering,
Ashby Building, Stranmillis Road,
Belfast. BT9 5AH.
United Kingdom
TEL: +44-1232-274142

T.S.Martin@ee.qub.ac.uk

Abstract. Local Multipoint Distribution Service is a solution to the "last mile problem" for broadband digital service access systems. A two-layer cellular network architecture can be used to increase signal coverage. In such networks, a Multiple Access Control (MAC) protocol is needed to manage the two-way communications between LMDS providers and their users. A novel MAC layer has been proposed for use in the EU/ACTS project CABSINET. However, the MAC layer should also be able to bear multiple service classes in order to support future users with a range of applications such as voice and Internet access, as well as the video services. This paper presents an analysis of the CABSINET MAC layer performance when considered for use with multiple traffic types.

1. Introduction

The need for an enhanced multi-channel interactive TV service in Europe exists and is growing stronger. A broadband digital service access system addresses this need. Such a system must have enough bandwidth to supply users with high quality video and audio as well as data, and should be bi-direction in order to permit the use of interactive services. The main areas such a system may be applied include: entertainment, commerce, healthcare, and education. Typical applications are Video-on-Demand (VoD) and interactive television services; tele-shopping; remote learning; tele-conferencing; Internet based applications such as email, WWW browsing, file transfer, remote LAN access and network game playing; and traditional telephone services.

Access systems can be either wired or wireless. Wired access systems use co-axial cable or fibre-optic cable. The two biggest problems with wired systems are low flexibility and high installation costs particularly in more rural areas. Wireless or radio systems do not require expensive, time consuming and disruptive infrastructure installation work. Because of this, a much higher proportion of the capital investment is available for customer premise equipment. In addition, new customers can be added more easily. There is less physical infrastructure to maintain, thus increasing the potential for reduced running costs.

The two main types of wireless video distribution system are the Multi-channel Multi-point Distribution System (MMDS) and Local Multi-point Distribution System (LMDS).

An MMDS uses frequencies below 5GHz and a cell radius of up to 40 Km. The large coverage area means that an MMDS is suitable for transmission of video and broadcast services in rural areas. A disadvantage of the large coverage area is the potential for very large numbers of users per cell. This makes an implementation of a return channel for bi-directional communication unwieldy. This necessarily limits the return channel capacity of each wireless user, and requires the use of complex and inefficient MAC protocols. An example of a two-way MMDS is CyberStrean from New Media Communications [1] of Israel used by Antenna Hungaria. Its uplink channel is by ordinary telephone line.

An LMDS uses frequencies higher than 5GHz and a cell radius of less than 5Km. The higher frequencies used by an LMDS mean that the available bandwidth is higher and the smaller cell sizes makes a wireless uplink easier to implement. The first LMDS system to be implemented also uses ordinary telephone lines as the uplink channel. This was in Brighton Beach, New York and is owned by Cellular Vision [2].

Convergence of telecommunications services can be seen in cable TV companies that also provide telephony services and are introducing high speed internet access services to their customers. If it is to be successful any broadbnd digital service access system must be able to handle video, voice and data over two-way high performance connections.

2. CABSINET

The aim of the CABSINET project is to define and then demonstrate a solution to the "last mile" problem [10] found when implementing a broadband digital services access system with both cordless fixed and 'nomadic' terminals. CABSINET overcomes the "last mile" problem with a novel two-way wireless Two-Layer Network (TLN) implementation of an LMDS with Media Access Control (MAC) as its solution.

2.1 LMDS

An LMDS is characterized by high frequency microwaves and a small cell radius. The major disadvantage of a traditional LMDS is that the frequencies used require it to be "line-of-sight". The signal can be interrupted by hills, tall buildings, and trees. Also, meteorological phenomena particularly rain reduces the effective radius of coverage. The LMDS cell layout determines the number of transmitters used and hence the cost of transmitter construction and the percentage of users covered by the signal. Hilly and high-density urban areas, such as found in many European cities, are expensive to provide with good coverage, as more transmitters are required per unit area.

2.2 Two Layer Network

Coverage is the most important factor in implementing an LMDS. The two-layer network architecture, proposed by CABSINET, is a cost effective way of improving coverage. The first layer is called the macrocell layer. At the centre of each macrocell is a base-station transmitting on a 40 GHz frequency to a number of sub-base-stations. The sub-base-stations, also known as local repeaters act, as frequency exchange points. The size of a macrocell is up to 5 Km. The base station is linked to a central office or distribution centre by any appropriate means such as cable, microwave or satellite link.

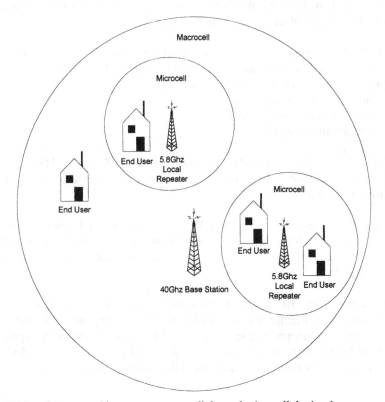

Fig. 1. TLN architecture with access at macrocellular and microcellular levels.

The second layer is called the microcell layer. Centred on the local repeaters, microcells are small with a typical radius of 50-300 m. Within these, terminals communicate using the 5.8 GHz frequency band. The 5.8GHz band permits omni-directional transmission and consequently allow more compact and lower cost tranceivers. Microcells can be used to service apartment buildings in urban areas and small villages and communities in more rural areas. Users connect via either a set-top-box or multimedia PC. Two types of access are possible: they can connect to a 5.8GHz microcell or connect to the 40GHz macrocell depending on their location and which signal is most convenient. Higher power microcells can be used, where appropriate, to service larger radius cells of up to 1 – 2 km. The flexibility of this approach allows the number and size of micocells to be tuned to the desired system capacity. Frequency reuse can be optimized and the transmitter power of microcells can be adjusted to compensate for microcell overlap.

2.3 MAC

The functions of a MAC protocol include: the data link layer part of call request and admission control; bandwidth allocation (i.e. scheduling of a specific time slot); resource allocation between different access modes like random access; and, depending on the type of traffic, reservation access.

The MAC layer handles bandwidth allocation, synchronization and access management in the down link and initialization, set-up and network management in the uplink. There are three types of MAC message:
(i)   physical link management.
(ii)   multiple access management.
(iii)   connection management.

CABSINET's MAC layer is based on the DAVIC standard[4]. DAVIC (Digital Audio Visual Council) is a nonprofit association set up to create a standard for support of interactive multimedia services.

Different types of application such as WWW, telephone, and video-conferencing place different demands on a network. The MAC system must be able to support CBR (Constant Bit Rate), VBR-rt (Variable Bit Rate real-time) and VBR-nrt (Variable Bit Rate nonreal-time) services.

All data sent through the downlink, including video, is carried in an MPEG-II transport stream. Currently the CASINET project can support 400 channels of MPEG-II transport stream in one macrocell. One microcell currently supports 14 channels of MPEG-II transport stream. The number of channels available and hence number of users supported can be increased if the available spectrum is increased.

3. Multiple Access Control Protocols

3.1 DAVIC Protocol

The application of a cellular broadband service and interactive TV with a number of terminals and a single base station involves the design of downlink and uplink channels. As in conventional point-to-multipoint communication systems, Time Division Multiplexing (TDM) can be used to allocate system capacity for requesting services. The uplink channel is designed to transmit information from multiple terminals which share a single channel to the base station. The problems in designing a uplink channel are much more critical, and a MAC protocol needs to be applied. The implementation of an efficient MAC protocol becomes extremely important and challenging when the wireless network and broadband transmission system has to provide a guaranteed Grade of Service (GoS) for CBR traffic, *and* Quality of Service (QoS) for VBR traffic as well as making full use of channel resources. Various MAC protocols have been proposed such as DAVIC and IEEE 802.14 [3].

The DAVIC1.3 specification [4] defines an "interactive channel" that is composed of downlink and uplink channels for MAC message transmission. MAC messages defined in DAVIC 1.3 include initialization, provisioning, sign on, connection establishment, termination and link management messages. The uplink MAC frame format is defined as in Figure 2. The MAC frame is a total of 68 bytes with 4 bytes sync header; a 53 byte MAC message body, a 10 byte Reed Solomon parity code and a one byte guard interval as shown in Figure 2.

The MAC protocol for the uplink channel is based on a contention-based (CB) / contentionless (CL) time slot assignment. Contention based slots are randomly accessed by active terminals without any prior allocation which means that collisions may occur. DAVIC suggests a backoff algorithm [5] which schedules retransmission to alleviate the collisions.

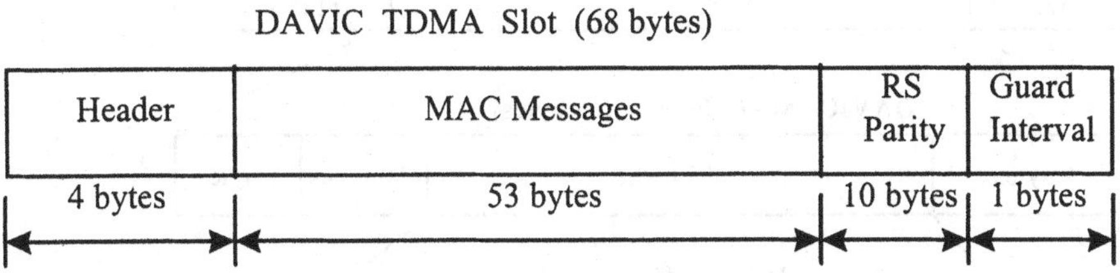

DAVIC TDMA Slot (68 bytes)

Header	MAC Messages	RS Parity	Guard Interval
4 bytes	53 bytes	10 bytes	1 bytes

Fig. 2. Uplink MAC Frame Format.

3.2 CABSINET Protocol

CABSINET's uplink system is used for TCP/IP, telephony, and client VoD requests. The MAC protocol is compatible with DAVIC, but does not strictly adhered to it. The MAC protocols as defined in DAVIC are for one-layer architectures, i.e., the signals are transmitted between a single base station and multiple terminals. In CABSINET's two-layer architecture, the local repeater acts as a transponder for the microcell. It receives incoming signals from terminals and simply retransmits them, point-to-point, to the base station. Thus the MAC protocol is used only between base stations and wireless terminals in the microcells.

The two main features of the CABSINET uplink system are its MAC system and the TDMA (Time Division Multiple Access) synchronization system. A classic TDMA multiple access control is used by the CABSINET system. The most critical part of any TDMA based protocol is the synchronization system that is used to avoid simultaneous access to the channel. For this, the MAC massages and synchronization information are transmitted using either an in-band or out-of-band signaling channel. In the case of in-band, the signaling channel sends MAC messages and synchronization information by inserting them into the downlink MPEG-2 TS (Transport Stream) with specific PIDs (Program IDentity numbers).

TDMA Frame structure. In regard to the wireless link and large macro-cell structure, the CABSINET MAC layer frame structure is extended to make the system more robust and safe by using a more flexible and longer framing of the time slot structure [6] as shown in Figure 3. The CABSINET TDMA frame consists of k DAVIC frames per slot and n slots per frame. A time margin ensures that two consecutive slots from different terminals do not overlap due to the propagation delay between base station and user terminal. The parameters of the TDMA frame, such as number of slots per frame and slot duration, are based on the traffic bit rate, number of terminals per frame, bit rate for each slot, channel transmission rate.

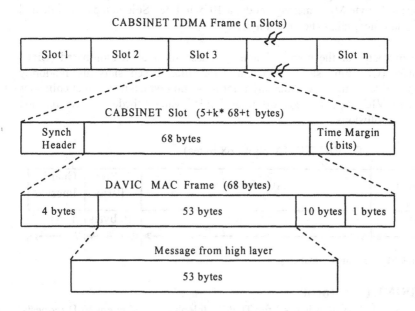

Fig. 3. CABSINET TDMA Frame Format.

Slot allocation procedure. This is based on dynamic bandwidth assignment. A TDMA frame (total bandwidth) consists of a number slots. At beginning, every slot is available for contention based access. Every terminal will receive one slot reserved after connection establishment. The slots are allocated so that the first terminal to connect to the base station will receive the first slot, the second one to connect will receive the second slot, and so on. Each terminal can request extra slots if its message length is longer than one frame. The extra slot will be granted when free slots are available. If there are no more slots free, and a new slot request is made then every terminal will lose all but one of its slots. This means that at least one slot is always available for contentionless access. This provides a minimum bandwidth, or grade of service, to all connected users.

Synchronization information. Synchronization signals allow terminals to locate the next starting upstream slot and its position (e.g. slot number) within the TDMA frame. These parameters are dynamically updated. Synchronization messages include frame start indicator, slot start indicator, next upstream slot number. The synchronization signal received from the base-station is sent together with the TDMA frame for uplink modulation.

4. MAC Layer Model and Simulation

In order to define a bandwidth allocation algorithm for multiple traffic and analyse the MAC performance, a computer-based model of the system was developed.

4.1 Uplink System

Total transmission Time. This figure is used to investigate the propagation delay and system transmission time and also to study the impact of the radius of macrocells and microcells on the system parameters, such as the time margin for a TDMA slot and the phase adjustment in the synchronization module. As shown in Figure 4, with a two-layer architecture, the propagation delay between the base-station and a local repeater is $T_{pmacro} = 20$ μs. The delay variance between two terminals in a microcell was found to be $T_{pmicro} = 2.5$ μs (using a 500m cell radius). Therefore, the total uplink propagation delay $T_p = T_{pmacro} + T_{pmicro} = 22.5$μ s.

As mentioned previously the slot transmission time $T_{iup} = 417$μs in the uplink, so that the uplink total transmission time is $T_{up} = T_p + T_{iup} = 439.5$ μs. In the downlink channel, the MPEG-2 TS packet size is 204 bytes which is compatible to DVB-T [7] with RS (204, 188, 8) encoding. The channel transmission rate is 34 Mbps which means that the transmission time of MPEG-2 TS is $T_{idown} = 48$ μs in the case of 4.5 km radius cell. Therefore, the total downlink transmission time is $T_{down} = T_p + T_{i\,down}$ = 70.5 μs.

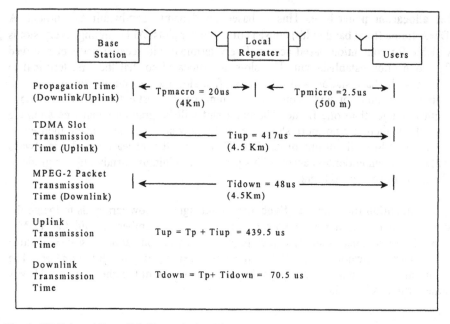

Fig. 4. Uplink and Downlink Transmission Times.

Time Margin. As seen in the discussion above, the propagation delay can cause an overlap of up to 2.5 µs between two slots. A time margin is introduced into the TDMA frame to overcome the channel propagation delay. The time margin is the duration between two slots, in which the data comes from different terminals via uplink in TDMA frame. In CABSINET, a 17 µs margin time is used which is about 6 times the propagation delay in the uplink in the case of only one DAVIC frame in a slot. This allows further enhancements of the MAC layer to support multiple DAVIC frames.

Multiple traffic types. For the services provided in CABSINET, the bandwidth assignment procedure can be extended to cope with multiple type of traffic. We propose a dynamic slot allocation protocol for multiple traffic types to make use of bandwidth efficiently. The TDMA frame is divided into two areas, contentionless (CL) for telephony (CBR) traffic and contention based (CB) for WWW/client commands (VBR) traffic as shown in Figure 5. A multi-priority mechanism is used. We assume that the CBR traffic has a higher priority than VBR traffic for slot assignment. For example, a total 2 Mbps is available for transmitting both CBR (voice) traffic and VBR (WWW) traffic. Consider, for example, 10 users who are making telephone calls simultaneously, 640Kbps of bandwidth is used (64 Kbps for each user), leaving 1360 Kbps for WWW/ VoD client command services.

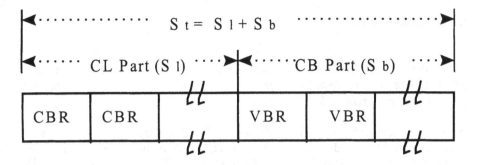

Fig. 5. Frame Structure for CBR and VBR Traffic.

ACK Messages. A logical link layer protocol is used to provide reliable uplink channel. For this purpose, it uses an acknowledgment algorithm between base station and terminals. In the model, we assume that:

(i)   There are no Acknowledgment (ACK) messages required for CBR (voice, video conference) services for which the major requirement is short transmission delay.

(ii)   ACK messages are required for VBR based (WWW) services.

(iii)   ACKs are required for VoD commands.

As may be observed, the link layer protocol will be different for each class of service.

4.2 The Model

A simulation model implements a dynamic TDMA slot allocation protocol, which accommodates CBR and VBR traffic. In this system:

(i)   All CBR traffic are assigned slots before VBR traffic as CBR traffic has priority over BR traffic when CBR and VBR traffic make requests simultaneously.

(ii)   A TDMA frame has St slots which consist of Sl slots in the CL, reserved for CBR traffic, and Sb slots in the CB part, reserved for VBR traffic.

(iii)   The VBR traffic can occupy some slots in the CL part when the CL part is not be fully occupied by CBR traffic.

(iv)   The CBR and VBR traffic randomly generate a number of requests which have a Poisson arrival interval.

(v)   The procedure of slot assignment for VBR and CBR traffic is first come first served.

(vi)   The CBR request will be discarded if there is no slot available so that a blocked call occurs.

(vii)   The VBR request will be buffered for retransmission so that there is no loss of data.

4.3 Simulation Results

The model employs CBR and VBR traffic sources distributed across all users in a cell. and these make requests for timeslots that are either granted, blocked or queued according to the current load.

In the simulation model, the CBR traffic and VBR traffic integration is implemented using the movable boundary L ($L = S_l / S_b$) scheme. A frame size of 24 slots was assumed and the L was initially set to 50%. With the CBR having priority over VBR traffic, the remaining slots in the frame are used by VBR traffic. CBR traffic is generated (CBR load), each with constant call arrival rate λ. Figure 6 shows the probability of blocked calls for CBR services, which represents a typical Grade of Service for an Engset distribution. The graph shows that a 50% S_l/S_b ratio will adequately provide an acceptable Grade of Service for CBR traffic. Further analysis of the VBR system shows it to be equivalent to a G/G/1 queuing system, where the service time varies according to the S_l/S_b ratio and the CBR loading at any time. However the results show that this may be approximated to an M/M/1 queue for simplification.

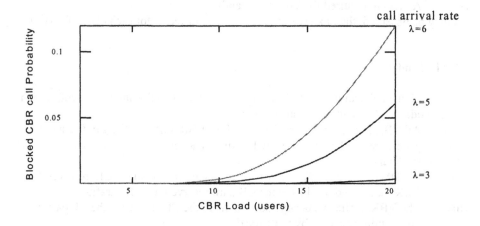

Fig. 6. Total Rejected CBR Users vs Average requested No. of CBR Users.

Figure. 7 shows that total VBR queue size increases with increase in the average VBR load (users). Moreover, the average queue size increases with increased CBR load (users). From the results, a tradeoff relationship between the VBR load and CBR load can be obtained, which is expressed by L= S_l / S_b. To achieve an acceptable CBR blocking probability (GoS) and maintain a certain level of queue size (QoS), a traffic controller (i.e. base station) can dynamically adjust L depending on the GoS and QoS required for the composite traffic mix in a cell.

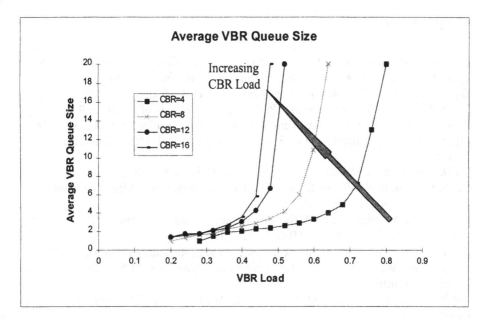

Fig. 7. The Average VBR Queue Size vs VBR Load with different CBR load (users).

5. Conclusion

LMDS with a Two Layer Network architecture is a novel way to solve the 'last mile' problem. Two-way communications are controlled though a Media Access Control protocol. This paper describes the CABSINET MAC protocol and its performance in dealing with multiple traffic types. The key feature of the MAC protocol is its ability to dynamically allocate bandwidth according to the traffic types. It is also compatible with the DAVIC specification.

The protocol uses a dynamic TDMA algorithm in the uplink to assign a available bandwidth according to the type of traffic (CBR or VBR). Simulation results show that the average VBR queue delay is proportional to the VBR traffic loading and total available bandwidth (number of slots). The results also show that there is a trade-off between the average number of CBR users and the average number of VBR users with allowed maximum VBR queue delay. This relationship can be used by the MAC controller (the base station) to dynamically allocate bandwidth to each type of traffic class.

6. References

[1]New Media Communications , CyberStream, LMDS1 "Fast Internet & Push System for LMDS Networks", http://ww.nmcfast.com/, Tel. +972-3-623-622

[2] George Gilder, "The New Rule of Wireless", Forbes ASAP, March 29th 1993.

[3] H. Kokkinen, M. Grundström, "Performance Analysis of Random Reservation Protocol in ETS 300 800 Standard and DAVIC 1.3 Specification", GLOBOM, 1998.

[4] DAVIC 1.3 Specifications: Part 8, Lower Layer Protocols Physical Interfaces, Sept. 1998.

[5] D. Bonarrigo, M. De Marco, R. Leonardi, D. Melpignano, Monza, "A Comparason of Back-off and Ternary Tree Collision Resolution Algorithm in HFC Access Networks", GLOBCOM, 1998.

[6] A. Jamin, T. Sukuvaara, P. Mähönen, A. Sitomaniemi, T. Saarinen, "DAVIC Compatible MAC for 40 GHz LMDS-system", ICT 98.

[7] "ETS 300 744: DVB-T", European Telecommunication standard, March 1997

[8] M. Celidonio, "A new LMDS Architecture based on TLN", The European Microwave Conference, 1998.

[9] P. Mahonen, E. Russo, M. Carolmagno, "40 GHz LMDS-System Architecture Development", ICT 98.

[10] CABSINET (Cellular Access for Broadband INTeractive Television), EU/ACT Project AC236, 1996-1999.

Integrating MPEG-4 into the Internet

Christine Guillemot [1], Stefan Wesner [2], Paul Christ [2]

[1] INRIA/IRISA, Campus Universitaire de Beaulieu, 35042 RENNES, FRANCE
Christine.Guillemot@irisa.fr

[2] RUS University of Stuttgart, Allmandring 30, 70550 Stuttgart, Germany
Stefan.Wesner@rus.uni-stuttgart.de
Paul.Christ@rus.uni-stuttgart.de

Abstract. The standard MPEG-4 (ISO/IEC 14496), initially made available as version 1, in October 1998, was published as an International Standard in January 1999. In addition to new compression algorithms for video and audio, the MPEG-4 standard covers new features such as VRML-like scene description together with advanced streaming and user-interaction functions. By not targeting any particular delivery technology, MPEG-4 is open to all kinds of transport or delivery mechanisms. However, when it comes to integrating MPEG-4 with Internet technology, there are still some unresolved issues that this paper is addressing. Firstly, transport solutions for MPEG-4 over IP-based networks, including the Internet, are addressed. The paper then examines the problem of application signalling and describes solutions for Stream Control, especially within the Internet context. Finally, the possibility for integrating MPEG-4 clients with an RTSP server is examined.

1 Introduction

Within the process of convergence of interactive multimedia applications - ranging from entertainment to engineering, our goals are to realise an interoperable multimedia platform on the fast growing and competitive Internet, based upon a set of new paradigms introduced by recent and on-going innovations in ISO/MPEG-4/VRML[1] and the IETF.

By developing a complete framework for integrating MPEG-4 into the Internet, our objectives are to demonstrate and validate, from the targeted residential users as well as professional application perspectives, the usefulness and added value of new and attractive functions:

---

[1] VRML : Virtual Reality Modeling language

- *All-media integration* aimed at in a virtual 3D catalogue which integrating digital high quality multimedia with video, photo-realistic images and high quality sound.
- *Increased interactivity* with content such as objects contained in motion pictures, audio tracks, 3D objects; i.e. not just restricted to clickable icons, buttons or hypertext links (already available on Internet)
- *Real-time streaming* of all media onto the user-sided scene, facilitating navigation and allowing at the same time a better adaptation of the content presentation process to available Internet network resources.
- *QoS management,* from best-effort to predicted QoS (Quality-of-Service), encompassing scaleable services on a variety of access networks, from narrow-band to broad-band Internet,

These targeted features are essential steps in the direction of enhanced user-friendliness and content realism, for reinforced audio-visual and interactive dimensions in multimedia applications, and taking into account the evolution of Internet access from PSTN/ISDN towards HFC, xDSL and others.

The proposed architecture for integrating MPEG-4 over the Internet should lead to an interoperable functional platform, and contribute to the development of *open, standardised Web-centred technology* and service environments. The developments, presented in this paper, should lead to bridging actions between ISO and IETF such as

- Placing **MPEG-4 *within the context of the Internet*,** in the spirit of ITU-H.225 and the IETF Audio-Visual Transport Group.
- Bringing an **application-signalling framework**, encompassing Internet application signalling concepts (e.g. RTSP[2] [1]), into the MPEG-4 framework.

Additional goals in the architectural design and in the proposed solutions include the issue of **QoS monitoring** in heterogeneous, and possibly time-varying, network environments.

2 MPEG-4 Overview

2.1 MPEG-4 System Overview

The MPEG-4 dynamic-scene description framework is inspired by VRML. However, the content of an MPEG-4 scene is identified in terms of media objects. The spatio-temporal location of each object, as well as its content, if it is synthetic and static, is defined by a format called BIFS (Binary Format for Scene) [2]. The scene description is conveyed through one or more Elementary Streams (ES). Natural and animated synthetic objects may refer to an Object Descriptor (OD) that points to one or more

---

[2] RTSP : Real Time Streaming Protocol.

Elementary Streams that carry the coded representation of the object or its animation data. The object descriptors are conveyed through one or more Elementary Streams. An OD groups, while defining their hierarchical relations and properties, one or more Elementary Stream Descriptors referring to a single media object. A complete set of ODs can be seen as an MPEG-4 resource or session description. The Elementary Stream Descriptors provide an information set relative to the stream, such as the compression scheme used. By conveying the session (or resource) description as well as the scene description through their own Elementary Streams it is made possible to change portions of scenes and/or properties of media streams separately and dynamically at well known instants of time.

2.2 DMIF for Session Configuration and Control

The Delivery Multimedia Integration Framework (DMIF)[3] aims at ensuring transparent access to MPEG-4 content irrespective of the delivery technology (e.g. the Internet, an ATM infrastructure, a broadcast or local storage technology). It defines mechanisms to manage sessions, transport channels and the flow of streams through these channels. Management of sessions and transport channels is visible to MPEG-4 only through the DAI (DMIF Application Interface). An application using this interface does not need to know how the underlying modules interpret the commands. Each network (i.e. delivery layer instance) needs, for example, to define its own glue to map MPEG-4 ES_IDs to their transport channels. When considering the currently existing Internet, these functions need to be mapped to appropriate protocols, i.e., to SDP[3] [4] and RTSP[4][1].

DMIF also aims at delivery QoS monitoring by providing mechanisms for bundling multiple Elementary Streams into a single network connection (TransMux) and for computing the QoS for the network connection, using the QoS parameters as defined by the network infrastructure. When considering the Internet, this function tends to substitute multiplexing mechanisms currently being specified by the IETF AVT – Audio-Visual Transport Group. In our architecture, additional multiplexing functions are considered at the transport level, using RTP multiplexing mechanisms, as defined in [5], without relying on the FlexMux layer.

3 Transporting MPEG-4 ES over RTP

In addition to the best-effort service, as in today's Internet, our design goals include networks with managed QoS and 'controlled load' classes, as considered in the context of Integrated Services (IntServ), as well as networks with differentiated services (DiffServ).

---

[3] SDP: Session Description Protocol.
[4] RTSP: Real-Time Streaming Protocol.

Due to the real-time nature of the envisioned data streams, multimedia delivery usually makes use of so-called unresponsive transport protocols, i.e. the User Datagram Protocol (UDP) and/or Real-time Transport Protocol (RTP)[6]. Both UDP and RTP offer no quality-of-service control mechanisms and therefore do not guarantee any level of QoS, despite the companion Real-time Control Protocol (RTCP)[6]. The latter is indeed somehow an empty shell for multimedia data bits, with respect to traditional transport features; e.g. flow control or reliability. RTP provides end-to-end transport functions without offering reliability mechanisms. It has no notion of connection and is usually implemented as part of the application. RTCP provides only minimal monitoring of the objective quality of transmissions.

3.1 Alternative Transport Solutions

The MPEG-4 Sync Layer (SL) defines an encapsulation of Elementary Streams carrying media or control (ODs, BIFS) data that serves primarily to convey stream synchronisation. The SL Layer organises the Elementary Streams in Access Units (AU), the smallest elements for which individual timestamps can be attributed. Integer or fractional AUs are then encapsulated in SL Layer PDUs (SL-PDU). The interface between the compression layer and the Sync Layer is called Elementary Stream Interface (ESI). Thus far, the ESI is informative.

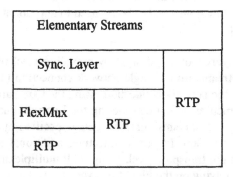

Fig. 1. Alternative Solutions for Transport of MPEG-4 ES over RTP.

At this point, several design choices, as shown in Fig. 1, can be made for the transport of MPEG-4 contents over IP: One solution may consist of encapsulating SL-PDUs into RTP packets. In this case, RTP is used as a transport mechanism only, the timing information contained in the RTP header being used only for de-jittering, and for generating the RTCP reports. The media synchronisation relies on the MPEG-4 sync layer. The major advantage of this approach is inter-operability with other delivery mechanisms (other than IP). Indeed, synchronisation of MPEG-4 content can be performed in the same way as it is performed in other environments (e.g. local retrieval, DAB), and there is in this case no need for system translators between different delivery mechanisms. On the other hand, a few drawbacks can be listed:

- This approach relies on the assumption that error resilience is handled by proper mechanisms in the compression layer and that the encapsulation process is media unaware. This supposes that the compression layer is network aware. But, even if techniques for error resilience have been designed in the compression layer, they will not be able to satisfy every possible scenario, if not complemented with an optimal management of the delivery technology. And what about the scenario where the compression layer is network unaware for applications using pre-encoded/stored streams?
- It turns out to be difficult to synchronise MPEG-4 contents with non-MPEG-4 contents.

The second alternative consists in relying on RTP mechanisms, not only for de-jittering but also for media synchronisation. Further ES multiplexing could then be performed by using generic-multiplexing mechanisms as currently discussed within the IETF AVT group[5]. The major advantages foreseen in this approach are:

- Saving in bandwidth due to less overhead,
- A media-aware mapping process leading to a better error resiliency against packet losses.
- A possible usage of MPEG-4 elementary streams in non-MPEG-4 presentations.

The only drawback for such an approach resides in the need for a system layer transcoder in the context of heterogeneous environments relying on mixed IP based and non IP-based delivery mechanisms.

Targeting applications over IP-based delivery infrastructures, including today's Internet, it is proposed to adopt here the second scenario, for the major advantages mentioned above. Let us examine in more detail the requirements and design goals.

3.2 Motivation and Rationale

MPEG-4 applications may potentially require many types of elementary streams, namely MPEG-4 video, BIFS, MPEG-4 audio streams encoded with CELP, parametric, or time/frequency encoders, face and body animation streams, and even existing material (e.g. MPEG-1 video). Thus, one question that may arise is: Do we need to design and support a payload format for each type of Elementary Streams?

Different solutions for increased error resiliency exist, either based on reliable transport protocols for highly sensitive and high priority data [7], or relying on error control mechanisms. Reliable transport increases overall latency and delay, which can be incompatible with delay requirements of real-time multimedia. Open loop error control mechanisms consist of transmitting redundant data. Thus, so far, the payload formats used for transporting audio-visual streams over RTP incorporate dedicated mechanisms for increased error resiliency [8][9][10][11]. These mechanisms, often consisting in repeating the picture header information, are conceptually closed. The payload formats are hence tailored to specific compression schemes. A specific payload format has also been defined for redundant audio [12]. The error control mechanism incorporated is based upon repetition of the media data being encoded at lower data rates in consecutive packets.

Packets can have additional protection by applying FEC (Forward Error Correction) - e.g. parity data or data encoded using block codes - mechanisms over the entire media packet [13]. The FEC packets are sent as a separate stream from the media packets, so that some of the original lost data can be recovered from the redundant information. In applications where the number of streams can be potentially high (e.g. MPEG-4 applications), this approach may lead to extra connection management complexity.

The potential of the different error control mechanisms depends upon the characteristics of both the packet loss process, and of the compressed media streams. In addition, compressed streams are usually characterised by bit segments containing information with different priority levels, in the sense that the loss of these segments will lead to different impacts, from decoder no-start, to a whole range of quality impairments, including loss of entire frames. Similarly other types of streams, such as scene description streams (in the VRML/MPEG-4 sense) require a very high level of protection, possibly reliable transport. Therefore, it seems natural to envisage different levels of protection for stream segments to improve resiliency against packet loss, motivating the design of a payload with a flexible support for a range of error control mechanisms that could be adapted to the stream segments types. The different priority levels considered here are defined according to three main criteria:

- Impact on decoder initialisation.
- Quality degradation due to packet loss.
- Delay requirements.

This motivates the design of a payload that would provide support, with a single mechanism, for a range of error control solutions such as:

- Redundant data of different types (e.g. lower rate secondary data, duplicated vital information, etc.)
- FEC – Forward Error Correction - based on parity data or block codes
- No protection.

Therefore, in summary, our design goals are:

- To avoid defining and supporting a specific payload format for each type of stream.
- Provide a fine   error correction control with a set of possible mechanisms ('no', redundant data, duplicated headers, FEC, etc.) to be used possibly in conjunction with congestion control;

- To possibly allow for selective protection of segments of streams in the direction of Unequal Error Protection (UEP);
- For small-encoded frames and for non-monotonically increasing Presentation Time Stamps (PTS), allow the grouping of several AUs in one packet. Note that the grouping mechanism will also allow to group in the MPEG-4 video hierarchy header information with raw data. e.g. group GOV (Group Of Video object planes) header information, considered as an AU. It is indeed vital to be able to group the GOV header information with the data encoding the first VOP (Video Object plane) in the GOV, the resulting entity identifying a random access point in the stream.

Since, most of these requirements apply to the different types of streams, why not 'factorise' the common features?

3.3 Further Design Considerations

Two Internet-drafts have been submitted to the IETF towards delivering media generically over RTP[14][15]. Building upon these initial proposals, the model proposed here relies on three layers, as shown in Fig. 2: the compression layer which may be network aware (MTU – Maximum Transfer Unit, loss rate, etc.) or network unaware. This layer will support a media-aware fragmentation into independently decodable entities called Access Units (AU's) or into fragments of AU's, i.e. into PDU's – Protocol Data Unit – (e.g. VOP header, Video Packet, audio frame header, etc.).

A network adaptation layer will choose the protection mechanism for different AUs and possibly for different segment types, which could be adapted to varying network conditions during the session. The selection of a protection mechanism could also be made dependent upon a degradation priority coming from the compression layer (e.g. via the ESI). This layer, on the sender side, will compute and add the FEC, and/or redundant data. It may also possibly support additional 'media unaware' fragmentation if the compression layer is not MTU aware. Note that the notion of 'independently decodable' entities supposes for the video ES that all spatially predictive information is confined within the given entities or PDUs. On the receiver side, if the previous packet has been received correctly, it will filter out the redundant information, in order to pass only the relevant information to the decoders. In case of loss, it will pass the redundant data or recover the missing data by using the FEC data.

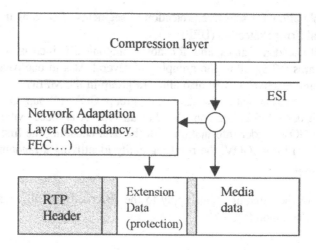

Fig. 2. Delivery Model.

3.4 Brief Overview of the RTP Payload Format

The approach proposed here consists of 'factorising' protocol features common to the different streams in order to derive a single payload format in which only the error resiliency would be parametrisable. This leads to a format combining a generic grouping and fragmentation mechanism together with adaptive error control signalled dynamically in-band via an extension data type.

Grouping and Fragmentation: The grouping mechanism concerns the possibility of:
• Concatenating several AU's or PDUs within one packet
• Aggregating extension data, if present, and AU or PDU in the same packet, as proposed in [14].
Although it is not the main goal of this grouping mechanism, it may possibly be used for grouping 'fragments' of PDU's within one packet, in the scenario where the compression layer producing these PDU's is not MTU aware, and the PDU size is smaller than the MTU size. The decision for grouping fragments of PDUs can depend on loss rate and available bandwidth.

RTP Header Usage:
• Marker bit (M bit): The marker bit of the RTP header is set to 1 when the current packet carries the end of an access unit AU, or the last fragment of an AU.
• Payload Type (PT): The payload type shall be defined by the RTP profile for this class of applications, or chosen from the dynamic range.

- Timestamp: The RTP timestamp encodes the presentation time (composition time) of the first AU contained in the packet. The RTP timestamp may be the same on successive packets if an AU (e.g. audio or video frame) occupies more than one packet. If the packet contains only 'extension' data objects (see below), then the RTP time-stamp is set at the value of the presentation time of the AU to which the first extension data object (e.g. FEC or redundant data) applies.

Payload Header:

A variable length payload header has been defined [16]. It supports the generic fragmentation and grouping mechanism as well as the signalling of the type of extension data, if present. This extension data will contain the redundant data or FEC for increased error resiliency in case of high loss rates on the network. An out-of-band mechanism, such as SDP [4], is proposed for announcing at the beginning of the session the list of extension data types supported. During the session, different extension data types (e.g. for supporting different error protection mechanisms) can then selected to be adapted to stream segments types or/and to network characteristics with the XT in-band signalling mechanism.

Note that in the MPEG-4 framework, in the payload type the indication of the compression scheme is not necessary, since this information is provided by the decoder-configdescriptor delivered with the Object Descriptors (OD) or, for the case of the Initial OD, via an out-of-band mechanism such as SDP.

Several solutions can be envisaged to transport the IOD: the first solution would be to convey the IOD in a textual form inside an SDP record. An alternative solution would be to use the multipart/related mime type for the transmission of the IOD in a binary form together with additional SDP records.

3.5 Towards a Standardised MPEG-4 Elementary Stream Interface

A widely and standardised usage of a direct transport of Elementary Streams over RTP, or other transport protocols may require a normative ESI. Currently, the MPEG-4 system proposes only an informative ESI [2]. Within this context and to support our model of a media and network aware adaptation layer, we propose an extended ESI. In Fig. 2, the compression layer will deliver PDUs to the network adaptation layer. A PDU can contain a whole access unit or a fragment of an AU, such as a video packet, e.g. as for header information. The interface to receive elementary stream data – in a unified way from the synchronisation layer or from another network adaptation layer – contains a number of parameters that reflect additional information retrieved together with the PDUs. Note that in order to support protection mechanisms in the spirit of [8],[9],[10],[11] for, respectively, H.261, H.263, H.263+ and MPEG1/2 streams, it is necessary to access the headers in the syntax hierarchy defined for audio and video streams. Hence the notion of a PDU defined as a fragment of AU data. Note also that, in the case the PDU contains the whole AU then, the same interface can be used both between the compression layer and the network adaptation layer, and between the compression layer and the synchronisation layer.

The interface on the receiver side is defined as (the loop() construct is used to represent an unbounded array of elements.):

```
ESI.receiveData (DTS⁵, CTS⁶, OCR⁷, IdleFlag,
loop(AUSegment))
```

A similar interface is considered on the sender side:

```
ESI.sendData (DTS, CTS, OCR, IdleFlag, loop(AUSegment))
```

The loop range is implementation dependent and could even vary at runtime in order to optimize the trade-off between OS overhead and real-time performance.

The AUSegment type above is defined as follows:

```
class AUSegment

{

        bit(1) randomAccessFlag;

        bit(1) AUStartFlag;

        bit(1) AUEndFlag;

        byte[] Esdata;

        bit(32) dataLength;

        bit(8) degradationPriority;

        bit(16) segmentType;

}
```

---

[5] DTS: Decoding Time Stamp.
[6] CTS: Composition Time Stamp.
[7] OCR: Object Clock Reference

The segmentType parameter indicates the type of the AU segment, for example if the segment contains header information, such as decoder configuration parameters that are vital for the decoder. Similar to the approach followed for H.261/263/263+ and for MPEG1/2, this mechanism allows to better protect vital segment of streams, such as decoder configuration parameters contained in the different headers in the video and audio syntax hierarchy.

The other parameters are defined as in ISO/IEC JTC 1/SC 29/WG 11 N 2501.

4 Application Signalling - Control of MPEG-4 Streams over IP

In VRML/MPEG-4, the syntax and semantics of the nodes of a scene determine and confine the characteristics of possible interactions. This is true for the parameters available both in 'media-playing nodes' such as MovieTexture, and in 'structure related' nodes such as Inline.

In VRML, application specific procedural logic and state management can be implemented via Script nodes - which will be - together with Prototypes - provided only in MPEG-4 Version 2. MPEG-4 Version 2 will introduce an advanced Interactivity Model (MPEG-J). This should lead to application specific procedural code at the terminal side, allowing e.g. for the local construction/encoding/decoding of BIFS updates. As the script code probably would be read as part of the scene description, the Browser could (probably) remain generic, i.e. independent of any specific application.

However, even with future Proto and Script nodes, the expressiveness of signalling, (e.g. with respect to media streams) will be confined by such to the corresponding nodes in the scene. Hence, all interactivity and in turn all application signalling has to be constructed in accordance with syntax and semantics of the relevant nodes.

4.1 Architecture

An MPEG-4 client-server application scenario, as illustrated in Fig. 3, can be characterised as follows: from the terminal side and driven by events from user interactions with the scene, a generic MPEG-4 Browser via Application Signalling requires from the Server, MPEG-4 compliant streams of scene descriptions. This constitutes the very application and their companions e.g. Audio-Video streams.

4.1.1 Generating the stream control commands: A walkthrough

The different steps for deriving, from user interaction with a sensor node, the command to be stored in the URL bearing node is as follows:

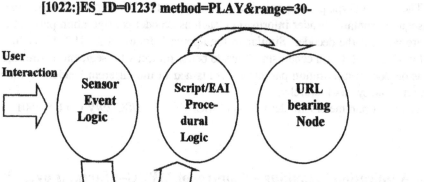

Fig. 3. Deriving the command to be stored in the URL-bearing node

- Results from user interactions with sensor nodes in the scene are used by procedural capabilities of the EAI[8] or Script nodes to construct extended 'URLs'. In the spirit of a query string ?-connected to URLs (e.g. in CGI), these URLs are augmented by Methods and Random Access Points (RAP). RAPs can be further used to specify ranges.
- While interpreting scene nodes bearing such URLs, the browser passes them to an Application Signalling Module (AS-Module).
- The AS-Module converts the query string into a set of RTSP-like commands - using ES_Ids for the identification of the streams.

The procedure is shown in Fig.3.

The communications between the client AS-Module, parsing the URL extensions stored in the URL bearing node, and a counterpart on the server side, is done using the UserCommand DAI primitives.

The commands are interpreted on the server side and a reply to the command is sent back to the client. Additional actions on the server side depending on the command itself can be e.g. the start of transmission or a jump to another Random Access Point in the stream.

---

[8] EAI: External Authoring Interface

4.1.2 Handling of non-stream control application signalling commands

The proposed mechanism allows the generation, transmission and handling of any kind of stream control related commands. MPEG-4 applications with a more complex interactivity than stream control e.g. e-commerce applications can be realised using the mechanism of AnchorNodes. These nodes are prepared to carry HTTP URLs. With this possibility of linking MPEG-4 scenes with HTTP all non-stream control functionality like "add item to a shopping basket" can be implemented using for example the Common Gateway Interface (CGI), Servlets or Active Server Pages. These technologies also allow the use of existing security mechanisms such as X.509 certificates based authentication.

4.1.3 Integration with an RTSP server

Following our approach, integration with existing Internet technologies is easy and requires virtually no changes to the MPEG-4 browser. As mentioned above, the MPEG-4 client application interacts with the remote peer using DAI primitives. An RTSP service module on the client side (cf. figure 4) can implement this interface, between the application and the control and delivery mechanism. The tasks of this module are

- Receive and handle the DAI messages from the MPEG-4 application.
- Send the replies received from the network to the MPEG-4 application.
- Interpret the DAI primitives for SessionAttach and Detach and send DESCRIBE and ANNOUNCE commands for session set-up with the RTSP server.
- Interpret the DAI primitives for ChannelAdd and Delete and send the appropriate SETUP and TEARDOWN commands to the RTSP server.
- Catch the StreamControl commands sent through the DA_UserCommand and add the missing elements to get full RTSP commands. This can be easily done because the only missing parameter is the number of the session gained from the SETUP command sent before.
- The URL to use for accessing the data streams is constructed from the IP-address of the server and the ES_ID as an identifier of the stream.

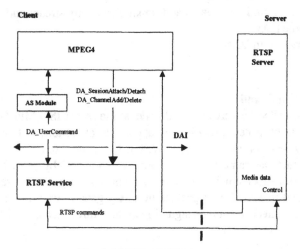

Fig. 4. MPEG-4 RTSP interactivity

Adding the RTSP service module as a translation instance between the DAI and the network allows the interaction of an MPEG-4 browser client with an RTSP server. The advantages of integration rather than replacing are:
- The possibility to reuse existing software and infrastructure.
- The ability to mix MPEG-4 content with other media. A possible scenario could be an ordinary web-browser running 3 frames. One frame contains an MPEG-4 browser applet/plug-in, the second an HTML page used to show the results of user interaction (e.g. shopping) inside the MPEG-4 browser and the third running a video/audio conference system.

4.2 Other solutions for remote interactivity

4.2.1 The command descriptor framework

Another architecture for adding support for user interaction in MPEG-4 systems was proposed in [17]. The command descriptor framework consists of three elements, a CommandDescriptor, a CommandROUTE and a Command. The CommandROUTE is part of the scene description and routes user interaction to one or more CommandDescriptor objects. These objects are processed on the client side, requiring some parameter generation, with the Command's command identifier being sent to the server. The Object descriptors are sent as a separate ES. The exchange of the commands between the client and the server is also done using the DAI UserCommand primitives.

This approach has several disadvantages when compared with the latter:
- Adds additional nodes to the scene description graph.
- Full integration of the interactive functionality within MPEG-4 makes it impossible to use existing technology for StreamControl and Additional Interactivity.
- Re-invents existing functionality.
- Command information is sent as an additional elementary stream and is therefore opaque below the DAI.
- Nothing comparable in VRML

4.2.2 The ServerCommand

Introducing the so-called ServerCommand node, at the recent ISO MPEG-4 meeting in Seoul, March 1999, a new proposal in support of client-terminal-to-server remote interactivity was brought forward. Within this framework, "commands" are possibly to construct the same way as in our own proposal by procedural means (script nodes). Using upchannel elementary streams to carry server related commands encapsulated in Sync Layer packets in a very generic way, the new solution seems to be but not suited to emulate signaling architectures such as RTSP.

5 Summary

Targeting remote interactive client-server MPEG-4 applications in the "homogeneous" IP-based best-effort Internet, in this paper we have made the following assumptions and proposed the following solutions: Firstly, in the Internet environment, the MPEG-4 Compression Layer together with the Sync Layer do not provide sufficient functionality with respect to error protection and congestion control. Therefore, replacing the Sync Layer, a media- and network-aware adaptation layer was proposed. Through an extended and possibly normative Elementary Stream Interface, this adaptation layer receives the necessary information concerning media structures and their respective priorities. Taking into account (RTCP) feedback from the network, the network adaptation layer then provides error and congestion control via a generic RTP payload format. Providing for grouping, fragmentation and extension data, this format factorizes in an economic way a possible open set of corresponding mechanisms. Adapted to the related time scale, extensions data types are signaled both out-of- and in-band. Secondly, application signaling, not present in MPEG-4 Version 1, is derived from urls in media bearing scene nodes. In the spirit of queries in HTTP, these urls are augmented by command strings. This solution is compatible with the present VRML semantics and allows for inter-working with existing RTSP infrastructures.

Acknowledgements

This work is partly funded by the European Union within the framework of the ACTS program through the project COMIQS, involving several European companies: CCETT-France, CSELT-Italy, DMI-Finland, FilmakademieLudwigsburg - Germany, FINSIEL-Italy, GIE-échangeur - France, INRIA-France, Philips-LEP-France, RUS-Germany, Traumwerk-Germany.

References

[1] H. Schulzrinne, A. Rao, R. Lanphier, 'RTSP: Real-Time Streaming Protocol', RFC 2326, April 1998.
[2] Information Technology - Coding of Audiovisual Objects, System, ISO/IEC 14496-1, Dec. 18, 1998.
[3] Information Technology - Coding of Audiovisual Objects, DMIF, ISO/IEC 14496-2, Dec. 18, 1998.
[4] M. Handley, V. Jacobson, 'SDP: Session Description Protocol', RFC 2327, April 1998.
[5] M. Handley, 'GeRM: Generic RTP Multiplexing', draft-ietf-avt-germ-00.txt, Nov. 1998
[6] H. Schulzrinne, S. Casner, R. Frederick, V. Jacobson, 'RTP: A Transport Protocol for Real-Time Applications', RFC 1889, December 1997.

[7]   M. Reha Civanlar, G.L. Cash, B.G. Haskell, 'AT&T Error Resilient Video Transmission Technique', draft-civanlar-hplp-00.txt, July 1998.

[8]   T. Turletti, C. Huitema, 'RTP payload for H.261 video', RFC 2032.

[9]   C. Zhu, 'RTP payload format for H.263 Video Streams', RFC 2190.

[10] C. Borman, L. Cline, G. Deisher, T. Gardos, C. Maciocco, D. Newell, J. Ott, S. Wenger, C. Zhu, 'RTP payload format for the 1998 version of ITU-T Rec. H.263 video (H.263+)', draft-ietf-avt-rtp-h263-video-02.txt, 7-May-98.

[11] D. Hoffman, G. Fernando, V. Goyal, M. Civanlar, 'RTP Payload format for MPEG1/MPEG2 video', RFC 2250, January 1998.

[12] C. Perkins, I. Kouvelas, O. Hodson, V. Hardman, M. Handley, J. Bolot, A. Vega-Garcia, S. Fosse-Parisis, 'RTP Payload for Redundant Audio Data', draft-ietf-avt-redundancy-revised-00.txt, 10-Aug-98.

[13] J. Rosenberg, H. Schulzrinne, 'An RTP Payload Format for Generic Forward Error Correction', draft-ietf-avt-fec-03.txt, 10-Aug-98.

[14] 14. 9. A. Klemets, 'Common Generic RTP Payload Format', draft-klemets-generic-rtp-00, March 13, 1998.

[15] A. Periyannan, D. Singer, M. Speer,' Delivering Media Generically over RTP', draft-periyannan-generic-rtp-00, March 13, 1998

[16] C. Guillemot, P. Christ, S. Wesner, 'RTP generic payload with scaleable and flexible error resiliency', draft-guillemot-genrtp-01.txt, Internet-Draft, December 1998.

[17] H.Kalva and A. Eleftherioadis, Using Command Descriptors, ISO/IEC JTC1/SC29/WG11, M4269, Dec. 1998

New Services on an Advanced Internet

Rui L. Aguiar, José Luís Oliveira

Dep. de Electrónica e Telecomunicações, Universidade de Aveiro, 3810 Aveiro, Portugal,
Tel.: +351.34.370200, Fax: +351.34.381128
E-mail: ruilaa@ua.pt, jlo@ua.pt

Abstract. This document presents some new network operator services possible to deploy on an advanced Internet. These new services are placed in the context of current standardization activities under development in the IETF (Internet Engineering Task Force). In particular, both quality of service and PSTN (Public Switched Telephone Network) interoperation are discussed, and emphasis is placed on multimedia applications. Final comments present some operational and management issues in this new environment.

1   Introduction

As the Internet evolved from academic-research to a global data network, new requirements and expectations were laid upon it. These expectations included the ability to provide multimedia interactive services, and faster, more efficient, data transport [1].

Multimedia (MM) communications have gone through an enormous progress in the application part, through the development of adaptive methods. However, the lack of confidence on minimum network quality assurances had always impaired the reliable use of interactive MM communications on the net. This has become a problem, similar to the more general need for increasingly differentiated data transport: the progressive commercialization of the Internet is changing the nature of the Internet access paradigm, from "equal access to everybody" to "better service to privileged customers". Both issues became a related problem: there is a need for controlling the quality of service being provided in the Internet. ˙

The new generation of Internet protocols, IPv6, already introduces some sort of *quality assurance*, through the Resource Reservation Protocol (RSVP) and the Integrated Services framework, and also incorporates protocols for real time multimedia communications (Real Time Protocol, RTP, and Real Time Control Protocol, RCTP) [2]. However, it was found that the RSVP approach suffers from a major problem: it is not scalable due to its "per-flow" approach [3], which precludes its usage in links with many flows, such as the core inter-ISPs (Internet Service Provider) connections. The RTP cannot assure by itself any kind of quality assurance in the network. Thus several approaches for MM communication (such as buffering, variable quality coding, etc.) were developed to avoid this problem, and became widely deployed by popular applications, such as RealAudio.

In this moment, new approaches circumventing the scalability problem presented by RSVP are being taken to solve this lack of quality on the Internet. If multimedia interactive communications are possible in the Internet, then the interoperation between the Internet and the Public Switched Telephone Network (PSTN) becomes naturally an important area of interest. This has also been a motivation behind recent protocol developments in the Internet.

This paper presents some of the Internet developments being discussed along these lines in section II, with special emphasis on IETF approaches. Section III researches new network operator services which may be provided above this new Advanced Internet, presenting clues for their possible implementation and usage. Section IV presents some comments on operational issues and network evolution, while section V summarizes our conclusions. This work aims to present some views on end-to-end services to be deployed in this Advanced Internet, and show their relationship with on-going technical developments.

This work is being developed under the framework of ACTS project AC.207 DIFFERENCE (http://www.det.ua.pt/Projects/difference). The project's main objective is to facilitate the integration of several different architectures arising in ACTS with those coming from several industry groups (OMG, TMF, EURESCOM, DAVIC, TINA-C, IETF) in order to support an European Open Service Market.

2   The (Near-)Future Internet?[1]

The development of new services is always dependent on the technical possibilities being provided by the network. A good understanding of network capabilities is helpful; thus we will quickly review current network topics in three categories, selected by their special relevance for the support of network-wide MM services: multimedia transport; interoperation with non-data networks; and the provision of Quality of Service (QoS) in the Internet.

2.1   Multimedia

Multimedia support was a major factor in the development of IPv6 protocols. Multimedia applications have been deployed over the Internet, both interactively and non-interactively [4]. Internet multimedia applications are now able to adjust their transmission rate, by changing the quality of the video/audio under transmission, by using different coding schemes, or both. Thus they are able to adjust themselves to the ever-changing conditions of the Internet. Unfortunately, even with all these intelligent methods, a more efficient transport mechanism was still desirable to support interactive multimedia in the Internet. RTP, and its associated control protocol RTCP[2], were the protocols developed to support this type of applications over IPv6.

RTP does not define the coding method being used in the data. Thus RTP acts as the transport framework for the coding method being used in the application. For

---

[1] *Note*: Many of the issues described in the following sections are still under development inside the IETF. For updated information related with the effective status of these developments, check the IETF web site (http://www.ietf.org/)

[2] RTP control is done through RTCP messages. Both protocols are inseparable.

instance, RTP has already embedded support for audio coding ranging from PCMA to G728, and video ranging from JPEG to H261 (see Fig. 1). The protocol is not closed, allowing other coding schemes to be supported in the future.

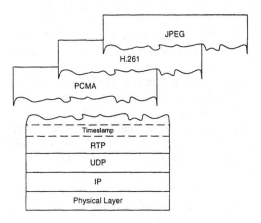

Fig. 1. RTP protocol suites.

RTP does not resort to any control of the transmission, although it provides its own timestamp mechanism (as most multimedia standards require some form of timing reference). It uses UDP, and streamlines network resources usage. It has also been designed with multicast and adaptability objectives, allowing different stations to be connected to (e.g.) the same broadcast transmission, with different quality levels: RTP was developed already targeting future broadcast services in the Internet.

Simple Internet telephony is an area where standards have likewise been proposed. Multimedia work is now proceeding on the issues of multisession control. Some protocols (notably SIP, Session Initiation Protocol) have already been described for initiating, distributing, controlling, and assuring security in multi-party teleconferencing [16]. This is being done in close cooperation with ITU activities (H.323, H.332), in order to facilitate future interoperation; close interaction with the multicast addresses activities is also being pursued, as these are a fundamental part of the IPv6 multimedia broadcast reference architecture [2].

2.2 Interoperation with non-data networks

Led by the voice and video activities, some efforts have been made to define proper interoperation with non-data networks (such as PSTN and IN, Intelligent Network). Although several techniques are already being used for transporting voice and video traffic in the Internet, there is no defined method for the Internet to exchange information with PSTN networks. IETF is defining a whole set of protocols for supporting signaling information and conveying information between both networks. The several working groups approaching different aspects of this (pint, iptel, sigtran) are focusing especially on these control aspects.

Regardless of the specific details and protocols, all interfaces between the Internet and the PSTN will require a gateway, as both networks have quite different architectures. This gateway (or gateways) may potentially support a vast range of functions, from simple voice coding and decoding, to complex signaling procedures. It can provide service interoperation from a data network to a non-data network, or even improve the services available on both types of networks. For instance, the PSTN/Internet interface can support services where the Internet requests a service from the PSTN (such as the so called Click-to-Dial or Click-To-Fax-Back) [5,6]. Thus it effectively mixes facilities from both networks to create new user services.

Some issues must still be handled regarding this reference model. The key issues at this moment are the choice of the proper gateway (for the interface between the PSTN and the Internet) and the definition of the call control syntax inside the network. Work has also recently started on generic transport of packet-based PSTN signaling over IP networks, taking into account functional and performance requirements of the PSTN signaling. This work is required for generic usage of PSTN/Internet interoperation. These tasks as expected to be completed by the year 2000.

2.3 Quality of Service: Differentiated services

The Integrated Services approach exploited the potentialities of RSVP to introduce QoS assurances in the network. But RSVP is non-scalable, as has already been mentioned, which impairs the overall deployment of QoS over the Internet. To handle this problem, a scalable mechanism for the introduction of QoS in the network is been developed inside the IETF Differentiated Services (DS) group, and is briefly described in the following paragraphs [7-8].

Differentiated Services define two main types of services being provided over the network: quantitative and qualitative services. For quantitative services, DS requires both the ingress and egress points in the network to be known in advance, in order for proper network provisioning to be done. Qualitative services are defined in function of relative network behavior, and do not suffer this constraint.

Services by themselves are not defined in the DS work; a clear separation is made between the services and the network methods supporting these services. A customer is issued a Service Level Agreement (SLA); the service provider will convert it in a Traffic Conditioning Specification (TCS), implementable in the network equipment. This TCS will have two major components: a router behavior description; and network boundary functions (comprising classification, marking, dropping and shaping traffic).

DS uses a specific field in IP packet headers (Fig. 2). This field (the DS field) describes the type of "network behavior" (regarding delay and drop probability) the packet should expect. This "network behavior" is only defined between hops, and is thus called the Per-Hop-Behavior (PHB). In the core network, internal routers will forward different packets with different behaviors, according to the PHB set in their DS field. In terms of implementation, routers will have to support different queues, for different types of PHBs, and will process these queues with different policies. Adequate queuing strategies for these environments are still a source of argument, and clearly will have an immediate impact on how the mapping between SLAs and TCSs will be performed.

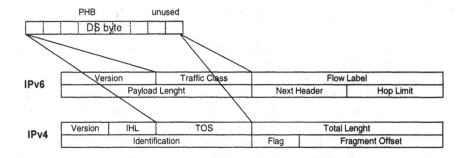

Fig. 2. The differentiated services byte in IP packet headers

More complex routers are required at the network boundaries (known as boundary routers, BR), as some complex functions have to be implemented: [9]

- Classification - the selection of packets according to some rules. Two types of classifiers exist, the Boundary Aggregate (BA) classifiers, which make the classification based on the DS field only; and the Multi-Field (MF) classifiers, which may use all the information in the IP packet.
- Marking - setting (or resetting) the DS field code.
- Dropping - discarding packets. Dropping is a key policing activity.
- Shaping - delaying packets in order to make the global traffic conform to a SLA.
- Metering - the measurement of specific characteristics of the traffic.

Boundary routers fulfil two different functions: protection of the DS network; and traffic (TCS) validation control. These routers can implement traffic classification, policing (using droppers) and shaping. They may also apply metering, and mark the packets with the proper DS field, according to the service subscribed by the customer. As the complexity of the network is placed at the boundaries, only relatively low bandwidth connections will have to go through complex operations, thus making the network scalable (with proper network management and provisioning!).

At this moment, two different PHBs (besides the default "best effort behavior") have already been approved for Proposed Standard status [10-11]. The first, known as EF (expedited forwarding), defines a top priority packet; internal routers should always forward these packets without reordering and without undue delay. These packets may throttle other types of traffic. This PHB is targeted to the implementation of quantitative services. (A small variation has also been discussed, known as Bounded Delay [12]. It basically defined an EF PHB with maximum round-trip delay, but possible implementation problems have dissuaded further developments of this PHB). The second PHB being proposed is oriented towards qualitative services: the AF (assured forwarding) PHB. This defines a set of four classes, and three drop-precedences in each class. The internal router behavior will be such that in each class the probability of dropping packets will change according to each drop-precedence. Current views about the relationships between classes suggest implementations where different classes behave as seeing different bandwidths (when lines get congested), with different drop probabilities according to the drop precedence in each packet.

3   New Internet Services Provided By Network Operators

There are no clear service definitions in the developments above described. Companies choose the "end-user services" they create, according to the way they are able to use the resources provided by the network. The existence of these new technical possibilities will furthermore bring increased differences on services being provided by ISPs. Both ISPs and telecom operators will expand their transport service offerings, increasing their client base and their profit [1]. Of particular interest to network operators are those services connected with quality of service and interoperation with telephone networks. Both are of special interest to these operators, as MM traffic (and in the near-term, most specially voice telephony) is one of their primary targets – and both quality of service and PSTN interoperation are key aspects for the successful introduction on MM traffic in the network [1].

The current framework for differentiated services will potentiate the appearance of new transport services. These could be clustered around three main areas, in accordance to the QoS they are able to provide: quantitative, qualitative and variable QoS transport services. Note that these services can be used to provide "generic" quality of service in the *transport* - independent of the type of traffic being carried by the network (which may, or may not, be multimedia data).

Notice that billing and management can be combined to provide end-user with quite different services, all based on these basic transport services. Moreover, other types of new Value-Added Services can be deployed in the near future, concerning both associated services related with transport, and interoperation services with the PSTN.

3.1   Quantitative QoS Transport Services

These services characterize themselves by a SLA where a minimum QoS (measured in bandwidth availability, delay, or drop probability[3]) is assured to the customer. Generally this will require both sender and receiver addresses, in order for the service provider to be able to provision the network for the contracted QoS parameters. These services will not be generally able to achieve large multiplexing gains, and will require heavy in-core network provision.

a) *VLL service* - The Virtual Leased Line service can be described basically as an assured bandwidth line between two points. All traffic above that bandwidth threshold will be discarded, and the network guarantees the delivery of all traffic below the threshold without reordering.

This service would present a usage profile quite similar to current leased lines, and its usage with MM traffic is obvious. Network implementation could be done by using simple EF PHB [10], with an ingress traffic shaper that would discard out-of-profile traffic (or subject this to very smooth shaping). Provisioning of the network is clearly a major issue for this service.

---

[3] No discussion will be made on the precise nature and measurement of these concepts. The intuitive idea suffices for our purposes.

b) *Minimum assured bandwidth (MAB) service* - this is a service similar to the VLL service, but would allow out-of-profile traffic to go into the network, with "best-effort" constrains.

DS implementation would resort to an EF PHB (for the minimum contracted bandwidth), and the ingress traffic shaper would mark all excess traffic as "best-effort". Network management could be more complex here: several pricing schemes could be envisaged where requirements for detailed per-class traffic measures would be required (see also section 3.4). However, a flat rate approach may also be feasible in this case in properly designed networks.

This service would be of interest to clients with occasional traffic peaks (e.g. the automatic teller machines connections), but could also prove to be an economic method to support MM connections in the network. A minimum bandwidth would be permanently reserved (able to assure minimum quality parameters), but end-user applications could still achieve increased quality, depending on general network traffic. MM diffusion would benefit from this service, assuring a minimum QoS to each connection, while being able to improve transmission quality according to the global network load.

c) *Multimedia interactive service* - this is a bonded-delay VLL service, with assured round-trip delay for the minimum assured bandwidth.

This transport service may be used for multimedia interactive traffic (multi-party conferencing e.g.) and its implementation will follow the EF PHB, with a traffic shaper that will discard out-of-profile traffic. Once again, network provisioning is paramount. A further problem is the definition and assurance of the total line delay: no specific methods are already defined. Possibilities under consideration are the methods developed initially for the Integrated Services approach of Guaranteed Service, but with some adaptation to the DS environment. Implementation of real DS networks is expected to bring some insights for implementation details of this service.

3.2 Relative QoS Transport Services

These services characterize themselves by providing the customer with a relative priority assurance regarding its own traffic in every situation. For MM traffic, these services present the advantage that current Internet MM applications could be directly used without any modifications– and from the end-user point of view, the perceived network quality would increase significantly.

d) *"Premium"*[4] *service* - probably one of the simplest services to be provided in DS networks. This is a simple "preferential service", where clients (mostly companies) would pay for preferential treatment in the network. This implies that the network will become congested for "lower class" traffic first; "premium" traffic will suffer congestion only after non-priority traffic becomes (heavily) congested.

Usage of this service is evident: every company that wishes to have better treatment in the network, and is willing to pay the extra cost for it. Implementation can be done with AF-based PHB classes, and proper traffic shaping and marking in

---

[4] "Premium" service has been often confused with the VLL service. We preferred to adopt a nomenclature that should be nearer real service implementation.

the network boundaries. Network service management is mainly based on edge-routers policing and accounting.

e) *"Olympic" services* - an extension of the Premium service, allowing graceful degradation of the traffic treatment, following several different service levels [3]. A SLA may provide different treatment (priority) to different traffic, according with contracted usage parameters (bandwidth or time of day, e.g.).

As an example, a customer may subscribe for a 6Mb/s access, divided as 2 Mb/s of "green" traffic, 3 Mb/s of "yellow" traffic and 1Mb/s of "red" traffic. In case of congestion, the "red" traffic will start to suffer heavy droppings, while the "green" should remain virtually unaffected. As the congestion increases, "yellow" traffic will also suffer increasing losses, while the 2Mb/s "green" traffic will remain with a low drop probability.

This may be also an attractive service for companies, providing them with preferential treatment under heavy traffic conditions. MM diffusion could use this service also, depending on the traffic profiles in each class.

Implementation of this service should resort to AF-based PHB, plus proper boundary functions at the BR. Network management could have variable complexity, according to the specific assurances provided by the SLA, and the corresponding TCS in place.

These "Olympic-style services" could be implemented in several ways, generating different customer services. For instance, a "Traffic-depended variable bandwidth", where different types of QoS would be provided in function of the type of traffic: the network will set a different AF class depending on the type of traffic being transported. (As an example, email would be in a lower priority class than voice; in the nomenclature above, voice would then be marked "green", and email would be marked "red").

f) *Privileged location connection* - a normal best-effort service, but providing higher QoS for specific locations or domains.

Companies may wish to use this service for connections between their offices and customers, while general traffic would still be "best-effort". The net result is the creation of a kind of Virtual Private Network (VPN) over the ISP core network; however, this "VPN" would not have any strict traffic guaranties. Implementation can be done using AF PHB; the quality of this "VPN" will strongly depend on network provisioning and control.

g) *Unassured, Regular or best-effort service* - what we have today. Traffic is handled without priority, without guaranties, without any QoS contract. This is the service existing today, and probably the default being provided by the future network operators.

3.3 Variable QoS Transport Services

These services present a variable QoS, dependent on characteristics (or requests) of the customer traffic. The customer will be able to request/change QoS parameters for its packets, according to its needs.

h) *"Pay-per-Request" service* - this service will provide the client with the choice of different QoS transport services, from which the client can request the service that better suits his needs at that moment.

It can be implemented as an "Olympic" service, but now the customer has the responsibility of dynamically choosing which traffic should be marked with each class, in a per-flow (or per packet) base. This is the most versatile form of non-assured service, but will place some control of traffic types outside the operator network. As a consequence, it brings increased complexity to network management and provision, as traffic forecasts will be more difficult to make.

i) *Fast connection event-based VLL* - this service will act as a VLL service, but with increased bandwidth of the connection according to a particular event (e.g. during nights, or in peak traffic hours, or according to the traffic level in the client network). The customer will have several VLLs available, but most of these will be "dormant", and will be activated according to the triggering event.

This service could present applications quite similar to current usage of ISDN access routers (fast connection routers, which increase the number of connection lines in use according to the requested traffic; sometimes voice is already multiplexed with this traffic).

Basic support for this service would be an EF PHB. A dynamic implementation of this service across the network would be quite complex, with signaling (for dynamic change of the EF-traffic bandwidth) being exchanged across the network. A much more reasonable approach for an ISP to introduce this service is related with the possibility of increasing its own multiplexing gains (in contrast to the basic VLL service). The ISP will provision the network with the maximum bandwidth, but will know that its multiplexing gains (for other types of traffic) will be much better than with a simple VLL service.

3.4 Pricing and Measurement Related Services

Many variants of the above services are possible, according to market demand, tariff policies, and management flexibility in the ISP network. Service pricing is a fundamental tool for end-user service differentiation. Simple time-based and amount-of-traffic-depended services can be found even today, when proper management software is available [13]. In future networks, concepts such as "time-based variable tariffs" or "time-based variable service" (for instance), can be applied to most services described above, with more complex boundary functions.

"Time-based variable tariffs" will need to register the traffic being processed, and calculate total costs in function of the time of the day. "Time based variable service" will allow different QoS according to the time of the day (e.g. changing either AF class or AF-drop-precedence in function of the time of the day, or changing queue characteristics inside routers). Thus some basic flexibility on the boundary functions can support the implementation of quite different end-user services.

Furthermore, some more complex measurement facilities in place at the boundary routers may increase the flexibility of network services being provided to the end user. E.g. the *Pay-per-Request* service does require permanent traffic measurements in a per-class base. Furthermore, some types of Variable Services may require dynamic adjustment of the boundary functions (such as policing). If all these facilities are in place, then complex end-user services can be envisaged, where billing and QoS parameters can be changed according to several other parameters (such as total customer traffic, hour of the day, service class being requested).

Naturally, these services will only appear if future market demand for DS network usage justifies their deployment, and will certainly change from ISP to ISP.

3.5   Support Services

Supplying these transport services requires in many cases proper marking of the packets according to a specific policy. This policy is usual chosen by the ISP customer; thus marking (as well as traffic shaping) is a function naturally done by the customer. At the network boundary, the ISP has to perform conformance policing, for proper control and network reliability. This implies that the network, by itself, only requires simple marking and/or dropping functions. *More complex functions are actually services being provided to the customer.*

Several of the services presented above will require MF classifiers, i.e. a classification entity that will select the packets according to different fields of the packets. Some will require complex (parameter dependent) markers, where the DS byte will be set according to several global service parameters (e.g. peak bit rate, or time of the day). Furthermore, it may be convenient to have traffic shaping in many services, in order to adapt traffic variations to the agreed traffic profile, and thus decrease drop probabilities.

All these functions can be setup at the customer interface of the ingress router, and thus can be provided to the customer as a service. Many customers may prefer to implement these functions themselves, in their own equipment, either by security measures, or by internal traffic control. Nevertheless, other customers will prefer to have these functions bundled in their Internet access packet as a value-added service.

3.6   Interoperation Services

PSTN/Internet interoperation originates several new services, many of MM nature. Even at this moment, fax-service providers are operating in the Internet with extremely low rates, and some voice-over-IP products can be found. As PSTN/Internet interoperation becomes standardized in an Internet with QoS characteristics, PNOs (Public Network Operators) can provide new services, supporting fax transmission from the Internet to the PSTN, voice calls between both networks, or other types of services (e.g. mixed Internet/PSTN voice conferences). These services can be classified in several classes:

- interoperation of PSTN services with data networks (e.g. the establishment of a voice call between an Internet-based phone and a traditional phone);
- interoperation of data services with the PSTN network (e.g. paging/phoning a user on the reception of an email)
- new services based both on PSTN and Internet facilities (e.g. a WEB-based helpdesk, able to fax-back some of the documentation)

Although several of these services already exist, its widespread usage in the Internet (potentiated by the global introduction of QoS in the network) will greatly increase its usage, and create more complex problems. For instance, a voice call can be placed through the Internet to a PSTN gateway near the (phone) receiver; this situation will change from (the now existing) locally available gateway, to a (in the future) widespread set of gateways which may cooperate to decide where to route that call to. This increased dimension will enlarge its usage and applicability, and both ISPs and PNOs are bound to exploit this type of services, probably only limited by regulatory constraints. Market demands will became the final law for the definition of the specific interoperation services that will become successful.

3.7 Example: An Advanced Scenario

As an example, we can present an advanced scenario with a DS network providing both voice services and PSTN/Internet interoperation services to special clients. Fig. 3 concisely presents the network structure required to provide this interoperation over a DS-enabled Internet.

In this figure, we present a possible application of this network with a simple phone call communication. John wants to call Suzy from his office (logical connection A). There are two ways of establishing this connection: the regular PSTN (path B); and the data DS network (path C). Due to the receiver location, price structures are such that the intelligent PABX in John's company decides to use the C path. For doing that, it first issues a request to the PSTN/Internet internetwork, trying to figure what should be the proper phone gateway near Suzy's phone. (There is no need to resort to a specific phone gateway in John's location, as its company PABX already includes an Internet gateway.) After determining the far-end gateway, it requests a "Multimedia Interactive" transport service between his location and that gateway. This request is done by contacting the Bandwidth Broker (BB), responsible by managing all SLAs inside the DS network. The BB will accept the request (if possible), define the proper TCS in order to fulfil this new SLA, and adjust the DS network parameters in order to provide (and charge for) the requested service. The PABX will then establish the connection between John and the target network gateway, using RTP-based protocols, and from there the call will reach Suzy's telephone through the PSTN network.

This target scenario, although highly desirable, is not possible to implement in the near term, in this exact form. Some of the supporting protocols for these tasks are still under consideration, but nevertheless there is a major technical problem in providing all this flexibility: time! The total time generally required for the connection setup, with current protocols, would be too large. So early implementations of the above described framework would probably have to skip some of the steps described, at a loss of generality (e.g. John's locations has a VLL-alike service permanently set-up with Suzy's location; or John's PABX is able to determine immediately what is the destination gateway; or this would be a fax transmission, instead of a voice call, and thus the fax software would be designed to cope with this long setup phase; or proper signaling would be generated in John's PABX to support these longer call establishment procedures).

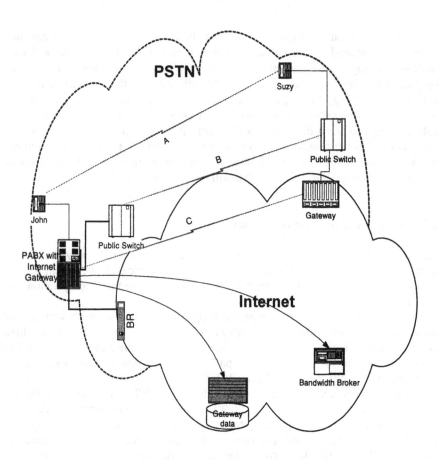

Fig. 3. A DS network with PSTN interoperation, comprising a *boundary router (BR)*, a simple *Gateway*, a *PABX with an internal network gateway*, and a *Bandwidth Broker* and G*ateway data* management units, connected to a PSTN switch

Notice that in this scenario, there are several tasks that are performed either by network operators, or by John's company. In a real-world scenario, the situation could be even more complex. For instance, the "interoperation provider" could be distinct from the DS-network ISP provider; this last one could be distinct from the telecom provider; or we could have different transport and access service providers; or we could even have competing, or cooperating, providers for some of these services; or we could have variable tariffs in all these services, and cross billing amongst operators; or John's company could subscribe to several different service offering, each including a whole set of transport and value-added providers in a bundle pack. These possibilities bring a new complexity layer to the problem, concerning management, billing, and auditing - and John's PABX would have to take fairly complex decisions.

4 Operational Issues

Although much work is still required for a complete implementation of the potentialities described in the previous sections, IETF working groups are already handling many of the major problems still pending. However the efficiency of these approaches for Internet-wide usage is still an issue that will have to be settled by future real implementations. And clearly its ability to provide end-user services will depend strongly on technical details still under discussion (such as the ability to provide and dynamically control a differentiated services network).

Key to the success of its deployment will be the management topics associated with these new services. The emergence of differentiated services into the Internet (or generically QoS sensitive services) will increase management problems. Current Internet networks are mainly data based networks, with asynchronous communications and best-effort policies (i.e. "no policy"). Nowadays the typical user accepts well this *status quo*; the next generation user will claim for increasingly complex QoS services, as his MM applications will be sensitive to QoS performance. Internet reliability, management reliability, will be a very important issue for the widespread adoption of new protocols in the near future [1].

The introduction of new equipment, services and increasing bandwidths will raise to unavoidable levels the overall available management information (our previous example already points some of those management needs). Present management architectures suffer from several shortcomings to answer those new requirements. Traditional management approaches inside IETF were mainly oriented towards (device) management information definition and management protocols. Topics such as service management have not been considered relevant and have been delegated as a company problem. Thus we may reach a situation where management related issues preclude the wide diffusion of advanced MM services in the network.

Clearly new management paradigms must be implemented in order to cope with the limitations of current frameworks, which are mainly based on the manager-agent model and on polling access methods. The arrival to the net of Integrated/Differentiated services is increasing the visibility of this problem. New drafts that aim to facilitate the introduction and management of QoS services are under way. Network managers must be able to define access policies based upon criteria such as user identity, applications, bandwidth requirements, security considerations, etc. [14]. Characteristics such as scalability through distribution, an approach tailored to organisational structures (hierarchies), and "off-line" operation reliability, will be required for successful management strategies, and are being pursued inside the IETF working group on Distributed Management. These issues will become fundamental for practical implementation of an Advanced Internet. We have already seen that the management facilities in place can change significantly the end-user services offered by the ISPs.

New management paradigms are furthermore fundamental for network development: current telecommunication liberalization will promote new competitors that must cooperate for achieving a working differentiated services network. New trends are expected in management area to solve these issues, where service providers will work in a closely coupling fashion in order to explore the best the network they have, with different control of operational levels of network equipment. These developments will become essential to maintain the overall cohesion of the Internet, and creating worldwide services with controlled quality of service. Lack of concerted effort in these areas may lead to a network where services are not universally available, impairing increasing Internet widespread usage.

5 Conclusions

The Internet has become a major communication infrastructure on nowadays life. Internet robustness has cope adequately on the past with the massive growth of services and users. Just considering the infrastructure, there are already companies (e.g. MCI) testing IP switching at 2.4 Gb/s and expectations are that soon IP routers can handle 30 to 40 Gb/s [15]. An increasing Internet-based business will help to grow even more this dependency on Internet and its impact on the society. New demands are underway considering the globalization of communications market (services and architecture integration - PSTN, Cable TV, Internet, etc.). These demands aim to achieve a global MM network, able to support most communication needs.

This paper has highlighted some recent outcomes from IETF working groups that are providing solutions for this increasing network complexity, with special focus on two key issues that currently constraint network-wide multimedia support and development: quality of service and PSTN interoperation. Based on this background, we have proposed some new network services that exploit these near-future technological solutions and allow providers to push this evolution. These services have been arranged in several classes, according to their global characteristics, and several issues concerning their implementation have been presented. We have illustrated some new service potentialities and limitations in an QoS-enabled Internet, able to run MM traffic and interoperate with the PSTN.

The early provision of these services would accelerate network development and usage. Considering the technical developments progress under way inside IETF, we have alerted to the fact that operational issues (especially service management) may become key aspects in the early implementation/limitation of new services. These issues should be considered for a successful QoS capable network to be deployed.

References

1. Aguiar R.L., Oliveira, J.L.: Issues on Internet Evolution and Management, ICEIS'99, International Conference on Enterprise and Information Systems (1999), pp. 563-571
2. Thomas, S.: IPng and the TCP-IP Protocols, John Wiley and Sons, (1996)
3. Baumgartner, F., Braun, T., Habegger, P.: Differentiated Services: A New Approach for Quality of Service in the Internet, HPN'98, IFIP Conference on High Performance Networking, (1998)
4. Huitema, C: IPv6, the new Internet Protocol, Prentice-Hall, (1996)
5. Petrack, S., Conroy, L.: The PINT Profile of SIP and SDP: a Protocol for IP Access to Telephone Call Services, Internet Draft <draft-ietf-pint-profile-04.txt>, (March 1999)
6. Lu, H. (ed.): Towards the PSTN/Internet Internetworking -Pre PINT Implementations, Internet RFC 2458, (November 1998)

7. Bernet, Y., et all: A Framework for Differentiated Services, Internet Draft <draft-ietf-diffserv-framework-02.txt>, (February 1999)

8. Blake, S., et all: An Architecture for Differentiated Services, Internet RFC 2475, (December 1998)

9. Bernet, Y., et all: Requirements of Diff-serv Boundary Routers, Internet Draft <draft-bernet-diffedge-01.txt>, (November 1998)

10. Jacobson, V., et all: An Expedited Forwarding PHB, Internet Draft <draft-ietf-diffserv-phb-ef-02.txt>, (February 1999), approved for Proposed Standard status in March 99

11. Heinanen, J., et all: Assured Forwarding PHB Group, Internet Draft <draft-ietf-diffserv-af-06.txt>, (February 1999), approved for Proposed Standard status in March 99

12. Carter, S. et all: A Bounded-Delay Service for the Internet, Internet Draft <draft-carter-bounded-delay-00.txt>, (November 1998)

13. Billing for Internet usage, in Telecommunications News, 16, Hewlett Packard European Edition (1998)

14. Yavatkar, R., Guerin, R., Pendarakis, D.: A Framework for Policy-based Admission Control, Internet Draft <draft-ietf-rap-framework-01.txt>, (November 1998)

15. Lange, L.: The Internet", IEEE Spectrum, (January 1999) pp.36-40

16. Handley, M. et all: SIP: Session Initiation Protocol, Internet RFC 2543, (March 1999)

Adaptive Video on Demand Service on RSVP Capable Network[1]

Carlos Veciana-Nogués, Jordi Domingo-Pascual

Computer Architecture Department
Advanced Broadband Communications Center
Polytechnic University of Catalonia
Campus Nord. Mòdul D6. Jordi Girona 1-3. 08034 Barcelona.
{carlosv, jordid}@ac.upc.es

Abstract. At present, the provision of quality of service is one of the most relevant research topics. The Integrated Services approach defined by IETF and based mainly on the resource reservation protocol (RSVP [1]) is one of the issues that attracts many research work. On the other hand, research on adaptive applications [2] is another research topic. In this paper, we present a proposal that combines the features of RSVP and adaptive applications altogether. We put into work two protocols, RSVP and SVA[2] to get an optimum resource usage for a video on demand transmission. RSVP helps to maintain a given network bandwidth available, while SVA adapts video flow taking into account not only the network impairments but the client resources variations as well. We think that it is very important to cope with the resource availability at the end systems to provide a QoS to the final user. Once a flow is being transmitted, RSVP may renegotiate the reservation to adjust the bandwidth usage. Flow adaptation is done at the video server by reducing video flow size. We choose MPEG1 format because it has a good compression factor and allows a good quality. Our mechanism may work on other video formats with hierarchical relationships among frames. SVA[3] is a protocol that interchanges information between the client and the video server. The client informs the server about how many frames per second it is able to decode and to display, then the video server adapts the video source rate while it maintains frame synchronization and sequence dependencies. The experiences we present demonstrate that a good collaboration of reservation and adaptation procedures may provide a given QoS.

Introduction

Delivering interactive multimedia information across a packet switched network with a best effort service is not a simple task. There are a lot of factors to take care of such as packet losses, synchronization among flows, error recover, scalability, admission

---

[1] This work has been partially funded by the Spanish Research Council under grant CICYT TEL97-1054-C03-03.
[2] SVA stands for the Spanish name "Servicio de Video Adaptativo"; in English "Adaptive Video Service"

control, bandwidth usage optimization and so on. Many proposals have been presented in order to "introduce" network quality of service. Both, the Integrated Services and Differentiated Services approaches are well known proposals with a lot of research work being carried out. From the user's point of view, QoS is a non-quantifiable characteristic about the "goodness" of the application [4](i.e. the video being displayed in the terminal). Usually, a range of "acceptable" quality is defined or allowed. QoS applies to all layers in a communication process: application, transport, network, link and physical medium. We will focus on the network, transport and application layers.

Usually, real time video communications work on a connectionless transport service (RTP/UDP) [6] over network service (IP), and they appear to the application layer as one service. QoS at network layer must allow video flows to maintain a given bit rate, a maximum delay and a delay jitter between a maximum and minimum value that allow the decoders to keep the synchronization.

At application layer, QoS must keep flow synchronization while decoding and displaying the video on the terminal. At this point resource management within the terminal (which includes the OS, the decoding process, inter process communication, etc.) affects the overall QoS perceived by the user. Resource reservation in the network (or providing different classes of services [5]) is necessary to provide QoS but it is not sufficient. Resource reservation at the end system is necessary as well.

Our scenario considers the following assumptions. There exists a resource reservation in the network (RSVP). A video server may deliver video flows to an heterogeneous set of terminals; each of them has its own properties and resources (i.e. hardware or software decoding). The end system may not be dedicated exclusively to receive and to process the video flow and thus the internal resources available at a given time may vary (i.e. CPU or memory). Most proposed adaptive applications take into account network losses and react according to network performance. We propose that the adaptation process must include the terminal performance as well.

We implemented an adaptive mechanism that monitors the terminal performance as well as the network performance. We tested it in an experimental platform [7] using the RSVP protocol to maintain QoS at network layer and SVA protocol to monitor and to adapt the client performance at application layer.

The paper is organized as follows. The first section introduces the framework for adaptive applications in real time communications. Section 2 gives a brief description of RSVP and explains how it fits in our QoS management architecture. The third section presents our proposal for the SVA protocol. Section four and five include a detailed description of our selective frame discard algorithm, how it applies to MPEG1 flows, and how it maintains frame quality while reducing flow volume. Section 6 presents the details of the application and the scenario for the tests including RSVP, heavy traffic and the video server, the client and SVA protocol. Finally, some results that show the behavior of the overall system and its adaptation properties.

1 Simple QoS Framework

Layered frameworks help developers and designers to simplify their job. QoS management must be present in all layers. However, layered frameworks are not the "best" solution to manage QoS in an effective way. Timing restrictions are the most important QoS characteristics for interactive multimedia applications. Information about QoS parameters must be interchanged and managed. The management plane controls certain aspects of several layers together.

Usually QoS requirements at each layer have been defined [4]. These definitions allow designers to get control of QoS per Layer. Nevertheless, the mapping of QoS parameters between Layers is a complex task.

Simplifying the QoS framework for a certain kind of application makes QoS parameters management simpler. We can see in [8] and [9] how, with a set of a few parameters (one per layer), a Video distribution application may provide some kind of QoS control.

In our proposal, we consider three Layers: Network, System and Application. We manage these parameters together (as a control plane) to get a good frame quality. The video stream is optimized taking into account the client performance, the server and the network load. The parameters considered are the following: packets per second (pps) at Network Layer, complete frames per second (cfps) at System layer, and visualized frames per second (vfps) at Application layer.

We consider Network Layer includes all the layers below IP layer. System Layer includes all the processes between Network layer and Applications layer, such as flow streaming, segmentation and reassembling. Application Layer includes stream decoding, synchronization and presentation. On top of them, the User Layer reflects the set of parameters related to user perception. Figure 1 shows our simplified framework.

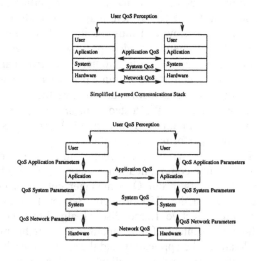

Fig. 1. Simple QoS framework

Parameters pps cfps and vfps are directly related. Variations in received packets/second (pps) affect the number of complete frames/second available (cfps), and this affects the number of displayed frames/second (vfps). CPU load variations, concurrent network traffic, and concurrent processes affect vfps too. A feedback mechanism is used to inform the Server about the Client performance. The Client will send periodically the value of vfps to the server. Then, the Server will modify video flow, by discarding frames (or by including more frames) to fit in the free resources of the client. It is a self-regulated mechanism as shown in Figure 2.

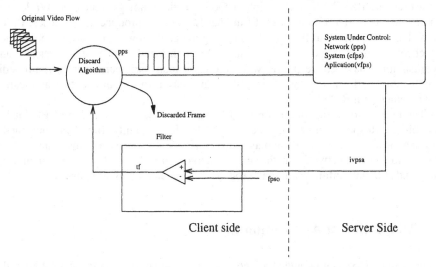

Fig. 2. Self-regulated system based on a feedback parameter and discarding frames

2 Allocating Bandwidth with RSVP

The Reservation Protocol, RSVP [1], is an IETF's proposal to standardize a mechanism to reserve resources along the path within the network. We use RSVP over IP network protocol to reserve bandwidth for unidirectional connectionless transmissions (UDP).

The server advertises its session with a PATH message. The PATH message contains a list of parameters that specify the flow characteristics (mean bandwidth, peak bandwidth, MTU size...). This information and some other added by intermediate routers allow the client to ask for a reservation. Reservation message (RESV) is sent back to the server, creating a "soft state" at all intermediate routers that will allow to keep free resources to maintain the QoS for this flow. The soft state at the routers is refreshed via periodically PATH and RESV messages [10].

Mapping multimedia application parameters into Tspec (PATH parameters) and Rspec (RESV parameters) is too complex to leave this task for the user of the application. Some authors [11] propose a new layer above RSVP to simplify this task. They propose the definition and use of a database of well-known sources and their corresponding reservation parameters. This requires a lot of experimentation to find the "optimal" set of parameters for each application and configuration. We use a similar method by using only the bandwidth parameter for the reservation.

Nevertheless, RSVP forces all transmission systems (routers and end systems) to support this protocol. Soft-state per-flow management is too complex to be implemented at core routers. Core routers deal with large amounts of flows and data and require high speed and simple algorithms. Scalability is one of the main issues to be solved. For backbone high-speed routers, it is envisaged to use differentiated-services oriented mechanisms to guarantee QoS.

Moreover, RSVP helps to maintain QoS but does not guarantee it. While it is maintained between routers, shared Ethernet LANs may produce packet loses. RSVP may help to protect a flow from other aggregated flows so that the adaptation mechanism gives a good performance. As mentioned above, end systems and workstations may behave poorly when the CPU load varies and affects multimedia applications performance too. This is the main reason to use an adaptive application [2] together with RSVP.

The reservation re-negotiation procedure can take a while due to high CPU load at the client. Response time may be critical for high quality flows in multimedia applications. Another problem may arise if RESV messages are lost due to high congestion in the network. In this case, response time for new reservation may be long and soft state information in the routers may be cleared by timeout.

3   Adaptation at Application Layer

Once a given QoS is guaranteed at network layer, the application layer must keep the quality specified at this layer. In the case of a video-based application, QoS at application layer is a good frame quality and timing, but not frame rate in most cases. Video degradation usually comes from the loss of frames at network layer or from a poor performance at application layer. Trying to maintain a given frame rate when the resources are not enough is not a good approach. There are several possible alternatives to reduce the bit rate of a video flow to fit in the available resources. Re-coding the video flow in a simpler format is one option. Another solution may be based in a discrete quality reduction, such as removing color. We discard these two alternatives because re-coding is too expensive in time and resources, and the reduction of colors is not scalable; once color has been removed from a flow no other simple treatment is possible.

Our approach is to reduce the number of frames per second because it allows smooth variations. As far as the frames are completely recovered, the quality is acceptable while the sensation of continuity is maintained at least until the frame rate is reduced to a half of the nominal rate. Most high quality video flows are coded at 25 or 30 frames per second. Displaying 12 or 15 frames per second gives a good continuity feeling if frame quality is maintained. Even in the case the bandwidth of the transmission channel is very narrow or the server/client resources are very scarce, less than 10 frames per second may be acceptable in some cases.

Using RSVP packet losses will not be frequent. However, loss of frames at the server or the client is possible because of overload of these systems. We will not discuss the Server system because we assume stored video flows distribution with enough resources. With this assumption, video coding is already done and files accesses and distribution on the network are the main tasks of the server. The Client at the receiver terminal must decode the video flow, and perhaps more than one flow if it is listening to a multiparty session. Lack of specific hardware, for example an MPEG decoder card, could be an important handicap when considering CPU usage in the client. Other software and Operating System processes may slow down the video decoding process.

3.1 Adaptation mechanism in the Client

Several factors limit the decoding rate. The first factor is the number of packets per second (pps) that are delivered by Network Layer. As we are using RSVP for allocating sufficient bandwidth, pps will be the same at Server and Client side. However, loss of packets is still possible, for example during reservation renegotiations. The loss of certain kind of information could produce the loss of a part of some frames and even the loss of whole frames, depending on the video format. The sequence of the received packets is the result of segmenting a certain number of frames per second into packets of a size according to the Network MTU. It will be a variable value because most video formats generate variable bit rates.

The client will receive these packets and reassemble them to build the complete frames. This process will give us the number of complete frames per second (cfps). The value of cfps may not be the same at the client and at the server side because of several reasons. The lack of CPU, buffer overflow at the Application Layer, the system layer being unable to deal with that frame rate may be some of the problems. In summary, all these factors directly affect the upper layer parameter perceived by the user: the number of visualized frames per second (vfps).

In an ideal situation where there are neither packet losses nor frame losses, cfps vfps are constant values. The Vfps is the Application Layer QoS parameter. It is the one that gives the end user the feeling of a good visualization. We may deal with pps, cfps and vfps together to manage the control plane, but we have decided to use only the vfps parameter because it comprises the overall performance of the client.

Table 1. QoS mapping, related parameters

QoS Layer	QoS parameter	Acronym
Network	Packets per second	Pps
System	Complete frames per second	Cfps
Application	Visualized frames per second	Vfps

The vfps parameter will be monitored during video presentation. Then, varying values in pps and cpfs parameters will be detected at Application layer. As stated above, the main factors that contribute to a certain vfps value are:
- Packets lost at network
- Too late arrival packets
- Client buffer overflow
- Client insufficient capacity

3.2 Adaptation mechanism

Periodically, the client sends feedback information to the Server. This information includes the current value of vfps (cvfps). The server compares this value with the original vfps of the stored flow (ovfps). Then, the server computes the frame reduction it must apply to fit the Client resources.

$$\text{Transmission Factor} = \text{cvfps/ovfps} \qquad (1)$$

The Transmission Factor parameter (TF) means how much the server should reduce the flow, in frames per second, to adapt to current client resources.

Next step is to decide how to use the TF. For example, if we have a video coded at 30 fps (ovfps) and our client is displaying 10 fps (cvfps), TF is 0,33. It means that we should drop 20 frames out of 30.

The TF means the frame transmission probability too. If we calculate TF every transmission time and accumulate it, when the accumulated value is greater than 1, we should transmit a frame.

Pause time between consecutive frames transmission varies to according to cvfps variable. Then synchronization is maintained. Table a in Figure 7 shows this example. The whole system (Client cvfps, Server ovfps, TF, and the related parameters pps and cfps) is self-regulated. It means that it gets the optimal transmission rate taking into account both the channel and the client performance.

4 MPEG-1 principles

MPEG-1[12] format gets a high compression rate thanks to intraframe and interframe redundancy reduction. Intraframe compression does not affect our mechanism because we remove complete frames. If a packet loss occurs, the whole frame will be discarded. Interframe compression affects directly our mechanism because of inter-frame dependency.

MPEG-1 codification generates three kinds of images. Type I images (Intraframe codified) are stand-alone and do not depend on any other. Type P images (Predicted) depend on previous complete decoded P or I image. Type P images only code the parts of the image that have changed from the previous P or I image respectively. Finally, type B images (Bi-directional predicted) code differences between previous and future type I or B images. Compression rate for B images is higher than for P images, and P compression rate is bigger than that of I images. MPEG-1 combines these three kinds of images to get the best ratio between complexity and compression. Figure 3 shows inter-frame relationships.

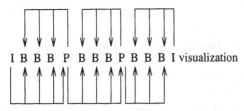

Fig. 3. Inter-frame relationships. Arrows means that source frame is used to generate destination frame.

Because of this interframe relationship, frames are stored in a different order to optimize the decoding speed and to reduce buffer requirements. Figure 4 shows store/transmission order and visualization order.

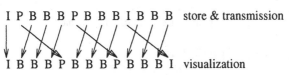

Fig. 4. Store and transmission order

Discarding certain kind of images produces different effects on the rest of the video flow. Discarding B images do not affect video sequence decoding, B images errors are not propagated. Discarding P images affects past and future (in the order they are displayed) type B images, and future type P images. Discarding I images affects all images until the next I image arrives. Figure 5 shows and example of how P image discard/lost affects displayed flow. Frame loses produce some block error decoding in related frames and visualized frame may contain non sense square areas.

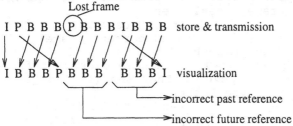

Fig. 5. Lost frame effects

5 Selective Frame Discard for MPEG-1 Video Flows

In the previous section, we have seen a mechanism to decide how to reduce a video flow by dropping frames. However, frame discard affects the quality of the following frames. In order to maintain frame quality and sequence selective frame discard algorithm must be applied. This selective discard must maintain inter-frame relationships [3].

In order to maintain interframe relationships we introduce a queue in the server. This queue will contain dropped frames with potential importance. We can send correct sequences combining the Transmission Factor with the current frame type to be sent and the frames stored in the queue.

A high-level code description, which implements this process, is presented next. Note that cvfps and TF are constants in this piece of code, but they are updated in parallel by a monitoring process.

```
Loop
wait(1/cvfps)
send_prob=send_prob+TF        // recalculate send
probability

if TF<1   then // it's time to drop a frame

   if current_frame_type=B then
                           drop_frame

   if current_frame_type=P then
                           put_queue(q,current_frame)

   if current_frame_type=I then
                           empty_queue(q)
                           put_queue(q,current_frame)

 else // TF>=1, it's time to send a frame
   send_prob=send_prob-1    // remember left probability
   if current_frame_type=I then
                           empty_queue(q)
                           send(current_frame)
   if current_frame_type=B then
          if queue_lon=0    then send(current_frame)
          if queue_lon>0    then send(extract_first(q))
 if current_frame_type=P then
                           send(extract_first(q))
                           put_queue(q,current_frame)
   if current_frame_type=I then    empty_queue(q)
                           send(current_frame)
 end if
loop
```

A careful look at this algorithm shows that not all types of frames are dropped with the same probability. B frames first ones to be dropped, followed by P frame, and finally I frames. Then, a reduction in a percentage of frames does not contribute in the same way to reduce the flow. This is because I frames are larger than P and B, while the discard probability is in reverse order. A queue to store and recover the last important P or I dropped frames is necessary. Figure 6 shows this modification.

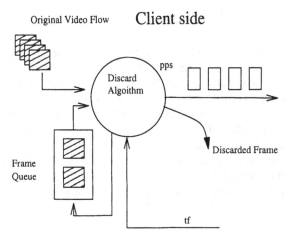

Fig. 6. Client side with selective discard algorithm

Figure 7 shows an example of the application of the selective discard algorithm, compared to raw discard. We can see how frame relationships are maintained, while some images are sent later. Images are never delayed beyond next displayed I time. MPEG-1 must transmit at least one I image per second. In the most greedy discard application this delay will always be not greater than a second and it will be transparent to the users most of the time.

$$\text{Transmision Factor} = \frac{\text{Current Frame Rate}}{\text{Real Frame Rate}}$$

Frame Number	1	2	3	4	5	6	7	8	9	10	11	12	13	14	15	16	17	18	19	20	21	22	23	24	25	26	27	28	29	30
Decoding Order	I	P	B	B	P	B	B	I	B	B	P	B	B	P	B	B	I	B	B	P	B	B	P	B	B	I	B	B	P	B
Presentation Order	I	B	B	P	B	B	P	B	B	I	B	B	P	B	B	P	B	B	I	B	B	P	B	B	P	B	B	I	B	B
Transmission Factor	1	.66	.32	.98	.64	.3	.9	.62	.28	.94	.6	.26	.92	.58	.34	.9	.56	.22	.88	.54	.2	.86	.52	.18	.84	.5	.16	.82	.48	.4
Not Transmited		⊠		⊠		⊠			⊠			⊠			⊠			⊠			⊠			⊠			⊠			

Table a

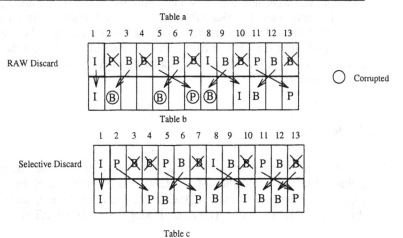

Table b

Table c

Fig. 7. Selective Discard example

6 Application Architecture

Our test application SVA is MPEG-1 video server. It serves an MPEG-1 video flow over an unreliable UDP connection. We use RTP [6][13] for segmenting and synchronizing video frames. The feedback control channel is a reliable TCP connection that the client uses to send the feedback information (visualized frames per second) to the server. The server implements the selective frame discard algorithm described above to reduce the video flow (number of frames sent). The client uses the Berkeley mpeg_play [14] decoder to visualize video. Mpeg_play code has been modified to share some parameters that the client uses to calculate the number of visualized frames per second.

An RAPI [15] front-end application [7] is activated at the same time to make a reservation along path from server to client.

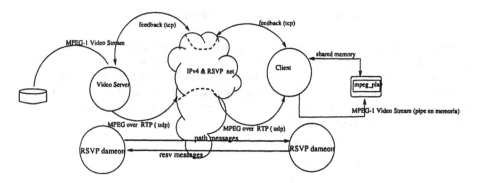

Fig. 8. Application components and communication channels

A point to point transmission is established in the experiment. The proposal may be extended using multicast transmission. Scalability may be improved by using a hierarchy of active nodes [16], which apply the selective discard algorithm. In this way, the server can feed video flows for a group of clients with the QoS adaptation for each of them. In this case, the feedback information must be sent to the nearest active node, not to server in order to avoid control information overhead in the server. Active nodes must interchange feedback information too, to know which video rate they can receive.

7 Results

Our test environment is based on a real deployment of the Internet architecture including the implementation of the RSVP test application and the SVA mechanism (figure 9). There is a router (CISCO 7026) interconnecting three nets: CCABA (Ethernet 10Mbps), SABA (Ethernet 10Mbps) and SABA-ATM (ATM 155Mbps).

This configuration allows us to send interfering traffic straight through the router. Router performance is affected while there are no collisions on the Ethernet segments.

WS1 (SunUltra-1) is the server and WS2 (SunUltra-1) is the receiver (client). RSVP reserves resources at the router for this UDP flow. Then, WS1 serves a video flow to WS2 on the reserved channel.

WS3 (SunUltra-1) stresses the router interface by sending traffic with Mgen traffic generation application to WS4 (PC486). The router must route this traffic from SABA-ATM network to SABA segment.

In this scenario, the frame-rate transmission is adapted to the client free resources only, because the network bandwidth is maintained in the router by using RSVP.

Two additional workstations WS5 (SunUltra-1) and WS6 (SunSparc20) are used to perform traffic measurement and run tcp_dump to collect statistics about sent and received packets on both the source and the destination Ethernet LANs.

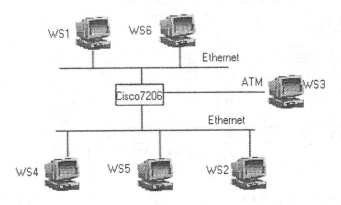

Fig. 9. Network interconnection scenario

The following tables show the effects of the selective discard algorithm on some video transmission. WS1 is Video Server and WS2 is the client and includes the video decoder. Table 2 shows the video characteristics: frame size, sequence type, decoding frame rate and number of each type of frames.

Table 2. Video characteristics

Video	Frame size	Sequence	Fps	frames	I	P	B
Rnm	320x240	IBBBBBBBBBPBBBBB BBBBPBBBBBBBBBB	25	1211	41	81	1089
ToEdge	160x120	I	30	1730	1730	0	0
Bbima	160x112	IBBPBB	30	13126	3751	1875	7500
Work1	382x288	IBBPBBPBBPBBPBB	25	1390	110	390	920
Team1	160x120	IBBPBBPBBPBBPBB	30	820	69	137	614
Team2	160x120	IBBPBBPBBPBBPBB	30	2694	225	450	2019
Valk	160x120	IBBPBBPBBPBBP	30	1684	141	281	1262

Table 3 shows how the video flow adaptation works in the server. Reduction of video flow depends on the decoding complexity. Decoding complexity varies due to the image size, sequence type and intraframe compression factor. Most videos do not reach original fps value because of the decoding process being made by software. Note that image dropping is done with different percentages depending on the image type. As mentioned before, the image type most affected by the discard algorithm is a B type frame, followed by P frames and finally I frames.

Several MPEG-1 video sequences have been used in the experiments. Those experiments labeled by number 2 correspond to a second scenario where additional CPU load is present in the client workstation. Work1(*2) is executed while another local mpeg_player is active. Valk(*2) is decoded with 24bit depth color, while valk(*1) is decoded with 8bit depth color.

Table 3. Selective discard algorithm results

Video	Fps	Frames	I	P	B
Rnm	22	1089	35	75	979
ToEdge	28	1638	1638	0	0
Bbima	20	12451	3687	1742	7022
Work1(*1)	23	1291	100	339	852
Work1(*2)	15	743	74	237	614
Team1	30	820	69	137	614
Team2	30	2692	225	450	2019
Valk(*1)	30	1684	141	281	1262
Valk(*2)	23	1269	114	230	925

Valk(*1) can reach original fps without client CPU overload, but it decreases fps value if 24 bit depth decoding is applied. Figure 10 shows the client vfps (visualized frames per second) parameter and figure 11 shows frames per second served. A transient effect may be observed during the first seconds due to the empty buffer effect. Service speed changes are modulated by client buffer occupation. This effect will be removed by reducing the buffer and modifying the Mpeg_play to process strict time-stamp information.

Figures 12 and 13 show the same parameters but with a more complex decoding process Valk(*2). Application adaptation is done at a lower service rate.

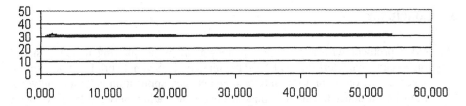

Fig. 10. Client frame rate during simple decoding process

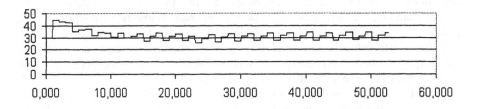

Fig. 11. Server frame rate during simple decoding process

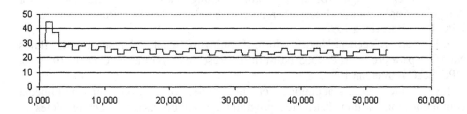

Fig. 12. Client frame rate during complex decoding process

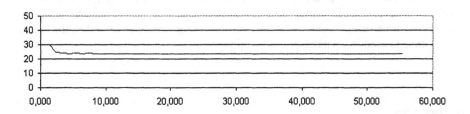

Fig. 13. Server frame rate during complex decoding process

8 Conclusions

The RSVP protocol will help in QoS management by simplifying the QoS stack. Mapping stream characteristics on RSVP parameters, QoS at network layer and below is managed. However, parameters interchange between application layer and network layer must be introduced. This information interchange allow network layer to adapt to application performance, and application to adapt to network layer resources.

Selective frame discard algorithm allows us to reduce smoothly and gradually MPEG flows. Some approaches reduce flow volume by reducing frame quality and maintaining frame rate. These solutions display fast poor images. Selective frame discard maintains frame quality but reduces frame rate. Frame rate reduction in high quality videos can be done without affecting QoS perception in most of the cases. High frame rate reduction not decreases user QoS goodness perception as reducing frame quality does, especially in video-presentation and cooperative work applications, where users pay attention to audio and slides.

Response time of the RSVP and the feedback protocols must be improved to correct calculation of the global system configuration (server-network-client). Period of the feedback messages and the reservation refresh must be tuned jointly.

Adaptive applications must take care of QoS parameters in layers above network too. CPU load, as network congestion, can reduce severely application performance. Transmission of video streams larger than the client cant deal with is a waste of network resources. QoS management at application layer must help to optimize overall resource usage. Operating System re-design for networked multimedia applications is need for general-purpose computers.

References

[1]   R. Braden, L. Zhang, S. Berson, et al. "Resource ReSerVation Protocol (RSVP) – Version 1" Functional Specification. RFC 2205, 1997.

[2]   Josep Mangues-Bafalluy, Jordi Domingo-Pascual. "A framework for Adaptive Applications". Research report n° UPC-DAC-1998-7 (to be published). UPC-DAC Barcelona 1998.

[3]   Carlos Veciana-Nogués, Jordi Domingo-Pascual. "Adaptación de flujos MPEG-1 para protocols de QoS best-effort". Research report n° UPC-DAC-1998-10. UPC-DAC Barcelona 1998.

[4]   Daniel G. Waddintong et al. "Specifying QoS for multimedia communications within distributed programming environments". Lecture Notes in Computer Science, 1(1185):75—103. 3rd Cost 237 Workshop, Barcelona 1996.

[5] Network Working Group, "An Architecture for Differentiated Services". RFC 2475, December 1998.

[6]   Audio Video Transport Group. "RTP: A Transport Protocol for Real-Time Applications". RFC 1889, 1997.

[7] Esteve Majoral, "Multimedia Applications evaluation and implantation over new Internet protocols", Final Project Degree. Facultat d'Informàtica - Polythecnic University of Catalonia, February 1999.

[8]   Shanwei Cent, Calton Pu, et al. "A distributed real-time mpeg video audio player". Lecture Notes in Computer Science, 1(1018):151—162. Proc. Of NOSSDAV, Durham 1995.

[9]   Carlos Veciana-Nogués and Jordi Domingo-Pascual. "Transmisión de flujos multimedia con gestión de la Calidad de Servicio". Proc. Yuforic'97, pages 13—20, Barcelona, April 1997.

[10]   L. Zhang, S. Deering, D. Estrin, et al. "RSVP: A New Resource Reservation Protocol." IEEE Network, September 1993.

[11]   Bob Lindell. "SCRAPI: A Simple 'Bare Bones' API for RSVP, Version 2", draft_lindell_rsvp_scrapi-01.txt (expires May'99)

[12]   Joan L. Mitchell, et all. "MPEG Video Compression Standard". Champman & Hall, 1986. ISBN 0-412-08771-5.

[13]   Audio Video Transport Group. "RTP: Payload Format for MPEG1/MPEG2 Video". RFC 2038, 1997.

[14]   MPEG player. University of Berkeley. "MPEG utilities". Available at: http://bmrc.berrkeley.edu/ftp/pub/multimedia/mpeg/, 1997.

[15]   R. Braden and D. Hoffman. RAPI "An RSVP Application Programming Interface. Version 5". Internet draft, draft-ietf-rsvp-rapi-00, 1997.

[16]   R. Wittman and M. Zitterbart. "Amnet: Active Multicasting Network". Proc. Of the 4th COST237 Workshop, pp. 154—164. Lisboa, Portugal, December 1997.

An Engineering Approach
to QoS Provisioning over the Internet*

Raffaele D'Albenzio, Simon Pietro Romano and Giorgio Ventre

Dipartimento di Informatica e Sistemistica, Università di Napoli "Federico II",
Napoli, Italy
Email: {rafdalb, sprom, ventre}@grid.unina.it

Abstract. Existing communications systems are rapidly converging into an ubiquitous information infrastructure that does not distinguish between computing and communications, but rather provides a set of distributed services to the user. The research community must be prepared to foresee these changes and to deal with them, enlarging the space of technical possibilities so as to make available to society's needs new valuable choices. In this scenario the capability of the network to provide the applications with end-to-end Quality of Service (QoS) becomes a central issue. An engineering approach is needed in this research field in order to incrementally build the next-generation network. This paper focuses on some of the hot topics related to end–to–end QoS provisioning over the Internet and aims at exploiting the current proposals of the research community, while looking at them from a critical point of view and providing actual implementation of some of the discussed ideas. Thus, we propose a QoS-capable architecture aiming at providing flexible and effective implementation of the Integrated Services model via a Weighted Fair Queueing scheduling mechanism, while defining a new service class capable of giving long-term rate guarantees to Internet flows.

Keywords: Quality of Service, Integrated Services, Scheduling Disciplines.

Introduction

The computer and communications revolution has occurred. The Internet is rapidly becoming ubiquitous and we can look forward to a scenario in which everything communicates and communication is everywhere. Yet we have only begun to see the fundamental implications of these and of the forthcoming changes. Apart from some enthusiastic and somewhat fanciful assessments, a number of issues remain still open and need further investigation. The research community must be prepared to deal with these issues and to propose new effective solutions which enable us to cope with the astonishing growth of the network, both in scale and capability, and with the new kinds of applications that it must be prepared to support.

---

* This work has been partially supported by the Ministero dell'Università e della Ricerca Scientifica e Tecnologica (MURST), Italy, in the framework of project MOSAICO. Simon Pietro Romano's work was supported by a Telecom Italia research fellowship for the project "Cantieri Multimediali".

The need for new architectural and technical approaches is under everybody's eyes and the directions in which networking and telecommunications will evolve are very much shaped by the key lessons we learned so far. Based on these assumptions, in this paper we try to apply an engineering approach to networking research in the field of Quality of Service (QoS) provisioning over the Internet. Starting from the observation that, although network designers stress the point that the network is more than its applications, it's the applications themselves that drive its evolution and deployment, we try to propose a framework in which new kinds of applications get from the network adequate support in terms of the available services. Such a framework aims at exploiting the current proposals of the research community, while looking at them from a critical point of view and providing actual implementation of some of the discussed ideas, in order to make available an experimental infrastructure that will permit the proposed technologies to be tested. We claim that the time is ripe for filling the gap between what we envision and what is actually available. To our knowledge, in fact, there currently exist no implementations of the ideas we discuss. What we do need is to carry on actual experiments in real environments in order to better understand which are the hot topics the research community has to cope with in the near future.

Among the main issues related to the effective pursuit of QoS mechanisms we definitely see the development of efficient traffic management modules, primarily based on some of the queueing disciplines which have been proposed and studied to date by a number of researchers. In fact, the only way to provide performance bounds concerning bandwidth, delay, jitter and loss, thus meeting real-time applications requirements, still remains that of making available sophisticated queueing policies in the inner part of network elements (both hosts and routers). Several disciplines [2][15] exist which might satisfy, more or less efficiently, network traffic management requirements, but no one is widely used since it is somewhat difficult to implement them into the existing network equipment. We chose to start by designing and building a QoS-capable router which makes use of the Weighted Fair Queueing [1] scheduling algorithm. The queueing engine of our experimental router is implemented as an extension to ALTQ (ALTernate Queueing) [3], that allows the utilization of a set of queueing disciplines, such as CBQ, RED and SFQ (Stochastic Fairness Queueing). In this paper we will present our system architecture and will provide some insight and preliminary results of the testing.

The paper is organized as follows: Section 2 describes the state-of-the-art in the field of QoS over the Internet together with some hints concerning future development trends; Section 3 goes into the most relevant details concerning the Integrated Services model; Section 4 contains a proposal for a new service class for the Internet aiming at dealng with efficiency in bandwidth management over the network; Section 5 is a brief overview of the Differentiated Services Model; Section 6 introduces QUEUE-NET, a project under development at the University of Naples relating to effective implementation of mechanisms for QoS provisioning over heterogeneous networks; finally, Section 7 provides conclusions and directions for future work.

The QoS problem : state of the art and future trends

Experiences over the Internet have showed the lack of a fundamental technical element: real-time applications do not work well across the network because of variable queueing delays and congestion losses. The Internet, as originally conceived, offers only a very simple quality of service: point-to-point best-effort data delivery. Thus, before real-time applications can be broadly used, the Internet infrastructure must be modified in order to support more stringent QoS guarantees, mostly relating to the provision of some kind of control over end-to-end packet delays. The goal is not to design new solutions from scratch, but rather to find the appropriate extensions to the framework currently available.

Real-time cpmmunication is not the only open issue for next generation Internet traffic management policies: the ability to control the sharing of link bandwidth among different traffic classes is another point which is worth further investigating. Based on these assumptions, in the past several years work on QoS-enabled networks has led to the developement of the Integrated Services Architecture, where the term *Integrated Services* (IS) is used to denote an Internet service model that includes best-effort service, real-time service and controlled link sharing. Such an architecture, together with an appropriate signalling protocol like RSVP (*Resource reSerVation Protocol*) enables applications to demand per-flow guarantees from the network. However, as work has proceeded in this direction, a number of basic limitations have emerged which impede large-scale deployment of QoS mechanisms in the Internet: the reliance of IntServ protocols on per-flow state and per-flow processing schemes, in fact, brings to a level of granularity too fine to avoid scalability problems on large networks, thus raising the need to define a scalable architecture for service differentiation. Such an architecture is the subject of the studies conducted by the *Diffserv* working group in the IETF. A differentiated-services network achieves scalability by means of aggregation of traffic classification state conveyed in an appropriate DS field set by IP-layer packet marking.

The Integrated Services Model

IP has been playing for several years the most important role in global internetworking. Its surprisingly rapid growth makes it the dominating protocol in the scene of networking research. However, IP choice does not only rely on the fact that the vast majority of applications has been conceived for it. The connectionless nature of IP has proved to be a key feature to support integrated services networks.

Based on this assumption, the IETF Integrated Services working group has specified a control QoS framework [4] in order to provide new applications with the appropriate support. Such a framework proposes an extension to the Internet architecture and protocols which aims at making broadly available integrated services across the Internet. The main features of the QoS framework are:

- the definition of a reference model for the integrated services architecture;
- the specification of a *reservation protocol* compatible with the assumptions of the reference model;
- the definition of a number of *service classes* satisfying the needs of the different kinds of network applications;
- the design of an appropriate service model for all of the defined classes.

The reference model

The key assumption on which the reference model for integrated services is built is that network resources (first of all its bandwidth) must be explicitly managed in order to meet application requirements. The overall goal in a real-time service, in fact, is that of satisfying a given set of application-specific requirements, and it looks clear that guarantees are hardly achieved without reservations. Thus, resource reservation and admission control will be playing an extremely important role in the global framework. The new element which arises in this context, with respect to the old (non-real-time) Internet model, is the need to maintain flow-specific state in the routers, that must now be capable to take an active part in the reservation process.

Based on these considerations, the components included in the reference framework are (¡Error!Argumento de modificador desconocido.): a packet scheduler, an admission control module, a packet classifier and an appropriate reservation setup protocol.

HOST   **ROUTER**

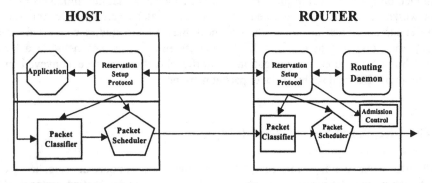

Fig. ¡Error!Argumento de modificador desconocido.. The Integrated Services Model

In today's Internet, all packets of a given flow receive the same quality of service and are typically forwarded using a simple FIFO queueing discipline. As ¡**Error!Argumento de modificador desconocido.** shows, for the integrated services paradigm, a router is compelled to implement an appropriate function to guarantee QoS on a per-flow basis. Such a function, with the associated implementation mechanisms, is called *traffic control*, which is in turn made up of three different building blocks: the packet scheduler, the packet classifier and the admission control module.

The packet scheduler takes into account the forwarding of different packet streams by appropriate management of a set of queues together with other related mechanisms like timers. It must be implemented as a link-layer protocol at the output driver level of the operating system. The function of the classifier is to perform the mapping of incoming packets into some service class, in order to achieve the twofold goal of traffic control and accounting. All packets belonging to the same class get the same treatment from the packet scheduler. Finally, admission control is invoked at each node throughout the network at the time a host requires a real-time service along a specified path. It has the responsibility to determine, on a local basis, whether a router or host can grant a new flow the requested QoS without impacting earlier guarantees to previous flows.

The last block showed in the figure refers to the reservation setup protocol needed to create and manage state information along the whole path that a specific flow crosses between two network end-points. One of the features required to such a protocol is that of carrying the so-called *flowspec* object, that is a list of parameters specifying the desired QoS needed by an application. At each intermediate network element along a specified path, this object is passed to admission control to test for acceptability and, in the case that the request may be satisfied, used to appropriately parameterize the packet scheduler. RSVP [5] is the resource reservation protocol recommended by IntServ.

¡Error!Argumento de modificador desconocido. shows the role of the packet classifier and packet scheduler in the context of an Intserv-capable network element.

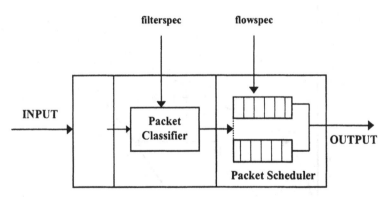

Fig. ¡Error!Argumento de modificador desconocido.. The role of the packet classifier and packet scheduler

Service classes

IntServ service classes define a framework for specifying services provided by network elements and available to applications, in an internetwork capable of offering multiple, dynamically selectable qualities of service.

Each definition specifies the characteristics that must be possessed by a network element (e.g., a router) to support a particular service, defines the invocation parameters specific of each available service and characterizes the end-to-end behavior obtained by utilizing the same kind of service along all the hops of a specific path. The goal of these services is that of bypassing the current limitations of the traditional, best-effort service made available by the Internet by providing different qualities of service to different applications, allowing them to request network packet delivery characteristics according to their perceived needs.

Two different service classes have so far been defined: *guaranteed quality of service* and *controlled load quality of service*.

The Guaranteed Service (GS) class provides the clients data flow with firm bounds on the end-to-end delay experienced by a packet while traversing network [6]. It guarantees both bandwidth and delay. The GS emulates the service that would be offered by a dedicated communication channel between the emitter and the receiver. Two parameters apply to this service: TSpec and RSpec.

The former describes the traffic characteristics for which service is being requested. It is composed of a token bucket (b) plus a peak rate (p), a minimum policed unit (m), and a maximum datagram size (M). The RSpec specifies the QoS a given flow demands from a network element and it takes the form of a clearing rate R and a slack term S. The clearing rate is computed to give a guaranteed end-to-end delay and the slack term denotes the difference between desired and guaranteed end-to-end delay after the receiver has chosen a value for R.

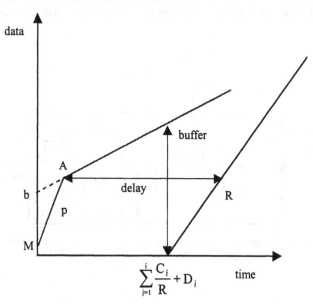

Fig. ¡Error!Argumento de modificador desconocido.. The traffic envelope for a (b,r,p) flow.

During the reservation phase [7] each intermediate network element i computes C_i and D_i which represent the deviation from a fluid server which operates at the clearing rate R demanded by a potential receiver for a given flow. Thus, the delay encountered by any bit of the flow in network element i is required to be no more than the one it would be subject to in an hypothetical system that first delays the flow by $C_i/R + D_i$ units of time and then serves it at the reserved rate R. C_i and D_i are accumulated into the C_{tot} and D_{tot} fields within the ADSPEC object of a PATH message. So, given a (b,r,p) flow (to which a "service curve" like that showed in ¡**Error!Argumento de modificador desconocido.** is associated), the following equation applies to the end-to-end delay bound computation for a network element with MTU size equal to L:

$$Delay = \begin{cases} \dfrac{(b-M)(p-R)}{R(p-r)} + \dfrac{M}{R} + \sum_{j=1}^{N}\left(\dfrac{C_j}{R} + D_j\right) & \text{if } p > R \\[4mm] \dfrac{M}{R} + \sum_{j=1}^{N}\left(\dfrac{C_j}{R} + D_j\right) & \text{if } p \leq R \end{cases} \tag{1}$$

Similarly, the buffer requirement at network element i is given by:

$$Buffer = M + \frac{(p-X)}{(p-r)}(b-M) + \sum_{j=1}^{N}\left(\frac{C_j}{R} + D_j\right)\cdot X$$

$$\text{where} \quad X = \begin{cases} r & \text{if} & \dfrac{(b-M)}{(p-R)} \leq \sum_{j=1}^{N}\left(\dfrac{C_j}{R} + D_j\right) \\[4mm] R & \text{if} & \dfrac{(b-M)}{(p-R)} > \sum_{j=1}^{N}\left(\dfrac{C_j}{R} + D_j\right) & \text{and} \quad p > R \\[4mm] p & \text{otherwise} \end{cases} \tag{2}$$

The actual procedure used to determine the value of the clearing rate to be inserted in the RESV message is the following: (i) substitute R = p in the second of the above formulae and compute the corresponding value of the upper bound on the end-to-end delay (D*); (ii) if D* is less than the desired end-to-end delay bound, then insert the known values of the flow characterization parameters and desired end-to-end delay bound into the first formula to determine the corresponding value of the clearing rate R; (iii) otherwise, use the second formula.

Controlled-load (CL) service [9] may be thought of as a "controlled best-effort" service, i.e. a service which has the same characteristics of best-effort delivery in the case where the network is not overloaded, but is able to avoid QoS degradation when the load increases. To guarantee such a behavior, CL service makes extensive use of admission control algorithms. CL is best suited to applications that have been developed taking into account the limitations of today's Internet, but are highly susceptible to overloaded conditions. A typical example is given by adaptive real-time applications, which have proved to work well when there is little or no load on the net, but to immediately come into crisis under overloaded conditions.

A client that wants to request controlled-load service provides the intermediate network elements with a *TSpec* object containing a description of the data traffic it is going to generate. This object, as already seen in the case of GS service, takes the form of a bucket rate (r) and a bucket depth (b), plus a peak rate (p), a minimum policed unit (m), and a maximum datagram size (M). The peak rate field is present only for compatibility with other QoS control services, but may always be ignored by CL service. Given this traffic characterization, policing techniques must force the packets of the flow to not exceed, over a specified time period T, the threshold value of rT+b.

Fundamental, with CL service, becomes the role of admission control, for which multiple approaches are feasible. The most conservative approach is to reject new flows requests whenever they exceed the capacity of the network element, which must be able to maintain the delay and loss characteristics conformant with those typical of unloadead best-effort service. Another possibility is to permit some kind of oversubscription of the available resources. This is a good approach when network elements make use of some measurement-based algorithm which allows them to be sure that actual resources utilization is less than that computed by simply adding the token bucket values of the flows they manage.

The Differentiated Services Model

The keyword in describing Internet history is out-of-doubt *growth*: growth in the number of hosts, routers, applications, in the capacity of the network infrastructure and the variety of user requirements. The need arises to define a scalable architecture capable of coping with this continued growth.

This architecture [10] must address many different requirements. First of all, it has to take into account a wide variety of service behaviours, decoupled from any particular application, while relying only upon a small and efficient set of forwarding mechanisms. Second, it must decouple these mechanisms from traffic conditioning and service provisioning functions. Finally, it must avoid per microflow or per-customer state within the routers in the core of the network and must be able to accommodate incremental deployment and interoperability with non-QoS-capable network nodes.

Based on these assumptions, the differentiated services architecture can be contrasted with the Integrated Services model, which relies upon traditional best-effort delivery in the default case, but allows sender and receiver applications to exchange signalling messages (typically via RSVP) which establish classification and state information in the routers along the network path between them, thus triggering the reservation setup process. If utilized without any form of state aggregation, such a model quickly leads to scalability problems, primarily due to the excess of granularity implied.

The differentiated services architecture, on the other hand, is based on a much simpler model, where traffic entering the network is subjected to a conditioning process at the network edges and then assigned to one of different behaviour aggregates, identified by means of a single DS codepoint. Furthermore, each DS codepoint is assigned a different per hop behaviour, which determines the way packets are treated in the core of the network. Thus, differentiated services are achieved through the appropriate combination of traffic conditioning and per-hop behaviour forwarding.

Dealing with efficiency: a proposal for a new class of service

Guaranteed Service results in a fairly low utilization of the link bandwidth since the reserved rate R is always much greater than the average rate of the flow. Some solution should be found to allow other flows to exploit the unused bandwidth. Such flows should present less stringent requirements than GS flows. A proposal which goes in this direction is contained in [8], that defines a **Bandwidth Recovery (BR)** service aiming at recovering the unused bandwidth while giving flows some long-term rate guarantee. The introduction of a service class fulfilling these requirements could prove very useful in an integrated services architecture. As an example, the traffic generated by web applications could greatly benefit from this kind of service.

To implement this new service class, a WFQ scheduling mechanism with separate queues for each GS and BR flow is used. For each GS flow a weight is assigned that determines the reserved clearing rate for it. Assuming M GS flows characterized by the envelope (b,r,p) and a link capacity of C_l, to guarantee their end-to-end delay bounds the following inequality must be satisfied:

$$\sum_{i=1}^{M} R_i \leq C_l - \Delta_{BR} - \Delta_{SIG} \tag{3}$$

Δ_{BR} and Δ_{SIG} in the above equation represent, respectively, the portions of bandwidth reserved to BR and signalling flows . Nevertheless, the weight associated to each BR flow, and thus the reserved bandwidth, is purposely chosen very small and it does not represent the minimum rate required by the flow. The function of the weight is to merely allow the flow to gain access to the residual bandwidth left by the GS flows without giving any guarantees in terms of delay bounds.

Considering M' BR flows with average rate equal to r', to guarantee their minimum rate on a long-term basis the following inequality applies:

$$\sum_{i=1}^{M} r_i + \sum_{i=1}^{M'} r_i' \leq C_l - \Delta_{SIG} \tag{4}$$

The equation above ensures that given that GS flows respect their traffic contract or a suitable policing mechanism is used, BR flows will receive a guaranteed minimum rate over a reasonable period of time.

A simulation-based implementation of the above service discipline may be found in [8]. Based on the results contained in the cited work, we decided to put our hands on the real thing and so here we propose an actual implementation of an integrated-QoS framework which supports both the standard services proposed by the IETF and this new kind of service by means of an intelligent traffic control mechanism based on a Weighted Fair Queuing scheduling algorithm. The next section will cover this topic.

The QUEUE-NET Project

At the University of Naples we're currently working on a project called QUEUE-NET (QUality of service Environment Underway for Enhancing NETworks) whose main purpose is to represent an implementation-oriented approach to the problem of QoS provisioning over large and heterogeneous networks. The theoretical foundations which such a project relies upon are to be found in the generic integrated/differentiated services framework we just depicted. Most of the work presented in the literature is either theoretical or simulative. To our knowledge, in fact, there currently exist no implementations of the ideas we discussed in the previous sections. Yet, we believe that, for an exhaustive understanding of the behaviour of these proposals, it is needed to carry on actual experiments in real environments in order to better understand which are the issues the research community has to cope with in the near future.

Among the main issues related to the effective pursuit of QoS mechanisms we definitely see the development of efficient traffic management modules, primarily based on some of the queueing disciplines which have been proposed and studied to date by a number of researchers. In fact, the only way to provide performance bounds concerning bandwidth, delay, jitter and loss, thus meeting real-time applications requirements, still remains that of making available sophisticated queueing policies in the inner part of network nodes (both hosts and routers). Plenty of disciplines [2] exist which might satisfy, more or less efficiently, network traffic management requirements, but no one is widely used since it is somewhat difficult to implement them into the existing network equipment. We chose to start by designing and building a QoS-capable router which makes use of the Weighted Fair Queueing scheduling algorithm.. The scheduling mechanism it implements is one of the most famous variants of WFQ, known as *Virtual Clock* [12]

Weighted Fair Queueing

The WFQ discipline emulates the ideal (but unimplementable) *Generalized Processor Sharing* (GPS) scheduling discipline [13], that serves packets as if they were in separate logical queues, visiting each non-empty queue in turn and serving an infinitesimally small amount of data from each queue, so that in any finite time interval, it can visit every logical queue at least once. It can be demonstrated that the GPS provides a fair allocation of the available bandwidth among different data streams. The WFQ approximates the GPS discipline, by computing the '*finishing time'* for each packet, that is the time it would take to completely serve a packet with a GPS server, and then by transmitting packets in order of these finishing times. Finishing times are more appropriately called *finish numbers*, to emphasize that they are only service tags that indicate the relative order in which packets are to be served, but they have nothing to do with the actual times at which packets are served. Very much like in WFQ, a *Virtual Clock* (VC) scheduler stamps packets with a tag, called *virtual transmission time*, and packets are served in order of their tags. These tags are computed so to emulate a time-division multiplexing. VC can not be inserted among the algorithms providing GPS emulation, yet it guarantees the same delay bounds as WFQ [2].

Comparison between WFQ and CBQ scheduling disciplines

To our knowledge, the only existing implementations of non-FIFO scheduling disciplines for RSVP-capable routers, besides the one we already mentioned (contained in [3]), are based on the Class Based Queueing (CBQ) algorithm [14]. CBQ relies on bandwidth partitioning and sharing techniques which make extensive use of hierarchically structured classes. A single queue and a well defined share of the total available bandwidth are assigned to each and every class and, provided that excess bandwidth is available, a child class can borrow a fraction of it by its parent class. Such an approach is well suited to scenarios in which the total bandwidth is divided among different organizations, which in turn manage their resources on the basis of local policies.

We argue that, in an RSVP-based environment, in which QoS requests are made on a per-flow (or per/application) basis, a WFQ scheduling discipline is more indicated to meet bandwidth management requirements. Furthermore, as far as we could notice, no current release of RSVP relying on CBQ traffic control modules makes a differentiation in the way guaranteed and controlled load services are treated, in the sense that no computations are made relating to ADSPEC object updating in the case where there exist specific bounds on the delay which the packets belonging to a GS flow can tolerate.

Implementation of the scheduler

Our scheduler may either be run as a privileged user program (which may be in turn configured by means of an ad hoc configuration file) or as a traffic control module used by the RSVP protocol to reserve network resources on a per-flow basis. In order to make the last point feasible, we implemented the standard Traffic Control primitives required by the RSVP specification document [5], including the more relevant parts concerning the treatment of the guaranteed service case, with the associated ADSPEC updating operation.

The queueing engine of our experimental router is implemented as an extension to ALTQ (ALTernate Queueing) [3], a flexible queueing framework that allows the utilization of a set of queueing disciplines, such as CBQ, RED and SFQ (Stochastic Fairness Queueing). ALTQ makes some minor changes to the FreeBSD kernel in order to implement a queueing interface which is nothing but a switch to a set of queueing disciplines, as shown in **¡Error!Argumento de modificador desconocido.**

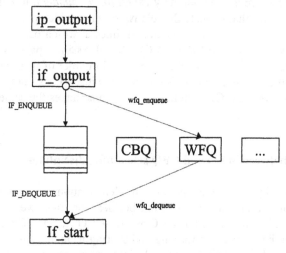

Fig. 4. Queueing operations in ALTQ

What we needed was a dynamically configurable scheduling module which could be used both to build an intelligent PC-based router capable of efficiently managing the available bandwidth and to provide an actual traffic control component for RSVP. Based on these considerations, we implemented WFQ as a new minor device of the original ALTQ character device: such a device is dynamically configurable by means of *ioctl* system calls.

We carried out a number of experiments aiming at testing the effectiveness of our proposal for the Bandwidth Recovery class of service, which fully confirmed the results we had already obtained in our simulation environment.

A simple scenario for the experimental testbed

For our first experiments, we set up a simple scenario, whose purpose is that of verifying the correct behaviour and the stability of our WFQ-based router, while demonstrating the correctness of our assumptions as far as it concerns the Bandwidth Recovery service class.

As **¡Error!Argumento de modificador desconocido.** shows, we have two hosts connected by means of the WFQ router: one of the interfaces of the router is a 100Mb/sec ethernet card, while the other is a simple *slip* interface.

This solution has been adopted in order to evaluate the behaviour of our scheduling policy in an extreme situation, in which the incoming traffic has to be routed over an output link characterized by a much lower bandwidth capability.

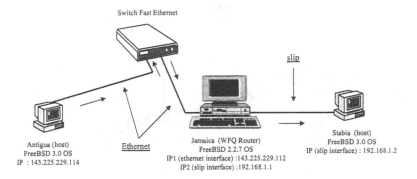

Fig. 5. Our simple test scenario

In order to effectively saturate the link, we generated, on the ethernet side of the whole path, five different flows, whose characteristics are summarized in ¡Error!Argumento de modificador desconocido.

Service Class	Traffic characteristics	Assigned weight
GS	(b,r,p)=(20kb,8kb/sec,∞)	88
BR	r=30kb/sec	4
BR	r=20kb/sec	3
BR	r=20kb/sec	3
BR	r=12kb/sec	2

Table 1. Flows generated to carry out experiments

¡Error!Argumento de modificador desconocido. and ¡Error!Argumento de modificador desconocido. show the measured delay values for the flows contained in the table.

Specifically, ¡Error!Argumento de modificador desconocido. demonstrates that GS packets are not affected by BR flows since the desired end-to-end delay bound is always respected for all of them. On the other side, ¡Error!Argumento de modificador desconocido. , which is related to the delay behaviour of BR flows, confirms our expectation that their packets endure a much greater delay than the one experienced by GS packets.

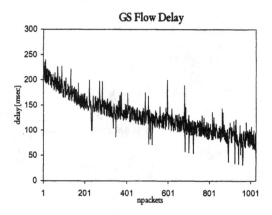

Fig. 6. Measured delay for the GS flow

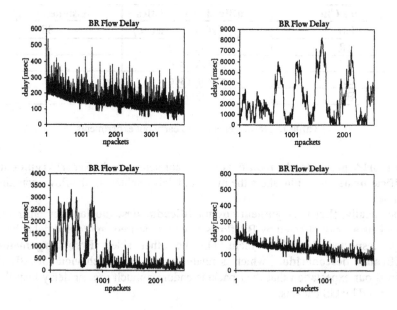

Fig. 7. Measured delays for the four BR flows

Curves in ¡Error!Argumento de modificador desconocido. and ¡Error!Argumento de modificador desconocido. show that the average rate is guaranteed for all of the flows, including the BR ones, that converge quite rapidly to the desired values.

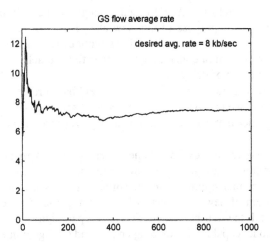

Fig. 8. Measured average rate for the GS flow

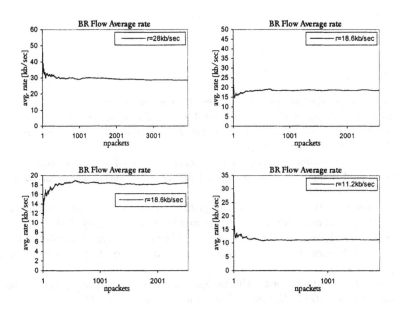

Fig. 9. Measured average rate for the BR flows

Conclusions and future work

The contribution of this paper is twofold. First, we propose a QoS-capable architecture that mainly aims at providing flexible and effective implementation of the Integrated Services model via a WFQ-based strategy, while defining a new service class for the Internet. The purpose of this new class is that of recovering the unused portion of the bandwidth reserved to GS flows without affecting their delay bounds and while giving long-term rate guarantees to other flows (such as web traffic) which are less sensitive in terms of delay.

Second, we provide actual implementation of a PC-based router which conforms to the conceptual model we propose. Such a router represents the very basis of a testbed used to carry out experiments on QoS provisioning over heterogeneous networks in a "real" environment .

Based on the encouraging results obtained after the first expermentations, the next steps in our research work are primarily concerned with:

- router performance optimization and software porting issues;
- imlemention of new mechanisms for the integration between the Integrated Services and the Differentiated Services paradigms, in order to build a scalable model capable of providing end-to-end QoS guarantees.

Work related to the last issue is already in progress and we hope we will be able to provide a prototype version of the complete framework in the near future.

References

1. A. Demers, S. Keshav, and S. Shenker. Design and Analysis of a Fair Queueing Algorithm. Proceedings of ACM SIGCOMM '89, Austin, September 1989.
2. H. Zhang and S.Keshav. *Comparison of Rate-Based Service Disciplines.* Proceedings of ACM SIGCOMM '91, pp 113-121, 1991
3. K. Cho. "A Framework for Alternate Queueing: Towards Traffic Management by PC-UNIX Based Routers." In Proceedings of USENIX 1998 Annual Technical Conference, New Orleans LA, June 1998.
4. R. Braden, D.Clark, and S. Shenker. Integrated Services in the Internet Architecture: an Overview. Technical Report RFC 1633, Request For Comments, July 1994.
5. R. Braden, L. Zhang, S. Berson, S. Herzog, S. Jamin. Resource ReSerVation Protocol (RSVP) -- Version 1 Functional Specification. RFC 2205, Request For Comments, September 1997.
6. S. Shenker, C. Partridge, and R.Guérin. Specification of Guaranteed Quality of Service. Technical Report RFC2212, Request For Comments, September 1997.
7. J. Wroklawsky. The use of RSVP with IETF Integrated Services. RFC 2210, Request For Comments, September 1997.
8. S.P. Romano, J. F. de Rezende, C. Deleuze, and S. Fdida. Integrated QoS Architecture for IP Switching. In Proc. of 7th Workshop on High-Speed Networks (HSN' 97), Stuttgart, Germany, October 1997.
9. J. Wroklawsky. Specification of the Controlled-Load Network Element Service. RFC 2211, Request For Comments, September 1997.

10. S. Blake, D. Black, M. Carlson, E. Davies, Z. Wang, W. Weiss. An Architecture for Differentiated Services. RFC 2475, Request For Comments, December 1998.

11. Yoram Bernet, James Binder, Steven Blake, Mark Carlson, Srinivasan Keshav, Elwyn Davies, Borje Ohlman, Dinesh Verma, Zheng Wang, Walter Weiss. A Framework for Differentiated Services. Internet Draft, Differentiated Services, October 1998. draft-ietf-diffserv-framework-01.txt

12. L. Zhang. Virtual Clock: A New Traffic Control Algorithm for Packet Switching Networks. Proceedings of ACM SIGCOMM '90, Philadelphia, September 1990.

13. A. K. Parekh. A Generalized Processor Sharing Approach to Flow Control in Integrated Services Networks. Ph. D. Dissertation, issued as Technical Report LIDS-TH-2089, Massachusetts Institute of Technology, Cambridge, MA 02139, February 1992.

14. S. Floyd and V. Jacobson. Link-sharing and resource management models for packet networks. IEEE/ACM Transactions on Networking, 3(4), August 1995

15. H. Zhang and E. W. Knightly. RCSP and stop-and-go: a comparison of two non-work-conserving disciplines for supporting multimedia communication. ACM/Springer-Verlag Multimedia Systems Journal n.4, pp 346-356, 1996

A Charging Model for Sessions on the Internet

Nadia Kausar, Bob Briscoe[1], Jon Crowcroft

Department of Computer Science, University College London
Gower street, London WC1E 6BT, UK
[1]BT Labs, Martlesham Heath Ipswich IP5 3RE, England
n.kausar@cs.ucl.ac.uk, rbriscoe@bt.com, jon@cs.ucl.ac.uk

Abstract. A chargeable session on the Internet may consist of more than one underlying chargeable service. Typically there will be two, one at the network layer and one at the session layer. Since different applications can have different demands from the Network, a generic charging scheme has to separate the service provided by the network from the service provided by an application/service provider. In this paper we propose a pricing model which is session based and we look at the impact of this on real-time multimedia conferencing over the Internet. In this model, we are trying to allow for the optional integration of charging at the network layer with charging at the session layer, while keeping the underlying technologies still cleanly apart. This paper also highlights the fact that the main problem of pricing application on the Internet is not just a simple case of analyzing the most technically feasible pricing mechanism but also making the solution acceptable to users. We take the position that session based pricing is easier for end users to accept and understand and show why this is the case in this paper.

1 Introduction

As the popularity of the Internet grows, the number of services offered over the Internet grows with it. Users normally pay a flat fee to join the Internet and are forced to get used to a service which is not guaranteed and prone to variable delays. However, different applications have very different service requirements. For instance, some applications like email, can tolerate significant delay without users expecting discernible performance degradation, while other applications, such as audio and packetised video degrade perceptibly with even extremely small delays[Cocchi93]. With rapidly diverging types of tasks the need for traffic characterization on the Internet is becoming very obvious. Cocchi et al[Cocchi93] have argued that, in order to produce performance incentives it is necessary to support service-class sensitive pricing for any multi-class service discipline. Using this paradigm it is possible for the user to prioritize their applications to conform to what they perceived to be acceptable QoS values. In this situation the user has an option to pay a higher price for the higher quality.

The services on the Internet have a two level matrix for charging. One is from the application perspective, and the other is from the network perspective. Research has been done to provide better than best-effort QoS in the network and provide a corresponding charging model for the added QoS (e.g., charge for throughput, bandwidth, delay etc.). Whereas, Application related pricing, i.e., charging certain fee for an application has been left to different application/service providers. These applications can have either a fixed fee or could be usage based (i.e. charge the users if they have used the application over a certain time period). In this paper, *the term "pricing" is used to refer to the process of setting a price on a service, a product, or on content. Whereas, "charging" determines the process of calculating the cost of a resource by using the price for a given record, i.e. it defines a function which translates technical values into monetary units*[Stiller98].

As previously mentioned, different application can have very different demands from the network Therefore, in order to provide a comprehensive service for an application, a user must be able to deal with separate charges for both the network and the application QoS. For example, in a video conference, participants may just want to listen to a conference and may not require a guaranteed bandwidth. In this case, these users can be charged to join the conference (e.g. obtain password to join the conference) but pay nothing for reserving network resources. However, if the network resource is scarce then a price will combine both the (minimum amount of) network resource required to transmit the conference and the facility to join the conference(obtaining password – an access key).

Therefore, it is best to provide a charging scheme that is not directly integrated with network QoS and specific applications. *In this paper, we propose a session based pricing, we use the term "session" to define the lifetime of activities of a single/group of users.* The aim is to provide protocol independence, in the sense that, different sessions(e.g. multimedia conferencing, multiplayer games or e-commerce activities) from the application layer can be charged independent of any different basis for charging network resources.

A number of approaches have been proposed for control of usage and explicit allocation of resources among users in time of overload, both in the Internet and in other packet networks[Clark95]. RSVP [RSVP], in combination with the Integrated Service model, can be used to explicitly reserve a path or flow between end points in a network Recent research has focused on a more generalized means of providing network QoS based on tagging packets where 'out' tagged packets receive congestion indication first and will be dropped when congestion occurs(diff-serv)[Clark95](b). The goal of session based pricing is to allow Internet service provider (ISP) to charge applications that can use a variety of network reservation mechanism; such as RSVP, diff-serv, or DRP[White98].

Note that, a session can use multicast to achieve N-to-N communications at the network layer, or it could use an IPtelephony gateways to interwork PSTN phone sets with an IP based conference. Therefore, this paper looks at the issues concerned with commercial model for Multicast, different service aggregation model, and uses session based pricing approach to price gateways. The sections in this paper are organised as follows: section two reviews different basis for charging in the network layer, section three looks at various ways services can be aggregated(bundling) for session based pricing, section four looks at the design approach and possible user interfaces for session based pricing, section six highlights the commercial model for multicast, and the last section concludes the paper.

2   Review of basis for charging in the network

The main reasons for charging on the Internet are: a) to cover the cost for providing the service by service providers b) make a profit (Service providers) c) control the behaviour of users or limit the usage to benefit higher paid traffic. Different mechanisms have different types of technical and economical advantages and disadvantages. In [Cos79], it was shown that users repressed their usage of the network when faced with usage-based charging. The complexities of understanding the criteria the users are paying for have an affect on payment as well. That is to say, if a user is presented with a complex bill that shows different criterias, and how different schemes they subscribed have different prices, there is a likelihood the user will prefer the flat -rate option.

The charging policy in telephone networks has existed for a long time and it works very well. Telephone companies offer a menu of local calling plans, some usage-based (e.g., metered service), some capacity based (e.g. unlimited service), and some a combination of both (e.g. a certain number of free minutes per month, plus a metered rate for calls in excess of this number). It is likely that the same will happen in computer networks, with some users choosing usage based and others choosing capacity based charges, and many being somewhere between[Shenker96].

The two most discussed pricing schemes which can be implemented vary easily for the Internet traffic are a) Capacity pricing and b) Usage based pricing. In **capacity based pricing**, a user would purchase a profile, called an expected capacity profile, based on the general nature of his/her usage. For example, a user exploring the web would need a very different profile from a scientist transferring a sequence of large data sets[Clark95].
Expected capacity pricing has the advantage of stable budgeting for network use. Also, expected capacity gives the providers a more stable model of capacity planning. If users are permitted to install and use different profiles on demand, the provider must provision somewhat more conservatively, to deal with peaks in demand. However, the biggest drawback of this scheme is that to this point the description of bandwidth allocation has been in terms of sender of the data, when the sender may be generating data because the receiver initiated it (e.g. in ftp case, where the server may be sending data when the user has requested the file).

In **usage based pricing**, the users pay for the volume of traffic (as well as length of time) they are interested in. The argument could be that if the resource is limited and the existing resource are used in different ways, service classes could be applied to differentiate its use appropriately. The biggest argument against this scheme is that usage based charges change the user perception and may decrease user's usage.

TCP Based pricing Edell et al[Edell97] have demonstrated a charging system based around TCP. This system charges for bandwidth but triggers who to charge per TCP connection. It does not reflect congestion costs as the pricing information is based on time of day rather than actual network loading. The authors claim it should work for UDP. UDP and TCP impose different traffic flows on the network and it is not clear how this will be reflected in the pricing structure. Oeschlin et al[Oesc98] modified the behaviour of TCP which reflects congestion based billing which does not work easily for constant rate traffic. Also users or software developers can get round MulTCP charging by opening multiple TCP connections to achieve the same end.

Edge Pricing Shenker et al have suggested a method to price the traffic where congestion costs are estimated using the expected congestion (e.g. time of day) along the expected path. Therefore, the resulting prices can be determined and charges are assessed locally at the access point (i.e. the edge of the provider's network where the user's packet enters), rather than computed in a distributed fashion along the entire path. Edge pricing has the attractive property that all pricing is done locally. Interconnection here involves the network providers purchasing services from each other in the same manner that regular users purchase service[Shenker96].

Paris Metro Pricing (PMP) Another way to deal with congestion in packet networks is provided by the PMP model[Odl97]. Odlyzko suggests that an end-user should be required to pay more to use a particular queue, although its architecture would be identical to a cheaper queue. The idea is that the queue that is more highly priced would attract less traffic and therefore suffer from less congestion than the queue with the lower price. PMP does not deal with more than one dimension of QoS. There would need to be a number of bands for each combination of bandwidth differentiation, latency differentiation and reliability differentiation. It is not true that all high bandwidth application also needs high reliability and latency.

Table 1. Summary of advantages and disadvantages of some basis of charging

Name of pricing scheme	Payment for	Pros[*]	Cons	Technical aspect
Smart Market	Pay for speed	Provide user with the highest price	Would be worth only when the network is congested	Difficult to implement
PMP	Different queue	Simple model,	Multiple profiles	Simple to

---

[*] pros – mainly economical advantages, not technical

	priority	traffic will get through	have to be defined at each differently congested bottleneck, doesnt provide different dimensions of QoS	implement if traffic is not traversing to many congested bottlenecks
Quota	Quota of usage	Easy to establish long term contract	Sender based/ need priory knowledge of how busy the network is	Relatively easy to implement
Usage	Time of connection	Better than flat-fee, incentive not to use the network for too long	The basis of the bill can be very variant(e.g. duration, amount of resources, no. Of cells, priority etc.), disincentive to use the network at all	Depending on what is being charged implementation can be very difficult. Multicast traffic billing can be very difficult.
Session based	Session (e.g. application)	Simple and effective,easier itemised bill for users.	A lot of market research is required to set a suitable, profitable session price	Simple from session layer but network necessarily has no handle on sessions. So in the context of networking, session charging introduces huge complexity
TCP	Bandwidth	Most traffic on the Internet uses TCP, so it has a huge customer base	Cannot use for other traffic	Technically very easy to implement.

Smart Market proposal : One of the most ambitious pricing proposals for best effort traffic is the "smart-market" proposal for Mackie-Jason and Varian described in [Mackie95].

In this scheme, each packet carries a "bid" in the packet header; packets are given service at each router if their bids exceed some threshold, and each served packet is charged this threshold price regardless of the packet's bid. This threshold price can be thought of as the highest rejected bid; having the packet pay this price is akin to having them pay the congestion cost of denying service to the rejected packet. This proposal has stimulated much discussion and has significantly increased the Internet community's understanding of economic mechanisms in network. However, there are

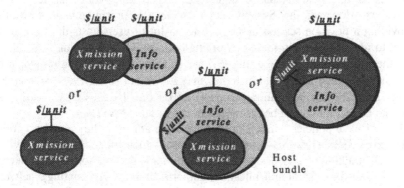

The framework for charging to use different services with different quality on the Internet is quite complex. The parameters charged can be very dynamic and variable. For example, in the telephone system, all calls require the same network capacity and the same quality of service, whereas flows in the Internet can differ widely in their need for capacity, control of delay, or other features. Especially in the context of associating value with enhanced services, it must be possible for the users to describe the service they require. The features that can be charged are: throughput, speed, accuracy(assertions connecting QoS to the ability of the search engine for example to deliver the requested information), accessibility and reliability. Therefore, for the novice type of users, there may be a requirement to set the session price for them, otherwise they have to be educated through the process of quality of service aspects of the Internet.

In this section we look at different service aggregation methods, i.e. various ways a user can be billed for a particular service he/she used over the Internet. These mechanisms have to be easily understood by the people so that they will be interested in using them. We would like to propose that there will be mainly two ways to bundle.

There are:

1. ISP bundling .
2. Session owner bundling

And there is always another approach which is based on

3. User's choice

1. ISP bundling – In this scenario, the ISPs will set a price for a given session and the hosts and the participants directly pay their ISP for that session. This is probably not a very attractive option for the ISPs because they have to work out separate prices for interconnecting with different providers for each session, how many people possibly want that service and work out a set price for every session they are providing. ISPs providing Internet telephony services should pay access charges to the local telephone companies as do other long-distance service providers. However, the ISPs can actually make a sufficient amount of profit by providing a price on session based, because a lot of users/hosts do not actually want to go through the trouble of working out a price for a session. In order to bill the users for that session, the ISP has to take into consideration that users may pay into their account (which may/may not exist , so for every session they have to create separate billing account) or by credit card or by e-cash. As mentioned that it may not be the most attractive option for ISPs.

    ISPs will have policies which can be exchanged among policy-enabled entities. DIAMETER[Rubens98] is currently a proposal which for example, can be used for ISP bundling. It is designed as a common platform for several Internet services, such as AAA(authentication, authorization and Accounting), network-edge resource management and VPN (virtual private network). So for example, when a caller (e.g. a SIP proxy server) is being notified to set up a call for a user, it first initiates a DIAMETER request command to its policy server with all the information about the user. The server, in turn, checks the request against admission control policy database, and returns the findings in a DIAMETER response message[Pan98]. [Pan98] attempts to cater only for ISP bundling, but it is unlikely DIAMETER would be the preferred solution for non-ISP bundling. Therefore a more general solution would be beneficial.

2. Session owner bundling – In this scenario, the master of ceremonies (e.g. an organiser of a conference) sets the price for individual user or mainly an organization, where the novice users do not have to know the implications. For example, user A decides to host a conference in UCL, 1999 for 2 days. This conference requires access to the Mbone[Mbone] in order to multicast the session. So the host has to work out what is the minimum bandwidth required to transmit video(frame rate) and in order to deliver audio what is the bit rate required. After that the session owner sets a common price for all that absorbs and hides peaks and throughs in costs for each participant. A slight premium allowance above the expected average cost involved underwrites the host's risk. This might either turn a profit for the host or be returned to all participants in equal shares (co-op dividend). Each participant's cost to the host will depend on their ISP's price, but the host is wholesaling (hiding) this to participants. This may be a lot of work for the host to work out a suitable price. This scheme will be attractive for a type of host who holds a lot of sessions like that a year and the host is likely to be a big organization. As for the user is concerned, they do not have to worry about the technical aspects of the conference and it makes it definitely simple for them to just pay the host and participate in the conference. The question remains, will a user be interested in paying a fixed amount for which they are confined to the policy the host/session owner has set?

3. User - In this scenario, the user has the choice to go either with the "best-effort service" for a session or can pay their ISP directly for guaranteed service. Normally for all of the above option as well, the frame rate for video and for audio the required bandwidth will be advertised on SDR(see section 4 for further discussion). Therefore, it is up to the user to pay a certain fee for a certain amount of guaranteed service. For novice users, they do not necessarily need to know the technical details. There will be the option in the form of a sliding bar marked with values (either monetary values or other forms of prices), and increasing the value of the sliding bar will increase the quality.

With this option, the host or the ISP do not have to set certain prices for everyone for different sessions. Also, it gives the user the flexibility to go with their own policy, i.e. they are not confined to ISP's or the host's policies.

For all of the models of payments above strong security is necessary both between routers and policy servers and between policy servers and the billing system that connects policies to economics because their interaction implies financial transactions. Whatever the bundling scenario is and whether an ISP or a user is setting the price, they can use a session based pricing interface (as discussed in the section below) to serve their purpose.

4 Model for application driven session pricing

This section proposes a possible example of user interface that could be used for any of the bundling scenarios discussed in section 3. An important aspect of the problem of designing a model to price real-time applications on the Internet is that the Internet architecture is based on the network layer not knowing the properties of the applications implemented above it. Therefore, in this model the knowledge of underlying resource management and network implications of providing a guaranteed service is not necessary and has been separated from the applications. ISPs or the bandwidth broker sets a certain price for each session that can be accessed from the session layer. While in this paper and in this model we have focused on monetary values to participate in a session, the underlying accounting structure and pricing architecture should allow the use of these other incentive forms if they are locally applicable.

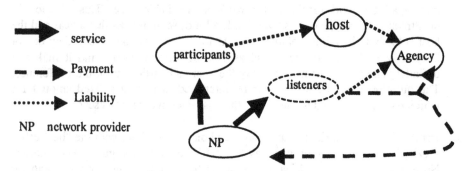

Fig. 2. Model of interaction between participants and agency

The design philosophy of this model is quite simple. Let us take a multimedia conference for example, there will be few participants among which some are just listeners. This session is advertised by some arbitrary means (e.g. SDR [Kirst97] or a web page), with the session's price being a fixed priori. As discussed in section 3, the user driven system where the user has the choice of either paying a certain fee for guaranteed QoS or not paying. So there will be an "agent" who will be responsible for collecting the payment. The session based pricing comprises a "back-end" , whose job is to inform the service provider or the initiator (depending on who is charging and what the policy is) that the specific session is being paid for and a guarantee for that service for that price is required. Each router, on receiving a packet, must able to determine whether the router is within the paid region. There are only two ways that a router can have access to information about a flow. Either it is stored in the router (this is not the preferred option), or in the packets of the flow. The second part is a "front-end" which allows a client to provide inputs in the selection process. In this scenario we have used multimedia conferencing as an example where there are different classes of participants. So the participants who are just listeners can choose to pay a flat fee whereas a speaker will pay an additional amount for that session. However, for example, if the speaker is an invited speaker then he/she may pay nothing. Floor control [Kausar98] for the session plays a very useful part for this pricing scheme.

If a user initially chose the option not to speak then the floor control option is not enabled. However, we realized that a listener may have a question at the end of a session, but the amount of traffic that will be generated by this question may have an impact on the network if the resource available is scarce. For most of the existing conference tools there is a facility to use the chat option where the users can type in their question. A possible example of front end could look as shown in Figure 3:

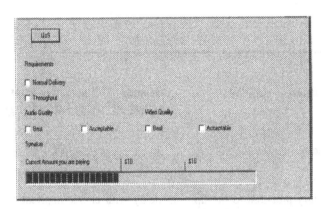

Fig. 3. An example of front end of payment service

An Mbone session directory SDR[Kirst97] is used to advertise multimedia conferences, and to communicate the session addresses (whether multicast or unicast)and conference-tool- specific information necessary for participation. This would be an ideal tool to advertise the prices associated with the sessions. Currently the user interface looks like as shown in Figure 5. An extra option with QoS details which will show the sliding bar for payment can be added to enhance the features of SDR.

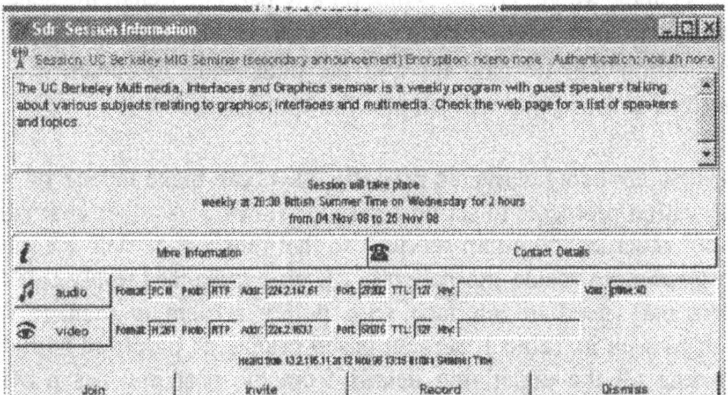

Fig. 4. Session directory would need an option for payment

5 Support from Network layer

The Internet today offers a single class of service, where all packets are serviced on a best effort, First-in–First-Out (FIFO) basis. Disrupted audio and video due to packet losses make multimedia conferencing less efficient and less effective. The applications that generate traffic can be located on a continuum (see Figure 5) which also represents the delay tolerance. As the amount of real-time traffic increases there may be a corresponding need to define a richer set of QoS parameters for these traffic types[Bouch98].

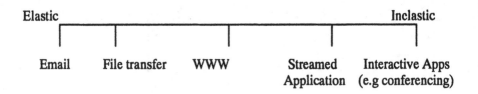

Fig. 5. Relative traffic elasticity

Although users are normally prepared to put up with delay with elastic applications because it is expected to be delivered later in the day and picked up some other time, one may send an urgent email which can be treated as a real-time or inelastic application (for example, an email informing someone to join a conference immediately).

In order to guarantee the service that is chosen from the session based application pricing interface, the network has to provide enough resources. Since an RSVP API[Stevens] is currently available, we suggest to integrate RSVP with the different models of session based pricing. However, as discussed in section 2 there are other ways to reserve the resources or characterise the packets that are being paid for in network layer. In this paper, we are not focussing on any particular charging scheme for network or service, any number of combinations can be used. We are assuming the commercial application will be paid for and the underlying resources will be reserved or characterized in a way that will support the application.

To ensure voice and data are being delivered properly, users can make the use of end-to-end resource reservation protocols to set up reserved "flows". Another alternative is to mark the packet header as "premium service" so that they can be delivered with low delay and rate guarantees inside the network. Both approaches imply that the network-edge routers may need to interface with policy servers to manage link resources. However, as seen in Table 1, session based pricing as proposed here, has the advantage of hiding all the underlying details from the user and has a better chance of being accepted by users.

6 ISP's perspective

One of the attractive schemes which perhaps allows a great encapsulation and therefore compact characterization of application specific QoS parameters is known as 'User share Differentiation' (USD) [Wang97]. USD involves, not the separate reservation of bandwidth for each flow per session but the sharing of a pool of bandwidth among multiple users. The user is given a minimum amount of individual bandwidth, according to the user-ISP contract, and a minimum share of bandwidth over this bandwidth. It is argued that this scheme strikes the correct balance between aggregation and isolation of sources. Its additional benefits may be:

- The definition of 'user' is flexible: this entails that the level of aggregation of traffic is flexible. For example, the ISP is free to implement multiple classes of traffic to reflect the needs of different users; some users may only require a best-effort service.
- A hierarchical management structure is provided: The ISP allocates bandwidth to the user, the user then allocates among its applications. The user can choose to mark it s applications to reflect loss or delay priorities. This has important implications for traffic classifications at different levels of the market structure[Bouch98].
- Incentives are provided for users to control their traffic sending rates. This fits perfectly well with "user bundling" system described in section 3.

7 Multicast Model

It is held that multicast offers significant advantages to the Internet community. Multimedia real-time applications which are being multicast pose more of a challenge to be priced and different access rates need to be considered carefully when pricing the senders/receivers. A multicast address is merely a logical name, and by itself conveys no geographic or provider information. Multicast routing identifies the next hop along the path for packets arriving at an interface, multicast routing does not identify the rest of the tree. Thus, estimating costs in the multicast case requires an additional piece of accounting infrastructure. One approach to price the receivers is to introduce a new form of control message – an accounting message – that would be initiated when the receiver sends its multicast join message[Shenker96]. These accounting messages would be forwarded along the reverse trees towards each source, recording the "cost" of each link it traversed and summing costs when branches merged.

With the User bundling scenario, the session based pricing solves the problem of charging receiver/sender in a multicast session. As discussed previously, the user can pay a set price regardless their position in a multicast tree. If the receiver wishes to receive a session with a certain guarantee, they just have to pay. In user bundling system, the price to be paid for a session's quality is upto the user, so whether the user is a multicast receiver or not, does not really affect the pricing scheme. If the multicast tree is organised in a hierarchical structure, then the host or the ISP (if it is a host or ISP bundling system being used to pay for services) can negotiate or set a price for a particular branch of the tree. Then, if one of the child nodes join a session which needed to be paid for, the node can obtain the price from the nearest parent node.

Another issue to be addressed is: which party (content provider, ISP or receiver) does multicast transport offer the most intrinsic value compared with unicast transport? In overall, one can say that multicast access and peering agreements are likely to be placed on a very different financial basis from the existing unicast agreements. The figures below compare multicast and unicast data delivery, for a simple case in which both the content provider and subscribers buy access from the same ISP.

As seen in Figure 6, the multicast sender (e.g. content provider) benefits greatly from multicast, since access costs are drastically reduced. There is little multicast benefit to the receiver. To the receiver it makes little difference whether multicast or unicast is used (assuming, received bandwidth is charged at the same rate unicast or multicast). By default, the ISP should charge multicast senders (e.g. content providers) more for multicast access bandwidth (sent into the network) than for unicast access bandwidth.

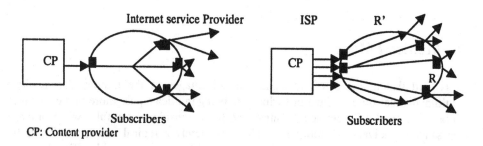

Internet service Provider   ISP   R'

CP

CP

Subscribers   Subscribers
CP: Content provider

Fig. 6. Comparison of (a) multicast and (b) unicast delivery

If the multicast sender is charged more, the increase in access bandwidth tariff should be in some way be related to the degree of replication (actual, average etc.) performed by the network, but should be less than would have been charged for unicast access to N clients. One of the main difficulties with charging multicast senders according to the degree of replication is that it is likely to be a considerable overhead for the ISP to measure the actual degree of replication on a per-session basis. If the multicast access tariff for senders is based on an average degree of replication (averaged across sessions), then this will not cater for different ranges (tens to thousands of participants).

8 IP Telephony issues

Most charging for transportation system in our day-to-day life (e.g. train fare, plane fair etc.) is based around geographic distances. On the Internet, distance related charging does not apply because the sender may not necessarily know where the receivers are, especially in multicast scenario (even in unicast case, IP addresses of hosts do not represent the "geographic distances" between each other). Therefore, a video conferencing that is taking place between a host on the Internet to a PSTN phoneset or another host on the internet becomes tricky to charge.

There are mainly three types of billings that can take place for a conference:
1. PC to PC billing
2. PC to phone billing
3. Phone to PC billing

The physical location of a PC on the Internet cannot be used to price the connection that takes place in either of the above cases. If it is a PSTN to IP pricing (case c) scenario, then the user will pay the local phone company for using the service and it is upto the phone company to locate the IP telephony gateway and complete the call. Currently different standard committees (c.g. IETF E.164 BOF and DTS TIPHON) are going through the process of assigning E.164 numbers to machines on the Internet. The gateways can then use the "dial plan" to price the call that takes place from the gateway (end of PSTN) to the PC (over IP). So for example, if user A wants to video conference a machine named B, it will be assigned an E.164 number, which may start with 00 44 171, which represents a UK number. Therefore the caller will be charged accordingly.

The other alternative of the model above, is to use session based pricing. The users will be divided into different regions who are serviced by different ISPs. The local region marked as R in Figure 6 will have a set session price than the one which is marked as R'. Although, in the Figure they are both clients of the same ISP, in reality they may have used different ISPs with different subscription to different telephone companies. It is up to the service provider to set a price to interconnect PSTN to IP.

9 Conclusion

Different types of traffic sent into the network may have different QoS requirement associated with them. The satisfaction a network user derives from their network access depends on the nature of the application being used and the quality of service received from the network. Since the nature of the Internet architecture is based on the network layer not knowing the properties of the applications implemented above it, we have proposed a session based pricing model that operates over existing network reservation/pricing schemas and augments it to take into consider additional needs of applications.

Thus, we view existing network reservation/charging schemas as providing a baseline set of services to a user. Subsequent or value-added services and refinements of the network. Services is accomplished with a session-based pricing schema. One example of its realization could be in SDR, which is aimed at users and thus can provide a simple and straightforward way of conveying price-to-function relationship.

Setting a session price that will profit the ISP or the content provider, and yet still be price-competitive with their competition, can be difficult to predict. The complexity to predict and implement a profitable price for session based pricing is still an open issue and a subject for further research. However, session based pricing has the attractive features of providing a more direct way of communication costs to the user and the flexibility to implement it with any different basis for charging network resources. The proposed work is currently under implementation.

Acknowledgements

Special thanks go to Ken Carlberg and Orion Hodson of UCL and Ian Marshall of BT Labs for their useful comments and suggestions on this paper.

References

[Bouch98] Bouch A., " A user cnetered approach to the design and implementation of Quality of service and charging mechanisms in Wide-area Networks" – 1st year report, http://www.cs.ucl.ac.uk/staff/A.Bouch

[Clark95](a) Clark D. "Adding service discrimination to the Internet " September 1995, presented at MIT workshop on Internet Economics

[Clark95](b)Clark D.(MIT), A model for cost allocation and pricing in the Internet, presented at MIT workshop on Internet Economics, Mar 1995 "http://www.press.umich.edu/jep/works/ClarkModel.html"

[Cocchi93] Cocchi R., Shenker S., Estrin D., Zhang L. "Pricing in computer Networks" – Motivation, formulation and Example , IEEE/ACM Transactions on Networking, vol. 1, Dec. 1993.

[Cos79] Cosgove J., Linhart P. "customer choices under local measured telephone service" Public utilities fortnightly, 30, pp 27-31, 1979

[Edell97] Edell R J, McKeowen N and Varaiya PP "Billing users and pricing for TCP". IEEE Journal on selected areas of Communication 1997

[Kausar98] Kausar N., Crowcroft J. – " Floor control requirements from reliable IP multicast" 8th IFIP Conference on High Performance Networking (HPN'98) The Millennium Push of Internet, Vienna September 21-25, 1998

[Kirst97] Kirstein P., Whelan E. "SAP - Security using public key algorithms"Internet draft http://www.ietf.org/internet-drafts/draft-ietf-mmusic-sap-sec-04.txt

[Mackie95] Mackie-Mason J., Varian H. "pricing the Internet" – In brian kahin and James Keller, editors, Public access to the Internet. Prentic –Hall, New Jersey 1995, URL: ftp://gopher.econ.lsa.umich.edu/pub/papers/Pricing_the_Internet.ps.Z

[Mbone] Mbone information site, http://www.mbone.com/techinfo/

[Oec98] Oechslin P., Crowcroft J. "Weighted Proportionally Fair Differentaited Service TCP", accepted for ACM CCR, 1998

[Odl97] Odlyzko A. "A modest proposdal for preventing Internet congestion" 1997, http://www.research.att.com/~amo/doc/recent.html

[Pan98]Pan P., Schulzrinne H. "DIAMETER: policy and Accounting Extension for SIP" Internet draft, Internet Engineering task Force, July 1998

[RSVP] Internet draft –A Framework for Use of RSVP with Diff-serv Networks http://search.ietf.org/internet-drafts/draft-ietf-diffserv-rsvp-01.txt

[Rubens98] Rubens A., Calhoun P "DIAMETER base protocol" Internet draft, Internet Engineering task Force July 1998

[Shenker96] Shenker., Clark d., Estrin D., Herzog S. " Pricing in computer networks" ACM Computer
Communication Review, vol. 26, pp. 19-43, Apr. 1996.

[Stevens]Stevens "Advanced Programming in the Unix environment"

[Stiller98] Stiller B., Fankhauser G. "Charging and Accounting for Integrated Internet Services – state of the art, problems and trends", INET 1998, Switzerland, July 21 – 24, 1998

[Wang97] Wang Z., Internet draft User-Share Differentiation (USD) Scalable bandwidth allocation for differentiated services 1997

[White98] White P. and Crowcroft J.. A Dynamic Sender-Initiated Reservation Protocol for the Internet. 8th IFIP Conference on High Performance Networking (HPN'98) The Millennium Push of Internet, Vienna September 21-25, 1998

COMIQS System for Commercial Presentations on the Internet

Irek Defée, Jami Kangasoja, and Mika Rustari
on behalf of the COMIQS consortium

Digital Media Institute Tampere University of Technology
P.O. Box 553 FIN-33101 Tampere, Finland
{defee, jami, mpr}@cs.tut.fi

Abstract. Commercial presentations can be one of the main applications of multimedia in the Internet world. ACTS COMIQS project develops a networked multimedia system for the Internet to facilitate the commercial applications of new multimedia tools and systems. The COMIQS system is based on the MPEG-4 standard and new Internet protocols. MPEG-4 DMIF part is used as the communication architecture model in which applications are separated from underlying transport network details. The RTP protocol is used for transporting time sensitive data and RTCP is used for QoS monitoring. The application signalling is based on the RTSP. COMIQS builds and integrates complete system including media servers, networking and MPEG-4 terminal. Two applications will be used in technical trials over the Internet.

1 Introduction

Development of Internet into a networked multimedia platform for the presentation of rich interactive content is faced with several technical problems. Multimedia uses mostly streaming data and requires strict timing and synchronization. Because of this, system resources need to be reserved in order to guarantee the QoS (Quality of Service). Traditionally the Internet has been developed only for best effort QoS and applications were tuned to it. Changes to the Internet architecture are thus needed in order to provide support for multimedia content. In parallel, new methods of organisation of multimedia data are needed to realise the full potential of the Internet.

These challenges are currently being solved in several standardisation bodies. The ISO MPEG has recently finished first version of the MPEG-4 standard. MPEG-4 covers all issues related to the compression, encoding and presentation of video, 3-D graphics, images and other data types. MPEG-4 is very flexible and efficient which makes this standard ideal for Internet multimedia applications.

Fully networked MPEG-4 applications could play a major role on the Internet. Networking of MPEG-4 is the current topic of work in the IETF (Internet Engineering Task Force) and ISO MPEG. This work aims for specifying network system components for running MPEG-4 applications with the necessary QoS.

The ACTS project COMIQS plays active role in these developments. COMIQS (Commerce with MPEG-4 over the Internet with Quality of Service) builds a networked system for running the MPEG-4 applications over the Internet. The project develops a framework for such a system by contributing to the IETF and MPEG standardisation process while simultaneously aiming for the implementation of a testbed system.

Electronic commerce over the Internet is growing quickly and it is clear that it will demand for even more tools to attract consumers. Presentation of products and services using multimedia will undoubtedly enhance the appeal of electronic shopping. Due to these considerations the COMIQS project implements a demonstrator for its technical platform directed to commercial presentation. One application deals with multimedia catalogue of a department store and another one with an interactive city guide.

In this paper the COMIQS project developments are presented in detail. COMIQS develops complete platform as well as system components, software, and applications. In the following these elements are described with the emphasis put on architectural solutions which are required in order to synthesise networked multimedia system for the Internet.

2 Project objectives

2.1 COMIQS main objectives

COMIQS main objective is the technical and service validation of a set of new paradigms introduced by recent and on-going innovations in international standardisation bodies like ISO MPEG, Web3D, and the Internet IETF.

More specifically, COMIQS objectives are to demonstrate and validate, the usefulness and added value of new and attractive multimedia functionalities:
- *All-media integration* for digital high quality multimedia with video, 3D graphics, photo-realistic images and high quality sound
- *Increased interactivity* with content such as objects contained in motion pictures, audio tracks, 3D objects i.e. not restricted to clickable icons or buttons or hypertext links which are already available on the Internet
- *Real-time streaming* of all media over the Internet to the clients, facilitating navigation and allowing at the same time better adaptation of the content presentation process to available network resources
- *QoS management*, from best-effort to predicted QoS (Quality of Service), encompassing scaleable services on a variety of access networks, from narrowband to broadband Internet

These functionalities targeted by COMIQS are essential steps in the direction towards enhanced user-friendliness and content realism for interactive multimedia over the Internet.

2.2 COMIQS technical approach

COMIQS works towards achieving its main objectives by the following technical approach:

- Defining user and service requirements, design scenarios and create content for trials
- Developing the multimedia client/server architecture on IP-based transport systems using real-time protocols like RTP/RTCP to support realtime streaming of synchronized media and QoS management from narrowband to broadband Internet [4].
- Verifying services over a variety of IP-based networks

COMIQS develops complete technical and service platform. The technical platform is build upon the recent MPEG-4 standard developed by ISO MPEG. MPEG-4 multimedia data encoding is used for presentation. The DMIF (Delivery Integration Multimedia Framework) part of the MPEG-4 standard is used as the model for client-server architecture in the Internet context [2]. For these developments COMIQS is undertaking the following steps which are explained in detail in this paper:

- Specifying and implementing the mapping of the MPEG-4 buffer, timing and multiplexing model over the RTP protocol, and RTP payload for the transport of MPEG-4 [1], [4], [10].
- Specifying and implementing network signalling. This covers DMIF network interfaces at different levels, MPEG-4 System TransMux Instance able to create RTP connections, or MPEG-4 System FlexMux Channels multiplexed in a single connection [1], [2], [4].
- Specifying and implementing application signalling between peer applications.
- Investigating and specifying mechanisms to support dynamic bandwidth negotiation and for managing QoS. This encompasses interpretation and translation of generic QoS parameters (to be defined by DMIF) requested by the application into network specific QoS traffic parameters.
- Specifying and implementing the complete terminal architecture integrating the network and application signalling, de-multiplexing and network adaptation, developed by the project, with MPEG-4 audio/video decoding, 3D rendering and presentation modules.
- Specifying and implementing the complete server architecture supporting the developed applications.

3 MPEG-4 Application Components

MPEG-4 is a newly developed ISO MPEG standard with a broad set of functionalities for developing interactive networked multimedia applications.

As illustrated in Fig. 1., the MPEG-4 framework enables to:

- Represent units of audio, visual or audio-visual content, called audio/visual objects or AVOs. These AVOs can be of natural (from camera or microphone) or synthetic (from computer) origin.
- Compose those objects together to create compound audio-visual objects that form audio-visual scenes; to multiplex and synchronise the data associated with AVOs, for transport over network channels providing a QoS appropriate for each AV Object.
- To interact at the terminal side with the audio-visual scene.

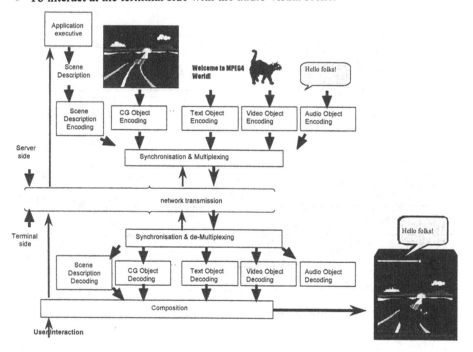

Fig. 1. MPEG-4 Application components

4 COMIQS System Architecture

The deliverable "COMIQS System Architecture Specification" [6] specifies the architectural framework of the COMIQS project. The general architecture of the main components of the COMIQS system is shown in Fig. 2. It is a client-server system providing necessary mechanisms for running MPEG-4 interactive multimedia applications. The DMIF communication system, the MPEG-4 media server and the MPEG-4 terminal are described in the next sections.

The COMIQS network delivery is based on the Internet. Transport mechanism uses the RTP (Real Time Protocol) proposed for time sensitive multimedia data. The RTP protocol does not provide guarantees for data delivery but only encapsulates data packets with time stamps. The accompanying RTCP (Real Time Control Protocol) can be used for the monitoring of QoS of RTP transport. There is not yet a common network resource reservation mechanism for the Internet. In this situation COMIQS will rely on networks with sufficient bandwidth and on adjusting bandwidth demands based on the RTCP reports [4].

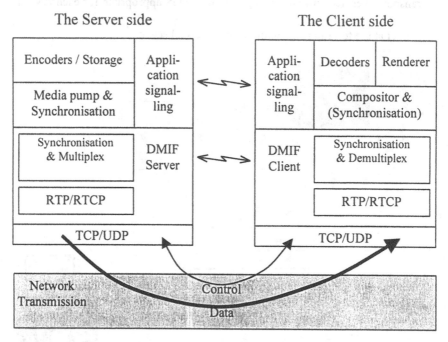

Fig. 2. COMIQS system architecture

5 COMIQS DMIF

DMIF (Delivery Multimedia Integration Framework) is a part of the MPEG-4 standard describing networking concept for MPEG-4 applications [2]. As indicated by its name DMIF is only a framework that can be adapted to a variety of underlying networks. Basic idea of DMIF is to separate applications from the details of underlying networking in other words to make applications 'network indifferent'.

COMIQS is developing concrete DMIF instance relying on the RTP/RTCP/IP protocol stack [4]. Also, WWW URL connectivity mechanisms are used since it is assumed that COMIQS applications will be running in WWW-browsers.

5.1 The DMIF Control Plane

When operating over interactive networks, DMIF defines a purely informative DMIF-Network Interface (DNI): this interface allows to highlight the actions that a DMIF peer shall trigger with respect to the network, and the parameters that DMIF peers need to exchange across the network. Through reference to the DNI it is possible to clearly identify the actions that DMIF triggers to e.g. set-up or release a connection resource. The DNI primitives are mapped into messages to be actually carried over the network. A default syntax is defined (DMIF Signalling Messages -DS-), which in practical terms corresponds to a new protocol.

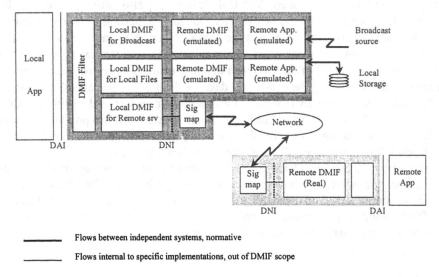

Flows between independent systems, normative

Flows internal to specific implementations, out of DMIF scope

Fig. 3. DMIF communication architecture

Fig. 3. represents the overall DMIF concepts. Applications (e.g. an MPEG-4 player) access data through the DMIF-Application Interface (DAI), irrespectively whether such data comes from a broadcast source, from local storage or from a remote server. In all scenarios the local application only interacts through a uniform interface (DAI). Different DMIF instances will then translate the local application requests into specific messages to be delivered to the remote part of the application, taking care of the peculiarities of the involved delivery technology. Similarly, data entering the terminal (from remote servers, broadcast networks or local files) are uniformly delivered to the local application through the DAI.

Different, specialised DMIF instances are indirectly invoked by the Application to manage the various specific delivery technologies: this is however transparent to the

Application, that only interacts with a single "DMIF filter". This filter is then in charge of directing the particular DAI primitive to the right instance. DMIF does not specify this mechanism, it just assumes it is implemented. This is further emphasised by the shaded boxes in the Fig. 3., which show what are the borders of a DMIF implementation: while the DMIF communication architecture defines a number of modules, actual DMIF implementations only need to preserve their appearance at those borders.

5.2 The Data Plane

In the MPEG-4 standard no assumption is made on the delivery technology, and no complete protocol stack is specified in the generic case. The multiplexing facilities offered by the different delivery technologies (if any) are exploited, avoiding duplication of functionality: mappings to various existing transport protocol stacks (also called TransMuxes) are defined. MPEG-4 Systems [1] also defines a tool for the efficient multiplexing of Elementary Stream data, to be applied in particular at low or very low bitrates. This tool is named the MPEG-4 FlexMux, and allows up to 256 Elementary Streams to be conveyed on a single multiplexed stream: by sharing the same stream, the impact of the overhead due to the complete protocol stack can be reduced without affecting the end-to-end delay. This implies a so-called 2-layer multiplex, that could be roughly represented with a FlexMux Layer as the MPEG-4 addition to a TransMux Layer which gathers the multiplexing facilities provided by specific delivery technologies (e.g. IP addresses and ports, ATM VPs and VCs, MPEG-2 PIDs, etc.). This structure of MPEG-4 streams is shown in Fig. 4.

The separation between FlexMux and TransMux Layers is however somewhat artificial, since the delivery technology peculiarities might influence the FlexMux Layer configuration as well. The details of particular arrangement in this case are handled by DMIF, which is responsible for configuring the Data Plane and determination of the protocol stack, including both the FlexMux and TransMux Layers.

5.3 QoS

Quality of Service (QoS) is a term used in several contexts, with similar but technically very different meanings. Sometimes it means the quality (subjective) perceived by the end user, other times it means the objective quality provided by the transport network. Different transport networks use different parameters to characterise and measure the QoS.

In the Internet, a couple of technologies provide mechanisms to manage QoS: the RSVP (Resource ReSerVation Protocol) for reserving network resources in advance, the RTCP (Real Time Control Protocol) of the RTP (Real Time Protocol) for monitoring the objective quality of transmissions [4], [5].

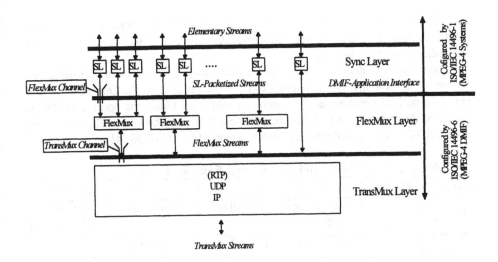

Fig. 4. The MPEG-4 System Layer model

5.3.1 DMIF QoS Model

The QoS aspects of DMIF specification deserve particular attention. Ability of the standard to adapt to different service scenarios is affected by its ability to consistently manage QoS requirements. Different delivery technologies may implement different techniques for QoS provisioning, including guaranteed QoS, statistically controlled QoS, best effort; tools for the monitoring of the perceived QoS in the delivery may be exploited for providing feedback to the sender and receiver, and allow upper layer applications to react accordingly.

Current techniques on error resilience at the compression layer are already effective, but are not and will not be able to satisfy every possible scenario, if they are not complemented with optimised management of the delivery technology (including the notification of low quality conditions). The ability to model this behaviour keeping separated the compression and delivery aspects, is a challenge to the MPEG-4 layered architecture.

The QoS that is requested to the Delivery Layer is named "transport QoS", since it describes the requirements for the transport. The mechanism used by the Delivery Layer to fulfil the requirements depends on the specific delivery technology. In particular, the Delivery Layer will process the requests, determine whether to bundle multiple Elementary Streams into a single network connection (TransMux) and compute the QoS for the network connection, using the QoS parameters as defined by the network infrastructure. Two QoS Descriptors are defined in ISO/IEC 14496: one is used at the DAI, another one is used at the DNI. Both are intended to specify the "transport" Quality of Service for an individual Elementary Stream, however only the traffic parameters (e.g., bitrate) have been specified, not the performance parameters (e.g., delay, loss probability). The QoS_Descriptor is able to carry a number of QoS metrics. The currently defined set of metrics and their semantics is summarized in table 1. This QoS concept is named "network QoS", since it is specific for a particular network technology.

In some types of networks, it is possible that during the delivery of an Elementary Stream, changes in the network conditions cause a variation in the QoS actually provided. In such circumstances the Delivery Layer shall notify the application of the perceived degradation, so that the appropriate actions may be taken. This is the case of RTP/RTCP on IP-based networks, which are used by COMIQS [4].

Table 1. ISO/IEC 14496 (MPEG-4 DMIF) defined QoS Metrics.

QoS_QualifierTag	Description	Unit	Type
MAX_DELAY	Maximum end to end delay for the stream	Microseconds	Long
AVG_DELAY	Preferred end to end delay for the stream	Microseconds	Long
LOSS_PROB	Allowable loss probability of any single AU	Fraction (0.00 – 1.00)	Double
MAX_GAP_LOSS	Maximum allowable number of consecutively lost AUs	Integer number of access units (AU)	Long
MAX_AU_SIZE	Maximum size of an AU	Bytes	Long
MAX_AU_RATE	Maximum arrival rate of AUs	AUs/second	Long
AVG_AU_SIZE	Average size of an AU	Bytes	Double

6 COMIQS Server

COMIQS server specified by the deliverable "Media Server Architecture Specification" [8] acts as a repository and Mediapump for delivering MPEG-4 content to clients. The server is composed of several basic modules.

6.1 Basic Operating Scenario

The operation scenario of the COMIQS server describes how the server co-operates with the client according to the scheme shown in Fig. 5. The client application is running inside a WWW-browser.

The client accesses the service from the WWW-browser. On the service WWW-page there is a special DMIF-URL [2] for the desired MPEG-4 application. The following operational scenario is executed:

• The client retrieves the DMIF-URL from the WWW-server.

- The client sends the DMIF-URL in a service request to the COMIQS server DMIF via a TCP connection to start the DMIF operation [2].
- A sequence of commands between the client and server for establishing required communication links as required by DMIF take place.
- The server sends the MPEG-4 IOD (Initial Object Descriptor) to the client [1].
- The server responds to the application signalling commands from the client.
- Server delivers data required by the application, especially streams and manages communication resources.
- Server adapts the communication links and applications to the required QoS.
- Server releases connections when the application is finished or links are broken.

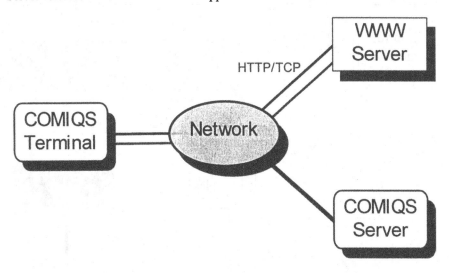

Fig. 5. Basic Operation Scenario

6.2 Server Architecture

The architecture of the COMIQS server, shown in Fig. 6., implements two different servers on two different platforms, Windows NT and Sun Solaris. The main difference between the servers is in the Synchronization-Multiplexing-Transport mechanisms used as can be seen in Fig. 6.

Control module
Server control is related to the functionalities needed for operation with many simultaneous users and applications. The main task of the Control module is session handling. It is the end point of the session establishment at the server side. The Initial Object Descriptor (IOD) [1] is sent in the server's response to the session request to conclude the session establishment. Control module is connected to the DMIF module via the DMIF Application Interface (DAI) [2].

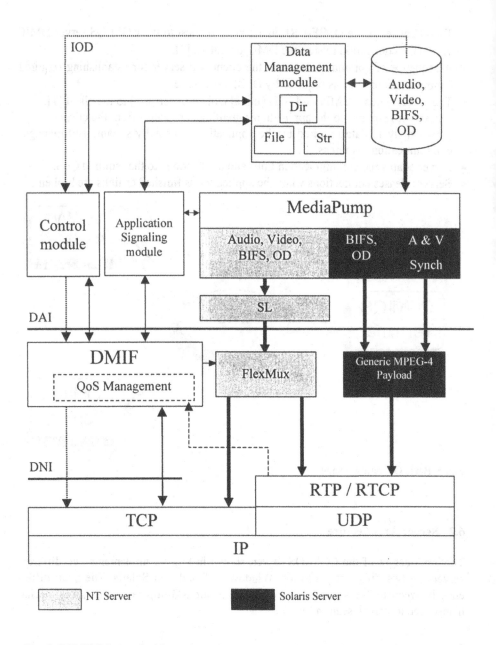

Fig. 6. COMIQS Server Architecture

Application Signalling module
COMIQS proposed to both ISO and IETF and is about to implement an URL-centred application signalling approach [9]. Application signalling messages in the COMIQS system are conveyed through the DAI.

The AS methods are a subset of RTSP (Real-Time Streaming Protocol) methods with some additions and modifications [3]. The methods are OPTIONS, PLAY, PAUSE, R-MUTE and RESUME.

The Application Signalling module includes an instance of a state machine for each active session. The Application signalling module commands the Mediapump. These commands are defined by the combination of the current state and the received method.

Data Management module

Data Management module manages all the different types of the application data residing in the storage system. It maps the logical data entries to the physical files in the file system. The Mediapump uses the Data Management module to resolve the file names of the desired content.

Mediapump

The Mediapump retrieves the desired content i.e. the application data from the storage system and passes it to the DMIF module through the DAI (DMIF Application Interface) [2].

In general Mediapumps for MPEG-4 system can be complicated due to the fact that handling and multiplexing of numerous data streams in real time might be necessary. Mediapump handles two types of data: data, which may require synchronization (audio and video), and data, which might not require synchronization, e.g. BIFS (Binary Format for Scenes) and OD (Object Descriptors).

There are two possibilities to perform the synchronization. One possibility is to perform the synchronization in the Mediapump. In COMIQS this solution is implemented in the Solaris Server and it is inline with the IETF approach. The other possibility to perform the synchronization is to implement the SL (Synchronization Layer) and the FlexMux layers in which case there is no need to deal with the synchronization in the Mediapump [1]. In COMIQS this solution is adopted in the NT Server and it is inline with the MPEG-4 approach.

DMIF module

The DMIF module implements the DMIF part of the MPEG-4 standard. The DMIF module separates the rest of the Server from the network, since both the signalling and the data transmission goes trough it.

The interface between the DMIF module and the Control and the Application signalling modules is the DAI. The signalling interface to the network is the DMIF Network Interface (DNI). The data flows from the Mediapump through the DAI to the DMIF module and from the DMIF module to the appropriate network interface [2].

6.3 Server Platforms

The following lists describe the development and minimum demonstration platforms for the two different COMIQS servers.

Solaris Server development platform
- Sun Ultra Enterprise 2 Server
- Sun Sparc StorageArray A5000 diskarray
- Sun Solaris 2.6 OS
- SunATM SBus Adapter (155 or 622 Mb/s)
- Java and C++ compilers

Solaris Server minimum configuration for testing and demonstration purposes
- Sun Ultra 2 Workstation
- Sufficient disk space on local disk
- Sun Solaris 2.6 OS
- SunATM SBus Adapter (155 Mb/s)

NT Server development platform
- Pentium 133
- Windows NT 4.0 Service Pack 3 OS
- Ethernet Adapter (10 Mb/s)
- ATM Adapter (25 Mb/s)
- Microsoft Visual C++ 6.0 compiler

NT Server minimum configuration for testing and demonstration purposes
- Pentium 133 or higher
- Sufficient disk space on local disk
- Windows NT 4.0 Service Pack 3
- Ethernet Adapter (10/100 Mb/s)
- ATM Adapter (25 Mb/s)

7 COMIQS Terminal

The COMIQS terminal, specified by the deliverable "Terminal Specification and Architecture" [7], is an MPEG-4 compliant interactive terminal with the following capabilities:
- BIFS/VRML decoding for: 3D scene description, 2D scene description and mixed 2D/3D scene description [1]
- 2D/3D viewer for the presentation of the scene [1]
- JPEG/GIF decoder for still images
- MPEG-4 video decoder
- MPEG-4 audio decoder
- Network access (multiplexing and synchronization) using RTP, UDP, TCP, IP protocols and related adaptation layers with respect to MPEG-4 FlexMux or MPEG-4 generic payload format for RTP [1], [4]
- DMIF compliant media access layer for all media types (audio, video, BIFS) [1], [2]
- Local interaction and network interaction

The user of the terminal is able to navigate a 2D or 3D scene where audio and video content is being played. Typical media controls available are play and pause. Changes in the scene (BIFS-update and BIFS-anim) can be triggered either from the server or from a local interaction, resulting in a request to the server [1].

7.1 Terminal Platform

The target platform is a high-end PC, typically a >450 MHz Pentium processor with a minimum of 128 MB of RAM. A 3D accelerating board compatible with OpenGL may also be needed.

The network interface is either an Ethernet card (10 Mb/s) or an ATM card (typically Virata 25 Mb/s), or a V90 modem (56 kb/s) depending on the targeted media quality. All network interface adapter hardware will be accessed by software through the BSD Socket interface and must therefore come with the relevant IP protocols drivers (Winsock2). The operating system is Windows NT.

7.2 Terminal Modules

Fig. 7. presents the different modules involved in the terminal. Main parts of the terminal are:
- Compositor [1]
- Media decoders (Audio and Video)
- Network adaptation layers (synchronization layers, FlexMux, generic MPEG payload, RTP stack [1][4])
- The DMIF control plane composed of the DMIF Client and DMIF Manager [2]
- The Application Signalling module

7.2.1 Compositor
The BIFS browser is written in Java (JDK 1.0.2) except for the rendering part which makes use of C-coded native library (Open GL). In general, the interface to native code is not a problem although it may require a wrapper in case of complex C++ structures. An executable Java class such as an Applet can be downloaded and launched from the BIFS browser. This functionality is not originally provided by the BIFS specification [1].

The Java BIFS viewer will be running on a Java virtual machine running on the Pentium processor. The compositor is the core application in the terminal. It receives the data through the different network layers and passes it to the media decoders [1].

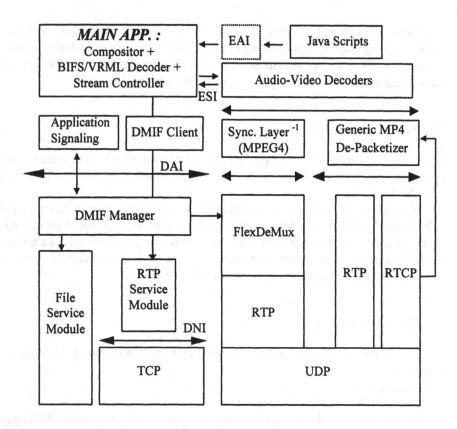

Fig. 7. COMIQS Terminal Configuration

7.2.2 MPEG-4 Video Decoder

The video decoder is MPEG-4 compliant and implements a subset of the core profile of the MPEG-4 standard with the following capabilities:

- Handling of arbitrary number of objects
- Handling object of arbitrary shapes
- Handling arbitrary image sizes (recommended image sizes are CIF - 352x288 pixels and QCIF - 176x144 pixels)
- Arbitrary frame rates up to 30 frames per second for a rectangular CIF image (real time decoding is possible only for a limited number of objects)
- No constraints on the number of inter images between intra images.
- Decoding of intra frames
- Decoding of P-frames
- H.263 quantization
- AC/DC prediction
- OBMC (Object Block Motion Compensation) for motion compensation
- Random Access Point with GOV (Group of VOP) marker
- Grey level transparency
- Zoom-in and zoom-out
- Object interaction (translation)

MPEG-4 video decoder was developed in the context of ACTS EMPHASIS project and is provided to the COMIQS project as background work.

7.2.3 Audio Decoders

The MPEG-4 audio decoder available so far is a Wide-Band CELP decoder. It is well designed for speech since it is based on human voice characteristics and it has the following features:

- 16 or 24 kbits/s bitrate
- mono
- frames of 10 ms
- sampling frequency = 16 kHz

MPEG-2 BC Audio Decoder has a very good quality at large variety of bitrates. It can perform mono, stereo and multiple channels decoding for music. The characteristics of the decoder in a classical usage are the following:

- 192 kbits/s bitrate
- mono
- frames of 24 ms
- sampling frequency = 48 kHz

MPEG-2 BC is preferred for its Random Access functionalities. Like the video decoder also the audio decoders are provided as background work.

8 COMIQS Applications for Trials

In addition to the MPEG-4 networked multimedia system COMIQS develops two applications aiming for illustrating the possibilities offered by MPEG-4 standard and using them in testing the technology over the Internet. The first of these applications called Virtuguide is a city guide. The second, Virtucat, is a commercial catalogue with navigation capabilities. Both applications are nontrivial and have several interesting aspects.

8.1 VIRTUGUIDE

The concept for the Virtuguide is based on a modern travel video documentary, which presents to young people "insider" information from locals rather than the usual information about sightseeing, opening times of museums etc.

The viewer is presented with a 360-degree camera image, but only a portion of it can be seen at the time. This visible frame can be turned "around" (i.e. changed), panning the whole 360 degrees.

The user is guided by five different guides. Each guide concentrates on one of the special areas of interest: Art & Galleries, History, Shops & Clothes, Coffee-Houses, Bars and Clubs. Communication with the guides is done in a reduced way, by asking questions or giving answers to their questions. Answers are given by text lines with different options, which are displayed interactively, depending on what is appropriate for the actual scene.

The existing technique for still frames, QuicktimeVR™ (QTVR™), allows the viewer to look around inside a panorama picture, to choose the point of view and to select a link, that is contained in the image, for example a door or person. The user's point of view, the virtual camera, is in the centre of a cylindrical panoramic picture. The viewer can't move away from the centre, but revolve. There is also a possibility to zoom.

MPEG-4 offers among other things the functionalities of the QTVR™. In MPEG-4 these functionalities can also be extended to moving images. In Virtuguide these extended functionalities are used to create an interactive video scene.

8.2 VIRTUCAT

VIRTUCAT is a virtual shopping centre consisting of several 3D towers. The shopping centre can be divided into the following elements and sub-elements:
- departments: correspond to the towers
- shops: correspond to the floors of the towers
- stands: correspond to areas on the floors of the towers
- articles, which are either at the normal price or on special offer

Users are guided towards the appropriate points of sale according to their interests. Rapid access to the desired products is enabled; resulting in navigation strictly reduced to the search for a specific product. The application is able to present associated products to the customer. The creation of advertising banners in three dimensions allows products to be presented and encourages impulse purchases.

The application offers the sale of products made up of several articles or accessories. Consumers select the elements, which interest them and build up the product to suit them in real time. The application handles a three-dimensional view of the accessories, assembly of the final product, dynamic suggestion of associated articles and implementation of special offers.

During their visit to the virtual shopping centre, consumers can get help from a virtual assistant. The duty of this three-dimensional character is to guide customers through the shopping centre, offering them associated articles, providing appropriate video sequences and giving additional explanations of products. The application ensures on-line sales assistance by presenting the profile of products whose functions customers can explore in a three-dimensional world. Fig. 8. shows an example scene from a bike shop.

Fig. 8. Example screenshot of the Virtucat application

9 COMIQS Partners

The following list contains all the COMIQS partners and the names of the contributors to this paper.

- CCETT Rennes France: Christian Bertin (the project leader), Dominique Curet, Carlos Islas-Pérez
- CSELT Turin Italy: Guido Franceschini
- Traumwerk GmbH München Germany: Benjamin Seide, Christian Ganzer
- Digital Media Institute, Tampere University of Technology Tampere Finland
- GIE Echangeur Paris France: Yves du Boisrouvray
- Laboratoire d'Electronique Philips Paris France: Laurent Herrmann
- RUS University of Stuttgart Stuttgart Germany: Paul Christ, Stefan Wesner
- Filmakademie Ludwigsburg Germany: Jürgen Karg
- Finsiel Pisa Italy: Michele Re
- INRIA Rennes France: Christine Guillemot

9 Conclusion

COMIQS integrated complete architecture for a network multimedia system running over the Internet. The architecture builds on the most recent achievements in the MPEG and Internet standardisation. MPEG-4 terminal allows for all media integration including video, audio and 3D graphics interactive objects. Networking architecture is realised using DMIF part of the MPEG-4 standard for effective separation of applications from underlying network details. The system offers the first comprehensive solution for handling advanced multimedia content over the Internet.

10 References

1. ISO/IEC 14496-1, Information technology, "Generic coding of moving pictures and associated audio information", Part 1: System, (FDIS at Now 1998).
2. ISO/IEC 14496-6, Information technology, "Generic coding of moving pictures and associated audio information", Part 6: Delivery Multimedia Integration Framework, (FDIS at Now 1998).
3. H. Schulzrinne, A. Rao, R. Lanphier, RTSP: Real-Time Streaming Protocol', RFC 2326, April 1998.
4. H. Schulzrinne, S. Casner, R. Frederick, V. Jacobson, RTP: Transport Protocol for Real-Time Applications', RFC 1889, January 1996.
5. R. Braden, L. Zhang, S. Berson, S. Hertzog, S. Jamin, RSVP: Resource ReSerVation Protocol', RFC 2205, September 1997.
6. COMIQS: deliverable AC322/CCT/DS/P/04.b1. "COMIQS System Architecture Specification", CCETT, (December 1998), http://www.ccett.fr/comiqs/welcome.htm.
7. COMIQS: deliverable AC322/LEP/DS/R/06.a1. "Terminal Specification and Architecture", LEP, (November 1998), http://www.ccett.fr/comiqs/welcome.htm.
8. COMIQS: deliverable AC322/DMI/DS/P/07.b1. "Media Server Architecture Specification", DMI, (September 1998), http://www.ccett.fr/comiqs/cmx_del.htm.
9. P. Christ, Ch. Guillemot, S. Wesner, 'RTSP-based Stream Control in MPEG-4', draft-christ-rtsp-mpeg4-00.txt, 16 November 1998.
10. Ch. Guillemot, P. Christ, S. Wesner, 'RTP-Generic Payload with Scaleable & Flexible Error Reciliency', draft-guillemot-genrtp-00.txt, 13 November 1998.

The CATI Project:
Charging and Accounting Technology for the Internet

Burkhard Stiller[1], Torsten Braun[2], Manuel Günter[2], Bernhard Plattner[1]

[1] Computer Engineering and Networks Laboratory TIK, ETH Zürich, Switzerland
[2] Institute of Computer Science and Applied Mathematics IAM, University of Bern
[1] E-Mail: [stiller I plattner]@tik.ee.ethz.ch, [2] E-Mail: [braun I mguenter]@iam.unibe.ch

Abstract

The objectives of the CATI project (Charging and Accounting Technology for the Internet) include the design, implementation, and evaluation of charging and accounting mechanisms for Internet services and Virtual Private Networks (VPN). They include the enabling technology support for open, Internet-based Electronic Commerce platforms in terms of usage-based transport service charging as well as high-quality Internet transport services and its advanced and flexible configurations for VPNs. In addition, security-relevant and trust-related issues in charging, accounting, and billing processes are investigated. Important application scenarios, such as an Internet telephony application as well as an Electronic Commerce shopping network, demonstrate the applicability and efficiency of the developed approaches. This work is complemented by an appropriate cost model for Internet communication services, including investigations of suitable usage-sensitive pricing models.

1 Introduction and Motivation

The CATI project covers the design and implementation of charging and accounting mechanisms based on currently available protocols of the Internet protocol suite. Efficient protocol support for collecting and handling accounting and charging information is developed to deliver a solution to communication services capable of handling cost-related information. This is extended by a design and implementation of a Virtual Private Network (VPN) management and configuration system, where charging mechanisms form the basis for the cost recovery in VPNs. The implemented network charging and accounting system is used within a test-bed (Internet and VPN) to evaluate its real-life behavior.

The Internet is known as an open and heterogeneous networking infrastructure. To support open Electronic Commerce, a myriad of service providers, users, and networking equipment has to be integrated. However, besides the technical provision of services, charging and accounting issues have never been solved in the Internet. This is due to a very strong component of public funding of Internet infrastructure and operation and the presence of many non-commercial services on the Internet (*e.g.*, Universities, Libraries). However, commercially operated IP (Internet Protocol) networks, *e.g.*, the one connecting Swiss universities and research centers are running out of central funding. Therefore, operating cost has to be fully recovered by usage fees. In the past, mostly volume-based pricing schemes for IP services have proven to be somewhat beneficial, but they have caused suboptimal usage of the network. The advent of new IP service classes will require more fine-grained accounting and control.

From a commercial point of view charging and accounting must take place where most of Electronic Commerce traffic can be accounted for to allow service providers to receive feedback about the usage of their services and to recover communication costs. Two pre-studies [15], [17] have determined that such traffic will be based on the Internet and that Internet customers constitute the fastest growing and largest community in Electronic Commerce. Therefore, research focuses on the well-known hour-glass-model (cf. Figure 1) which describes the relationship between network technology, Internet protocols, and value added services.

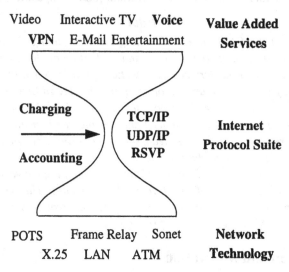

Figure 1. Hour-glass Model of the Internet

On one hand, a huge variety of network technology, such as Frame Relay, Sonet, ATM (Asynchronous Transfer Mode) technology, is available. On the other hand, value added services as offered from providers show a broad range as well, such as with video, interactive television (TV), or entertainment. The questions to be answered is now: How can these services be supported over the range of network technology? The Internet Protocol (IP) suite serves as a common interface. In particular, the Internet Protocol (IP) serves as a robust, connectionless network protocol. It is completed with the User Datagram Protocol (UDP) or the Transmission Control Protocol (TCP) for different degrees of required reliabilities and traffic management control functionality. Depending on the overall network model, the Resource Reservation Protocol (RSVP) allows for the network-wide reservation of resources required for guaranteed services in the Integrated Services (IntServ) approach. The hour-glass now is due to the fact that purely a very limited set of protocols forms the common denominator for applications and network technology.

The integration of resource reservation protocols and their employment for charging and accounting information as well as flow aggregation approaches are required to offer a future-safe Internet being prepared for commercialization within open Electronic Commerce platforms and limited funding for operating public networks. Commercial Internet users require integrated services [2] and differentiated services [1]

Internet technology for advanced applications, *e.g.*, based on the Internet Protocol Next Generation [3], [4]. While products for both enhanced service concepts are appearing, provisioning of enhanced services is currently unsupported, due to lack of appropriate charging, accounting, and billing mechanisms. Users must be ensured that accounting and charging data is secured. Managing accounting data in the Internet involves two groups of applied security. This covers the (1) secure collection and transmission of data related to accounting and charging and (2) a secure payment system allowing for transferring funds allocated for paying communication and information services. Furthermore, Internet charging protocols must support flexible payment modes (sender/receiver) to accommodate for applications such as reverse charging, advertising, or emerging push technologies.

In the highly competitive Internet Service Provider (ISP) market it is mandatory that a provider is able to respond quickly to changing market conditions. One important difference can be a flexible customer management and billing system that allows the quick and easy deployment of new service bundles and aggressive pricing plans. Besides today's traditional Web access and e-mail services it is foreseeable that new services like Internet Telephony will become part of ISPs' service offering. This trend is incompatible with today's undifferentiated pricing schemes and will require fine-grained accounting information from the network infrastructure.

The ISP connecting Swiss universities and research centers currently applies a simple volume-based charging scheme to recover costs from connected organizations. While this has proven mostly beneficial, it has caused suboptimal usage of the network. As the connected sites have expressed a need for better cost attribution within their respective organization and the advent of new service classes will require even more fine-grained accounting and control, cost and pricing models for IP-based networks and the Internet in particular are required.

Networks for electronic commerce are required to support secure and flexible communication within a dynamic set of users originating from different companies. In addition, the communication technology must be widely available such that it provides a common basis for as many people as possible in order to support as many business processes as possible. Internet technology is currently the only networking technology which fulfills this requirement of being widely available. In addition, there is currently a tremendous growth of Internet technology usage in order to establish intra- and inter-company networks such as Intranets and Extranets. The technological basis for Intranets and Extranets are Virtual Private Networks (VPN). VPNs are used to build temporary or permanent networks for distributed inter-/intra-company working groups and virtual companies/enterprises. Appropriate concepts must cover several issues, not only data transfer volumes, but also other factors such as costs for server access or VPN management.

Therefore, the emerging need for providing a basis for accounting and charging schemes in today's and tomorrow's Internet requires protocols and mechanisms capable of defining, collecting, charging and accounting information being utilized to determine resource and service usage. In addition to the reservation-based approach, the target scenario for the proposed project is based on a best-effort Internet. Customers decide to establish a VPN, *e.g.*, in order to run secure business applications. Currently, VPNs are established by manual configuration of IP tunnels. Dynamic reconfigurations for adding or deleting tunnels and the support for Quality-of-Service (QoS) are not possible today. Routers provide features in order to support QoS, such as sophisticated filtering and scheduling mechanisms, allowing to provide bandwidth reservations for aggregated flows through an IP router network. However, since filtering and scheduling parameters must be configured manually, dynamic and flexible QoS support is hard to achieve in larger networks.

This paper is organized as follows. Section 2 determines the detailed project objectives. In addition, Section 3 discusses the work in progress on charging and accounting protocols, the VPN configuration and management design, the development of a demonstrator, and evaluation principles. Finally, in Section 4 currently available results are summarized and preliminary conclusions are drawn.

2 Project Objectives

The feasibility and customer acceptance of such new charging protocols/schemes can be best verified with Internet Telephony, for several reasons. Firstly, users are already accustomed to pay for such a service in a usage dependent way, *e.g.*, per-minute. Secondly, desktop based telephony is an elementary service recurring in many envisaged Internet and Electronic Commerce scenarios. IP Telephony charging can be viewed as an important initial step in establishing pricing in the Internet. Expanding Internet usage scenarios should more easily follow, given Telephony as a well understood crystallization point.

Within the CATI project, a demonstrator will be established implementing a basic Electronic Commerce scenario. It will allow the use of the WWW to make a product offer and include Internet Telephony as a means for interested parties to contact the supplier for clarifying aspects of a possible product purchase. While the focus will be on pricing issues relating to Telephony itself, considering a whole usage scenario shall help to understand how a solution can fit into an overall approach regarding pricing.

Based on the introductory motivation of the CATI project, its working goals include the following ones:

- Design and implementation of charging and accounting mechanisms based on currently available protocols of the Internet protocol suite, focussing on secured, reservation-based approaches.
- Design and implementation of a VPN configuration service including charging and accounting functions, best-effort and differentiated services, fairness and congestion control mechanisms to ensure that customer traffic is handled fairly and securely.
- Development of generic support functionality in terms of Application Programming Interfaces (API) for Internet-based open Electronic Commerce.
- Development and demonstration of an IP Phone, which employs the implemented charging and accounting functionality and makes use of QoS-support in existing Internet protocols.

- Investigation and definition of business models for Internet services for the Internet, which include Internet Service Provider network costs and pricing schemes with respect to traditional, best-effort IP services and the integrated/ differentiated services Internet architecture.

- Evaluation of developed Internet charging and accounting mechanisms based on Internet services business models for the Internet, which include Internet Service Provider network costs and pricing schemes, the demonstrator application as well as regular traffic.

3 Work in Progress

The work undertaken in CATI concentrates on charging and accounting protocols which are based on the current IP technology and Integrated Services (IntServ) architecture to allow for the implementation of a demonstrator. Recent developments in the Differentiated Services (DiffServ) architecture are closely considered in the design process as well. In addition, the design and implementation of a flexible and efficient VPN configuration and management architecture for IP-VPNs is considered essential. Based on a demonstrator application, which will be an IP telephony, the progress made for usage-based charging of transport services can be shown in the open Internet as well as the VPN environment. A set of closely related evaluations in terms of technical and economic performance metrics complements the work.

3.1 Charging and Accounting Protocols

The design of a family of protocols will complement existing ones used on the Internet by adding charging and accounting mechanisms. The Internet protocol suite is easy to implement using existing network protocols, such as TCP/IP, and it results in the smallest possible overhead. This defines naturally an initial demonstrator to be assessed. Other desired features are that the extended protocols work with local control, make efficient use of existing resources, and scale naturally as the network grows. Thus, enabling the enlargement of the initial demonstrator to support more realistic scenarios, where non-uniform communication costs, among others, are taken into account. Furthermore, the development of such a demonstrator within the project on "Management, Evaluation, Demonstrator, and Business – MEDeB" delivers a tool of broader applicability; in particular for applications, where the control of the distribution of information and the avoidance of duplication may help in saving resources.

The implementation of project tasks covers as basic end-system protocol mechanisms consumer interface and feedback aspects, network-internal monitoring, resource reservation, admission control techniques, and protocol support for the pricing model. In particular, this includes the implementation of protocols for accounting, charging, and controlling. Assuming a distributed, unfair, insecure, and unfriendly (=commercial) environment, the implemented solution includes wide-spread protocols and environments as far as required features for fair charging and accounting can be solved. Mechanisms to provide fairness are important in addition to charging methods. Identifying these mechanisms which act locally to restrict aggressive flows, need to perform without an overall view of the network. Assuming a minimum of information about the network (obtained indirectly) approximate global fairness in these places have to be warranted. In this sense, fairness determines the basis for fair charging. Charging for a service makes fair customer handling necessary. In all networks, *e.g.*, the Internet, the traffic in congested points (bottlenecks) should receive fair treatment as in the future, available bandwidth in the Internet will grow, but the demand of bandwidth will increase even faster according to several reasons: (1) The amount of users will continue to grow. (2) Applications, such as multimedia applications need more and more bandwidth to satisfy acceptable information transfer quality, *e.g.*, for pictures or movies. There will never be too much bandwidth. Congestion will not disappear. However, QoS is essential for business applications, since business users cannot tolerate service degradation as occurring in the Internet today. In addition, in contrast to home users, business users are willing to pay for better services. Therefore, there is an urgent need for chargeable Internet services providing better QoS than today.

In the Internet, the Transport Control Protocol (TCP) runs on top of the Internet Protocol (IP). Conform TCP traffic is defined as a well-behaving traffic, if it slows down, when congestion occurs. During congestion packets are dropped. Missing acknowledgments provide to the protocol TCP this information which acts by reducing the amount of unacknowledged data, it allows in the network. In addition, misbehaving traffic (aggressive flows) already exists. Applications like Web-browsers start with several parallel connections for Web-page downloading as opposed to one because they can steal more resources from others. Other applications, such as real time radio, do not slow down in the face of congestion, i.e. they will continue to send at the same rate. Various applications increase their rate to try to ensure their required rate is obtained. All these applications use network resources at the expense of well-behaving traffic. Well-behaved charged traffic needs protection, and thus misbehaving traffic needs restriction and control at bottleneck points, i.e. where congestion occurs. Fair treatment/fairness can be considered at many different levels, two of which are fundamental - local and global fairness. For local fairness, allocation and control is restricted to information at this point. Parameters and, in the case of networks, congestion information from other places are not available or considered. This can lead to wasted network resources. The achievement of global fairness is more difficult, but more important, since it suppresses the waste of network resources. New mechanisms have to be found to warrant approximate global fairness.

Based on the availability of protocols and systems in support of IntServ, the Crossbow toolkit [8] provides a suitable design environment. IntServ mechanisms such as a packet classifier or packet filtering and scheduling on the host's and router's implementation platform are available, as well as an preliminary version of the Resource Reservation Protocol RSVP. Figure 2 depicts the simple IntServ architecture enhanced with a charging interface where applications are able to access reservation services and they will be offered with additional accounting and pricing information on the return.

Since current RSVP implementations do not support the exchange of charging or accounting information, standard RSVP objects have been extended by appropriate pricing and payment objects. Figure 3 depicts necessary objects. The price object allows for the exchange of market prices between senders and receivers. The payer object delivers the possibility to implement split payments between sender and receiver within a single connection. The bid object carries information for highly dynamic pricing models, such as the bid for the currently requested service.

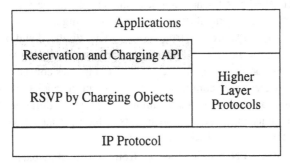

Figure 2. IntServ Protocol Architecture

3.2 Virtual Private Networks for the Internet

VPNs emerge from the need to securely interconnect private networks. The Internet is a promising platform for that task, because of its global reach and cost effectiveness. However the Internet is intrinsically insecure. Internet VPN technologies (IP-VPN) therefore add access control and privacy mechanisms to ensure the desired level of privacy.

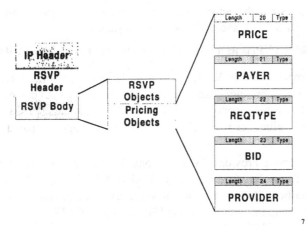

Figure 3. RSVP Object Extensions

3.2.1 VPN State of the Art

IP-VPNs use tunnelling to decouple the internal addressing scheme and the routing mechanisms from the ones used in the underlying Internet. Access control, authenticity and confidentiality of the VPN traffic is typically ensured by cryptography. The Internet Engineering Task Force (IETF) proposes a variety of Protocols capable of supporting VPNs for the Internet, some of which are specialized for different types of VPNs.

IPSec is a transparent security architecture that handles tunneling and cryptography on a per packet basis, while PPTP and L2TP support remote users connecting to a VPN. These protocols enable the setup of logical and secured networks over the public Internet and thus form the basis for new applications namely in the area of e-commerce. E.g. a VPN can consist of computers of a company offering a service over the Internet such as soft products (software, electronic newspapers, digitized audio and video) and the customers using the service. An upcoming application of VPNs is the support of virtual organizations or virtual companies. Virtual companies consist of single specialists residing at different real companies. The different specialists shall complement each other in order to collaborate in a common project which duration is limited. Thus the involved companies must securely open parts of their private networks for collaboration. This scenario is often called an Extranet.

However, today's VPN solutions suffer from several drawbacks. On one hand, VPNs are a significant management burden, they require additional network equipment and trained staff. If VPNs are not managed properly either the connectivity or the security of the VPN will be affected. On the other hand, VPNs using the Internet suffer from the inherent lack of quality-of-service (QoS) of the Internet. These problems can be addressed by outsourcing the VPNs to Internet Service Providers (ISP), since they have the knowledge and the resources to manage VPNs and may use QoS ensuring technology. Furthermore the ISPs are eager to offer new value added services such as VPNs to survive in the ever increasing competitiveness of the data forwarding market. The CATI project designs an architecture to deploy such services, and to account and charge for them. It focuses on the on-line configuration of VPN services and automatic price calculations, since the automation of the service installation, configuration and management is crucial for a successful service offering.

3.2.2 QoS Enabled VPNs as a Value-Added Service: Using IPSec with DiffServ

A major competitor of IP-VPNs are private leased lines (Frame Relay, ISDN). While the leased lines are more expensive because the user has to pay even when not using the line, they usually come with guaranteed QoS. Enhancing todays VPN solutions with QoS will eliminate the VPN's only real disadvantage compared to the leased line solutions.

An Internet Service Provider (ISP) has control over a part of the Internet. Using emerging traffic forwarding technologies such ATM, MPLS or RSVP it can offer QoS guarantees for traffic in its own domain. However, a customer wants to be able to purchase a VPN spanning more than just one ISP. Therefore the ISPs need an automated way to link their individual QoS solutions together to form one supply chain.

Differentiated Services (DiffServ) seem to be the technology that is simple enough to enhance VPNs without restricting the global reach of the Internet. Thus the most promising technologies for a service bundle combining VPN with QoS are DiffServ and IPSec. DiffServ and VPNs have various concepts in common:

- VPNs are traffic aggregations with known traffic destination points. DiffServ also operates on traffic aggregations. The known destination points can furthermore ease the specification of necessary service level agreements.

- DiffServ and VPNs both need enhanced functionality of border routers of the ISP but not of intermediate routers. Both share some similar functionality in the border routers, e.g. the traffic classification.

It was pointed out before that in order to bundle services spanning multiple ISPs such as a QoS VPN the ISPs must use an automated and flexible mechanism to collaborate and sell services to each other, allowing them to partially configure the peer's network. Since this does not exist up to date, the CATI project proposes a generic architecture for that purpose.

3.2.3 An Architecture for Configurable Internet Services

Todays Internet is made of the interconnection of multiple autonomous networks (domains). Some of these networks are driven by business companies such as ISPs. We can assume that the future ISPs and their services will have the following features:

- A network which is fully remotely controllable (configurable) by the ISP and whose hardware is able to support the new service.
- Intra-domain resource management that is able to provide service guarantees. This can be a fine grained mechanism (e.g. per flow) if the domain is small.
- Application level interfaces for service requests by customers.

In order to produce the complete revenue of these investments, the ISPs need to collaborate. Today the collaboration is done by human network administrators communicating with each other by phone or fax. However, with automatically configurable networks and appropriate communication protocols, an automated approach is much more favorable. We envision the following requirements:

- Between each adjacent ISP there are electronic service level agreements (SLAs), describing the service delivered and its duration and price.
- Also, there is an inter domain resource management procedure which allows the new services to span multiple ISPs. In order to be scalable to large backbone networks, this management must handle aggregations of the intra domain resource management entities; it must be coarse grained.

The following goals for an architecture allow the automatic provision of new services spanning multiple ISPs based on the mentioned assumptions.

- The architecture shall consist of generic components that are specialized for the given purpose.
- It shall not limit the ISP to a given business model.
- The architecture shall be open and interoperable in the sense that component interfaces are declared.
- The architecture focusses on security issues (robustness and prevention of abuse).
- The new services we are focussing on are the support of QoS based on DiffServ and VPNs. However, the architecture shall be service independent.

Service Brokers as Basic Components

A service broker accepts service specifications for the specific service it sells. It can query the cost of the service and negotiate its price with a customer. Upon agreement, the broker can setup the service. The broker keeps the knowledge about the services provided in the form of electronic service level agreements (SLA). It can thus accept requests to change the service specifications for a given customer. Note that the service broker may synchronize and coordinate multiple service requests. Furthermore, a service broker is an autonomous entity. It can pro-actively change an SLA. For such decisions, it needs access to various policy databases.

In general, services can be classified regarding two criteria:

(1) The *range* of the service: local to a single machine, local to ISP or affecting multiple ISPs.

(2) The service can be implemented by hardware configuration *orthogonally* to other services or it must be coordinated with configuration of other services.

For each orthogonal service we propose a component hierarchy following criterion (1). This situation is depicted in Figure 4: The machine-dependent configuration local to a network equipment is handled by a configuration daemon (CD). An Internal Service Broker (ISB) is used to manage an ISP's service that is solely supported local to the ISP. The ISB can configure the ISP's network via secured connections to configuration daemons of each relevant network equipment (e.g. border routers). The ISB manifests the fine grained resource management. Its implementation is in the responsibility of the ISP and does not need standardization. If the service needs the collaboration of other ISPs we propose the External Service Broker component (ESB). The ESB has knowledge of the adjacent ISPs and can negotiate the necessary services of the adjacent ISP through its peer ESB broker. The ESB controls the corresponding local ISB in order to trigger local service configuration.The ESB manifests the coarse grained resource management mentioned before.

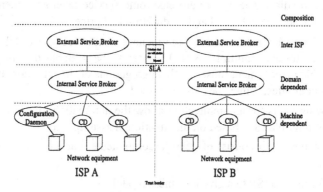

Figure 4. Broker Hierarchy

The bandwidth broker (BB) for differentiated services [13] is an example for an external service broker. It is often neglected how the BB interacts with its network. In our case, the BB would not only interact with BBs of other domains but also with an ISB that could for example match DiffServ to ATM configurations. Note that ESB and ISB represent a two class hierarchy which allows for a scalable solution. The separation matches the topology found in todays Internet. The case of non-orthogonal services (see previous classification) must be handled by servers that are specially designed to offer a service combination. Such composite service servers (CoSS) can use and coordinate several ISBs and ESBs (of the different services influenced by this special service). Note that the management of such services is very complex. In general such a service can only be automated if the different 'sub'-services interfere in very few specific areas.

An example of such a service combination is the provision of VPNs with QoS guarantees with DiffServ. Such a service is very useful for the branch office scenario: the headquarter of a company is connected to its trusted ISP, the branch office to another ISP. The headquarter requests a VPN with QoS from its ISP using the QoS - VPN composite service server of the ISP. The QoS-VPN server (Composite Service Server) negotiates with the local ESBs (VPN ESB and DiffServ ESB) that they negotiate with the next domain and so forth. Finally, the ISBs on the route between the headquarter and the branch office will configure their network to support the requested QoS, and the ISBs of the border ISPs will configure their border routers for the VPN tunnel.

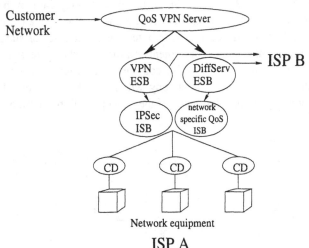

Figure 5. Combined Services

Conceptionally, there are only external service brokers interacting between two ISPs. At least in the case of a customer network it is desirable, that also a human can interact with a foreign service broker. We propose a simple GUI supporting service server to translate between a human and an ESB.

Charging and Accounting between Brokers

The electronic SLAs established between ESBs describe how the use of services is charged between ISPs. The same mechanism can be used to charge customers of ISPs. The SLAs are negotiated using a signalling protocol between the brokers, which is a topic of current research. The service price is dependent of three basic components: (1) The one time charge, which has to be paid upon service establishment, (2) the reservation based fee, which is dependent of the amount of reservation needed for a given service and (3) a usage based fee. Given that brokers calculate these prices semiautonomous this opens a field for simulation and optimization of business strategies.

3.3 Demonstrator

As a demonstrator for CATI Internet telephony is being developed. It determines an emerging service based on packet–based delivery of voice data. Today's IP Phone products neglect real-time network transport issues and charging for such voice calls. Being currently positioned as a low–end service with these deficiencies, pricing is intermixed with the ISPs pricing policy or specialized voice carriers offer the service via gateways and charge per minute. However, if these services are going to be as dominant as described in [16] solving the problem of usage–based charging is of utmost importance. Models being developed and studied at MIT predict that voice and data traffic will share equal bandwidth in 1999. Due to the traffic networks higher growth rate, a significant transition will happen in the following years (cf. Figure 6).

At the same time, and related to this, the Internet is expected to evolve from a best-effort network service to one that offers a range of service qualities in order to support more applications and to allow for more differentiation in the market. Besides the technical problems that have to be solved, this will involve an adaptation of the commercial interrelations between customers and service providers as well as among service providers. Internet telephony is considered an interesting test case for such an architecture: it poses significant quality requirements on the underlying network service, and the economics of the traditional, while complex, are reasonably well understood. Charging models for an Internet telephony will probably look very different from those for traditional telephony, but many of the concepts will be common to both.

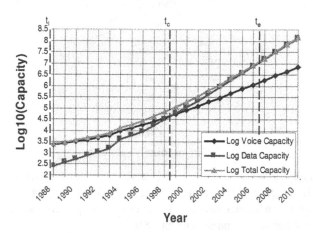

Figure 6. Transition to Multiservice Integrated Networks

Within this project an IP Phone will be utilized to facilitate and demonstrate the various aspects of charging and accounting in the Internet. The IP phone determines in this case a basic and Internet-integrated application in an Electronic Commerce environment, since on-line support during a shopping transaction or a pre-sales advertisement activity supports one-to-one marketing and facilitates business transactions in general. On one hand the IP Phone will make use of the (reservation-based) network service used to set up connections for real-time data transfer between telephony end users. Also, it will provide for the required signaling (e.g., ringing, busy phone signaling) between end-systems. In addition, it will make use of the charging and accounting functions offered to applications which form an integrated part of the Electronic Commerce platform. In a first step, the IP Phone will be provided as a stand-alone application making charging and accounting information directly available at the user interface. In a second step, the IP Phone will be integrated into a basic Electronic Commerce scenario, where electronic offers are made to allow users to contact the party making an offer. This setting takes into account requirements regarding pricing and accounting which emerge from various forms of Telephony usage, for instance for allowing for charging the sender or receivers for calls, including telephony charging into an overall Electronic Commerce service scheme, for instance by considering the content of the offer to be a pricing factor. This basic scenario will also be a basis for the development of various business models for charging IP telephony.

The basic infrastructure for the demonstrator to be developed, the newly established SWITCHng forms an excellent basis. With SWITCHng, each Swiss university can get two kinds of services: either an IP service or an ATM service. For the network that will interconnect the project partners, the ATM service will be used. The various routers and end systems of the partners will be interconnected via direct ATM connections. This allows to control the bandwidth available for the experiments.

3.4 Evaluations

The economic and technical performances are measured for different ranges of environments. This will validate decisions and show their practical usability made in other projects and work packages of the compound-project proposal. The performance analysis is likely to be used for tuning the implemented solution and reach an attractive trade-off, economically acceptable for Internet Service Providers (ISPs) and clients and technically sound to be incorporated harmless in the Internet. Besides the tuning of the solution, the analysis should give birth to a rating system guiding ISPs to define their pricing policies and helping ISPs' customers in their search for the optimal service adapted to their needs. In addition, VPN configuration and management systems are rated in terms of configuration overhead, performance, and seamless integration of charging and accounting mechanisms. Flow aggregation and Quality-of-Service support in routers for VPNs and their provision are investigated in detail.

The preparation of a performance analysis, *e.g.*, in terms of natural metrics of Internet distance, in this particular framework is itself a challenging task, because it will encompass both the pricing model and the communication aspects of networking. Therefore, performances must be expressed in terms of:

- Economic metrics, such as the kind of service the most requested, the average connection time, the average duration of the client's subscription to an ISP, the kind of payment, *e.g.*, totally electronic payment with banks on the Internet, fund-transfer orders processed by a back-end office.

- Usual computing metrics, such as net latency, response time, or bandwidth consumption.

Moreover, these metrics and the resulting analysis are also likely to be exploited in the commercial context of ISPs in order to determine marketing and pricing policies for their own product line, particularly Internet services. Henceforth, testbed and metrics have to be as meaningful as possible to suit the real market requirements. The performance analysis needs to be designed also in order to measure the overhead introduced by accounting at application level in terms of the number of exchanged messages, logging records, or account management.

To add the perspective of an Internet Service Provider (ISP), insight into technical and commercial interrelations of the networks that form the Internet is essential. The different accounting and charging mechanisms developed are being used. The participation in the definition and evaluation of new charging schemes and in the support of accounting and charging protocols for the Internet will lead to significant improvements in current schemes. In particular, this is a refinement of the cost sharing model to optimize resource usage for Internet services. It devises methods to provide customers with sufficient accounting information for cost distribution within their local organization. Finally, it develops pricing models aware of integrated and differentiated Internet services and for multicast traffic.

3.5 Related Work

Related work with respect to the CATI objectives corresponds to the technical area as well as the economic area and their interoperation. Therefore, pricing models and their application to service integrated networks are important. This subsection briefly sketches a small number or other related approaches. Refer to the book [11] for a good overview of related work approximately until 1997.

A priority-based multiple service class network architecture with separate fixed prices set for each class is proposed in [5] and [7]. Another model has been developed that calculates prices by conducting second price auctions for packets arriving at a congested router [12]. The goods available are the time and processing slots in the queue of the output interface. This model has been made technically efficient by applying auctions to reservation requests for reservation periods [10]. An additional pricing model as proposed in [6] is based on a contract between user and provider for a specified bandwidth, the expected capacity. Some of those ideas were revisited for a new proposal termed Edge Pricing [14].

4 Results and Conclusions

Concerning the status of the work in progress the results achieved so far are of an intermediate nature. Therefore, the following details will be extended further and elaborated with respect to a number of metrics that are being developed currently. With respect to the charging and accounting protocol the flow of relevant information and their messages between senders and receivers are defined for reservation-based charging methods. In addition, the employment of electronic payment systems for a full electronic handling of payments for Internet flows is being investigated. Furthermore, basic issues of a trust model for participating players in an Electronic Commerce environment have been discussed including the definition of suitable assumptions of trusted or untrusted relations between the roles of Internet-hosts, routers or Internet Service Providers, banks, and public certification infrastructures. An Internet telephony scenario has been designed to act as a demonstrator. The description of a business model for Internet service provisioning and service differentiation has been initiated.

A number of VPN concepts has been evaluated in terms of configuration approaches, charging mechanisms, and QoS-support. Basic mechanisms, such as IP tunneling or Class-of-Service mechanisms, are provided by many hardware vendors. However, pure hardware solutions for VPN management are inflexible and lacking Application Programming Interfaces (API) do not facilitate VPN management tasks. Therefore, the CATI project aims to support a highly efficient and flexible system for charging and accounting of Internet services as well as a feature-rich VPN configuration service.

Acknowledgments

This work has been performed in the framework of the project Charging and Accounting Technology for the Internet – CATI (CAPIV 5003-054559/1 and MEDeB 5003-054560/1) which is funded by the Swiss National Science Foundation, SNF, Berne, Switzerland. The authors like to acknowledge contributions of their project colleagues from the following organizations: Computer Engineering and Networks Laboratory, ETH Zürich: G. Fankhauser, G. Joller, P. Reichl, N. Weiler; IBM Research Laboratory, Zürich, Communication Systems: G. Dermler, L Heusler; Institute for Computer Communications and Applications, EPF Lausanne: F. Dietrich; Institute of Computer Science, Informations and Communications Management, University of Zürich: H. Kneer, C. Matt, U. Zurfluh; Institute of Computer Science and Applied Mathematics IAM, University of Bern: F. Baumgartner, M. Kasumi, I. Khalil; SWITCH, Zürich: S. Leinen; and Teleinformatics and Operating Systems Group, University of Geneva: D. Billard, N. Foukia.

References

[1] S. Blake, D. Black, M. Carlson, E. Davies, Z. Wang, W. Weiss: *An Architecture for Differentiated Services,* RFC2475, December 1998.

[2] R. Braden, D. Clark, S. Shenker: *Integrated Services in the Internet Architecture: An Overview,* RFC1633, June 1994.

[3] T. Braun: *Internet Protocols for Multimedia Communications, Part I: IPng – The Foundation of Internet Protocols;* IEEE Multimedia Magazine, Vol. 4, No. 3, July-September 1997, pp. 85-90.

[4] T. Braun: *Internet Protocols for Multimedia Communications, Part II: Network Transport and Application Protocols;* IEEE Multimedia Magazine, Vol. 4, No. 4, October- December 1997.

[5] R. Cocchi, D. Estrin, S. Shenker, L. Zhang: *A Study of Priority Pricing in Multiple Service Class Networks;* ACM Computer Communication Review, Vol 21, No. 4, September 1991, pp 123-130.

[6] D. D. Clark: *A Model for Cost Allocation and Pricing in the Internet;* MIT Workshop on Internet Economics, March 1995, also in an updated version available in [11].

[7] R. Cocchi, S. Shenker, D. Estrin, L. Zhang: *Pricing in Computer Networks: Motivation, Formulation and Example;* IEEE/ACM Transactions on Networking, Vol. 1, No. 6, December 1993, pp. 614-627.

[8] D. Decasper, M. Waldvogel, Z. Dittia, H. Adiseshu, G. Parulkar, B. Plattner: *Crossbow - A Toolkit for Integrated Services over Cell-Switched IPv6;* Proceedings of the IEEE ATM'97 Workshop, Lisboa, Portugal, June 1997.

[9] G. Fankhauser, B. Stiller, B. Plattner: *Arrow - A Flexible Architecture for an Accounting and Charging Infrastructure in the Next Generation Internet;* Accepted for publication in Netnomics, Baltzer, The Netherlands, Vol. 1, No. 2, March 1999.

[10] G. Fankhauser, B. Stiller, B. Plattner: *Reservation-based Charging in an Integrated Services Network;* 4th INFORMS Telecommunications Conference, Boca Raton, Florida, U.S.A., March 1998.

[11] L. W. McKnight, J. P. Bailey: *Internet Economics;* The MIT Press, Cambridge, Massachusetts, U.S.A., 1997.

[12] J. K. MacKie-Mason, H. R. Varian: *Pricing the Internet;* Technical Report, University of Michigan, Michigan, U.S.A., February 1994.

[13] K. Nichols, V. Jacobson, and L. Zhang: *A Two-bit Differentiated Services Architecture for the Internet;* ftp://ftp.ee.lbl.gov/papers/dsarch.pdf, November 1997.

[14] S. Shenker, D. Clark, D. Estrin, S. Herzog: *Pricing in Computer Networks: Reshaping the Research Agenda;* ACM Computer Communication Review, Vol. 26, No. 2, April 1996, pp 19 – 43.

[15] B. Stiller, G. Fankhauser, B. Plattner, N. Weiler: *Pre-study on "Customer Care, Accounting, Charging, Billing, and Pricing";* Computer Engineering and Networks Laboratory TIK, ETH Zürich, Switzerland, Pre-study performed for the Swiss National Science Foundation within the "Competence Network for Applied Research in Electronic Commerce", February 18, 1998.

[16] D. Tennenhouse: *From Internet to Active Net;* INFOCOM 98 Panel Session, San Francisco, California, U.S.A., April, 1998.

[17] U. Zurfluh, A. Meier, M. Holthaus: *Pre-study on "Security;* BI – Research Group, Uetikon am See, Switzerland, Pre-study performed for the Swiss National Science Foundation within the "Competence Network for Applied Research in Electronic Commerce", February 24, 1998.

A Conceptual Framework to Support Content-Based Multimedia Applications

E. Hartley, A. P. Parkes and D. Hutchison

Distributed Multimedia Research Group
Computing Dept.
Lancaster University
{e.hartley@lancaster.ac.uk, dhlapp@comp.lancs.ac.uk}

Abstract. Future applications will require content-based representations of multimedia. This paper elaborates on what is meant by the term "content", when applied to multimedia. The engineering view of content as "the bits in the stream" is contrasted with the linguistic view of content as "meaning". A linguistic model of content is described and expanded to incorporate the needs of digital multimedia. The model is used to clarify existing spatial and temporal segmentation terminology used for multimedia. The importance of the model to standardisation activities, particularly MPEG-7, is discussed. It is argued that the model provides a clear separation of content from the display, transmission and compression technologies used in the creation and distribution of the content. The application of the model is illustrated by discussing its application to an example scenario.

1 Introduction

The use of narrow band telephony networks for multimedia content delivery has increased substantially alongside the widespread adoption of digital technologies within the broadcast sector. This has resulted in growing interest in multimedia content management and retrieval. Most applications being developed will rely on some form of metadata or annotation scheme. This metadata may equally be applied to compressed, uncompressed or legacy analog archive material.

This paper compares and contrasts the engineering viewpoint on content with that of a linguistic-oriented approach. We discuss the extensions that need to be made to the linguistic model of content, in order to support digital multimedia. A conceptual framework to support analysis, description and manipulation of multimedia content is presented in terms of the definition of "planes of representation" and their associated terminology. We demonstrate that our model can clearly separate the content of multimedia from the technologies used in its creation and distribution.

In order to develop our model, we begin by presenting an example scenario. A user is browsing a video database of sequences relating to the 1960s space race. She selects and plays a sequence. She pauses the video, leaving a still image on display such as that shown in Figure 1.The images from the video feature active "hot spots", as do many applications. Some questions now occur to her: "what type of rocket was this?";

"was this a successful launch?"; "was this launch part of a series?"; "was the mission manned?", and so on.

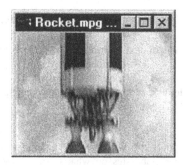

Fig. 1. Rocket Launch

Consider an alternative scenario: a video clip is being played by someone selecting archive video footage for a documentary on engineering activities in space. A number of clips are required showing different space engineering activities. Can suitable footage be collated without the archivist having to view all the material? What information would be needed to make such selection possible? Will the sequence from which the still image shown in figure 2 is taken be suitable?

Fig. 2. Moon Surface.

The above potential scenarios are representative of applications being considered by those concerned with the development of multimedia content description standards. (ISO SC29 WG11, 1999-1 and SMPTE/EBU 1998) The two scenarios require that the "system" delivering the video has knowledge about the content of the viewed sequences. This leads to the question: what is content? The view advanced in this paper is not identified with that of signal and image processing approaches, where content analysis is taken to mean the derivation of image characteristics by numerical methods. (Chen, Pau & Wang, 1993). Nor do we take the view that multimedia content can be determined from consideration only of the syntax of the bit stream.

The model of content proposed in this paper diverges significantly from these two approaches in that it adopts the assumption from linguistics that the content of a text, or artifact, is its meaning (Crystal, 1985). This view is developed within the linguistics field concerned with the study of signs and sign systems; namely *semiotics*. In this paper, we describe the linguistic model of content and show how the model can be extended to incorporate multimedia. In addition, we show how the application of the model helps to resolve ambiguities that can develop in discussions of multimedia content and its representation.

In its traditional linguistic context the content of an artefact is taken to be the mental sensations invoked in the viewer or reader when experiencing that artefact. Content was therefore understood to be the domain of those creating the material and of those linguists and critics for whom content analysis was important. Moreover, traditionally the content was communicated and manipulated through the use of analogue recording, storage and reproduction technologies.

Improvements in technology mean that a growing proportion of new material is now generated in digital form. This poses new problems since any descriptions of content that have been created may refer to compressed, uncompressed digital media or analogue material. The descriptions may in fact refer to different instances of the same content with different access and segmentation characteristics.

2 A Linguistic view of content

Semiotics has developed an analytical methodology allowing sign systems to be studied. This methodology distinguishes, for text (Pierce, 1932; 1960, Saussure, 1960 and Eco, 1977) and pictures (Sonesson, 1989), between the *expression* and *content* of a piece of a work. Thus, in the case of the text you are reading, the page and the marks upon it making up the letters and words are the *expression*. In contrast, the content is the ideas that are being invoked in the reader's mind. In a linguistic context the *content* and *expression* aspects are referred to as planes.

Similarly, in the case of Figure 1, for example, the greyscale dots on the page are in the *expression plane*, whereas the *content plane* contains the ideas invoked in the viewer's mind. This terminology has been adapted for application to film and video (Eco, 1977, Metz, 1974 and Parkes, 1988). The terminology is thus applicable irrespective of the medium used for expression. The separation of the mechanism used to express a sign system (*the signifiers*), and the mental sensations invoked in the reader or viewer (*the signified*), does not provide for the unique requirements of digital multimedia.

There has been some effort to consider the implications of information theory on the Semiotic model (Eco, 1977). However the necessary extensions to the semiotic model, to the knowledge of the present authors have not been completed. Extensions to the semiotic model enabling it to be applied to digital multimedia will now be considered.

3 Extending the semiotic model

The semiotic model, as expounded by other authors, is insufficiently rich to deal with digital multimedia. To this end, we propose the consideration of specific aspects of multimedia by extension of the semiotic model. Additional terminology is introduced to facilitate a clear separation of multimedia material, in terms of how it is perceived, how it is encoded, and in terms of its content. Note that, at this stage, our analysis is not exhaustive. Nor are any assumptions made about the number of dimensions within the defined planes themselves; the multimedia environment is considered to be implicitly multidimensional.

3.1 Expression Plane

This plane contains what is displayed to the viewer and sonified to the listener, independent of the storage, coding, display and transmission medium and technology. This definition is intended to be sufficiently broad to encompass text, film, and any other medium. The term is introduced to emphasise the distinction between what is played to the recipient and what the recipient perceives.

3.2 Data Plane

This is the plane in which recorded images and sounds are captured for transmission, storage and retrieval. It is the domain of analogue and uncompressed digital video, and would normally be present only when material was captured and digitised after some performance.
Technologies for synthetic video and audio creation allow for the creation of video and audio material without any prior sonification, display or capture phases.

3.3 Transformed Data Planes

These are the planes in which compression for storage efficiency and bit stuffing for transmission resilience takes place and in which digital signal processing for image analysis occurs. They are the domains of MPEG-1, 2, 4 and JPEG, etc. This definition is intended to be sufficiently broad to encompass compressed text.

3.4 Content Plane

This comprises what is perceived by a "normal" viewer to be contained in the expression plane. If the expression plane is textual then the content plane and the expression plane may be considered to be identical or isomorphic. Implicit in this definition is a distinction between the denotative and connotative aspects of content (these terms are discussed further below). Note that a more formal definition may be available based in semiotics. For a critique of the existing usage of connotation and denotation in visual semiotics see Sonesson (1989).

3.5 Description Plane

This plane will contain the descriptions of the content plane. This is the concern of a number of standards related-activities including MPEG-7. The contents of this plane are often referred to as Metadata.

3.6 Transformed Description Plane

This plane was introduced to allow compression of the content of content description. In the authors' view, the ability to extend the model illustrates the power and flexibility of the terminology.

3.7 Relevance of the Planes Terminology to MPEG

The following discussion will help to justify the introduction of the above terminology. MPEG-1 and MPEG-2 have been concerned with the efficient compression of digitised audio and video. These two standards have been concerned with the transformation from the *data plane* into the *transformed data plane*, and the efficiency of the coded representation. An additional objective of MPEG-1 and 2 was that the *data plane* should be preserved with levels of loss acceptable within the *expression plane* requirements of the target applications. MPEG-4 has introduced synthetic mechanisms for expression and a new paradigm for the transformation from the *data plane* into the *transformed data plane*; namely objects. MPEG-4's interest in content continues to be in terms of accuracy, fidelity and loss level.

MPEG-7 is concerned with the content plane, i.e., what a "normal" person perceives to be represented by the material in the expression plane, and with standardising descriptions of the content plane. This leads to the introduction of the *description plane*. There is growing evidence to support the view that MPEG-7 may also be interested in the transmission and storage efficiency of the content descriptions. This leads to the introduction of yet another plane, this being the *compressed description plane*.

In more general terms, MPEG-7 is in the process of developing a standard for multimedia content description. As a result of this it is now becoming recognised that a description of multimedia content may be referenced to multiple instances of the data in either the data or transformed data planes.

Finally, it could be added that the success of MPEG-1 and MPEG-2 has already resulted in the development of recording technology that allows direct transformation

of information from the "real world" into the *transformed data plane*. This suggests the need for future refinements, but this is left for further discussion.
We will now further refine the planes terminology to include more details of the semiotic model.

4 Refinement of Terminology

The following discussion introduces several semiotic terms defines them and demonstrates their application in the analysis of multimedia content.

4.1 The Sign

The term *sign* is used in semiotics to provide a mapping between the *expression* and *content planes*. Parkes (1988) and Nack (1996) have extended the use of the term "sign" to encompass film and video. We propose the *sign* as the basic unit of spatial segmentation in the expression plane. A working definition of the term follows. A sign stands to somebody for something in some respect or capacity. Implicit in this definition is the notion of denotation versus connotation. Further detailed analysis of these issues in a textual context is given in Pierce (1932 ;1960) and in a filmic context in Stam, Burgoyne & Flitterman- Lewis(1992). The sign can be further categorised as iconic, symbolic or indexical. These may be defined as follows.

Iconic sign
A sign which represents its object mainly through its similarity with some properties of the object, based on the reproduction of perceptual conditions. A zebra, for example, can be identified from at least two characteristics - four leggedness and stripes.

Indexical sign
A sign that represents it's object by an inherent relationship with the object. Examples: a man with a rolling gait can indicate drunkenness, a sundial or clock can indicate the time of day, a wet spot on the ground indicates spilt liquid, etc.

Symbolic sign
A sign with an arbitrary link to its object (the representation is based on convention). Examples: the traffic sign for a forbidden route, and the cross as an iconographic convention.

4.2 Diegesis, Mimesis and Meaning

Following Sebeok (1986), in English, the term "diegesis" derives from two expressions; in French these are indicated by the usage diègèsis as opposed to mimèsis, and diègése referring to the spatiotemporal universe designated by the narrative text. Care needs to be exercised when using these terms in English. The French structuralists adopted for use in narratology the diegesis versus mimesis dichotomy as a pair of equivalents to the difference between showing and telling as used in criticism. This is the distinction between narrative of events (diegesis) and narrative of words (mimesis). The other English meaning of diegesis as the spatiotemporal universe derives from the expression diègése, which originates in Metz's film theory (Metz, 1974) and it is this sense in which the term is used in the definition of connotation quoted below. This is significant because it points to the need to have representation structures capable of representing the narrative structures of multimedia as distinct from descriptions of images. This issue is discussed further in Parkes (1988, 1989, 1992), and Nack & Parkes (1997).

4.3   Denotation and Connotation

These are terms have been applied within linguistics and semiotics to distinguish between the base meaning attributed to an element in the *expression plane* and subsidiary meanings that may be invoked by the base meaning. We will give a definition of these terms as they are used in a linguistics context (noting the dangers of linguistic analogy) then as they are used when applied to film and video. This linguistic account follows that of Cruse (1990).

The use of the terms "denotative" and "connotative" arise within linguistics from the need to discuss the meanings of words that do not immediately refer to anything, examples of which are "however" and "concerning". Further problems arise because it is not clear what a particular concrete noun such as "cat" refers to. "cat" does not refer to some particular cat, nor does it refer to the class "cat", for it cannot be said that "cat has many members". This problem may be overcome by introducing the terms "*denotation*" and "*connotation*". That is to say, the meaning of cat is not what it refers to but what it *denotes* and/or what it *connotes*. The denotation of a word is the class of things to which it can be correctly applied; so the denotation of cat is the class of things of which it can be correctly said: "This is a cat". The necessary and sufficient set of properties that must be possessed by something for the word cat to be applied to it is the connotation of cat. The definitions given above are satisfactory for linguistic purposes, where the basic units of meaning are taken to be words. To arrive at suitable definitions for their use when applied to moving images, it is useful to consider the following:

> In the cinema the word diegesis refers to the film's represented instance, the sum of the film's DENOTATION, i.e. the narration itself, plus the fictional space and time dimensions implied in and by the narrative (characters, landscapes, events etc.), and even the story as is it is received and felt by the spectator. (Stam, Burgoyne & Flitterman-Lewis, 1992, p38)

Further discussion of these issues is given in the work cited and in Barthes (1964). It follows from the discussions above that attempts to apply the techniques of transformational grammar to film and video have been of limited success. We feel there are considerable problems associated with the use of these techniques in domains for which there is no clearly defined "language", in the technical sense of the term.

5 The Methodology and Standardisation Activities

Both MPEG and SMPTE/EBU are engaged in activities associated with the standardisation of mechanisms to exchange multimedia metadata. These approaches are described in (ISO SC29 WG11, 1999-2) and (SMPTE/EBU 1998). The approach adopted by MPEG is to develop a standard for the interchange of multimedia content description.

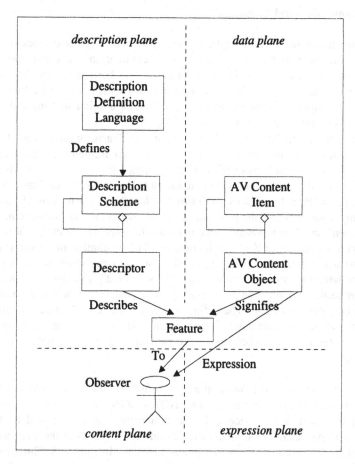

Fig. 3. MPEG-7 Framework annotated to show the planes

The SMPTE/EBU task force have seen metadata from the viewpoint of programme material exchange as bitstreams. It will be noted that the UML representation of the

MPEG frame work illustrated in the MPEG documents and derived from an MPEG input document by one of the present authors (ISO SC29 WG11, 1998) very closely follows the methodology we have described.

The basic MPEG-7 framework is illustrated using the UML notation in figure 3 with annotations to show the planes of representation. It should be noted that MPEG have substituted the term *feature* for the term *signifier*. The *description plane* and *data planes* are readily apparent the *expression* and *content planes* are represented abstractly. This framework can be readily extended to include the *transformed data* and *description* planes as shown in figure 4 which omits the *expression* and *content planes* for clarity.

The SMPTE/EBU task force metadata activities have largely concentrated on the categorisation of metadata and how it can be associated with content through the use of what are termed wrappers. The metadata categories that have been identified are; transport, essential, access, parametric, composition, relational, geospatial, descriptive, other and user defined. Wrappers provide a mechanism by which metadata might be streamed or stored together with data or transformed data. As such wrappers provide a mechanism for combining together material from one or more of the planes we have described.

The SMPTE/EBU terminology does not make a strong distinction between data and data that is compressed both of which are included within the definition of the term *essence*. A distinction is made, however, between different types of essence, these types are; audio, video and data essence. This distinction is made irrespective of whether the data is in the *data* or *transformed data planes*. Data essence is defined as any material that can stand alone from other forms of essence, examples given include closed captioning text or material contained in a programme guide. In our terminology this would be text in the *data plane*.

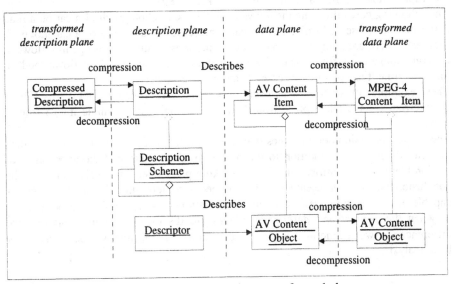

Fig. 4. MPEG-7 Framework extended to show transformed planes

6 Spatial and Temporal Segmentation Terminology

In the course of this discussion so far the term "plane" has been introduced, and a distinction made between the expression plane, the data plane, the transformed data plane, the content plane, the description plane and the transformed description plane as distinct representations of multimedia content. Some new terminology was introduced and will be used in the subsequent discussion of the spatial and temporal segmentation terminology being considered by MPEG and elsewhere. The discussion shows that existing terminology for segmentation in the planes' temporal axes is a source of ambiguity. There is also a need to provide a clear separation of the concepts of segmentation in the time dimension from those in the spatial dimension. The analysis will be carried out on each aforementioned plane in turn, during which additional terminology will be introduced and the ambiguities resolved.

6.1 Expression Plane Segmentation

The expression plane was defined above as what is displayed to the viewer and sonified to the listener, independent of the storage, coding, display and transmission medium and technology. Therefore, using the semiotic terminology introduced above, this plane contains the *signifiers* that will evoke what is *signified* to the viewer, listener or reader. This plane has been introduced into the discussion to highlight the distinction between the *signifiers* and the *signified*.

Introducing the signifier and signified is useful because these terms provide a basis for distinguishing between what Parkes has referred to as "a single image in its own right" e.g. a photograph, decompressed JPEG file, or MPEG picture, and "an interrupted moment from a moving film" (Parkes, 1989).

The following cases illustrate the above distinctions. A photograph of a car on a road could be both (case 1) "a picture of a car" and (case 2) "a picture of a car moving". Similarly, there are many films that feature time lapse sequences of opening flowers. A single image taken from one of these sequences would be (case 3) "a flower bud" at the same time it is a picture of (case 4) "an opening flower".

These examples illustrate how an event may (cases 2 & 4) or may not (cases 1 & 3) be inferred to have taken place from both a still image and a single image from a movie.

The above discussion demonstrates that from a mere succession of images more than motion is signified. In addition to the objects in the picture and the appearance of motion there is the signification of events taking place over time. This reinforces the conclusion that the representation of multimedia content should provide structures capable of representing events and temporal relationships. This point will be returned to when the *content* and *description planes* are discussed. The discussion of the differences between time as it is portrayed in film and real time will be set aside for later analysis.

6.2 Data Plane Segmentation

The data plane supports the analogue and digital recording of material in the expression plane. In the analogue domain, with the exception of temporal division into frames, there is little natural spatio-temporal segmentation. As a consequence, much of the terminology applied naturally to the content plane is also applied to recorded material. We take this to be a reflection of the traditional close coupling between content and data. The same applies to the digital domain, but here there is additional segmentation associated with the discrete nature of the sampling process.

6.3 Transformed Data Plane Segmentation

This plane may be segmented according to the following schema.

Object
The object-oriented approach adopted by MPEG-4 introduces into the discussion of the transformed data plane the notion that images may be decomposed into objects. The MPEG-4 documents strictly define an "Audio Visual Object" or AV-Object. The approach adopted by Ibenthal, Siggelgow and Grigat (1996) is illustrative of the segmentation algorithms being adopted. The intention is that AV-objects should be combined within an MPEG-4 terminal to form "scenes". In this terminology, MPEG-1 and MPEG-2 elementary audio or video streams are defined as AV- objects. In addition, AV-objects may be synthetically produced. The MPEG-4 AV-object is similar in concept to the VRML node. The use of the term AV-object here is distinct from the use of the term object in the content plane. This distinction is developed below in the discussion of terminology for use in the content and description planes.

Picture
The term *picture* is used in MPEG-1 & 2 as the coding plane equivalent of the frame. A summary of the definitions from ISO/IEC 11172-2 and ISO/IEC 13818-2 is given here.

> A source, or reconstructed picture, consists of three rectangular matrices of numbers, a luminance matrix (Y) and two chrominance matrices (Cr and Cb). The size of the matrices, the bit length of the numbers and relative amount of chrominance information to luminance information is dependent on the specific requirements of the target application.

Group of Pictures
The term "group of pictures" is specific to MPEG-1 and 2, so we take the view that the use of the term should remain restricted to this context. The term is defined in ISO/IEC 11171-2 (ISO/IEC 11172-2, 1993).

Sequence

The term "sequence" is used in MPEG-1 and MPEG-2. Comparing the definition below (ISO/IEC 11172-2, 1993) with that used in a cinematographic context makes explicit the problems of extending the use of the term into the content plane.

A coded sequence commences with a sequence header and is followed by one or more groups of pictures and is ended by a sequence end code. Immediately before each group of pictures there may be a sequence header.

Scene

MPEG-4 and VRML use the term "scene" to describe the result of composing several MPEG-4 AV-objects or VRML nodes. The VRML term "scene graph" adequately distinguishes the VRML usage from the everyday and cinematographic usage. The distinction is needed because an MPEG-4 scene could be made up of primitive AV-objects such as icons and menus which has little in common with the cinematographic "scene" which is discussed in more detail below. MPEG-4 appears to be somewhat deficient in this area and for this reason we would propose that a scene generated by an MPEG-4 compositor be referred to as an AV-scene.

6.4   Content Plane Segmentation

Object

An object in the content plane provides the basis for spatial segmentation. It may map a polygonal shape in a succession of frames or be a separately coded entity such as an MPEG-4 object.

Frame

The term "frame" has a clear meaning when applied in the content plane of cinema and video for which this definition is adequate. The term refers to an individual photograph recorded on motion picture celluloid or individual image recorded on videotape. The frame is not necessarily equivalent to the MPEG-1 & 2 term, picture that is used in the coding plane because of the well known use of I-picture information in B and P pictures. The frame apparently forms a natural base for the temporal segmentation hierarchy of moving pictures. It is well known that while a single frame can convey a sense of motion, it cannot portray motion actually taking place over time. This dichotomy stems from the issue of inference that was introduced in the discussion of the expression plane above.

The individual frame is included in the segmentation hierarchy because it provides the minimal temporal segmentation unit in non-object based systems.

Setting

Parkes (1988) introduced the term "setting" to describe the base unit of a temporal hierarchy for the content representation of video. The setting formalism was introduced as a solution to the problems of descriptive ambiguity that arise if an attempt is made to use the shot, the scene or the sequence as the base of the content plane temporal hierarchy. A discussion of the terms shot, scene and sequence follows a definition of the setting.

An initial definition was given in Parkes (1988) and later became elaborated to:

> A setting is essentially defined as being a group of one or more still images which display the same objectively visible "scene". Effectively, the objectively visible dimension of an image consists of the physical objects represented in an image and the relationships between those physical objects which can be seen and are not inferred to be present, as it were. Still images have a continuum of meanings (Parkes, 1988) ranging from the objectively visible (what they effectively "show"), through event ambiguous where a member of a set of events could be assigned as being what the image could be inferred to be displaying a "moment" of, and finally to event determined, where some other information beyond that contained in the actual image itself leads the viewer to infer that a particular event is represented (in "snapshot" form). The author's contention is that descriptions applied to the image itself should be as objective as possible, because it is only by doing this that the maximum flexibility of use of the arbitrary image can be guaranteed.
> (Parkes, 1989)

Shot

Of the remaining terms being considered in the expression plane the shot is the least problematic because shots can generally (with notable exceptions) be distinguished in a finished programme on the basis of objectively visible discontinuities. This analysis follows that of Parkes (1992). The following definitions of "scene" and "sequence" show that placing the shot within the temporal hierarchy shot: scene: sequence is problematic. Various authors define the shot, notably Wurtzel and Rosenbaum (1995), Beaver (1994) and Monaco (1981). Analysis of the definitions given by these authors shows that the unit is problematic, since a shot can be a single frame, or a whole programme, or be of any duration in between. A further point of note is that reliance on the idea of an objective optical transition as a delineator of a shot arises as a result of production activities and is not necessarily present until after a complete program has been produced. This indicates the further need to introduce a plane for terminology referring to the production space-time of a work. Consideration of this will be set aside for the time being.

Other definitions provide greater independence of the number of frames that make up the shot and also introduces the notion that the set-up of the recording device is of importance (cf. Silverstone, 1981; Katz, 1994). These discussions ignore the need to make the definition independent of the technical device used to achieve the objectively visible optical transition. Spottiswoode (1935, 1955) achieved this independence, but his definition remains deficient due to its dependence on film media and other sequential recording technologies. Indeed, many current definitions are dependent on a frame-based recording and reproduction paradigm. Therefore, the following refinement to Spottiswoode's definition is proposed (while noting the problems of applying video terminology to audio) for use in the content plane.

> *Shot:* A collection of frames, and their associated streams without perceivable spatial or temporal discontinuity.

Extending the use of the definition to an object oriented paradigm presents further difficulties. We feel that the term "shot" continues to lack objectivity and its use should be avoided.

Scene

To the knowledge of the authors, there is no definition of the scene that does not resort to references to the content of the material. The term is discussed here due to its ambiguous meaning outside of the theatre and its frequent use in common parlance. The imprecision of the term becomes apparent on considering the following definitions of the scene (and that of sequence, in the discussion of the content plane, below). This is problematic in attempting to define description schemes, for collections of frames can only be classed as a scene by reference to descriptions of their content (giving rise to recursive definitions). The definition given in Beaver (1994) is typical of this type of dependency on content:

> *Scene:* A unit of motion picture usually composed of a large number of interrelated shots that are unified by location or dramatic incident.
> (Beaver, 1994, p304)

The temporal problems inherent in the definition of a shot have already been noted above. They are reintroduced in definitions by Katz (1994). The following definition is the most satisfactory and one that emphasises the problems associated with its use:

> A complete unit of film narration. A series of shots (or a single shot) that take place in a single location and that deal with a single action. A relatively vague term.
> (Monaco, 1981, p451)

In conclusion, the use of the term "scene" for logical or formal units of material should not be adopted. The accepted use of the term to refer precisely to particular physical locations in film and theatre scripts suggests that further investigation of the relationship between this supplementary textual material and the audio-visual material is needed.

Sequence

Comparison of the use of the term "sequence" in MPEG-1 and MPEG-2 with the following definitions shows that there is no effective mapping that can be made between the use of the term in the coding plane and the use of the term in the content plane. The term is defined variously in Beaver (1994), Katz (1994) and Monaco (1981) These definitions all show a subjective aspect when applied to segmentation of the content plane. Moreover, the sequence is defined in terms of the scene in all but one of the definitions. The following definition is the most satisfactory:

A succession of shots forming, in the complete film, a subordinate unity of conception and purpose" (Spottiswoode, 1935; 1955)

However, we caution against the use of this term in formal segmentation schemes.

Event
Event descriptions have for some time been used to represent content (Schank and Abelson, 1977, Schank and Reisbeck, 1981). Parkes (1989) introduced their use in the representation of film content. Events can be considered to be represented in a collection of images, during the course of which an entity performs some action, on itself or other entities, that results in, or is accompanied by, state changes.

6.5   Description Plane Segmentation

Though many terms have been discussed above, none should be regarded as redundant at this stage. This is because no consideration has hitherto been given to the applicability of temporal segmentation approaches to particular types of content description. There are two major approaches to content representation that have been adopted to date. These are:

- Those involving a combination of free text and keywords. Examples of this approach include Aguierre-Smith and Davenport (1992) and Lougher *et al.* (1997).
- Those that have taken a more structured approach based on knowledge representation schemes. (Parkes, 1988, 1989, 1992; Nack & Parkes, 1997)

Standardisation activities are insufficiently advanced at this stage to determine whether either, or a combination of both, of these approaches will be adopted in the future.   What can be added is a set of definitions for the terms in the content description plane that reflects the equivalent terms in the content plane.

Object Description
At present an object description may be taken to be one or other of the following.

- A description of the content of an MPEG-4 AV object.
- A description defining the content of a polygonal area in a number of frames of an elementary MPEG-1 or MPEG-2 stream which may in themselves be MPEG-4 AV objects.

Frame Description
There are problems associated with the use of the frame as the base element in a content description hierarchy. These stem from the difficulties in equating cinematographic frames with video frames and, further with the MPEG-1 and 2 picture definition. This problem becomes more acute when one considers the MPEG-4 environment where the "frame rate" will be dependent on the MPEG-4 terminal's

ability to render objects and scenes. We therefore recommend that the base element in the temporal hierarchy is the setting. This view does not preclude the use of the frame in less structured approaches. It should be noted, however, that the term "setting" applies to single frames as well as longer visual states, since a single frame also represents a *visual state*.

Setting Description

A setting description represents the objectively visible state shown by a setting. Formalisms based on knowledge representation have been applied in the description of settings. A setting is associated with an interval of time over which the logical propositions representing its description are held to be true, (cf. Parkes; 1989, 1992; Parkes and Nack, 1997; and Butler and Parkes 1997).

Scene Description

The ambiguities inherent in the definition of the scene that were discussed above lead us to the view that the term "scene" should be used with care by developers of content description schemes.

Sequence Description

A sequence description may be a formal or informal description of the content of a collection of frames having a defined start and end point. Examples of sequence descriptions using informal description structures can be found in Aguierre-Smith and Davenport (1992), Davis (1993) and Lougher, et al. (1997).

Event Description

An event description takes the form of a formal structure that represents the principal elements of the event. The principal elements of the event are the entities involved, any state changes, and the nature of, and relationships between, the entities (actor, instrument, object, and so on). These elements will be asserted to be occurring between a starting point and an ending point in the multimedia material. Structures for representing events in moving film are described and applied in Parkes (1988, 1989). The methodological and logical foundations of motion video event descriptions can be found in Parkes (1992).

6.6   Coded Description Plane Segmentation

Segmentation of the Coded Description Plane is not discussed further in this paper. We are unaware of any existing compression schemes for content description save for those based on existing text compression techniques.

7   Applying the methodology

As an example of the application of the planes consider again the first scenario from the introduction to this paper, that of the space vehicle, Figure 1, above, is a picture captured from an MPEG coded video file that existed in the *transformed data plane*. As the video was played it was decoded from the *transformed data plane* into *the data plane*. Each decoded picture was rendered on the video screen of a PC where it entered the *expression plane*. As the image was viewed, it invoked ideas in the viewer who generated the *content plane* in her mind.

In *transformed data plane* temporal segmentation terms figure 1 is derived from an MPEG Picture forming part of a Group of Pictures that was part of a Sequence. In data plane terms, it would be a frame taken from a shot or sequence. In *content plane* terms it would be a frame again taken from a shot or sequence. In terms of the content description plane, according to Parkes' methodology it would be a frame, which is described by a setting description, by virtue of it being a frame from the associated setting. In the *description plane*, individual frames could be spatially segmented into areas that are part of the rocket and those that are not. The setting description might contain more detailed information about what parts of the rocket are objectively visible examples of which are "fuel system" and "rocket motor". It can now be seen that the first question posed above ("what type of Rocket was this?") is answerable if the setting description contains sufficient detail. If there is not a setting showing the rocket exploding, a negative answer to the second question ("was this a successful launch?") can be inferred from this and other setting descriptions that are encompassed by an event description. Answering the third question ("was this launch part of a series?") requires that the "system" possesses further knowledge about other launches. This is the type of information that might be contained in cataloguing information, if several launch sequences are available to the system. The fourth question ("Was the mission manned?") can be answered by reference to other setting and event descriptions if any parts of the video show a crew either entering or in the launch vehicle.

8   Conclusion

A wide variety of terminology is used in MPEG, and elsewhere, to define spatial and temporal segmentation of multimedia. A clear distinction between temporal and spatial segmentation is required. Furthermore, a methodology to distinguish clearly between the different aspects of multimedia representation is needed. In this paper, we have attempted to achieve these aims by introducing the concept of "planes of representation", referred to, for convenience, as "planes". Adoption of this terminology enables an analysis of existing video terminology to be carried out. It is recommended that the planes terminology be adopted by standardisation bodies. Our argument is that a linguistically oriented model of multimedia content can provide a clear separation of content from the display, transmission and compression technologies used in its creation and distribution.

References

Aguierre-Smith T.G. and Davenport G. (1992) The stratification system: A design environment for random access video. MIT Media Lab Technical Report.

Beaver F. (1994) Dictionary of Film Terms: The aesthetic companion to Film analysis Beaver, Twayne's Filmmakers Series.

Barthes R. (1964) Elements of semiology 1.2.5 p 30 Barthes Cape Editions. Translated from the French Elements de Semiologie Editions du Seuil Paris, 1964.

Butler S., Parkes A.P. (1997) Film sequence generation strategies for automatic intelligent video editing. Applied Artificial Intelligence 11(4), 1997

Davis M. (1993) Media Streams: An iconic language for video annotation. Teletronikk 89(4), 59 - 71.

Chen C.H., Pau L.F., Wang P.S.P. (1993) Handbook of Pattern Recognition and Computer Vision, World Scientific.

Crystal D. (1985) A dictionary of linguistics, Blackwell.

Cruse D.A. (1990) Language, Meaning and Sense: Semantics. In An Encyclopaedia of Language, Ed. Collinge N.E. Routledge.

Eco U. (1977) A theory of semiotics, McMillan.

Ibenthal A., Siggelgow S., Grigat G. (1996) Image sequence segmentation for object orientated coding. Conference on Digital Compression Technologies and Systems for Video Communication, Berlin, Germany

ISO SC29 WG11 (1999-1) MPEG-7 Context and Objectives Document. Available from http:\\drogo.cselt.it/mpeg

ISO SC29 WG11 (1999-2) MPEG-7 Requirements Document. Available from the URL above.

ISO SC29 WG11 (1998) M4005 UML: A preliminary DDL for the MPEG-7 PPD, E. Hartley

ISO/IEC 11172-2 (1993) The generic coding of moving pictures and associated audio information Part 2 Video

ISO/IEC 13818-2 (1997) The generic coding of moving pictures and associated audio information Part 2 Video

Katz E. (1994) The Macmillan International Film Encyclopaedia: Harper Perennial.

Lougher R., Hutchison D., Parkes A., Scott A. (1997) A Hypermedia Model for the Organisation and Description of Video. Proceedings Ed-media/Ed-telecom 97, Calgary, Canada

SMPTE/EBU (1998) EBU Technical Review Special Supplement 1998, EBU/SMPTE Task Force for Harmonized Standards for the exchange of Programme Material a Bitstreams. Editeur Responsible P.A. Laven, Editor M.R. Mayers. (www.ebu.ch)

Monaco J. (1981) How to read a film: The Art, Technology, Language, History and Theory of Film and Media, Oxford University Press.

Metz C. (1974) Film language. Oxford University Press.

Nack F. (1996) AUTEUR: The application of video semantics and theme representation for automated film editing. PhD Thesis Lancaster University

Parkes, AP. (1992). Computer-controlled video for intelligent interactive use: a description methodology, in A.D.N. Edwards and S. Holland (Eds.), Multimedia Interface Design in Education, 97-116, New York: Springer-Verlag.

Nack F. & Parkes A.P. (1997) Toward the automatic editing of theme-oriented video sequences., Applied Artificial Intelligence, 11 (4).

Parkes A.P. (1988) An Artificial Intelligence Approach to the Conceptual Description of Videodisc Images. AP Parkes 1988 PhD Thesis Lancaster University

Parkes A.P. (1989) Automated Propagation of Networks for Perusing Videodisc Image States. Proceedings of ACMSIGIR 1989 NJ Belkin and CJ van Rijsbergen (Eds.).

Pierce C.S. (1932, 1960) Elements of Logic, Harvard, 1932 2.228 in Collected Papers of Charles Sanders Pierce. Ed. C Hartshorne and P Weiss, The Belknap Press of Harvard University Press LCCN 60-9172

Saussure F. (1960) Course in General Linguistics. Eds. C Bally & A Sechaye in collaboration with A Reidlinger. McGraw Hill.

Schank R.C.and Abelson R.P (1977) Scripts, Plans, Goals and Understanding. Lawrence Erlbaum 1977

Schank R.C.and Reisbeck C. (1981) Inside Computer Understanding. Lawrence Erlbaum

Sebeok T.A. (1986) Encyclopaedic dictionary of Semiotics, Mouton de Gruyter.

Stam R., Burgoyne R. & Flitterman-Lewis S. (1992) New Vocabularies in Film Semiotics: Structuralism Post-Structuralism and Beyond, Routledge.

Silverstone R. (1981) The Message of Television. Heinemann Educational Books

Sonesson G. (1989) Pictorial Concepts, Inquiries into the semiotic heritage and its relevance for the visual analysis of the visual world, Chartwell-Bratt Ltd.

Spottiswoode R. (1935, 1955) The grammar of the film: An analysis of film technique: Faber and Faber, London

Wurtzel A. and Rosenbaum R. (1995) Television Production. McGraw-Hill

High Level Description
of Video Surveillance Sequences

Patrick Piscaglia, Andrea Cavallaro[1], Michel Bonnet[2], Damien Douxchamps[3]

[1] Signal Processing Laboratory, Swiss Federal Institute of Technology (EPFL),
CH-1015 Lausanne, Switzerland
Andrea.Cavallaro@epfl.ch
[2] Laboratoires d'Electronique Philips, 22 avenue Descartes, BP 15,
94453 Limeil-Brévannes Cedex, France
bonnet@lep-philips.fr
[3] Telecommunications and Remote Sensing Laboratory, Catholic University of Louvain,
Louvain-la-Neuve, Belgium
douxchamps@ieee.org

Abstract. One of the goals of the ACTS project MODEST is to build an automatic video-surveillance system from a sequence of digital images. The overall system can be divided into the following sub-tasks which are of great interest in the representation of images, namely the automatic segmentation of the video-surveillance sequences, and the extraction of descriptors (such as those in MPEG-7) to represent the objects in the scene and their behaviors.

1 Introduction

The European ACTS project MODEST (Multimedia Objects Descriptors Extraction from Surveillance Tapes) aims at building an automatic video-surveillance system (http://www.tele.ucl.ac.be/MODEST). The input for the system is a sequence of digital images acquired by a number of cameras installed along speedways, in tunnels, at crossroad, and so on.

The global architecture of the application can be decomposed into three main parts:

1. Segmentation of the input images, extracting video objects from the scene;
2. Description of the video objects, delivering compact and high level descriptors that ease their manipulation;
3. Reasoning based on the descriptors received. This step generates statistics, classifications, alarms, etc., and provides the user with images. The engine of this reasoning is made of Intelligent Agents.

One key particularity of the MODEST approach is its link to standardization bodies. The segmentation stage is performed in relation with the COST [3] activities. The description scheme is developed together with the development of the MPEG-7 [6]

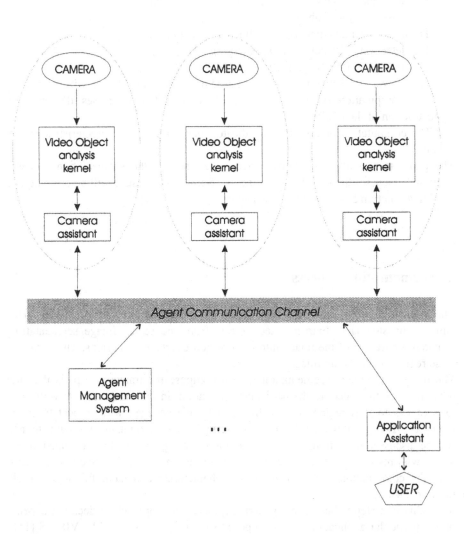

The overall tasks that the agents have to fulfill are, in the case of road monitoring:
- The detection of stopped or very slow vehicles
- The detection of vehicles driving opposite in direction.
- The classification of objects
- The tracking of a vehicle in a multiple camera environment
- The detection of vehicles driving in zigzag
- The detection of traffic jams and accidents
- The delivery of elaborated statistics, based on the results of the classification
- The computation of a global level of service (that expresses the state of obstruction of the road)
- The computation of a pollution indicator, based on some characteristics of the traffic.

The paper is structured as follows. Section 2 presents the segmentation process. Section 3 discusses the description extraction. Some visual results will be presented in Section 4. Section 5 will conclude the paper.

2 Segmentation Process

The segmentation process is the first step in the overall architecture of Modest. The aim of this step is to extract video objects from the scene. Image segmentation provides a partition of the image into a set of non-overlapping regions. The union of these regions is the entire image.

The purpose of image segmentation is to decompose the image into parts that are meaningful with respect to the particular application, in our case video surveillance. Our goal is to find regions in one frame that have changed with respect to some reference. Having a reliable reference (i.e. background) is a fundamental requisite that will be discussed in section 2.1. The detection of the regions that have changed in the image with respect to the reference is then described in section 2.2. Section 2.3 deals with the computation of the features that characterize a meaningful object mask (section 2.4).

Since this first step is based on a general segmentation approach, it does not depend on the particular application. Other proposed surveillance systems, like VIEWS [11], use parameterized 3D model-based approach able to adapt the shapes to different classes of vehicles. That choice leads to good performances but does not allow the method to be applied, for instance, to an indoor scenario.

2.1 Background Extraction

The background extraction is an iterative process that refreshes, at an instant $n+1$, the background obtained from n previous frames of the sequence with the incoming $(n+1)$ frame. All the frames of the video sequence do not need to be used in this process: in our case, we refresh the background every two frames (The refreshment rate is therefore half the video frame rate, e.g. 3.125 Hz if the frame rate is 6.25 Hz). The accretion method uses a *blending formula* that weights regions of the incoming frame, according to their chances to belong (or not) to the background (i.e. inlier/outlier discrimination).

As shown in Fig. 2 a first error map is generated by comparing the incoming frame *(n+1)* with the current background *n*. The error map is then filtered to get rid of isolated outliers pixels. But still, this error map is *pixel-based* and detects *outliers*, mainly at the borders of moving objects, as soon as these objects are not textured enough. Moving objects are therefore only partially detected as outliers. This is the reason why *Connected Operators* [9] are used: it is a straightforward method to solve this problem that filters an image by merging its flat zones without deteriorating objects boundaries. A straightforward spatial segmentation that leads to a tree representation and detects uniform areas, in addition to a labeling process based on the error map information, enables to apply a Viterbi algorithm to prune the tree and make the decision of weighting regions (Fig. 4). This final step makes the inlier/outlier decision on whole objects by "filling the holes" efficiently. The whole process leads to a *region-based* error map.

In our case, the tree structure that defines the spatial segmentation is built from the luminance image. The resulting so-called Max-Tree grows up from dark parts of the image (the root is a region of minimal pixels value) to bright regions defining the leaves of the tree (see [10] for more details on the tree creation process). The pruning process, when applied on such a tree labelled with the error map information, eliminates more easily bright than dark moving regions. That is the reason why Connected Operators are processed twice, once on the luminance image, once on the inverse luminance image. The two resulting maps are then merged in to a final region-based weight map that will be used for blending (Fig. 3).

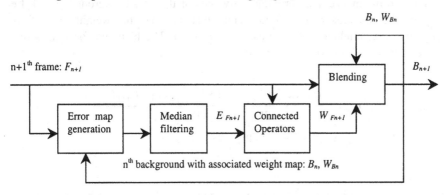

Fig. 2. Global iterative process for background extraction

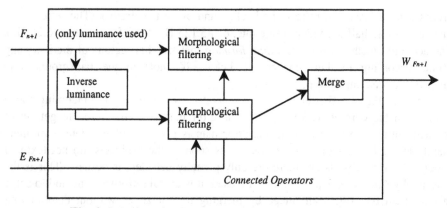

Fig. 3. Detail on the Connected Operators process (cf Fig. 2)

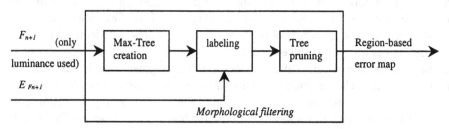

Fig. 4. Detail on the morphological filtering (cf Fig. 3)

To blend the frame *(n+1)* with the background *n*, a weighted mean formula is used to calculate the luminance and chrominance values of the new background *(n+1)*. Let $W_{F_{n+1}}$ be the previous region-based weight map and W_{B_n} the weight map of the background (accumulation of weights at each pixel). The blending formula is then given by (see Fig. 2 for notations):

$$\begin{cases} B_{n+1}(x,y) = \dfrac{W_{B_n}(x,y).B_n(x,y) + W_{F_{n+1}}(x,y).F_{n+1}(x,y)}{W_{B_n}(x,y) + W_{F_{n+1}}(x,y)} \\ W_{B_{n+1}}(x,y) = W_{B_n}(x,y) + W_{F_{n+1}}(x,y) \end{cases} \qquad (2.1)$$

Finally, the process is iterated to obtain a background that is cleaner and cleaner at each step.

An example of extracted background is shown on Fig. 8.

2.2 Change Detection Mask

A change detection mask is a first approximation of the segmentation mask. It is a binary mask: the value 0 represents, in first estimation, a point belonging to the background while a value 1 represents a point estimated as belonging to an object.

Two techniques are combined to obtain the change detection mask: a detection based on the changing from the next and previous frames, and a detection based on the difference with an automatically extracted background image.

Change from frame detection. Two *change_from_frame detection masks* are computed, using the same technique on different input images.

The change detection detects the changing between the current frame and a reference frame. At first, the reference frame is the previous one. For the second run, the reference frame is the next frame. This method imposes a delay of one frame, but gives a much more precise mask. The estimation of the difference between the current image and the reference image is based on the value of the pixel difference between both images. The point is supposed to be a part of an object if this difference is higher than a threshold. A median filtering removes the noise and smoothes the mask.

Two masks are computed:

- A *change_from_previous_frame*, that uses the current frame and the previous frame.
- A *change_from_next_frame*, that uses the current frame and the next frame.

Change from background. The technique used to estimate the *change_from_background* mask is similar to the one used to estimate the *change_from_frame detection masks*.

Combination of change masks. The *change_from_previous_frame mask* is too big at the rear of the vehicle. The *change_from_next_frame* is too big at the front of the vehicle. A logical AND between both masks gives a *change_detection_mask* that is precise.

Large homogenous areas of the vehicles are not taken into account by this detection technique, while parts of the vehicles that have a color similar to the road are not taken into account by the *change_from_background* mask.

A logical OR between the *change_detection_mask* and the *change_from_background* mask gives the *change_detection_mask*.

2.3 Feature Extraction

In this section features chosen as significant representatives of the characteristics of the images are presented. These features constitute the input for the clustering algorithm described in 2.4. The simultaneous use of many features has the advantage of better exploiting the correlation that exists among them. In addition, it is possible to avoid the need for an iterative refinement through different stage of segmentation.

The interest of a segmentation stage after the computation of the change detection mask is related to the intrinsic limits of the information provided by the change detector. The output of the change detector, indeed, is an image representing the pixels (grouped in blobs) which are changed with respect to the reference. In other words it is a binary information. If there is only one object inside a blob in the change detection mask, this blob has a semantic meaning, i.e. it represents a car or a pedestrian. On the other hand, if there are two or more objects closed one to each other, the change detector is not able to discriminate between them. It is therefore necessary to find a strategy to overcome this limitation. In our approach we have chosen to consider the features characterizing such a blob. By clustering (see the following section) it is possible to provide the upper level (Intelligent Agents) with a richer information. This information can be exploited to separate the objects inside the same blob.

We consider two kinds of features:
- *temporal information* obtained by the computation of the motion field;
- *spatial information* considering color, texture and position.

The choice of this set of features has been driven by the results obtained after extensive simulations.

Motion information is obtained by evaluating and post-processing the optical flow. The optical flow is estimated using the algorithm proposed by Lucas and Kanade [5]. A median filtering is then performed on the resulting motion field in order to avoid the effect of spurious vectors.

Among the different options for choosing the *color* space, the YUV coordinates have been selected since they allow a separate processing of the luminance (Y) information. The color information undergoes a post-processing stage (by a median filtering) that reduces the noise while preserving the edges. The use of the spatial coordinates (*position* feature) of each pixel helps in increasing the level of spatial coherence of the segmentation and thus the compactness of the resulting regions. A *texture* feature is finally taken into account. This value characterizes the amount of the texture in a neighborhood of the pixel and is defined as standard deviation of the gray level over a 3x3 window. The result is then post-processed to reduce the estimation error due to the presence of edges.

2.4 Object Mask

The extraction of regions is based on several features computed from the image as described in the previous section. Given the change detection mask (see section 2.2) and the set of features, we take into account only the pixels that have been classified as changed. The Fuzzy C Means algorithm [1] is used to identify regions that are homogeneous in the feature space. As said earlier, these regions can be grouped together by the Intelligent Agents to form objects.

3 Descriptions Extraction

The descriptions extracted by this section of the algorithm intend to be MPEG-7 compliant. At the time of this writing, MPEG-7 standard is not finalized yet. A Call for Proposals (CFP) [2] has taken place in February 1999, to which four description schemes have been submitted by MODEST, namely the TimeStamp, GlobalSceneParameters, Trajectory and XenoObject description schemes.

A geometric measure alone is not useful in the 2D-pixel image to describe accurately real dimensions in the scene. For instance, if a vehicle moves away from the camera, its size expressed in pixels decreases, while its real size of course does not change. A conversion from the 2D data to 3D world measures is then mandatory to have meaningful descriptions, which is why there is a lot of work in the field of 2D-pixel to 2D-meters coordinates mapping [8]. This conversion is only achievable if the camera has previously been calibrated, which is first discussed. The originality of our approach is the use of full 3D coordinates to describe the scene: not only we locate the object in real-world coordinates the ground plane, but we also determine its height and 3D-shape. We also use a non-model-based approach for generality, which differs from other research in the field [11]. The different descriptors are described in the following subsection, while the future work that the project is about to perform on the descriptions, is drafted in the last subsection.

3.1 Camera Calibration

The preliminary step before three-dimensional reconstruction of the scene is the camera calibration. The goal of this process is to compute the parameters of the central projection of the world on the image plane of the camera. One should note that this transform will not be enough to compute 3D coordinates: it is only able to give us the equation of the line (in world coordinates) passing through the image point and the focal center of the camera. Such a line is called a 'ray', and the process that will remove the last unknown (i.e. change the ray to a single 3D point) is discussed in the 2D-3D conversion section.

This world to image transformation (a central projection) is approximately affine, so that we need to find 12 parameters: 9 for the rotation matrix (the camera orientation) and 3 for the translation vector (the camera location in world coordinates). The equation that links 3D to 2D coordinates is then:

$$\begin{pmatrix} X \\ Y \\ Z \end{pmatrix} = \frac{1}{R} \left[\begin{pmatrix} x_i \\ y_i \\ 1 \end{pmatrix} - \begin{pmatrix} t_x \\ t_y \\ t_z \end{pmatrix} \right], \qquad (3.1)$$

where *(X,Y,Z)* are the world coordinates, *(xₚyᵢ)* the image coordinates, *R* the rotation matrix and *t* the translation vector. This equation can be used to find the *R* matrix and *t* vector providing that both world coordinates and image coordinates are available for some points, called calibration points. If such calibration points are delivered to the system, all the parameters are then the solution of a simple linear system.

When *R*, *t* and *(xₚyᵢ)* are known, the directing vector of the ray associated with a image point can be computed, the translating vector of the ray being always *t*.

3.2 2D to 3D Conversion

The classic way to convert two-dimensional pixel coordinates into three-dimensional world coordinates would be to use stereovision. However, in our case, there is only one camera for each observed scene.

In general, three-dimensional reconstruction is possible if several spatially different views of the same object can be obtained. In the case of a single camera, different views can be obtained in the way that the objects will move from one frame to another. The movement will cause the perspective to change, yielding the different views for the object.

The complete process consists in finding interesting points on the moving objects, matching them between two frames and deducing the three-dimensional coordinates from the two different locations of the feature point.

The feature detector used is the Moravec [7] operator. The detection of significant features is done by thresholding the resulting feature image and matching its neighborhood in the original image with a region in the next frame (special BMA algorithm, directed by an interest map). Inverting the first and the second frame in this process yields two sets of pairs of points. We then only select the pairs that are the same in the two sets. The selection of the best pairs further downsizes the set.

The three-dimensional reconstruction requires several hypotheses. Objects must be rigid and in motion (see above). The objects should also behave following a plane movement, i.e. each feature point has the same height in each frame. This height conservation hypothesis is combined with the supposition of the existence of points located on the ground to yield a set of equations determining the free parameter of the rays, and hence the three-dimensional points.

If we suppose Pg on the ground (see Fig. 5) and P above it, the true X-Y location Pr of P will be a function of the projection Pp of P on the ground plane. If we have two frames for this object, the distance conservation between the frames will yield a determined system for the Pr location of the three-dimensional point P:

$$\text{perspective equations for } t_1 \text{ and } t_2: \quad P_r = (1 - P(z)/t(z))P_r \qquad (3.2)$$

$$\text{rigidity equation: } \| P_r(t_1) - P_g(t_1) \| = \| P_r(t_2) - P_g(t_2) \| \qquad (3.3)$$

where P(z) is the altitude of point P and t(z) the altitude of the camera.

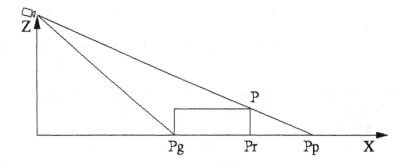

Fig. 5. Three-dimensional reconstruction: projected view of the 3D scenario

Results from this process are shown on Fig. 6. The bounding boxes show the reconstructed 3D limits of the vehicle, while the tails are the trajectories of the projection of the center of mass of the vehicle on the ground.

Fig. 6. Vehicles bounding boxes and trajectories

3.3 Descriptions

The descriptions are high level ways of representing the information contained in the scene. Once the objects are extracted, they can be characterized by their dimension, their speed, their position, their orientation, their color and their shape. The global conditions on the scene are also extracted to deliver to the reasoning agents a complete information.

The description schemes proposed at the MPEG-7 CFP, and mentioned at the beginning of section 3 are made up with a subset of the following descriptors.

Dimension. The descriptor for the dimension of the vehicle gives the 3D-dimension of the object along its main and perpendicular axis. Three values are delivered: length, width and height.

After the 2D to 3D conversion, the X dimension of the objects is the distance between the minimum and maximum X coordinates. The Y and Z dimensions are computed with the same rule.

Speed. The descriptor for the speed gives the (x,y,z) speed of an object from the previous frame. Three values are delivered: x,y,z motion.

After the 2D to 3D conversion, the speed vector is the difference between the position of the center of mass of the object at the current frame and at the previous frame, divided by the time separating both frames.

Position. The descriptor for the position gives the (x,y,z) position of the mass center of the object. The (x,y,z) position is delivered.

After the 2D to 3D conversion, the position is the 3D-position of the center of mass of the object.

Orientation. The descriptor for the orientation gives the orientation of the main axis of an object, defined as the angle between the main axis and the horizontal axis (using the standard trigonometric referential).

After the 2D to 3D conversion, the orientation of the vehicle is the angle given by

$$angle = \frac{1}{2}\arctan\left(\frac{m_{11}}{m_{20}}\right) \tag{3.4}$$

where m_{11} stands for the first order xy-momentum and m_{20} stands for the second order x-momentum.

Color. The descriptor for the color gives the colors of an object as a set of (H,S,V) values (one triplet of value for each dominant color of the object).

Shape. A lot of possibilities exist for describing the shape of an object. The simplicity, efficiency, speed and relevancy for higher levels of several algorithms have been under study. The contour has finally been chosen.

The description scheme that gives the contour of the object is a set of (x,y,z) points representing the approximation of the contour of the object if joined by a straight line.

Global conditions. The global conditions on the scene can be expressed by several descriptors or description schemes:

- The global color gives the global H, S and V values of the scene, and their variance. The global color can vary for example with the color calibration of the camera.
- The global motion of the camera gives the global motion (or tilt) of the camera. Despite the fact that the camera is supposed to be fixed, small motions or tilts can occur due to the wind, abnormal vibrations...
- The number of objects identified in the scene.

3.4 Future Work

The coding of the descriptors and description schemes is currently under study. Two coding scheme are developed:

- A textual coding scheme that represents the data as a text. An example of textual coding is given in section 4.
- An efficient coding. The aim is to obtain a bytecode as small as possible to describe the descriptors and description schemes. In the Modest application, the segmentation and description tools are located closed to the camera. The reasoning can be located in the central dispatching. The descriptions must be sent as fast as possible, on communication lines as cheap as possible.

4 Results

This section presents some results of the algorithms described in the sections 2 and 3. Fig. 7 presents a few snapshots of some of the sequences.

Fig. 7. Snapshots from the original sequences

Fig. 8 shows the background that is automatically extracted from the sequences.

Fig. 8. Background image

For the first snapshot, Fig.9a shows the Change Detection Mask obtained with the previous frame and Fig. 9b shows the Change From Background (CFB) mask. The combination of the two CDM and the CFB mask is represented in Fig. 9c to form, after segmentation and morphological filtering, the object masks presented in Fig. 10 for the two snapshots.

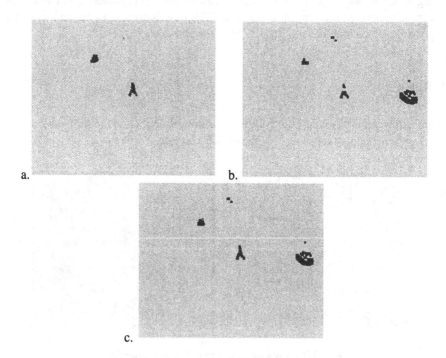

a.
b.
c.

Fig. 9. Change Detection (i, i-1), Change From Background, and final CD masks

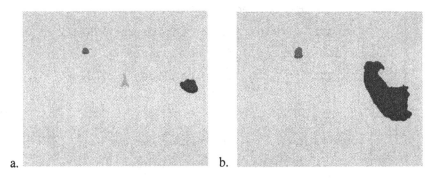

a.   b.

Fig. 10. Object Masks

Fig. 11 displays the real extracted objects. Objects that are very far in the field are not taken into account because they are too small. One can see that the segmentation is quite accurate for most of the vehicles of peoples, except for the load of the truck, that is a large homogeneous zone, with a color close to the background color. The 2D to 3D conversion will nevertheless find enough correct points to obtain the 3D shape of the truck.

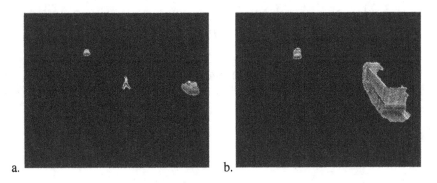

a.   b.

Fig. 11. Visual representation of the extracted objects

The second part of the algorithm computes the descriptions extracted from the object masks, in combination with the original images. The textual representation of the descriptors and description schemes is presented.

```
:object (
     :id 1
```

```
:size (     // Expressed in meters
        :length (:value 4.23 :confidence 0.93)
        :width (:value 1.56 :confidence 0.87)
        :height (:value 1.42 :confidence 0.81)
)
:trajectory (
        :position (     // Expressed in meters
             :X (:value 40.53 :confidence 0.91)
             :Y (:value -6.20 :confidence 0.86)
             :Z (:value 0.76 :confidence 0.65)
        )
        :speed ( // Expressed in meters/second
             :X (:value 29.12 :confidence 0.91)
             :Y (:value 0.11 :confidence 0.84)
             :Z (:value 0.02 :confidence 0.21)
        )
        :orientation ( // Expressed in radian
             :value 1.59
             :confidence 0.94
        )
)
:color (
  . . .
)
)
```

5 Conclusion

This paper has presented a representation scheme of images in two steps. The first step consists of an efficient segmentation of images in order to obtain object masks that ease the extraction of a high level description of the objects present on the scene. The second step consists of an extraction of high level descriptors and description schemes from the above object masks. The descriptions have been submitted to the MPEG-7 standardization group.

We have shown in the paper different techniques combined to obtain the object masks, from the previous, the current, the next frame, and from the background image. We have also shown the way to extract descriptions for the objects, containing the size, the position, the orientation, the speed, the color, and so on, and some trails for the coding/decoding of the descriptions for their transmission.

A third step, which is out of the scope of this paper, has been briefly presented. It describes the way the descriptions are used by the application developed in the framework of the ACTS project MODEST.

References

1. R. Castagno, T. Ebrahimi, M. Kunt. "Video Segmentation based on Multiple Features for Interactive Multimedia Applications". In IEEE Transactions on Circuits and System for Video Technology, Vol.8, No.5, pp.562-571, September 1998

2. ISO/IEC JTC1/SC29/WG11 N2469 "Call For Proposals for MPEG-7 Technology", October 1998, Atlantic City, USA

3. The European COST211quat Group home page (http://www.teltec.dcu.ie/cost211)

4. The Foundation for Intelligent Physical Agents (FIPA) home page (http://www.fipa.org)

5. B. Lucas, T. Kanade. "An iterative image registration technique with an application to stereo vision". In Proceedings of 7th International Joint Conference on Artificial Intelligence, pp. 674-679, 1981

6. The Moving Picture Expert Group (MPEG) home page (http://drogo.cselt.stet.it/mpeg)

7. H.P. Moravec, "Towards automatic visual obstacle avoidance", Proc. 5th Int. Joint Conf. Artificial Intell., vol. 2, pp. 584, August 1977

8. C.S. Regazzoni, G. Fabbri, G. Vernazza, "Advanced Video-Based Surveillance Systems", Kluwer Academic Publishers, 1999

9. P. Salembier, J. Serra, "Flat zones Filtering, Connected Operators, and Filters by reconstruction", IEEE Trans. On Image Processing, vol. 4, No 8, pp. 1153-1160, August 1995

10. P. Salembier, A. Oliveras, L. Garrido, "Anti-extensive Connected Operators for Image and Sequence Processing", IEEE Trans. On Image Processing, vol. 7, No 4, pp. 555-570, April 1998

11. The VIEWS project home-page (http://www.cvg.cs.rdg.ac.uk/views/home.html)

12. COST XM document (http://www.teltec.dcu.ie/cost211)

Enabling Flexible Services Using XML Metadata

Luis Velasco, Ian Marshall

BT-Labs, Martlesham Heath, SUFFOLK, IP5 3RE, UK

velascol@drake.bt.co.uk, marshall@drake.bt.co.uk

Abstract. Combining eXtensible Markup Language (XML) and Active Layer Networking may yield strong benefits for networked services. A Wide range of new Multimedia applications can be developed based on the flexibility of XML and the richness of expression afforded by metadata. XML is an emerging technology that will constitute the foundation of an Object Oriented Web. A system of network intermediaries based on caches, which are also active and driven by XML metadata statements, is described.

Keywords XML, Cache, Active Node, Proxylet, HTTP

1   INTRODUCTION

The characteristics and behaviour of future network traffic will be different from the traffic observed today, generating new requirements for network operators. Voice traffic will become another form of data, most users will be mobile, the amount of traffic generated by machines will exceed that produced by humans, and the data traffic will be dominated by multimedia content. In the medium term the predominant multimedia network application will probably be based around electronic commerce capabilities. Operators will therefore need to provide a low cost service, which offers an advanced global trading environment for buyers and sellers of any commodity. The e-trading environment will be equipped with all the instruments to support the provision of a trusted trading space. Most important is the ability to support secure transactions over both fixed and mobile networks. Networks will thus need to be robust, contain built in security features and sufficiently flexible to address rapidly evolving demands as other unforeseen applications become predominant.

2 MOTIVATION

Existing networks are very expensive, and the deployment of new communication services is currently restricted by slow standardisation, the difficulties of integrating systems based on new technology with existing systems, and the overall system complexity. The biggest cost is management. The network of the future will need to be kept as simple as possible by using as few elements as possible, removing duplication of management overheads, minimising signalling, and moving towards a hands off network.

The simplest (and cheapest) current networks are multiservice networks based on powerful ATM or IP switches. New transport networks are designed on the basis that nearly all applications will eventually use internet-like connectionless protocols. The difficulties of adding services such as multicast and QoS to the current internet demonstrate that even these simpler IP based networks will require additional mechanisms to enhance service flexibility. The simple transport network will thus need a flexible service surround. The service surround will provide a trusted environment, with security features (for users, applications and hosts), QoS support, application specific routing, automatic registration and upgrade for devices connected to the transport network. It will also enable Network Computing facilities such as secure gateways, application layer routers, cache/storage facilities, transcoders, transaction monitors and message queues, directories, profile and policy handlers. Such a service surround will likely be based on some form of distributed middleware, enabling the features to be modular and interoperable. The service surround must enable rapid introduction of new features by the operator. In order to minimise the management overhead clients will directly control which features should be used for a particular session, without operator intervention. The network will thus need to know nothing of the semantics of the session. To achieve this a middleware based on some form of active services or active networks will be required.

2.1 Active Networking Proposals

Active networking was originally [TENN] a proposal to increase flexibility by adding programmes to packet headers which run on forwarding devices that lie in the path of the packet. However service operators are unlikely to permit third party programmes to run on their equipment without prior testing, and a strong guarantee that the programme will not degrade performance for other users. Since it will be extremely hard to create interesting programmes in a language, which is simple enough to enable termination guarantees, we regard this approach as unrealistic.

A somewhat different flavour of active networking, in which the packets do not carry programmes but flags indicating the desirability of running a programme, has also been proposed [ALEX] based on a dynamic interpretation of programmable network ideas. This would enable the service operator to choose a programme to load, which matches the indicated need, but is sourced from his own database of tested programmes. We believe that this second approach may be valuable in the long term, however in order not to degrade router performance the number of flags will need to be small and the number of possible programmes will thus also be small. In addition it will not resolve the immediate need for increased flexibility, as it will require standardisation, which will take time.

We have proposed a third alternative, which we call application layer networking [ALAN]. A similar proposal [AMIR] was described as active services. In this system the network is populated with application level entities we refer to as service nodes, or dynamic proxy servers. These could be thought of as equivalent to the HTTP (HyperText Transfer Protocol) caches currently deployed around the Internet, but with a hugely increased and more dynamic set of capabilities. This approach relies on redirecting selected packets into the application layer device, where programmes can be run to modify the content, or the communication mechanisms. The programmes can be selected from a trusted data source (which is normally a cache and has minimal restoration overhead), and can be run without impacting router performance or requiring operator intervention. Packets are redirected on a session by session and protocol by protocol basis, so there is no need for additional flags or standardisation. Programmes are chosen using the mime type of the content (in the application layer header), so again no additional data or standards are required.

There is a further proposal [PEI98] that allows servers to supply cache applets attached to documents, and requires proxies to invoke the cache applets. Although this provides a great deal of flexibility, it lacks important features like a knowledge sharing system among the nodes of the network (It only allows interaction between the applets placed in the same page). The functionality is also severely restricted by the limited tags available in HTML (HyperText Markup Language). Most importantly the applets do not necessarily come from a trusted source, and clients do not have the option of invoking applets from 3rd party servers. Which may be trusted.

Using mime-types (as in ALAN) provides more flexibility than HTML tags, but still restricts the range of applications that can be specified by content providers, as, different operations are often required for content with identical mime types. It is therefore necessary to find a better way to specify new services. XML [WOO99] provides a very promising solution, since the tags are extensible and authors can embed many different types of objects and entities inside a single XML document. In this paper we present a design for a modified ALAN based on XML in order to enable an object-oriented approach to Web information [MAN98]. This will show how a range of services could be implemented. We demonstrate feasibility by implementing and measuring a simple example service. A brief introduction to XML is provided in Appendix 3 for those who are new to this technology.

3 ALAN & XML

Our design built in several layers based on existing technology:

The ALAN Platform is a Java RMI based system built by the University of Technology (Sydney) in collaboration with BT-Labs to host active services. It provides a host program (Dynamic Proxy Server) that will dynamically load other classes (Proxylets) that are defined with the following interface: Load, Start, Modify, Stop [ALAN].

The platform provides a proxylet that analyses the HTTP headers and extracts the mime-types of the objects passing through the machine (HTTP Parser). After determining the mime-type of the object, the program chooses a content handler, downloads the appropriate proxylet from a trusted host to handle that mime-type, and starts the proxylet with several parameters extracted by the HTTP parser. Using this model, a wide range of interesting services can be provided. However, this original model cannot support the whole range of services we plan to implement. There is a need for additional data (not included in the HTTP headers) to manage interoperability among the services and to expand the flexibility and range of applications that can be developed. XML provides a mechanism to implement these improvements and appears a perfect complement to the architecture [MORG99].

We have built a simple XML Parser in Java that will work in collaboration with an HTTP parser to utilise all the Metadata needed in the active applications. The HTTP Parser provided by the University of Technology (Sydney) has been completely rewritten in order to integrate the XML parser seamlessly into the processing.

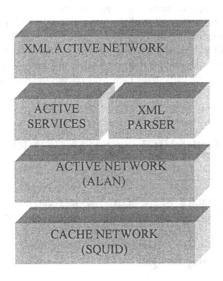

Fig. 1. shows the architecture or the prototype. The first layer is the cache network. For the prototype, we have used squid v1.19 [WESS97] for the cache. The second layer and the upper layers constitute the core of our system and will be discussed thoroughly within this paper. An Application Layer Active Network Platform (ALAN) implements the active services. One of these services is an XML parser that provides the functionality to handle the active objects and Metadata.

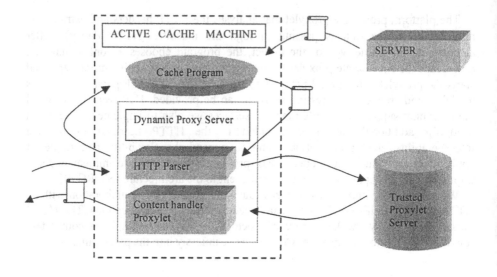

Fig. 2. Functionality of an active Node. The functionality of an active node (figure 2) is described as follows. Upon the arrival of an object into the node, the HTTP parser examines the header and gets its corresponding Mime-Type. If the object is an XML object, then the XML Parser is called and it will extract the Meta-Data. The metadata specifies which proxylets should be invoked, in which order, with which parameters, and under what circumstances. The parser then makes the appropriate calls to the DPS, which loads the proxylets.

4   MULTIMEDIA SERVICES ENHANCED BY THE ACTIVE NETWORK

We provide a set of examples where active services can be applied to give new functionality and versatility, together with outline designs for each service.

4.1   Alternate Path Routing for QoS.

In order to deploy Multimedia Applications over Internet, it is necessary to establish the mechanisms needed to guarantee QoS. QoS-based routing has been recognised as a missing piece in the evolution of QoS-based service offerings in the Internet. Alternate Path Routing algorithms allows the network, or end systems, to determine a path that supports the QoS needs of one or more flows across the network. Current Internet routing protocols, e.g. OSPF, RIP, use "shortest path routing", i.e. routing that is optimised for a single arbitrary metric, administrative weight or hop count. These routing protocols are also "opportunistic," using the current shortest path or route to a destination [CRAW98]. Our aim is to enable route decisions to be made on multiple metrics and fixed for the duration of the flow. For example a node could have a connection via landline with low latency, low bandwidth and high security, and a satellite connection with high bandwidth, high latency and low security. The choice of best route will be application, user and context specific. The XML Metadata is rich enough to express the application layer requirements and force a correct choice. . Using our scheme it also allows return traffic to be correctly routed using an appropriate proxylet at the head end of the satellite link. As part of our research program we plan to apply application layer active networking in a scenario like the one presented in Figure 3. The aim is to show how mobile multimedia applications can be deployed.

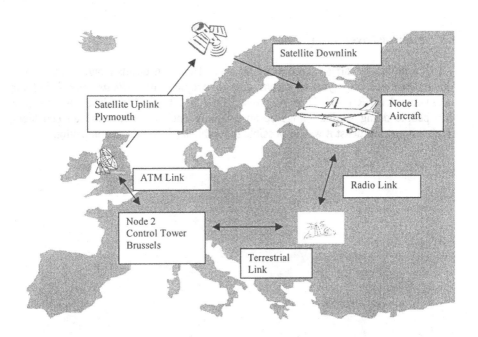

Fig. 3. The aircraft application is an excellent example that shows diverse communication paths based on different physical layers: Aircrafts (Node 1) will have a radio based bi-directional link to the control tower. Meanwhile, the control tower can use COIAS wide area connectivity to establish a high bandwidth link to the aircrafts using ATM and Satellite combined. Path selection is performed at the Control Tower by examining the meta-information of the packets, deciding which is the most appropriate path and adding security if needed. Users can use meta-information to mark their packets with their needs of bandwidth, latency, needed degree of security and needed degree of guarantee. This meta-information will help the system to classify the packets so a smart path selection. By doing this, the packets will be routed using the optimum path.

The design of the system is quite straightforward and involves tunnelling content between active nodes/end systems. By pushing an XML object, the source machine is able to provide the information needed to make correct routing decisions. The XML Object will be parsed, at any active nodes in the path, and the corresponding router proxylet will be downloaded and executed. A tunnel proxylet will then choose the best available route to a point near the client, which can support the remote end of the tunnel. Any downstream active nodes can obviously perform further local route optimisations in a similar manner

With respect to the XML object, it is quite straightforward to produce it from the template provided in Appendix 2. We need to change the proxylet to be loaded and provide the arguments relevant to the QoS required (basically maximum RTT and minimum Bandwidth, some security specifications and the IP address of the client requiring the service). Then the router proxylet will be able to check the available possibilities and choose the most optimum path.

4.2   Multicast over unicast lines

Using multicast carries some disadvantages. The main disadvantage is that many routers don't support it yet. As a consequence, people built *multicast islands* in their local networks [ERIK93]. Then, they discovered that it was difficult to communicate with people doing similar things because if only one of the routers between them didn't support multicast it was impossible to establish the multicast connection.

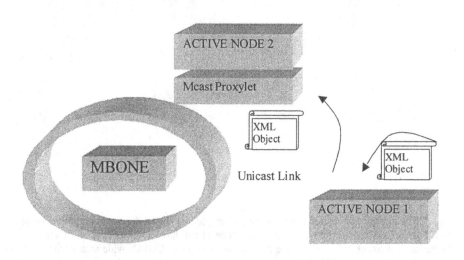

Fig. 4. Briefly, when an active node (Node 1) receives an XML-based request demanding the multicast service over a unicast link, it will download a multicast reflector proxylet. The Proxylet will obtain information about possible active nodes connected to the Mbone. With that information, the proxylet will be able to select an active node (Node 2) from the list and to forward a modified XML object demanding a reflection tunnel.

To overcome the difficulty of using Multicast over unicast lines, it has been shown [ALAN] that running a reflector (as shown in figure 4) at each end of a unicast link to tunnel the multicast over unicast is useful. Our system provides the same facility for XML based multicast, with the advantage that we can specify conditions requiring multicast in the Metadata rather than assuming multicast is always required for a particular mime type as in ALAN.

When the active node connected to the Mbone (Node 2) receives the XML object sent by the first node (Node 1), it will parse it and download a proxylet that will reflect the desired Multicast data onto the Mbone. Node 2 is thus a proxy for a multicast address, which actually originates at node 1. Reversing the order makes node 1 the proxy able to perform a local multicast of Mbone material.

The XML object needed to transmit the Metadata is very easy to build. Basically, we have to adapt the template in Appendix 2 by changing the name of the proxylet and the arguments we need to pass to it. In this case, the multicast group to be subscribed, the type of information that is going to be multicast (STREAM for example), the IP address of an active node connected to Mbone and the reflector proxylet that is required.

4.3 COOPERATIVE PROCESSING

There are several jobs and services, offered in the network that are carried out quite slowly. This is due to servers that cannot cope with the demand and transferring part of the load to other machines can help. This requires co-operation between nodes, which can take the form indicated by policies expressed in the XML metadata. Nodes need to have some knowledge of other nodes and this too can be conveyed in metadata or can be obtained by other means

An XML object specifying the different tasks to be performed by the nodes is sent to them. This XML object will transmit the semantics needed to establish the collaboration and interaction policies that are going to apply to rule the distributed process uses this approach. The active layer network can produce a distributed computation scheme that may help solve complex calculus. Search engines are an interesting example because they rely on physically distributed data, but physical location of an item needs to be computed in the shortest possible time to give a quick response.

The main XML object will be composed of a hierarchy of several objects like the one described in the Appendix 2. Each embedded XML will contain the needed proxylet and the task to perform and the active node where it must be used. In addition, it would contain metadata describing how to implement the interaction among the nodes.

4.4 ADVERT ROTATION

Studies show that among the most popular dynamic contents are advert banners that are dynamically rotated so the same HTML page can show different adverts for each request. These dynamically created HTML pages are just slight modifications of an original template page. The changes usually consist of sets of graphics of the same size that will appear consecutively in the same position of the page. To achieve this, the server executes a cgi program that generates the HTML text dynamically. This dynamic behaviour tends to make this content un-cacheable. It is preferable to make simple dynamic pages containing rotating banners cacheable since this will;

a) Allow a distributed service and eliminate the critical failure points.

b) Improve the usage of the existing bandwidth.

This task requires Meta-Data that is not provided in the HTTP headers. XML will enable information like the rotation policy, the adverts that are going to be rotated, and perhaps a watermark to protect copyright, to be embedded.

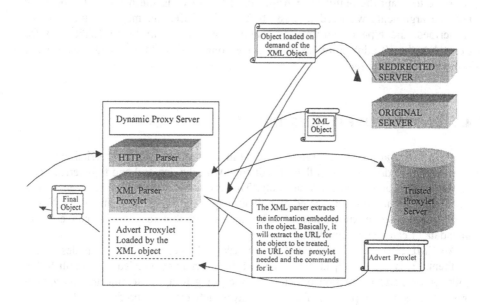

Fig. 5. As the object is requested and passes through the active node, it will be parsed in the http parser and then by the XML Parser. This analysis will extract the generic html page that is going to serve as a static template for the rotated adverts, the list of images which should be rotated and the rotation policy. The information is used as a parameter list in the invocation of a rotator proxylet, which will download the objects as needed. Subsequent requests for the page will be passed to the proxylet by the cache at the active node, and the proxylet will execute the rotation policy. The complete XML specification is provided in Appendix 2.

5   IMPLEMENTATION OF AN EXAMPLE & RESULTS

In order to get some preliminary performance measurements of the architecture we implemented the advert rotator example. The objectives are: Demonstrate the feasibility of the model and show the weak parts of the implementation in order to improve releases in the future.

First Request Time Distribution

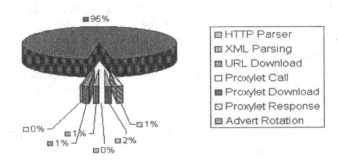

Further Requests Time Distribution

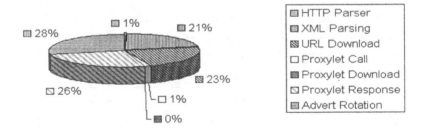

Fig. 6. The graphic shows the average distribution of times during the first ten experiments. It appears that most of the time is spent downloading and starting a new service (setting up a new proxylet in the node).

Fig. 7. Shows that once the active service is set up, we can use it for further requests and avoid that undesirable delay. Caching can perform a very important role in active networks.

Our experiment consisted of running an active node on a Sun Sparc Station 10 with 64 MB running SunOS Release 5.5.1. The Java version for both programming and testing was JDK 1.1.6. The active node program was started and was already running the Proxylets needed for HTTP and XML Parsing.

We conducted 20 experiments. For the first ten, the whole process ran each time a new advert rotation was requested, the advert proxylet was loaded. The subsequent ten utilised caching. When a new request arrived, a proxylet that was already running was used. We measured the times needed to accomplish the different tasks. The numerical results of these experiments are shown in the graph below.

The proportional results are illustrated in the figures 6 and 7.The analysis tries to show the times needed to perform the processes and tasks during the normal operation of the system. The functionality of these processes is described as follows:

1. HTTP Parsing. Time needed to determine analyse the HTTP header and determine the Mime-Type.
2. XML Parsing. Time needed to get the XML Object, parse it and extract all the Metadata Embedded.
3. URL Download. Time needed to download the HTML.
4 Proxylet Call. Time need to generate the query to load the Proxylet in our Active Node.
5 Proxylet Download. Time needed to download and start the proxylet; it requires a lot of time because of the ALAN platform design.
6 Advert Rotation. Time needed to perform the demanded task. In this case the advert rotation.

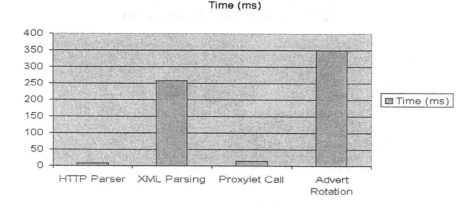

Fig. 8. The graphic in figure 8 shows the results of the experiments when the service was cached. The proportion of time spent downloading the proxy has disappeared. The URL download time can vary depending the object to be downloaded and the bandwidth to the server. In our testing, all the objects are available in our LAN so we can expect greater values for this part of the process in wide area tests. However this increment will only be important for the first request, thereafter the URL object is cached and is made locally available.

The most imporant variable is the times due to the additional processing of the proxylets. It appears that the XML-Parse Proxylet and the Advert Rotator Proxyler are taking most of the time. Nevertheless the total delay is below one second. We can expect better results if a faster computer is used as a server with a non-interpreted language. However the purpose of this paper was to demonstrate the feasibility of active caching nodes based on XML and throughoutput was not a priority. This proto-type shows that it is possible to provide active services with delays of just several hundred milliseconds.

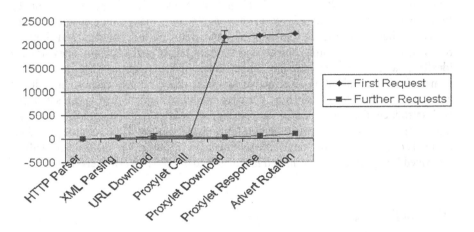

Fig. 9. ilustrates the diference in the delay between the experiments that needed the proxylet to be downloaded and started and the experiments where the proxylet was already downloaded and running in the active node.

6   FUTURE WORK

In the immediate future we intend to build and test all the services outlined in this paper. In addition there are three major longer-term issues, which we are concentrating our efforts on solving;

It would be beneficial to specify behaviour and other non-functional aspects of the programmes requested in the metadata, using a typesafe specification language. One possibility is to use SPIN], which is c-like and has some useful performance and time related primitives. The use of a language of this kind would provide greater flexibility and interoperability, and go some way towards solving our second issue.

For complex services it will be necessary to invoke several proxylets. At present the question of how multiple proxylets interact, and how interactions such as order dependencies can be resolved, is open. We anticipate attempting to use metadata specifications (using the language from issue a)) to maximise the probability of avoiding problems.

The performance and scalability of the DPS is currently far from ideal. Our colleagues in Sydney [ALAN] are addressing these issues, and we anticipate significant improvements will be available before our tests are complete.

7 CONCLUSIONS

Application layer active networks will play a crucial role in networked applications that can tolerate a delay of around a hundred milliseconds. They will extend the functionality and versatility of present networks to cover many future customer needs. HTTP caches help reduce the use of bandwidth in the Internet and improve responsiveness by migrating objects and services closer to the client. They are also ideally placed to evolve into the active nodes of the future. XML is a perfect complement to Application layer active networks based on http caches, since it will allow active nodes to be driven by enriched Metadata requests and at the same time will introduce the mechanisms for sharing knowledge between nodes. We have implemented a prototype, which demonstrates the feasibility of this approach and has enabled some initial performance measurements to be made. The results can easily be improved by using a non-interpreted language and a more powerful server.

REFERENCES

[ALAN] Application Layer Active NetworkM. Fry and A. Ghosh, "Application Level Active Networking" , Fourth International Workshop on High Performance Protocol Architectures (HIPPARCH '98), June 98. http://dmir.socs.uts.edu.au/projects/alan/prog.html

[ALEX] Alexander, Shaw, Nettles and Smith "Active Bridging" Computer Communication Review, 27, 4 (1997), pp101-111

[AMIR] E.Amir, S.McCanne, R.Katz "An active service framework and its application to real time multimedia transcoding" Proc SIGCOMM '98 pp178-189

[CRAW98]A Framework for QoS-based Routing in the Internet. E. Crawley. R. Nair. B. Rajagopalan. H. Sandick. Copyright (C) The Internet Society (1998). ftp://ftp.isi.edu/in-notes/rfc2386.txt.

[ERIK93]"MBone - The Multicast Backbone", Eriksson, Hans, INET 1993

[WOO99]Lauren Wood. Programming the Web: The W3C DOM Specification. IEEE Internet Computing January/February 1999

[MAN98]F. Manola, "Towards a Web Object Model", tech report, Object Services and Consulting Inc, 1998. http://www.objs.com/OSA/wom.htm

[MORG99]   JP Morgenthal. "Portable Data / Portable Code:XML & JavaTM Technologies", tech report. NC. Focus

[PEI98] Active Cache: Caching Dynamic Contents (Objects) on the Web P. Cao, J. Zhang and K.Beach University of Wisconsin-Madison, USA.
http://www.comp.lancs.ac.uk/computing/middleware98/papers.html#PCao.

[TENN98]"Towards an active network architecture". Computer Communication Review, 26,2 (1996) D. Tennenhouse, D.Wetherall.

[WESS97]"Configuring Hierarchial Squid Caches", Duane Wessels AUUG'97, Brisbane, Australia.

[XML]Extensible Markup Language (XML) W3C Recommendation 10-February-1998 http://www.XML.com/aXML/testaXML.htm.

APPENDIX 1

```
<?XML version="1.0" encoding="UTF-8" standalone="no"?>

<!DOCTYPE novel PUBLIC "-//ACTIVE-XML-VEL98//DTD
ACTIVE-XML//ES" "activeXML.dtd" []>

<dynamic initiator>

<front>

<title>active-XML</title><author>Luis Velasco</author>

</front>

<body>

<programms to load>

        <program>

          <name> activebann.Activeban </name>

          <orders>

          <load>

             <trusted program server>

             http://midway/proxylet/activebann.jar

             </trusted program server>

             <host machine>

             midway.drake.bt.co.uk:1998

             </host machine>
```

```
        </load>

        <start>

        <arguments>

    banner1 banner2 banner3 banner4 RANDOM

        </arguments>

        </start></orders>

        <orders_other_caches></orders_other_caches>

        </program>

    </programms to load>

    <redirect object></redirect object>

    </body>

    </dynamic initiator>
```

APPENDIX 2

	HTTP Parser	XML Parsing	URL Download	Proxylet Call	Proxylet Download	Proxylet Response	Advert Rotation
Average	7.6	257.4	278.0	14.9	21735.4	317.2	350.8
Standard Error	18.7	180.7	563.6	1.8	1307.6	198.5	63.1

Table 1. Numeric result table with the time in miliseconds It shows the results in milisecond for the different experiments deployed in the last part of the paper. It is important to note that the figures are in milliseconds and that the Proxylet download time only includes the values for the first ten experiments, then as this step is skipped, this time is reduced to zero.

APPENDIX 3

The Web community is increasingly targeting the W3C's Extensible Markup Language as its next generation data representation. XML defines a data format for structured document interchange on the Web and is a simple subset of Standard Generalized Markup Language.

XML is syntax for developing specialised markup languages, which adds identifiers, or tags, to certain characters, words, or phrases within a document so that they may be recognized and acted upon during future processing. "Marking up" a document or data results in the formation of a hierarchical container that is platform-, language-, and vendor-independent and separates the content from any environment that may process it.

1   Structure to model data to any level of complexity
2   Extensibility to define new tags as needed
3   Validation to check data for structural correctness
4   Media independence to publish content in multiple formats
5   Vendor and platform independence to process any conforming document using standard commercial software or even simple text tools.

The XML definition provides specifications for both XML documents and XML Document Type Definitions (DTD). A DTD is a formal definition of a document. It specifies the element tags that can appear in the document. XML documents have both a logical and physical structure. Physically, the document is composed of units called entities. An entity may refer to other entities to cause their inclusion in the document. It begins in a "root" document entity that is logically composed of declarations, elements, comments, character references and processing instructions. If both physical and logical structure merge well together, then the document is well formed.

XML is a key technology for increasing the Web's support of complex applications through the use of metadata, which describes or interprets other resources located either on the Web or elsewhere. XML can be interpreted as representing information in the form of properties and their values. This possibility of embedding behaviour associated to specific application elements using metadata makes XML the right technology to compliment active networking.

VIDAS Analysis/Synthesis Tools for Natural-to-Virtual Face Representation

Fabio Lavagetto

DIST – University of Genova
Via Opera Pia 13, 16145, Genova, Italy
fabio@dist.unige.it

Abstract. This paper describes the work carried on by the ACTS project VI-DAS[1] in the area of facial image analysis for the synthesis of 3D animated virtual faces. The proposed facial decoder is compliant to MPEG-4 standard and is capable of reproducing the characteristics of any real specific face and guaranteeing synchronisation of lip movements with speech. Evidence of the achievable performance is reported at the end of the paper by means of pictures showing the capability of the system to reshape its geometry according to the decoded MPEG-4 facial calibration parameters and its effectiveness in performing facial expressions. A variety of possible applications is proposed and discussed.

1. Introduction

One of the more exciting possibilities offered by the new MPEG-4 standard is that of mixing natural audio/visual data with synthetic objects like 3D computer generated graphics or structured audio. Among the most sophisticated audio/visual natural objects, the human face represents an ideal example of visual complexity, due to the non-rigid facial movement (i.e. facial expressions), and intrinsic acoustic/visual correlation between the speech output and the lip movements. Moreover, the human face is the audio/visual object most commonly represented in multimedia applications and the one currently deserving major attention in the MPEG-4 standardisation process. In the "Face and Body Animation" (FBA) MPEG "ad hoc group" the synthetic representation of human faces has been investigated deeply and has led to the standardisation of key parameters being the Face Definition Parameters (FDP) which characterise the somatic of a face, and the Face Animation Parameters (FAP) which encode at low level the movements of the head, of eyes, eyebrows, mouth, jaw and so on, and at

---

[1] The VIDAS consortium is coordinated by DIST-University of Genoa (I) and includes Matra-Nortel Communication (FR), Elmer (I), University of Linkoping (S), UPC (E), Irisa-Inria (FR), EPFL (CH), University of Geneve (CH), LEP-Philips (FR), NAD (IR) and Aristotle University of Thessaloniki (GR).

high level the coherent movement of the lips with speech and the emotional content associated to the face expressions. VIDAS is exactly aiming at applying this new technology to the field of videophone coding through the software composition of natural representation of the background with synthetic modelling of the speaker's face. For this reason a 3D mesh has been developed for suitable modelling of the speaker's head and face, capable to be adapted to any specific real face through FDPs and to be animated through FAPs.

VIDAS objective is twofold, oriented on one side to the implementation of a MPEG-4 decoder with 3D synthetic head modelling/animation and, on the other side, to the implementation of a corresponding encoder capable to encode a MPEG-4 bitstream including face parameters. For this purpose, suitable image/speech analysis tools are developed for the segmentation of the images, the detection of the speaker's head , the extraction of facial features and their tracking in time. The segmentation of the face texture allows the extraction of the related pictorial information which must be encoded and transmitted to the decoder where it will be decoded and warped on the 3D head model. Complementary information is also extracted for encoding FDPs and drive the adaptation of the generic 3D head model to the specific face. Dynamic facial feature extraction and tracking must be performed then on each frame grabbed at the encoder for FAP extraction, encoding and transmission. High level FAP (i.e the 65th and 66th FAPs) encode the "viseme" (shape of the mouth) and the "expression" so that the face can be animated in coherence with speech VIDAS videophone will allow the correct acoustic and articulatory reproduction of speech. The availability of anatomic facial models capable of speech-assisted synthetic animation, besides being interesting for applications like very low bit-rate model-based video-telephony, would be of dramatic impact also in the realisation of multimedia man-machine interfaces and for advanced applications in the fields of education, culture and entertainment.

After the successful organisation of the 1st Int. Workshop on "SNHC and 3D Imaging", Rhodes, 1997, VIDAS is organising the 2nd edition of the workshop, scheduled in Santorini (Greece) on September 15-17, 1999. (http://www-dsp.com.dist.unige.it/snhc/confer/santo.html).

2 The Head Detection Process

A statistical scheme has been adopted for detecting human faces under varying poses and for locating the mouth in a suitable normalized domain In our approach[2] the majority of the face is assumed to be modeled by a plane. The *eigen-space* decomposition has been exploited to approximate the face appearance using a reduced number of *eigen-images* in a Karhunen-Loeve transform [1-4]. A statistical matching criterion is optimized w.r.t. to an affine or a perspective transform (3D position of the head) by using a coarse-to-fine strategy combined with a *Simulated Annealing* (SA) algorithm.

---

[2] Image analysis tool developed at Irisa-Inria (FR), partner of the VIDAS project

The developed tool is able to robustly extract the speaker's head in adverse situations such as noise, partial occlusions of the face, rotation of the head. It requires no *a priori* knowledge about the initial position of the speaker in the image. The extraction of mouth features is finally confined to a mouth bounding box in a normalized domain obtained by compensating the estimated geometric transform. The method is adapted to the poor quality of the H263-coded QCIF images and is suited to a further real-time application.

The visual target (face or mouth) has been described by a set of 2D representative views. Given such a training set, the *eigen-space* analysis allows constructing a small set of basis images (*eigen-vectors* of the covariance matrix of training images) that characterize the majority of the statistical gray-level variation observed in the training set. This training step is performed off-line, yielding our *a priori* face model. Such a view-based technique on gray-level images yields a compact parametric form of the target appearance and has been proved very efficient in object detection/recognition. The unsupervised face/mouth detection is then formulated as a matching with a linear combination of *eigen-images*.

For the face detection task a robust matching criterion, based on the Generalized Likelihood Ratio, has been used where two adverse hypotheses are examined:

H1: presence of one face
H2: presence of no face

The visual learning of faces consists of building a distribution-based model of frontal view photographs of faces at fixed scale to capture the full range of permissible variations in patterns. The Olivetti Research Laboratory Database (see Fig. 1) is used for this purpose. A PCA is performed to identify the degrees of freedom of the « face class » on a low dimensional eigen-space. A tractable estimate of the probability distribution of face images is derived from the 3 most significant eigen-images. To build the « non-face » model, we propose to use a reduced number of significant negative images showing views of objects, which look like faces (see Fig. 2). A distribution-based model is built according to the previous visual learning procedure. Three eigen-images are considered in the modeling of the probability distribution.

The detection problem is based on the comparison of the 2 adverse hypotheses H1 and H0. Our matching criterion aims at estimating the similarity, affine or perspective transform that locates a local sub-image in one QCIF image containing the speaker's face. The specified criterion maximizes the ratio of probability distributions estimated respectively for the « face class» and the « non-face class » during the training step. This maximum is compared to a statistical threshold in order to validate the face detection.

The optimization of the statistical criterion requires an efficient coarse-to-fine strategy. For every training image in the two training steps, we construct a pyramid of images by spatial filtering and sub-sampling. The images at each level in the pyramid form distinct training sets and at each level a PCA is performed to construct the eigen-space description of that level. The QCIF images are similarly smoothed and sub-sampled. At the coarse level in the pyramid, only the spatial position and scale parameters are estimated using a fast version of *Simulated Annealing* algorithm. The solution is then refined at the next levels and the matching procedure stops when the affine or perspective transform is estimated at the finest resolution. An example of the achievable results is shown in Fig. 3-6.

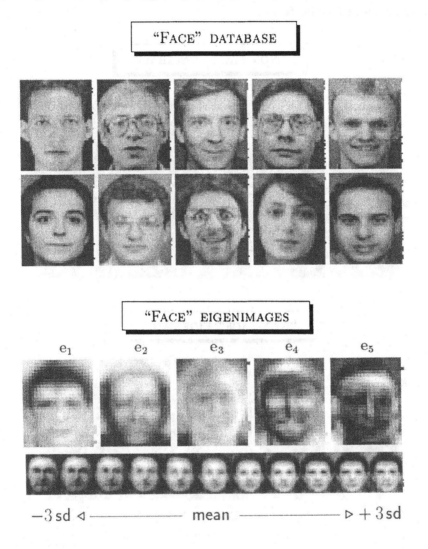

Fig. 1. The Olivetti Database used to train the head detection system to recognize images belonging to class H1

3. The Facial Region Segmentation Process

The sub-image where the presence of the head has been detected is further processed to segment the facial region through a merging process[3] that specifies which regions of the sub-image form the face.

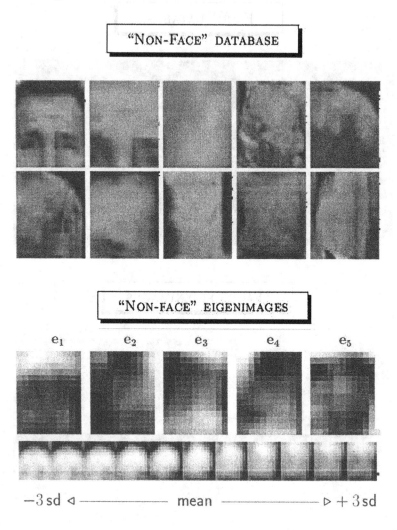

Fig. 2. Database of "non face" images used to train the head detection system to recognize images belonging to class H2.

---

[3] Segmentation tool developed at UPC (E), partner of the VIDAS project

The general merging strategy allows the implementation of segmentation algorithms and filters. The algorithm works on a region adjacency graph (RAG), a graph where each node represents a connected component of the image (regions or flat zones) and the links connect two neighboring nodes. A RAG represents a partition of the image. A merging algorithm on this graph is a technique that removes some of the links and merges the corresponding nodes.

Fig. 3: Multi-resolution search (3 levels) of the speaker's face on the first frame of the image sequence.

The merging is done in an iterative way. In order to completely specify a merging algorithm three notions have to be defined:

The merging order: it defines the order in which the links are processed. In the case of a segmentation algorithm the merging order is defined by a similarity measure between two regions, and is closely related to the notion of objects.

The merging criterion: each time a link is processed, the merging criterion decides if the merging has actually to be done or not. In the case of a segmentation algorithm, the merging criterion always states that two regions have to be merged until a termination criterion is reached.

The region model: when two regions are merged, the model defines how to represent the union.

Fig. 4: GLR face detection (affine transform) on 3 intermediate frames of a QCIF videophone sequence.

All the steps in the face detection process rely on this general merging algorithm. The main differences are the merging order and criteria used in each step.

The proposed technique [5] tries to avoid working at pixel level and, as first step, segments the image into homogeneous regions applying the merging algorithm described in the previous section. Color information is introduced in order to obtain more accurate contours. The region model used for each region is the median of each (y,u,v) component, computed recursively from the median of the two merged regions. The merging order is the relative squared error between region models, and the merging criterion (a termination criterion) is the final number of regions.

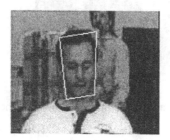

Fig. 5: GLR face detection (perspective transform) on 3 intermediate frames of a QCIF videophone sequence.

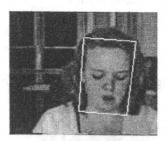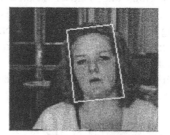

Fig. 6: GLR face detection (affine transform) on 3 intermediate frames of a QCIF videophone sequence.

Since a face contains a set of regions with chrominance homogeneity, the goal of this step is to merge some regions from the initial partition following this criterion.

The merging strategy discussed in the previous section is applied to the initial partition, using the same region model and merging order as before, but taking into account the (u,v) color components of the image. The merging is done until only one region remains, and the sequence of mergings is then analyzed.

The analysis is performed by associating the merging sequence to a binary partition tree, where the nodes represent the regions and the links connect two merging nodes.

Then a similarity measure between each node and a face class is computed. This measure is an estimation of a distance between the regions associated to the node and the face class. To calculate the distance, an auxiliary image (i_x) containing a scaled version of the region information from the original image is created. This image has the size of the tightest rectangle bounding the original region. In the areas outside the region, the data base background is introduced.

For each node in the tree, the distance between the auxiliary image (i_x) and the face class is estimated and the node with minimum distance is selected

The initial estimate of the face may lack of some regions that form the face. The use of a merging process based on a chrominance criterion allows the simplification of the face segmentation process. However, it does not ensure that the optimum region (in the sense of the likelihood) is present as a node in the Binary Tree. Nevertheless, once the core components have been detected, a refinement step can be applied to completely extract the face information, without largely increase the computational load.

This refinement is based on the same merging algorithm as before, but the process is constrained to merge regions to the core components of the face. The merging order is given now by the estimated distance between the union of two neighboring regions and the face class.

The face partition is not directly used for tracking purposes since its regions do not fulfill any fixed motion or spatial homogeneity. Instead, a second partition level is defined by re-segmenting the face partition. The re-segmentation yields a second partition whose objective is to guarantee the color homogeneity of each region (texture partition) while preserving the contours present in the face partition.

  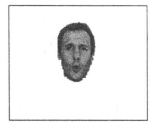

Fig. 7: Original images, bright face components, bright and dark face components and the final segmented faces.

The texture partition of the previous image is projected into the current frame to obtain the texture partition at the current image. The projection of the texture partition accommodates the previous partition to the information in the current image. An estimation of the region position in the current image is obtained by motion compensation of the previous texture partition. Compensated markers are fit into a finer partition to validate them. In a first step, compensated markers are reduced to the set of fine regions that are totally covered by them. Finer regions that are partially covered by more than one compensated marker are assigned to the uncertainty area. This step is purely geometrical and it yields the main connected components of each projected marker. Once the main components of every compensated region have been computed, neighboring regions from the fine partition can be added to them. This second step takes into account geometrical as well as color information and yields the core components of the face region. The final face partition is created by applying the refinement step based on the distance to the face space to these core components.

The face segmentation and tracking technique developed within this project successfully performs in a large set of sequences. Therefore, it can be used as a generic technique for applications that require the extraction of faces from sequences with human presence. Nevertheless, it has to be noticed that it relies on the quality of the initial segmentation. That is, since the final face partition is built up by means of a merging process starting from a fine partition, regions in this initial partition have to correctly represent the face boundaries. Some examples of the achieved results are shown in Fig. 7 and 8.

Fig. 8: Examples of the achievable results in facial region segmentation.

4 The Facial Feature Extraction Process

Facial feature extraction is defined as the process of locating a number of specific points or contours in a given facial image (like mouth corners or mouth outline) or to align a face model to the image (i.e., extract the face model parameters). In both cases, a set of two- or three-dimensional point coordinates are usually the output from the facial feature extraction. Sometimes, a set of deformations to a face model is the output, but since it is always possible to express those as a set of points coordinates, we lose no generality by this definition. When discussing facial feature extraction, it is assumed that a face is present in the image, and that its approximate location is known, i.e., it is preceded by a face detection process.

There is no clear definition on what a correct output is. A widely used quality measure of facial feature extraction is the average error in relation to a manual feature extraction process. Naturally, this is a quite unpleasant quality measure to compute, since it involves manually do all the work of the algorithm.

Another measure to use is how well the extracted face fits into a face space. The concept of a face space is also used for face detection and facial texture coding. In short, it is a low-dimensional subspace of the N-dimensional image space. Each image of the size pixels, where , is regarded as a vector, and all images of a face is assumed to belong to the M-dimensional face space. Usually the set of all face images is modelled as a M-dimensional Gaussian distribution, but this is misleading since the face set is obviously non-convex. However, there is a non-linear operation called geometrical normalization that transforms the face set to a presumably convex set.

The geometrical normalization is simply the process of aligning a wireframe face model to an image, capture the texture onto the model and reshape the model into a standard shape, e.g., the average human face shape. The resulting texture is called a normalized facial texture or a shape-free face image.

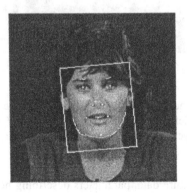

Fig. 9: Detected face and extracted facial features using a deformable template using edges, template matching and an iris-detecting function as attractors.

The geometrical normalization is dependent on the face model used as well as the standard shape, but also the quality of the alignment of the model to the image. Given the model and the standard shape, the optimal alignment of the model could be defined as the one resulting in the normalized facial texture that best fits in the normalized face set.

Typically, a face model consists of a quite large number (K) of vertices, and to find the optimal deformation of the model is a search in a 2K-dimensional space (since each vertex has 2 coordinates in the image). This search can be done with a stochastic search algorithm like simulated annealing. Another method is an optimization procedure where a manual alignment is refined to an optimal alignment.

The drawback with such global deformation algorithms is their high computational complexity due to a) a high dimensionality of the search space b)the computational complexity of projecting a remapped face image on the face space.

To reduce the computation time we can avoid projecting the entire face image onto the face space; important regions like eyes and mouth could be enough. We will then need a way to connect the features to project, so that only combinations possible to find in a human face are computed. For example, we would like the eyes to above the mouth, at approximately the same y-coordinate etc. A tractable way to do this is to connect selected features in the face with a deformable, face-shaped template. In [6] methods for such templates and computation of their deformations are be discussed. Also, a supporting algorithm for the robust detection of irises [7] is described, which has been used to improve the performance of the deformable templates leading to the quality shown in Fig. 9.

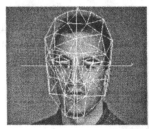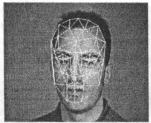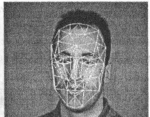

Fig. 10: The face-mask Candide adapted to the feature data. The allowed deformations were rotation around the z-axis (left), scaling (center) and translation (right). The distance between the eyes and the distances eyes-nose and nose-mouth were also allowed to change.

From the extracted feature data, parameters describing how to adapt a face model [8] to the face image is computed. Only a subset of the parameter space is used; the output should be possible to express using a set of "allowed deformations", thus reducing the influence from noise in the extraction process.

The goal is to provide an automatic segmentation of a human face and therefore to obtain a set of 3D facial features exploiting the CANDIDE model[4] [9]. The method consists in estimating 3D rigid and non-rigid parameters that correspond to the best matching with the 2D speaker face in the input image. The rigid parameters are limited to 3 global translations and 3 global rotations whereas the non-rigid parameters correspond to different weights, which control the principal eigen-shapes (we recall that the eigen-shapes describe non-rigid deformations on the 3D CANDIDE model). Some results of the projection of the 3D CANDIDE model on the image plane are shown in Fig. 10.

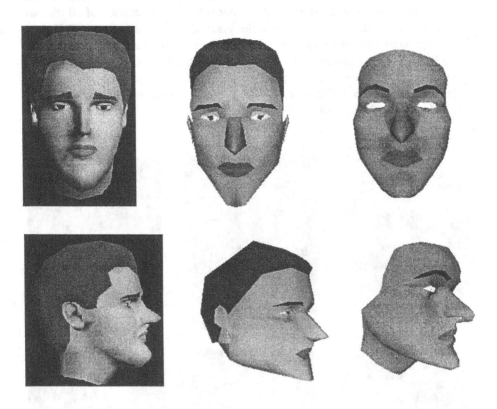

Fig. 11: (Left) Front and side view of "Cyrano"; calibration of the model "Mike" (center) and of the model "Oscar" (right) on the feature points extracted from "Cyrano". The version of the model "Oscar" employed in this calibration was still preliminary and still incomplete.

---

[4] Feature extraction/tracking tool developed at LiU (S), partner of the VIDAS project.

5 The Facial Synthesis Process

MPEG-4 defines a set of parameters for the calibration of a synthetic face, called FDP (Facial Definition Parameters), responsible of defining the appearing of the face.

These parameters can be used either to modify (though with various levels of fidelity) the geometry and texture of a face model already available at the decoder, or to encode the information necessary to transmit a complete model together with the criteria which must be applied to animate it. FDP are typically employed one time only when a new session is started while Face Animation Parameters (FAP) will act on the model to perform facial expressions. For a detailed description of all the parameters so far introduced, please refer to the Visual CD [10] and Systems CD [11].

Every proprietary model available at any decoder must be in a neutral position and all the FDP used for calibration are referred to a neutral face. The calibration of the model is achieved through a few iterations that reshape the 3D mesh geometry in dependence on the decoded calibration FDP, preserving in the meantime the smoothness and somatic characteristics of the model surface. A few examples is shown in Fig. 11-12.

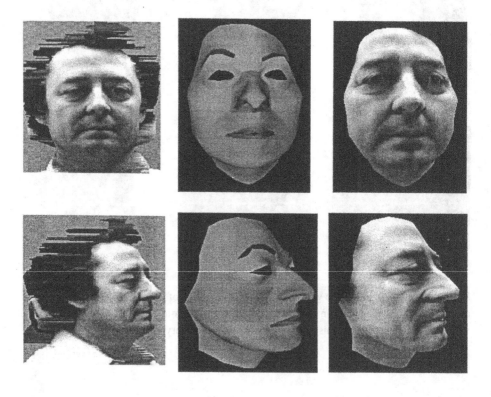

Fig. 12: (Left) Frontal and side views of the texture calibration target "Claude"; (right) model "Oscar" reshaped with feature points and texture of "Claude".

These calibration points are very few (around 80) with respect to the global number of vertices on the wire-frame which, depending on its complexity, can be as numerous as 1000 or more. In the following we report some results obtained using the data available in the TDS of the FBA "ad hoc" group of MPEG-4. The proposed algorithm has been employed to animate different models, like "Mike", "Oscar"[5] [12] or "Miraface"[6] [13]. After having calibrated the model geometry, also the texture information and the texture co-ordinates for each feature point can be mapped on the model surface. Model animation is achieved by supplying corresponding FAP information derived from the analysis of natural sequences by means of the algorithms described in the previous section. In Fig. 13 an example of the achieved results is reported.

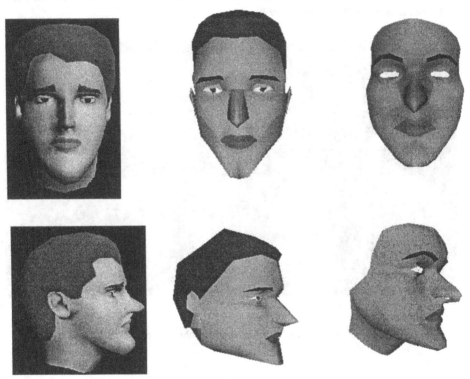

Fig. 12: (Left) Front and side view of "Cyrano"; calibration of the model "Mike" (center) and of the model "Oscar" (right) on the feature points extracted from "Cyrano". The version of the model "Oscar" employed in this calibration was still preliminary and still incomplete.

---

[5] The "Mike" and "Oscar" models have been developed at DIST (I), coordinator of the VIDAS project.

5. Conclusions

The technologies developed by the VIDAS project, as described in short in the previous sections, allow the effective representation of human faces by means of synthetic 3D models, calibrated and animated through a very limited set of MPEG-4 parameters. Besides straightforward application in very low bitrate videophone, as explicitly addressed by VIDAS, a variety of exploitations are foreseen in virtual/natural studio composition, computer gaming, multimedia title production and advanced man-machine interfaces.

Live demonstration has been given at IST'98 exhibition in Vienna, November 30 – December 2, 1998 and at the Conference for the launch of the 5th Framework Programme, Essen, 25-26 February, 1999.

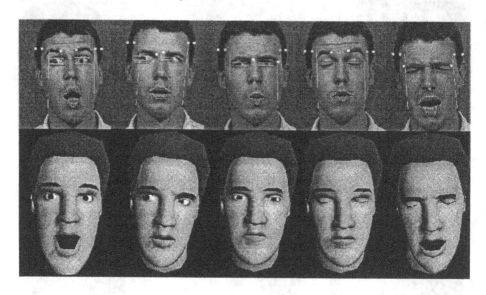

Fig. 13: Example of synthesis driven by analysis, obtained on the "Miraface" model.

References

1. Turk, M., Pentland, A., Eigenfaces for recognition, J. of Cognitive Science, Vol. 3, n. 1, (1991) 1-24
2. Moghaddam, B., Pentland, A., Maximum Likelihood detection of faces and hands, in ICCV95, (1995) 786-793

---

6 The "Miraface" model has been developed at the University of Geneve (CH) and EPFL (CH), partners of the VIDAS project.

3. Murase, H., Nayar,, S., Visual learning and recognition of 3D objects from appearance, Int. J. Computer Vision, Vol. 14, (1995) 5-24

4. Lanitis, ATaylor, C.J, T.F. Cootes, An unified approach to coding and interpreting face images, in ICCV95, Boston, (1995) 368-373

5. Salembier, P., Garrido, L., Binary partition tree as an efficient representation for filtering, segmentation and information retrieval, Proc. Int. Conf. on Image Processing, (1998)

6. Ahlberg, J., Escher, M., Li, H., Pardàs, M., Ström, J., Facial Feature Tracking Reference Model", VIDAS deliverable d35 (1998)

7. Daugman, J., High confidence visual recognition of persons by a test of statistical independence, IEEE Trans. on Pattern Analysis and Machine Intelligence, Vol. 15, n. 11, (1993) 1148 -1161

8. Nordgren, A., J., Scott, Model-Based Facial Feature Extraction Tech. report LiTH-ISY-EX-1926 (M.Sc Thesis), Dept. of Electrical Engineering, Linköping University, Sweden, (1998)

9. Rydfalk, M., CANDIDE, a parameterized face, Tech. report LiTH-ISY-I-0866, Dept. of Electrical Engineering, Linköping University, Sweden, (1987)

10. MPEG Video, "Text for CD 14496-2 Video", ISO/IEC JTC1/SC29/WG11/N1902

11. MPEG Video and SNHC, "Study of CD 14496-2 (Visual)", ISO/IEC JTC1/SC29/WG11/N1901

12. Ambrosini, L., Costa, M., Lavagetto, F., Pockaj, R., 3D Head Model Calibration based on MPEG-4 Parameters, IEEE 6th Int. Workshop on Intelligent Signal Proc. and Comm. Systems ISPACS-98 (1998) 626-630

13. Kalra, P., Mangili, A., Magnenat Thalmann, N., Thalmann, D., Simulation of Facial Muscle Actions Based on Rational Free Form Deformations" Proc. Eurographics (1992) 59-69

Face Location and Recognition for Video Indexing in the Hypermedia Project

Luis Torres[1], Ferran Marqués[1], Luis Lorente[1],
Verónica Vilaplana[2]

[1] Department of Signal Theory and Communications
Polytechnic University of Catalonia
08034 Barcelona, Spain
{luis,ferran,alorente@gps.tsc.upc.es}

[2]Departamento de Computación
Facultad de Ciencias Exactas y Naturales
Universidad de Buenos Aires, Argentina
veronica@dc.uba.ar

Abstract. There is an increasing interest to specify standardized descriptions of various types of multimedia information. This description will be associated with the content itself, to allow fast and efficient searching for material that is of interest to the user. This effort is being conducted within the activities of the new standard MPEG-7. It is in this context that Face Detection and Recognition acquire a renovated interest and there is a need to develop new tools that may help the user that browse a data base or a video sequence to find specific persons. The objective of this paper is to provide an updated information of the related activities done in the Hypermedia ACTS European project.

1 Introduction

Face recognition has been object of much interest in the last years [3] [4]. It has many applications in a variety of fields such as identification for law enforcement, authentication for banking and security system access, and personal identification among others. In addition to all these applications, there is an increasing interest to specify standardized descriptions of various types of multimedia information. This description will be associated with the content itself, to allow fast and efficient searching for material that is of interest to the user. This effort is being conducted within the activities of the new standard MPEG-7 (Multimedia Content Description Interface) [5]. It is in this context that Face Recognition acquires a renovated interest and there is a need to develop new tools that may help the user that browse a data base to answer the following type of query: Is there any face in this video sequence that matches that of Marlon Brando?

This work has been partially supported by the Hypermedia ACTS project and by grant TIC98-0422 of the Spanish Government

The automatic answer to this question is at this time very difficult, and it needs, at least, three stages: segmentation of the sequence in different objects, location of objects that correspond to human faces and recognition of the face. It has to be emphasized that almost all efforts in face recognition, have been devoted to recognize still images. A very few works have presented results on video sequences [6]. We are developing a face image analysis system that detects, tracks and recognizes a face in a video sequence. The main objective is to provide a tool to be used in the Hypermedia project to help video indexing activities. In the MPEG-7 standardization activities effort, the accepted test sequences are in MPEG-1 format what poses additional problems.

There is a need then, to develop efficient face detection and recognition schemes which may take into account the CIF format and the low quality present in MPEG-1 sequences.

We present in the following some preliminary results obtained in face detection and recognition of video sequences. We will present first the basic technical approach for face detection, segmentation and tracking. Then the face recognition technique will be introduced. Results will be presented for different video sequences. Please notice that the complete system has not been yet integrated. It will be at the end of the Hypermedia project.

The detection and tracking system has been developed by the Polytechnic University of Catalonia (UPC) in the VIDAS ACTS project. Part of the recognition system is UPC background information which has been improved and adapted to the requirements of the Hypermedia project.

2 Detection, segmentation and tracking of human faces

One of the basic approaches in face detection is that of view based Eigenspaces [10]. This approach assumes that the set of all possible face patterns is a low dimensional linear subspace within the high dimensional space of all possible image patterns. An image pattern is classified as a face if its distance from the face subspace is below a certain threshold. With this technique, the position of a face in an image can be detected.

The previous face detection method has been extended to directly deal with regions [11]. This way, the face is not only detected but correctly segmented. The proposed technique tries to avoid working at pixel level and, as first step, segments the image into homogeneous regions applying a merging algorithm. Color information is introduced in order to obtain more accurate contours. The region model used for each region is the median of each (y,u,v) component, computed recursively from the median of the two merged regions. The merging order is the relative squared error between region models, and the merging criterion (a termination criterion) is the final number of regions.

Since a face contains a set of regions with chrominance homogeneity, regions from the initial partition are merged following this criterion. The previous merging strategy is applied to the initial partition, using the same region model and merging order as before, but taking into account the (u,v) color components of the image. The merging is done until only one region remains, and the sequence of mergings is then analyzed.

The analysis associates the merging sequence to a binary partition tree, where the nodes represent the regions and the links connect two merging nodes. Then a similarity measure between each node and a face class Ω is computed. This measure is an estimation of a distance between the regions associated to the node and the face class. For each node in the tree, the distance between each node and the face class is estimated and the node with minimum distance is selected. To be able to detect faces with sizes different from the size of the faces in the data base, this distance should be minimized with respect to a geometrical transformation (ω) applied to the connected component.

The distance is related to the likelihood of an image of being a face. The class membership of the transformed component (x_ω) is modeled as a unimodal Gaussian density:

$$P(x_w / \Omega) = \frac{\exp\left[-1/2(x_w - \overline{x})^T \Sigma^{-1}(x_w - \overline{x})\right]}{(2\pi)^{N/2}|\Sigma|^{1/2}} \qquad (1)$$

where the mean and the covariance matrix are estimated using a training data set.

The Mahalanobis distance is used as a sufficient statistic for characterizing this likelihood:

$$d(x_w / \Omega) = \sum_{i=1}^{N} \frac{y_i^2}{\lambda_i} = \sum_{i=1}^{M} \frac{y_i^2}{\lambda_i} + \sum_{i=M+1}^{N} \frac{y_i^2}{\lambda_i} \qquad (2)$$

A computationally tractable estimate of this distance, based on the M first principal components of the covariance matrix, is

$$\hat{d}(x_w / \Omega) = \sum_{i=1}^{M} \frac{y_i^2}{\lambda_i} + \frac{1}{\rho} \varepsilon^2 (x_w / \Omega) \qquad (3)$$

The initial estimate of the face may lack of some regions that form the face. The use of a merging process based on a chrominance criterion allows the simplification of the face segmentation process. However, it does not ensure that the optimum region (in the sense of the likelihood) is present as a node in the Binary Tree. Nevertheless, once the core components have been detected, a refinement step can be applied to completely extract the face information, without largely increase the computational load.

This refinement is based on the same merging algorithm as before, but the process is constrained to merge regions to the core components of the face. The merging order is given now by the estimated distance between the union of two neighboring regions and the face class.

The face partition is not directly used for tracking purposes since its regions do not fulfill any fixed motion or spatial homogeneity. Instead, a second partition level is defined by re-segmenting the face partition. The re-segmentation yields a second partition whose objective is to guarantee the color homogeneity of each region (*texture partition*) while preserving the contours present in the face partition [12].

The texture partition of the previous image is projected into the current frame to obtain the texture partition at the current image. The projection of the texture partition accommodates the previous partition to the information in the current image. The motion between the previous and current images is estimated and the previous texture partition is motion compensated. Compensated regions are used as markers giving an estimate of the region positions in the current image.

Given that motion compensated markers may be erroneous, they are accommodated to the boundaries of the current image. Such boundaries are obtained from the so-called *fine partition*. Compensated markers are fit into the fine partition to validate them. In a first step, compensated markers are reduced to the set of fine regions that are totally covered by them. Fine regions that are partially covered by more than one compensated marker are assigned to the uncertainty area. Note that this first step is purely geometrical and it yields the main connected components of each projected marker. Once the main components of every compensated region have been computed, neighboring regions from the fine partition can be added to them. This second step takes into account geometrical as well as color information and yields the core components of the face region. The final face partition is created by applying the refinement step on these core components.

Some examples of the performance of this technique are presented in the results sections.

3   General face recognition system

Our system for face recognition is based on the representation of facial images using eigenfaces [1] [2]. In the eigenface representation, every training image is considered a vector of pixel gray values. The full image space is not an optimal space for face description, because all the face images are very similar, and therefore all the face vectors are located in a very narrow cluster in the image space. The goal of the eigenface representation is to find the basis that best represent the image faces. The solution is to apply a PCA analysis over the training faces. The main idea is to obtain a set of orthogonal vectors that optimally represent the distribution of the data in the RMS sense. Using these vectors, a good representation of the faces may be obtained.

Any training image can be obtained as a linear combination from the eigenvectors. These eigenvectors are usually referred to as eigenfaces because they look like faces. Furthermore, good representations of the face images can be obtained using only a low number of eigenfaces. Another feature of the eigenfaces is that they form a orthonormal basis, so it is very simple to compute the components of any face in the eigenface space. A inner product is simply needed. Once the corresponding eigenfaces are computed, they are used to represent the test and training faces to be identified. The test face (the one to be recognized) is matched to the training face whose eigen representation is the most similar.

In order to minimize the differences due to changes in size, expression and orientation a morphing technique is applied first to every image. The morphing process gives an image face in which the facial feature points have been moved to standard predefined positions. This is equivalent to a normalization of the shape of the faces. These standard positions correspond to a frontal view with neutral expression and a given fixed size. The morphing technique is based on texture mapping, a widely known technique in computer graphics [8]. The image of a face is split into triangular polygons (based on the Candide model) whose vertices are characteristic facial points. The texture of each original triangle is mapped to the triangle defined by the standard points. The points used in this synthesis stage are obtained from the Candide model [9] that has been previously matched to the face. Although some shape information is lost during this morphing stage, the recognition system greatly improves because the resulting images are normalized in size, expression, and above all in orientation. The morphing is applied to all the faces to be identified, independently of their degree of variation in expression or orientation. The morphing process also eliminates the image background and the hair. When a face includes significant portions of the hair, the available featural information can often give good short term recognition rsults. Howewer the hair is not invariant over periods of months during which a practical system must maintain useful recognition performance. Finally, the contrast of the images is normalized, adjusting the pixel values in order to occupy the range [0, 255].

To improve the recognition stage, in addition to the eigenfaces, we have also incorporated to the overall scheme some other eigenfeatures. As in [7], we have extended the eigenface concept to certain parts of the face: both eyes (left and right eigeneyes), the nose (eigennoses) and the mouth (eigenmouth) (Figure 1). We have also introduced the concept of eigensides (left and right), which are eigenfaces generated from the left and right sides of the face. This way, it is possible to avoid certain limitations of the eigenfaces, mainly when some parts of the faces are occluded, or when some conditions such as lateral lighting or facial expression change along the face. The key issue is to take advantage of the fact that the distortions caused by these difficult conditions affect more to some parts of the face than others.

In the recognition stage, the corresponding overall eigenfaces, right and left eigensides, right and left eigeneyes, eigennoses and eigenmouths are found for the training and test faces. The normalized Mahalanobis distance is applied between every eigenfeature of the test and training faces. The global distance between the test and the training image is the weighted sum of the different distances in such a way that the contribution of each eigenfeature to the recognition stage is the same. Weightings factors may be altered to give more importance to certain features than others. It is notable that the best results are obtained eliminating the contribution of the eigenfaces to the total distance and increasing the contribution of the eigensides. The system can also use some thresholds (of reconstruction errors) to decide if a part

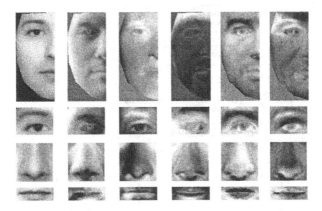

Figure 1. **Mean and first eigenfeatures of some parts of the face (left eigensides, left eigeneyes, eigennoses and eigenmouths).**

of the face is useful for the recognition. This should be useful in the cases in which the faces are partially hidden by an obstacle. Figure 2 shows the general face recognition system. Above training stage. Below test stage.

4   Face recognition of video sequences

One of the main problems in the adaptation of the system to recognize video sequences is the location of the facial points. The system needs the information of the location of the 44 facial points for the normalization stage. This information is used in a morphing proces that normalize face size variations and also can normalize succesfully orientation variations. An alternative facial model that only needs four facial points locations has been developed. However, the performance of the system decreases notably under changes in orientation conditions. Algorithms to improve these drawbacks are being studied. Two main approaches are being followed: First, with a bigger training set of images, in which there is more than one image per person in several different conditions. Secondly is the automatic location of the points of the model. This automatic location is limited by the size and quality of the MPEG-7 test sequences used until now. In addition, the introduction of color information in the recognition stage is being studied.

The original face recognition system uses a facial model with 44 points and 78 polygons (triangles), based on the Candide model. The location of the facial points was done manually. The use of the face recognition system with MPEG-1 sequences implies that the system must be able to work with small images. In addition, the final face recognition system must be fully automatic or semi-automatic, a difficult task with small face images with a significant noise level. For all these reasons we have developed a simplified model that only needs to know the location of four main facial points (center of both eyes, nose and mouth). The automatic location of these points is an affordable task even with small images. At the present stage of the development the points are located manually. An automatic location algorithm will

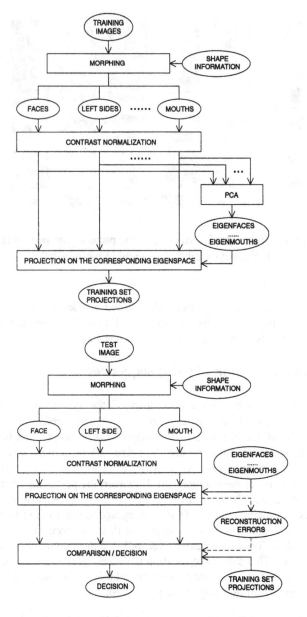

Figure 2. **General eigen approach for face recognition: Above: training stage; below: test stage**

be developed with the eigenfeature technology. The simplified model is built from the four main facial points. Thirteen additional facial points more are automatically estimated, so the model has 17 points. Figure 3 shows the simplified model.

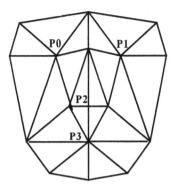

Figure 3. **The simplified face model.**

The results of the morphing process (included in the normalization stage) with the simplified model are good with small orientation variations (**Figure 4**). The aim is to synthethise a frontal view of the face in which all the points have been moved to a standard set of positions. With big rotations the normalized face is distorted and does not seem a frontal view. These bad results are due to the low number of points of the model.

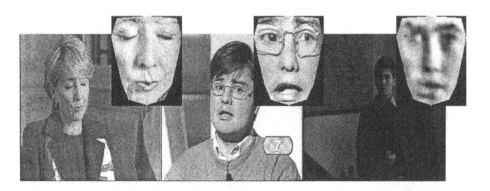

Figure 4. **Examples of normalization using the simplified model. With small face images the normalized images have bad quality**

5   Face detection results

Some examples of the performance of the face detection technique are presented here. The first example (Figure 5) shows the segmentation of the face in the first frame of the *Carphone* sequence. The first image is the original first frame, and the second and third images are the core component extracted from the Binary Partition Tree and the final face component, respectively. The second example (Figure 6) shows the tracking of the face in the *Foreman* sequence. Some examples using the MPEG-7 test sequences, are also shown (Figure 7).

Figure 5. **Detection and segmentation of the first frame in the *Carphone*
sequence**

Figure 6. **Tracking of the face in the *Foreman* sequence**

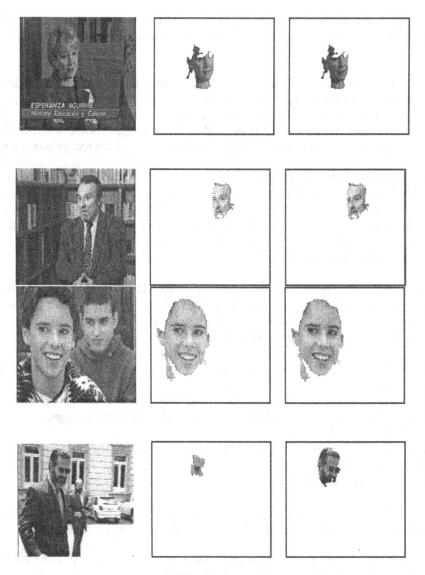

Figure 7. Detection and segmentation of the *MPEG-7* test sequences

6   Face recognition results

Tests using the four point model have been conducted with the MPEG-7 test sequences. In particular the sequences news12, news11, music, movie, drama and contest have been used. The images have been separated in two sets: the training set and the test set. The training images are the images known by the system, so the person ideally must recognize all the images of every face that has an image in the training set. The test set are other images of people represented in the training set. The training and test image of the persons have been always taken from differents shots of the sequences, although in a few cases some conditions are similar in both shots. Please notice that only a frontal view of the person has been used in the training set.

Several combinations of normalization operators have been tested. The standard normalization, the standard normalization plus the local contrast normalization and the standard normalization plus the mean and variance normalization have produced the best results. The training set contains 59 different images corresponding to 59 different persons and the test set 29. Note that the difficulty of the recognition is due to the number of training images. Results are provided in Table 1. It is interesting to comment that particular applications may require less number of training images, what will imply an improvement in the recognition system. One of the possible applications considers that the user is given a video sequence and an actor is detected and recognized. Then, for indexing purposes, it is required to find out where the same actor appears again in the same video sequence. In this case, the number of training images decreases a lot, what improves the recognition system.

It seems that every eigenfeature gives the best results with a different normalization process. If these results are consistent with larger test sets a different normalization process for every feature of the face might be done. The recognition results are far from the results obtained, with controlled databases. This is due to several reasons:

• The rotation and lightning conditions of the training images are not homogeneus nor controlled.
• The size of many images is too small and there is noise due to the MPEG compression (Figure 7). This problem is more critical in the training images.
• The high rotation angles
• The variations of rotation and lightning conditions come together in many images of the test and training set
• The presence of obstacles

The weights assigned for the partial distances of every feature in the test are all one. The fine tuning of these weights can lead to a slight improvement.

Although the results are still in a preliminary stage, they show that the taken approach will be helpful for the video indexing application.

Figure 8 provides some examples of correct and incorrect matches. The left incorrect match is due to two of the problems commented above. The test image is too small, while the training image has lateral illumination (like the test one) that fools the system. These kind of errors can be avoided if the conditions of the training set are controlled.

EIGENFEATURE	STANDARD NORM.	+ LOCAL CONT. NORM.	+ MEAN AND VAR. NORM.
GLOBAL	19/25 (76.00%)	19/25 (76.00%)	19/25 (76.00%)
EIGENFACE	18/25 (72.00%)	18/25 (72.00%)	18/25 (72.00%)
LEFT EIGENSIDE	14/25 (56.00%)	16/25 (64.00%)	15/25 (60.00%)
RIGHT EIGENSIDE	15/25 (60.00%)	15/25 (60.00%)	15/25 (60.00%)
LEFT EYE	11/25 (44.00%)	11/25 (44.00%)	9/25 (36.00%)
RIGHT EYE	14/25 (56.00%)	10/25 (40.00%)	11/25 (44.00%)
NOSE	13/25 (52.00%)	14/25 (56.00%)	11/25 (44.00%)
MOUTH	4/25 (16.00%)	6/25 (24.00%)	5/25 (20.00%)

Table 1. **Results of the face recognition system with training (59 images) and test (25 images) sets taken from the MPEG-7 test sequences and three types of normalization. Standard normalization: morphing with the simplified model + contrast (not local contrast) norm. The other two types are the combination of the standard normalization with the local contrast normalization and with the mean and variance normalization.**

Figure 8. **Examples of correct (superior row) and incorrect (inferior row) matches. For every couple of images, the left image belongs to the test set and the right one to the training set**

7   Conclusions

Preliminary results have been presented concerning a face detection and recognition scheme. The two schemes show quite acceptable performance for "normal" TV sequences although it is clear that needs some improvements. The schemes have not been integrated yet. The second phase to be developed in the Hypermedia project is the integration and improvement of the overall detection-recognition scheme. In particular, the following section provides some insight on further work to be carried on.

8 Further research

The main future research work is:

• **Adaptation to the case of coded images**: The fact that the sequences to be analyzed in the project have been previously coded using the MPEG1 standard introduces specific types of problems in the segmentation and tracking technique of the location stage of the overall face recognition system. Concretely, the face refinement step has been seen to present problems when dealing with MPEG-1decoded images. The way to solve these specific problems will be analyzed.

• **Selection of the most suitable face in a sequence.** The location algorithm algorithm is able to detect and track a (some) face(s) in a sequence but, for the given application, the relevant result is not only to detect and track the face(s) but to give to the face recognition step, the information about the frame that contains the face that best represents a given person. This way, a new method will be developed that, relying on the analysis of the complete series of faces detected in a sequences for a given character, will select the most suitable face for its posterior recognition (test stage).

• **Location of the points of the face model.** At its present stage, the points of the facial model are found manually. An automatic method based in the eigen-approach will be developed to find such points.

• **To study the assignment of a different weight for every eigenfeature.** The fine tuning of each weight can lead to a slight improvement of the overall recognition system.

• **Introduction of the color information in the recognition stage.** The actual face recognition system does not use the face color information. Studies will continue to find out the importance of the color information in the overall system.

• **Study and design of the best set of images for the training sequence.** As the test sequence may contain several views of the same person, the training stage should contain a preselected set of images that best fit the recognition scheme. To that objective, an algorithm that will select the best set of training images for the given application will be designed.

• **Test of the overall location and face recognition system.** Evaluation of the whole system will be made using the MPEG-7 test sequences.

References

[1] L. Lorente, L. Torres, "A global eigen approach for face recognition", International Workshop on Very Low Bit-rate Video Coding, Urbana, Illinois, October 8-9, 1998.

[2] M. A. Turk, A. P. Pentland, "Face recognition using eigenfaces", Proceedings of the IEEE Computer Society Conf. on Computer Vision and Patter Recognition, pp. 586-591, Maui, Hawaii 1991.

[3] R. Chellappa, C. L. Wilson, S. Sirohey, Human and machine recognition of faces: a survey, Proceedings of the IEEE, Volume 83, No. 5, pp. 705-740, May 1995.

[4] J. Zhang, Y. Yan, M. Lades, "Face recognition: eigenface, elastic matching, and neural nets", Proceedings of the IEEE, Vol. 85, No. 9, pp. 1423-1435, September 1997.

[5] ISO/IEC JTC1/SC29/WG11. MPEG Requirements Group. "MPEG-7: Context and Objectives", Doc. ISO/MPEG N2460, October 1998 / Atlantic City, USA.

[6] S. McKenna, S. Gong, Y. Raja, "Face recognition in dynamic scenes", British machine vison conference, 1997.

[7] A. Pentland, B. Moghaddam, T. Starner, "View-based and modular eigenspaces for face recognition", MIT Media Laboratory Perceptual Computing Section, Technical Report 245, 1994.

[8] D. Rowland, D. Perret, D. Burt, K. Lee and S. Akamatsu, "Transforming facial images in 2 and 3-D", Imagina 97 Conferences - Actes / Proceedings, Feb. 1997, pp. 159-175.

[9] The Candide software package", Image Coding Group, Linköping University, 1994.

[10] B. Moghaddam and A. Pentland, "Probabilistic Visual Learning for Object Representation", IEEE Transactions on Pattern Analysis and Machine Intelligence, Vol. 19. NO. 7, pp. 696-710, July 1997.

[11] V. Vilaplana, F. Marqués, P. Salembier, and L. Garrido, "Region-based segmentation and tracking of human faces", Proceedings of EUSIPCO'98 Conference on Signal Processing, Rodhes, Greece, September 1998.

[12] F. Marqués, J. Llach, "Tracking of generic objects for video object generation", International Conference on Image Processing, ICIP 98, October 1998, Chicago, USA.

Object Articulation Based on Local 3D Motion Estimation *

Ioannis Kompatsiaris, Dimitrios Tzovaras, and Michael G. Strintzis

Information Processing Laboratory, Electrical and Computer Engineering
Department, Aristotle University of Thessaloniki, Thessaloniki 54006, Greece,
ikom@dion.ee.auth.gr

Abstract. This paper describes a 3D model-based unsupervised procedure for the segmentation of multiview image sequences using multiple
sources of information. Using multiview information a 3D model representation of the scene is constructed. The articulation procedure is based
on the homogeneity of parameters, such as rigid 3D motion, color and
depth, estimated for each sub-object, which consists of a number of interconnected triangles of the 3D model. The rigid 3D motion of each
sub-object for subsequent frames is estimated using a Kalman filtering
algorithm taking into account the temporal correlation between consecutive frames. Information from all cameras is combined during the formation of the equations for the rigid 3D motion parameters. The parameter
estimation for each sub-object and the 3D model segmentation procedures are interleaved and repeated iteratively until a satisfactory object
segmentation emerges. The performance of the resulting segmentation
method is evaluated experimentally.

Keywords : *Multiview image sequences segmentation; 3D model-based
analysis; rigid 3D motion estimation.*

1   Introduction

The ability of model-based techniques to describe a scene in a structural way has
opened up new areas of applications. Very low bitrate coding, enhanced telepresence, video production, realistic computer graphics, multimedia interfaces and
databases and medical visualization are some of the applications that may benefit by exploiting the potential of model-based schemes [1], [2], [3]. One of the
major steps in model-based image analysis is the segmentation of the input 3D
model into an appropriate set of sub-objects, corresponding to semantic regions
in the 2D views (e.g. head, body, arms, e.t.c.). This is necessary, for example,
for the efficient estimation of rigid 3D motion of the segmented sub-objects.

---

* This work was supported by the European CEC Projects ACTS 092 PANORAMA,
  ACTS 057 VIDAS and the Greek Secretariat for Science and Technology Program
  YPER.

Segmentation methods for 2D images may be divided primarily into region based and boundary-based methods [4], [5]. Region-based approaches rely on the homogeneity of spatially localized features such as gray level intensity, texture, motion and other pixel statistics. Region growing and split and merge techniques also belong in the same category. On the other hand, boundary-based methods use primarily gradient information to locate object boundaries. Deformable whole boundary methods [6] rely on the gradient features of parts of an image near an object boundary. Methods for the segmentation of image sequences have been presented in, among others, [7], [8], [9], [10], [11]. In most of these methods, region growing and merging techniques are used, depending on the homogeneity of the 2D or 3D motion.

The present paper addresses a related, but considerably more difficult problem, which is the coherent simultaneous segmentation of two or more views of a scene. To this end, an unsupervised procedure for the segmentation of multiview image sequences using various sources of information, is proposed. The segmentation procedure is performed at the triangle level of a 3D model, as in [12], [13], [14], using characteristic properties of the triangle, such as rigid 3D motion, color and depth. Sub-objects consist of collections of one or more interconnected triangles of the 3D model, with similar parameters. Information from all cameras is combined to form the equations for the extraction of the rigid 3D motion parameters. Combined motion, color and depth information, extracted from multiview information is used, along with the 3D motion fields. The rigid 3D motion of each sub-object for subsequent frames is estimated using a Kalman filtering algorithm taking into account the temporal correlation between consecutive frames. The parameter estimation for each sub-object and the 3D model segmentation procedures are interleaved and repeated iteratively until a satisfactory object segmentation emerges.

The methodology used overcomes a major obstacle in multiview video analysis, caused by the difficult problem of determining and handling coherently corresponding objects in the different views. This is achieved in this paper by defining segmentation and object articulation in the 3D space, thus ensuring that all ensuing operations (for example rigid 3D motion estimation of each sub-object) remain coherent for all views of the scene.

The paper is organized as follows. In the following section, the three-camera geometry is described, and in The technique used for object articulation is examined in Section 4. In Section 5 the estimation of the segmentation parameters is described. In Section 6 experimental results are given evaluating the performance of the proposed methods. Conclusions are finally drawn in Section 7.

2 Camera Arrangement and Relation to the PANORAMA Project

The algorithm described in this paper was developed within the ACTS PANORAMA project (in fact only the local rigid 3D motion estimation was used for the purposes of the project). In this project a series of enhanced-telepresence videoconference sequences were used, in order to achieve telepresence by using multicamera setups (and auto-stereoscopic displays) and by permitting the transmission of complex scenes with gestures and motion and objects other than just heads and shoulders. The most practical of these multicamera setups uses three cameras, placed on either side and the top of the monitor [15].

The approach developed in the project will use a parametric 3-D scene description in order to model the scene (Fig. 1). This scene description is composed of model objects defined by their 3-D shape, 3-D motion and surface texture parameters. Each real object, like a person with a flexible surface or a table with a rigid surface, is represented by a model object. The parameters of the model objects will be estimated from trinocular input image sequences by means of image analysis. It is expected that the use of 3-D model objects will give a higher quality than using pixel-based methods. Also content-based manipulations will be possible using a parametric 3-D scene description. Whereas the image synthesis can be carried out in real-time on available graphics computers, image analysis must be carried out off-line in software.

All results of the present paper are derived assuming this camera geometry and are evaluated with real multiview sequences produced by precisely such an arrangement of cameras. However, the basic ideas and results of the paper may be easily extended to monoscopic, stereoscopic and arbitrary multiview systems using arbitrary arrangements and numbers of cameras.

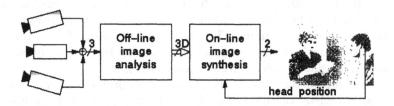

Fig. 1. Overview of the off-line image image analysis scheme.

3 Camera Model

A camera model describes the projection of 3-D points onto a camera target. The model used here is the CAHV model introduced in [16]. This model describes extrinsic camera parameters such as position and orientation and intrinsic camera parameters such as focal length and intersection between optical axis and image plane.

As mentioned in the introduction, in our multiview camera geometry, three cameras c are used : $c = left, top, right$. For each camera c the model contains the following parameters shown in Fig. 2 : a) position of the camera $\mathbf{C}_c$, b) optical axis $\mathbf{A}_c$, i.e. the viewing direction of the camera (unit vector), c) horizontal camera target vector $\mathbf{H}_c$ (x-axis of the camera target), d) vertical camera target vector $\mathbf{V}_c$ (y-axis of the camera target), radial distortion and sx,sy pixel size.

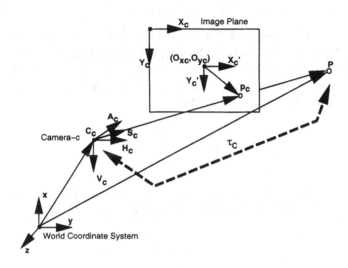

Fig. 2. The CAHV camera model.

In our camera model we shall assume that the radial distortion is compensated. The cameras setup is previously calibrated and maintained static. In this case, the projection of a 3D point $\mathbf{P}$, with coordinates relative to world coordinate system, onto the image plane (X'_c, Y'_c) is [16] :

$$X'_c = \frac{(\mathbf{P} - \mathbf{C}_c)^T \cdot \mathbf{H}_c}{(\mathbf{P} - \mathbf{C}_c)^T \cdot \mathbf{A}_c} \quad , \quad Y'_c = \frac{(\mathbf{P} - \mathbf{C}_c)^T \cdot \mathbf{V}_c}{(\mathbf{P} - \mathbf{C}_c)^T \cdot \mathbf{A}_c} \quad , \tag{1}$$

The coordinates (X'_c, Y'_c) are camera centered (image plane coordinate system) with the unit pel. The origin of the coordinate system is the center point of the camera. The coordinates of a point relative to the picture coordinate system (X_c, Y_c) is given by : $(X_c, Y_c) = (X'_c + O_{x,c}, Y'_c + O_{y,c})$, where $(O_{x,c}, O_{y,c})$ is the center of the image plane in the picture coordinate system.

Conversely, given its position (X_c, Y_c) on the camera plane, the 3D position of a point can be determined by :

$$\mathbf{P} = \mathbf{C}_c + \tau_c \cdot \mathbf{S}_c(X_c, Y_c) \, , \tag{2}$$

where $\mathbf{S}_c(X_c, Y_c)$ is the unit vector pointing from the camera to the point in the direction of the optical axis and τ_c is the distance between the 3D point and the center of camera c.

4 Object Articulation

A novel subdivision method based on characteristic descriptors of each triangle of the 3D model will be proposed for the articulation of the foreground object. The model initialization procedure [17] results in a set of interconnecting triangles in the 3D space : $\{T_k, k = 1, \ldots, K\}$, where K is the number of triangles of the 3D model. In the following, $S^{(i)}$ will denote an articulation of the 3D model at iteration i of the articulation algorithm, consisting of $\{s_l^{(i)}, l = 1, \ldots, L^{(i)}\}$ sub-objects. Each sub-object consists of $\{T_m^{(s_l^{(i)})}, m = 1, \ldots, M^{(s_l^{(i)})}\}$ triangles.

The object articulation procedure exploits the homogeneity of a set of characteristic descriptors based on known and estimated parameters, such as rigid 3D motion, color and depth, for each sub-object. The total descriptor value for each sub-object will in general be defined as :

$$p^{(s_l^{(i)})} = \sum_{j=0}^{P-1} a_j \bar{x}_j \ ,$$

where $\bar{x}$ is the value of a specific descriptor, normalized so as to lie between 0 and 1, P is the number of characteristic descriptors used and

$$\sum_{j=0}^{P} a_j = 1.$$

The choice of values for a_i depends on the weight given to each specific descriptor in each specific application. For example, if rigidly moving components must be found, the weights corresponding to the rigid 3D motion descriptors should be higher than the others.

The proposed iterative object articulation procedure is composed of the following steps :

Step 1 Set $i = 0$. Let an initial segmentation $S^{(0)} = \{s_l^{(0)}, l = 1, \ldots, L^{(0)}\}$, with $L^{(0)} = K$, $T_1^{s_i^{(0)}} = T_l$ and $M^{(s_i^{(0)})} = 1$. In this initialization step, each sub-object consists of one triangle of the 3D model. Set an initial threshold value : $th^{(0)} \ll 1$.

Step 2 Apply the segmentation parameters estimation algorithm to each sub-object $s_l^{(i)}$ in order to find $p^{(s_l^{(i)})}$ (Section 5).

Step 3 The initial object is merged into $L^{(i)}$ sub-objects i.e. $S^{(i)} = \{s_l^{(i)}, l = 1, \ldots, L^{(i)}\}$ using an iterative region merging algorithm. Two sub-objects $s_l^{(i)}, s_m^{(i)}$ will be merged if

$$\|p^{(s_l^{(i)})} - p^{(s_m^{(i)})}\| \le th^{(i)} \ .$$

Step 4 Using the histogram of $p^{(s_l^{(i)})}$ the new threshold $th^{(i+1)}$ is defined as the mean distance between two maximas of the histogram.

Step 5 If $\|th^{(i)} - th^{(i+1)}\| \le \epsilon$, where ϵ is a threshold affecting the number of sub-objects created, then stop. Else set $i = i + 1$ and go to Step 2.

5 Parameter Estimation for Each Sub-object

The subdivision criterion is based on the homogeneity of characteristic descriptors of each triangle of the 3D model. Though many such descriptors can be used for efficient segmentation, in this paper we focus on those based on the rigid 3D motion parameters, color and depth information.

5.1 Rigid 3D Motion Equation

For each sub-object, the rigid 3D motion parameters are estimated for a number of frames. In order to exploit temporal correlation between consecutive frames, a Kalman filtering approach is used. The system of equations describing the rigid 3D motion parameters is formed and is used to determine the Kalman filter for the estimation and tracking of the rigid 3D motion.

In the following, for the sake of notational simplicity, the sub-object $s_t^{(i)}$ will be simply denoted by s. This means that the procedure to be described is applied to all sub-objects at any iteration step of the object articulation algorithm. The rigid motion of each sub-object s is modeled using three rotation and three translation parameters [18] :

$$\mathbf{P}_{t+1} = \mathbf{R}^{(s)} \, \mathbf{P}_t + \mathbf{T}^{(s)} \;\; , \tag{3}$$

with $\mathbf{R}^{(s)}$ and $\mathbf{T}^{(s)}$ being of the form :

$$\mathbf{R}^{(s)} = \begin{bmatrix} 1 & -w_z^{(s)} & w_y^{(s)} \\ w_z^{(s)} & 1 & -w_x^{(s)} \\ -w_y^{(s)} & w_x^{(s)} & 1 \end{bmatrix}, \;\; \mathbf{T}^{(s)} = \begin{bmatrix} \tau_x^{(s)} \\ \tau_y^{(s)} \\ \tau_z^{(s)} \end{bmatrix} \tag{4}$$

where $\mathbf{P}_t = (x_t, y_t, z_t)$ is a 3D point on the 3D planes defined by the triangles $T_m^{(s)}$ of sub-object s. The rigid 3D motion parameters vector for sub-object s is : $\mathbf{a}^{(s)} = (w_x^{(s)}, w_y^{(s)}, w_z^{(s)}, \tau_x^{(s)}, \tau_y^{(s)}, \tau_z^{(s)})$.

At time t, each point $\mathbf{P}_t$ on s is projected to points $(X_{c,t}, Y_{c,t})$, $c = l, t, r$ on the planes of the three cameras. Using equations (1) and (3), the projected 2D motion vector, $\mathbf{d}_c(X_c, Y_c)$ is determined by

$$d_{xc}(X_{c,t}, Y_{c,t}) = X_{c,t+1} - X_{c,t} = \frac{(\mathbf{R}^{(s)} \, \mathbf{P}_t + \mathbf{T}^{(s)} - \mathbf{C}_c)^T \cdot \mathbf{H}_c}{(\mathbf{R}^{(s)} \, \mathbf{P}_t + \mathbf{T}^{(s)} - \mathbf{C}_c)^T \cdot \mathbf{A}_c} - \frac{(\mathbf{P}_t - \mathbf{C}_c)^T \cdot \mathbf{H}_c}{(\mathbf{P}_t - \mathbf{C}_c)^T \cdot \mathbf{A}_c} \;\; , \tag{5}$$

$$d_{yc}(X_{c,t}, Y_{c,t}) = Y_{c,t+1} - Y_{c,t} = \frac{(\mathbf{R}^{(s)} \, \mathbf{P}_t + \mathbf{T}^{(s)} - \mathbf{C}_c)^T \cdot \mathbf{V}_c}{(\mathbf{R}^{(s)} \, \mathbf{P}_t + \mathbf{T}^{(s)} - \mathbf{C}_c)^T \cdot \mathbf{A}_c} - \frac{(\mathbf{P}_t - \mathbf{C}_c)^T \cdot \mathbf{V}_c}{(\mathbf{P}_t - \mathbf{C}_c)^T \cdot \mathbf{A}_c} \;\; , \tag{6}$$

where $\mathbf{d}_c(X_c, Y_c) = (d_{xc}(X_{c,t}, Y_{c,t}), d_{yc}(X_{c,t}, Y_{c,t}))$.

Using the initial 2D motion vectors, estimated by applying a block matching algorithm to the images corresponding to the left, top and right cameras and also using equations (5) and (6), a linear system of equations for the rigid motion parameter vector $\mathbf{a}^{(s)}$ for sub-object s, between time t and $t+1$ is formed :

$$\mathbf{b}^{(s)} = \mathbf{D}^{(s)} \, \mathbf{a}^{(s)} \; . \tag{7}$$

Equation (7) define a system of $2 \times 3 \times L$ equations with six unknowns, where L is the number of 3D points contained in s, since for each 3D point $\mathbf{P}_t$, two equations are formed for the X and Y coordinates for each one of the three cameras. This system combines the rigid 3D motion parameters, with the camera parameters and the points of the 3D model, taking as initial values the 2D motion, using available information from *all* cameras simultaneously.

Whenever the value of L falls below a predefined threshold, neighboring triangles are also used, in order to enhance the stability and efficiency of the rigid 3D motion estimation procedure. In this case, the additional 3D points contained in triangles neighboring those of s, i.e. triangles sharing at least two common nodes with any triangle of s, are used in (7). This is normally necessary only in the initial step of the articulation procedure where each sub-object consists of only one triangle.

5.2 3D Motion Tracking Using Kalman Filtering

In order to exploit the temporal correlation between consecutive frames, a Kalman filter [19], [20] is applied for the calculation of the 3D rigid motion parameters at every time instant. In this way, the computationally complicated solution of (7) is needed only for the first of a sequence of F frames. In subsequent frames the estimation of the motion parameters is based on the initial frame estimation improved by additional observations as additional frames arrive. Omitting, for the sake of further notational simplification, the explicit dependence of the motion parameters to the sub-object $s_l^{(i)}$, thus writing $\mathbf{a}_t$, $\mathbf{b}_t$, $\mathbf{C}_t$ instead of $\mathbf{a}_t^{(s_l^{(i)})}$, $\mathbf{b}_t^{(s_l^{(i)})}$, $\mathbf{C}_t^{(s_l^{(i)})}$, the dynamics of the system are described as follows:

$$\mathbf{a}_{t+1} = \mathbf{a}_t + w \cdot \mathbf{e}_{t+1} \tag{8}$$

$$\mathbf{b}_{t+1} = \mathbf{D}_{t+1} \, \mathbf{a}_{t+1} + \mathbf{v}_{t+1} \; , \tag{9}$$

where $\mathbf{a}$ is the rigid 3D motion vector of each sub-object and $\mathbf{e}_t$ is a unit-variance white random sequence. The term $w \cdot \mathbf{e}_{t+1}$ describes the difference of consecutive frames and a high value of w implies small correlation between consecutive frames and can be used to describe fast-changing scenes, whereas a low value of w may be used when the motion is relatively slow and the temporal correlation is high. The term $\mathbf{v}_{t+1}$ represents the random error of the formation of the system (7), and is modeled as white zero-mean Gaussian noise, with $E\{v_n \cdot v_{n'}\} = \mathcal{R}_v \, \delta(n - n')$, where v_n is the $n - th$ element of $\mathbf{v}$.

The equations giving the estimated value of $\hat{\mathbf{a}}_{t+1}$ in terms of $\hat{\mathbf{a}}_t$ are [21], [22]

$$\hat{\mathbf{a}}_{t+1} = \hat{\mathbf{a}}_t + \mathbf{K}_{t+1} \cdot (\mathbf{b}_{t+1} - \mathbf{D}_{t+1} \cdot \hat{\mathbf{a}}_t) \tag{10}$$

$$\mathbf{K}_{t+1} = (\mathbf{R}_t + w^2 \, \mathbf{I}) \cdot \mathbf{D}_{t+1}^T \cdot \mathbf{k}^{-1} \tag{11}$$

$$\mathbf{k} = \mathbf{D}_{t+1} \cdot \mathbf{R}_t \cdot \mathbf{D}_{t+1}^T + \mathbf{D}_{t+1} \cdot w^2 \, \mathbf{I} \cdot \mathbf{D}_{t+1}^T + \mathcal{R}_v \tag{12}$$

$$\mathbf{R}_{t+1} = (\mathbf{I} - \mathbf{K}_{t+1} \cdot \mathbf{D}_{t+1}) \cdot (\mathbf{R}_t + w^2 \, \mathbf{I}) \tag{13}$$

where $\hat{\mathbf{a}}_{t+1}$ and $\hat{\mathbf{a}}_t$ are the predictions of the unknown motion parameters corresponding to the $t + 1$-th and t-th frame, respectively, $\mathbf{K}_{t+1}$ represents the correction matrix and $\mathbf{R}_t$ and $\mathbf{R}_{t+1}$ describe the covariance matrix of the estimation error $\mathbf{E}_t$ and $\mathbf{E}_{t+1}$, respectively

$$\mathbf{E}_t = (\mathbf{a}_t - \hat{\mathbf{a}}_t), \quad \mathbf{R}_t = E\{\mathbf{E}_t \cdot \mathbf{E}_t^T\}$$

$$\mathbf{E}_{t+1} = (\mathbf{a}_{t+1} - \hat{\mathbf{a}}_{t+1}), \quad \mathbf{R}_{t+1} = E\{\mathbf{E}_{t+1} \cdot \mathbf{E}_{t+1}^T\}$$

The initial value $\hat{\mathbf{a}}_0$ of the filter (first frame or $t = 0$) is found by solving directly Eq. (7). More specifically, since $2 \times 3 \times L \geq 6$ for all sub-objects (in the worst case s is composed of a single triangle with $L = 3$ and $2 \times 3 \times 3 = 18$), (7) is overdetermined and can be solved by the robust least median of squares motion estimation algorithm described in detail in [23]. Erroneous initial 2D estimates, produced by the block-matching algorithm, will be discarded by the least median of squares motion estimation algorithm.

The initial correlation matrix $\mathbf{R}_0$ is :

$$\mathbf{R}_0 = E\{\mathbf{a}_0 \cdot \mathbf{a}_0^T\}$$

In the above, w and $\mathbf{v}$ are assumed to be the same for the whole mesh, hence independent of the sub-object s. Notice that Eq. (7) is solved only once in order to provide the initial values for the Kalman filtering. During the next frames, $\mathbf{D}$ and $\mathbf{b}$ are only formed for use in the Kalman filter procedure.

The final rigid 3D motion descriptor characterizing each sub-object s is the sum of the rigid 3D motion parameters for frames $t = 0, \ldots, F - 1$, where F is the total number of frames used. More specifically we define for a rigid 3D motion vector $\mathbf{a}_t$ at time t the matrix :

$$\mathbf{M}_t = \begin{bmatrix} 1 & -w_{z_t} & w_{y_t} & \tau_{x_t} \\ w_{z_t} & 1 & -w_{x_t} & \tau_{y_t} \\ -w_{y_t} & w_{x_t} & 1 & \tau_{z_t} \\ 0 & 0 & 0 & 1 \end{bmatrix} \tag{14}$$

The total rigid 3D motion for a number of frames is described by :

$$\mathbf{M} = \prod_{t=0}^{F-1} \mathbf{M}_t \tag{15}$$

and the rigid 3D motion parameters for descriptor $\mathbf{a}^{(s)}$ are extracted from $\mathbf{M}$, which is of the form of $\mathbf{M}_t$. I.e. the motion descriptor

$$\mathbf{a}^{(s)} = (w_x^{(s)}, w_y^{(s)}, w_z^{(s)}, \tau_x^{(s)}, \tau_y^{(s)}, \tau_z^{(s)}) ,$$

is found from

$$
\mathbf{M} = \begin{bmatrix} 1 & -w_z^{(s)} & w_y^{(s)} & \tau_x^{(s)} \\ w_z^{(s)} & 1 & -w_x^{(s)} & \tau_y^{(s)} \\ -w_y^{(s)} & w_x^{(s)} & 1 & \tau_z^{(s)} \\ 0 & 0 & 0 & 1 \end{bmatrix} \; ,
$$

where $\mathbf{M}$ is determined using (14) and (15).

5.3 Color and Depth Descriptor Estimation

In addition to the rigid 3D motion descriptor of each triangle, other observations can be used for efficient segmentation. More specifically a color descriptor can be assigned to each sub-object s. For each triangle $T_m^{(s)}$, contained in s, let

$$
y^{(T_m^{(s)})} = \frac{1}{3} \sum_{c=0}^{2} \left(\frac{1}{N_c^{(T_m^{(s)})}} \sum_{i=1}^{N_c^{(T_m^{(s)})}} I_c(x_i, y_i) \right) , \tag{16}
$$

where $c = 0, 1, 2$ corresponds to $c = left, top, right$ cameras, $N_c^{(T_m^{(s)})}$ is the number of 2D projected points for each triangle for each view c and $I_c(x_i, y_i)$ is the intensity value of each projected view. The color descriptor for sub-object s is then defined by

$$
y^{(s)} = \frac{1}{M^{(s)}} \sum_{m=1}^{M^{(s)}} y^{(T_m^{(s)})} .
$$

Similarly, in order to assign a depth descriptor to each triangle, we define :

$$
d^{(T_m^{(s)})} = \frac{1}{3} \sum_{c=0}^{2} \left(\frac{1}{N_c^{(T_m^{(s)})}} \sum_{i=1}^{N_c^{(T_m^{(s)})}} d_c(x_i, y_i) \right) , \tag{17}
$$

where $c = 0, 1, 2$ corresponds to $c = left, top, right$ cameras, $N_c^{(T_m^{(s)})}$ is the number of 2D projected points for each triangle for each view c and $d_c(x_i, y_i)$ are the projected depth maps to each view. For each sub-object s the depth descriptor is then defined by :

$$
d^{(s)} = \frac{1}{M^{(s)}} \sum_{m=1}^{M^{(s)}} d^{(T_m^{(s)})} .
$$

6 Experimental Results

The proposed 3D model-based segmentation algorithm was evaluated for the segmentation of the 3D model created from real multiview image sequences. The interlaced multiview videoconference sequences of "Ludo3" of size 720×576 [1] were used. All experiments were performed at the top field of the interlaced sequences, thus using images of size 720×288.

The rigid 3D motion for each sub-object was estimated using the methods described in 5.2. The rigid 3D motion for each triangle (iteration $i = 0$ of the algorithm, where each sub-object consists of a single triangle) for the "Ludo3" sequence is shown in Fig. 4a,b. More specifically in Fig. 4a the translation parameters for each triangle are shown. The color of the triangle shows the magnitude of the translation vector, with darker areas corresponding to regions with greater motion. The vector shows the direction of the translation. In Fig. 4b the rotation parameters are depicted. The color of the triangle corresponds to the value of the angle of rotation (with darker areas corresponding to larger angles) and the vector shows the axis of rotation. The motion of the "Ludo3" sequence is a rotation of the head towards the right with almost no movement of the rest of the body. As can be seen, the estimated motion approximates the real motion quite accurately.

The histogram used in order to provide the decision for the threshold after the initial iteration is shown in Fig. 4c. The final articulation of the 3D model is shown in 4d. As can be seen, all characteristic sub-objects appear segmented. The table is separated from the body even though neither object moves. In these areas the motion descriptor is zero and the dominant descriptors are the color and depth ones, which are efficiently used for the separation of the body from the table and the arms from the rest of the body.

7 Conclusions

In this paper, an unsupervised procedure for the segmentation of multiview image sequences using multiple sources of information, was presented. The articulation is based on the homogeneity of parameters estimated for each sub-object, which consists of a number of interconnected triangles of the 3D model. The rigid 3D motion of each sub-object for subsequent frames is estimated using a Kalman filtering algorithm. Information from all cameras is combined during the formation of the equations for the rigid 3D motion parameters. The threshold used in the object segmentation procedure is updated at each iteration using the histogram of the sub-object descriptors.

The methodology used overcomes a major obstacle in multiview video analysis, caused by the difficult problem of determining and handling coherently corresponding objects in various views. This is achieved in this paper by defining segmentation and object articulation in the 3D space, thus ensuring that all ensuing operations (for example rigid 3D motion estimation of each sub-object) remain coherent for all views of the scene.

A further advantage of the algorithm is that the segmentation is defined at the triangle level, thus making possible to define the detail of the segmentation mask.

---

[1] These sequences were prepared by the CNET Rennes (formerly CCETT) for use in the PANORAMA ACTS project.

In cases where a coarse segmentation mask is needed, a 3D model consisting of large triangles may be used making the segmentation procedure much faster, whereas for highly detailed masks a finer mesh may be used. This is not possible with segmentation algorithms working at the pixel level.

The algorithm combines an arbitrary number of sub-object descriptors. Based on the available information and the type of application, different sources with different weights can be used.

The important connectivity constraint for each sub-object produced is implicitly imposed in the segmentation algorithm, since each sub-object is merged with only neighboring sub-objects. Thus no special post-processing is needed in order to fill "holes" in the resulting sub-objects. In fact the only post-processing procedure necessary, is the merging of very small regions with larger ones.

Possible applications of the algorithm (apart from segmentation) include *rigid 3D motion estimation* in model-based coding. The sub-objects defined in the algorithm, along with their estimated rigid 3D motion parameters can be used to update the model in the next time instance [14]. The only parameters that need to be transmitted are the rigid motion parameters since the 3D model is transmitted only at the beginning. In this manner significant bitrate savings may potentially be achieved. The rigid 3D motion of each triangle, used in iteration $i = 0$ of the algorithm, can be used in a manner similar to that in [24] for *non-rigid* or *flexible 3D motion estimation* of each node of the wireframe. A flexible 3D motion can be assigned to each node by taking into account the rigid 3D motion of all triangles having as vertex the specific node.

References

1. H. G. Musmann, M. Hotter, and J. Ostermann, "Object-oriented analysis-synthesis coding of moving images," *Signal Processing: Image Communication*, vol. 1, pp. 117–138, Oct. 1989.
2. S. Malassiotis and M. G. Strintzis, "Model based joint motion and structure estimation from stereo images," *Comp. Vision, and Image Understanding*, vol. 64, November 1996.
3. J.-R. Ohm and E. Izquierdo, "An Object-Based System for Stereoscopic Viewpoint Synthesis," *IEEE Trans. Circuits and Systems for Video Technology*, vol. 7, Aug 1997.
4. K. S. Fu and J. K. Mui, "A Survey on Image Segmentation," *Pattern Recognition*, vol. 13, pp. 3–16, 1981.
5. R. M. Haralick and L. G. Sapiro, "Image Segmentation Techniques," *Computer Vision, Graphics and Image Processing*, vol. 29, pp. 100–132, 1985.
6. M. Kass, A. Witkin, and D. Terzopoulos, "Snakes: Active contour models," *International Journal of Computer Vision*, vol. 1, pp. 312–331, 1988.
7. D. Tzovaras, N. Grammalidis, and M. G. Strintzis, "Object - Based Coding of Stereo Image Sequences using Joint 3-D Motion/Disparity Compensation," *IEEE Trans. on Circuits and Systems for Video Technology*, vol. 7, Apr. 1997.
8. M. Hötter, R. Mester, and F. Müller, "Detection and Description of Moning Objects by Stochastic Modelling and Analusis of Complex Scenes," *Signal Processing: Image Communication*, vol. 8, pp. 281–293, 1996.

9. L. Wu, J. Benois-Pineau, P. Delagnes, and D. Barba, "Spatio-temporal Segmentation of Image Sequences for Object-Oriented Low Bitrate Image Coding," *Signal Processing: Image Communication*, vol. 8, pp. 513–543, 1996.

10. N. Grammalidis, S. Malassiotis, D. Tzovaras, and M. G. . Strintzis, "Stereo Image Sequence Coding based on 3-D Motion Estimati on and Compensation," *Signal Processing : Image Communication*, vol. 7, pp. 129–145, Aug 1995.

11. I. Kompatsiaris and M. G. Strintzis, "Automatic 3D Model Construction for Rigid 3D Motion Estimation of Monocular Videoconference Image Sequences," in *International Workshop on Synthetic Natural Hybrid Coding and 3D Imaging*, (Rhodes, Greece), pp. 44–47, Sept. 1997.

12. I. Kompatsiaris, D. Tzovaras, and M. G. Strintzis, "3D Model Based Segmentation of Videoconference Image Sequences," *IEEE Trans. on Circuits and Systems for Video Technology, Special Issue on Image and Video Processsing for Emerging Interactive Multimedia Services*, vol. 8, Sept. 1998.

13. G. Martinez, "Automatic Analysis of Flexibly Connected Rigid 3D Objects for Object-Based Analysis-Synthesis Coding (OBASC)," in *Picture Coding Symposium (PCS'94)*, (Sacramento, USA), pp. 21–23, Sept. 1994.

14. D. Tzovaras, I. Kompatsiaris, and M. G. Strintzis, "3D Object Articulation and Motion Estimation in Model-Based Stereoscopic Videoconference Image Sequence Coding," *to appear, Signal Processing : Image Communication*, Nov. 1996.

15. F. Pedersini, D. Pelle, A. Sarti, and S. Tubaro, "Calibration and Self-Calibration of Multi-Ocular Camera Systems," in *International Workshop on Synthetic Natural Hybrid Coding and 3D Imaging* (M. G. Strintzis et al., ed.), (Rhodes, Greece), pp. 81–84, Sept. 1997.

16. Y. Yakimovski and R. Cunningham, "A System for Extracting 3D Measurements from a Stereo Pair of TV Cameras," *CGVIP*, vol. 7, no. 2, pp. 195–210, 1978.

17. T. Riegel, R. Manzotti, and F. Pedersini, "3-D Shape Approximation for Objects in Multiview Image Sequences," in *International Workshop on Synthetic Natural Hybrid Coding and 3D Imaging*, (Rhodes, Greece), pp. 159–162, Sept. 1997.

18. G. Adiv, "Determining Three-Dimensional Motion and Structure from Optical Flow Generated by Several Moving Objects," *IEEE Trans. on Pattern Analysis and Machine Intelligence*, vol. 7, pp. 384–401, Jul. 1985.

19. S. Lee and Y. Kay, "A Kalman Filter Approach for Accurate 3-D Motion Estimation from a Sequence of Stereo Images," *CVGIP: Image Understanding*, vol. 54, pp. 244–258, Sept. 1991.

20. J. Kim and J. W. Woods, "3-D Kalman Filter for Image Motion Estimation," *IEEE Trans. Image Processing*, vol. 7, pp. 42–52, Jan. 1998.

21. A. K. Jain, *"Fundamentals of Digital Image Processing"*, pp. 304–306. Enlewood Cliffs, NJ 07632: Prentice Hall, 1986.

22. A. P. Sage and J. L. Melsa, *"ESTIMATION THEORY with Applications to Communications and Control"*. McGraw Hill, 1971.

23. S. S. Sinha and B. G. Schunck, "A Two-Stage Algorithm for Discontinuity-Preserving Surface Reconstruction," *IEEE Trans. Pattern Anal. and Mach. Intell.*, vol. 14, Jan. 1992.

24. I. Kompatsiaris, D. Tzovaras, and M. G. Strintzis, "Flexible 3D Motion Estimation and Tracking for Multiview Image Sequence Coding," *Signal Processing: Image Communication, Special Issue on 3D Video Technology*, no. 14, pp. 95–110, 1998.

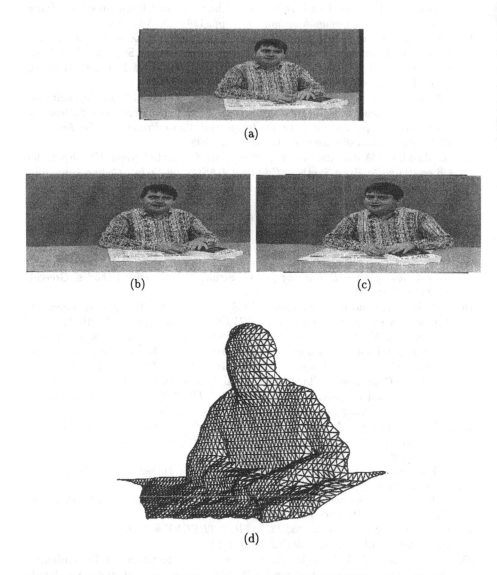

Fig. 3. "Ludo3 sequence" : (a) Top view. (b) Left view. (c) Right view. (d) The 3D model produced by the model initialization procedure.

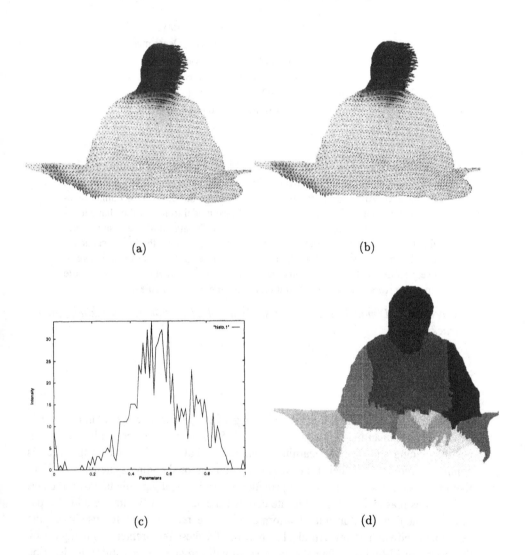

(a)

(b)

(c)

(d)

Fig. 4. "Ludo3" sequence : (a) 3D translation parameters of each triangle. (b) 3D rotation parameters of each triangle. (c) The histogram of the sub-object parameters after some few iterations. (d) The final segmentation of the 3D model.

Three Dimensional Model Adaptation and Tracking of a Human Face

Nikolaos Sarris, Georgios Tzanetos and Michael G. Strintzis

Information Processing Laboratory
Electrical and Computer Engineering Department
Aristotle University of Thessaloniki
Thessaloniki 54006, Greece
phone: +30 (31) 996349, fax: +30 (31) 996398
e-mail: {nikos, gtza}@dion.ee.auth.gr

Abstract. This paper develops a methodology consisting of improved previously known methods and novel techniques for the model based coding of a human face. An image scene is analysed to locate the position of human faces and transform a generic three dimensional face model to reflect the characteristics extracted from the particular image. A set of feature points necessary to define the position and posture of the face is tracked through the image sequence and the three dimensional model is continuously adapted to the facial image of every subsequent frame. Results are shown for every individual module, while on going work aims to the integration of the component modules.

Keywords: *3D model-based analysis, 3D model adaptation, face tracking, feature tracking*

1 Introduction

We present a system for the efficient coding of image sequences containing scenes where only a human facial image is of interest. Such scenes are frequently met in videoconferencing and distance learning applications; however the bandwidth which is commonly required for their transmission by conventional coding systems is prohibitive for use over the internet, which provides a very low and variable bandwidth channel. For this reason, a very low bit rate coding scheme is needed with the added capability of caching the transmitted information at the receiver end for use when the available bandwidth is low. An ideal framework for these requirements is being set by the emerging MPEG-4 coding standard which will provide the possibility to describe changes in facial expressions with arithmetic parameters: the Face Definition Parameters (FDPs) and the Face Animation Parameters (FAPs). The first set allows a detailed definition of the shape, size and texture of the face, while the second allows the description of all naturally possible facial expressions [1]. This is accomplished by exploiting a three dimensional face model which is initialised by the FDPs and subsequently modified by the FAPs. Although the MPEG-4 standard will provide the framework and the scene synthesis module, it will not provide any support for the scene analysis method which will have to identify the human face in the scene, track its movements and translate them into definition and animation parameters. The method presented here aims to fill this gap by combining previously known and novel algorithms into a common efficient framework. More specifically, this paper addresses the issues of adaptation of a three dimensional (3D) face model on a two dimensional (2D) face image and tracking of the face image in the 3D space using 2D image information and knowledge of the 3D model. The proposed system combines novel neural network techniques for the initial analysis of the scene, photogrammetry and geometric deformation methods for the continuous adaptation of the 3D model, and fast image analysis techniques for the tracking of the 2D features. The facial features which are identified and tracked comply with the FDP and FAP parameter sets, and thus, the system can be easily updated to be fully MPEG-4 compatible when the standard is finalised.

2 System Overview

The proposed system is completely modular and the sections that follow describe each module separately. For the initial model adaptation the scene is analysed and the position and orientation of the face are determined by locating a number of characteristic feature points. These are automatically chosen from a set of candidate feature points which lie on the circumferences of the face, eyes and lips. The exact positions of the chosen feature points are found with the use of neural network and geometric image analysis techniques as described in section 3. The initial model adaptation involves rigid and non-rigid transformations of the 3D model so that it depicts in the best possible way the particular characteristics of the given face. This process is described in detail in section 4. The feature points are tracked in the next 2D image frame using a modified version of the Lucas-Kanade-Tomasi (KLT) tracking algorithm [2], as described in section 5 and their positions are used to readapt the 3D model under certain constraints as described in section 6. The scene reconstruction at the receiver end is a module handled entirely by the MPEG-4 standard which has already presented the first version of viewers for face and body animation. Finally, experimental results and conclusions are in section 7.

3. Scene Analysis

In this module it is necessary to identify the position of the human face by locating a number of characteristic points in the given image, which must correspond to existing nodes of the 3D facial model used. Several methods have been proposed for this task ([9]-[14]) and many of these involve the use of neural networks ([9], [10]). However, the presented technique improves on previous work by introducing a Neural Network with a two dimensional structure in all its layers and a direct association of local observations in neighbouring 2D areas. This way, even in complex scenes, the rectangular areas within which lie the head, eyes and mouth are successfully located, while gradient based methods combined with geometric constraints are proposed to locate the exact positions of the required points within these areas. At least 5 feature points, covering the whole area of the face, are needed for accurate rigid adaptation; but more may be needed, as will be seen in the sequel, to determine the non-rigid transformation needed to adapt the model to the precise characteristics of the face.

The method developed for the location of the rectangular areas of the head, eyes and mouth, involves the use of a 2D neural network which is based on a local processing of its input and a special topology (succession) of its input layer characteristics. This neural network is first called upon to decide whether the input image contains a face or not. Having decided that the image does contain a face, this is located and within its area a similarly structured neural network, (which, however, is differently trained), is used to locate the eyes and mouth.

The proposed neural network is based on the Backpropagation topology having as input the image under investigation as a vector of its pixels in lexicographic order. If Ω is a 2D image and x is the corresponding vector at the input layer then the conventional way for a neural network to operate on this input is shown in Fig. 1a, where if w_i is the weight of the i_{th} neuron, its output will be $y_i = f(x\, w_i)$

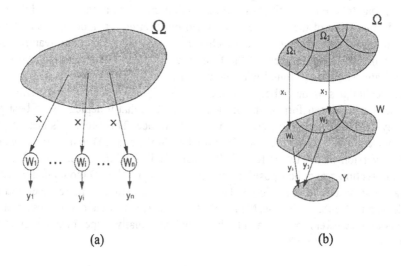

(a)   (b)

Fig. 1. Conventional and proposed ways of mapping the input image

However, we believe that the human visual system perception and understanding of an image is based on associating local observations along the surface of the whole image. Based on that observation we propose the structure shown in Fig. 1b where the initial 2D representation Ω is split into local areas Ω_i and corresponding vectors x_i with $i=1, \dots ,K$ where K is the maximum number of local areas. These local areas in the general case need not be disjoint and may overlap, simulating the local associations performed by the human visual system. The weights are also not independent;

they are spread on a 2D representation W similar to Ω and with similar local areas W_i. In the same way, the output is a 2D representation **Y**, of which every element y_i corresponds to a pair (Ω_i, W_i) and is given by the formula: $y_i = f(\Omega_i \cdot W_i)$

In Fig. 2 we show the structure of the proposed neural network which implements the scheme described above: the input is a 2D image, the hidden layers have 2D inputs outputs and weights, and every output of a hidden layer corresponds to a local area (window) of the corresponding input or upper hidden layer and the set of these outputs constitutes the input to the next hidden layer. The size and moving steps of these windows, which may vary from layer to layer, determine the number of layers as well as the number of neurons in each layer. The training algorithm is similar to that of the Backpropagation topology, suitably modified to adapt to the altered structure.

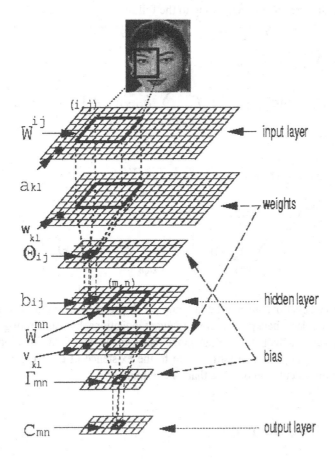

Fig. 2. Structure of the proposed neural network

Thus, if the network has one hidden layer and W^{ij} and W^{mn} are the windows used on the input and hidden layer correspondingly, the equations describing the network are as follows:

The outputs of the network are given by:

$$c_{mn} = f\left(\sum_{kl \in W^{mn}} b_{kl} \cdot w_{kl} + \Gamma_{mn}\right),$$

where b_{ij} are the calculated values in the hidden layer, given by:

$$b_{ij} = f\left(\sum_{kl \in W^{ij}} a_{kl} \cdot v_{kl} + \Theta_{ij}\right)$$

and the weights are updated according to the following:

$$\Delta w_{kl} = \beta \cdot b_{kl} \cdot d_{mn} \quad , \quad k, l \in W^{mn}$$

$$\Delta \Gamma_{mn} = \beta \cdot d_{mn} \tag{1}$$

$$d_{mn} = \left(c_{mn}^{k} - c_{mn}\right) \cdot f'\left(\sum_{kl \in W^{mn}} b_{kl} \cdot w_{kl} + \Gamma_{mn}\right)$$

$$\Delta v_{kl} = \alpha \cdot a_{kl} \cdot e_{ij} \quad , \quad k, l \in W^{ij}$$

$$\Delta \Theta_{ij} = \alpha \cdot e_{ij}$$

$$e_{ij} = \left(\sum_{kl:\{i,j \in W^{kl}\}} d_{kl} \cdot w_{ij}\right) \cdot f'\left(\sum_{kl \in W^{ij}} a_{kl} \cdot v_{kl} + \Theta_{ij}\right)$$

In the above equations all but the last one are deduced by a straightforward extension of the standard backpropagation relevant equations by substituting the one-dimensional vertices with two-dimensional matrices. In the final equation, for the calculation of e_{ij}, the first sum term is due to the existence of the weights w_{ij} which contribute to the calculation of more than one output.

4. Initial Model Adaptation

The purpose of this module is to transform the 3D model in such a way so that it adapts to the characteristics of the face in the 2D image. In theory, any 3D model of the human face may be used. In practice however, the closer the characteristics of the model are to the characteristics of the image (e.g. model of female face for a female face) the fewer feature points will be needed for accurate adaptation.

In order to project the coordinates of the feature points to the 3D space, more information is needed than that provided by the single 2D image frame. In the proposed scheme we utilise the combined information from two views of the face at right angles to each other. These may be obtained either by a stereoscopic system of two cameras at right angles to each other (as can be seen in Fig. 3), or by a rotating single camera. It is emphasised, however, that the second view is only needed at the beginning of the procedure, when the 3D model is initialised to adapt to the given face image. After the initialisation, a monoscopic image sequence suffices, as will be detailed in section 6.

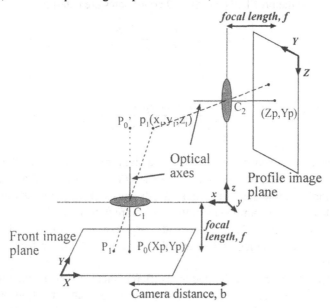

Fig. 3. Image acquisition layout

We shall assume the use of a perspective projection camera system which is shown in Fig. 4. The 3D points with coordinates (x, y, z) are projected on two image planes, the front and the profile, with perspective rays passing through the two corresponding projection centres C_1 and C_2, which lie within the physical camera and are at a distance b from each other. The focal length f is the distance of the image planes from the corresponding centres of projection, while the point where the optical axis of the camera intersects the image plane is called the principal point. For the front image plane the principal point coordinates are (Xp, Yp) and for the profile (Zp, Yp); in our experiments these were fixed to the centres of the corresponding projection images. Finally, X and Y are the projections on the frontal view, while Z and Y the projections on the profile view of the 3D image.

The projection coordinates for the front image can be computed from the similar triangles $P_1C_1P_0$ and $p_1C_1P_0'$, shown in Fig. 3, and in the same way, the projection coordinates for the profile image may be determined:

$$X = f\frac{-b+x}{z} + Xp$$

$$Y = f\frac{y}{z} + Yp \qquad (2)$$

$$Z = f\frac{b-z}{x} + Zp$$

From this system of equations, given the projections of the feature points $(X\ Y\ Z)$ on the frontal and the profile views, the 3D coordinates are determined:

$$x = \frac{bf(X - Xp) + bf^2}{f^2 + (Z - Zp)(X - Xp)}$$

$$y = \frac{(Y - Yp)z}{f} \qquad (3)$$

$$z = \frac{-bf(Z - Zp) + bf^2}{f^2 + (Z - Zp)(X - Xp)}$$

The adaptation procedure continues with a rigid transformation of the model (i.e. such that each node of the model undergoes the same scaling, rotation and translation transformation) with the aim to minimise the distances of the 3D model feature nodes from the calculated 3D coordinates of the 2D feature points. Finally, a non-rigid transformation ensures that the feature nodes are displaced to their exact calculated positions, dragging their neighbours in a way that does not deform the facial model in an unnatural way.

The model is first stretched (scaled by a different factor for every axis) to match the dimensions of the real face. The rotation and translation transformations are then calculated by a slight modification of the 'spatial resection' problem in photogrammetry [5]: The relation between the initial model and the transformed model is described by a translation and a rotation as follows:

$$\begin{bmatrix} x' \\ y' \\ z' \end{bmatrix} = \mathbf{R} \begin{bmatrix} x \\ y \\ z \end{bmatrix} + \mathbf{T} \qquad (4)$$

where x', y', z' are the coordinates of the transformed nodes, $\mathbf{R}$ is a 3x3 rotation matrix and $\mathbf{T}$ is a 3D translation vector. We shall assume a left-hand coordinate system, and let ω be the angle of rotation around the x-axis of the camera reference frame, φ the angle of rotation around the y-axis, and κ the angle of rotation around the z-axis. Then the rotation matrix $\mathbf{R}$ will be given by [5]:

$$\mathbf{R} = \mathbf{R}(\omega)\mathbf{R}(\phi)\mathbf{R}(\kappa), \text{ where:}$$

$$\mathbf{R}(\omega) = \begin{bmatrix} 1 & 0 & 0 \\ 0 & \cos\omega & \sin\omega \\ 0 & -\sin\omega & \cos\omega \end{bmatrix}$$

$$\mathbf{R}(\phi) = \begin{bmatrix} \cos\phi & 0 & -\sin\phi \\ 0 & 1 & 0 \\ \sin\phi & 0 & \cos\phi \end{bmatrix} \qquad (5)$$

$$\mathbf{R}(\kappa) = \begin{bmatrix} \cos\kappa & \sin\kappa & 0 \\ -\sin\kappa & \cos\kappa & 0 \\ 0 & 0 & 1 \end{bmatrix}$$

Our purpose is the minimisation of the following sum of squares by appropriate selection of the 6 unknown parameters (3 translation coefficients and 3 rotation coefficients):

$$\sum_{i=1}^{N} \left(\begin{bmatrix} x \\ y \\ z \end{bmatrix} - \begin{bmatrix} x' \\ y' \\ z' \end{bmatrix} \right)^2 \qquad (6)$$

where N is the number of feature points located in the front and profile image frames by the image analysis module, x, y, z are their positions in the 3D space calculated from equations (3) and x', y', z' are the positions of the model 3D nodes after the transformation (4). A modification of the Levenberg - Marquardt algorithm using 5 feature points was used in our experiments.

In the second step of the adaptation process the model is transformed in a non-rigid way so that the feature nodes are displaced to their exact calculated positions. The remaining vertices are moved so that the final deformed model adapts to the particular characteristics implied by the feature points (e.g. bigger nose or smaller eyes) keeping the generic characteristics of a human face (e.g. smoothness of the skin and symmetry of the face). This is achieved by imposing the same feature-node displacement on every node within a three node distance and exponentially dampen this displacement for the farther nodes. The dampening is done according to the distance from the feature node and is recursively spread to the whole of the model. The reason for maintaining the same displacement in the close neighbourhoods of the feature node is the preservation of the original smoothness of the generic model across local areas, while the decaying of the displacements further away aims to smoothen the connection of these displaced local areas. Current results show that the model adapts to the characteristics required and retains the natural smoothness of a human face. Alternative approaches are the Free Form Deformation (FFD) [6] method and its extensions, Rational FFD [7] and Dirichlet FFD [8].

5. Feature Tracking

This module aims to track the positions of feature points in subsequent frames. Our first task is to select the 2D image feature points to be tracked. It is necessary that every such feature point on the 2D image corresponds to a node (vertex) of the 3D model (e.g. we may decide to track the position of the "tip of the nose" only if the 3D model used has a node on the tip of the nose). In addition, every feature point has to be characteristic in a way that will make it visible to the scene analysis module and 'trackable' by the tracking module (e.g. the corner at the inside of an eye is much easier to locate and track than the point in the middle of the forehead). To measure the 'trackability' or 'goodness' of a feature we use the metric established and described in [2]. In this way the 'best' M feature points are determined in the first 2D image frame and are tracked in subsequent frames of the sequence. In this case 'best' characterises points which correspond to vertices in the 3D model, belong to a set of characteristic features which are possible to locate by image analysis and have a 'goodness' value above a predetermined threshold.

The minimum number of feature points that are required by the rigid adaptation algorithm is 5 (therefore M>5), but the use of more feature points produces better adaptation accuracy. However, care must be taken so that the feature points used for the adaptation have been accurately tracked. Being in the list of the 'best' feature points does not guarantee that every one of these features will be accurately tracked in every frame, as unpredictable difficulties in the tracking procedure, like occlusions, may occur. Therefore, it would be beneficial to use only the N feature points (N<M) which have been more accurately tracked in the present frame. To measure tracking accuracy we use the 'dissimilarity' metric established and described in [2]0 and [3].

The tracking of the feature points is performed by the KLT algorithm[2], [4], modified so as to adhere to the restrictions described in the previous paragraphs.

6. Face Tracking

Having tracked the number of N feature points in the next frame, the 3D model has to be readapted, undergoing both a rigid and non-rigid transformation. The rigid adaptation is performed by minimising the distances of the projections X, Y of the 3D feature nodes (given by (2)), from their actual positions determined by the tracking process. To perform the minimisation the same modified version of the Levenberg – Marquardt algorithm has been used. After the initialisation of section 4, this adaptation is very fast since the initial values of the rigid parameters are those of the previous frame and hence the algorithm converges in far fewer iterations. In order to calculate the non-rigid motion of the face however, 3D information of the non-rigid feature nodes is required and as it was also pointed out earlier, information from only one image frame is not enough to define the 3D position of a point. However, now we only need to determine a minimal displacement caused by a change in the facial expression. Since the facial deformation of the model between two frames is small and based on the nature of the minimal deformations of a human face, we may assume that, having calculated the rigid motion, when a feature node moves from one frame to the next its new position lies on the plane which was tangent to the mesh, at the node's initial position (i.e. perpendicular to the node's normal), as shown in Fig. 4.

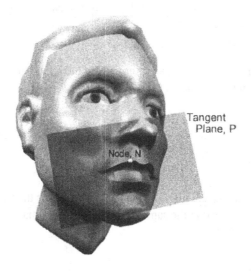

Fig. 4. The plane P, tangent to the mesh, at the node N

Therefore, by knowing only the projection of a feature point on the 2D image plane we may calculate its 3D position, which will be the intersection of the position vector of the projection point with the plane P tangent to the model at the previous 3D position of the node.

Thus, if x_0, y_0, z_0 are the coordinates of the previous position of the node N and **n** is the normal vector of the mesh at the location of this node, the equation of the plane P tangent to the mesh at this location is given by:

$$\begin{pmatrix} x_0 \\ y_0 \\ z_0 \end{pmatrix} \bullet \vec{n} = d \tag{7}$$

We require that the node remains on this plane, i.e. the new coordinates x_1, y_1, z_1 of the node satisfy:

$$\begin{pmatrix} x_1 \\ y_1 \\ z_1 \end{pmatrix} \bullet \vec{n} = d = \begin{pmatrix} x_0 \\ y_0 \\ z_0 \end{pmatrix} \bullet \vec{n} \tag{8}$$

The projection ray which connects the centre of projection (origin), with the new position of the node and intersects the image plane on the projection point (X, Y), is defined by the equation:

$$\begin{pmatrix} x \\ y \\ z \end{pmatrix} = \lambda \begin{pmatrix} X + Xp \\ Y + Yp \\ f \end{pmatrix} \qquad (9)$$

where (Xp, Yp) is the principal point and f is the focal length of the camera.

Since X and Y are known (8) and (9) give:

$$\lambda = \frac{x_0 n_x + y_0 n_y + z_0 n_z}{(X - Xp)n_x + (Y - Yp)n_y + fn_z}, \quad \text{where } \vec{n} = \begin{pmatrix} n_x \\ n_y \\ n_z \end{pmatrix} \qquad (10)$$

Following the calculations of the 3D positions for the tracked N feature points, the model is transformed in the same rigid and non rigid manner described in section 4.

7. Results

The neural network scene analysis technique was found to give reliable results in any type of image containing a human face, with or without a background. Fig. 6 demonstrates the results of locating the rectangular areas containing the face eyes and mouth in various images.

Fig. 5. Locating the areas of the face, eyes and mouth

The feature tracking algorithm also exhibited robustness as seen in Fig.7, through the 10 first frames of the Miss America image sequence:

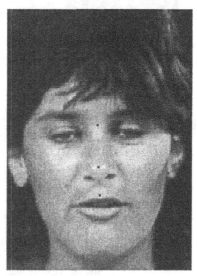

Fig. 6. Tracking the feature points through the Miss America image sequence

The model adaptation method based on given positions for the feature points has worked well in rigidly transforming the 3D model so that its projection fits to the 2D image, and non-rigidly deforming it to adapt to a synthetic closing of the mouth, as shown in Figure 7.

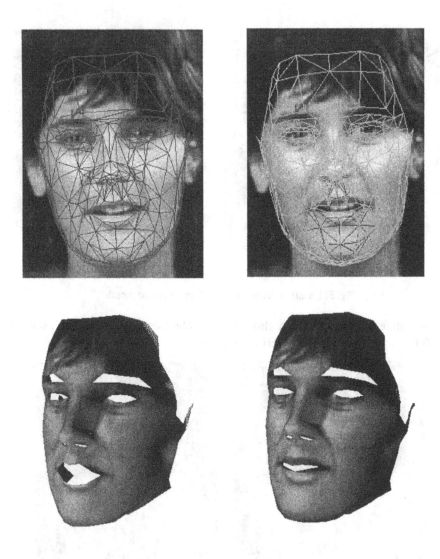

Fig. 7. Rigid and non-rigid Model adaptation

Top left: Rigid transformation of the face model
Top right: Non rigid transformation to close the mouth
Bottom: Texture mapping of the above image on the 3D model

8. Conclusions

A method has been proposed for the model-based coding of human face images. The method is based on the analysis of the scene using a-priori knowledge of the scene content by means of a predefined 3D model of the human face. The model is adapted to the 2D image scene and its motion is tracked in subsequent frames. Thus, the position of every 3D node for every frame is known and a direct translation into MPEG-4 compliant FAPs and BAPs can be realised.

9. Acknowledgements

This work was supported by the EU CEC Project ACTS VIDAS (Video Assisted Audio Coding and Representation, ACTS project 057)

References

1. "The MPEG-4 Final Draft, part 2:visual", tech. Rep. ISO/IEC JTC1/SC29/WG11 N2502, October 1998.
2. J. Shi and C. Tomasi, "Good Features to Track", in Proceedings, IEEE Proceedings, IEEE Conference on Computer Vision and Pattern Recognition, pp. 593-600, 1994.
3. C. Tomasi and T. Kanade, "Detection and Tracking of Point Features", Carnegie Mellon University Technical Report CMU-CS-91-132, April 1991.
4. B. D. Lucas and T. Kanade, "An Iterative Image Registration Technique with an Application to Stereo Vision", in 7th International Joint Conference on Artificial Intelligence, pp. 674-679, 1981.
5. R. M. Haralick and L. G. Shapiro, Computer and Robot Vision, Volume II, pp.125-150, Addison Wesley, 1993.
6. MacCracken R., Joy K. I., "Free Form Deformations with Latices of Arbitrary Topology", Computer Graphics Research Laboratory, University of California, Technical Report CSE-96-7
7. Kalra P., Mangili A., Magnenat Thalmann N., Thalmann D., "Simulation of Facial Muscle Actions Based on Rational Free Form Deformations", Computer Graphics Forum, 2, 3, Blackwell Publishers, pp. 65-69, 1992
8. Moccozet L., Magnenat-Thalmann N., "Dirichlet Free-Form Deformations and their Application to Hand Simulation", Computer Animation '97, 1997.
9. Rowley R., Baluja S., Kanade T., "Human face detection in visual scenes", tech. Rep. CMU-CS-95-158R, November 1995.
10. Sung K. and Poggio T., "Example-based learning for view based human face detection", IEEE Transactions on Pattern Analysis and Machine Intelligence, Vol. 20, No1, pp 39-50, January 1998.
11. Yuille A., Hallinan P., Cohen D., "Feature extraction from faces using deformable templates", Int'l Journal of Computer Vision, vol. 8, no 2, pp 99-111, 1992.
12. Essa I, Darrell T., Pentland A., "Tracking Facial Motion", Proceedings of the IEEE Workshop on Nonrigid and Articulate Motion, Austin, Texas, November 1994
13. Zhang L., "Tracking a face for knowledge based coding of videophone sequences", Signal Processing: Image Communication 10 (1997) 93-114.
14. Sobottka K., Pitas I., "A novel method for automatic face segmentation, facial feature extraction and tracking", Signal Processing: Image Communication 12 (1998) 263 - 281

H.323 Videoconference over Native ATM

António Grilo, Mário Nunes

INESC, Switching and Terminal Equipment Group, R. Alves Redol, N° 9,
1000 Lisboa, Portugal
{amg, msn}@cris.inesc.pt

Abstract. This document presents an architecture for native ATM videoconference based on H.323, which takes advantage of ATM QOS characteristics. The ATM addressing scheme is used, and the transport functions are performed by ATM related protocols. This architecture allows the definition of different QOS requirements for audio and video, using the RTP/RTCP mechanism to adapt media quality to the capabilities of the terminals. The audiovisual data distribution in a multipoint-to-multipoint videoconference is decentralised, and based on ATM point-to-multipoint connections without requiring an MCU. This architecture was the framework for the development of a prototype videoconference application, whose performance measurements are presented and discussed.

1   Introduction

Due to its Quality of Service (QOS) capabilities, ATM is being regarded as a suitable network technology to carry multimedia real-time services, namely videoconference.

In parallel with the development of ATM, the world has been watching the fast growth of the Internet. Due to the increase in LAN speed and processing capacity of personal computers, these can now be used as a platform for multimedia communication services. This motivated ITU-T to define the H.323 standard for videoconference and telephony over LANs and Internet.

Nowadays, one of the main applications of ATM is as a WAN technology for carrying Internet Protocol (IP) traffic. In this way, its main capability, QOS, is not used. On the other hand, as a LAN technology, ATM has currently to face the competition of well-established technologies such as Ethernet. Nevertheless, access network technologies such as ADSL, HFC and HFR are likely to decrease its cost in the near future, encouraging the development of native ATM applications, specially multimedia communication applications. The main advantages of native ATM applications towards multimedia communications are the following:

- Direct use of ATM allows the definition and maintenance of QOS, which is crucial for multimedia real-time services.
- Multimedia communication services, such as videoconference, are inherently connection-oriented, which simplifies the mapping to native ATM.

The H.321 [1] and H.310 [2] recommendations defined by the ITU-T for videoconference in the B-ISDN do not present the flexibility of H.323 [3].

H.321 simply adapts the H.320 N-ISDN recommendation [4] to the ATM environment, using the AAL1 CBR service to emulate 64 Kbps N-ISDN channels. This approach presents the same drawbacks of the N-ISDN standard, namely the limitation to H.261 CIF resolution video. Although H.262 (MPEG-2 video) is optional, the high cost of encoding equipment discourages its use for desktop videoconferencing. Anyway, support to AAL1 is nowadays scarce in ATM terminal equipment, AAL5 being preferred.

H.310 is the recommendation for high-resolution videoconference in the B-ISDN, besides keeping compatibility with H.321. Nevertheless, it is also based on MPEG-2, which as already said is nowadays very expensive for desktop videoconferencing.

The H.323 recommendation for videoconference in LANs and the Internet, presents more flexibility. The use of the Real Time Protocol (RTP) [5], [6] for media encapsulation and synchronisation has the following advantages:

- Audio and video streams are carried in different RTP sessions, which allows independent handling of QoS.
- The Real Time Control Protocol (RTCP) associated with RTP, offers a flow control mechanism that allows the sender to adapt the transmission bit-rate to the processing capacity of the receiver, an interesting feature in computer based desktop videoconferencing.

The presence of these mechanisms in H.323 is mostly due to the fact that H.323 systems were originally designed to work over networks that offer no QoS guarantees. Although QoS capabilities are likely to be added to IP in the near future, in order to reduce overhead and to provide direct use of ATM QoS in IP/ATM networks, a specific annex was added to the original specification. The new annex, H.323 annex C, is an optional enhancement to allow H.323 endpoints to establish QOS-based media streams on ATM networks using AAL5. The protocol stack can be seen in Fig. 1. It keeps the IP-based stack for the parts that do not need QOS (control protocols and T.120), and uses native ATM for the transport of audiovisual streams.

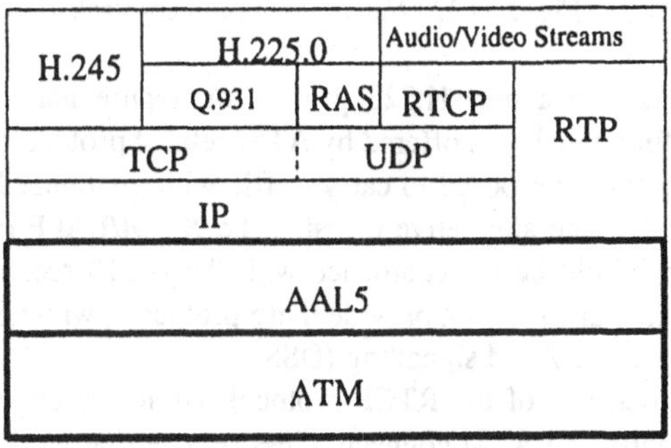

H.245	H.225.0		Audio/Video Streams	
	Q.931	RAS	RTCP	RTP
TCP		UDP		
IP				
AAL5				
ATM				

Fig. 1. H.323 Annex C protocol stack

The ATM Forum is presently studying efficient ways for audiovisual transmission over native ATM (v. [7]). The compatibility of the control aspects of annex C with H.323 for the LAN simplifies the adaptation of existent H.323 applications to ATM.

These aspects turned H.323 into a de facto standard for desktop multimedia communications in ATM networks. Although H.323 annex C remains an IP-oriented stack, it joins the ATM QoS with the H.323 flexibility, deserving our attention as a basis for the definition of a true native ATM videoconference architecture. Nevertheless, it still depends on IP addressing, which is limited to 32 bits in IPv4. With IPv6 deployment still frozen, the future growth of the Internet is becoming a problem. This does not happen with the N-ISDN and B-ISDN where the E.164 address format allows for a network of world scale. It is thus legitimate to think that in the near future an additional H.323 profile should be added for complete native ATM operation, i.e. an architecture that makes exclusive use of ATM addressing and transport protocols. This paper proposes such an architecture, which is named H.323 Native ATM.

2 Description of H.323 Native ATM

H.323 Native ATM can be obtained with the following changes to H.323 annex C:

- Replacement of the Q.931 Call Control protocol by the ATM DSS2 protocol [8].
- Removal of the IP layer, not needed in a native ATM environment.

The resulting architecture is named H.323 ATM, with the protocol stack shown in Fig. 2.

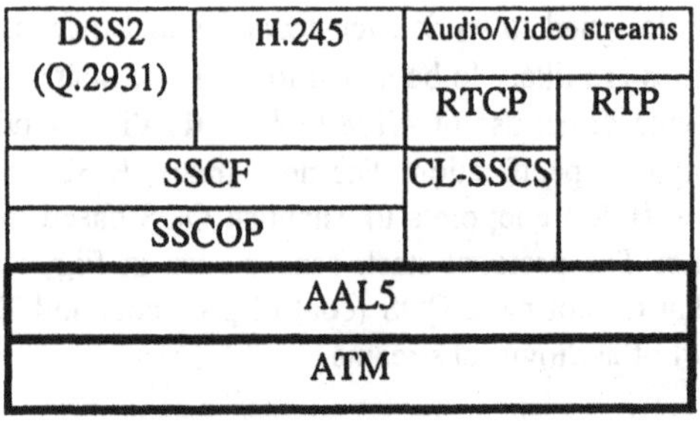

DSS2 (Q.2931)	H.245	Audio/Video streams	
		RTCP	RTP
SSCF		CL-SSCS	
SSCOP			
AAL5			
ATM			

Fig. 2. H.323 Native ATM protocol stack.

H.323 ATM represents a new H.323 profile for a pure native ATM environment, where all transport functionality is offered by ATM related protocols.

The SSCOP protocol is proposed to carry traffic with guaranteed delivery (H.245 and T.120), replacing TCP. The alternative of using the X.224/LAPF (with FR-SSCS as the AAL5 SSCS) stack, would be in accordance with the H.310 recommendation, however the ATM card manufacturers do not provide these protocols, while SSCOP is always present in order to support the ATM signalling (DSS2).

Concerning the transport of the RTCP protocol, while the connectionless UDP/IP is used in H.323, we define an ATM connectionless service that works over AAL5. Details of this service can be found later in this paper.

All videoconference recommendations for ATM (including H.323 annex C), only consider a centralized topology for multipoint-to-multipoint videoconference (Fig. 3), although recommendation F.732 [9] presents some decentralised topologies.

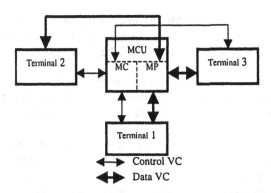

Fig. 3. MCU-based multipoint-to-multipoint topology in B-ISDN.

This centralised topology is based on a special unit, the Multipoint Control Unit (MCU). The MCU comprises two main modules:

- **Multipoint Controller (MC):** Controls the videoconference, ensuring mutual knowledge between terminals and a common communication mode (i.e. common media encoding formats, etc.).
- **Multipoint Processor (MP):** Receives and processes the audiovisual streams from all terminals, in order to select or mix the data into output media streams that present a lower global bandwidth than the original. The processed streams are sent to each terminal, allowing the terminals to present lower processing capacity and complexity, at the cost of increasing those factors at the MCU.

Terminals are connected to the MCU through bi-directional point-to-point VCs, both for control and data.

Centralised topologies present availability problems, as the MCU is a limited network resource that must be allocated before starting a multipoint-to-multipoint videoconference. With the increasing processing power of personal computers, decentralised multipoint-to-multipoint becomes possible. In H.323 for the LAN, this is achieved through IP multicast. In ATM, a multicast mechanism is achieved by the point-to-multipoint signalling, which can also be used to provide decentralisation. The decentralised multipoint-to-multipoint topology proposed in this document is shown in Fig. 4.

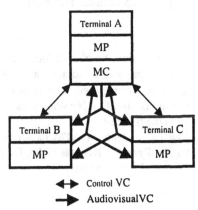

Fig. 4. Decentralized multipoint-to-multipoint topology.

In this topology, both MC and MP functions of the MCU are moved to the terminals. Each terminal comprises an MP unit for selection and mixing of audiovisual data received from the other participants. This data is efficiently carried in unidirectional point-to-multipoint VCs.

On the other hand, the MC functionality is easier to implement in a centralised way. As such, it will be performed by one of the terminals (e.g. the terminal that starts the video-conference), named the MC terminal. Like in the MCU case, control data is carried in point-to-point VCs.

In H.323 ATM, the encapsulation of RTP is done in the same way as in H.323 annex C, i.e. directly in AAL5 CPCS-PDUs. In the H.323 recommendation, RTCP reports between each pair of sender/receiver are carried by UDP/IP, whose connectionless characteristics simplify the control of the multiple connections, as RTCP reports need only to be sent to the correct UDP/IP port/address. In connection-oriented ATM, a simple solution would be to use a point-to-point VC between each sender/receiver pair, however the number of VCs would grow rapidly with the number of participants $((n-1)*n/2)$. A better solution consists on using a native ATM connectionless service (ATM CLS), which is currently under specification by the ATM Forum [10]. In the absence of a final standard specification, a proprietary CLS solution was implemented, which allows connectionless operation among the participants of a videoconference. Connectionless traffic is sent through bi-directional point-to-point VCs, which are established between each terminal and a CLS Server located in the MC terminal, together with the control of the videoconference. This does not present any performance problems, because RTCP traffic has a low intensity.

As already stated, connectionless traffic is carried over AAL5. A special SSCS layer was defined, the CL-SSCS. The CL-SSCS PDU is called an ATM datagram, and its proposed format is depicted in Fig. 5.

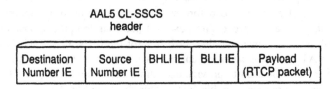

Fig. 5. AAL5 CL-SSCS PDU format.

The **Source Number** and **Destination Number** Information Elements (IEs) have the same format of the DSS2 IEs **Calling Party Number** and **Called Party Number**, respectively. **BLLI** and **BHLI** IEs are also required to completely identify an ATM Service Access Point (SAP). Note that the **Destination Number** goes ahead of the **Source Number** in order to be transported in the first cell.

Table 1 and Table 2 show the contents of ATM datagrams that carry respectively RTCP **Sender Reports (SR)** and **Receiver Reports (RR)**, for an RTP session in which terminal B is the sender and terminal C the receiver.

Table 1. Datagram field coding for an RTCP SR sent by terminal B to terminal C.

Field	Coding
Source Number	ATM address of B.
Destination Number	ATM address of C.
BHLI	Port number of the RTP session, at the receiver.
BLLI	Still undefined for H.323 ATM.
Payload	RTCP SR.

Table 2. Datagram field coding for an RTCP RR sent by terminal C to terminal B.

Field	Coding
Source Number	ATM address of C.
Destination Number	ATM address of B.
BHLI	Port Number of the RTP session, at the sender.
BLLI	Still undefined for H.323 ATM.
Payload	RTCP RR.

In Table 3 the ATM VCs required for an H.323 ATM videoconference are identified, considering a videoconference with one audio session and one video session.

Table 3. ATM virtual channels in H.323 ATM.

Function	Topology	Direction	Bit-rate	ATM Service Class	AAL
H.245	PP	Bi-directional	64 Kbps	CBR	SSCOP / AAL5
CLS	PP	Bi-directional	–	UBR	CL-SSCS / AAL5
Audio emission	PMP	Unidirec-tional	Depends on encoding	CBR or VBR (e.g. G.723)	Null-SSCS / AAL5
Video emission	PMP	Unidirec-tional	Depends on encoding	VBR, ABR or UBR	Null-SSCS / AAL5

H.245 traffic is carried in point-to-point VCs, there being 1 for a non-MC terminal and $n - 1$ for an MC terminal, where n is the number of participants. Recommendation H.245 specifies that the transport protocol should have guaranteed delivery, which is assured by SSCOP in H.323 ATM, using a CBR service with 64 Kbps guaranteed bit-rate.

For a total number of n participants, a terminal will be the receiver of $n - 1$ terminals and send its audio and video streams to the same $n - 1$ terminals. As such, for each audio or video session, a terminal will be the root of 1 point-to-multipoint VC and the leaf of $n - 1$ point-to-multipoint VCs.

Audio streams are important in a videoconference, however system performance is usually dictated by video, which requires much more bandwidth and processing power than audio. In computer based videoconferences the RTP/RTCP mechanism is useful to adapt video resources dynamically, taking into account that terminals can run several applications simultaneously. In a decentralised multipoint-to-multipoint environment, this is even more justified, because the number of participants – and hence the needed resources – can vary dynamically. Video encoding usually generates a variable bit rate stream. On the other hand, due to the conservative characteristics of ATM traffic control, enough bandwidth is left free to use at application discretion [11]. In this situation, the service categories more suitable to RTP/RTCP are VBR or ABR. ABR can be used to assure minimum quality by defining a minimum bit-rate, allowing an efficient use of spare bandwidth to dynamically increase quality. It should be pointed that the amount of spare bandwidth is subject to unexpected variations, and thus it must be used carefully, otherwise reception quality can greatly be affected. Nevertheless, the ABR specification is recent, and it is still not implemented in most ATM cards and switches. In the absence of VBR and ABR, UBR can be used with RTP/RTCP instead, although it does not assure any quality at all.

3 Multipoint-to-multipoint

Decentralised distribution of audiovisual data presents some control problems. In a centralised topology the MCU is the only entity that knows all participants in order to mix/select audiovisual streams. This is not the case with a decentralised topology, where all terminals must know the addresses of all participants in order to send/receive audiovisual data to/from all the others. In H.323 for LAN the problem is solved with IP multicast. Audiovisual data is sent to group addresses, and implicitly received by all terminals that belong to the group.

This is in contrast with ATM multicast, which due to its connection-oriented nature, each point-to-multipoint VC root must know the ATM addresses of the leafs to join. In H.323 ATM, the MC terminal must have a way to notify the other terminals about the ATM addresses of all participants. As the current H.245 specification (see [12]) does not include this functionality, we propose the addition of two H.245 messages **AddMultipointParty** and **DropMultipointParty**, together with their acknowledgement messages **AddMultipaintPartyAck** and **DropMultipointPartyAck** respectively. The syntax of these messages is shown in Fig. 6 in ASN.1 notation.

```
AddMultipointParty          ::= SEQUENCE
{
  terminalLabel             TerminalLabel,
  h245Channel               TransportAddress,
  sessionTable              SET SIZE(1..256) OF SessionChannelTableEntry,
  ...
}
AddMultipointParty Ack      ::= SEQUENCE
{
  terminalLabel             TerminalLabel,
  ...
}

DropMultipointParty         ::= SEQUENCE
{
  terminalLabel             TerminalLabel,
  ...
}

DropMultipointPartyAck      ::= SEQUENCE
{
  terminalLabel             TerminalLabel,
  ...
}

SessionChannelTableEntry    ::= SEQUENCE
{
  sessionID                 INTEGER (1..255)
  dataType                  DataType
  mediaChannel              TransportAddress,
  mediaControlChannel       TransportAddress OPTIONAL,
  portNumber                INTEGER (0..65535),
  ...
}
```

Fig. 6. ASN.1 syntax for AddMultipointParty, DropMultipointParty and respective acknowledgements.

The **AddMultipointParty** message is sent by the MC terminal to notify a participant about the ATM SAPs dedicated to each session in another participant. In this way, the notified terminal can join those ATM SAPs as leafs of its outgoing point-to-multipoint VCs (see Fig. 7).

The **DropMultipointParty** message has the opposite purpose, i.e. to notify about the disconnection of a participant.

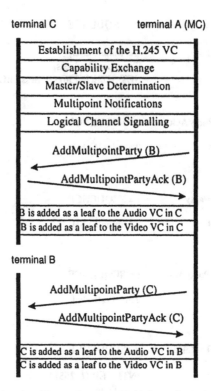

Fig. 7. Terminal C is added to the videoconference, of which terminals A and B are already participants.

4 H.323 ATM application

A videoconference application was developed in order to demonstrate the feasibility of H.323 ATM. The selected operating system is Microsoft Windows (95 and NT4 versions), due to the native ATM support offered by the WinSock 2 API, as well as the Video For Windows multimedia device control interface. The application architecture is depicted in Fig. 8.

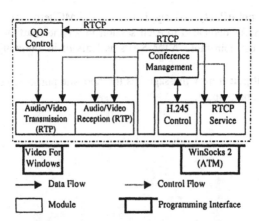

Fig. 8. Architecture of the H.323 ATM application.

Below is a brief description of each application module:

- **Conference Management:** This is the core of the application. It is responsible for the initialisation and coordination of the other modules, taking into account both the user options and the H.245 Control notifications.
- **H.245 Control:** It implements H.245 signalling and the MC functions. In case of a non-MC terminal, it has only one H.245 instance (H.245 Agent) and the MC function is deactivated. In the MC terminal, the MC function is activated and there is one H.245 instance connected to each of the other participants.
- **Transmission:** This module performs local capture, compression, RTP encapsulation and transmission of audiovisual data.
- **Reception:** This module receives, decompresses and displays audiovisual data from only one remote sender. Therefore, in a multipoint-to-multipoint environment with n participants, there are $n - 1$ instances of this module in the application. It also sends RTCP **RRs** periodically, in order to be processed by the QOS Control module at the sender.
- **QOS Control:** Based on the RTCP **RRs** sent by remote receivers, this module evaluates overall reception quality, and tries to improve it by adjusting capture parameters in the Transmission module.
- It uses a QOS control algorithm for multicast environments similar to the algorithm presented in [13]. It is also responsible for sending RTCP **SRs** periodically.
- **RTCP Service:** The internal architecture of this module is depicted in Fig. 9. It implements the CLS Service for the transport of RTCP messages. In case of a non-MC terminal, it has only one CLS instance (CLS Agent) and the CLS Server function is deactivated. In the MC terminal, the CLS Server function is activated and there is one CLS instance connected to each of the other participants.

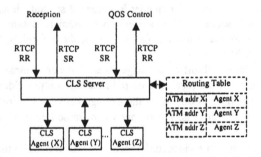

Fig. 9. Architecture of the RTCP service.

In order to evaluate the feasibility of the proposed architecture with currently existing equipment, the developed application was tested in a local ATM network with three PCs, each equipped with 25 Mbps ATM card and connected to the ATM switch.

In order to verify the effectiveness of the dynamic QOS adaptation, as well as to evaluate the performance of H.323 ATM multipoint-to-multipoint videoconference, a heterogeneous environment was created deploying PCs with different hardware support and operating systems. The PC characteristics are presented in Table 4and Table 5.

Table 4. PCs used for testing the H.323 ATM application.

PC	CPU	Memory	Operating System
PC1	Pentium 166 MHz MMX	64MB	Windows 95
PC2	Pentium II 233 Mhz MMX	64MB	Windows 95
PC3	Pentium 166 MHz	32MB	Windows NT 4.0 Server

Table 5. Multimedia devices used in the tests.

PC	Video capture card	Video camera	Audio card
PC1	Intel Smart Video Recorder III (MMX support)	Philips VCM7510	Sound Blaster 16
PC2	Intel Smart Video Recorder III (MMX support)	SONY EVI-D31	Crystal AV320
PC3	No H/W support for video	Connectix QuickCam B/W	Crystal AV320

The tests were performed with the INTEL Indeo format for video and G.728 (16 Kbps LD-CELP) format for audio.

The following parameters were used for the QOS Control algorithm presented in [13] and explained in the Appendix: $\alpha = 0.7$; $\lambda c = 0.4$; $\lambda u = 0.1$; $Nd = 0.1$; $Nh = 0.1$; $\mu = 0.8$; $\nu = 1$ frame/s; interval between RTCP Sender Reports = 3 seconds; interval between RTCP Receiver Reports = 3 seconds. This conservative parameterisation was chosen experimentally in order to prevent erroneous oscillations of the algorithm, while allowing efficient use of available bandwidth.

Two tests were made with different image sizes, in order to measure the performance of the system in terms of the receiver loss ratio and the output video frame rate. In the results, the frame loss ratio of one PC is the average between the frame loss ratios of all received audio and video streams. The output video frame rate is measured in frames per second (fps).

PC1 was chosen to start the videoconference, and thus it became the MC terminal. The videoconference establishment sequence corresponds to the signalling example described above:

1. PC1 creates a videoconference with PC2;
2. PC1 adds PC3 to the videoconference.

It should be noted that the measurements are only presented from the end of step 2 onwards. This means that although all PCs start with the same output video frame rate, during the interval between steps 1 and 2 (a few seconds), the QOS control algorithm in PC1 and PC2 is already responding and adjusting the video frame rate.

The first test was done with the Indeo small image size (160×120 pixels). The initial frame rate was 20 fps. The connection setup delay was of 2 seconds. As the measurements gave similar results in all PCs, only the measurements taken in PC1 are shown, and can be seen in Fig. 10. A null loss ratio in all PCs prompted the QOS control algorithm to gradually increase the output frame rate, until the maximum (30 fps) was reached.

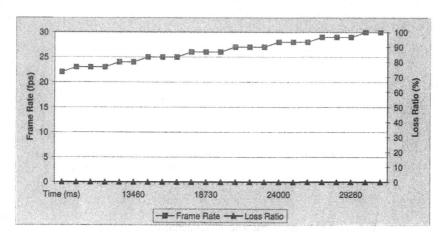

Fig. 10. Frame rate and loss ratio in PC1 during the first test.

Table 6 shows the output bit-rate for each PC, once the maximum video frame rate is reached. The videoconference termination delay was of 3 seconds.

Table 6. Output bit-rates after the QoS control algorithm reaches equilibrium during the first test.

PC	Minimum bit-rate (Kbps)	Average bit-rate (Kbps)	Maximum bit-rate (Kbps)
PC1	302	338	360
PC2	292	377	441
PC3	52	65	78

The second test was performed using the Indeo large image size (320×240 pixels). This time, all the PCs started with an output video frame rate of 15 fps. As can be seen in Figs. 11-13, before PC3 was added to the conference, PC1 and PC2 already reached an steady state. Although not shown in the figures, PC1 had a few frame losses during initialisation, inducing PC2 to slightly decrease the frame rate below the initial 15 fps. At the moment PC3 was added, PC1 had already recovered and PC2 was slowly increasing the frame rate again. After the videoconference was completely established (delay of 7 seconds), the loss ratio in PC3 started to increase and urged PC1 and PC2 to decrease their output frame rates. Equilibrium was reached between 3 and 10 fps, where PC3 had a small or null loss ratio. On the other hand, PC1 and PC2 registered null frame loss ratios, allowing PC3 to increase the video frame rate until the maximum of 30 fps was reached.

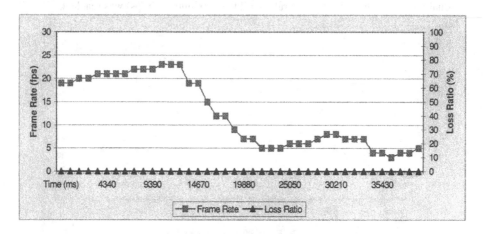

Fig. 11. Frame rate and loss ratio in PC1 during the second test.

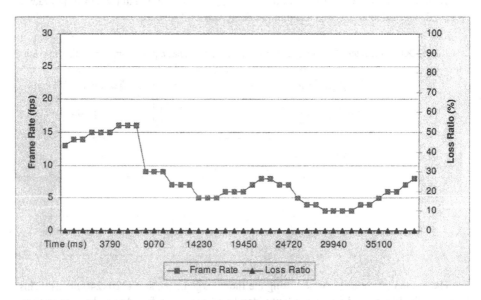

Fig. 12. Frame rate and loss ratio in PC2 during the second test.

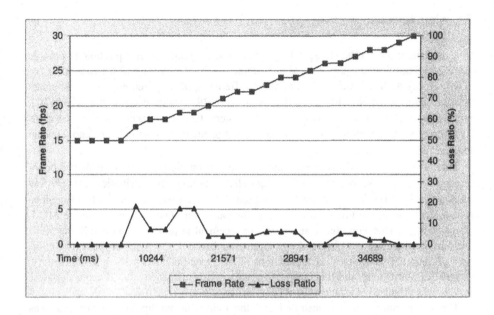

Fig. 13. Frame rate and loss ratio in PC3 during the second test.

Table 7 shows the output bit-rate for each PC, once equilibrium is reached. The video-conference termination delay was of 3 seconds.

Table 7. Output bit-rates after the QoS control algorithm reaches equilibrium during the second test.

PC	Minimum bit-rate (Kbps)	Average bit-rate (Kbps)	Maximum bit-rate (Kbps)
PC1	122	437	738
PC2	194	408	788
PC3	57	164	343

5 Conclusions

This paper proposes the H.323 ATM architecture, showing that it is possible to provide the H.323 flexibility in a native ATM environment, taking advantage of the capabilities of ATM. H.323 ATM allows the definition of different QOS requirements for audiovisual streams. In association with the VBR, ABR or UBR service classes, the RTP/RTCP mechanism makes video transmission more efficient, taking into account reception quality in order to dynamically adapt the video output bandwidth to the network and terminal load and characteristics.

The advantages of a decentralised architecture for multipoint-to-multipoint videoconference were also discussed. H.323 decentralises audiovisual distribution using ATM multicast, which is based on point-to-multipoint VCs. Videoconference control functions remain centralised, but this time inside a participating terminal, not in a separate MCU, simplifying the videoconference setup and management in private networks. Some problems arise, which are not observed by current standards. H.323 ATM proposes the addition of four new messages to the current H.245 specification: **AddMultipointParty**, **DropMultipointParty** and their respective acknowledgements. An ATM connectionless service was proposed to manage the RTCP traffic.

The architecture was demonstrated and the multipoint-multipoint performance was measured in a heterogeneous environment with three participants. The results show that current technology allows H.323 ATM decentralised multipoint-to-multipoint videoconference, with some trade-off between video quality and the number of participants, a situation that can only improve in the future, with the increasing processing power of the terminals.

The presented work is partially funded by the European Union in theframework of the ACTS program, project AROMA (AC327). The authors alone are responsible for the content of the paper.

References

1. ITU-T Recommendation H.321: Broadband Audiovisual Communication Systems and Terminals. ITU-T, 1995.
2. ITU-T Recommendation H.310: Broadband Audiovisual Communication Systems and Terminals. ITU-T, 1996.
3. ITU-T Recommendation H.323: Visual Telephone Systems and Equipment for Local Area Networks which Provide a Non-Guaranteed Quality of Service. ITU-T, 1996.
4. ITU-T Recommendation H.320: Narrow-band ISDN visual telephone systems and terminal equipment. ITU-T, 1995.
5. H. Schulzrinne: RTP Profile for Audio and Video Conferences with Minimal Control. IETF RFC 1890, January 1996.
6. H. Schulzrinne, S. Casner, R. Frederick, V. Jacobson: RTP: A Transport Protocol for Real-Time Applications. IETF RFC 1889, January 1996.
7. ATM Forum: H.323 Media Transport Over ATM Baseline Text. ATM Forum BTD-SAA-RMOA-01.03, 1998.
8. ATM Forum: User-Network Interface (UNI) Specification Version 3.1. ATM Forum User-Network (UNI) Specification Version 3.1, 1994.

9. ITU-T Recommendation F.732: Multimedia Conference Services in the B-ISDN. ITU-T, 1996.
10. ATM Forum: Proposed Requirements for Native ATM Connectionless Service (CLS). ATM Forum RTD-SAA-CLS-01.00, 1998.
11. N. Antunes, R. Rocha, P. Pinto: Analysis and Simulation of a Traffic Management Control Scheme for ATM Switches with Loose Commitments. In Int. Conf. On Networks and Distributed Systems Modeling and Simulation, Phoenix, 1997.
12. ITU-T: Control Protocol for Multimedia Communication. ITU-T Recommendation H.245, 1996.
13. I. Busse, B. Deffner, H. Schulzrinne: Dynamic QOS Control of Multimedia Applications based on RTP. In Computer Communications, 19, Number 1, January 1996.

Appendix: Dynamic QoS Control in Multipoint Environments

The algorithm for dynamic QoS control of RTP based multipoint multimedia applications is presented in [13]. This algorithm comprises the following three phases:

- **RTCP Analysis.** The RTCP Receiver Reports of all receivers are analysed and statistics of packet loss, jitter, etc. are computed.
- **Network State Estimation.** The actual network congestion state seen by every receiver is determined as unloaded, loaded or congested. This is used to decide whether to increase, hold or decrease the bandwidth requirements of the sender.
- **Bandwidth Adjustment.** The bandwidth of the multimedia application is adjusted according to the decision of the network state estimation. The user can set the range of adjustable bandwidth, i.e. specify the minimum and maximum bandwidth.

For **RTCP Analysis**, the source provides a record for each receiver containing the most recent receiver reports. In the current scheme only the loss rate is used as a congestion indicator. Statistics are smoothed by a filter in order to avoid QoS oscillations. The smoothed loss rate λ is computed by the low-pass filter $\lambda \leftarrow (1 - \alpha)\lambda + \alpha b$, where b is the most recent value and $0 \leq \alpha \leq 1$. In our case, λ corresponds to the average between audio and video loss.

As a measure of congestion, the **Network State Estimation** algorithm uses the smoothed loss rate observed by the receivers. The network congestion state is determined and used to make the decision of increasing, holding or decreasing the bandwidth through the use of a linear regulator with dead zone. Two thresholds are used to determine the network state seen by each receiver as UNLOADED, LOADED or CONGESTED according to the distinction in Fig. 14.

The upper threshold λ_c should be chosen so that the data transmission may suffer from the losses but is still acceptable. The dead zone must be large enough, i.e. λ_u must be low enough to avoid QoS oscillations.

In the unicast case the network congestion state can be directly mapped to decrease, hold and increase, respectively. In the case of a point-to-multipoint connection, a large number of receivers are receiving multicast real-time data and are sending back receiver reports. Should the bandwidth of a video session be decreased only because one link on the other end of the world suffers from high packet loss? One possible solution is to count

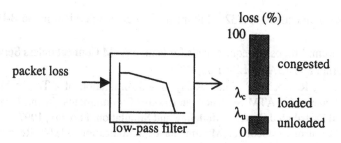

Fig. 14. Receiver classification.

the network congestion states as seen by the receivers and to derive the adjustment decision from the proportion of unloaded, loaded and congested receivers. Firstly, all receivers are classified as described above, and the algorithm proceeds to the calculation of the
number of receivers in the unloaded state n_u, in the loaded state n_l and in the congested
state n_c as well as the total number of receivers n. The decision (d) is taken according to
the following algorithm:

```
if        n_c/n ≥ N_d   then        d ← DECREASE

else if   n_l/n ≥ N_h   then        d ← HOLD

else                                d ← INCREASE
```

Another important aspect is how the **Bandwidth Adjustment** is performed. In our
case, only the video bandwidth is changed. Video bandwidth is measured as a frame-rate
in frames-per-second (fps). In the case of congestion the application should rapidly reduce
its bandwidth. This behaviour can be obtained by using a multiplicative factor μ for the
DECREASE decision and an additive factor ν for the INCREASE decision. If the decision is HOLD, no changes take place. Bandwidth is always kept within the interval [b_{min},
b_{max}]. The bandwidth adjustment algorithm is the following:

```
if       d = DECREASE    then       b_a ← max{b_r * μ,
b_min}

else if  d = INCREASE    then       b_a ← min{b_r + ν,
b_max}
```

where b_r is the reported bandwidth and b_a is the allowed bandwidth, with $b_a, b_r \in$ [b_{min},
b_{max}]. The former is the actual bandwidth as reported in the most recent RTCP Sender Report (in our case it corresponds to the current video output frame-rate), while the latter is
the allowed output bandwidth that can be used by the application.

Some Design Issues of SRMTP, a Scalable Reliable Multicast Transport Protocol

Stephan Block[1], Ken Chen[2], Philippe Godlewski[1], and Ahmed Serhrouchni[1]

[1] ENST and CNRS URA 820, Paris, France
[2] L2TI, Institut GALILEE, Université Paris 13, France

Abstract. In this paper, we propose a transport layer protocol for one-to-many multicast that is designed to have good scalability properties in large receiver groups and provides reliable transmission. Reliability is achieved using forward error correction (FEC) in combination with selective repeat NAK-based ARQ. Using FEC can significantly reduce the necessity for retransmission requests or make them totally unnecessary, which is important in wireless and satellite communicaton environments, as well as for delay-sensitive multimedia applications. The protocol uses one multicast group address for the original transmission and a second group address for the handling of retransmissions, which helps in significantly reducing the network load on branches with low loss and facilitates usage in the context of satellite communications. We hope that our work will be useful and encouraging for the development of group communication applications.

1 Introduction

Communication between people is not limited to one-to-one conversation. Being able to talk in groups is an important feature across all communication media. In computer networks, however, much research is still needed in the field of group communication. The demand for group-aware applications and network technology is growing. Some examples for applications are data distribution (software upgrades, electronic newspapers, database replication, etc.), and multimedia applications like the transmission of radio or TV programs. For many of these applications, there are software products available. But since the standard network protocol stacks dont't provide versatile, reliable, easy-to-use group communication, developers are forced to implement their own group communication protocols into their applications. This certainly leads to non-interoperable protocols and duplicate development efforts. To help remedy this situation, we are proposing a scalable, reliable, transport layer Multicast protocol that can be adapted to suit a broad range of applications and network structures. We have carried out a simulation to study the behavior of the protocol for different scenarios, and we are currently working on an implementation in C for various UNIX platforms.

The remainder of this article is organized as follows. In Sect. 2 we introduce related work. Section 3 describes the problems associated with reliable multicast and the solutions we propose with our protocol. In Sect. 4 we present our simulation model and derive some formulas for timers and memory capacity for the retransmitter. Section 5 presents and discusses some numerical results of the simulation. Section 6 concludes the article with some remarks and an outlook on future work.

2 Related Work

A general introduction to multicast and associated problems under various aspects is given in [3].

The authors of [8] examine many-to-many group communication protocols and compare different group topologies (tree, ring) and sender-initiated vs. receiver-initiated protocols. They find that in general receiver-initiated protocols in a tree topology perform better than all other reviewed classes.

In [16], the authors compare the throughput of sender-initiated and receiver-initiated reliable multicast protocols. Their analysis shows the general superiority of a receiver-based approach.

The backoff mechanisms we use in our protocol proposal are described in [14].

A performance comparison of a multicast tree with one log server and a hierarchy of local log servers is carried out in [11]; the authors show that the performance of the latter is better. They also find that the use of parity information (i.e., one retransmitted data packet can repair different losses at different receivers[1]) can increase performance close to that of a protocol with multiple local log servers. This is also discussed in [4,6].

Multicasting retransmissions to all receivers generates a certain overhead because all receivers have to process the packets and decide whether they are interested or not. This effect can be reduced if there is a separate multicast address associated with the retransmissions for every block of n data packets. This topic is discussed in [7]. The authors find that with a relatively small number of retransmission groups the desired effect can be achieved. On the other hand, overhead is created by the join and leave operations and multicast group setup.

In [12,13], the author shows that FEC implemented in software is reasonably fast even on today's available desktop PCs.

Some thoughts on where to use FEC are presented in [10]. The authors discuss different multicast tree topologies, different degrees of loss, and different multicast group sizes. They find that FEC is used profitably, especially for big multicast groups, when FEC is applied to all links of the multicast tree.

3 Reliable Multicast

3.1 Problems

One of the major problems in reliable multicast is the risk of *implosion*. Ensuring reliable data transfer implies that there is some exchange of state information

---

[1] which is essentially the effect of using Forward Error Correction (FEC)

between sender and receivers, i.e. the sender must have some way of knowing if the data has arrived at all receivers. Whether we use positive confirmation for received data packets or negative confirmation for lost packets, the risk that these messages arrive all at the same time at the sender (they "implode" onto the sender) exists in both cases. This is the case notably with very large multicast groups.

A very important issue of a multicast transport protocol is its scalability, i.e. its ability to support groups of different sizes without major degradation of the quality of service. The traditional way to ensure reliability in unicast is to have the receiver send positive acknowledgment messages (ACKs) back to the sender whenever it has successfully received some amount of data. This approach, however, is not suitable in a multicast context where the multicast groups can be very large. One problem is that the sender has to keep state information about every single participating receiver so that it knows when it is safe to flush the send buffers. For large groups, this can represent an important load in terms of CPU and memory usage.

Another problem with this approach concerns the network load. In the case of large groups, the impact of the ACK messages on the network is not negligible. This holds especially true if the multicast tree is dense. What's worse, the ACK messages are not equally distributed over time, but they arrive at the sender in bursts. The consequence can be network congestion, which can seriously affect the performance of the whole transmission group.

Because of these inconveniencies associated with positive acknowledgments, most proposals for reliable multicast protocols are promoting another solution: instead of confirming positively the reception of data, the receivers send *negative acknowledgment messages* (NAKs) back to the sender whenever they are missing some data. The rationale behind this is that generally the data packets will not be lost in the network, so in the general case it is not necessary to send positive ACKs for the data. Instead we will send negative acknowledgements for the case that is supposed to be the rare one. This means actually a transfer of responsibility from the sender to the individual receivers. From a fairness point of view, this can also be justified: since it is the receiver that wants to get something from the sender, it seems logical that the receiver should be responsible for correct delivery.

However, this approach has some weak points, too:

Impossibility to obtain total reliability. The sender can never be sure if all receivers have successfully captured the sent data. If several consecutive packets are lost for a particular receiver, it will take a long time for it to detect the loss and request retransmission. So, in theory, the log server must have an infinite memory to store the data for possible retransmissions, because it is always possible that it receives a retransmission request for a packet it just purged from the buffer.

Risk of implosion. Even if the risk of implosion is very much reduced, it does not completely disappear. It is still possible that several receivers experience packet loss quasi-simultaneously, notably in situations where the packets are routed in a tree-like topology. If the packet loss occurs near the root of the tree, the consequence is a very large part of the multicast group sending their NAK messages to the sender at the same time. This then leads to the same problems as described in the ACK-based case.

Packet loss detection delay. Packet loss can only be detected by noticing a gap in the packet sequence numbers. In other words, a receiver can detect a loss only after again having received a packet correctly. If the transmission often contains longer periods of silence, the time it takes to detect a loss is significantly increased. For certain applications (e.g. "live" audio or video transmission), this is inacceptable.

Despite these weak points, the reduction of the server load by employing the NAK-based scheme is in most cases significant. Analytical studies [16] have shown the superiority of this scheme in contrast to the ACK-based approach in terms of maximum throughput. So we have selected this approach for our protocol proposal.

3.2 Our Solution

Contractual Group Membership. As we have seen, the ACK-based ARQ approach for ensuring reliability is not appropriate in the context of group communication, especially with very large receiver groups. For this reason we have chosen to use the NAK-based scheme where a receiver requests the retransmission of lost packets. We have also stated that with this mechanism, it is impossible to guarantee total reliability in all cases. But, as we will demonstrate, it *is* possible to guarantee reliability for a class of receivers that fulfill certain criteria. These criteria define some QoS parameters, like the minimum bandwidth or the maximum packet loss rate. The idea behind that is to put the receivers into groups that are relatively homogeneous so that no receiver will overly obstruct the communication by requesting retransmissions frequently (this is often referred to as the "crying baby" problem).

We call this mechanism "contractual group membership" because each receiver has to "sign a contract" before being granted access to the multicast group. If a receiver "violates" the conditions imposed by the contract, it has to leave the group. The specific contract parameters are announced periodically by the sender, and an interested receiver can decide if it wants to join the transmission after having examined these announce messages.

As there is no explicit session opening handshake between sender and receivers, it is not possible for the sender to reject interested receivers that are not capable of fulfilling the "contract". Instead, it also lies in the receiver's responsibility to obey the rules and not try to follow such a transmission.

The conditions that constitute the contract are based on constraints imposed by the network, such as the bandwidth, the round trip time (RTT), the packet loss rate (as measured by the number of retransmissions being requested during a certain period of time). Based on these parameters, we can dimension the sender's send buffers so that we can assure contractual reliability if the receivers fulfill their contracts.

The "contract" and resource management is subject to an external group and resource management protocol, which in IP networks could be based e.g. on RSVP [1]; similar mechanisms exist for other network types, e.g. ATM. This external protocol is not discussed here. It could also provide mechanisms for authorization, host-based or user-based access control, accounting, and key management (if the data transmission is to be encrypted[2]).

Separation of Transmission and Retransmission. As we have stated earlier, NAK messages are generated by receivers that have detected a problem, i.e. they are missing one or more data packets. These NAK messages, as well as the retransmitted data packets, are of interest only to those receivers that do experience packet loss. This leads us to the conclusion that it would probably be a good idea to separate the retransmission handling from the original transmission. We try to accomplish this by creating a secondary transmission group (called a "channel") for NAK and retransmission handling. In other words, we are creating a *formal group* of potential NAK sources. The primary channel is reserved exclusively for the original data transmission. Only receivers that have experienced packet loss are listening to the secondary channel; the other receivers are freed from the burden of processing messages on the secondary channel. This also minimizes network load on branches with no packet loss. Another benefit from the separation of original transmission and retransmissions is that it facilitates the use of different physical networks for the two channels; e.g. the original transmission could be distributed via satellite, while retransmissions could be handled over a dial-on-demand modem or ISDN link.

Figure 1 shows the communication relations used by the protocol. As stated above, the primary and secondary channel do not necessarily have to be transmitted by the same network.

Minimizing Costs for NAKs. The NAK-based error control scheme helps reducing the risk of implosion, but it can't avoid it in all cases, notably when packet loss occurs near the root of the multicast tree. There is an algorithm, proposed by Santoso and Fdida [15], which uses a backoff technique to suppress multiple NAKs requesting the same data packets. Its principle is the following. Whenever a receiver notices a packet loss, it joins the secondary channel, but it does not immediately send a NAK. Instead it starts a backlog timer. The value of this timer is the greater, the fewer packets will be requested by this NAK. While the backlog timer is counting down, the receiver monitors the secondary channel for NAKs from other receivers that request the same (or more) missing packets. If such a NAK is seen while the backlog timer runs, the receiver cancels

---

[2] encryption etc. are tasks of the application layer and are not handled by our transport protocol

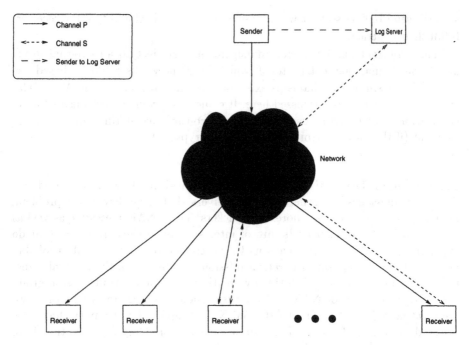

Fig. 1. Relations between the communication partners

the transmission of its own scheduled NAK.[3] This algorithm reduces the number of NAKs in an effective manner, as far as it is *statistically provable* that only one of the affected receivers will transmit a NAK by carefully determining the backoff timer values.

As mentioned earlier, there is a certain overhead associated with the join and leave operations that occur when employing the mentioned algorithm. Depending on the actual loss in the network, this could become a problem if receivers frequently join and leave the secondary channel. There are two possible solutions. One consists in adapting the FEC parameters so that receivers can recover from loss without needing to request retransmissions frequently. Another solution would be to delay the leave operation after a successful retransmission, in order to keep the set of receivers that are members of the secondary channel persistent. The appropriate timer values could be determined by the individual receivers themselves, by measuring the time between two join operations for the secondary channel.

Forward Error Correction. The methods and algorithms we have introduced so far have the goal of reducing problems that arise with packet loss and retransmissions. By using the principle of Forward Error Correction (FEC), it is

---

[3] Actually, the backlog timer for the cancelled NAK is just reset, in case the "other" NAK is lost in the network afterwards.

possible to drastically reduce or even eliminate the need for retransmission. FEC uses Reed-Solomon codes to encode the data. These encode a message consisting of k data packets into n data packets so that it is possible to reconstruct the original message out of *any* k received packets. In other words, we add redundant information. This means that the amount of data to be actually transmitted is increased by $(n-k)/k$. Since this amount is known in advance, it can be allowed for in network resource management procedures. This, obviously, is not the case for NAKs and retransmissions.

Using FEC with an appropriate ratio n/k can *totally eliminate* the need for NAKs and retransmissions, i.e. it can eliminate the causes for implosion. It also avoids the high delays associated with retransmission requests. For certain classes of applications, like live audio or video transmission, this is a crucial requirement. There are other scenarios where it is very difficult or expensive to use a secondary feedback channel, like e.g. satellite or mobile communications. Applications in these environments can certainly take advantage from the use of the FEC mechanism.

The usage of FEC imposes a processing charge on the sender and receivers, but recent studies (e.g. Rizzo [13]) show, FEC can be done reasonably fast in Software on today's available desktop computers.

As a sidenote, the FEC procedure contributes to the scalability of the protocol because there is no dependency on the number of receivers.

A Dedicated Retransmission Server. The task of managing retransmissions can be a heavy burden for a sender. In order to face this situation, the use of a special retransmission server (*log server*) has been proposed by Holbrook et al. [5]. A log server for a multipoint communication is a separate entity, usually (but not necessarily) located on a separate machine, that keeps a copy of the data transfer. It receives this copy from the sender via a reliable point-to-point connection (e.g. TCP).

Implementing the idea of a log server is made easy by our proposition of two distinct multicast channels. In fact, it is sufficient for the log server to be member of the secondary channel. The original sender can be completely disconnected from the secondary channel.

We are not limited to using just one log server; for large, geographically wide distributed groups it would probably be a good idea to introduce local log servers. The protocol can easily be extended to use multiple local log servers simultaneously.

Limiting Error Detection Time. As we have seen earlier, the choice of the NAK-based error control mechanism is essential to obtain a scalable protocol. However, this choice also arises several problems. One of these is that the sender can never be sure whether all receivers have correctly received a data block, because they only give feedback if they experience packet loss. Packet loss is detected by a receiver if it notices a gap in the sequence numbers of arriving data packets. This implies that loss can only be detected after again having successfully received a data packet after a loss. For smooth data transfers, this is not a problem since the time intervals between packets are relatively small and equally distributed. But if we have bursty traffic and longer periods of silence, a receiver is not able to distinguish if the silence is intentionally or if there really is a problem in the network. We can avoid this uncertainty on the receivers' side if we ensure a maximum time interval between two packets. In the case where there is no application data available for transmission, the sender transmits "heartbeat" packets to indicate that the transmission is still "alive". So, a receiver can reliably detect that there is a problem, and thus will schedule a NAK, if it receives nothing for this maximum time interval. In other words, by limiting the maximum time interval between two packets, we effectively create an upper limit for the error detection time.

Limiting Log Server Storage Requirements. Another problem with the NAK approach to reliable transfer is that, to achieve 100% reliability, the log server must have infinite storage capacity. This becomes clear if we think about multiple packets that are lost consecutively. Thanks to the "heartbeat" we have an upper time limit to detect one lost packet. If two packets in a row are lost, this time limit is doubled; for three lost packets it is tripled, and so on. The log server has no means of knowing if a particular receiver experiences packet loss of, say, 100 or 1000 consecutive packets. So, in theory, to be 100% reliable, it has to store all data for ever. It can never reclaim its buffers for new data.

It is clear that there must be some mechanism to limit the amount of stored data. We propose the following solution. Starting from the QoS contract, we have a given probability for the loss of an individual packet. We define a probability q which expresses the probability that more than m consecutive packets are lost. We are willing to accept that with this probability q, a transmission can be aborted due to packets requested for retransmission that are already purged from the log server's memory. Based on this, we can calculate the maximum acceptable number m of consecutively lost packets, and in turn the maximum time it takes to detect and repair (by retransmission) this condition. From the knowledge of this maximum time we can then calculate the required memory size of the log server. In other words, we can guarantee a successful transfer on the condition that no more than m packets are lost consecutively. Since this condition is part of the contract a receiver has to "sign" when joining the transmission, we can state that we can provide a reliable, NAK-based transport with a limited log server capacity.

The detailed calculations can be found in Sect. 4.

3.3 Implementation Details

The protocol provides layer 4 multicast functionality. Like unicast TCP, it offers reliable virtual-circuit transport. It builds on top of the available layer 3 multicast capabilities, e.g. IP Multicast [2].

Figure 2 shows a block diagram of the cooperating layer 4 functions of the communicating parties and the data flow between them.

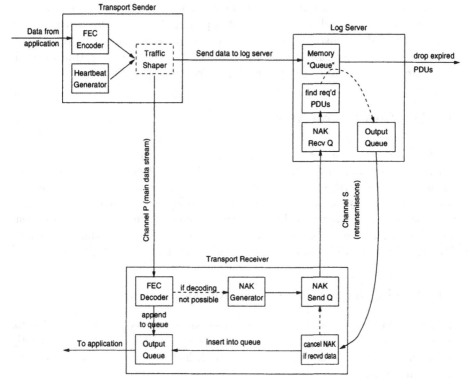

Fig. 2. Layer 4 Functions Block Diagram of Sender, Log Server and Receiver

During idle periods, when the application temporarily does not send data, the transport sender generates a "heartbeat", small packets that are sent at fixed intervals, so that the receivers know that the network connection is still operational. Status information, such as the current position in the data stream, changes in FEC parameters, etc., can be transmitted with the heartbeat.

The proposed NAK suppression mechanism has a potential weak point: If there are several receivers experiencing identical loss patterns, they generate identical NAK messages. The consequence is that their NAK backlog timers also have the same value and thus will expire at the same time. In this (rare) case, duplicate NAKs are sent out. We address this problem by adding a random period of time to the NAK backlog timer, so that the probability for two timers expiring simultaneously is reduced.

Due to varying network traffic, leading to a certain jitter in end-to-end transmission times, it is in practice impossible to avoid all redundant NAKs by the proposed timer-based NAK backlogging. So we use a similar technique at the log server. Incoming NAKs are kept in a waiting queue, and the log server tries to merge arriving NAKs with the NAKs already in the queue. This bears the potential to avoid many unnecessary multiple data retransmissions.

These backlogging techniques help reducing the network load, but at the same time they increase the application end-to-end delay. Choosing the values for the backlog timer algorithms implies making a trade-off between the network load and the end-to-end delay, and what is preferable or acceptable depends on the nature of the transmission, on technical network issues, on network access policies, etc. In either case, it is probably the best to try to avoid retransmissions in the first place by adjusting the FEC parameters appropriately.[4]

4 The Simulation Model

We have implemented the protocol in a simulation environment to evaluate the behavior under different scenarios. In contrast to most of the previous work on the performance of reliable multicast, we use the Full Binary Tree as the underlying routing topolgy for our simulation, as shown in Fig. 3, which Nonnenmacher and Biersack have shown to be a realistic model [9]. In a tree, losses on one branch can affect more than one receiver. This is unlike e.g. the mostly-used Multihop Fanout, where losses on one branch affect only a single receiver.

4.1 Backlogging NAKs and Data Retransmission

To avoid NAK implosion and retransmission storms, we try to make sure that for a sequence of missing packets there is exactly one NAK generated and exactly one retransmission issued. We try to accomplish this by backlogging NAKs and retransmissions.

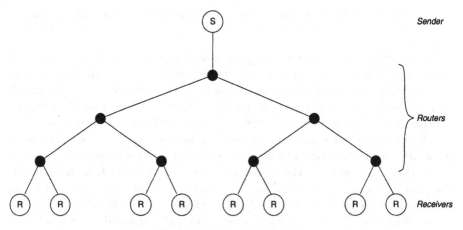

Fig. 3. Multicast Tree Model

If, e.g., receiver A requests 4 packets from the last transmission block and receiver B requests 3 packets, then the backlog time for receiver B has to be

---

[4] Implementations of this protocol could provide dynamic adjusting of these parameters.

longer than the time for receiver A in such a way that B has a chance to hear A's NAK before its own backlog timer expires. B then restarts its own backlog timer (in case A's NAK or the response are lost).

Timings in a packet switched network do vary, so that it is still possible that multiple NAKs requesting the same data packets are being sent. Furthermore, NAKs too can be lost on the way from one receiver to another while getting through to the log server. So, to avoid unnecessary multiple data retransmissions in these cases, we backlog the incoming queue at the log server and try to merge the incoming NAKs.

We now derive the formulas to compute the backlog times and the maximum capacity that is required for storage at the log server.

We assume knowledge of the following parameters:

- the (maximum) probability p that a packet is lost on one hop,
- the (maximum) time t_{SR} a packet needs to travel through the multicast tree from the sender to a receiver (and vice versa),
- the (maximum) number of hops h a packet makes from the sender to a receiver[5] (and vice versa),
- the (maximum) interval Δt_{gen} between two consecutive data (or heartbeat) packets sent by the sender on channel P.

We further assume that p is equal for all links and for all packet types, and that losses occur independently. Sender and log server are located on the same network node, and the two channels are transmitted using the same network. The (maximum) time t_{RR} a packet needs to get from one receiver to another receiver is assumed to be

$$t_{RR} = 2t_{SR} \ . \tag{1}$$

We define the probability q as the probability of the occurrence of a non-recoverable transmission error, i.e. the log server sees a NAK requesting data packets that have already been deleted from its memory, and thus this particular receiver must leave the transmission since reliable data transfer is no more possible. The value for q can be chosen arbitrarily at connection setup. Smaller values mean a larger storage capacity at the log server.

This probability q can be expressed in terms of the number of consecutive packets m that are lost on the way from the sender to a receiver (or vice versa):

$$q = \left(1 - (1-p)^h\right)^m \ . \tag{2}$$

Solving for m yields

$$m = \left\lceil \frac{\ln q}{\ln(1 - (1-p)^h)} \right\rceil \ . \tag{3}$$

Since $0 < p \ll 1$, the right hand side can be approximated as follows:

---

[5] i.e. the number of routers' incoming queues it passes on its way

$$m = \left[\frac{\ln q}{\ln(h \cdot p)} \right] \tag{4}$$

$$= \left[\frac{\ln q}{\ln h + \ln p} \right] \; . \tag{5}$$

This means that with the given probability $1 - q$, no more than m consecutive packets are lost for a particular receiver. This is valid for packets sent by the sender (and log server). For NAKs generated by the receivers, the worst-case scenario is that they traverse the tree up to the first router and then down again to the leaves, thus making $2(h - 1)$ hops. We define

$$m_{SR} = \frac{\ln q}{\ln(1 - (1 - p)^h)} \tag{6}$$

for the route sender $\leftrightarrow$ receiver, and

$$m_{RR} = \frac{\ln q}{\ln(1 - (1 - p)^{2(h-1)})} \tag{7}$$

for the route receiver $\leftrightarrow$ receiver, respectively.

The NAK backlog time can then be calculated to

$$t_{BR} = \text{MAX}(m_{RR} - l, 0) \cdot t_{RR} \tag{8}$$

where l is the actual number of requested data packets for retransmission.

If two receivers request the same number of data packets, the backlog timers of those receivers will have the same values. To circumvent this, we add a random element to the NAK backlog timer:

$$t_{BR} = (\text{MAX}(m_{RR} - l, 0) + d \cdot r) \cdot t_{RR} \tag{9}$$

where r is a random value in the range $[0 \mathinner{\ldotp\ldotp} 1]$, and d is a scaling factor for r.

The lower bound for t_{BR} is ($l \geq m_{RR}; r = 0$):

$$t_{BR \, \text{min}} = 0 \; ; \tag{10}$$

the upper bound is ($l = 0; r = 1$):

$$t_{BR \, \text{max}} = (m_{RR} + d) \cdot t_{RR} \; . \tag{11}$$

Thus, the maximum time difference at which NAKs requesting packets from the same block can arrive at the log server is

$$\Delta t = t_{BR \, \text{max}} = (m_{RR} + d) \cdot t_{RR} \; . \tag{12}$$

In order to be able to handle these NAKs with one retransmission, the NAK incoming backlog at the log server must be at least

$$t_{BS} = \Delta t = (m_{RR} + d) \cdot t_{RR} \; . \tag{13}$$

4.2 Log Server Capacity

Based on these results, we can now determine how many packets the log server must store that with a probability of $1 - q$ a retransmission request can be fulfilled.

The time a data packet has to be stored in the log server before we can say that with a probability of $1 - q$ it will no more be requested for retransmission is

$$t_{\text{expire}} = m \cdot \Delta t_{\text{gen}} + k \cdot t_{\text{BR max}} + 2t_{\text{SR}} \; , \tag{14}$$

where Δt_{gen} is the (maximal) interval of data transmission of the sender on channel P, k is (with a probability of $1 - s$) the maximum number of NAK packets that are lost in a row (derived analogously to m above), and t_{SR} is the time a packet needs to traverse the tree from root to leaf. Assuming that $s = q$, from which follows that $k = m$, we get

$$t_{\text{expire}} = m \cdot (\Delta t_{\text{gen}} + t_{\text{BR max}}) + 2t_{\text{SR}} \; . \tag{15}$$

We can now calculate the minimum number of data packets the log server must store in order to fulfill the requirements of the contractual reliability:

$$c_{\text{LS}} = \frac{t_{\text{expire}}}{\Delta t_{\text{gen}}} \tag{16}$$

$$= m + k\frac{t_{\text{BR max}}}{\Delta t_{\text{gen}}} + 2\frac{t_{\text{SR}}}{\Delta t_{\text{gen}}} \tag{17}$$

$$= m \cdot \left(1 + \frac{t_{\text{BR max}}}{\Delta t_{\text{gen}}}\right) + 2\frac{t_{\text{SR}}}{\Delta t_{\text{gen}}} \; . \tag{18}$$

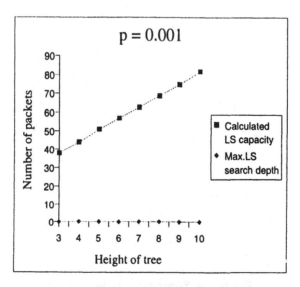

Fig. 4. Log Server capacity for $p = 0.001$

5   Numerical Results

The following diagrams present some results of our simulation runs. Graphs are shown for link loss probabilities of $p = 0.001$, $p = 0.010$ and $p = 0.050$. The tree height h that is given on the x axis includes the first hop from the sender to the top router (see Fig. 3), so that the number of receivers is actually $n_R = 2^{(h-1)}$. Thus, the graphs show multicast trees from 4 to 512 receivers. Note that the "end-to-end" loss probability increases with the tree height because packet loss occurs independently in each router's and receiver's incoming queue.

The FEC parameters are kept constant with a message size of $k = 12$ data packets and a redundancy of $n - k = 4$ packets, so that a total loss of 4 packets can be compensated without the need for retransmissions.

In the first graph series (Fig. 4 through 6), the calculated capacity of the log server is compared to the actually needed log server capacity. The lower absolute capacity numbers in Fig. 6 result from a lower packet sending rate (1 packet/sec instead of 10 packets/sec for the other graphs); this was necessary because of restrictions in the simulation environment.

As can be seen, the log server is able to fulfill all retransmission requests in all cases. Furthermore, the storage capacity that is needed is approximately proportional to the logarithm of the number of receivers. At first glance, it seems that the protocol does not scale well. But closer investigation reveals that this dependency exists because in the simulation model the round-trip time increases

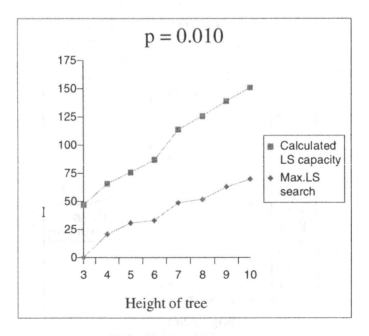

Fig. 5. Log Server capacity for $p = 0.010$

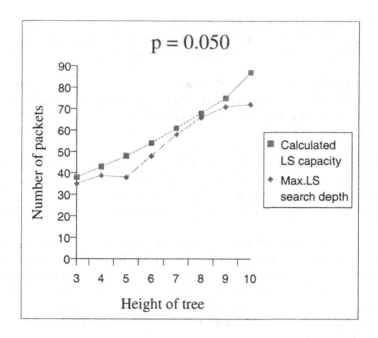

Fig. 6. Log Server capacity for $p = 0.050$

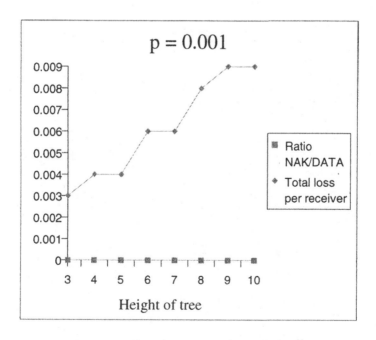

Fig. 7. NAK/data and total loss for $p = 0.001$

with the tree height (we have assumed a constant time per hop). The log server capacity depends directly on this round-trip time, so the graphs show an increase of needed capacity with the growing number of receivers.

In the case of high packet loss, the "safety margin" becomes very thin. A solution would be to increase the FEC redundancy. The increase in bandwidth usage by the additional FEC redundancy is compensated by the decreasing number of retransmissions.

The second graph series (Fig. 7 through 9) shows the ratio "NAKs seen at the log server" to "total number of data packets sent by the sender", as well as the average total packet loss experienced by the receivers (i.e. the total percentage of packets that were lost somewhere on the way from the sender to the receiver).

For networks with a high packet loss probability, the ratio NAK/data is very high. This high number of retransmissions implies higher latencies for the data transmission. It is clearly visible that in environments with potentially high loss rates, a protocol based only on NAKs and retransmissions is not suitable. The FEC solution proves its superiority especially in these cases. An implementation could contain dynamic adjustment of the FEC parameters, depending on the loss rate observed by the log server.

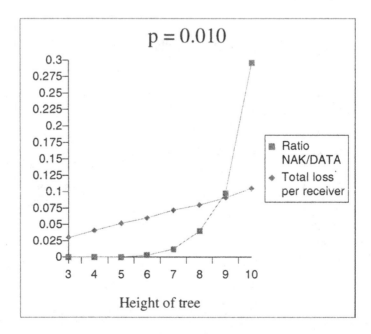

Fig. 8. NAK/data and total loss for $p = 0.010$

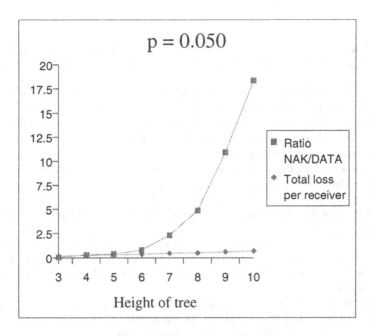

Fig. 9. NAK/data and total loss for $p = 0.050$

6 Conclusions and Further Work

We have presented some thoughts on the design of a scalable, reliable, one-to-many multicast transport protocol. The basic ideas behind our proposal are establishing a homogeneous receiver group, the use of backlogging techniques to avoid NAK implosion, a combination of FEC and ARQ for ensuring reliability, and using two separate multicast group addresses for the original transmission and for retransmissions.

The results of the simulation are encouraging. Our simulation has shown that the protocol scales well to large receiver groups. Due to the use of FEC, the amount of retransmissions can be drastically decreased or even totally eliminated. This makes the protocol applicable in fields where a feedback channel is very expensive or not available, e.g. satellite or mobile communications.

Further research could be directed to the following areas:

- optimizing retransmission handling,
- studying the effect of dynamic adjustment of FEC parameters,
- examining the use of a hierarchy of local retransmission servers,
- building a framework for the multicast group management ("contract" management, subscription and connection management, etc.)

References

[1] E. Braden, L. Zhang, S. Berson, S. Herzog, and S. Jamin. Resource ReSerVation Protocol (RSVP) – Version 1 Functional Specification. RFC 2205, September 1997.

[2] S. Deering. Host Extensions for IP Multicasting. RFC 1112, August 1989.

[3] Christophe Diot, Walid Dabbous, and Jon Crowcroft. Multipoint Communication: A Survey of Protocols, Functions, and Mechanisms. *IEEE Journal on Selected Areas in Communications*, 15(3):277–290, April 1997.

[4] Markus Hofmann, Torsten Braun, and Georg Carle. Multicast communication in large scale networks. In *Proceedings of Third IEEE Workshop on High Performance Communication Subsystems (HPCS)*, Mystic, Connecticut, August 1995.

[5] Hugh Holbrook, Sandeep Singhal, and David Cheriton. Log-based receiver-reliable multicast for distributed interactive simulation. In *ACM Computer Communication Review*, pages 328–341, August 1995.

[6] Sneha K. Kasera, Jim Kurose, and Don Towsley. A comparison of server-based and receiver-based local recovery approaches for scalable reliable multicast. Technical report, Department of Computer Science, University of Massachusetts, Amherst, November 1997.

[7] Sneha K. Kasera, Jim Kurose, and Don Towsley. Scalable Reliable Multicast Using Multiple Multicast Groups. Technical report, Department of Computer Science, University of Massachusetts, February 1997.

[8] Brian Neil Levine, David B. Lavo, and J. J. Garcia-Luna-Aceves. The case for reliable concurrent multicasting using shared ack trees. Technical report, Department of Computer Engineering, University of California, Santa Cruz, September 1996.

[9] Jörg Nonnenmacher and Ernst Biersack. Performance Modelling of Reliable Multicast Transmission. Technical report, Institut EURECOM, Sophia-Antipolis, France, December 1996.

[10] Jörg Nonnenmacher and Ernst W. Biersack. Reliable Multicast: Where to use FEC. Technical report, Corporate Communications Department, Institut EURECOM, Sophia-Antipolis, France, 1996.

[11] Jörg Nonnenmacher, Martin Lacher, Matthias Jung, Ernst W. Biersack, and Georg Carle. How bad is Reliable Multicast without Local Recovery. Technical report, Institut EURECOM, Sophia-Antipolis, France, January 1998.

[12] Luigi Rizzo. Effective erasure codes for reliable computer communication protocols. *ACM Computer Communication Review*, 27(2):24–36, April 1997.

[13] Luigi Rizzo. On the feasibility of software FEC. Technical report, Dip. di Ingegneria dell'Informazione, Università di Pisa, January 1997.

[14] Harry Santoso and Serge Fdida. An Efficient Error Control for Statistical Reliable Multicast. Technical report, August 1993.

[15] Harry Santoso and Serge Fdida. Transport Layer Statistical Multicast based on the XTP Bucket Algorithm. *Annales des Telecommunications*, November 1994.

[16] Don Towsley and Jim Kurose. A Comparison of Sender-Initiated and Receiver-Initiated Reliable Multicast Protocols. Technical report, Dept. of Electrical and Computer Engineering, University of Massachusetts, Amherst, October 1996.

A Multicast Gateway for Dial-In Lines *

Christoph Kuhmünch

Lehrstuhl für Praktische Informatik IV, Universät Mannheim,
L15,16, D-68 131 Mannheim, Germany,
cjk@pi4.informatik.uni-mannheim.de

Abstract. With the increasing number of MBone sessions the interest of home users to participate in multicast sessions is also increasing. Unfortunately the cost for the hardware necessary to participate in multicast sessions over a high speed link are still prohibitively high. This paper discusses technical problems and solutions for users who wish to participate in multicast sessions over dial-in lines and presents our approach, the *Dial-In Multicast Gateway*, which meets the requirements for an application layer multicast router with a restrictive broadcasting policy and a dynamic tunneling mechanism. The Dial-In Multicast Gateway allows the transmission of selected multicast sessions over dial-in connections such as modems, ISDN or even new network access technologies like ADSL by providing a mechanism to configure a multicast tunnel dynamically. For each selected media stream the desired quality of service parameters can be set interactively, e.g. a certain share of the available bandwidth can be reserved. In order to allow a graceful scaling of video we integrated a simple scaling mechanism for H.261 video streams that controls the temporal resolution of the video.

Keywords: *Dial-In lines, PPP, ISDN, MBone, media scaling*

1 Introduction

The MBone technology [4] made significant progress within the last two years and now allows a relatively dependable transmission of media streams via multicast. This technology allows new types of multimedia applications: Beside from multi-point video conferencing and video broadcasting services synchronous teleteaching [7] proofed to be an important application of the Internet and the MBone. A number of public domain tools for the transmission of media streams have been developed. Important applications are the MBone tools vic, vat and wb [18][17][13][14] which have triggered the development of many other applications like the dlb [8], the MBone VCRoD [12], sdr and rat from UCL and videophone from Nizza. But there are also a number of commercial tools available (e.g. IP-TV from Cisco, and Microsoft's Netshow). Java-Soft provides the Java Media Framework (JMF), a Java API for the development of multimedia tools.

This variety of applications attracted a large number of users who are responsible for an increasing number of sessions transmitted over the MBone. At the same time the number of

---

* This project is supported by the BMBF (Bundesministerium für Forschung und Technologie)

home users of the Internet — i.e. those users who are connected to the Internet via dial-in lines — increased enormously due to the rapidly falling costs for dial-in connections of Internet service providers (ISP). Low bandwidth dial-in connections such as modems or ISDN are now widely available and used. Unfortunately these network access technologies provide only a very low bandwidth between 28.8Kbit/s and 128Kbit/s. Nevertheless even the bandwidth of a modem with 28.8Kbit/s is sufficient for the transmission of a (low quality) audio stream and with ISDN lines (128Kbit/s) the transmission of a single session consisting of audio, video and whiteboard data is possible. For the near future new network access technologies like ADSL and cable modems, which allow a much higher bandwidth of up to 8Mbit/s, can be expected to replace the old low bandwidth techniques.

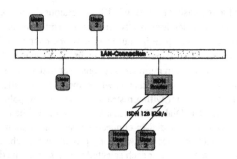

Fig. 1. An interactive home user scenario (IHU): A Multicast scenario with three users connected via highspeed LAN and two users connected via ISDN. Each participant is sending media streams via multicast and receives the media streams of all other participants via multicast.

For many of these home users multipoint video conferencing or participation in teleteaching lectures would be an interesting application but so far the transmission of multicast streams via dial-in lines is not possible for the following two reasons:

1. Typically, participants in a multicast session are connected over network technologies with different bandwidth, e.g. some users use highspeed LANs or ATM connections while other users are connected via modem or ISDN with low bandwidth. Figure 1 depicts a scenario with three users who are connected via LAN and two users connected via ISDN. Since the three LAN users have high bandwidth available they can communicate via media streams of good quality, e.g. high resolution video with 25 frames per second. The ISDN users on the other hand only have a bandwidth of 128Kbit/s available and thus can only handle media streams of low quality, e.g. video with only 4 frames per second and a lower resolution. Thus the quality of the media streams must be somehow adapted to the available bandwidth.

2. With dial-in connections direct transmission of multicast packets is not possible for the following reason: Usually the Point-to-Point-Protocol (PPP)[19] with dynamic IP addresses is used over dial-in lines for authentication. In other words the users machine is always assigned with a new temporary IP address after each dial-up process. Thus multicast packets cannot be routed directly to the user. Besides from that dial-in nodes usually are not capable to handle multicast IP. Therefore tunneling is necessary to overcome the non multicast capable dial-in connection but there is no mechanism in the Internet protocol architecture to set up tunnels dynamically of PPP links.

In this paper we discuss these technical problems and propose our solution, the *Dial-In Multicast Gateway*. This gateway meets the requirements for an application layer multicast routing demon with a restrictive broadcasting policy and a dynamic tunneling mechanism. It allows tunnels to be set up dynamically and selected multicast sessions to be transmitted through channels without multicast capabilities.

The remainder paper is structured as follows: The next section summarizes related work. Section 3 describes in detail the technical problems that have to be overcome in order to send high-bandwidth multicast data streams via low-bandwidth unicast connections. Section 4 presents our approach, the Java-based reflector and scaling tool, and is followed by a summary of our experimental results in an example scenario. Conclusions and an outlook in Section 6 finish the paper.

2 Related Work

Peter Parnes et al. [21] propose a modified multicast routing demon called *"mTunnel"* which allows user-based dynamic tunneling of multicast packets. The tunnel is set up by a special routing demon at either end of the tunnel. Beside the tunneling mechanism the system also provides user-influenced QoS: A data stream can be piped through a translator that can scale the data stream or change the encoding method. The last function to be mentioned here is the mTunnel's ability to prioritize data streams. This is especially useful in teleteaching scenarios because good audio quality in a lecture is much more important than high video quality.

However, the mTunnel does not exactly match the requirements of a scenario as described in figure fig:ihu-scenario because the tunneling mechanism connects only two participants. This means that each participant would have to set up his/her own tunnel in order to participate in the lecture. Our scenario needs a mechanism that connects several participants.

An earlier approach is *CU-SeeMe*, developed at Cornell University [6]. This system uses a special server called a "Reflector". Figure 2 explains the reflector technique: Clients communicate with each other via a reflector server. Each client sends its media streams to the server, which sends a copy to all other clients connected to the server. Clients can either use unicast addresses or multicast addresses. The drawback with CU-SeeMe is that it uses its own conferencing tools and that it does not allow media scaling.

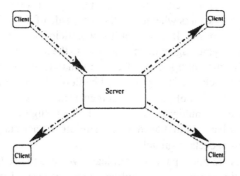

Fig. 2. The CU-SeeMe Reflector technique

Another alternative the *"RTP Gateway"* was developed by Amir et al. [2]. It allows to rescale the audio and video stream of a MBone session. The gateway consists of two tools, the audio gateway (agw) and the video gateway (vgw). The vgw receives a video stream (sent by the video tool vic), decodes the pictures in the stream, recodes them with a chosen encoding algorithm and in a chosen quality, and sends them to the output stream. The input and output streams can be either multicast or unicast packet streams.

The RTP Gateway solves the scaling problem mentioned in Table 1. Furthermore, it can be used to translate a multicast group address into a unicast address. Unfortunately it fails to exactly match our needs for the following two reasons:

1. The current implementation supports only one output stream so that one gateway has to be started for each ISDN receiver.
2. As the name suggests, the RTP Gateway relies heavily on the RTP protocol. The wb tool, currently the standard shared whiteboard application on the MBone, does not run over RTP, and therefore is not supported by the RTP Gateway.

We conclude that each of the existing systems solves one specific part of our problem, but there is no integrated solution and just pasting those components together would obviously not work. We claim that multicast routing, scaling and tunneling are closely related, and only an integrated architecture can provide an optimal solution for multicast to heterogenous end systems.

3 Technical Challenges

The transmission of MBone sessions via low bandwidth dial-in lines is much more complicated than the transmission over LANs or leased lines for the following reasons:

1. As already described in Section 1 the low bandwidth of most dial-in lines causes a number of problems for the transmission of multicast streams. Besides from the scaling problem in a heterogenous network environment (s. Figure 1) and the fact that multicast is not supported by ISDN routers, or modem dial-in nodes the low bandwidth causes another problem: Multicast routing protocols such as the Distance Vector Multicast Routing Protocol DVMRP [5][4] are based on a flooding and pruning policy, i.e. when a network node receives multicast packets on a link they are flooded into all other network links whether on the other side of the links exist participants in the multicast group or not. If there aren't any participants on the other side of the link eventually a pruning message will be send back to the node and it will stop transmitting the packets of this multicast group. After a certain time the pruning will be nullificated and the multicast packets of the group will be flooded again. This behavior causes an unrestricted transmission of packets at unregular intervals on the network link. Since the data rate of these multicast streams can be quite high they will soon exhaust the capacity of a low bandwidth dial-in line. Therefore the normal policy of dial-in nodes to drop multicast packets is suitable.
2. Since dial-nodes are not capable of multicast, we have to use the multicast tunneling mechanism for the transmission of multicast media streams. The tunneling mechanism was integrated into IP multicast in order to cross wide area network lines and routers

within the Internet without multicast capabilities as is depicted in Figure 3. Tunnels are currently the only possibility to introduce multicast routers to each other in a WAN. In order to accomplish this a multicast router (Router A) encapsulates multicast packets in unicast packets with the destination address of the next multicast router (Router B). When such an encapsulated packet arrives at the destination multicast router it is unpacked and routed like a normal multicast datagram. Tunneling is a static mechanism

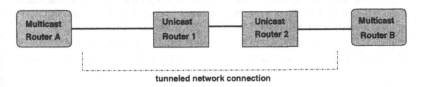

tunneled network connection

Fig. 3. Principle of the tunneling mechanism

where each tunnel has to be set up manually. In our scenario in Figure 1, we have to set up a tunnel to each home user's machine. If a home user disconnects the tunnel will break down and has to be set up again manually when the user reconnects. Dial-in connections usually use the Point-to-Point Protocol (PPP) [19] with dynamic IP addresses for authentication. Thus the IP address of a user is not known in advance. Additionally even if the tunnel could be set up dynamically during the login process the dynamic IP addresses will cause problems. Consider an example scenario where a user connects via a dial-in line and joins a multicast session. Now the user disconnects without leaving the multicast group and simultaneously a new user connects and is assigned with the dynamic IP address of the previous user. Now this new user will receive (unwanted) packets from the multicast group.

To summarize, the multicasting problem can only be handled by a tunneling mechanism with much more restrictive pruning algorithms.

Table 1 summarizes the major problems of the scenario.

According to these problems we define the following requirements which must be met by a multicast gateway for dial-in lines:

- Dynamic IP addresses demand that a dynamic tunneling mechanism must be provided.
- The tunneling mechanism must be robust against errors, e.g. if a user disconnects without logging out correctly. This case must be detected rapidly and all multicast sessions transmitted to this user must be canceled.
- Due to the low bandwidth of some dial-in lines a restrictive forwarding policy must be developed. It must be safeguarded that only multicast packets are transmitted which were requested by the user.
- It would be desirable to integrate a Quality of Service negotiation process: for example a flow control mechanisms can safeguard that the network connection leaves some bandwidth for other applications and control information. A buffer reservation within the multicast router can be used to smooth peak bit rates caused, for example, by whiteboard applications. A priorization mechanism would allow to prioritize certain media streams if a bottleneck in the network connection occurs. Since the human perception is much more sensitive to audio errors than to video errors it is desirable to reserve a minimum share of the available bandwidth for the audio signal.

No.	Problem
1	**Dynamic Tunneling** – Tunneling is a static routing mechanism but the students connect and disconnect dynamically through the universities' PPP/ISDN ports. – Multicast routing demons are not available for all platforms, and their administration is difficult. In the current protocol implementation a multicast demon is required to set up a tunnel. – Tree pruning has to be implemented more strictly than in other environments.
2	**Priorities, Flow Control, and Scaling** – In contrast to the ATM connection between lecture rooms, the bandwidth of ISDN is limited to 128 Kbit/s (2 B-channels). – The media streams have to be scaled to the bandwidth of ISDN. – Some media streams are less important than others; e.g. in teleteaching in computer science a good audio quality is more important than good video quality. – The transmission of large postscript files by the wb causes high peak bit rates.

Table 1. Major problems with the Home Learning scenario

– Scaling mechanisms must be integrated which scale down the media streams to the available bandwidth. Most importantly it must be possible to scale video since this media produces the highest bandwidth demands. Additional services which allow the filtering of packets from certain users are desirable. E.g. in a video conference it can be desirable to transmit only the video of the person who is currently talking.

4 Dial-In Multicast Gateway

Since none of the tools described in section 2 solves our problem, we developed our own solution. Our *"Dial-In Multicast Gateway"* enhances and combines the features of the approaches mentioned above and thus provides the services demanded in the previous section. Our intention is to create an integrated service that can even be handled by those users with little experience with computers.

The gateway basically follows the architecture of a reflector [6] that receives packets from a multicast group and forwards them via unicast to home users. Vice versa, packets from home users are forwarded to the multicast group and to the other home users.

4.1 Functionality

Dynamic Tunneling The gateway adopts the functionality of a multicast router, whose tunnels can be configured dynamically by the user. With the help of a graphical user interface, home users can notify the gateway server. The server verifies login and password and assigns a non-ambiguous identifier to the client. This identifier is then always used to authenticate the client. After this authentication process the server sends a list of session announcements — according to the Session Description Protocol SDP [9] — to the client, where they are displayed in a list box. The user may now choose several sessions from the list box to be joined. Each packet stream from a session can be assigned with a priority according to which a certain share of the total bandwidth of the dial-in line will be reserved for the data stream.

At the client end decoder tools such as vic, vat and wb are started automatically with the necessary parameters. Once established the tunnel works bidirectionally: the user may actively participate in the session. Media streams are transmitted unicast from the home user to the server and the server forwards them to the multicast group and to other home users.

In order to implement error robustness a client component a the home user's machine has to transmit "alive" signals containing its identifier to the server component in regular terms. If the server does not receive alive signals for certain time all sessions requested by this user are canceled.

Priorities and Flow Control Priorization and flow control are realized by means of Priority Queues (PQ). A PQ implements a FIFO queue with a priority parameter p that stands for the bandwidth reserved by a certain home receiver for a certain media stream and is measured in bits per second. A PQ is assigned to each pair of home receiver and media stream to be transmitted and incoming packets from the multicast group are enqueued in the appropriate PQ of each receiver. After a datagram has been dequeued, a deadline for this PQ is calculated, thus at any given time the deadline for the first packet of all PQs is known. In the next cycle a datagram is dequeued from the PQ with the earliest deadline (EDF= earliest deadline first scheduling). Empty PQs are skipped. The deadline d (a timestamp in the future) is calculated in the following way: Let B be the total bandwidth of the connection to the client (e.g. 128 Kbit/s) and p the priority value reserved for a media stream (e.g. 64 Kbit/s for audio). Furthermore let $| pkt |$ be the size of the datagram, that currently has to be transmitted, and $timestamp$ the current value of the "system-clock".

$$d = timestamp + \frac{| pkt |}{p} \qquad (1)$$

Furthermore, for each home receiver an interval timer is instantiated. Scheduled by this timer the packets are dequeued from the PQs of this receiver and sent. The calculation of the wake-up interval t of the timer is similar to the calculation of the deadline of a PQ:

$$t = \frac{| pkt |}{B} \qquad (2)$$

Since empty priority queues are skipped the unused bandwidth that has been reserved for a media type is distributed among the other media types.

Figure 4 depicts an example scenario where a receiver has joined a session with the typical three media types audio, video and whiteboard.

The algorithm described so far assigns priorities above the minima in proportion to the minimum values, i.e. a 32Kbit/s stream will get higher priority than a 16 Kbit/s stream when all minimum requirements are fulfilled. We are currently developing models for more sophisticated priority algorithms.

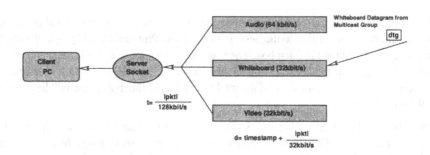

Fig. 4. Priorization, flow control and filtering through priority queues

Consider an example scenario where a home receiver has joined a session with an audio, a video, and a whiteboard stream through a 128 Kbit/s connection. For audio the user has reserved $p_{audio} = 64Kbit/s$ while whiteboard and audio both receive $p_{wb} = p_{video} = 32Kbit/s$. Incoming packets are inserted into one of the three queues according to its media type. The packets are removed in a process scheduled by an interval timer. In each cycle of the process a packet is removed from the PQ with the earliest deadline; i.e. when a packet has been removed from the video queue, its deadline is equal to $d = timestamp + (| pkt | /32kbit/s)$ and the timer interval is set to $t =| pkt | /128kbit/s$. In other words, the effect will be that video and whiteboard will get 25% of the bandwidth each; audio will get 50%.

Scaling and Filtering When a new packet from a media stream arrives it is inserted into the corresponding PQ of each receiver. Since the dequeuing rate is typically lower than the rate of arrival rate, scaling of media streams becomes necessary in order to prevent the overflow of the priority queues. For each media type a scaling (i.e. packet discarding) algorithm has to be devised. For the first prototype of our gateway we have concentrated on video scaling. The quality of video is defined by its three dimensions color resolution, spatial resolution and temporal resolution. The color resolution is defined by the number of bits used to represent the color of a single pixel, the spatial dimension is defined by the width and height of the video, and the temporal resolution is represented by the number of frames per second. Several approaches have been developed in order to scale video in any of these three dimensions [16][3][1][17][20][11].

For simplicity and due to performance we decided to use a simple scaling mechanism that reduces the temporal resolution [15] of intra-encoded H.261 video streams by relying on the RTP header information [24][23] as it is produced, e.g. by the video conferencing tool vic: If the length of a PQ reaches a certain upper limit all packets, carrying data from the latest video frame are removed from the queue, and packets of this video frame arriving later will also be discarded. Information about the frame number and encoding type is taken from the RTP header. This method gracefully reduces the bandwidth of the video signal. Other more complex scaling algorithms will be integrated into future versions of the gateway. Furthermore we plan to integrate transcoding and multiplexing strategies for audio streams.

An additional filtering service makes it possible to discard packets from a certain user in RTP streams. In order to accomplish this the SSRCS field of the RTP header is used to identify the user who sent a packet.

Additional Services Our experiences with the MBone proofed that the reliability is still low compared to the reliability of unicast IP. Multicast communication usually works fine within local area networks but if wide area networks have to be overcome the reliability often develops reverse proportional to the distance. This especially holds true for trans-European networks. While the loss rate of unicast transmissions is often acceptable even for video conferencing applications multicast communication between the same partners is often almost impossible due to high packet losses.

In order to overcome this problem we integrated a gateway-to-gateway communication, i.e. it is possible to set up a tunnel between two dial-in gateway servers. Figure 5 depicts an example scenario.

With the gateway-to-gateway communication protocol it is possible to join two multicast sessions in two different LANs. So far the tunnels must be set up manually through a configuration file. Future developments shall allow it to connect two multicast sessions via a graphical user interface.

4.2 Overall Architecture

The Dial-In Multicast Gateway system consists of a server and a client component. The client component, programmed in Java, mainly provides a graphical user interface for the communication with the server component. The server component carries out the scaling, filtering and reflecting of the data streams: it is implemented in C++ to ensure good performance. In principle it works in the following way: Users can connect to the server through the client application via a dedicated port number. Once a user has logged in the client will receive a list of sessions available for transmission. The user will then choose a session to join. A request for the selected session will be sent to the server, which then will transmit and rescale the media stream according to the bandwidth available.

The following list summarizes the features of the Dial-In Multicast Gateway:

- distributed client-server oriented architecture,
- integrated solution with an-easy-to-handle graphical user interface,
- client is implemented in Java and therefore platform-independent,
- support of the most popular MBone Tools (audio, video and whiteboard).

Technical Outline of the Server Component The server consists of the components indicated in Figure 6:

- Client Communication Manager,
- Session Announcement Protocol Listener (SAP-Listener),
- Reflector Service, and
- Media Filtering Service.

The Client Communication Manager is the central management component of the server. It provides the service interface for the clients and starts and stops reflection and scaling services. Clients communicate with the server by transmitting control protocol data units

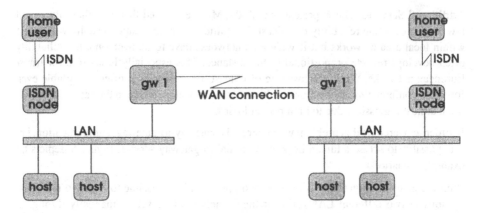

Fig. 5. Gateway-to-Gateway-communication: In this scenario a number of hosts communicate via multicast. The hosts are distributed over two LANs. In each LAN two hosts are connected directly to the LAN and a home user participates via ISDN. Furthermore a dial-in gateway is installed in each LAN which is used by the home user in order to receive the multicast packets. The dial-in gateways in the two LANs can communicate with each other. It is possible to set up an application layer tunnel between the two gateways which is used to connect the two multicast sessions in each LAN.

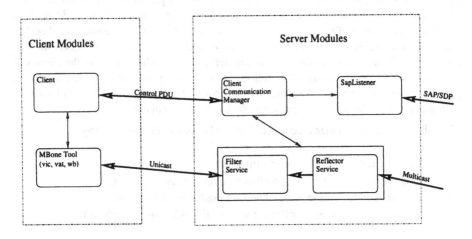

Fig. 6. The Dial-In Multicast Gateway.

(PDUs) to the remote site. A PDU holds a command token along with parameters. The token and the parameters are transmitted in a single datagram as character strings separated by zero-bytes. Table 2 summarizes the most important PDUs we have defined so far.

The Session Announcement Protocol Listener receives MBone session descriptions, described according to the session description protocol SDP [10] and announced in conformance with the session announcement protocol SAP [9]. Received session descriptions are stored in a local cache and transmitted to the client upon demand.

The Reflector Service is the central component and the most time-critical part. When a client requests a multicast session, the client communication manager adds the requesting

PDU	Parameters	Description
ConReq	login, password, bandwidth	Connect Request PDU is sent by a client in order to connect to the server.
ConConf	ctrl-id	Connect Confirm PDU is sent by the server if a connect request of a client is accepted. The server sends a unique identifier (ctrl-id) to the client.
SesInf	SDP-description	A SesInf PDU is sent by the server if a new session description is received by the SAP-Listener component. The PDU contains the new session description.
SesReq	ctrl-id, sdp-id, media-id, bandwidth	A Session Request PDU is sent by the client in order to request the transmission of a media-stream of a certain session.
SesAck	port	A Session Acknowledgment PDU is sent by the server. The PDU holds the information on the port to which the data is sent.

Table 2. Control PDUs of the Dial-In Multicast Gateway

client to the list of receivers of the corresponding Reflector Service. Multiple clients can participate in a reflected session. The Reflector Service is created when a client requests a session for the first time and destroyed when the last of its customers leaves the session. Its task is to broadcast incoming multicast packets to all of its customers. In order to be as platform independent as possible timers and IO-multiplexing are implemented by using the C API provided with Tcl/Tk.

The Media Filtering Service receives incoming data stream packets and either enqueues them to a PQ or discards them as described above. In the current version only video streams are scaled down and we use the very simple temporal scaling mechanism described in Section 4.1.

Technical Outline of the Client Component The client component is available both as a stand-alone Java application. Currently we are developing an additional Tcl/Tk based client. When a client connects to a server it receives the announcements of those MBone sessions [1] currently available. The user may then choose the sessions to be received. The client sends the request back to the server process which then transmits the requested data stream to the client. At the client site the MBone tools are started automatically.

Figure 7 illustrates the graphical user interface of the client.

5 Experiences

During the summer term 1998 we extensively tested the Dial-In Multicast Gateway in our Interactive Home Learning scenario [2]. In this scenario 12 students received our teleteach-

---

[1] announced for example with the sdr-tool

[2] Information about the project can be found in: http://www.informatik.uni-mannheim.de/informatik/pi4 /projects/IHL/

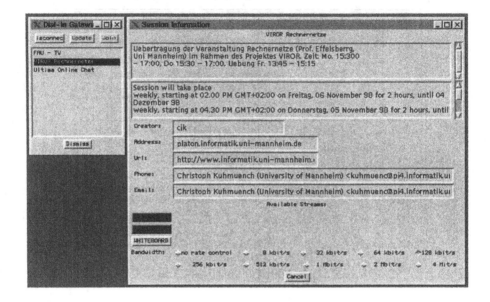

Fig. 7. The graphical user interface of the client

ing lecture in computer science through an ISDN access node. The server component of the dial-in gateway was installed on a Sun Ultra-1 workstation running Solaris 2.6. Simultaneously the lecture was transmitted to lecture halls of our partner university in Freiburg. The multicasted video stream had a bandwidth of about 600Kbit/s with about 12 frames per second. In order to transmit the video to the students at home we had to set the priority factor of the video PQs to 64Kbit/s which resulted in a low quality video signal with only a few frames per second.

Conclusively for the IHL scenario we have to consider two groups of participants: The first group is connected by high-bandwidth Internet connections, uses Unix workstations and is connected directly to the MBone via ATM and Local Area Networks. The second group uses PCs with Linux or Windows 95/98, participates through ISDN at a bandwidth of 128 Kbit/s, and the Point-to-Point-Protocol (PPP) is used to transfer IP datagrams through the ISDN channels. As shown in Figure 8, audio, video, and whiteboard packets are sent via multicast IP from the local lecture room to the remote lecture rooms. This mixed data stream were scaled to the bandwidth of ISDN (max. 128Kbit/s) and transmitted to the student's PCs.

For the transmission of the data streams we were using the MBone tools. Figure 9 depicts the protocol stack of the most popular MBone tools vic vat and wb. While vic and vat are using RTP as transport protocol wb relies on a Reliable Multicast Protocol (RMP). These packets are encapsulated in IP multicast datagrams which can be transmitted on any network type, e.g. a LAN or ATM.

The proband home learning students judged the quality of the video as sufficient. The voice of the lecturer was transmitted in GSM compressed format which resulted in a data stream with about 15Kbit/s. The students found the quality of the audio acceptable for a lesson in computer science although they mentioned that they found it hard to concentrate for

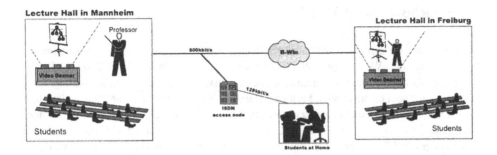

Fig. 8. The synchronous Home Learning Scenario

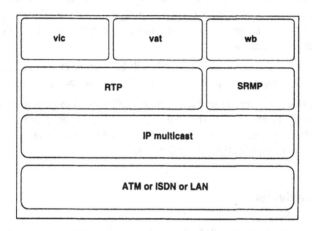

Fig. 9. The protocol stack of the most popular MBone tools vic, vat and wb

more than 60 minutes and a better audio quality would be appreciated. The whiteboard data stream could only be received by 6 students who used Linux on their PC at home. We had no problems to transmit the whiteboard data stream with a priority value of 32 Kbit/s although it sometimes took quite some time to transmit large postscript files.

Further on we found out that the dial-in gateway caused only a very low CPU-load (always below 10% on the Sun). A test on a Linux PC (Pentium Pro 200) showed a much higher CPU-load on this machine (25%). Since the filtering mechanisms of the gateway are quite simple the reason for this phenomenon must caused by the better network performance of the Sun operating system.

Conclusively our evaluation proofed that even low bandwidth connections such as ISDN allow the participation in a multicast session with media streams. In a future project we plan to make use of new dial-in connections like ADSL which provide a higher bandwidth for users at home.

6 Conclusion and Outlook

In this paper we discussed technical problems of the transmission of multicast streams over dial-in lines. We then presented our approach, the *Dial-In Multicast Gateway*. It implements an application layer multicast routing system with built in media scaling. The client component of the Dial-In Multicast Gateway is implemented completely in Java using JDK1.1 and thus works on every platform. The server component is written in C++ and was ported successfully to several different platforms (SUN Solaris 2.6., Linux, and Irix). The system fulfills not only the requirements of the Interactive Home Learning scenario but can also be used for other services, such as Media-on-Demand servers and multimedia databases.

Future work will comprise more complex scaling algorithms for video, which will allow a more graceful scaling. Additionally we are investigating the use of RTSP [22] as control protocol, which would allow a more facile integration of the Dial-In Multicast Gateway into other types of application.

New network access technologies like ADSL will be another area of research. In a future project we plan to integrate our protocol into ADSL network access nodes.

Finally we consider to move our multicasting protocol for dial-in lines from the application layer into a lower layer, i.e. into the network layer. We expect a performance increase from this step because packets do not have to be moved from the operating systems kernel address space into the application layer address space.

7 Acknowledgment

This project is supported by the BMBF (Bundesministerium für Forschung und Technologie/ Federal Minitstry of Research and Technology).

References

1. Elan Amir, Steven McCanne, and Martin Vetterli. A layered dct coder for internet video. In *Proc. of IEEE International Conference on Image Processing ICIP '96, Lousanne Switzerland*, pages 13 – 16. IEEE, September 1996.
2. Elan Amir, Steven McCanne, and Hui Zhang. An application-level video gateway. In *ACM Multimedia, San Francisco*, pages 255 – 265, November 1995.
3. Peter Burt and Edward Adelson. The laplacian pyramid as a compact image code. *IEEE Transactions on Communications*, 1983.
4. Stephen Deering. *Multicast Routing in a Datagram Internetwork*. PhD thesis, Stanford Univerity, California, USA, 1991.
5. Stephen Deering, C. Partridge, and D. Waitzmann. Distance vector multicast routing protocol. Internet Request For Comments, IETF, RFC-1075, August 1989.
6. T. Dorcey. Cu-seeme desktop video conferencing software. *Connexions*, March 1995.
7. Andreas Eckert, Werner Geyer, and Wolfgang Effelsberg. A distance learning system for higher education in telecommunications and multmedia – a compound organizational, pedagogical and technical approach. In *Proc. ED-MEDIA/ED-TELECOM'97, Calgary, Canada*. AACE Association for the Advancement of Computing in Education, 1997. [on CD-ROM only].

8. Werner Geyer and Wolfgang Effelsberg. The digital lecture board — a teaching and learning tool for remote instruction in higher education. In *Proc. ED-MEDIA/ED-TELECOM'98*. AACE Association for the Advancement of Computing in Education, 1998. [on CD-ROM only].

9. Mark Handley. Sap: Session announcement protocol. Internet draft, IETF, Multiparty Multimedia Session Control Working Group, draft-ietf-mmusic-sap-00, January 1997. Expiring date May 25th, 1997.

10. Mark Handley and Van Jacobson. Sdp: Session description protocol. Internet draft, IETF, Multiparty Multimedia Session Control Working Group, Internet draft draft-ietf-mmusic-sdp-03, February 1997. Expiring date September 26th, 1997.

11. Don Hoffmann and Michael Speer. Hierarchical video distribution over internet-style networks. In *Proc. of the IEEE Conference on Image Processing*, pages 5 – 8, Lousanne, Switzerland, September 1996.

12. Wieland Holfelder. Interactive remote recording and playback of multicast videoconferences. In *Proc. 4th International Workshop on Interactive Distributed Multimedia Systems and Telecomminication Services (IDMS '97)*, 4, pages ?? – ?? IDMS, September 1997.

13. Van Jakobson and Steven McCanne. Video conferencing tool (vic). Lawrence Berkeley Laboratory, ftp://ftp.ee.lbl.gov/conferencing/vic, 1996.

14. Van Jakobson and Steven McCanne. Visual audio tool (vat). Lawrence Berkeley Laboratory, ftp://ftp.ee.lbl.gov/conferencing/vat, 1996.

15. Christoph Kuhmünch, Thomas Fuhrmann, Gunther Schöppe, and Dieter W. Herrmann. Java teachware - the java remote control tool and its applications. In *Proc. ED-MEDIA/ED-TELECOM'98*. AACE Association for the Advancement of Computing in Education, 1998. [on CD-ROM only].

16. Christoph Kuhmünch and Gerald Kühne. Efficient video transport over lossy networks. Technical Report 7-98, University of Mannheim, http://www.informatik.uni-mannheim.de/ cjk/publications/, April 1998.

17. Steven McCanne. *Scalable Compression and Transmission of Internet Multicast Video*. PhD thesis, University of California, Berkeley, Ca, USA, 1996.

18. Steven McCanne and Van Jacobson. vic: A flexible framework for packet video. In *MultiMedia '95 (San Francisco)*, pages 511 – 523, New York, November 1995. ACM, ACM Press.

19. G. McGregor. The ppp internet protocol control protocol (ipcp). Internet Request For Comments, IETF, RFC-1332, May 1992.

20. Michael Merz, Konrad Froitzheim, Peter Schulthess, and Heiner Wolf. Iterative transmission of media streams. In *Proceedings of the conference on Multimedia '97*, pages 283–290. ACM, 1997.

21. Peter Parnes. mtunnel: a multicast tunneling system with a user based quality-of-service model. In *Proc. 4th International Workshop on Interactive Distributed Multimedia Systems and Telecomminication Services (IDMS '97)*, 4. IDMS, September 1997.

22. H. Schulzrinne, A. Rao, and R. Lanphier. Real time streaming protocol (rtsp). Internet draft, IETF, Multiparty Multimedia Session Control Working Group, draft-ietf-mmusic-rtsp-09, February 1998. Expiring date August 2nd, 1998.

23. Henning Schulzrinne. Rtp profile for audio and video conferences with minimal control. Internet Request For Comments, IETF, RFC-1890, January 1996.

24. Henning Schulzrinne, Stephen Casner, Ron Frederick, and Van Jacobson. Rtp: A transport protocol for real-time applications. Internet Request For Comments, IETF, RFC-1889, January 1996.

Fast Multimedia Encryption in JAVA
Using Unbalanced Luby/Rackoff Ciphers

Rüdiger Weis[1]* and Stefan Lucks[2]**

[1] Praktische Informatik IV
University of Mannheim, 68131 Mannheim, Germany
rweis@pi4.informatik.uni-mannheim.de
[2] Theoretische Informatik
University of Mannheim, 68131 Mannheim, Germany
lucks@th.informatik.uni-mannheim.de

Abstract. Multimedia applications often serve high-bandwidth channels. Thus, if encryption is required, cryptographic security often conflicts with efficiency. In the current paper, we consider the efficiency of *unbalanced Luby-Rackoff ciphers*. Such ciphers can operate very fast on large blocks of data and can easily cope with flexible block sizes.
Anderson and Biham proposed two unbalanced Luby/Rackoff ciphers: *LION* and *BEAR*. An even faster algorithm is BEAST (Block Encryption Algorithm with Shortcut in the Third round). Like BEAR and LION, BEAST is assembled from a key–dependent hash function and a stream cipher. BEAST it is *provably* secure if these building blocks are secure. We evaluate the JAVA performance of BEAR, LION, and BEAST. For the sake of comparison, we also evaluate the performance of some well-known proven 64-bit block ciphers.

Keywords:
Performance, block cipher, JAVA, Luby-Rackoff ciphers, BEAR, LION, BEAST.

1 Introduction

Multimedia encryption is a difficult and interesting research problem, since real-time applications need high throughput and low latency. Commercial demands and technological requirements make this conflict between security and efficiency even more difficult to resolve. The software should be portable to different hardware environments without much work. Thus a machine-independent high-level application of the software is desirable, which prohibits machine-specific optimizations. Secure multimedia applications require highly efficient encryption. It is controversial whether a high–level language such as JAVA is fast enough for this purpose.

* Supported by the Landesgraduiertenförderung Baden–Würtemberg
** Supported by Deutsche Forschungsgemeinschaft (DFG) grant KR 1521/3-1

Most existing multimedia applications neglect security issues. Many use no encryption, some only DES. DES is hardware–oriented, slow and not secure against exhaustive search attacks. Anyway, victimizing security to save on efficiency is always dangerous. The easy availability of pirate decoders for many pay-TV standards and the resulting commercial damage should be a lesson to everyone contemplating this. In this paper, we evaluate techniques for having both: efficiency and high cryptographic security.

1.1 Cryptography in JAVA

JAVA is a portable, object oriented programming language with many interesting security features (e.g. sandbox paradigm, bytecode verification). Initially, JAVA was designed for *set-top boxes*. Today, JAVA is highly portable and can be used in different environments like phones, computer networks, and smartcards.

The JAVA Security API [SUN97] from SUN is a widely known cryptographic package in JAVA. It is still under construction and provides standard interfaces for different cryptographic protocols. Other packages are from RSA [RSA98] and Microsoft [Wiew96]. A freeware alternative to these packages without export restrictions is the Cryptix library [Cryt97], which we use in our tests.

Implementing a block cipher often involves certain bit-fiddling operations best done in hardware or in assembler. If one restricts oneself to a high–level language such as JAVA and does no low–level optimization, this limits the speed of encryption. On the other hand, for practical applications a cipher needs to be *fast enough* for the specific purpose, not as fast as possible.

We are interested in the efficiency of a *platform-independent* high-level implementation. Because of this we compare the performance of the interpreted JAVA bytecode.

1.2 Related Work

Publications exploring the performance of ciphers are surprisingly rare in the literature. Some years ago, Roe published benchmark results [Roe94], followed by an update one year later [Roe95]. More recently, Schneier and Whiting counted the number of machine cycles required by some cryptographic operations on a Pentium [ScWh97]. They concentrated on low–level optimizations for a specific machine. An overview of the performance of modern block ciphers (focused on smartcard systems), including some early submissions for the Advanced Encryption Standard (AES), can be found in [WeLu98a]. Some results about the performance of unbalanced Luby/Rackoff ciphers can be found in [AnBi96].

1.3 Organization of this Paper

In Section 2 we present our results for a couple of well–known and widely used ciphers. In Section 3 we present Luby-Rackoff ciphers and provide some theoretical background. In Section 4 we describe our implementation, our testing environment and the performance results, concluding with an outlook in Section 5

2 Modern 64-bit Block Ciphers

In section we concentrate on established 64-bit block ciphers, published at least some years ago, carefully examined by the cryptographic community and widely used today.

DES Family. The famous DES [FIPS46] encryption algorithm, originally designed for confidential but non–classified data, is used in many applications today (e.g. electronic banking). Internally, the DES is based on the so–called Feistel structure, in which a simple round function is repeated several times (in the case of DES, exactly 16 times). This allows inexpensive hardware implementations of DES.

Due to its key size of only 56 bits, DES must be considered weak. So since DES has been cracked by a brute force attack by the nonprofit organisation "EFF" in only 56 hours ([DESC97] – see also [EFF98]) we suggest to use Triple-DES [SiBa97] or DESX [Roga96]. (The key length today should be at least 75–90 bits [Blea96].)

Blowfish and CAST. In spite of having been developed independently, the basic structures of the block ciphers Blowfish [Schn94] and CAST [Adam97b] are very similar.

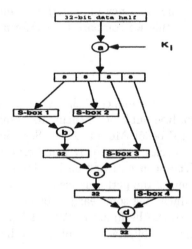

Fig. 1. Generalized CAST–round, using operations a, b, c and d [Adam97b].

In the case of CAST we analyze CAST-128 [Adam97a] which is proposed for standardisation. CAST was designed with resistance to differential cryptanalysis, linear cryptanalysis and related–key cryptanalysis in mind. CAST possesses a number of other cryptographic advantages compared to DES, e.g. no complementation property and the absence of weak and semi-weak keys. No such strong results regarding known cryptanalytic techniques have been published for Blowfish. On the other hand key–dependent S-boxes seem to have fine resistance against unknown cryptanalytic attacks. To conclude: no attacks of any practical relevance are known on either CAST or Blowfish.

IDEA. The IDEA block cipher [Lai92] has a strong mathematical foundation and possesses good resistance against differential cryptanalysis [Lai91]. Many cryptographers consider IDEA to be the strongest public algorithm [Schn96]. IDEA was the preferred cipher in the PGP versions (Pretty Good Privacy) until version 2.6.3.

SAFER-SK128. SAFER [Mass94] is a freely available block cipher which does *not* depend on the Feistel structure. It was designed with small processors (i.e., eight–bit microprocessors) in mind and thus is of special interest with respect to smartcards. We concentrate on the SAFER variant SAFER-SK 128/R 13 with an improved key schedule, 128 key bits, and 13 rounds. This variant is proposed for OpenPGP [CDF98] standardization (e.g. dlb[GeWe98]).

3 Luby/Rackoff ciphers

Based on random functions, Luby and Rackoff [LuRa88] described provably secure block ciphers. This theoretical break-through is of practical interest, since it enables us to assemble a secure cipher from secure components.

In this paper, the hash function SHA-1 [FIPS180] and the stream cipher ARCfour [NN94] are considered to be components, though other choices would do as well [Luck96a].

BEAST, like Luby-Rackoff ciphers in general, is a Feistel cipher similar to DES. While DES requires 16 rounds, BEAST needs only three. On the other hand, BEAST's round functions must be cryptographically stronger than those of DES.

Due to its construction, BEAST performs best when operating on large blocks. This bodes well for a possible use of BEAST in multimedia security applications, when a high throughput is required from the cipher, and the overall data volume is huge, too.

3.1 Theoretical Background

Encrypting with a block cipher means to apply a key-dependent permutation g to the plaintext, decrypting to apply the inverse g^{-1} to the ciphertext; g is computed by the 'encryption engine' and g^{-1} by the 'decryption engine'. A block cipher is *secure* if g appears to be a randomly chosen permutation to anyone not knowing the key.

The type of attack we consider is a *chosen plaintext attack*, in which the attacker chooses a plaintext x_1, injects x_1 into the encryption engine and gets the ciphertext $g(x_1)$. This is repeated for x_2, x_3, ... (see Figure 2). After a number of plaintext injections the attacker has to decide whether or not g is a random permutation.

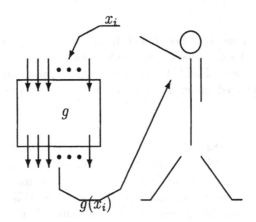

Fig. 2. Chosen ciphertext attack.

Similarly one can consider *chosen ciphertext attacks*. We only consider block ciphers where the ciphertexts are as long as the blocks, so in this case, we can simply use the inverse permutation g^{-1} for encryption and the straight permutation g for decryption.

Resistance against such attacks is commonly accepted as a sufficient security criterion for block ciphers.

Every cipher is designed to be resistant against certain attacks, but fails in the face of others. Among the advantages of using a cipher with a proof of security (under a reasonable assumption) is the simplicity of finding out which attacks the cipher is designed for – and which not. Overstretching the security of any cipher is tantamount to using an insecure one.

BEAST is not secure against *combined chosen plaintext/chosen ciphertext attacks*, in which the attacker accesses both the encryption and the decryption engine. It is very dangerous, anyway, to allow the enemy to decrypt and encrypt with the secret key. In most multimedia applications this kind of attack is not feasible.

Let f_1, f_2, and f_3 be random functions $f_1, f_3 : \{0,1\}^r \longrightarrow \{0,1\}^l$ and $f_2 : \{0,1\}^l \longrightarrow \{0,1\}^r$. By '$\oplus$' we denote the bit-wise XOR. We compute values $S, U \in \{0,1\}^l$ and $T \in \{0,1\}^r$ by

$$S := L \oplus f_1(R)$$
$$T := R \oplus f_2(S)$$
$$U := S \oplus f_3(T)$$

This defines a permutation $\psi(f_1, f_2, f_3)(L, R) = (U, T)$ over $\{0,1\}^{l+r}$. This is represented in Figure 3 – just start with L and R and follow the arrows. Similarly, $\psi(f_3, f_2, f_1) = \psi^{-1}(f_1, f_2, f_3)$ is the inverse.

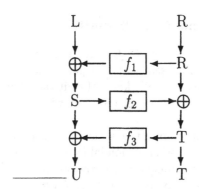

Fig. 3. The permutation $\psi(f_1, f_2, f_3)(L, R) = (U, T)$.

Luby and Rackoff showed in their famous paper [LuRa88] that $\psi(f_1, f_2, f_3)$ is indistinguishable from a random function if $l = r$ and f_1, f_2, and f_3 are random or pseudorandom functions. If a permutation p is indistinguishable from a random function, it also is indistinguishable from a random permutation. Maurer [Maur92] gave an amazingly simple proof of Luby's and Rackoff's theorem. Neither Luby and Rackoff nor Maurer regarded $l \neq r$.

Theorem 1. *Let* $g : \{0,1\}^{r+l} \longrightarrow \{0,1\}^{r+l}$ *be either a random function or* $g = \psi(f_1, f_2, f_3)$, *where* $f_1, f_3 : \{0,1\}^r \longrightarrow \{0,1\}^l$ *and* $f_2 : \{0,1\}^l \longrightarrow \{0,1\}^r$ *are random functions. Let* $n \leq \min\{l, r\}$ *be a security parameter.*

Let A *be a distinguisher. Given a 'black box' which is able to compute* g, A *outputs either 1 or 0. By* P_{RAND} *and* P_{PERM} *we denote the probabilities for* A *to output 1 if* g *is randomly chosen, resp. if* $g = \psi(f_1, f_2, f_3)$.

A accesses the 'black box' at most k *times, i.e.* A *chooses at most* k *inputs* $(L_1, R_1), \ldots, (L_k, R_k)$ *and receives the corresponding* $(U_1, T_1), \ldots, (U_k, T_k)$ *with* $(U_i, T_i) = g(L_i, R_i)$. *Then*

$$|P_{\text{RAND}} - P_{\text{PERM}}| < \frac{k^2}{2^n}.$$

Informally spoken, there is no reasonable chance for an attacker to distinguish between $\psi(f_1, f_2, f_3)$ and a random function, except if the attacker has chosen close to $\sqrt{2^n}$ blocks and has got the corresponding ciphertexts. The proof is based on Maurer's proof for $l = r = n$ and is given by Lucks [Luck96a].

Lucks also found a 'shortcut' for the third round: If $r > l$, the function f_3 can be replaced by $f_* : \{0,1\}^l \longrightarrow \{0,1\}^l$ which only uses any l of the r input bits to f_3 and ignores the remaining $r - l$ bits. If $r \gg l$, one can expect to evaluate f_* much faster than f_3.

Theorem 2. *Let the function* $f_* : \{0,1\}^l \longrightarrow \{0,1\}^l$ *be a random function. If – except for* $f_3(T) = f_*(T \bmod 2^l)$ *– the conditions of theorems 1 are satisfied, then* $|P_{\text{RAND}} - P_{\text{PERM}}| < \frac{k^2}{2^n}$.

3.2 Pseudorandomness and 'Security'

If the functions f_1, f_2 and f_3 are not random but pseudorandom, $\psi(f_1, f_2, f_3)$ represents a pseudorandom permutation – and a practical three-round Feistel cipher as well. We know that if the pseudorandom functions are secure, the block cipher is secure, too. But what is meant by 'secure' in this context?

In theoretical cryptography, the 'security' of a scheme often is reduced to the non-existence of probabilistic polynomial time algorithms capable of breaking it. Our theorems are much stronger! Recall the distinguisher A and the probabilities P_{RAND} and P_{PERM} in theorem 1. By P_{PSEU}, we denote the probability that A outputs 1 if A accesses the function $g = \psi(f_1, f_2, f_3)$ with pseudorandom f_i at most k times. If

$$|P_{\text{RAND}} - P_{\text{PSEU}}| \geq p + \frac{k^2}{2^n}$$

holds for $p > 0$, then it is straightforward to use A as a test for the randomness of f_1, f_2, and f_3. The distinguishing probability is at least p:

$$|P_{\text{PERM}} - P_{\text{PSEU}}| \geq p.$$

In other words, attacks on Luby-Rackoff ciphers are at least as hard as attacks on the underlying pseudorandom function generators, except for possibly increasing their probability of success by $k^2/2^n$:

> Let $g = \psi(f_1, f_2, f_3)$ be an encryption function. Let f_1, f_2, and f_3 be generated by a pseudorandom function generator which is secure in the following sense: 'There is no algorithm which in time t (i.e. the time required to encrypt t blocks) distinguishes between random and pseudorandom f_1, f_2, and f_3 with probability p or more.'
> Then the block cipher defined by g is secure in the following sense: 'There is no algorithm A to distinguish between g and a random function in time t with probability $p + k^2/2^n$ or more, where A chooses exactly k inputs x_1, x_2, ..., x_k and gets the corresponding outputs $g(x_1)$, $g(x_2)$, ..., $g(x_k)$.'

Note that the computation of the k ciphertexts takes time k and is a part of A's overall run time.

3.3 The block ciphers BEAR and LION – and BEAST

If $l \neq r$, 'compressing' (pseudo-)random functions f_i (with more input bits than output bits) and 'expanding' $f_{i\pm 1}$ (fewer input bits than output bits) alternate in Figure 3. For compressing, cryptographic hash functions are well suited – Anderson and Biham [AnBi96] suggested to use SHA-1[FIPS180]. For expanding, they considered the stream cipher SEAL[RoCo94].

Cryptographic hash functions such as SHA-1 are authentication tools. We may use them as building blocks for our ciphers, but then we have to demand that the hash functions be pseudorandom. Being pseudorandom is a widely accepted security-related design goal for cryptographic hash functions, anyway. [Ande95] describes some risks of using non-pseudorandom hash functions for authentication.

SEAL is a stream cipher explicitly designed by its authors to be a pseudorandom function, too. This is a much stronger requirement than just being a secure stream cipher, or, as a theorist would put it, than being a pseudorandom bit generator.

Anderson and Biham proposed two block ciphers for flexible but large blocks: BEAR and LION, both similar to Figure 3 with $(l + r)$-bit Blocks. BEAR was based on the choice $l = 160 \ll r$, with two SHA-1 r-bit to l-bit compression steps and one SEAL l-bit to r-bit expansion step, similarly LION on $l \gg r = 160$ with two expansion steps and one compression step. For large blocks (i.e. blocks greater than about 6 Kbyte), LION is faster than BEAR [AnBi96].

Anderson and Biham only considered a very weak type of attack, and their security proof for BEAR and LION is not valid for chosen plaintext attacks. But thanks to theorem 1 both ciphers are as secure as any block cipher based on Figure 3 – if the underlying pseudorandom functions are secure.

Theorem 2 enables us to define the BEAST ('Block Encryption Algorithm with Shortcut in the Third round', see Figure 4), a variant of BEAR, but faster than both BEAR and LION.

Since the round functions of Luby-Rackoff ciphers have to depend on a key[1], we need keyed variants Hash_K and Stream_K of Hash and the stream cipher Stream:

$$\text{Hash}_K(x) = \text{Hash}(K \oplus x) \text{ and } \text{Stream}_K(x) = \text{Stream}(K \oplus x). \quad (1)$$

Note that the input size for the keyed hash function is known in advance, otherwise we could use e.g.

$$\text{Hash}_K(x) = \text{Hash}(K||x||K),$$

where '||' stands for the concatenation of bit strings. BEAST can be described by the following equations:

$$S := L \oplus \text{Hash}_{K_1}(R),$$
$$T := R \oplus \text{Stream}_{K_2}(S)$$
$$U := S \oplus \text{Hash}_{K_3}(T^*) \text{ with } T^* = \text{'first } l \text{ bits of } T'.$$

Here, K_1, K_2, and K_3 represent the round keys of BEAST. It is easy to generate them from a smaller master key K_M using Stream_{K_M}.

---

[1] Actually, the second round of BEAR and LION does not depend on a key. This is theoretically sound, but does not simplify or speed-up the ciphers significantly.

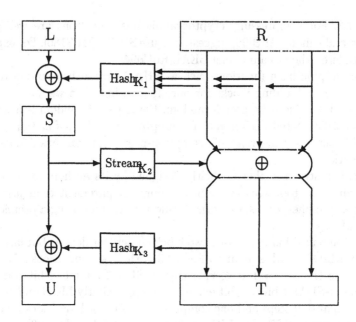

Fig. 4. The block cipher BEAST.

3.4 LIONESS - four–round variant

For an application to be secure against an adaptive combined chosen plaintext and ciphertext attack, Anderson and Biham [AnBi96] suggest to add a forth round. These attacks are similar to the attack on the balanced Luby/Rackoff construction [LuRa88].) An alternative to LIONESS is GRIFFIN [Luck97], which we estimate to be faster than LIONESS, although it is a nine-round cipher.

LIONESS Encryption

$$T := R \oplus \text{Stream}_{K_1}(S)$$
$$U := L \oplus \text{Hash}_{K_2}(T)$$
$$V := T \oplus \text{Stream}_{K_3}(U)$$
$$W := V \oplus \text{Hash}_{K_4}(V)$$

3.5 Modes of Operation

In [AnBi96] the authors discuss using the above ciphers with the following modes of operation:

Encrypting a single block. The whole message can be treated as a single block. This has several advantages:

- Each ciphertext bit depends on all the plaintext bits in a very complex manner, which contributes to cryptographic strength;

- The standard security proofs hold since only one block is encrypted under the same key.
- This mode prevents both differential [BiSh93] and linear [Mats94] cryptanalysis since the attacker cannot get more than one block encrypted under the same key.
- Easy key management.

Standard modes. The four–round cipher LIONESS can also be used with the standard modes of DES. We can divide the message into several blocks of some fixed length and use the standard modes of [FIPS81].

3.6 Choosing building blocks for unbalanced Luby/Rackoff ciphers

Keyed Hash Functions can be built based on an unkeyed hash function H and a key K. For simplicity reasons we should use the *envelope mode*:

$$\text{Hash}_K(x) = \text{Hash}(K||x||K),$$

The envelope technique is simple, but its theoretical implications are not well understood. While we actually expect no security problems, one may consider other techniques to define key–dependant hash functions based on conventional hash functions. Such are are MDX-MAC [PrOo95] and the HMAC/NMAC construction [BCK96],provably secure under reasonable assumptions regarding the underlying hash function.

We consider SHA-1 [FIPS180] and RIPEMD-160 [Doea96] to be secure hash functions with 160-bit output [Weis98b]. HAVAL [Zhea93] is an interesting alternative if we want to have a flexible round number and output up to 256 bit.(Our Haval version uses 3 rounds and 256-bit output.)

Hash Function	SHA-1	RIPEMD-160	Haval
1k packet size	183.5	140.8	244.5
100k packet size	200.2	151.6	286.8
1000k packet size	200.6	151.7	286.9

Performance in kB/s

MD4[Rive90] and MD5[Rive92] are still interesting pseudorandom functions, but only produce 128 bits of output and suffer from security problems showed by Dobertin. "Where MD4 is still in use, it should be replaced! An exception is the application of MD4 as a one-way-function" [Dobb96]. If we want to have 128-bit output we suggest to use RIPEMD-128 [RIPE93]. MD2 [Kals92] was designed for 8bit processors and is terrible slow on other systems.

Hashfunction	RIPEMD-128	MD5	MD4	MD2
1k packet size	209.6	203.2	473.9	24.6
100k packet size	227.0	228.6	524.9	25.4
1000k packet size	227.0	228.8	524.9	25.4

Performance in kB/s

Stream Ciphers are widely used in hardware encryption. Recently, interesting new software-oriented stream ciphers have been also developed [Weis98a]. Stream ciphers have to be secure against key recovery attacks and expansion attacks.

RC4 is a fast software stream cipher designed by Ron Rivest. It is widely used e.g. in the Netscape browsers and included in many cryptographic libraries. RC4 has been published anonymously [NN94]. Since RC4 is a trademark we call it ARCfour.

One of the most interesting new approaches is the *SEAL* cipher[RoCo94]. It is a pseudorandom function developed by Phil Rogaway and Don Coppersmith. The encryption of a clear text byte requires approximately five elementary CPU operations. Unlike many other stream ciphers, SEAL allows random access to the data stream which facilitates synchronisation. SEAL is patented by IBM, hence it is not contained in most free libraries.

After Handschuh and Gilbert published an attack [HaGi97], the algorithm was modified and is now available in version 3.0 [RoCo97]. We strongly suggest to wait for more cryptanalytic work before using SEAL in applications with high security requirements.

4   Experimental Results

In this section we present our performance results for different Luby/Rackoff ciphers and compare them with the classical 64-bit block ciphers. In our experiments, we actually measure the encryption speeds (in **kilobytes per second**) for differently sized packets of 1, 100 and 1000 kilobytes.

4.1   Testing Environment

The test was performed on a PC with an Intel Pentium 200 MMX CPU under Linux 2.0.33. The main memory size was 64 megabytes, and we used the SUN JAVA implementation JDK 1.1.5.

All JAVA classes were compiled with compiler-optimization *disabled* because otherwise some of the self-tests failed. For the same reason, no just-in-time compiler was used. No native routines were used although some are shipped with the current version of Cryptix and would give an important speedup.

The test measured the encryption speeds of various algorithms depending on different block sizes in ECB mode. Particularly, 1k, 100k and 1000 kbyte packets were used.

Typically, ciphers first run the *key schedule*, and then start encrypting. Two numbers are crucial to performance: the *latency* and the *throughput*. Given key and plaintext, the latency is the time to wait until the first ciphertext block is known. The throughput is the speed at which huge blocks can be encrypted, ignoring the key schedule. (Depending on the actual application, either the latency or the throughput may be of greater importance.) Essentially, the latency allows to estimate at which speed small blocks are encrypted, and the throughput stands for the speed at which large blocks are encrypted.

We concentrate on the speed of *encryption*. Due to different key schedules for encryption and decryption, decryption speed can differ slightly from encryption speed. We did not find great differences, though.

4.2 64–bit block ciphers and ARCfour

Cipher	DES	Blowfish	CAST	IDEA	SAFER	Triple-DES	ARC4
1k packet size	78.77	39.36	146.29	80.38	51.41	23.80	250.63
100k packet size	80.46	170.29	146.29	85.33	53.84	23.89	306.56
1000k packet size	80.68	189.00	157.60	110.35	53.86	23.90	307.13

Discussion

The tested implementation of Triple-DES is not optimized, i.e., both the initial permutation and its inverse are evaluated for each of the three DES steps.

Blowfish and CAST are the fastest 64-bit block ciphers in our 32-bit environment. The Blowfish key schedule is more involved than the CAST key schedule, hence for small blocks, CAST is much faster than Blowfish. Our measurements indicate that for large blocks Blowfish is faster than CAST. This has something to do with the fact that the CAST round function uses key–dependent rotations, XOR-operations and additions/subtractions, while Blowfish only uses XOR and addition.

4.3 Luby/Rackoff with SHA-1 and ARCfour

Cipher	BEAST	BEAR	LION	LIONESS
1k packet size	95.1	66.3	75.6	52.5
100k packet size	118.7	74.8	85.7	60.2
1000k packet size	119.4	75.1	85.7	60.2

4.4 Luby/Rackoff with RIPEMD-160 and ARCfour

Cipher	BEAST	BEAR	LION	LIONESS
1k packet size	81.4	54.2	67.2	44.5
100k packet size	99.6	60.1	75.1	50.3
1000k packet size	100.1	60.3	75.1	50.37

4.5 Luby/Rackoff with HAVAL and ARCfour

Cipher	BEAST	BEAR	LION	LIONESS
1k packet size	111.5	80.3	84.7	61.0
100k packet size	144.7	96.0	98.5	73.4
1000k packet size	145.8	96.5	98.5	73.4

4.6 Luby/Rackoff with MD4 and ARCfour

Cipher	BEAST	BEAR	LION	LIONESS
1k packet size	150.4	117.8	98.0	80.2
100k packet size	187.2	138.3	115.7	95.0
1000k packet size	188.3	139.1	115.6	95.0

4.7 Luby/Rackoff with MD5 and ARCfour

Cipher	BEAST	BEAR	LION	LIONESS
1k packet size	102.2	70.0	78.4	54.9
100k packet size	129.3	82.6	90.0	64.9
1000k packet size	129.1	82.6	90.0	64.9

4.8 Luby/Rackoff with MD2 and ARCfour

Cipher	BEAST	BEAR	LION	LIONESS
1k packet size	20.5	11.4	20.7	11.0
100k packet size	23.4	12.1	21.6	11.6
1000k packet size	23.4	12.1	21.6	11.6

5 Conclusions and Outlook

In the case of multimedia encryption, we often have blocks of data that belong together, such as those encoding a single video frames. It makes sense to encrypt them as one large block. Due to compression, the size of such blocks may vary. Unbalanced Luby/Rackoff ciphers such as the ones discussed, are especially good at encrypting variable-size large blocks.

If security against chosen plaintext attacks is sufficient, as in many multimedia applications, the cipher BEAST is a good choice. Otherwise, one should *not* use BEAST, but consider conventional block ciphers such as Blowfish, CAST, the ciphers from the DES family (but not single DES!), or GRIFFIN [Luck97].

While the JAVA programming language is better at supporting machine–independent software development than its competitors such as C and C++, it does not support machine–oriented optimizations very well. As our results indicate, modern block ciphers can still be reasonably efficient.

When using a conventional stream cipher, it is very dangerous to re-use the same key to encrypt different plaintexts. To deal with this issue may involve solving difficult key-management issues or generating unique *initial values*. Ignoring this issue is quite a common protocol error in practically implemented systems.

Similar problems arise if one is using an ordinary block cipher with small blocks in one of the standard modes of operations [FIPS81]: CBC, OFB, or CFB. Things get even worse with the ECB mode of operation.

The situation is much better if we use unbalanced Luby/Rackoff ciphers. As long as any two bits of two plaintext blocks are different, the two corresponding ciphertext blocks are completely scrambled. Thus, block ciphers with huge blocks are invulnerable to such problems. The only thing an adversary can find out (without breaking the cipher itself, of course), is that the same block has been sent again – which is quite unlikely if the blocks are large and the application is optimized to save bandwidth, i.e., uses compression. Compression is a standard technique in multimedia applications, anyway.

Our research on this topic is still in progress. Specially we are evaluating different schemes for *Remote-Key-Encryption* (e.g. [LWH99],[LuWe99]). Since stream ciphers can be implemented very efficiently in hardware, we are considering developing BEAST-based ASICs for video stream encryption.

Acknowledgement

The authors want to thank Prof. Dr. Wolfgang Effelsberg for his helpful comments and critical remarks. We also would like to express thanks to Sascha Kettler of the Cryptix Development Team for his assistance in developing and performing the tests and to the anonymous reviewers for some useful remarks.

References

[Adam97a] Adams, C., "RFC2144: The CAST-128 Encryption Algorithm", May 1997.

[Adam97b] Adams, C, "Constructing Symmetric Ciphers Using the CAST Design Procedure", in: Designs, Codes and Cryptography, v.12, n. 3, Nov 1997, pp. 71-104.

[Ande95] Anderson, R.J., "The classification of hash functions" in Codes and Cyphers – Cryptography and Coding IV (IMA), 1995, pp 83-93.

[BCK96] Bellare, M., Canetti, C., Krawczyk, H., "Keying hash functions for message authentication", Advances in Cryptology - Crypto 96 Proceedings, Lecture Notes in Computer Science Vol. 1109, N. Koblitz ed, Springer-Verlag, 1996

[BiSh93] Biham, E., Shamir, A., "Differential Cryptanalysis of the Data Encryption Standard", Springer, 1993.

[AnBi96] Anderson, R., Biham, E., "Two Practical and Provable Secure Blockciphers: BEAR and LION", Proc. of Fast Software Encryption (ed. D. Gollmann), LNCS 1039, Springer, 1996.

[Blea96] Blaze, M., Diffie, W., Rivest, R., Schneier, B., Shimomura, T., Thompson, E., Wiener, M., "Minimal Key Lengths for Symmetric Ciphers to Provide Adequate Commercial Security", a report by an ad hoc group of cryptographers and computer scientists , January 1996.

[Cryt97] Cryptix - Cryptographic Extensions for Java, 1997. http://www.systemics.com/software/cryptix-java/

[CDF98] Callas, J., Donnerhacke, L., Finnley, H., "OP Formats - OpenPGP Message Format", Internet Draft, 1998.

[DESC97] RSA-Challenge'97. http://www.rsa.com/des/

[Dobb96] Dobbertin, H., "Cryptoanalysis of MD4", Proc. of Fast Software Encryption (ed. D. Gollmann), LNCS 1039, Springer, 1996, pp. 53-69.

[Doea96]   Dobbertin, H., Bosselaers, A., Preneel, B., "RIPEMD-160, a strengthened version of RIPEMD", Proc. of Fast Software Encryption (ed. D. Gollmann), LNCS 1039, Springer, 1996, pp. 71-82.

[EFF98]   Electronic Frontier Foundation, "EFF press release (July 17, 1998): EFF Builds DES Cracker that proves that Data Encryption Standard is insecure", http://www.eff.org/descracker/

[FIPS46]   National Bureau of Standards, NBS FIPS PUB 46, "Data Encryption Standard", January 1977.

[FIPS81]   National Bureau of Standards, NBS FIPS PUB 81, "DES Modes of Operation", December 1980.

[FIPS180] National Bureau of Standards, NBS FIPS PUB 180, "Secure Hash Standard", Washington D.C., April 1995.

[GeWe98]   Geyer, W., Weis, R., "A Secure, Accountable, and Collaborative Whiteboard", Proc. of IDMS'98, Oslo, Springer LNCS 1483, 1998.

[HaGi97]   Handschuh, H., Gilbert, H., "χ^2 cryptoanalysis of the SEAL encryption algorithm", Proc. of Fast Software Encryption 1997, Haifa, Israel, LNCS, Springer, January 1997.

[Kals92]   Kalski, B.S., "RFC3129: The MD2 Message Digest Algorithm", Apr 1992.

[KiRo96]   Kilian, J., Rogaway, P., "How to protect DES against exhaustive key search", Proc. of Crypto'96, Advances in Cryptology, Springer, 1996.

[Lai91]   Lai, X., "Markov ciphers and Differential Cryptoanalyis", Proc. of EUROCRYPT'91, Advances in Cryptology, Springer, 1991.

[Lai92]   Lai, X., "On the Design and Security of Blockciphers", ETH Series in Information Processing, v. 1, Hartmut-Gorre-Verlag, Konstanz, 1992.

[LuRa88]   Luby, M., Rackoff, C., "How to construct pseudorandom permutations from pseudo random functions", SIAM J. Computing, Vol 17, No. 2, 1988, pp. 239-255.

[Luck96a] Lucks, S., "Faster Luby-Rackoff ciphers", Fast Software Encryption (ed. D. Gollmann), LNCS 1039, Springer, 1996.

[Luck96b] Lucks, S., "BEAST: A fast block cipher for arbitrary blocksize", (ed. Hoprster, P.), Proc. IFIP'96, Conference on Communication and Multimedia Security, Chapman & Hall, 1996, pp. 144–153.

[Luck97]   Lucks, S., "On the Security of Remotely Keyed Encryption", Fast Software Encryption, Springer LNCS, 1997.

[LuWe99]   Lucks, S., Weis,R, "Remotely Keyed Encryption Using Non-Encrypting Smart Cards". USENIX Workshop on Smartcard Technology, Chicago, May 10-11, 1999

[LWH99]   Lucks, S., Weis, R., Hilt, V., "Fast Encryption for Set-Top Technologies", Multimedia Computing and Networking '99, San Jose, 1999.

[Mass94]   Massey, L.J., "SAFER K-64: A Byte-Orientated Blockciphering Algorithm", Fast Software Encryption, Cambridge Security Workshop Proccedings, LNCS Springer Verlag, 1994, pp. 1–17.

[Maur92]   Maurer, U., "A Simplified and Generalized Treatment of Luby-Rackoff Pseudo random Permutation Generators", EUROCRYPT 92, Springer LNCS 658, 1992, pp 239-255.

[Mats94]   Matsui, M., "The first experimental cryptanalysis of the Data Encryption Standard", CRYPTO 94, Springer LNCS839, 1994, pp 1-11.

[NN94]   Nomen Nescio, "SUBJECT: RC4 Source Code", 1994.
           ftp://idea.sec.dsi.unimi.it/pub/crypt/code/rc4.revealed.gz,

[Pren93]   Preneel, B., "Analysis and Design of Cryptographic Hash Functions", Ph.D. Thesis, Katholieke Universiteit Leuven, 1993

[PrOo95]   Preneel, B., van Oorschot, P.C., "MDx-MAX and building fast MACs from hash functions" Advances in Cryptology - Crypto'95, LNCS 963, D. Coppersmith, Ed., Springer-Verlag, 1995, pp.1-14.

[RIPE93]   Race Integrity Primitive Evaluation (RIPE), RACE 1040,1993.

[Rive90]   Rivest, R., "RFC 1186, The MD4 Message Digest Algorithm", Oct 1990.

[Rive92]   Rivest, R., "RFC 1321, MD5 Message Digest Algorithm", April 1992.

[Roe94]   Roe, M., "Performance of Symmetric Ciphers and One-way Hash Functions" Fast Software Encryption, Cambridge Security Workshop Proceedings, LNCS Springer Verlag, 1994, pp. 83-86.

[Roe95]   Roe, M., "Performance of Block Ciphers and Hash Functions - One Year later", Fast Software Encryption, 4th International Workshop Proceedings, LNCS 809, Springer Verlag, 1994, pp. 359-362.

[Roga96]   Rogaway, P., "The Security of DESX", CryptoBytes, Volume 2, No. 2, RSA Laboratories, Redwood City, CA, USA, Summer 1996.

[RoCo94]   Rogaway, P., Coppersmith, D., "A software-optimized encryption algortithm", Proceedings of Cambridge Security Workshop on Fast Software Encryption, (ed. R. Anderson), LNCS 809, Springer, 1994, pp. 56-63.

[RoCo97]   Rogaway, P., Coppersmith, D., "A software-optimized encryption algorithm", recised version Sept. 5, 1997.
             http://www.cs.ucdavis.edu/ rogaway/papers/seal.ps

[RSA98]   www.rsa.com/rsa/products/jsafe or www.baltimore.ie/jcrypto.htm, RSA inc. 1998.

[ScBl94]   Schneier, B., Blaze, M.A., "McGuffin: an unbalanced Feistel network block cipher", Fast Software Encryption (ed. Preenel, B.), LNCS 1008, Springer, 1994.

[Schn94]   Schneier, B., "Description of a New Variable-Length Key, 64-Bit Block Cipher", Proc. of Cambridge Security Workshop on Fast Software Encryption, LNCS 809, Springer, 1994, pp. 191-204.

[Schn96]   Schneier, B., "Applied Cryptography Second Edition", John Wiley & Sons, New York, NY, 1996.

[ScWh97]   Schneier, B., Whiting, D., "Fast Software Encryption: Designing Encryption for Optimal Speed on the Intel Pentium Processor", Fast Software Encryption, 4th International Workshop Proccedings, LNCS Springer Verlag, 1997, pp. 242-259.

[SiBa97]   Simpson, W. A., Baldwin, R., "The ESP DES-XEX3-CBC Transform", Internet-Draft, July 1997.

[SUN97]   Java Security, 19.11.1997, See: http://www.javasoft.com/security/

[Vaud95]   Vaudenay, S., "La Securite des Primitives Cryptographiques", These de Doctorat, Laboratoire d'Informatique de l'Ecole Normale Superieure, 1995.

[Weis98a]   Weis, R., "Modern Streamcipher" (in German), in: "Kryptographie", Weka-Fachzeitschriften-Verlag, Poing, 1998.

[Weis98b]   Weis, R., "Cryptographic One-Way-Functions" (in German), in: "Kryptographie", Weka-Fachzeitschriften-Verlag, Poing, 1998.

[WeLu98a]   Weis, R., Lucks, S., "The Performance of Modern Block Ciphers in JAVA", CARDIS'98, Louvain-la-Neuve, to appear in: LNCS , Springer, 1998.

[Wiew96]   Wiewall, E., "Secure Your Applications with the Microsoft CryptoAPI", in Microsoft Developer Network News, 5/96,3/4, 1, 1996.

[Zhea93]   Zheng, Y., Pieprzyk, J., Seberry, J., "HAVAL-A One-Way Hashing Algorithm with Varable Length of Output", Proc. AUSCRYPT'92, Springer, 1993.

Watermarking in the MPEG-4 Context

D.Nicholson[1], P.Kudumakis[2], J.-F. Delaigle[3]

[1] THOMSON-CSF COMMUNICATION, 66 rue du Fossé Blanc, 92230 Gennevilliers, France
didier.nicholson@tcc.thomson-csf.com

[2] Central Research Labs, Dawley Road, Hayes, MiddleSex, UB3144, United Kingdom
pkudumakis@crl.co.uk

[3] Laboratoire de Télécommunication et Télédétection, Université Catholique de Louvain,
Bâtiment Stévin - Place du Levant, 2, B-1348 Louvain-la-Neuve, Belgium
delaigle@tele.ucl.ac.be

Abstract. This paper presents the constraints involved by MPEG-4 to copyright protection systems based upon watermarking technology. It proposes also an assessment methodology in order to evaluate such systems in terms of robustness to compression and quality.

1 Introduction

MIRADOR European ACTS project was set up to evaluate and upgrade existing watermarking techniques developed within the MPEG-2 framework, to the new issues arising within the MPEG-4 standard. The project's objectives are to:

- integrate MPEG-2 watermarking technologies into MPEG-4 for both video and audio
- assess how these technologies behave in this new environment
- optimise the techniques to the new MPEG-4 constraints
- actively participate in the MPEG-4 IPMP (Intellectual Property Management and Protection) Ad Hoc Working Group to push forward the use of watermarking in MPEG-4

It must be stressed that the project is intended not only to be innovative with the watermarking algorithms, but to work closely with the standards body to ensure that watermarking is integrated and recognised as a key enabling technology for content protection of MPEG-4 objects. Consequently, the project has as an important objective to analyse and actively participate to the MPEG-4 ad hoc working groups so that the technology is accepted and integrated at the level of the MPEG-4 system and that associated hooks for coupling watermarking and monitoring are specified.

The major applications for watermarking in MPEG-4 are :

- monitoring of multimedia object usage (usually to monitor copyright liability)
- fingerprinting (to create an audit trail showing transfer of media objects)
- copy control (to facilitate authorised access to, and copying of, media objects)

The major application segments involving IPR are: interactive television and multimedia to set top boxes, infotainment and streaming media over Internet. This wide spectrum of applications segments, together with the new technologies for encoding objects in MPEG-4, make the issue of watermarking far more complex than with MPEG-2.

As watermarking techniques become more widely known, quite complete lists of basic requirements have been made. Such lists can be found in ACCOPI, TALISMAN [2] for classical coding schemes. However, since MIRADOR wants to deal with new MPEG4 coding schemes in the new interactive multimedia environment, new requirements clearly appear for watermarking techniques. Watermarking should not alter the quality of a work but should resist to a number of manipulations: cuts, scaling, new compression schemes, etc. This document will overview the way how the major issues identified in MIRADOR D1 document, publicly available on MIRADOR web site [1], should be evaluated with existing watermarking technologies, regarding the new MPEG-4 constraints. The evaluation process specification describes the system used for determining the visual quality of the protection mechanism developed into the project.

The items covered are :

- Watermarking robustness evaluation process. The process for the verification of the degree of resistance offered by the watermark present into an object towards its re – encoding.

- Watermarking audibility/visibility evaluation process. The process of verification on a subjective basis the audibility/visibility of a watermarked decoded object into its different representations. Audibility/Visibility constraints will be specified in relation with the concerned applications. Quality of embedding is less constraining for non-professional applications.

2   Rights holder requirements and technical constraints

This Chapter briefly overviews the MPEG-4 underlying concepts to establish the pre-requisites for the IPR requirements analysis.

2.1   The Requirements of Creators and Rights Holders for Associating IPR Identifiers within Digital Content

The control mechanisms required to manage the activities of licensing, monitoring and tracking, and the enforcement of legitimate usage within the distribution chain will rely on the implementation of four key infrastructure tools.

2.2   Persistent Identification

Perhaps the most important of these tools is persistent identification, which should be interpreted as the ability to manage the association of identifiers with digital content [4]. This will achieve the critical link between the one or more component creations that may exist within a piece of digital content and the environment which stores the related descriptive data, current rights holders, license conditions and enforcement mechanisms. The association of the identifier with each creation must be both persistent and resistant. Digital content can and will be modified, whether legitimately or not, and so the persistence of association between identifiers and their creations is a critical requirement. As the imprinting of identifiers into digital content provides the key to associate creations with the control mechanisms required managing intellectual property rights they must also be resistant to attack and removal.

Among the best candidates, we can list
ISAN, ISBN/ISSN/BICI/SICI, ISRC, ISWC-T, ISWC-L, ISMN

2.3   Global Resolution for Identifiers

We see from the above definition of persistent identification that its function is to provide the link between component creations within digital objects and the metadata associated within them. A structure such as the International DOI [4] Foundation provides the necessary level of trusted neutrality to establish routing services for all types of digital content and their associated metadata.

2.4   Information Management Standards

The resolution of identifiers with the storage of associated metadata will present a range of information, in both a numerical and textual format, which will describe amongst other things the information about the creation, its rights holders and licensing terms and conditions. The organisation of this information in a standardised form is a critical requirement if the community it is designed to serve is to benefit from the common interpretation of the information and therefore derive maximum benefit from this level of integration. The Common Information System (CIS) [5] is a clear example where a community of interest has established such an initiative.

2.5   Trusted Certification Authority services

The role of the certification authority is probably the least well defined within an architecture for conducting electronic commerce as its activities cannot easily be associated with equivalent services in the world of physical commerce. The conceptual diagram of the IMPRIMATUR Business Model [9], to which we refer in MIRADOR, implies the certification authority provides a validation service to support transactions between the creation provider, the media distributor and the purchaser. On this basis it operates as an independent trusted third party to manage identification certificates which can uniquely identify the purchaser and the media distributor by using a system of public and private keys. To participate in this trading environment, the Media Distributor and the Purchaser must first register themselves with the Certification Authority where they will be assigned a unique name and identification number. These parameters can be watermarked or imprinted into the purchased Creation to enable the Purchaser to prove it was purchased according to predetermined rules. Consequently, any content that violates these rules can, in principle, be more easily detected because the imprinted keys will either be missing or show some evidence that tampering has taken place.

Based on this broad definition the function of the certification authority can be introduced wherever there may be a requirement to enforce variable 'rules' or 'conditions' to control transactions between different roles.

2.6 Protection of IPR

The ability of rights holders to track and monitor the usage of their intellectual property is an essential requirement in both a physical and virtual trading environment. Electronic distribution, however, presents a different set of problems to physical distribution models which will require different solutions. The predicted high volume of transactions to be conducted by consumers combined with frequency of use, ease of digital reproduction, and at low cost, present new challenges to the task of intellectual property rights protection.

As a summary, for an efficient protection scheme, the following functionalities should be guaranteed:

- Automated monitoring and tracking of creations
- Prevention of illegal copying
- Tracking object manipulation and modification history (i.e. persistent identification)
- Support transactions between Users, Media Distributors and Rights Holders

2.7 Licensing

The IMPRIMATUR Business Model proposes that the action of issuing a licence constitutes a transaction between the rights holder and one of the other roles that wish to acquire rights in a creation depending upon the type of usage which is required. The most likely roles to seek a licence from the rights holder are the creator, creation provider and the media distributor. Purchasers will also require a licence and these will form part of the terms and conditions of use encompassed by the acquisition from the media distributor.

To effectively control the activity of licensing and to be capable of determining the terms and conditions specified by a licence in a timely manner, licence metadata must be stored in an electronic environment and be accessible to:

- The parties who are signatory to the licence
- The party responsible for enforcing the terms and conditions of the licence

The Rights Holder is the most suitable candidate for managing the responsibility for the control and maintenance of a licence repository for the storage of licence metadata. It is the party closest to the source of the metadata and therefore is able to provide the most authoritative information. The licence Repository will require an interface with the IPR database to establish a link with the identity of the current rights holder. The Rights Holder is also the main source of data supplied to the IPR Database and so it is logical that they also take responsibility for the management of the licence metadata within the repository.

Licence Repositories can provide an archive for storing information about licences, which have been issued to specify the licensing conditions for any types of creation. It may be convenient to manage such a repository in a centralised way on behalf of a number of organisations that have a collective interest in sharing this information. Alternatively, a number of repositories may be managed independently by different rights holders, perhaps covering different geographical areas, but conforming to standards to achieve interoperability between them. Rights societies already maintain their own repositories but these are largely maintained for their exclusive use. Increasingly, societies are discussing the need to share certain information about their licensing activities and the need to introduce greater interoperability between their licensing systems. So the need for a global repository of licence information will increase.

The purpose of a licence repository is to provide essential knowledge about licences to enable:

- Identification (a mechanism by which licences for all types of rights can be uniquely identified)
- Enforcement (by the Certification Authority, according to the parameters which are specified by the licensee in a trust management system)
- Monitoring and Tracking (to verify the quantity of actual sales against the amount specified in a licence according to its period of validity).

To achieve these objectives it is essential that information about each licence is stored in the licence repository and it is **accessible**. A licence repository may be administered in either a centralised or a distributed environment depending upon the organisation of the rights holders who contribute the licensing data. Once a licence can be identified uniquely, routing devices can be implemented (such as DOI) to provide the navigational infrastructure to pinpoint its exact location.

2.8   Enforcement

The licence number can be embedded within a digital object as part of the process of certification in order to provide the enquiry reference identifier for the Monitoring and Tracking Authority to consult the licence repository. It will use the Licence Repository to carry out its primary activity of accurately collating usage information for the Rights Holder. In addition, however, the certification authority can verify that the type of use falls within the terms and conditions of the licence. The licence number provides the key which links to all the other pieces of metadata which are required in order to issue a licence. This will include the identification of the creation, its associated creators, the current rights holder, and other creations and interested parties to which it may be related (i.e. the sound recording of a musical work).

3   New concepts introduced by MPEG-4

The MPEG group initiated the MPEG-4 standardisation process in 1994 (ISO/IEC JTC1 SC29/WG11) with the mandate to standardise algorithms and tools for coding and flexible representation of audio-visual data to meet the challenges of future multimedia applications [10].

MPEG-4 addresses the need for :

- Universal accessibility and robustness in error prone environments
- Interactive functionality, with dynamic objects rather than just static ones
- Coding of natural and synthetic audio and visual material
- Compression efficiency
- Integration of real time and non-real time (stored) information in a single presentation

These goals were to be reached by defining two basic elements:

- A set of coding tools for audio-visual objects capable of providing support to different functionalities such as object-based interactivity and scalability, and error robustness, in addition to efficient compression.
- A syntactic description of coded audio-visual objects, providing a formal method for describing the coded representation of these objects and the methods used to code them.

The coding tools have been defined in such a way that users will have the opportunity to assemble the standard MPEG-4 tools to satisfy specific user requirements, some configurations of which are expected to be standardised. The syntactic description will be used to convey to a decoder the choice of tools made by the encoder.

Audio-visual scenes are composed of several Audio Visual Objects (AVOs), organised in a hierarchical fashion. At the leaves of the hierarchy, we find primitive AVOs, such as :

- A 2-dimensional fixed background,
- The picture of a talking person (without the background)
- The voice associated with that person;

MPEG standardises a number of such primitive AVOs, capable of representing both natural and synthetic content types, which can be either 2- or 3-dimensional. In addition to the AVOs mentioned MPEG-4 defines the coded representation of objects such as:

- Text and graphics;
- Talking heads and associated text to be used at the receiver's end to synthesise the speech and animate the head;
- Animated human bodies.

In their coded form, these objects are represented as efficiently as possible. This means that the bits used for coding these objects are no more than necessary to support the desired functionalities. Examples of such functionalities are error robustness, allowing extraction and editing of an object, or having an object available in a scaleable form. It is important to note that in their coded form, objects (aural or visual) can be represented independently of their surroundings or background.

3.1 Scene description

In addition to providing support for coding individual objects, MPEG-4 also provides facilities to compose a set of such objects into a scene. The necessary composition information forms the scene description, which is coded and transmitted together with the Audio Visual Objects (AVOs).

In order to facilitate the development of authoring, manipulation and interaction tools, scene descriptions are coded independently from streams related to primitive AV objects. Special care is devoted to the identification of the parameters belonging to the scene description. This is done by differentiating the parameters that are used to improve the coding efficiency of an object (e.g., motion vectors in video coding algorithms), and the ones that are used as modifiers of an object (e.g., the position of the object in the scene). Since MPEG-4 should allow the modification of this latter set of parameters without having to decode the primitive AVOs themselves, these parameters are placed in the scene description and not in primitive AV objects.

4 New technical constraints introduced by MPEG4 coding

The robustness of watermarking within Visual objects is extremely sensitive to all manipulations that may be applied to the objects. This was already true for JPEG and MPEG-2 but becomes even more relevant and more complex with MPEG-4 capabilities.

4.1 Visual objects

4.1.1 New coding tools

MPEG4 is specifying new coding tools for natural and synthetic visual objects. The robustness of watermarking technologies to the loss of information introduced by lossy compression has to be guaranteed. Watermarking technologies are efficient protection tools if and only if they resist to a compression ratio such that the quality of the compressed image and thus its commercial value is low. So, tests have to be conducted with the new MPEG4 coding tools, even if they are close to the ones specified in MPEG2. The same tests have to be performed for wavelet compression, EZW specified for still images. The tests already achieved by MIRADOR are presented in section 6.

4.1.2 Objects with arbitrary shapes and sizes

After MPEG4 encoding, two different entities carry information: the shape of the object and its texture. The watermarking may be embedded into both entities. In the case of the shape watermarking, the edge BABs or their transparency could be slightly modified. However, the possibility of objects merging (for instance when transcoding takes places) and of shape modification by the user (for instance the deformation and cropping) should be borne in mind.

Although watermarking the texture enables the use of more classical methods, the problem of synchronisation when attempting to retrieve the watermark is crucial, since a reference is always necessary. Difficulties start when the shape of the object has been modified, for instance when compressed with loss. Besides, practical difficulties also occur because of the arbitrary shape, since most algorithms are designed to work on rectangular images. In addition to this, it is obvious that a minimal size is required for the object to carry watermark information.

4.1.3 Geometric transforms

Geometric transforms concerning sprites objects are defined by the MPEG-4 standardisation:

- Translation (which may involve cropping of the object)
- Rotation
- Rescaling
- Generic affine transform

Moreover, taking into account the interactivity possibilities offered to the user, all kind of objects may be affected by geometric transforms. Thus, the watermarking techniques have to deal with this constraint. On the one hand, the watermark has to resist the deterioration introduced by the transformations. On the other hand, the watermark has to be associated with a so-called "re-synchronisation mechanism", which allow to look for the watermark in the good location. Finally, the watermark must be sufficiently redundant so as not to suffer from the loss of information introduced by cropping. It is important to mention that cropping is often associated geometric transformations.

4.1.4 Multiscale objects

Concerning scalability, the main issue is the degree of protection that must be provided by the watermark. The available bandwidth at each level, as well as the picture quality (directly connected with its commercial interest), must be taken into account.

Temporal scalability is not a problem with today's methods, since the message is repeated in each image; but it may be quite disturbing when the small size of the objects has to be compensated for by disseminating the message on several pictures. An interesting approach may consist of using temporal wavelet transforms in order to spread the message over several components (DC components corresponding to the static parts of the image as well as AC components connected with the moving parts of the sequence).

Regarding the spatial scalability, the main question is: what actually has to be protected, taking into account the fact that it will be very difficult to write a message in the lowest layer without visibility problems ? It could be interesting to have a hierarchical message with a hierarchy on the message quality or its content. For instance, the message could be split into sub-messages corresponding to the Authors' Society reference, to the author, to the work, etc., and each message hidden in a different layer. This would enable a partial but pertinent decoding of the message at the lowest level of scalability. The watermarking method should also be compliant with the wavelet.

4.1.5 Transcoding problems

The problems involved do not seem to be overwhelming as long as we stay in the original MPEG-4 bitstream (accepting some minor modifications). The transcoding of a MPEG-4 bitstream into another MPEG-4 or MPEG-2 bitstream seems to be much more critical. It can be regarded as a multiple watermarking problem, with different messages coming from the merged objects. When reading the watermarks, synchronisation might therefor be much more difficult. Due to the difference in size of the objects, the message carried by a small one may be hidden by another message.

5 Watermark usage in MPEG4 environment

5.1 IPMP

Versions of MPEG prior to MPEG-4 have not included the mechanisms to allow Rights Holders to adequately protect their works. With this in mind, as a part of the MPEG-4 standardisation process, a separate committee was set up to discuss how best to provide these facilities. This became known as the IPMP Group (Intellectual Property Management and Protection Group).

Initially, in the MPEG-4 IPMP, it was thought that it may be possible to include facilities such as encryption and watermarking within the MPEG-4 Standard. However, because of the need to finalise the standardisation process quickly, the large range of potential MPEG-4 applications combined with their widely differing IPMP requirements, and finally the legal implications of recommending particular techniques which could later be proven inadequate, it was decided not to take this major step. Nevertheless, in order to meet the needs of the creative industries and to encourage them to use MPEG-4, it was considered necessary to provide a mechanism whereby IP could be protected if required in any given application. MPEG-4 IPMP standardises a generic interface to (possibly private) IPMP tools. This interface is referred to as the IPMP interface.

The main issue is that MPEG-4 Version 1 was offering no IP protection and could have presented a "back-door" route to persons attempting to "attack" a protected work. This situation was resulting from the general MPEG versioning philosophy, which maintains that backward compatibility with Version 1 is essential. This implies that Version 2 works should be playable on Version 1 players, albeit without any "advanced features" introduced by Version 2.

In order to cope with these requirements and not to offer a "back-door" route to persons attempting to "attack" a protected work, it has been decided to include an interface to non-MPEG-4 Standard IP protection systems. Such systems will almost certainly be different for different applications but, as they are not part of the Standard, this does not present a problem. In fact this is seen as an advantage because the IPMP system can be optimised for individual applications.

The Dublin meeting saw the introduction of the IPMP "hooks" (control points) architecture. This represented a significant step in the development of IPMP infrastructure within MPEG. The group consensus after the May 1998 New York IPMP *ad hoc* meeting, and the subsequent evolution of the New York proposal at Dublin led the Convenor and others to suggest that IPMP should be considered for inclusion in MPEG-4 version 1.

MPEG-4 provides the facility to establish an IPI Data Set (Intellectual Property Identification Data Set). This provides no protection as such, but does allow a complete set of IP information to be included within the MPEG-4 bit stream. For further information please refer to WG11/N1918. The IPI Data Set can be used by IPMP systems as input to the management and protection process. For example, this can be used to generate audit trails that track content use. The IPI Data Set includes:

Type of Content	e.g. audio visual, book, musical work etc.
Type of Content Identifier	e.g. ISAN, ISBN, ISRC etc.
Content Identifier Code	i.e. a unique number identifying the content.
Supplementary Data Items	i.e. other data as required (not defined).

The aims of the IP Protection & Management, previously planned to be included in the Version2, were reviewed with a view to coping with the following issues:

- Persistent protection of IPI Data Sets.
- Management of intellectual property, conditional access permissions, transactions, user authentication and addressibility.
- Audit trails and modification history.
- Integrity and authenticity of intellectual property information, modification history information and payload.
- Real time issues and synchronisation.
- Interfaces between MPEG-4 and external systems (e.g. CORBA, DCOM, COM etc.).
- External security systems, watermarking and cryptography.

In order to provide appropriate solutions for the wide range of applications the MPEG-4 IPMP Group have proposed a modular IPMP System. A clear point of separation is defined between non-normative IPMP systems and the normative part of MPEG-4. This point of separation is the IPMP interface, on one side, being part of the Standard and on this other side, specific to an application and not part of the Standard. It should be emphasised that the interface is common to all applications and is part of the MPEG-4 Standard. This approach allows the design of application specific IPMP-S's (IPMP Systems).

While MPEG-4 does not standardise IPMP systems, it standardises the MPEG-4 IPMP interface. This interface was designed to be a simple extension of basic MPEG-4 systems constructs. It consists of *IPMP-Descriptors* (IPMP-Ds) and *IPMP-Elementary Streams* (IPMP-ES). IPMP Elementary Streams are like any other MPEG-4 elementary stream and IPMP Descriptors are extensions to MPEG-4 object descriptors. The syntax of these constructs is described in great detail in ISO/IEC 14496-1.

IPMP-Ds and IPMP-ESs provide a communication mechanism between IPMP systems and the MPEG-4 terminal. Certain applications may require multiple IPMP systems. When MPEG-4 objects require management and protection, they have IPMP-Ds associated with them. These IPMP-Ds indicate which IPMP systems are to be used and provide information to these systems about how to manage and protect the content.

Communication between the IPMP-S and the MPEG-4 unit is by means of IPMP-D's (IPMP-Descriptors) which may arrive via the MPEG-4 bit stream or through a side channel connected to the IPMP-S (such as a smart card). In the case of communications using the interface the IPMP-D's will be contained in either an IPMP ES (Elementary Stream) or in other ES's. The IPMP-S will communicate with the other ES handlers whenever objects in those streams have IPMP-D's associated with them. The IPMP-S is responsible for managing access to objects in protected streams.

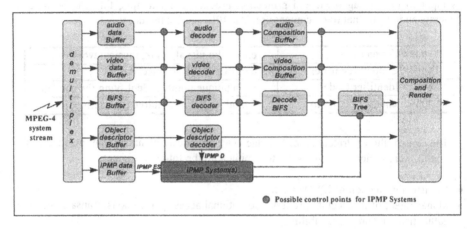

Figure 1: MPEG-4 IPMP framework

Watermarking is an emerging technology that aims at protecting IPR of diverse kinds of contents, such as sound, Still images, video, text or even 3D objects. The principle of watermarking is to embed invisibly (hide) IPR data directly into the Content. In other words, the Content is imperceptibly modified in order to carry IPR data. The embedding process is generally parameterised by a secret key. At the other end, the retrieval process extracts IPR data from watermarked contents with the use of the secret key. Without this key, it must be impossible to retrieve and thus remove IPR data. In certain cases, the above mentioned IPR data can be only a few bits and the retrieval process only checks the presence of a watermark. Watermarks can be applied before (Classical watermarks) or after MPEG4 encoding (bit-stream watermarks).

There are mainly three scenarios in which the watermark can be used:

- *Proprietary watermark search.* Typical uses of watermarks consist in monitoring contents on the Internet or on broadcast networks. The idea is to look for a proprietary watermark in order to detect illegal usage of a particular Content. This kind of application does not absolutely require any interaction with the MPEG4 playback, since it can be achieved after decompression and must be possible after decompression or re-encoding in any other formats. The major goal of this watermarking based monitoring is to deal with the leaks of encryption based security systems, which are no more efficient once the protected contents have been decrypted, copied, possibly re-encoded and eventually redistributed.

- *Copy Control.* The copy Control problem into MPEG4 player is primarily covered by the descrambling actions (IPMP). The idea is to use the watermark retrieval as an additional tool (additional to the scrambling) for copy Control. This can be done verifying whether the watermark read out from the object and the IPR data are coherent. This implies the existence of an IPR data flow providing copyright ownership of the objects being decoded. So the copy Control mechanism of the player should take advantage of two tools:

1. Mutual identification of client and server: if the identification fails the copy Control acts on the descrambler to avoid the copy.

2. Coherence check between the IPR data conveyed with the stream and the watermark: if the check fails the copy Control mechanism acts on the player to avoid the copy or the rendering.

Fingerprinting. Fingerprinting consists in associating the identification of the copying consumer device or the identity of the consumer with the copied Content, via a watermark insertion. Embedding fingerprints in consumer devices is a difficult challenge that absolutely needs interaction with MPEG4 playback platform.

The watermarked object must replace the decoded object in the rendering chain into the player.

To insert the watermark conveying the identities of the consumer are needed the following information:

- identity of the user
- key

6 Proposed Evaluation protocol for visual watermarking assessment

6.1 Introduction

MIRADOR evaluation methodology is the description of the way how watermarking experiments have been conducted in the context of MPEG-4. The evaluation process has two different parts, the robustness evaluation and the invisibility evaluation named quality evaluation. In order to establish an assessment protocol, it is necessary to overview what kind of evaluation has been made previously in other projects and domains. TALISMAN ACTS project has set up the first methodology to evaluate watermarking algorithms, and in order to analyse the robustness of the watermarks, it is totally possible to use the robustness evaluation process of TALISMAN. Concerning the quality evaluation, it is important, because the usage environment is different of the TALISMAN environment, to analyse what are the quality assessment used to conduct experiments regarding the quality of compression algorithms.

6.2 Robustness to compression measurement

The goal of the MIRADOR project is to test the behaviour of the watermarking techniques [3] within the MPEG-4 framework and MIRADOR targeted applications. The MPEG-4 encoder / decoder used in the project is the MoMuSys software. In this software, only MPEG-4 natural video objects tools are available. Therefore the working domain of the MIRADOR project is limited to the natural image content tools (still image and video). Watermarking / monitoring efficiency with regard to SNHC objects or graphics objects will be not tested in the context of this framework. It means that, if application targeted by the MIRADOR project, requires SNHC tools and natural tools, only the behaviour of the watermarking in the context of the natural content tools will be tested. However, by testing the behaviour of tools such as EZW (wavelet compression), synthetic objects watermarking is partially treated. By partially treated, we mean that we don't watermark « animation parameters », e.g. motion vectors in animated 2D meshes, facial animation parameters, ... but, by the study of still image watermarking, we deal partially with the problem of texture mapping watermarking in synthetic applications. Through the MIRADOR project, first efficient evaluations will be carried out.

From MIRADOR targeted applications, described in MIRADOR D1 document [1], useful objects types profiles and levels have been listed. From these object types, profiles and levels have been chosen and for every application, a set of parameters / tools has been proposed.

For each video object, a watermark is embedded in each frame. It is a 64 bits binary message. Robustness results will show the percentage of wrongly monitored embedded bits as well as the percentage of incorrectly protected frames. A frame is considered as not protected if at least one bit among the 64 bits message is wrong.

Error correcting code or time integration tools have not been used in these experiments. Even if these tools would enable to improve watermarking robustness, they could mask watermarking fine behaviour. When robustness results are given with error correction or post-processing, they must also be given as bare results, without any processing. This allow to analyse precisely the behaviour of watermarking algorithms, in order to be able to realise improvements.

6.3 Robustness measurement results

6.3.1 Still images

Concerning still images, the relevant robustness tests consist in using DCT and wavelet compression schemes recognised by MPEG4. For this purpose, we used JPEG and EZW at different bit rates to compress the images. We then made the statistics of watermarking retrieval after decompression.

Robustness assessments toward JPEG compression has been carried out by using a 50 still images database. This database regroups diverse images having different characteristics, from low textured images to highly textured images or even synthetic images. The JPEG baseline algorithm has been used and watermarking robustness is expressed with regard to JPEG quality factor. This parameter varies from 1 (high compression and very poor image quality) to 100 (low compression and lossless image encoding). For our experiences, it varies from 10 to 90 with a step of 10. It enables to obtain a great variety of compression rates. After compression, each image has been decompressed and a monitoring stage has been conducted, that is to say a statistics of watermarking retrievals.

Quality factor	10	20	30	40	50	60	70	80	90
images correctly monitored	0%	0%	0%	0%	5.8%	51.2 %	59.6 %	76.9 %	86.5 %
bits incorrectly decoded	50	39.8	29.2	22.5	16	12	8.2	5.5	3.7

Table 1 : Watermarking robustness toward JPEG compression

The table presents for each quality factor, the mean percentage of wrong bits with regard to the quality factor, the percentage of images perfectly monitored (the percentage of wrong bits is null) and the mean PSNR of the compressed images luminance.

A deeper analysis of the results show that except for some synthetic images, the watermark can be considered as robust toward JPEG. As a matter of fact, the watermark becomes inefficient at low quality percentages. The corresponding decompressed images have lost a lot of commercial value.

As for the JPEG evaluation, robustness assessments toward EZW compression has been carried out by using a database of 50 still images. The EZW algorithm is coming from the MoMuSys ACTS project. The encoding parameters used for this evaluation are:

- filter type : default filter of the algorithm
- Number of wavelet decomposition levels : 5
- wavelet uniform
- encoding mode : Multi-quantization level
- zero tree scanning : band by band
- spatial scalability level : 1
- SNR spatial scalability : 1

The parameters that enable to modify compression ratio is the quantization step of the AC coefficients of the wavelet decomposition. Quantization steps used are : 2, 4, 8, 16, 32. It enables to obtain a great variety of compression rates. The following table summarises the obtained results. It presents according the quantization step of the wavelet decomposition AC coefficients, the mean PSNR of the images decompressed, the mean percentage of wrong bits at the monitoring stage, obtained after EZW encoding.

AC quantisation step	32	16	8	4	2
average PSNR (dB)	31.27	34.65	39	43.8	48.54
average % of wrong bits	36.12	11.9	1	0	0
average bits rate (bit/pixel)	0.4	0.8	1.48	2.53	4

Table 2: Robustness toward EZW compression

The same conclusions can be drawn for EZW. When the efficiency of the watermrak decreases, the quality becomes much lower.

6.3.2 Moving Images

All along the project, experiments have been conducted with the following MPEG4 sequences : Akyio, Sean, News, Weather, Stephan, Flower and Table Tennis. Akyio and Sean are class A sequences (few motion), News is a class B sequence (intermediate motion), flower, tennis table and Stephan are class C sequences (lot of motion), weather is a class E sequences (Hybrid natural and synthetic). Each sequence consists in 300 images.

Sequences formats are QCIF (176 by 144 at 30 Hz), CIF (352 by 288 at 30 Hz) and ITU-R BT.601 (720 by 486 at 30 Hz or 720 by 576 at 25 Hz). QCIF and CIF sequences are progressive sequences and ITU-R BT.601 sequences are interlaced.

Several applications have been considered for the tests:

- Broadcasting ;
- Digital Television Set-Top Box ;
- Infotainment ;
- Streaming Video on the Internet/Intranet .

Each application requires different sets of MPEG-4 tools and parameters, which include :

- Rectangular video encoding with different images formats : QCIF, CIF, ITU-R BT.601;
- Arbitrary shape Video Object encoding ;
- Temporal and spatial scalability for video sequences encoding ;
- Progressive and interlaced encoding tools ;
- Still texture encoding with EZW (Embedded Zero tree Wavelet) ;

For each of them, experiments have been conducted. Analysis of the obtained results will allow to identify and highlight problems on the current algorithm , and then to set out new ways of research in order to solve those encountered problems. Consequently, only crude results (percentage of wrong monitored bits and wrong monitored images) will be given in this document Bare results are the results obtained without the use of data post-processing. In a real implementation, it is obvious that clever spatial and temporal redundancy should taken into account through the use of error correcting codes.

Sequence Name	targeted bit rate (Mbit/s)	Obtained bit rate (Mbit/s)	% of wrong bits	% of wrong images
Akyio	0,25	0,27	0,062	4
Akyio	0,5	0,52	0	0
Akyio	1	1,01	0	0
Akyio	2	2,00	0	0

Table 3: effects of the compression on CIF sequences : Akiyo

Sequence Name	targeted bit rate (Mbit/s)	Obtained bit rate (Mbit/s)	% of wrong bits	% of wrong images
Weather	0,5	0,55	19,3	100,0
Weather	1	1,05	9,4	99,67
Weather	2	2,02	4,2	94,67

Table 4: effects of the compression on CIF sequences : Weather

The tables above gather some of these results. The results are very good with these type of sequences. An improvement is needed when dealing with sequences having an important motion. As a consequence, we have worked in order to improve the algorithm. The new results are already promising, but they are too recent to be published. Moreover, this upgrading work is still on progress.

6.3.3 Arbitrary shapes objects

The algorithm has been modified in order to take into account arbitrary shape objects. Each of the objects is watermarked using a different value (identifier) and key, with regard to the binary shape. As the image sizes are quite small, few blocks are available to embed watermark . Moreover, as video objects are extracted and independently watermarked (one message associated with one video object), the number of blocks available is still more reduced . Each of the objects after watermarking is compressed separately. On the output of the decoder, each of the object is monitored separately.

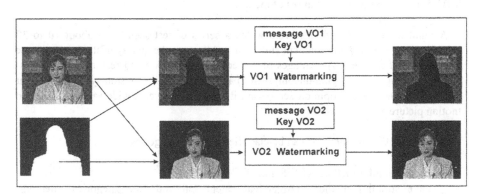

Figure 2: Watermarking of Arbitrary shape

Sequence Name	Bit rate (VO1) Mbits/s	% of wrong monitored images (VO1)	% of wrong bits (VO1)	Bit rate (VO2) Mbits/s	% of wrong monitored images (VO2)	% of wrong bits (VO2)
Akyio	0,19	0	0	0,74	12,7	0,218

6.4 Visual quality assessment protocol

Lots of work has been done on how to evaluate under standardised conditions the picture quality, necessary for the introduction of new television systems. For the moment, as far as the evaluation of codecs is concerned, only subjective assessments give confident results. Subjective measurements are the result of human observers, providing their opinion of the video quality.

Existing assessment methods have been developed and refined over years and have provided the reliable and sensitive test procedures, which have guided specification and design of actual television services. Formal subjective testing, as defined by ITU-R BT.500, has been used for many years with a stable set of standard methods. The current state of practice defines the best methods available and provides advice for the non-specialist on issues concerned with the choice of :

- basic methodology
- viewing conditions
- selection and screening of observers
- scaling method
- reference condition
- presentation timing
- test picture sequences
- analysis of voting
- presentation of results

In order to standardise subjective image quality evaluation, ITU Recommendation ITU-R BT.500 has been prepared and is regularly reviewed, to provide instructions on what seems the best available methods for the assessment of picture quality. In particular, ITU-R BT.500 defines common features of the tests.

A number of non-expert observers watch a series of test scenes for about 10 to 30 minutes in a controlled environment and are asked to score the quality of the scenes in one of a variety of manners. Advantages of subjective testing are valid results for both non-compressed (analog or digital uncompressed) and compressed television systems. A scalar mean is obtained (mean opinion score) and it works well over a wide range of still and motion picture applications.

The ITU-R BT.500 methods can be classified in three categories :

- Double stimulus methods (DSIS and DSCQS)
- Single stimulus methods (Adjectival categorical and Non-categorical methods, SSNCS, SSCQE)
- Stimulus comparison methods (Adjectival categorical judgement and Non-categorical methods)

These methodologies have been detailed in the MIRADOR D2 Deliverable, publicly available. As explained, in this document, in order to assess the quality of watermarked material and to discriminate small differences between the original and the modified pictures, the Double Stimulus Continuous Quality Scale (DSCQS) method is recommended.

6.4.1 Double Stimulus Continuous Quality Scale (DSCQS)

In the Double Stimulus method with a continuous quality scale, all the sequences are presented unimpaired (assessment reference) and impaired. The basic principle is to assess pairs of sequences.

One of the two sequences is a reference, the other has been subject to processing by the watermarking system being assessed. Observers are not informed of the position of these two images in the sequence and they allocate a score to each individual image using a continuous quality scale. This couple of sequences is repeated once. The sequencing of this method is summarised in the following figure :

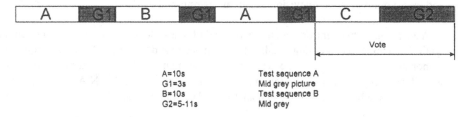

A=10s	Test sequence A
G1=3s	Mid grey picture
B=10s	Test sequence B
G2=5-11s	Mid grey

Figure 3 : Presentation sequence for the DSCQS method

The scoring sheet includes pairs of scales. Each scale is divided into five segments, but only on the left-hand side, are the appropriate descriptions (excellent, good, fair, poor and bad). Observers express their opinion by marking the scales.

The Grading scales corresponds to the following notes:

5	excellent
4	good
3	fair
2	poor
1	bad

Table 5: Grading scale and quality note correspondence

The marks on the graphical scale are converted into numbers by taking the upper scale boundary as 5 and the lower as 0. They are read for A and B, separately. For each combination of sequence, the average over observers of these difference scores is calculated as well as the standard deviation and the 95% confidence interval. Finally for each processed case, the average over observers and sequences of difference score is calculated, together with the appropriate standard deviation and 95% confidence interval.

At least 15 observers should be used. It has been found that means become stable when at least 15 observers are used. They should be non-expert, in the sense that they are not directly concerned with television picture quality as part of their normal work, and are not experienced assessors. Assessors should be introduced to the method of assessment, the types of impairment or quality factors, the grading scale, the sequence and timing. Training sequences demonstrating the range and the type of the impairments to be assessed should be used with illustrating pictures other than those used in the test.

In a subjective experiment, a large amount of data is collected. These data must be condensed by statistical techniques to present results, which summarise the performance of the system.

6.4.2 Quality assessment results

The conditions described in the ITU-R BT.500 have been respected. From the two types of environment, (laboratory or domestic environment), we chose the domestic environment which has the advantage of not requiring a special and standardised room for the assessments. Twenty-six observers respectively to the assessment conditions participated to the MIRADOR quality evaluation. They were between 25 and 45 years old, and were not involved in television as part as their normal work.

Assessor have been introduced to the method of assessment, the types of impairment or quality factors, the grading scale, the sequence and timing. Training sequences demonstrating the range and the type of the impairments to be assessed have been used with illustrating pictures other than those used in the test. TALISMAN ACTS project test sequences have been used for the explanation and training phase.

The training phase has the main objective of giving instructions to the assessors. During this phase a trial with two presentations has been done, to get the assessors used to the timing and the quality range shown during the test. It is very convenient for the observers to have a sequence identifier; it avoids confusion between sequences A and B. The sequence identifier has been inserted (for example, A or B) in the centre of a mid-grey frame, before the corresponding sequence.

The following sequences have been used for the quality assessment, respectively to this presentation order :

Sequence number	Title	Duration	Source library tape
1	Mobile and calendar	30s	EBU
2	Flower garden	30s	EBU
3	Akyio	10s	MPEG-4
4	News	10s	MPEG-4
5	Weather	10s	MPEG-4
6	Bream	10s	MPEG-4
7	Scan	11s	MPEG-4
8	Silent	18s	MPEG-4
9	Foreman	16s	MPEG-4

Table 6: Video sequences used for MIRADOR quality assessment

For our experiments we are using a PC platform with professional video boards with components (YUV) and ITU-R BT.656 Digital video outputs. The sequences stored on a disk array and rendered by the system are not compressed.

The display monitor used has been adjusted as described in the methodology. The Monitor is connected through its YUV inputs to the PC video system. The height of the screen is 40 cm. In a domestic environment assessment type, the viewing distance corresponds to the preferred viewing distance PVD (according to ITU-R BT.500-8), which is 6H (6 times the height of the screen) in our case, i.e. 2.4m.

Average value

	Calendar	Flower	Akiyo	News	Weather
original	3.577	3.452	3.837	3.875	3.808
watermarked	3.587	3.471	3.885	3.846	3.779
difference original- wk	-0.010	-0.019	-0.048	0.029	0.029

	Bream	Sean	Silent	Foreman
original	3.863	3.904	3.583	3.577
watermarked	3.844	3.865	3.525	3.587
difference original- wk	0.019	0.038	0.058	-0.010

Standard deviation

	Calendar	Flower	Akiyo	News	Weather
original	0.657	0.542	0.460	0.445	0.375
watermarked	0.693	0.506	0.515	0.519	0.435

	Bream	Sean	Silent	Foreman
original	0.509	0.361	0.609	0.532
watermarked	0.504	0.394	0.618	0.528

95% Confidence interval

	Calendar	Flower	Akiyo	News	Weather
original	[3.324, 3.829]	[3.244, 3.660]	[3.660, 4.013]	[3.704, 4.046]	[3.663, 3.952]
watermarked	[3.320, 3.853]	[3.277, 3.666]	[3.687, 4.083]	[3.647, 4.046]	[3.612, 3.946]

	Bream	Sean	Silent	Foreman
original	[3.668, 4.059]	[3.765, 4.043]	[3.349, 3.817]	[3.373, 3.781]
watermarked	[3.651, 4.038]	[3.714, 4.017]	[3.287, 3.763]	[3.384, 3.789]

The obtained results are very closed together, having similar values for both average and standard deviation value. Even the quality notes distributions curves doesn't allow to separate original and watermarked sequences. We can conclude that at the preferred viewing distance, 6 times the height of the screen in our case (6H=2.4m), there are no perceived differences between original and watermarked sequences.

7   Conclusion

This document overviewed the constraints involved by MPEG-4 to watermarking algorithms. It presented the evaluation methodology followed in MIRADOR Europeen ACTS project in order to assess robustness to compression and quality of the watermarked material. The performance of an algorithm issued from previous work has been evaluated. The robustness results are quite promising and, concerning the quality assessment, the standardised evaluation process applied on the test sequence library in formal conditions did not allow to establish any difference between the original and the watermarked material. The invisibility of the potential watermarking artefacts has been demonstrated.

More information is available on http://www.tele.ucl.ac.be/MIRADOR/

8   References

1. http://www.tele.ucl.ac.be/MIRADOR/
2. http://www.tele.ucl.ac.be/TALISMAN/
3. V Darmstaedter, JF Delaigle, D Nicholson, B Macq "A block based watermarkingTechnique for MPEG2 signals: optimization and validation on real digital TV distribution links", proceedings ECMAST 98, Springer, pp 190-206
4. http://www.doi.org
5. http://www.doi.org/workshop/minutes/CISoverview/
6. OCTALIS project, http ://www.octalis.com
7. http ://www.tele.cl.ac.be/CAS
8. CISAC organisation http ://www.cisac.org
9. IMPRIMATUR: http://www.imprimatur.alcs.co.uk
10. MPEG4 IPMP overview document W2614, available at http://www.cselt.it/mpeg/
11. F. Hartung and B. Girod, "Watermarking of Uncompressed and Compressed Video",in *Special Issue on Watermarking, Signal Processing*, vol. 66, N°3, pp 283-302, Elsevier, May 98
12. Recommendation ITU-R BT.500-8, Methodology for the subjective assessments of the quality of television pictures

Protecting Intellectual Proprietary Rights through Secure Interactive Contract Negotiation

Carlos Serrão, José Guimarães

ADETTI / ISCTE, Av. Forças Armadas
1600-082 Lisboa, Portugal

{Carlos.Serrao, Jose.Guimaraes} @ adetti.iscte.pt

Abstract. Protection of Intellectual Proprietary Rights is currently one of the most important barriers to electronic commerce of digital contents over networks. Authors and content providers understand the immense advantages of the digital world but show some reserve. However, technologies and techniques to protect IPR in digital content exist, their deployment in a coherent way is still in an early stage. In this paper, we describe the approach followed by the OCTALIS Project towards and effective electronic commerce of digital images. After describing briefly enabling technologies, the emphasis is on contract negotiation over Internet through a secure dialog between the Service Provider and the User.

1. Introduction

The trade of digital content through networks is an area that is receiving strong investments in research and development.

The problem is complex because digital content is possible to copy without any quality loss, thus the associated Intellectual Property Rights (IPR) are easily violated through unauthorised reproductions.

Authors, copyright owners and content providers in general face a crucial dilemma: profit from the immense advantages of exposing their work through digital mediums, or adhere to other business models and have higher costs to reach wide audiences.

In fact digital networks, like the Internet, provide the means to reach world-wide audiences with costs that can be considered inexpensive when compared with other types of media. However, the difficulty to protect IPR in digital content, to enforce them and to verify the correct usage of the content, is preventing the faster deployment of the electronic commerce of digital contents.

Electronic Commerce of any type of goods can be considered broadly under two main aspects: marketing and contracting [1]. While the first focuses on promoting company products and services to customers, the second focuses on negotiation of the terms and conditions of the contract and the monitoring of contract performance.

In this paper, we will focus on the second aspect.

The work that is described in this paper was developed in the framework of Project OCTALIS – Offer of Content through Trusted Access LinkS[1]. It implements the OCTALIS model, including on-line contract negotiation of the usage terms and conditions for electronic commerce of digital images.

2. Approach and objectives

Technology and tools for protecting digital content, such as conditional access systems, digital labels and watermarks already exist. Some are still incipient, but the main problem is that they are mostly used in an isolate way, without establishing a common framework for solving the real problem: the effective protection of the Intellectual Proprietary Rights - IPR [2].

The OCTALIS Project [11] addresses an open architecture for secure content negotiation, delivery and protection, trying to solve some problems raised by the IPR protection. One of the goals is to protect the access to valuable information through the establishment of a secure contract negotiation scheme. The project provides a framework that has been successfully tested for protecting the Intellectual Proprietary Rights for interactive database access and broadcast services [2]. In this paper we will only focus on the first architecture.

The OCTALIS project inherits results from other R&D European projects, in order to fulfil some of the needs identified by the consortium. This is the case of OKAPI[2], which provided the kernel for the conditional access system, and TALISMAN[3] with technologies for invisible watermarking and labeling of images.

The OKAPI Project developed a security kernel, which ensures interoperability, openness, equity and user privacy. It aims at an evolution towards an open multimedia market.

The purpose of the TALISMAN Project is to provide standard copyright mechanisms to protect digital images against large-scale commercial piracy and illegal copying. With this purpose, TALISMAN defined an evolutive and open framework based upon a group of entities requirements (author's societies, content providers and broadcasters) allowing the integration of a hierarchy of effective solutions for protecting video and still image contents [3]. Technologies that have been developed include *labeling*, which is directly associated with the bit stream and *invisible watermarking*, a sophisticated undetectable system.

Other sources concerning IPR protection where also consulted, and there was a special emphasis on the use of standards, such as those that address embedded content description for digital images.

---

[1] OCTALIS ACTS Project AC242 is partially financed by the European Commission - DGXIII.

[2] OKAPI - Open Kernel for Access to Protected Interoperable interactive services, ACTS Project (AC051), partially financed by the European Commission – DGXIII.

[3] TALISMAN - Tracing Authors rights by Labeling Image Services and Monitoring Access Network, ACTS Project (AC019).

3. OCTALIS Common Functional Model

In order to evaluate and test the reliability and robustness of the solution proposed by OCTALIS, two field experiments were set-up. One of these experiments focused on the primary distribution network for broadcast television, and the second one focused on the interactive access to high value professional image databases through Internet. In this paper we will concentrate on this last experiment.

The experiment implements the Common Functional Model (CFM) defined in an early stage of the project. The CFM, shown in Fig. 1, represents a multimedia chain and its actor's, together with a copyright and IPR protection mechanisms flow, from the content creator to the final user.

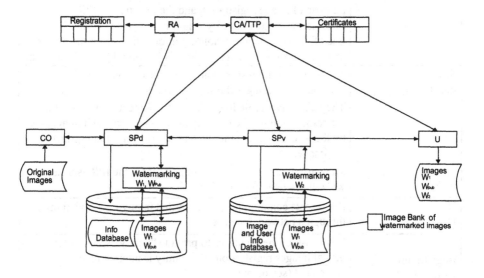

Fig. 1. OCTALIS Common Functional Model.

OCTALIS defined a set of different entities across the multimedia chain, establishing the necessary mechanisms for conditional access and copyright and IPR management [4]. These entities are shown in Fig. 1 and briefly described in Table 1.

It should be noted that the CA and the RA entities might not perform their main task on-line. In fact, it is even desirable to avoid security breaches.

Content flows in the CFM have implicit a set of procedures necessary to manage content itself and associated IPR. We will describe these procedures in the following sections.

Entity	Description
CO Copyright Owner	Represents the creative people contributing with content. For the purpose of the work described in this paper (digital images) they represent artists, like painters, ceramists, etc., as well as photographers, either as reproducers of the formers work or representing themselves with their own original works. We also include in this class an agent that may act a representative of artists in those aspects concerning IPR.
SPd Service Producer	Represents an entity that takes charge of preparing the artistic work to be made available in a digital format. Their task includes the interface with a RA (see below) for the purpose of image registration and the insertion of IPR information in the image by watermarking (see below). Each SPd has a database holding information about the images that were produced. This database is important for IPR tracking.
SPv Service Provider	These entities are responsible for the provisioning and distribution of images through networks. They also have a role in the IPR management flow, since they are responsible for the contract negotiations for each image, and by the insertion of another watermark (buyer's fingerprint) in the image. They also manage a database important for the IPR aspects, as we will see later in this paper.
U User	Represents common people interested in buying a digital image through a network (Internet).
RA Registration Authority	It is a task of these entities to provide "notary" services for digital images registration. This entity is internationally accredited (see below). They receive the original image together with associated information, namely IPR information, and perform a registration by assigning it a universally unique identification number, according to the SPIFF specification [5]. As we will see later, this entity also manages a database important for the IPR flow.
CA Certification Authority	Entity that is responsible for issuing certificates to all the other players. These certificates will be necessary to the on-line transactions. The model does not preclude the existence of multiple CA entities due to the role of the TTPs (see section 3.1).
TTP Trusted Third Party	Trustworthy entity that manages conditional control. Contributes to the establishment of a Secure Authenticated Channel (SAC) between the User and the SPv.

Table 1. Actors in the Common Functional Model.

3.1. Entities certification

One of the basic pre-requisites normal in conditional access systems is the certification of the involved entities. Two entities are responsible for this functionality in the CFM: the CA and the TTP.

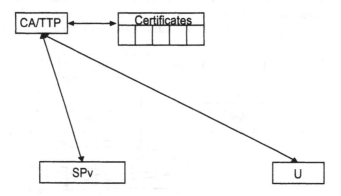

Fig. 2. Certification process.

The CA issues digital certificates for both the User and the TTP. It is normally available offline.

The TTP certificate is obtained from a CA and stored in the TTP database.

The User certificates are inserted into an Access Control Unit[4] (ACU), which, accordingly to the model, can be obtained by a person (the real user) in a store[5]. Public information corresponding to each ACU is forwarded off-line to all TTPs that hold a certificate issued by that CA. When acquiring an ACU, the real user receives a pin-code that will be necessary to initiate transactions.

This mechanism of distributed security allows a TTP to trust User's certificates obtained from diverse CAs.

The SPv certificates are obtained off-line from a TTP and stored in a database. A TTP has the possibility to register multiple SPvs and a SPv can be registered in multiple TTPs, ensuring a true interoperable solution and allowing the different TTP registered Users to be trustworthy at different SPvs and vice-versa.

---

[4] The ACU is a tamper resistant device fundamental to the OKAPI kernel (see section 4.4.), it is normally a smart-card however, since smart-card readers are not yet a standard peripheral on normal personal computers, an emulation based on a diskette and associated software was developed. Conceptually there are no differences between the smart card and the diskette based ACU, both are tamper resistant (the former by hardware, the later through content encryption) and protected by a pin-code.

[5] In the case of the emulation diskette, it can be obtained on-line through an interactive process at http://ra.adetti.iscte.pt.

3.2. Original images deployment

Images are delivered off-line to the SPd with the corresponding contractual terms for licensing and copyright and IPR information (see Fig. 3). Whenever it becomes necessary, it is assumed that the SPd is in possession of the technical means (e.g.: high-quality image scanner, software) to produce digital images from the original physical image and generate pertained information necessary for the SPv to accomplish an effective negotiation of contracts and licensing agreements.

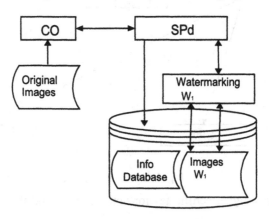

Fig. 3. Original image delivery process.

It is a task of the SPv to introduce a first approach to IPR management, by producing a digital image signature and embedding it in the image as an invisible watermarking. Relevant information for IPR purposes, namely the value that was watermarked in the image, is stored in the SPd database.

This process will allow at a later stage, if necessary, to enforce IPR in case the image is illegally reproduced.

Accordingly to the CFM notation, this watermark is designated as the first *private watermark* (W_1).

3.3. Images registration

An internationally accredited Registration Authority is responsible for performing image registration. This authority is defined in ISO/IEC 10918-4 as REGAUT and is in charge of producing and delivering unique identifiers, or *License Plates* (LP). The *License Plate*, together with other information about the image and its IPR, build sets of Directory Entries that constitute part of the SPIFF[6] format (see section 4.1).

---

[6] SPIFF (Still Picture Interchange File Format) is a standard approved by ITU-T and ISO/IEC to include metadata (data about data) information inside an image file. Annex F of document ITU-T T.84 | ISO/IEC IS 10918-3 "Digital Compression and Coding of Continuous-Tone Still Images" specifies the SPIFF format.

In the CFM, a SPd submits images to REGAUT, who issues an LP for each image. This LP is used by the SPd to embed a second *public watermark* in the submitted digital image (W_{pub}) thus identifying the entity that has the trusted repository of IPR information about the image.

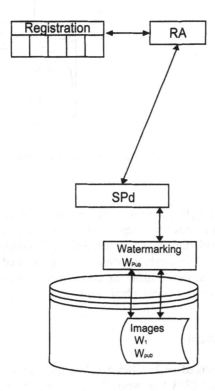

Fig. 4. Image registration processes.

As described before, the LP is world-wide unique for each image, therefore each image can be registered only once. This LP contains information about the REGAUT ISO country code, a unique JURA[7] identifying number and a sequential number for each of the registered images (e.g.: PT-98-1023).

3.4. Images provisioning

Once W_1 and W_{pub} watermarks have been introduced in the original image, the SPd produces several resolution levels for the same image. These levels constitute the pyramidal representation designated as JTIP (see sections 4.1. and 5).

It is the set of different resolutions, together with copyright and IPR information that is delivered off-line to a SPv.

---

[7] JURA - JPEG Utilities Registration Authority, http://jura.jpeg.org.

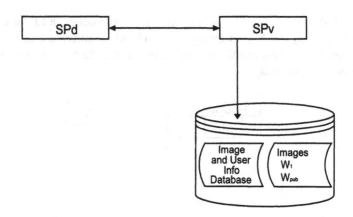

Fig. 5. Images provisioning process.

A database at the SPv location holds different levels of the images, resulting from JTIP, which include low-resolution reproductions adequate for web browsing. Images are displayed along with their copyright and technical information. For each available resolution, technical and copyright information is also showed.

The contractual terms for licensing are also stored, in order to allow the future on-line contract negotiation that is described in section 5.

3.5. Images acquisition

Images can be acquired on-line through Internet. The establishment of a Secure Authenticated Channel (SAC) between the User and the SPv is necessary for the secure download of images (see Fig. 6). The OKAPI kernel provides the necessary authentication and cryptographic features needed to fulfil the security requirements.

The ACU (see section 3.1) plays an important role by securely storing User secret information and certificates. Through this device the User can be authenticated to the OKAPI/OCTALIS system and therefore allowed to securely negotiate an image with the SPv.

This action and the subsequent image download are accomplished through a special application that calls the OKAPI security kernel through its API.

Before sending an image to a User a new invisible watermark is inserted. This watermark is obtained from the identification of the User, which is stored in the ACU and was previously sent during the process of establishing the SAC.

In the CFM this watermark is identified as the *second private watermark* (W_2), and corresponds in fact to a fingerprint of the User buying the image.

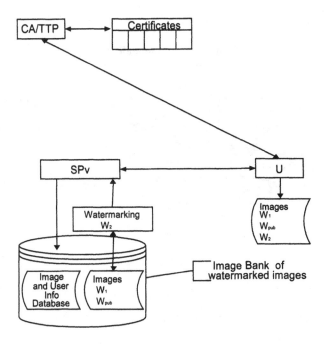

Fig. 6. Contract negotiation and image acquisition.

4. IPR protection

The OCTALIS system uses four different mechanisms for achieving IPR protection: standard image formats JTIP and SPIFF, REGAUT license plates, watermarking and the OKAPI kernel.

4.1. Standard image formats JTIP and SPIFF

The JPEG Tiled Image Pyramid (JTIP) format is an extension of the JPEG standard. This format defines a pyramidal tiling methodology to produce multiple resolutions of an image (pyramidal approach), and store higher resolution levels in different files (tiling approach).

The two lower resolution levels, A and B in the pyramid (see Fig. 7), are used at the ODISS site for web browsing. Higher resolution levels, including C (see Fig. 7), can be considered as having commercial value thus subject to licensing contracts.

Levels below C are tiled and stored in different files having the same dimensions as in C level. The purpose is to optimize downloading in case an error occurs during transfer. In this case it is only necessary to retransmit the file corresponding to the damaged tile. This is important considering that a professional image can have several hundreds of megabytes if stored in a single file.

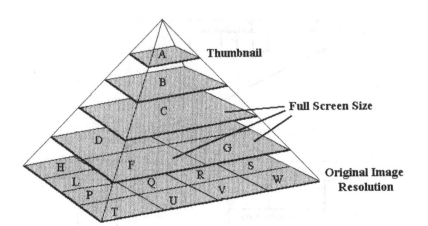

4.2. REGAUT License Plates

An image Registration Authority is defined in ISO/IEC 10918-4. It is in charge of delivering unique identifiers to be inserted inside image files for identification and copyright protection of contents. As stated in the scope of this standard, due to the fact that a very large number of registration applications are foreseen, the PTSMCR[8] authority will delegate the task of certifying such Registration Authority to the National Bodies [5].

This mechanism allows a National Body, on behalf of the PTSMCR authority, to deliver a certificate of validity to the registrant upon receipt of the input form duly completed and checked. The information contained in the input form is then disseminated to users. Multiple REGAUT allocations are possible inside a given country, provided that the registrants fulfil the exploitation conditions. A collective right society, an image agency, a public or private institution may apply for qualification as a REGAUT.

To become a National Body and receive a REGAUT Identification number, an organisation can apply to the JPEG Utilities Registration Authority (JURA) [7], meeting the following criteria:

i) Unique - it must not duplicate a REGAUT ID already defined:

ii) Correct submission - the syntactically and technically correct submission of SPIFF files produced by the applicant, along with all appropriate explanations;

iii) Suitability - the applicant must be a well-known institution recognised as a professional in the digital imagery domain. Furthermore, this institution must be willing to fulfil its obligation as a Registration Authority.

After a trial period using a temporary REGAUT number where all the necessary requirements must be fulfilled (both technical and legal) by the applicant, the definitive REGAUT is issued, and the organisation is accredited as a valid image Registration Authority, capable of issuing *License Plates*.

A *License Plate* contains information about the Registration Authority:

i) ISO country code;

ii) REGAUT Identification: the unique number assigned by JURA[9];

iii) A sequential number assigned by the REGAUT to each image that is registered.

4.3. Watermarking

An invisible watermark consists in a pattern of bits inserted into a digital image, audio or video file identifying uniquely the media copyright information (author, rights, etc.). The name comes from the faintly visible watermarks imprinted on stationery that identify the manufacturer of the stationery. The purpose of digital

---

[8] PTSMCR are the JURA items. P - JPEG and SPIFF profiles; T - SPIFF tag; S - SPIFF colour space; M - APPn marker; C - SPIFF compression type; R - Registration Authority.

[9] In Portugal an existing REGAUT is PT-1098.

watermarks is to provide copyright protection for IPR in digital formats. Unlike the printed watermarks, which are intentionally visible, digital watermarks are designed to be completely invisible or, in audio clips, inaudible. Moreover, the actual bits representing the watermark must be scattered throughout the file in such a way that they cannot be identified or manipulated. The watermark should be robust enough so that it can withstand normal changes to the file, such as reductions from lossy compression algorithms [3].

The OCTALIS CFM uses three different invisible watermarks: two private watermarks (W_1, W_2) a one public watermark (W_{pub}). Table 3 shows the purpose for each of these watermarks.

W_1	The first private watermark W_1 corresponds to the digital signature of the image. It will allow to prove if the image has been changed from its original
W_{pub}	The public watermark W_{pub} corresponds to the License Plate. It will contribute to establish the copyrights on an image, based on the entity that registered the image.
W_2	The second private watermark W_2 corresponds to the fingerprint of the User that licensed the image. It will allow tracing the responsibility for eventual unauthorised reproductions.

Table 3. Watermarks in OCTALIS.

4.4. OKAPI kernel

The OCTALIS system relies on the OKAPI security kernel to provide security for applications in open environments. It extends the normal functionality of an operating system for securing communications at the application level, ensuring authentication, privacy and integrity of the communications [9].

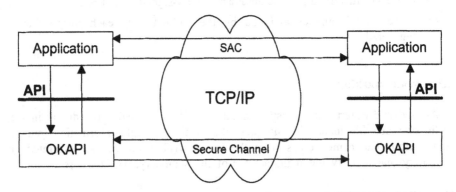

Fig. 9. Secure communications enabled by OKAPI.

Software developers can access the security kernel through an API (see Fig. 9). The API allows the design and implementation of non-proprietary and interoperable solutions for conditional access to multimedia services. Through the API, developers of conditional access systems can establish a Secure Authenticated Channel (SAC) between Users and SPv to achieve secure transactions over insecure channels.

Authentication is enabled through the infrastructure provided by the CAs and the TTPs (see Fig. 1 and Table 1).

Security is enabled through the use of public key cryptography and smart cards to store secret parameters.

5. Contract Negotiation

Like in the real world, establishing the conditions of an on-line digital contract satisfying all the involved parties is not always an easy task. Electronic Commerce can be considered in two main aspects [9]: marketing and contracting. While the first focuses on promoting the products and services to customers, the other focuses on negotiation of the terms and conditions of contracts and the monitoring of contract performance.

It is normally a difficult task to establish a generic model of digital contract for use on the Internet, considering that geographically distributed jurisdictions have different rules about the contents and legal establishment of a digital contract. Such a model should consider several aspects in order to develop a formal representation of electronic contracting:

i)   Represent several different trade scenarios, specifying the temporal sequence of the inter-organisational document exchanges for a given transaction;

ii) Be computable, allowing for fully automated computer-to-computer trade transactions;

iii) Be customisable to fit very specific contracting situations, while yet retaining the legal and control qualities of the generic version;

iv) Friendly end-user interface, whereby the terms, rules and procedures of the trade scenario can be easily read and understood by the contracting parties (as well as judges, arbitrators).

Generically a contract should define the following aspects [10]:

i)   **Parties**: the certified identity of two or more parties. Usually it should be possible to distinguish who originated the contract. The Copyright Owner must be clearly identified. In the case of shared copyright, all the copyright owners must be specified;

ii) **Validity**: a data interval specifying when the contract will be valid (or a starting date and duration). One of the most sensitive points is the electronic contract validity according to the agreed jurisdiction (country, state, or community);

iii) **Clauses**: one or more description items, which constitute the actual body of the contract, specifying the terms in the contract. These clauses can include, for example: privacy and sub-license conditions;

iv) **Jurisdiction**: the law governing the contract;

v) **Allowed or possible operations**: to each of the intermediary entities in the exploration chain and, if possible, over each of the specific work components, including commercial conditions (sold units, time limit, ...);

vi) **Signatures**: by all the **parties**, specifying agreement to honor the **clauses** of the contract during the **validity** period of the contract, in respect with its **jurisdiction**.

Considering the electronic contract clauses and the legislation gap that exists in most of the countries, both contracting entities must define specific own laws in order to fill this gap. The established electronic contract between the contracting parts must at least contain the following clauses: transmitted rights, remuneration, access warranty, work integrity, end of contract, offence compensation, end of contract consequences, and adopted legislation.

Contract information should be described in a language that is understandable to all parties: this is the information that is signed and will be retrieved during an eventual dispute resolution.

In OCTALIS the subject of contracts are digital images.

The rights associated with a digital image can vary accordingly to the terms expressed by the Copyright Owner (CO in Fig. 1). This system supports a wide range of hierarchical terms, providing the capability to define terms and conditions of the contract through an on-line negotiation. Once the buyer (User in Fig. 1) is satisfied with the contract that defines the image usage conditions, digital signatures will authenticate the business and the contract is established.

A demonstration Internet site (http://odiss.adetti.iscte.pt) implementing the on-line contract negotiation has been developed in the framework of the OCTALIS Project [11]. The site represents the SPv in the CFM model (see Fig. 1) previously described.

Throughout this section we will describe in detail the relevant aspects of the negotiation and measures aiming at contract enforcement.

5.1. IPR provisioning

In section 3 we introduced the notion that each image in the data bank would be available in different resolutions. The main purpose for this set of resolutions is to allow the buyer to select the option that best fits into his business needs, and pay accordingly.

As described in the business model adopted by OCTALIS, the CO must address a Service Producer (SPd in Fig. 1) who will produce a set of different resolutions corresponding to the different JTIP levels (see section 4.1). Each file is produced using the SPIFF format, which contains in the same file the image data and additional information concerning IPR (see section 4.1).

One of the important aspects in IPR is the unique registration number assigned by a Registration Authority (RA in Fig. 1). This number will be designated *License Plate* and relates the image, with its Author and Copyright Owner. Thus, before producing the SPIFF files for each JTIP level, the SPd must address a RA, providing it with all relevant information concerning IPR, in order to register the image and obtain a *License Plate* (see section 4.2).

Now the SPd can effectively produce the different image resolutions corresponding to the JTIP levels. Each file produced accordingly to the SPIFF format will contain specific standardised Directory Entries (see section 4.1) to accommodate the *License Plate* and other information such as image descriptions, IPR, date of registration, etc. Though resolutions are different, the original registered image is the same, thus information will be common to all SPIFF files.

5.2. Contract Terms definition

Naturally, each resolution of the same image, hence JTIP level, has a different commercial value, and possibly different associated contractual terms. Thus the terms and conditions must be established.

It is a task of the SPd in conjunction with the CO to define the Contractual Terms and deliver them, together with the SPIFF files, to a Service Provider (SPv in Fig. 3). The SPv will store all information in its image bank and provide the infrastructure that will enable the on-line contract negotiation, and the inherent electronic commerce of the images.

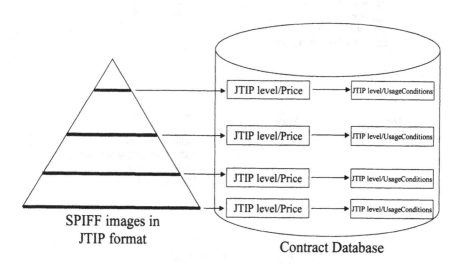

Fig. 10. Image contract database.

The system allows the storage of the Contractual Terms and Contractual Conditions that will be proposed to the buyer. Both contractual aspects are organised on a per resolution basis, as shown in Fig. 10.

5.2.1. Database model

The number of Contractual Terms for each image resolutions is unlimited, meaning that CO and SPd can define any terms that are reasonable and store them in the SPv database.

The structure adopted for the database allows the insertion of new terms or conditions at any time, without compromising contracts that were previously established for that same image resolution.

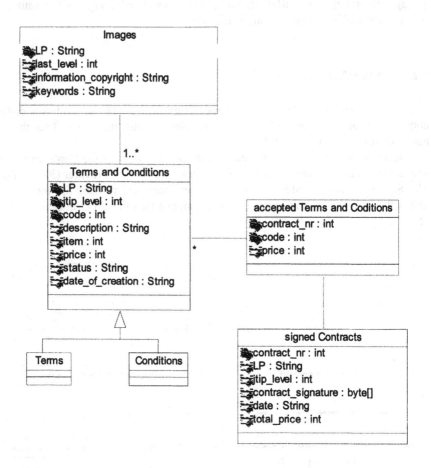

Fig. 11. Basic UML model.

A simplified UML model of the database is shown in Fig. 11.

Each Contractual Term has a *price* tag, and an *item* tag. Both are used in the contract negotiation, as described in section.

Terms can be negotiable or non-negotiable. This characteristic is defined through the *item* tag: a term that has a single tuple for a certain item number, is implicitly a non-negotiable term. Non-negotiable terms are imposed to the User and the system does not allow them to be removed. The price value can be negative to accommodate situations of discounts.

Table 4 shows some possible Contractual Terms, and how they can be related through the *item* tag.

Code	Contractual Term description	Price	Item
1	To be used in web pages	10	1
2	To be used in books	100	1
3	To be used in newspapers or magazines	1000	1
4	Not allowed in outdoor advertising	0	2
5	Can only be used once	0	3
6	Can be used an unlimited number of times	100	3
7	Image can not be edited	0	4
8	Rights granted for a period of 3 months	100	5
9	Can be used immediately	1000	6
10	Can be used only after 20/05/1999	500	6
11	Can be used only after 20/07/1999	-50	6

Table 4. Examples of Contractual Terms.

In addition to the Contractual Terms, the database also supports Contractual Conditions (see Fig. 11), which are normally associated with payment and delivery aspects.

A structure similar to the above has been adopted. Table 5 shows some possible Contractual Conditions.

Code	Contractual Conditions description	Price	Item
1	On-line immediate payment	0	1
2	Payment upon invoice	50	1
3	Payment upon invoice (30 days credit)	100	1
4	Image secure download	0	2
5	Image sent in CD-ROM through surface mail	10	2
6	Image sent in CD-ROM through air mail	20	2

Table 5. Examples of Contractual Conditions.

5.3. Establishing an On-line Contract

The process of establishing an on-line contract defining the usage terms and conditions for a digital image starts with the selection of the image.

5.3.1. Browsing the image bank

In the ODISS demonstration site http://odiss.adetti.iscte.pt there are two possibilities of selecting an image: i) searching by keywords or ii) browsing through thematic or artist collections.

Once the image is selected, it is necessary to choose the resolution adequate for the User's application.

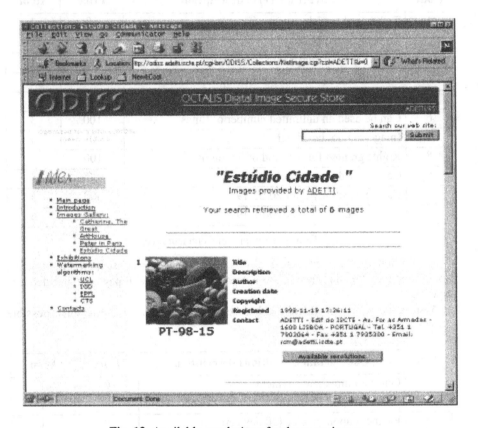

Fig. 12. Available resolutions for the same image.

The web page shown in Fig. 12 allows displaying of available resolutions for the image. The universal identification number, which was referred before as *License Plate*, is shown below the thumbnail image.

The approach followed in the development of this application allows the negotiation of several predetermined terms and conditions, defined by the CO. The purpose of the negotiation is to establish, upon input from the User, a contract defining the terms and conditions the User is willing to accept and comply with, for that particular image.

5.3.2. Contract negotiation

The Contract negotiation is performed on-line through a web page (see Fig. 13).

This page presents, on the left window, the terms that apply to the selected image. The right window proposes default terms to the User.

The User can accept or reject the default terms, by moving them from one window to the other, with the exception of non-negotiable terms.

Fig. 13. Web page for the Contract negotiation

Each term belongs to an item family, which aggregates terms that are interrelated.

The User is free to choose the terms that best suite the intended usage for the image, provided that one term for each different item is present in the right window, when the Contract is submitted to the SPv server at the ODISS site.

The next stage is the negotiation of the Contractual Conditions. Since these Conditions are related to payment and delivery issues, they are defined by the SPv.

Establishing the Contractual Conditions is a procedure that follows steps similar to the Contractual Terms negotiation. The web page shown in Fig. 13 is again used to display on the left window the available conditions and the default conditions on the right window.

Once the User has accepted one condition for each *item* present on the left window, the negotiation is finished and the Contract is ready to be signed.

5.3.3. Contract signature and transaction security

The process of signing the Contract uses some of the features present in the OKAPI Conditional Access System to ensure Contract authentication and non-repudiation, as well as security in the transaction.

In fact all the Contract negotiation that we have been describing is accomplished through the exchange of secure messages between the User application and the SPv server. The Secure Authenticated Channel (SAC), which was previously established when the User started the OKAPI User Application, provides security for those messages.

In the process of establishing a SAC, the User and the SPv have already exchanged their public keys. Selecting the OK button, shown in Fig. 14, the User application signs the final Contract and sends it securely through the OKAPI enabled SAC to the SPv.

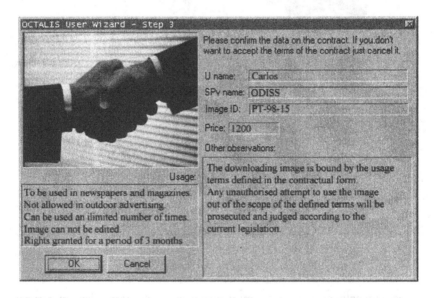

Fig. 14. On-line Contract signature.

A verification procedure takes place in the SPv server, ensuring those Contractual Terms and Conditions have not been tampered, and correspond to the image previously selected. Upon completion the SPv signs the Contract and sends it back to the User through the same channel.

5.3.4. Contract storage

The Contract is stored in two different places with different purposes: i) for administrative purposes, it is stored in the database and ii) for protection of IPR purposes it is written in a specific Directory Entry of the SPIFF file that will be delivered to the User.

Though it is easy to remove Directory Entries from a SPIFF file, or change their contents, the User is informed that tampering any information in the acquired file is not allowed, thus SPIFF entries should always accompany the image file.

5.3.5. Contract payment

Currently OCTALIS does not define a model for on-line payment. Integration with payment systems already existing is a possible and desirable evolution.

The fact that OCTALIS relies on the OKAPI security kernel to establish a SAC between the User and the SPv potentially provides the capabilities for diverse on-line payment forms.

5.3.6. Delivery of the image

Delivery of the contracted image can be accomplished through multiple channels.

As we have seen before, during the Contract negotiation the User is allowed to select the desired delivery channel, based on the possibilities previously defined by the SPv.

In case of on-line immediate delivery, the image will be sent to the User though the OKAPI enabled SAC. A protocol, using specific session keys negotiated between User and SPv, is established to encrypt the SPIFF file that is subject of the Contract, and send it across the network to the User.

6. Conclusions

The work developed in the OCTALIS Project demonstrates an approach to IPR protection through on-line negotiation of digital contracts that regulate digital content transactions.

Conditional access and watermarking technologies, together with the extensive use of standards provided the means to preserve IPR aspects over the Internet.

Several aspects contribute to an effective electronic commerce of digital images enabled by OCTALIS:

i) The CO can be assured that images will be used according to the licensed terms, furthermore the means to prove that the image is being misused are available;

ii) The User is assured that the origin of the image is from a certified image vendor (SPv) that the image itself is certified and that no one can intercept the image while the downloading process is in progress;

iii) The SPv is assured that the User has succeeded in establishing his identity towards the system and has the means to prove that the User signed a digital licensing contract for a certain image;

iv) In case of illegal copies the responsible entities can be identified and copyright information can be retrieved from the image;

v) Negotiation of the terms and conditions of a different licensing contract for each images and for each image resolution, with on-line price establishment.

An important aspect partially solved through the solutions deployed by OCTALIS is the insurance to authors and content owners that a User signs a contract on the licensing conditions they defined for their work.

However, there are other aspects related with legal issues that are not in the scope of the project. Technologies deployed provide the means to effectively define, trace and prove IPR over a digital content, but the possibility to enforce those rights depends on legislation that differs from one country to another. Digital signatures are not yet widely valid for document authentication and there is still much legal work to do until copyright violations on digital content can be effectively prosecuted.

References

1. *Standing Committee on Copyright and Related Rights – First Session*, WIPO – World Intellectual Property Organization, November 1998, http://www.wipo.org
2. Burnett, M., Jan, M., D10: Rights identification and management specifications, OCTALIS - AC242, April 1997
3. Delaigle, J-F, "D12 – Common Functional Model", TALISMAN, March 1996
4. Arnold, M., Koch, E., D11: OCTALIS Trial Specifications, OCTALIS – AC242, July 1997
5. Digital Compression and coding of continuous-tone still images: Registration of JPEG profiles, SPIFF profiles, SPIFF tags, SPIFF colour spaces, APPN markers, SPIFF compression types and Registration Authorities (REGAUT), ISO/IEC DIS 10918-4.2:1997
6. Information technology – Digital compression and coding of continuous-tone still images: Extensions, ISO/IEC 10918-3.
7. JURA – JPEG Utilities Registration Authority, http://jura.jpeg.org.
8. Serret, X., Boucqueau, J., Mas Ribés, J., "D19 – OKAPI specific tools design", January 1998
9. Lee, R. M., "Towards Open Electronic Contracting", International Journal of Electronic Markets, Vol. 8, No. 3, 1998.
10. Marques, J., "Protecção de Direitos de Autor no meio digital e seu impacto no Comércio Electrónico", Master Thesis, Mestrado em Gestão de Sistemas de Informação, ISCTE 1999.
11. OCTALIS – Offer of Content through Trusted Access LInkS, http://www.tele.ucl.ac.be /OCTALIS and http://adetti.iscte.pt/RSI/OCTALIS/CD-ROM.

Multimedia Dialogue Management in Agent-Based Open Service Environments

Olle Olsson[1], Fredrik Espinoza[1]

[1]Swedish Institute of Computer Science, Box 1263, SE-164 29 Kista, Sweden
{olleo, espinoza}@sics.se

Abstract.

Multimedia-based interfaces to complex services are difficult to create and maintain. An architecture for multimedia presentation systems has been developed in the KIMSAC project, based on a sharp separation between the services and their associated multimedia interfaces. The architecture supports flexibility in designing the multimedia dialogues for individual services, ranging from dialogues that are designed in great detail, to dialogues that are specified only in intentional ways and for which their presentations can be generated or adapted to the context of their use. Specific attention has been given to the needs that characterize open service environments exposed to the public at large. In such environments potentially independent services are accessed in parallel, introducing problems in managing the interleaving of dialogues with several services. The resulting architecture is compared to existing models for UIMS, highlighting the needs to refine these models when applying them to open service environments.

Introduction

Information technology is rapidly permeating all of our society. The Internet, when accessed as the World-Wide-Web, has proved itself to be attractive to large parts of the population. This has had two effects: on the one hand the average citizen is now familiar with the idea of finding information and accessing services through information technology infrastructures, and on the other hand, information and service providers are realizing that they need to offer their services via easily accessible information technology. We are now noticing a change in the picture. Previously IT systems were built to offer specific supports to narrow slices of the population, typically support to people in their professional role. We are now witnessing that the users of a service are no longer easily characterized, and they cannot be trained in accessing a specific service. Hence we see increasing demands on how services are packaged/presented to make them accessible to the ordinary citizen, through interfaces that exhibit more intelligence in their behavior.

Intelligent interfaces are notoriously difficult to build because of the complexities involved [Myers-93]. Complexities arise from a number of sources. The services provided may exhibit inherent complexity. Another reason is the wide spectrum of multimedia technologies that are now available. Yet another source is the diversity of the interface devices.

We will use the terminology "core service" to stand for the actually implemented service (application) that is being delivered (the semantics of the service), and by "interface component" we mean the implementation of the user interface.

The design of an interface must in practice be constrained by factors like:

- It must be possible to maintain the core service without disrupting the interface component.
- It must be possible to improve the dialogue behavior without having to reengineer the core service.
- It must be possible to adapt the exhibited dialogue to the characteristics of the individual user.
- It must be possible to adapt the dialogue to the characteristics of the interface device.

To aid in the practical development of intelligent user interfaces one must rely on two main cornerstones; a model that defines the concept of an intelligent dialogue system, and an implementation framework for such a system.

This paper describes an approach to modeling multimedia presentations, associated presentation system architecture, and the application of these in a specific project, the ACTS project KIMSAC. Within this project a generic presentation system for multimedia-based interaction was developed, and using this system, a number of multimedia-based applications were developed. The approach rests on the separation between knowledge-rich multimedia assets, adaptive presentation mechanisms, and knowledge-based application services.

The paper is organized as follows:

- Relevant models of presentation systems. Models of interactions and presentation systems have been proposed. Some of these will be characterized, which enables the technical results described in this paper to be related to state-of-the-art.
- The concept of an open service environment. The fundamental problem of "open service environments" is described, a problem that has been focussed on in the KIMSAC project.
- The KIMSAC system, it applications and their multimedia presentations. The context of the KIMSAC system and its application is described. These applications have explicated real-world requirements on open service environments, and have formed a driving force in the project.
- Assets as descriptions of multimedia presentations. The concept of knowledge-rich multimedia assets is introduced, a concept that is fundamental to the generic nature of the KIMSAC presentation system.
- The KIMSAC presentation system architecture. The actual architecture is described.
- Relationships between models of presentation systems and the KIMSAC presentation system. The KIMSAC architectural approach is compared to standard models.

In this paper the term "presentation system" is used as a generic term for a user interface management system. It covers all that is involved in materializing and managing a dialogue with a user, using whatever technology is available to create the mechanisms that enable the user and the system to communicate. By "a presentation" we mean the objects rendered for one step of a dialogue.

Models

There are a number of models of the interaction between users and services. Most of them are based on the idea of separability [Hartson-89][Szekely-88]; that the dialogue aspects can be separated (in a coarse-grained or fine-grained manner) from the actual service (often called "application"). The implication is that dialogue design issues can be separated from the service functionality and its implementation.

This section briefly introduces three high-level models, two of which will later in the paper be compared to the KIMSAC architecture. The first well-known model was the so-called Seeheim model [Pfaff-85]. The main components of this model are:

- The *presentation component*, describing the visual interaction objects
- The *dialogue component*, describing the elements of the dialogue and the behavior of interaction objects.
- The *application interface*, describing the dialogue in the application context

The Seeheim model is widely known, and refinements to the basic model have been proposed (e.g. [Dance-87]). The best way, though, is to understand the Seeheim model as a conceptual model (a paradigm), not necessarily having any specific implementation implications.

Another well-known model is the Arch model [UIMS-Dev-Workshop-92]. It provides, compared to the Seeheim model, a more fine-grained architectural view, consisting of the following components:

- The *domain-specific component*, manages domain data and performs domain functions
- The *interaction toolkit component*, provides physical interaction with the user
- The *dialogue component*, describing performs task-level sequencing and mapping of domain-specific formalisms to user-interface-specific formalisms
- The *presentation component*, maps toolkit-independent objects to toolkit-specific objects
- The *domain adapter component*, triggers domain-initiated dialogue tasks, reports and detects semantic errors

The Arch models has been adapted in different ways, e.g. "the Arch model for an adaptive intelligent human-machine interface" [Hefley-93], or the PAC-Amodeus [Coutaz-94].

A different set of models originates in strictly more implementation-oriented work. Models based on an implementation view come in two forms; micro-models and macro-models. A micro-model is more or less a tool-box of widgets (implemented or specified) that enables dialogues to be implemented using the widgets as encapsulated interaction objects, thereby isolating the dialogue manager from the details of atomic physical interaction events. In some cases the paradigm provided by a widget toolbox can be extrapolated in some natural way, offering a modeling and design approach to more application-specific components. An example is the Model-View-Controller concept [Krasner-88] [Burbeck], that originated as a pure software design approach for object-oriented systems, but has been adopted on a macro-scale for the design of interactive systems. Due to the character of the micro-models, they do not give major guidelines as to global system design..

A macro-model describes the implementation architecture of the interaction part of a system. Under this heading falls implemented UIMS systems (see [Myers]), as well as "reference models". An example of the latter category is the "Standard Reference Model for Intelligent Multimedia Presentation Systems" [Bordegoni-97]. The "Standard Reference Model" consists of a number of layers, and a set of knowledge servers. The layers are:

- *Control Layer*: handles incoming presentation goals and presentation commands.
- *Content Layer*: performs goal refinement, content selection, media allocation, and ordering
- *Design Layer*: transforms communicative acts to specifications of media objects and presentation layout
- *Realization Layer*: creates media objects and their layout
- *Presentation Display Layer*: performs actual rendering of media objects

The knowledge servers are:

- *Application Expert*: has application-specific knowledge
- *Context Expert*: has knowledge about the context
- *User Expert*: has knowledge that constitutes the user models
- *Design Expert*: has general knowledge about multimedia design

In a later section we revisit the models and compare them to the architecture that manages presentations in the KIMSAC system, with the aim of highlighting possible weaknesses in these models.

Multimedia-based open service environments

Methodologies, UI design techniques, and implemented frameworks have focussed on the situation where an application is to be provided with an interactive user interface. The emphasis is on one application. An *open service environment*, on the other hand, is clearly distinguishable from the single-application case. The characterizing property of an open service environment is that the user may during one session access several services (i.e. interact with several applications), services that can be provided by different service providers. This is not catered for in any of the approaches mentioned above, and introduces new difficulties of both a conceptual and an implementation nature.

Multimedia is now establishing itself as *the* way to realize the interface between the user and the system. Multimedia promises a large improvement in the potential at offering rich presentations to the user, thereby increasing the understandability of the services offered. The drawback is that the undisciplined use of multimedia may confuse the user instead of improving the communication between system and user. This especially holds in multi-service environments, where the user may access "in parallel" services from different service providers, and the diversity in how individual services are presented may cause great difficulties for the user.

The challenge posed by open service environments is: How to model and implement multimedia interfaces to a set of services potentially provided by independent service providers, constrained by the goal that the user should experience a uniform look-and-feel across different services?

The KIMSAC system and its application areas

The KIMSAC ("Kiosk-based Interactive Multimedia Service Access for Citizens") project is an ACTS project, aiming at developing an open service architecture for intelligent delivery of multimedia based distributed services (for an early overview, see [Charlton-97a]). Service access is provided via public kiosks based on multimedia PCs, while the actual services are provided from other hosts on a distributed network. The project has, among other things, developed architectural solutions in the technological areas of heterogeneous agent-based service access, representations of multimedia assets, and presentation system environments.

The project has passed through two major phases, each resulting in a multimedia-based system accessing different services. The application functionality and the use of multimedia as described in this paper refers to the result of the second phase of the project. Some of the technical approaches described in this paper originates in the third, minor phase of the project, during which technical extensions have been made and certain parts of the architecture has been reengineered.

The domains in which the KIMSAC architecture has been tested ("the KIMSAC trials") include services like job offerings for the unemployed and social benefits. These domains are complex, and corresponding services need to be continuously (e.g. available jobs) or regularly (e.g. changed rates for social benefits) adapted to changes in the environment. Such maintenance is simplified if the core application is clearly separated from the dialogue parts.

Services are, from an implementation point of view, provided by service agents, software agents that embody knowledge about the services and how these services relate to the users needs. E.g. the implementation for the trial domains include an Unemployment-Benefit agent, an agent having specific knowledge about the conditions, rules and rates for the social welfare service formally called "unemployment benefits".

Interaction with the user is in terms of multimedia assets, which includes graphics, video clips, audio clips and video conferencing. The following figure highlight the fact that service provisioning is done from hosts that are separated from the kiosks, and that a user at a kiosk can simultaneously access several independently provided services.

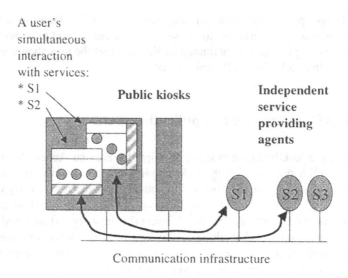

A user's
simultaneous
interaction
with services:
* S1
* S2

Public kiosks

Independent
service
providing
agents

Communication infrastructure

Fig. 1. The KIMSAC kiosks and the service agents.

The KIMSAC kiosks are "off-the-shelf" kiosks, based on PC/NTs with touch-screen, loudspeakers, handset to be used by the user for privately listening to audio output, printer to make it possible for the user to take away a persistent copy of results obtained, a card-reader for magnetic card, to enable the user to be identified to a service. The kiosk is connected to a network, and the actual services are available on servers present somewhere else on the network.

The kiosks in the KIMSAC trials are to be used unsupervised in public places (libraries, public offices, railway stations, etc), and to be used by anyone who feels like it. As they are not supervised, and as the KIMSAC trial applications covered services that are based on the user providing detailed personal information, the system must try to protect the privacy of the user. For this reason we have introduced the *session* as a first-class concept. The system is initially in a waiting mode, showing some multimedia to attract a user. Once the user touches the screen, a *user-session* starts. The user will enter into a dialogue that will lead to identification of a service to be accessed, and once this service is first accessed, an embedded *service-session* starts. Accessing several services within the same user-session causes the corresponding number of service-sessions to be created, and they will stay alive until the end of the user-session. The user-session ends when either the user explicitly requests a termination (touching a button dedicated for this purpose), or when the system has not detected any user action for a while (which the system interprets as an indication that the user has left the kiosk, and hence his user-session should be terminated).

A screen dump of a state of a KIMSAC user-session is shown in the following figure.

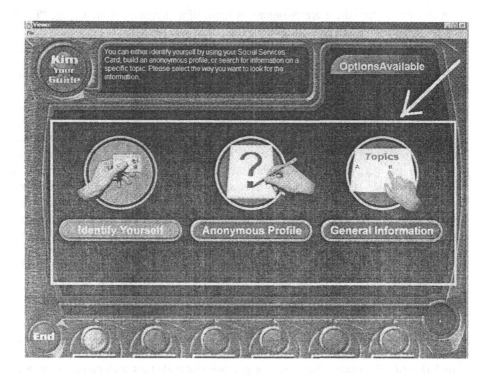

Fig. 2. A screen dump from the KIMSAC application. Note that the white rectangle and the white arrow have been added for references in the text below.

This screen dump illustrates some aspects of the way the KIMSAC applications are provided to the user in terms of multimedia presentations. The screen consists of two main parts:

- The *framework* area, which is the part of the screen outside of the white rectangle.
- The *service* area, which is the part of the screen inside the white rectangle.

The framework area is the stable part of the presentation, which has an existence and a structure that is independent of what service is actually being accessed. Along the top we see, from left to right, three distinct presentation items:

- Kim, the assistant to the user. It has two rendering modes. In one mode it is rendered as a video clip, showing a face that through audio output provides information to the user about the current state of the dialogue with a service and what he can do in this state of the presentation. In the other mode, which is the one actually shown in the screen dump above, Kim is only seen as an icon. By pushing this icon, the system changes into a help-and-guidance mode, where the user is offered an interactive presentation that gives assistance to the user about the kiosk and the services.
- A textual description of the state of the dialogue, containing a summary of the important points of the spoken instructions.
- A label that indicates where in the service dialogue the user presently is.

Along the bottom there are presentation items of a navigational nature; the "Exit" that terminates the users session, buttons that are bound to short-cuts to other parts of this or other visited services, and, at the right, a service-specific request button.

The framework area is visible during the entire user-session, even though actual items in the framework area changes values to reflect the state and the history of the user's interaction with services.

The dialogues with the services are performed in the service area of the screen. Different services have different requirements on dialogues, and this determines what is actually rendered in the service area. The screen dump above shows the "options available" state of a dialogue with a social benefits service. In this state the user may chose one of three options available: interact with the social benefit service in "identified mode" (the service may access stored data describing the client when evaluating whether the user is entitled to this benefit), interact in "anonymous mode" (the user has to provide personal details interactively so that the service can evaluate available entitlements), or look for information concerning how this benefit is defined (entitlement conditions, rates, etc.). So the content of this presentation in the service-area is really three buttons, each causing progress in the dialogue towards the indicated goal.

Assets

The KIMSAC approach is based on the premise that dialogues with complex services may need to be designed in some detail if inexperienced users are to access the service. I.e. complete dialogues between system and user cannot in practice be fully generated automatically. The policies for choosing a presentation may critically depend on being able to evaluate the usability of both individual presentation items as well as the consistency of (temporal and atemporal) configurations of presentations. This leads to an architecture of the presentation system that permits the use of packages of presentations as realizations of (a part of) dialogue. These packages are the results from a separate, manual asset design task.

An *asset* is defined as a concrete configuration of renderable multimedia objects. The flexibility of an individual asset is constrained by the need to provide enough information in the asset for the primitives of the presentation system to be able to materialize it. This requirement is in conflict with another requirement; that the results of the asset design task should be possible to reuse in a set of different contexts. A context can e.g. be described in terms of the characteristics of the user and characteristics of the physical interaction device. Hence we need a certain degree of flexibility in the use of predesigned assets. This is achieved in the KIMSAC approach by not designing concrete assets but rather *asset descriptions* (see [Charlton-97b] for more details). Looking at asset descriptions as templates with variables, a concrete asset is obtained by defining values for these variables. An asset descriptions is, formally speaking, a set of constraints that defines the contexts in which it is reasonable to generate an asset from this asset description, and in what way variables can be instantiated to values for this context.

An asset description contains three categories of descriptions:

- Preferences concerning multimedia properties, e.g. sizes, colors, graphics, and audio.
- Preferences concerning applicability; e.g. in what domain it can be used, for what service, for what task.
- Service-oriented behaviors it supports; e.g. what type of domain data it can render, what user requests it can support.

All these are embedded in a representational formalism, the KIMSAC asset description notation, which exhibits both the structural aspect of the asset as well as all the properties that can characterize it. This representation is created during asset design, but the representation is preserved during its flow through the system, to enable different components to adapt the asset to specific circumstances at hand. At the point at which the asset is to be physically rendered this representation is interpreted and the actual physical rendering is created. An effect of this approach is that as long as a representation of this type is available to the basic presentation system functions that create the physical presentation, it does not matter at all where this representation was actually created. This has been utilized in experiments with the KIMSAC applications, in terms of creating presentations based partly on pre-designed asset descriptions, and partly on assets that are constructed dynamically. The dynamically constructed assets are the result of having domain/service/task information at hand, and from these and from the context of the current dialogue, the actual assets are constructed from scratch.

A KIMSAC multimedia asset has a hierarchical structure, consisting of "composite" objects with parts that are themselves assets, and of "atomic" objects. Atomic objects will be rendered by specific content handlers, e.g. TextCH (for rendering text), HtmlCH (for rendering HTML-represented information) and ButtonCH (which has a visual appearance but also can be associated with a behavior/and effect).

At the extreme front-end, assets will be rendered by instantiating appropriate content-handler objects and feeding them a sufficient set of descriptive parameter values, so that they can create the desired look-and-feel.

The KIMSAC asset handling approach rests heavily on a separation between the multimedia aspects of an asset and the service/domain-oriented aspects. From the pure service-perspective, the only semantically important aspects of the dialogue are (a) what domain data needs to be presented to and/or obtained from the user, and (b) what requests for actions (often called "goals") can be offered to the user. In the asset description these are only indirectly described, in terms of the ontology that describes the domain and the service. In contrast to the multimedia properties, the asset description cannot provide possible values for the semantical properties, which means that these values have to be specified by some component in the asset flow prior to the physical rendering of the asset. This process is called *asset binding*, which means that the semantical properties of the asset are bound to specific values so that the behavior of the rendered asset is smoothly integrated into the behavior of the rest of the presentation system. E.g. presentation objects that render data values are bound to an object-property slot in a database, and presentation objects trapping user actions are bound to scripts that define the effects of that user action (see [Olsson-forthcoming] for more details.)

The KIMSAC presentation system architecture

The architecture of the KIMSAC presentation system is based on two main types of components: *permanent* components, and *session* components. The permanent components reside in the presentation system permanently (i.e. for as long as this presentation system instance is "up-and-running"), and their purpose is mainly to provide support for the session-components. Session components concern an individual user and his interactions with different types of services.

In the KIMSAC trials, there is a further subdivision in the terms of the roles of session components. As indicated earlier, the KIMSAC trial applications are based on two types of assets; the framework area of the interface which is the rendering of framework assets, and the service area which is where individual service assets are rendered. Whenever a user starts a session (*user-session*), the framework is set up, enabling navigation to find a service to access. Whenever a service is accessed and there is to be communication between the user and that service, a *service-session* is created. As the service-session is part of the entire user-session, it is materialized in a way that respects the constraints set up by the user-session. Specifically this implies that the resources needed by a service-session are requested from the user-session. This introduces a critical type of component in the system; the *resource manager*. Initially there is a fixed resource manager that has knowledge about the resources that are available to the presentation system. This covers things like screen-space, resolution, audio properties, externally connected functionality (e.g. card-reader, printers), and the type of content handlers that may be used. The user-session resource manager requests resources from the fixed resource manager, and it will provide resources to both the user-session components and to service-sessions. When a new service is accessed, a corresponding service-session is created, and it needs resources for its interaction. These resource needs are requested from the user-session, and it may now have to resolve a resource conflict (e.g. screen space may be occupied). This conflict is resolved either by the user-session resource manager based on priorities/preferences provided by the existing service-sessions, or by on-the-fly negotiation between service-sessions.

Another important type of component is the *session manager*. This manager has responsibility for over-all management of what goes on in the session, mainly in terms of managing the state of the session, and handling events that no other component in the session handles. Examples of states of a session are "in-focus" (the user is presently interacting with this session), "foreground" (the session is making itself known to the user, e.g. by being visible on the screen), and "background" (the session is still present, but at the moment not directly visible by the user). Examples of events handled by the session manager are "printer break-down", "session-abort", "service-agent-failure".

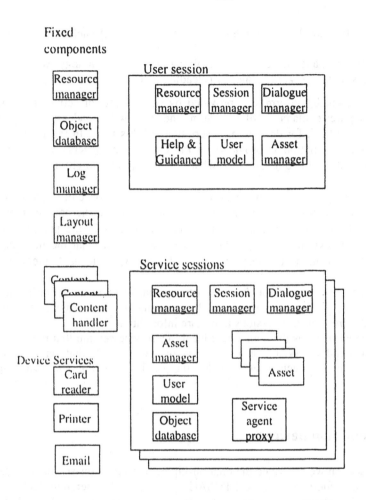

Fig. 3. The functional structure of the presentation system.

To provide support for adaptation to the user's characteristics, there is a user model component in the KIMSAC system. Each session (user-sessions as well as service-session) may need to access a user model in order to determine how and when to adapt the presentation. As services may have specific needs, and we are supporting an open service architecture, it is not feasible to define a single canonical user model. Rather we see each session as requiring (at least) one user model. But to avoid redundancy and the ensuing risk of inconsistency, the user models are coordinated via the user model managed by the user-session. In this way each service-session may add whatever service-specific user characteristics it needs to its own user model, and by announcing these to the user model in the user-session, this knowledge can be distributed to other service-sessions if they can make use of it.

The user-session contains a *Help&Guidance* (H&G) component. The aim of this shared component is that it should assist the user in his interaction during sessions. The H&G in the KIMSAC system provides assistance to the user about:

- the generalities that are defined at the user-session level (which includes the H&G itself!).
- service-specific assistance in terms of explaining domain terminology, what state the user is in, what the on-going dialogue is leading to, etc.

The H&G is driven by information provided by components of active sessions. E.g. if the user requires explanation of some term, the H&G will broadcast a query to other components and ask for definitions/descriptions of this term. In the KIMSAC applications, such information is provided by the dialogue managers, who knows about the current state of the dialogue, and what the queried term might mean in this state.

The *dialogue manager* is the component that navigates in the space of interactions, driven by events originating at the user, by events originating in the corresponding service agent, or by events originating from other components in the presentation system (e.g. from a session manager). Based on the event and what the next step should be, asset descriptions are inspected to determine how the next interaction should be rendered.

The *object database* is used for data consistency management and coordination within a service-session. But it can also be used as a mechanism to coordinate the data views between different service-sessions that share information.

The *service agent proxy* is the component local to a service-session that represents the actual "back-end" service agent. It is this component that is directly communicating with the agent that provides the service, sending and receiving messages.

Virtual presentation devices

In the previous section we described the relationship between the user-session and the service-sessions as a hierarchy. In the KIMSAC applications the hierarchy had only two levels; the user-session and underneath it a layer of service-sessions. This can be generalized in two ways:

- Viewing the set of fixed components as the real root node of the tree, with the user-session as the only subnode of this node.
- Adding trees underneath the service-sessions.

A way of conceptualizing this is in terms of *virtual presentation devices* (cf. [Hovy-96]). Each node of the hierarchy defines a virtual presentation device, providing resources to subnodes of that node, and acting as a presentation device to these subnodes (embedded presentations). In a way, nested virtual presentation devices imposes increasingly sharper constraints on embedded presentations, especially in terms of resources being used by nodes higher up in the tree. A concrete example of this is the screen-space resource. In the KIMSAC application the set of components managing the framework area acts as a virtual presentation device to the service-sessions, but as it occupies physical screen-space, the screen-space available to the embedded service-sessions is noticeable smaller, imposing corresponding constraints on the way service-sessions can generate presentations. On the other hand, a virtual presentation device can offer additional functionality to its embedded presentations. This can be seen in the KIMSAC applications in terms of the framework components offering presentation mechanisms for information like instruction texts and state indications (second and third item at the top of the framework), and additionally a way for the user to inform the service-session about a request (the rightmost item at the bottom of the framework). The implication is that the service-sessions do not have to bother about rendering and management of the corresponding presentation items in the framework area; from their point of view these are basic functionalities of the presentation device that is being used.

Separability based on knowledgeable interaction

The concept of separability (application from dialogue) has a natural correspondence in the KIMSAC approach, a consequence of services being provided by service *agents*. Agents communicate in terms of messages expressed in a representation-independent formalism (the ontology, see [Gruber-91]). Compared to ordinary application programs, agents are by definition capable of communicating with other agents, requesting services from other agents, and delivering services to other agents. Furthermore, when agents interact with each other, they do this on the assumption ("knowledgeable interaction hypothesis") that the other agents know what services they need, and how to communicate in order to obtain these services. I.e. the communication model for agent-to-agent communication is completely based on the semantics of the services provided.

When a service agent interacts with a user, and the user not completely familiar with this service, the assumption about knowledgeable interaction does not hold. When a human user is communicating with an agent, the dialogue takes a different form compared to agent-to-agent communication.

Multimedia-based human-agent communication involves not only service-related information, but also multimedia-related information. This may be a problem to the agent, as it might have to understand not only *what* service-information is being communicated, but also *whom* the agent is communicating with. In the worst-case scenario, the agent will have to be knowledgeable about fine-grained details of multimedia management, about presentation devices used, etc., something that will pollute the service agent and make it difficult to maintain.

The solution is to avoid exposing the details of the user dialogue to the service agent, by wrapping dialogue management in a component (user-assisting agent) that interacts with the service agent *as if it is knowledgeable agent*. From the service agent's point of view the user-assisting agent is just another agent that wants to utilize the services of the service agent.

This imposes two requirements; firstly the user-assisting agent (which in the KIMSAC approach is a complete service-session) must be able to model the dialogue in terms of the ontology of the service domain. Secondly, the user-assisting agent's interaction with the service agent is performed via message exchange, where these messages are expressed in the ontology of the service. Both of these requirements are fulfilled in the KIMSAC system, as (1) assets and dialogues have ontological descriptions, and (2) the service agent proxy embodied the "agentification" of the service-session, as it is the only front-end component that communicates with the core service.

When a service-providing agent needs to communicate with the user, it requests an asset from the asset manager (AM). The AM manages a repository of asset descriptions, described previously. The request for an asset is expressed in ontological, service-related terms, and the AM retrieves suitable assets descriptions from the repository. Then the AM and the service agent perform a dialogue through which an asset description is selected, and this asset description (seen as a template) is instantiated with values that are dependent on the current state of the interaction between the user and the service agent. After completing the instantiation of the template, the resulting asset is sent by the service agent to the service-agent-proxy in the presentation system, where the asset will now be rendered.

Relating the KIMSAC architecture to standard interaction models

In an earlier section a number of models of user interaction systems were described. We will now identify in what ways the KIMSAC architecture correlates to these models, and in what ways it introduces additional concepts in order to support open service environments.

The ARCH model

In terms of the ARCH model, we see clear correspondences, but it is important to emphasize that the ARCH model is coarse-grained, which means that certain distinctions noticeable in the KIMSAC architecture have no correlation to the ARCH model.

ARCH Interaction Toolkit corresponds to the KIMSAC multimedia content handler. These content handlers are responsible for creating rendered assets, as well as trapping whatever events the user causes by direct interaction with the physical device.

ARCH Presentation Component corresponds to the KIMSAC Layout Manager. This manager takes as input an asset description and creates the necessary content handlers. During this process it resolves certain media-specific resource-adaptations, based on current media-constraints (e.g. screen-space).

ARCH Domain Adaptor Component corresponds to the KIMSAC Service Agent Proxy and Object Database.

ARCH Domain Specific Component corresponds to the KIMSAC Service Agent (actually residing on some other host), Service Agent Proxy, and certain aspects of the Object Database.

ARCH Dialogue Component corresponds to the KIMSAC Dialogue Manager (for the dialogue structure), the Object Database (for translations of domain data) , and the Asset Manager (for mapping domain interactions to presentations).

Comments

What is missing from the ARCH model (given its level of abstraction!) is the session concept, the hierarchical structure of sessions, and the concept of parallel interactions with (semi-) independent services. The reason for this is of course that the ARCH model was defined at a time when each application was an independent entity, only co-existing with other applications by being processes run in the same operating system.

The Reference Model for Intelligent Multimedia Presentation Systems

The Reference Model for Intelligent Multimedia Presentation Systems (RM for short) is more recent, and has a stronger ambition compared to other efforts at abstractly modeling UIMSs. Hence we might expect that the RM might subsume the KIMSAC architecture. Mapping the "layers" and "experts" of the RM to KIMSAC gives the following result:

RM Control Layer's concern with determining the presentation goals is mainly covered by the KIMSAC Dialogue Manager. The typical input to the DM is a request to perform a communicative task. The DM will perform goal formulation (including determining whether there are task preconditions that are not fulfilled, in which case such precondition tasks are added to the agenda) and goal selection (determining what task to perform).

RM Content Layer: the Dialogue Manager performs the goal refinement task, by applying knowledge about the current state and history of the dialogue. Content Selection is supported by the asset descriptions. Media allocation is supported by the asset descriptions (resources needed) and by the resource manager (resources available). The ordering is partly statically determined (in the asset descriptions) and partly dynamically (state dependent).

RM Design Layer and RM Realization Layer: These are in the KIMSAC trial applications not present in full functionality. This depends on the fact that asset templates are predefined, which implies that RM design and realization tasks are performed during the asset definition phase. But as asset templates are to a certain degree under-specified (they admit presentation parameterization) there is in the KIMSAC architecture the task of determining values for these parameters. This is done by the Layout Manager, based on constraints specified in assets. The KIMSAC architecture does admit, though, assets to be defined dynamically, a task done by the Asset Manager.

RM Presentation Display Layer: This corresponds to the KIMSAC Layout manager that creates content handlers and allocates resources to them, and by the Content Handlers themselves, based on the description of what they should render.

RM User Expert: This correlates to the KIMSAC User Model.

RM Application Expert: The KIMSAC Service Agent Proxy fulfills this role, supported by the Object Database.

RM Context Expert: Knowledge about the state is managed by the Dialogue Manager, the Object Database has knowledge about what domain data is available, and it and the Content Handlers have knowledge about the relationships between domain data and the media objects.

RM Design Expert: The fixed KIMSAC component Resource Manager has knowledge about available media handlers, and about device characteristics. It should be noted though, that as we have a hierarchical structure of sessions, we do not necessarily fall back on a central resource description. The description of current technological characteristics is actually adapted by the superior session.

Comments

A critical issue in an open service environment is how to handle the switching between concurrently accessed independent services. The RM does not explicitly cover this. It should be possible to model it in RM terms, by mapping the hierarchical structure of KIMSAC sessions to a corresponding hierarchy of RM instances. But then the interdependencies/conflicts/etc between different sessions are not adequately modeled. Alternatively, a hierarchy of RM Knowledge Servers could be created, one for each session, but then again the interdependencies are not modeled.

The RM Design and Realization layers are not actually used in the KIMSAC applications. The reason for this is that the KIMSAC applications are the result of providing a balance between on the one hand the need for dynamic flexibility and adaptation at the front end, and on the other hand the desire to carefully design multimedia assets for envisioned interaction tasks. Some flexibility is admitted in the asset descriptions, which provides a decision space for dynamic decisions concerning multimedia presentations, and alternative assets can be provided for an interaction task, each tagged with descriptors declaring the conditions under which it can be used (e.g. the difference between expert and novice users, or the difference between the first time a certain interaction task is performed in a session, and subsequent times this task is to be done).

The KIMSAC system implementation

The KIMSAC presentation system is based on a generic Java-implemented platform [Espinoza-98], with a communication layer that permits communication with applications residing on other hosts on a network. The platform admits new content handlers to be easily added, to support new types of multimedia content. E.g. commercial AVI viewers and HTML viewers have been wrapped as content handlers. Content handlers execute asynchronously, communicating via message passing. To enable dynamic tailoring of the rendering of assets and of the behavior of assets, an interpreted scripting language is provided. The KIMSAC presentation system architecture is implemented by adding a few Java objects to support specific needs, but mainly in terms of embedding a Lisp execution subsystem on the platform. The intelligent components of the presentation system are implemented as objects within this Lisp-space, which means that they have access to a complete Lisp evaluator, something that is of extreme utility when implementing the reasoning processes required for adaptive intelligent behavior.

The service agents (and many other supporting components) are implemented in different technologies (C, C++, Java, Prolog). This heterogeneity does not cause any problems, as communication between the components (including the Presentation System) is realized in terms of representation-independent standardized KQML messages [KQML].

Further work

The KIMSAC presentation system is a concrete example of a generic presentation environment. In the KIMSAC applications, a large part of the dialogues were supported by pre-designed assets. This had the effect that the components that design assets dynamically have only been developed in a rudimentary form, to support experimentation with dynamic generation. Further work is required to explore the ways in which parts of assets or entire assets can be generated from intentional descriptions.

The goal of the asset description notation is to be independent of the actual rendering functionality (the content handlers) available in the presentation system. This implies that asset descriptions are actually independent of the presentation system used. The generic character of the asset notation should be verified by porting the higher level components to another set of ToolKit components. Some work has been done on relating the asset notation to standards like XML [Charlton-99], something that opens up to the use of an XML rendering platform as a presentation framework.

Summary

The KIMSAC presentation system is designed to support multimedia interaction with services in an open service environment. This necessitated the introduction of new concepts for management of user-system interaction; the hierarchical session concept. This concept and the way it has been realized in KIMSAC, also enables the concept of virtual presentation devices, whereby the presentation of a service-session can utilize shared functionality of an enclosing framework (e.g. Help&Guidance and navigation support). New services can easily be made available to the user in the form of new service-sessions. Uniformity in look-and-feel is achieved by adapting multimedia assets to the policies controlled by the user-session, and by reuse of media-handlers and asset templates.

The presentation system can handle pre-designed multimedia assets as well as assets generated on-the-fly. The separation of dialogues from the core service, a key feature for intelligent presentation systems in open service environments, follows naturally from the fact that core services are provided via software agents.

Acknowledgements

This paper is based on work performed in the KIMSAC (Kiosk-based Interactive Multimedia Service Access for Citizens) project (ACTS 030). Partners in the KIMSAC project consortium are Broadcom Éireann Research Ltd (IE), Centro Studi E Laboratori Telecomicazioni Spa (IT), Trinity College University of Dublin (IE), Digital Equipment Ireland Ltd (IE), Social Welfare Services (IE), Cap Gemini Telecom France (FR), Teltec Ireland (IE), Swedish Institute of Computer Science (SE), Imperial College of Science Technology and Medicine (UK), and Foras

Áiscanna Saothair (IE). Special thanks to the participating design and development personnel of Broadcom, Trinity College, SICS, and Imperial College, who formed the team that produced the technical solutions described here.

References

[Bordegoni-97] Bordegoni, M., Faconti, G., Maybury, M.T., Rist, T., Rugieri, S., Trahanias, P., Wilson, M.: A standard reference model for intelligent multimedia presentation systems. In: Computer Standards & Interfaces 18:6/7 (December 1997) North-Holland, pp. 477-496.

[Burbeck] Burbeck, S.: Applications Programming in Smalltalk-80: How to use Model-View-Controller (MVC). http://st-www.cs.uiuc.edu/users/smarch/st-docs/mvc.html.

[Charlton-97a] Charlton, P., Chen, Y., Mamdani, E., Pitt, J., Espinoza, F. Olsson, O., Waern, A., Somers, F.: Open agent architecture supporting multimedia services on public information kiosks, in Proceedings of Practical Applications of Intelligent Agents and Multi-Agent Systems, London (April 1997)

[Charlton-97b] Charlton, P., Chen, Y., Mamdani, E., Pitt, J., Espinoza, F. Olsson, O., Waern, A., Somers, F.: Using an asset model for integration of agents and multimedia to provide an open service architecture, in Proceedings of ECMAST'97, Milan (May 21-23, 1997)

[Charlton-99] Charlton, P. Fehin, P., McGuigan, R.: XXXX. (submitted)

[Coutaz-94] Coutaz, J.: Software Architecture Modeling For User Interfaces. In: J. J. Marciniak, (ed)., Encyclopedia of Software Engineering, pp. 38-49, Wiley, Chichester, (1994).

[Dance-87] Dance, J.R., Granor, T.E., Hill, R.D., Hudson, S.E., Meads, J., Myers, B.A., Schulert, A.: The run-time structure of uims-supported applications, Computer Graphics 21:22 (1987) 97-101.

[Espinoza–98] Espinoza, F.: sicsDAIS – Managing user interaction with multiple agents. Lic. Thesis 98-007, Department of Computer and System Sciences, Stockholm University (October 1998)

[Gruber-91] Gruber, T.R.: The role of common ontology in achieving shareable, reusable knowledge bases. In: Proceedings of the Second International Conference on Principles of Knowledge Representation and Reasoning (1991) pp 601-602.

[Hartson-89] Hartson, H.R., Hix, D.: Human-computer interface development: Concepts and systems for its management. ACM Computing Surveys, 21:1 (1989) 5-92.

[Hefley-93] Hefley, W.E., Murray, D.: Intelligent user interfaces. In: Gray, W.D., Hefley, W.E., Murray, D. (eds): Proceedings of the 1993 International Workshop on Intelligent User Interfaces. ACM Press 1993.

[Hovy-96] Hovy, E.H., Arens, Y.: Virtual Devices: An approach to standardizing multimedia system components. In Faconti, G.P. & Rist, T. (eds): Towards a standard reference model for intelligent multimedia systems, Proceedings of ECAI96 workshop, (1996).

[Krasner-88] Krasner, G.E., Pope, S.T.: A cookbook for using the model view controller user interface paradigm in Smalltalk-80. Journal of Object-Orientated Programming, 1:3 (August/September 1988) 26-49

[KQML] KQML Advisory Group: An overview of KQML – A Knowledge Query and Manipulation Language. http://retriever.cs.umbc.edu:80/kqml/.

[Myers] Myers, B.: User Interface Software Tools. http://www.cs.cmu.edu/~bam/toolnames.html

[Myers-93] Myers, B.J.: Why are Human-Computer Interfaces Difficult to Design and Implement? CMU-CS-93-183, Computer Science Department, Carnegie-Mellon University (July 1993)

[Olsson-forthcoming] Olsson, O.: The port/event model of reusable multimedia assets. (Forthcoming)

[Pfaff-85] Pfaff, G.E., ten Hagen, P.J.W. (eds): User Interface Management Systems, Springer Verlag (1985).

[Reynolds-97] Reynolds, C.: A Critical Examination of Separable User Interface Management Systems: Constructs for Individualization. SIGCHI 29:3, (July 1997), http://www.acm.org/sigchi/bulletin/1997.3/reynolds.html.

[Szekely-88] Szekely, P.: Separating the user interface from the functionality of the application program. PhD Thesis, Carnegie-Mellon University (1988).

[The UIMS Developers Workshop-92] The UIMS Developers Workshop, A Metamodel for the run-time architecture of an interactive system, SIGCHI Bulletin 24:1 (January 1992) 32-37.

MEMO: The Specification of a Hybrid System for Interactive Broadcast and Internet Access Using DAB and GSM

James Alty[1], Adam Bridgen[1], Iain Duncumb[1], Johan Ebenhard[2], Per Ruottinen[3]

[1]Loughborough University, Computer Science Department, Loughborough, LE11 3TU, UK
{J.L.Alty, A.L.Bridgen, I.P.Duncumb}@lboro.ac.uk
[2]Ericsson Mobile Data Design AB, S:t Sigfridgatan 89, S-412 66 Gothenberg, Sweden
Johan@erv.ericsson.se
[3]Teracom Svensk Rundradio AB, PO Box 17666, S-118 92 Stockholm, Sweden
pru@teracom.se

Abstract. The MEMO (Multimedia Environment for Mobiles) system has been developed in an ACTS project (AC064) and is built upon Digital Audio Broadcasting (DAB) and GSM networks. It is a hybrid network offering both interactive broadcast services and personal services with a much higher downlink bandwidth than GSM alone. A number of interesting problems have been solved resulting in an object-oriented service model for service providers and an extension of the socket API paradigm to facilitate access to broadcast services by mobile terminals. In addition, a cellular DAB network is proposed with mobility management based on Mobile IP, and TCP extensions to optimise the transport over the combined DAB downlink and GSM uplink. The MEMO specifications are open and are managed by the MEMO Forum, launched in March 1999.

1 Introduction

Digital Audio Broadcasting (DAB) was developed by a collaborative project known as Eureka 147. The specification for the system has been standardised [1] and provides broadcasters with the ability to deliver high quality, flexible audio services to listeners in a way that maximises the use of the available spectrum. DAB uses digital audio compression techniques developed by MPEG in combination with a high reliability 'digital pipe' to deliver this audio. However, this digital pipe may also be used for other types of data service to support the radio broadcasts, to provide a richer experience for the listener, and even to provide unrelated multimedia information services.

The MEMO project (Multimedia Environment for Mobiles) is a research and development project within the ACTS programme of the European Commission. It has developed and demonstrated an interactive multimedia platform for mobile and portable use based upon DAB. In their original form, DAB systems offered only a one-way, high bandwidth, down-link broadcast facility. The MEMO project extends DAB by providing end user interaction through the provision of an interactive channel using GSM [2]. Thus a MEMO DAB terminal allows users to interact with the DAB system by using the GSM link (for example, requesting more detail about broadcast information). The combination of DAB and GSM therefore offers an asymmetric high bandwidth down-link and low bandwidth interactive channel. Such a combination is ideal for many services, where the user wants to receive large quantities of information (e.g. maps of road systems, details of hotels, complete newspapers), but only wants to send relatively simple return messages (e.g. book this room for me, send me these details). Interestingly, Internet browsing can also be characterised by high down-link / low up-link activity.

Some initial results of the projects were published in [3]. More recently the emphasis of the project has been on the development of systems and mobile terminals for trials, [4]. In the last year, the results of these developments and trials have been drawn together in an overall specification of the MEMO system.

This paper introduces the MEMO specification and focuses on some of the interesting problems that have been solved in order to provide an integrated broadcast and telecommunications system. The following section (2) gives an overview of the MEMO system, providing a definition of terms used in the remainder of the paper. After this, section 3 identifies the technical challenges that needed to be addressed. The solutions to these challenges are presented in section 4. In conclusion, section 5 presents Release 1 of the MEMO specification and describes the process followed. The final section (6) describes future plans.

2 The MEMO System: A Definition of Terms

2.1 Reference model

The MEMO system reference model is shown in the figure below.

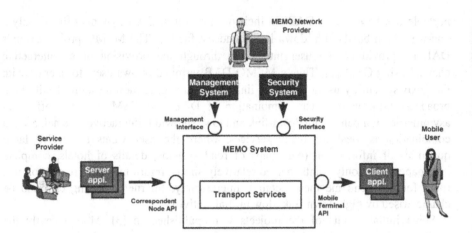

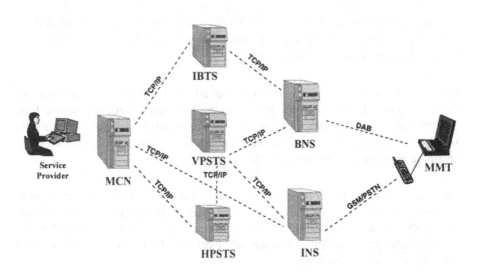

VPSTS. The Visited Personal Service Transport Server is one of the two core system entities for personal service transport. It includes: protocol peers for communication with other system entities, including routing of IP traffic for communication over the two channels (DAB via BNS and GSM via INS); the MEMO Foreign Agent function block with a location information database; and the Mobility Management Agent for exchanging roaming and security information with MMTs. It also encrypts individually addressed messages to be broadcast over DAB.

HPSTS. The Home Personal Service Transport Server is the second core system entity for personal service transport. It includes: protocol peers for communication with other system entities, including TCP split of end-to-end TCP connections and a re-transmission function for the MEMO side of the connection; and the MEMO Home Agent function block with a location information database. It also provides Mobile IP authentication of calling MMTs.

BNS. The Broadcast Network Server contains all DAB specific function blocks on the transmitter side of the system. It receives payload and control information from the VPSTS and IBTS and encapsulates this information in DAB protocols for broadcast to MMTs. It may also provide conditional access to the DAB broadcast by obtaining encryption information over the Security Interface.

INS. The Interactive Network Server is the equivalent to the BNS when it comes to encapsulating the traffic on the GSM return channel. It acts as a bridge from the GSM/PSTN network to the TCP/IP network connecting the VPSTS and MCNs. The INS may also perform PPP authentication of calling MMTs and is more or less a standard Network Access Server.

MMT. The MEMO Mobile Terminal contains all the functionality needed to enable a Mobile Terminal to access a MEMO system by receiving information from BNSs and exchanging information with INSs. The MMT also offers the Mobile Terminal API to the mobile user. It includes: protocol peers necessary for end-to-end communication and signalling to other system entities, including signalling of roaming information (mobility management); GSM and DAB network interfaces and functions to merge the two communication channels in order to present an integrated transport service at the Mobile Terminal API; and security functions such as decryption, de-scrambling, authentication and key exchange

3 Problems to be Solved

The hybrid nature of the MEMO system involves multiple transport media between the service provider and the mobile user. The MEMO network appears to the users of the network as an efficient digital transport between server and client. However, in the case of the personal service transport, the broadcast element of the network places particular stress on a protocol (TCP) that is not designed for this type of physical layer. In addition locating a mobile user, routing of data, submission of fixed services and setting transport protocol parameters (particularly those of DAB transmission) must all be handled internally if a seamless network interface is to be provided by the MEMO network. The following summarises the more interesting issues that must be addressed.

- For interactive broadcast services, the service provider is only really concerned with the service content, coverage and quality of service and not the underlying structure of the MEMO network and the ensemble/service structure of the DAB transmission. An abstract representation of the MEMO network is required, along with a submission mechanism to enable the service provider to readily interact with the network and control the content, structure and broadcasting parameters of the service
- Client applications at the mobile terminal require a simple means for finding, selecting and accessing services from the DAB transmission stream. This should be achievable without recourse to the uplink or interactive channel. This problem is reduced to one of finding and selecting content from a continuous digital stream. Similar problems are routinely solved in the lower layers of a protocol stack, with a suitable metaphor presented to the calling application. For the MEMO network the selection of content must form part of the metaphor presented to the calling application at the mobile terminal.
- The Memo system must support the mobility of the terminals for personal services. Although mobility management is an integral part of the GSM service it is still necessary for the network to independently keep track of where the mobile terminal is to be able to direct traffic to the right DAB cell.
- To provide personal services, TCP must be used as a transport protocol. The combined GSM/DAB network is asymmetric in nature and involves long round trip delays with high download bandwidth. In this situation fundamental TCP performance problems arise which require a number of extensions to be used.

The solutions to these issues are described in the next section.

4 Solutions Adopted

4.1 Service Modelling and the Service Provider API

The service provider interacts with the MEMO network by means of a service model. The model presents abstractions of the network to the service provider as elements within the model. Thus broadcast areas are not given as a set of BNSs but are abstracted into area addresses. In a similar way, transmission parameters are abstracted to a quality of service (QoS) metric. Both sets of possible values are provided by the network provider.

The service itself is modelled as a tree structure: a Service object is the root of the tree; ServiceComponent objects and ObjectCollection objects are nodes of the tree; and ObjectDescriptor objects are the leaves. Service components and object collections contain a set of object collections and/or objects descriptors. By manipulating the model, the service provider submits content to the network.

This structure is similar but not identical to the structure of a service within an ensemble of a DAB transmission. The Service object, ServiceComponent object and ObjectDescriptor object have realisations within the DAB transmission. The Service object and ServiceComponent object are described by the service and service component elements of the Fast Information Channel (FIC). The ObjectDescriptor is realised as an MOT [6] object within a given service component of the transmission. However, the ObjectCollection object, does not have a direct realisation in the DAB transmission. It is used to group ObjectDescriptor objects and other ObjectCollection objects within the model.

Each node and leaf of the service model has a set of attributes which describe that node or leaf. Attributes are inherited from the root to the leaves. These attributes can be grouped into three distinct types:

- **Constraints**. These constrain the transmission characteristics of the objects and are inherited from the root (i.e. service object) to the leaves. Constraints given at nodes and leaves are refinements on inherited constraints and cannot override these inherited constraints.
- **Directives**. These direct the transmission characteristics of the service objects. The directives must conform to the constraints imposed upon an object. Directives are inherited from the root to the leaves and can be overridden or redefined within the bounds of any inherited or imposed constraint.
- **Description**. A description of the object. This currently takes the form of a label, common to all objects, and on one class an external reference, indicating the data content to transmit

It is important to note that the constraints in themselves do not control the transmission of an object/set of objects/service. It is the directives which control how, where and when an object is to be transmitted. Thus, when an equality constraint is placed at a node in the service model hierarchy, it would be usual to find that a complementary directive would be placed there. An example would be an equality constraint on a geographical address (maybe a city or a single transmitter) placed at the service level. This would indicate that the service may only be transmitted to the given location. However, this is not sufficient to direct the service to be transmitted to this location. Thus a complementary directive is provided at the service level to indicate the geographical area in which to transmit.

An example of a service model is given below.

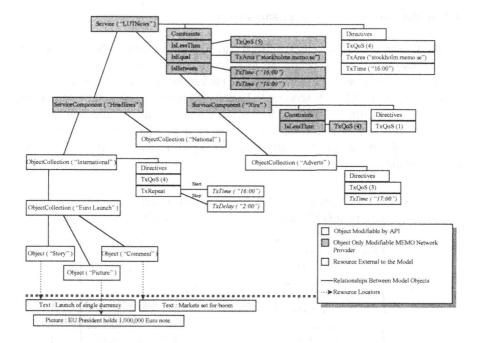

Fig. 3. Instance Diagram : A Simple Service Model

The above diagram represents a simplistic service labelled 'LUTNews'. This service has two components 'Headlines' and 'Xtra'. The labels given on these three elements are the labels that appear in the FIC description of the service.

Considering the constraints on the service object, these indicate that transmission can only take place between 16:00 and 18:00 to the geographical address 'stockholm.memo.se' and the requested QoS of transmission must be less than '5'. These constraints are inherited by all elements of the model, thus it would not be possible to set a QoS of '7' as a transmission directive on any element of the service. The constraints do not initiate transmission, so the directives at the service level are configured in symmetry with the constraints. Unless overridden at a lower level, resources will be transmitted with a QoS of '4', to the geographical address 'stockholm.memo.se' at '16:00'.

Moving to the lower levels of the model, the service component 'Headlines' consists of two object collections labelled 'International' and 'National'. The elements contained within the 'International' collection are to be transmitted at '16:00' for two hours and because the repetition delay and count are not set, the objects are transmitted as often as possible within this 2 hour period.

4.2 Addressing of sockets, and name service

'Sockets' offer a simple, well-established paradigm for accessing transport services. Sockets may be bound or connected to local or remote transport addresses. If we consider DAB addresses (physical or logical) to be analogous to transport addresses, then we can select different services to be received through a socket, by associating the socket with different DAB addresses. This novel form of addressing allows a selection mechanism to be present at the API level. In addition, a unified interface for both personal and interactive broadcast services is presented to the applications at the mobile terminal.

Use of sockets for 'connecting' to broadcast services: The following figure illustrates the concept of DAB addresses with which sockets may be associated.

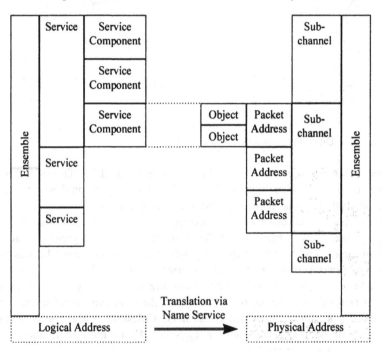

Fig. 4. The Concept of DAB Addresses

The logical addresses, on the left-hand side of the figure above, are intended to be understandable by humans and are based on the labels or identifiers (IDs) of ensembles, services and service components; logically, an ensemble may be considered to be a bundle of services. Note that the same service, as identified by its label and ID, may be present in more than one ensemble. The Name Service API (described in the next section) provides applications with a 'database' that can be browsed or searched, in order to locate services of interest. The Name Service also provides a physical address (in binary form) that is used to connect to the service component of interest. Corresponding logical and physical addresses are shaded in the figure.

Internet applications typically use sockets to communicate using TCP/IP and UDP/IP protocols. The MEMO Personal Services will provide support for Internet applications via GSM and DAB, and so a socket API will be needed at the terminal. Winsock 2 [7] extends the socket paradigm for multiple communication protocols and enables applications to use remote services without knowledge of the transport medium being used. It is proposed to extend the paradigm a little further to allow objects broadcast over DAB to be delivered via appropriately addressed sockets.

Broadcast objects can be identified (addressed) by a combination of parameters such as their sub-channel, packet address and transport ID. We consider such addresses to be analogous to the combination of a remote host and service (e.g. an IP address and a port number). If we 'connect' a socket to such an address, we expect to receive the selected service or component within it.

The following table compares the DAB addressing concept with TCP/IP addressing (for which sockets were originally defined).

Table 1. Comparison of proposed DAB addressing with TCP/IP addressing.

Concept	Description	Use in DAB	Use in TCP/IP
Logical transport address	An address in a form that makes sense to humans	Identifies a service (component)	Identifies an Internet host and service (via the port number)
Name Service	Translates logical addresses to physical addresses	Provides the physical address with which a socket can be associated	Provides the physical address with which a socket can be associated
Physical address (ascii)	A human readable physical address	Ascii representation of the address of an object or set of objects.	Network address and port number for a service at a host
Physical address (binary)	An address to which a socket may be bound or connected	Binary representation of the address of an object or set of objects.	Binary representation of the network address and port number

DAB data transport is connectionless. Datagram sockets are therefore used to receive datagroups and MOT objects. However a datagram socket *can* be connected, the effect being to filter out all datagrams not originating from the connected address. This property gives us the behaviour that we want. The DAB address may or may not refer to a unique object and can therefore be considered as a filter: all objects that match the filter will be made available through the socket.

One further extension to the paradigm is proposed where listening sockets are used to receive multiple objects. This involves binding (rather than connecting) the socket to the DAB address and then listening for connections (i.e. matching objects). An accept() call is then used to return a new socket, connected to a specific matching object.

DAB Name Service. The DAB Name Service enables applications to find broadcast services of interest within the DAB ensemble. One or more DAB Name Services may allow the DAB Namespace to be queried. The DAB namespace has dynamic properties and is driven by the DAB Fast Information Channel (FIC) see [1]. When a DAB ensemble is first received, the FIC is decoded and used to build the DAB Name Service. In addition, the Name Service will be updated if the FIC changes.

At its simplest, the Name Service needs to provide applications with the correct physical address for a known service and service component. In addition the namespace can be searched, based on a number of different attributes, or used to browse the contents of an ensemble (using a special type of query). The DAB Namespace is hierarchical and reflects the structure of DAB.

It is intended that the namespace lookup functions follow the example of the Winsock 2 API [7]. Here, the string representation of an ensemble and service can be used as a context for searches on the namespace using the *WSALookupServiceBegin(), WSALookupServiceNext()* and *WSALookupServiceEnd()* functions. As the MEMO services develop, service providers will register unique service classes, relating to different types of service component and this will provide a powerful high level search facility for the DAB namespace.

4.3 Cellular DAB networks and Mobility Management

The Memo system consists of a combination of two wireless systems: the GSM and the DAB networks. The GSM network is used as a bi-directional communication system with its own cell structure and mobility management. The GSM mobility management is viewed as a service from the Memo system point of view, which means that the mobility in the GSM channel is invisible to the Memo network entities. It is therefore not discussed further in this paper.

The DAB network is a unidirectional network designed for efficient information broadcast. The DAB broadcast system is also designed to provide regional broadcast with service handover using the DAB 'Other Ensembles' capabilities [1]. Both the Memo Interactive Broadcast service and the Memo Personal Service utilise the different DAB broadcast capabilities. The Memo personal service poses higher capacity requirements on the DAB network than the Memo broadcast services so the regional broadcasting is therefore extended with support for smaller broadcast cells.

The Memo network, consisting of both GSM and DAB cells is therefore highly scaleable depending on the need for capacity and coverage. The Memo network has a large benefit in the possibility to use large DAB single frequency networks to provide a high coverage with a limited capacity. The capacity may then be increased in areas with more users by adding further DAB cells, including BNS and VPSTS system entities. If necessary, further INSs and HPSTSs may also be added.

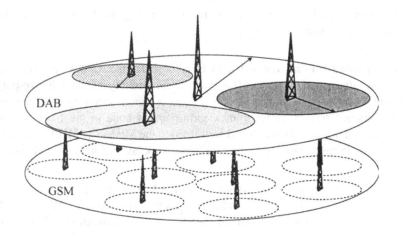

The functional blocks involved in mobility management are described in the following sub-sections.

Memo Mobile IP Home Agent. The MHA is located in the HPSTS system entity and maintains information on which MFA the MMT is currently attached. It is responsible for tunnelling the personal service traffic from a correspondent node to the current MFA. Personal service traffic from a correspondent node in the fixed network is always routed through the MHA and forwarded to the MFA. The MHA is responsible for performing authentication of the MMT's network layer address (IP address).

Memo Mobile IP Foreign Agent. The MFA in the VPSTS system entity decapsulates the personal service traffic that is forwarded from the MHA. The MFA forwards the traffic on to the Memo mobile Terminal through the DAB or GSM network. The Memo Mobile Terminal registers to the MFA through the Memo Mobility management agent using the Mobility management protocol when it wants to utilise the personal service.

Mobility Management Agent. The MMA resides in the VPSTS system entity and is responsible for translating and adapting between the Mobility management protocol and the standard Mobile IP protocol. It is responsible for the control of the personal service routing from the MFA to the MMT. The MMA maintains the lower layer addresses used by the lower layer bearer protocols (the DAB address and the MSISDN number for GSM) to be able to access the MMT. The MMA maintains the mobility management states of the MMT and uses the Mobility management protocol for synchronisation with the MMC

Mobility Management Client. The MMC in the Memo Mobile terminal (MMT) is responsible for the synchronisation of the Mobility management states with the MMA. It performs evaluation of the radio environment and decides/recommends the best available routing path to the MMT from the VPSTS. The MMP also conveys the authentication information and the encryption keys between the MMT and the Memo network.

4.4 TCP extensions

In the Personal Service Network the path between the HPSTS and the MMT (over the DAB radio link) operates with a large transfer rate (DAB ca $1.2*10^6$ bits/s) and with a large round-trip day (DAB ca 0,8 s). Network paths operating in a region where the product of the transfer rate and the round-trip delay is large (10^6 bits or more) are normally referred to as 'long fat pipes' in the Internet community, [8]. Networks containing long fat pipes are referred to as Long Fat Networks (LFNs).

The maximum throughput on a TCP connection is obtained when the 'pipeline' is kept full. The pipeline is full when the unacknowledged data is equal to the product of the transfer rate and the round-trip delay (the 'bandwidth' delay product [8]).

When a long fat pipe is kept full, a number of fundamental TCP performance problems arise, [8], requiring a number of extension options to be used:

- the Window Scale Option (required to fully utilise the DAB bandwidth)
- the SACK Option (required to improve the retransmission scheme and estimation of outstanding data)
- the TCP Time Stamp Option (required to obtain proper retransmission timeouts)

To enable the usage of these extensions, the TCP connection between the MCN and the MMT must be split in two parts. The split is necessary because we have no control over the TCP/IP stack in the MCN. The split is performed in the HPSTS. Thus both TCP connections are terminated in the HPSTS. This approach of splitting a TCP connection in two parts is in the Internet community refereed to as a 'TCP Split Connection'. Examples of a TCP Split Connection are described in the 'I –TCP' [9] and Mowgli [10] papers.

The inclusion of a TCP Split Connection removes the otherwise existing end-to-end semantics between the two TCP peers. The lost end-to-end semantics can introduce unwanted side effects that must be handled. For example, suppose that we have an established TCP connection between the MCN and the HPSTS and the HPSTS and the MMT. The MCN sends one TCP segment to the MMT, which is received by the HPSTS. The MMT's HPSTS receives the segment and acknowledges it towards the MCN. The HPSTS forwards the segment to the MMT over the wireless link. The segment is lost on the wireless link and the MMT never receives the segment, but the MCN believes that it has. To solve this and other problems caused by the lost end-to-end semantics the HPSTS must include functionality that can assure that the MMT/MCN receive the segments already acknowledged by the HPSTS. The following functions are required:

- The Segment Caching Function will cache segments not yet sent to the correspondent peer (i.e. the MCN or the MMT).
- The TCP Option Function will add the relevant TCP options to the segments sent to the MMT and remove the corresponding TCP options from the segments received from the MMT.

5 The MEMO System Specification

5.1 The specification process

The MEMO System Development Model aims to describe how the MEMO System is specified by decomposing it and describing it in pieces small enough to grasp. The pieces are basically gathered in three categories, as depicted below.

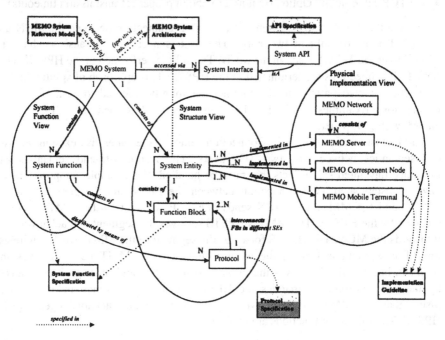

Fig. 6. Entities and relations in the MEMO System Development Model

The System Function View consists of a number of System Functions, each specifying a more or less easily distinguishable part of the total function offered by the MEMO System. Distribution is not visible in this view.

The System Structure View consists of a number of System Entities, each collecting sub-functions (Function Blocks) suitable to implement in a physical entity. In this view, distribution is visible.

The Physical Implementation View consists of the physical entities in a MEMO implementation. The entities are the end-to-end communication peers; MEMO Mobile Terminal and MEMO Correspondent Node and the MEMO Network, made up of MEMO Servers.

The process used for decomposing the MEMO System according to the development model has the following steps:

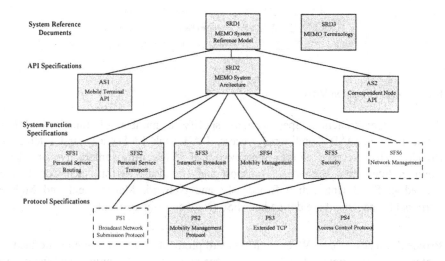

System Reference Documents

SRD1
MEMO System Reference Model

SRD3
MEMO Terminology

API Specifications

SRD2
MEMO System Architecture

AS1
Mobile Terminal API

AS2
Correspondent Node API

System Function Specifications

SFS1
Personal Service Routing

SFS2
Personal Service Transport

SFS3
Interactive Broadcast

SFS4
Mobility Management

SFS5
Security

SFS6
Network Management

Protocol Specifications

PS1
Broadcast Network Submission Protocol

PS2
Mobility Management Protocol

PS3
Extended TCP

PS4
Access Control Protocol

API Specifications. The two API specifications define the Application Programming Interfaces at the Correspondent Node and the Mobile Terminal. These are described in sections 4.1 and 4.2 of this paper.

System Function Specifications. Each of these specifications describes one or more system functions. Each system function is split into function blocks that are allocated to system entities and the protocols linking these function blocks are identified. The following figure shows the MEMO system functions.

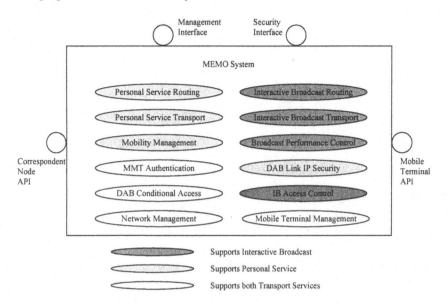

Fig. 8. System Function View

Some System Function Specifications specify a number of functions: MMT Authentication, DAB Conditional Access, DAB Link IP Security and Interactive Broadcast (IB) Access Control are defined in SFS5 (Security); Interactive Broadcast Routing, Interactive Broadcast Transport and Broadcast Performance Control are defined in SFS3 (Interactive Broadcast); and Network Management and Mobile Terminal Management are defined in SFS6 (Network Management).

Protocol Specifications. Where non-standard protocols are used, these are defined in protocol specifications. The protocol's functionality, data units and states are specified along with the service offered to higher protocol layers.

The Broadcast Network Submission Protocol is used to send service content and control data to the BNS, and the Access Control Protocol is used by the BNS over the security interface to obtain conditional access information generated outside the MEMO system. The Mobility Management Protocol and Extended TCP have been discussed in sections 4.3 and 4.4 of this paper.

6 Future plans

Three core MEMO partners (Bosch, Ericsson, Teracom) are preparing an open group - the MEMO Forum - of interested organisations which want to support the MEMO platform. An Interim MEMO Forum will start in January 1999 and is open for all current MEMO partners. The aim of this interim MEMO Forum is to prepare the MEMO Forum, which is planned to be launched in March 1999. At this date a first set of MEMO Specifications will be published for comments from outside. The MEMO Forum will be responsible for the continuation of the MEMO Specification.

References

1 ETS 300 401, Radio broadcasting systems; Digital Audio Broadcasting (DAB) to mobile, portable and fixed receivers, ETSI, Second Edition (1997-05)
2 GSM 01.02 or ETR 99, Digital cellular telecommunication system (Phase 2+), General description of a GSM Public Land Mobile Network (PLMN)
3 Rebhan, R. et al.: Multimedia Goes Mobile in Broadcast Networks. IEEE Multimedia Vol. 4, No. 2, April-June 1997. IEEE Computer Society, Los Alamitos (1997)
4 Klingenberg, W., Neutel, A.: MEMO - A Hybrid DAB/GSM Communication System for Mobile Interactive Multimedia Services. In: Proceedings of ECMAST '98, Berlin 1998. Lecture Notes In Computer Science Vol. 1425. Springer-Verlag, Berlin Heidelberg New York (1998)
5 RFC 2002, IP Mobility Support, IETF, October 1996
6 Draft EN 301 234: Digital Audio Broadcasting (DAB); Multimedia Object Transfer (MOT) protocol, ETSI, V1.2.1 (1998-09)
7 Windows Sockets 2 Application Programming Interface, Winsock Group, Revision 2.2.0, 10 May 1996
8 INTERNET DRAFT, TCP Extensions for High Performance, V. Jacobson, R. Braden, D. Borman, IETF, February 1997
9 I-TCP, Indirect TCP for Mobile Hosts, A. Bakre and B. R. Badrinath
10 Communications Interactive 97, Communications Services for Mobile Office in Wireless WAN Environments, T. Alanko, H. H. Kari, M. Kojo, H. Laamanen, M. Liljeberg, K. Raatikainen and M. Tienari Global

A Mobile Middleware Component Providing Voice over IP Services to Mobile Users

Michael Wallbaum[1], Dominique Carrega[2],
Michael Krautgärtner[3] and Hendrik Decker[3]

[1] Aachen University of Technology,
Department of Computer Science IV, 52056 Aachen, Germany
wallbaum@informatik.rwth-aachen.de
[2] Tesci SA, Tour Aurore, 18 Place des Reflets,
92975 Paris La Defénse Cedex, France
dominique.carrega@tecsi.com
[3] Siemens AG, ZT SE 2, 81730 Munich, Germany
hendrik.decker@mchp.siemens.de

Abstract. The ACTS project *MOVE* currently designs and develops a middleware architecture called Voice-Enabled Mobile Application Support Environment (VE-MASE). The VE-MASE enhances the middleware architecture, which was developed in the ACTS project OnThe-Move, by providing support for interactive real-time multimedia applications and integrated voice and data services. In preparation for future 3rd generation mobile networks, the aim is to enable a completely new class of interactive multimedia services targeted at, but not limited to, mobile devices that are equipped with the VE-MASE. This paper discusses the VE-MASE component called Audio Gateway, which is responsible for providing Internet Telephony services to mobile users.

1 Introduction

In the near future, wherever they are, people will want to use multimedia information services, whether global or local, on both fixed and mobile terminals, with comparable availability of services and quality of communication. The upcoming Universal Mobile Telecommunication System (UMTS) [SdS+] will lead to a convergence of the wireless network infrastructure and will provide mobile users with universal access to the entire communications space. Up to 27 million users of UMTS mobile multimedia services by the year 2005 are forecast by a European market analysis [Swai97].

Today's usage of wide area mobile networks is mainly limited to digital voice connections, fax services and short message services. Although undoubtedly useful, these services do not provide adequate support for multimedia applications because they do not well synchronise the different media, especially voice and data. In particular, no common interface between service providers and the different mobile and fixed network providers exists to support standard voice-enabled applications. Mobile applications based on the Internet Protocol (IP) include voice-based services only in a very simplified manner – by downloading small files containing speech data.

In contrast, IP-based speech services on fixed networks such as Internet Telephony are rapidly evolving and will be a part of the future telecommunication world. Also, multimedia electronic mail, hypermedia information browsers and video conferencing systems are on their way to everyday use. Nowadays, there exists already a large gap between services available on fixed networks and those available to mobile users.

This gap is addressed by the *MOVE* [Move] project. The main project objectives are:

– To design a middleware architecture - called Voice-Enabled Mobile Application Support Environment (VE-MASE) - that supports strong integration of voice and data over UMTS networks for interactive mobile multimedia services and applications.
– To evaluate emerging mobile multimedia protocols integrating voice and data communication and architectural approaches well suited for interactive wireless multimedia communication.
– To offer an Voice/Data Application Programming Interface (V/D-API) to content and service providers for rapid and flexible deployment and operation of voice/data services, supporting on-line user contextual assistance.
– To specify and prototype a demonstration service that demonstrates the benefits of the V/D-API.
– To define a demonstration on advanced Personal Digital Assistants (PDAs) or notebooks to demonstrate the V/D-API and VE-MASE architecture, and to show the value of the approach for service providers.

By achieving these objectives, *MOVE* will accelerate the use of voice-enabled mobile multimedia information services and assist the development of new applications and network-embedded mobility support.

This paper introduces the VE-MASE component which provides mobile users with the ability for real-time audio conferencing, namely the Audio Gateway. Section 2 introduces the *MOVE* project's approach and describes the architecture and design of the VE-MASE and its key components. Section 3 describes the design and functionality of the Audio Gateway. Specifically, its architecture and interworking with other VE-MASE components is introduced and issues related to signalling are discussed. An outlook on how the Audio Gateway will be integrated and deployed in a demonstrator testbed will be given in Section 4.

2 The VE-MASE Architecture

The proposed VE-MASE architecture enhances the Mobile Application Support Environment (MASE), that was developed in the course of the OnTheMove project [OTM]. The MASE provides for seamless integration of different bearers, carriers and terminal types with a focus on "static" multimedia services such as the delivery of textual information and images. It was assumed that the

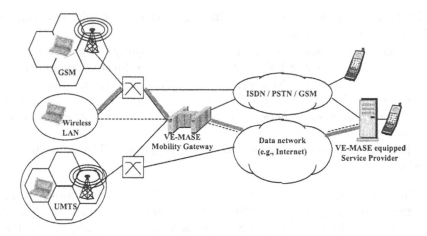

Fig. 1. Overview Of The *MOVE* Network Architecture.

mobile user only generates and sends a limited amount of data. The VE-MASE refines the existing MASE components and adds new components to create a true multimedia infrastructure enabling bi-directional, real-time services. Figure 1 illustrates the physical distribution of the VE-MASE.

The VE-MASE functionality is accessed through the Voice/Date Application Programming Interface (V/D API). Applications making use of the V/D-API may run partly on Gateway Servers located in the fixed network, partly on Information Servers located either within the mobile network or outside, and partly, on the mobile devices themselves.

Typically, application parts running on the Information or Gateway Server are service provider application parts relieving the mobile devices from complex operations. The VE-MASE will adapt to the specific transport capabilities of the underlying networks and supply a set of mobility and voice related management functions as depicted in Figure 2:

– The **Audio Gateway** on the Mobility Gateway provides for real-time audio conferencing between peers in a wireless access network and peers located in a fixed network environment.
– The **Collaboration Manager** on the Mobility Gateway enables the members of a conference to perform collaborative web browsing.
– The **Call Manager** is part of the distributed VE-MASE architecture and is responsible for the set-up and the termination of a voice/data conference between a mobile client and another client with voice/data capability. The call set-up is based on an existing IP connection; either a call is placed from the client terminal or call set-up information is delivered to the proxy gateway where the connection is set up to a Voice over IP based terminal, e.g., a call-centre. Depending on real-time changes of QoS parameters, the voice/data conference is possibly terminated or only the audio session is terminated.

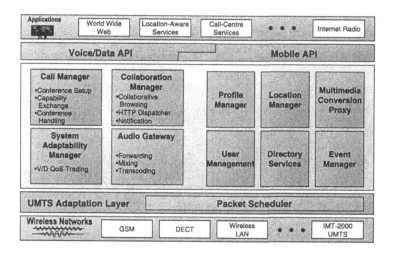

Fig. 2. The VE-MASE Architecture.

- The **Scheduler** ensures that real-time streams (e.g. audio) are not delayed by non real-time data (e.g. data created by collaborative web browsing). Incoming packets are classified according to their service class. Quality of Service (QoS) parameters are measured for each stream and signalled to the System Adaptability Manager.

- The *MOVE* extension of the **System Adaptability Manager** (SAM) collects events and measurements from the Audio Gateway, the Scheduler, and in principle also from the Collaboration Manager and the HTTP proxy. The quality of service (QoS) parameters are analysed in real-time for real-time audio and non real-time data and the result (e.g., QoS class cannot be guaranteed) is delivered to the Call Manager. The function of the SAM extension is to perform QoS trading for the complete transmission medium (e.g., voice and data), i.e. by co-ordinating per-stream QoS trading.

- The **Profile Manager** will give the service provider access to user-specific context information (e.g., to a history of HTML downloads preceding a particular information access).

The following sections will discuss the Audio Gateway and how it interworks with the other VE-MASE components.

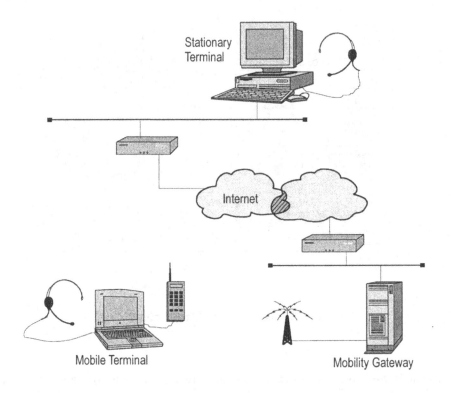

Fig. 3. A Simple Audio Gateway Scenario.

3   Audio Gateway

The Audio Gateway is a central component of the VE-MASE since it provides for real-time audio conferencing between peers in a low bandwidth wireless access network and peers located in the fixed network environment. Connected by one or more wireless access networks like GSM, DECT or Wireless LAN, mobile clients receive a possibly adapted Voice over IP (VoIP) stream from the associated Audio Gateway, which is located at the border between the wireless and the fixed network environment. Likewise the Audio Gateway forwards audio data from the mobile to the stationary client. The bi-directional and real-time properties of the gateway, which primarily differentiates the VE-MASE from its predecessor MASE, provides the basis for a number of new interactive mobile services and applications, such as the call centre demonstration service that will be prototyped and investigated by the *MOVE* project.

The Audio Gateway acts as a mediator between the participants in the fixed and wireless networks. Instead of just routing the media streams from one side of the gateway to the other by network layer protocols, the gateway intercepts the data streams on the application level. There it can manipulate the streams by means of intelligent operations such as transcoding, mixing, congestion control, etc. In principle, this scheme makes the Audio Gateway the endpoint of communication for the transport level entities of both parties engaged in a conference. Figure 3 shows a simple conference scenario with a stationary and a mobile terminal.

To achieve wide acceptance within the user community and in order to allow for simple implementation by reuse of existing code, the Audio Gateway makes use of standard protocols such as the Real-Time Transport Protocol (RTP)[Sch96a]. Thereby it can interact with standard VoIP clients, i.e. no assumptions are made concerning the client software used by the peer in the fixed network, except that it must use RTP to transport frames of encoded speech data over an IP-network.

The Audio Gateway is closely modelled on the Video Gateway that was implemented as part of the OnTheMove project [MSP97] [Kre+98]. Like the Video Gateway it is located at the border to the access network and performs operations such as forwarding and transcoding of media streams on the application level. But the Audio Gateway differs from the Video Gateway in three important aspects:

- In order to support interactive voice services such as those provided by the PSTN the Audio Gateway enables bi-directional, full-duplex transport of audio data.
- The Audio Gateway needs to consider the very strict delay and jitter requirements of interactive audio conferencing.
- The Audio Gateway is tightly integrated in the VE-MASE architecture, thus allowing integrated, adaptive transport and scheduling of voice and data packets.

Nevertheless, the conceptual similarities of the Audio and Video Gateways could ease a potential integration of these components in the future. The following section describes the Audio Gateway's architecture.

3.1 The Gateway Architecture

As the Audio Gateway acts as the endpoint of communication on the transport level for all parties taking part in the conference, its main task is to receive an audio stream from a sender and forward it to a receiver. The transport address of the actual receiver of a stream is conveyed to the gateway at session initiation time.

The Audio Gateway follows a layered architecture as shown in Figure 4. According to the prevailing quality of service (QoS) parameters, a channel selector determines which of the incoming media streams can be delivered to the output. If necessary, the next layer transcodes the data streams of the selected channels into a different format. The mixer merges the different channels to form a single audio stream, which is passed to the application framing entity. It subdivides the bit stream into application frames that allow limiting the amount of loss occurring during transmission. Furthermore, the network adaptation layer is responsible for adapting the bit stream to the form most suitable for transmission over the given network.

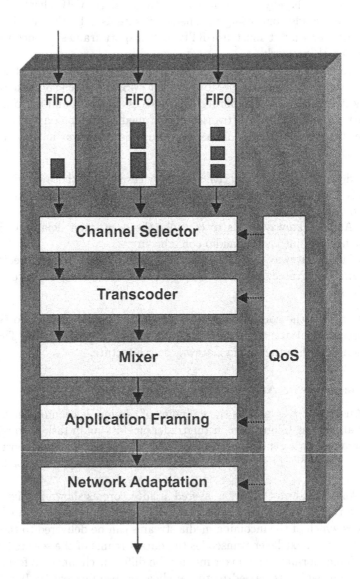

Fig. 4. The Layered Gateway Architecture.

The focus in the discussion of the gateway architecture is on the downlink (the direction to the mobile client), where channel selection and mixing are beneficial. For the uplink it is assumed that a mobile client will only generate one media stream, which will simply be forwarded to the client in the fixed network after potential transcoding.

Media And Channel Selection. The Media and Channel Selector is used in conjunction with the Video Gateway and plays a vital role in scenarios involving changing network conditions, e.g. caused by roaming, and in scenarios where the mobile user cannot influence the sender's output. The Media and Channel Selector obtains the current network configuration from the QoS Module, which comprises a characterisation of the input streams and the QoS characteristics of the currently employed wireless access network. The former includes the number of audio (and possibly video) channels and a description of each incoming bit stream, stating, e.g., bit rate and frames per second. According to the network conditions the selector will choose channel and media from the input stream and, if possible, configure available transcoders.

Transcoding And Codecs. The employed audio codecs dictate most of the QoS requirements. For example, a simple H.323 [ITU1] compliant conferencing system produces a stream of G.711 coded frames with a bit rate of 64 kbit/s. The Audio Gateway can transcode this audio stream, e.g. to G.723.1 [Cox97]. The latter is a newer format which allows to reduce the needed bandwidth to a bit rate below 5.6 kbit/s. A potential drawback of this scheme is the additional delay introduced by transcoding which, in fact, requires decoding and encoding each frame.

Though transcoding should be avoided when it is possible to inform the sender about the desired target encoding, it is a legitimate technique to enable mobile users to receive media streams, which do not require their interaction. Examples of this include lectures and conferences broadcast on the Internet or the reception of radio programmes.

Mixing. So far it was assumed that a conference consists of two participants – one in the fixed network and one in the wireless access network. But it is also conceivable to have more than two parties involved. If the media streams are not distributed by a multicast transport mechanism but by unicast, then the receivers will have one input stream from each sender. To meet the constraints of the narrowband wireless link, an application level relay called a mixer [Sch96a] is included in the Audio Gateway. The mixer resynchronises incoming audio frames to reconstruct the constant spacing between them and combines these reconstructed audio streams into a single stream. This scheme saves valuable bandwidth since the mixer's single output stream contains the audio information of all input streams, e.g. mixing together three G.723.1 streams into one G.723.1 stream reduces the amount of required bandwidth from 15.9 kbits/sec to 5.3

kbits/sec. A drawback of mixers is that receivers cannot control the playback of individual senders, i.e. they cannot mute or adjust the volume of a specific sender's data, which is contained in the mixed stream.

Application Level Framing. Application level framing [CT90] is closely related to the coding scheme. If knowledge about the syntax of the coder output is available, the bit stream may be segmented into frames at the application layer. The newly created segments form the smallest loss unit that can be encountered at the application layer. This is the basis for graceful degradation in case of transmission errors or losses. Because of the semantic knowledge of the bit stream, the error characteristics of the wireless network can be taken into account.

It is not envisaged to change the packetisation of the frames as they arrive from the stationary sender. Increasing the number of frames per packet would lead to more delay and would also increase the probability of packet losses. Decreasing the number of frames per packet is also not desirable, since it causes a greater packetisation overhead, though this effect can be partially avoided when IP/UDP/RTP header compression [CaJa99] is employed.

Network Adaptation. At this level, full knowledge of the semantic structure of the bit-/frame-stream should be available and may be exploited to enhance the loss or error properties: Possible methods include protection of vital information, commonly known as unequal error protection, by retransmission or forward error correction (FEC) codes. A form of forward error correction, that plays a role in VoIP, is the redundant encoding of audio data [Per+97]. Whilst FEC schemes are often overly complex and constantly require additional bandwidth, ARQ (automatic repeat request) schemes add additional delay. The choice of application controlled ARQ schemes nonetheless has its benefits. The application can decide if and when a retransmission is necessary. If only non-vital information is corrupted, the application can decide to use other methods to conceal the error.

By separating the error and loss protection from the network/transport layer and moving it to the application layer, content-based corruption handling becomes possible. This is in strong contrast to current transport protocols where all packets are handled the same way. The application only defines the guidelines and policies, while the application layer handles the rest to relieve the application and to provide a predictable behaviour.

3.2 The Gateway Client

The generic Audio Gateway architecture provides for a variety of possible realisations and configurations. Most importantly, the split between the wireless and the wireline network on the levels of transport and signalling makes it possible to employ different client software on both sites. This is especially useful, since both sites have different requirements:

- On the mobile client site efficient use of bandwidth is of utmost importance. Furthermore, an Audio Gateway client should have minimal storage and CPU resource requirements to meet the restrictions of today's mobile terminals such as notebooks and PDA's.
- On the stationary client site it is meaningful to employ legacy applications. The usage of legacy applications enables communication with hosts, which are not integrated into the VE-MASE architecture, thus raising the users' and providers' acceptance of the VE-MASE middleware and its applications.

Since RTP/RTCP is a widely acknowledged standard for the efficient real-time transport of audio and video data, differences are mainly reflected on the level of signalling. This issue will be discussed in the following section.

3.3 Signalling Issues

A goal of the *MOVE* project is to enable fixed network users to conduct VoIP sessions with mobile VE-MASE users by employing their regular client. The ITU standard H.323 [ITU1] for audio- and video conferencing is widespread among commercial client applications. It uses RTP/RTCP as a transport protocol, but includes a variety of other protocols for conference setup, control and termination. The following discussion of the relation of H.323 to the Audio Gateway is limited to the signalling required for Internet Telephony (H.245, Q.931) and does not include the conferencing protocol T.120 for data exchange.

Deploying an enhanced H.323 gatekeeper [ITU2] as part of the Audio Gateway is one possible way to perform call control. With this scheme standard Internet Telephony software can also be used on the mobile client, while an interception of the audio data at the mobility gateway is still required in order for the Audio Gateway to perform its tasks.

The gatekeeper, which is an optional component in an H.323 system, provides call control services to the H.323 endpoints. This entails address translation, admission control, bandwidth control, and zone management. Other optional functions are call authorisation, bandwidth management, call management, and call control signalling. For the interesting call control signalling mode, the gatekeeper may choose to complete the call signalling with the endpoints and may process the call signalling (Q.931) itself. The gatekeeper uses the ability to route H.323 calls, which can also be used to re-route a call to another endpoint.

Extending the call signalling capabilities beyond the standard is important if transcoding of the audio data by the Audio Gateway is necessary, e.g. due to different voice codecs at the two endpoints. Thus, a H.245 capability exchange has to be conducted. Using the Gatekeeper routed call signalling the H.245 Control Channel can be routed between the endpoints through the Gatekeeper.

The alternative to using end-to-end H.323 signalling is to employ lightweight signalling for the wireless link. This option is currently implemented in the *MOVE* project. In this scenario the mobility gateway acts as the termination point of the H.323 signalling for the H.323 compliant VoIP client in the fixed network. The VoIP client in the wireless network employs a lightweight signalling protocol for call control (e.g., audio conference with minimal control [Sch96b]). This scheme provides for small mobile devices with restricted storage and CPU capacities, since the Audio Gateway Client does not have to implement a full H.323 stack. Furthermore, it makes more efficient use of the access network's limited bandwidth than H.323, since the signalling overhead is kept to a minimum [Sch98].

For integrated conference control, i.e. target localisation, capability exchange, etc., the lightweight SIP protocol [HSSR99] can be deployed. It can signal the request for a combined data and voice session from the stationary or mobile client to the mobility gateway including the IP address of the mobile user to be called.

3.4   Interworking With Other VE-MASE Components

The VE-MASE components located on the Mobility Gateway provide several functions that are needed by the Audio Gateway. The most important component is the UMTS Adaptation Layer developed in OnTheMove which offers a uniform API to transport services provided by different access networks and bearer services. The API allows querying of complex QoS parameters and status information indicating the currently prevailing conditions of the installed access networks. The UAL is needed to allow a simplified transport access and to get QoS parameters needed for the calculation of e.g. filtering functions and transcoders.

Conversely, the Audio Gateway provides other VE-MASE components such as the System Adaptability Manager with vital information. The SAM monitors QoS parameters dynamically and delivers an overall voice/data QoS level to the Call Manager according to the QoS trading policy (usually, to always strive for an optimal QoS and to ensure the smoothness of quality degradation). More precisely, the SAM collects events and measurements from the Audio Gateway, the Scheduler, the Collaboration Manager, the HTTP Proxy and its multimedia conversion component. The QoS parameters are analysed in real-time for real-time audio and non-real-time data. The result (e.g., QoS class cannot be guaranteed) is delivered to the Call Manager, who also receives an adapted QoS class that actually can be guaranteed. In turn, the Call Manager instructs the Audio Gateway and the Collaboration Manager accordingly (e.g., to use a lower or higher bandwidth codec, or to shut down or resume web browsing).

4   Outlook

The Audio Gateway is currently being implemented and will be integrated into the *MOVE* demonstrator, which will serve the validation of the project's approach. The demonstrator scenario involves a mobile customer browsing through a Web site proposing a location-aware service for mobile users, and a "call-centre" agent providing vocal and multimedia assistance to the customer, with the help of a customer support application. The service designed for demonstration purposes consists of a hotel-search service for mobile customers.

With the help of this demonstrator a qualitative evaluation of the Audio Gateway will be possible in order to determine whether speech quality, delay, etc. are acceptable for the users. A quantitative evaluation using different access networks (e.g. DECT, Wireless LAN and GSM) will also be performed in order to determine actual values for the above quality of service parameters.

References

[CaJa99] S. Casner, V. Jacobson. *Compressing IP/UDP/RTP Headers for Low-Speed Serial Links*. IETF Request For Comments 2508 (February 1999).

[Cox97] R.V. Cox. *Three Speech Coders from the ITU Cover a Range of Applications*. IEEE Communications Magazine (November 1997).

[CT90] D. D. Clark, D. L. Tennenhouse. *Architectural considerations for a new generation of protocols*. SIGCOMM Symposium on Communications Architectures and Protocols , (Philadelphia, Pennsylvania), pp. 200–208, IEEE, Sept. 1990. Computer Communications Review, Vol. 20(4) (September 1990).

[HSSR99] M. Handley, H. Schulzrinne, E. Schooler, J. Rosenberg. *SIP: Session Initiation Protocol*. IETF Request For Comments 2543 (March 1999).

[ITU1] ITU-T Rec. H.323. *Packet-based multimedia communication systems*. (February 1998).

[ITU2] ITU-T H-Series Recommendations. *H.323 Version 2 – Packet based multimedia communications systems*. (1998).

[Kre+98] B. Kreller, A. Park, J. Meggers, G. Forsgren, E. Kovacs, M. Rosinus. *UMTS: A Middleware Architecture and mobile API Approach*. IEEE Personal Communications Magazine (April 1998).

[Move] ACTS *MOVE* Homepage. *http://move.rwth-aachen.de.*

[MSP97] J. Meggers, T. Strang, A. Park. *A Video Gateway to Support Video Streaming to Mobile Clients*. ACTS Mobile Communication Summit, Aalborg (October 1997).

[OTM] ACTS OnTheMove Homepage. *http://www.sics.se/onthemove.*

[Per+97] C. Perkins, et al. *RTP Payload for Redundant Audio Data*. IETF Request For Comments 2198 (September 1997).

[SdS+] J. Schwarz da Silva et al. *Evolution Towards UMTS*. ACTS Infowin, http://www.infowin.org/ACTS/IENM/CONCERTATION/MOBILITY/umts0.htm.

[Sch96a] H. Schulzrinne et. al. *RTP: A Transport Protocol for Real-Time Applications*. IETF Request For Comments 1889 (January 1996).

[Sch96b] H. Schulzrinne. *RTP Profile for Audio and Video Conferences with Minimal Control*. IETF Request For Comments 1890 (January 1996).

[Sch98] H. Schulzrinne, J. Rosenberg. *A Comparison of SIP and H.323 for Internet Telephony*. Network and Operating System Support for Digital Audio and Video (NOSSDAV), Cambridge, England (July 1998).

[Swai97] R.S. Swain. *Evolving the UMTS Vision*. Report of the Mobility, Personal and Wireless Communications Domain of the European Communities ACTS Programme (December 1997).

Introducing Mobile Multimedia Broadcasting Services

P. Christ and P. Pogrzeba, Deutsche Telekom Berkom GmbH
and MOTIVATE partners

Deutsche Telekom Berkom GmbH, Germany

Abstract

This paper presents the MOTIVATE project funded by the European Commission and will give first results of laboratory measurements, field trials and simulations of an optimised receiver in the framework of the MOTIVATE (Mobile Television and Innovative Receivers) project funded by the European Commission. These two major streams of innovation are expected from this project:

- Specification for an optimised DVB-T receiver for mobile reception,

- Implementation guidelines for planning of mobile DVB-T networks.

Finally, this paper should give an outlook on first mobile services that will exploit results of the MOTIVATE project. Applications designed for the specific needs of the car environment will be introduced with an outlook IFA'99.

Introduction

In the UK terrestrial television will stay the prevalent distribution media. The initial application of DVB-T is to provide more channels to increase choice. In other countries – such as Germany – there is a much higher penetration of cable and satellite: only 6.8 M of the 36 M German households rely on terrestrial broadcasting. DVB-T could overcome some of the limitations of analogue terrestrial TV but this alone would not guarantee a successful introduction of DVB-T services: added value services are needed to attract more users and increase revenues for broadcasters and network providers.

Mobile reception of video, Internet and multimedia data could be an attractive feature to help the launch of DVB-T in Germany. Only terrestrial broadcasting could bring mobility to the end user. A data rate up to 15 Mbit/s using one 8 MHz UHF channel seems to be possible with the 64QAM mode. Mobility is one of the advantages of the European DVB-T solution against competing standards.

The MOTIVATE project

In May 1998, after two years of feasibility tests of mobile reception by Deutsche Telekom, a consortium of 17 broadcasters, network operators, manufacturers of professional and domestic equipment and research centres launched the MOTIVATE project. It is funded by the European Commission in the ACTS (Advanced Communications Technologies and Services) Programme. MOTIVATE investigates the practical and theoretical performance limits of DVB-T for mobile reception. The optimisation of receiver algorithms for channel estimation, channel correction and time synchronisation will lead to the next generation of DVB-T receivers designed for the mobile environment. MOTIVATE will prepare guidelines for broadcasters and network operators on how to implement DVB-T networks for mobile receivers. The promotion of mobile television will be an essential part of the MOTIVATE project. Major Demonstrations are planned for IFA'99 and IBC'99. MOTIVATE builds on the strong consortium shown at the bottom of this page and has the backing of a number of sponsoring partners (TeleDanmark, RTÉ, DVB promotional module, TU-Munich, BMW and TU-Braunschweig). The collaboration with all broadcasters interested in mobility makes MOTIVATE the spearhead in promotion of mobile DVB-T services.

Partners in MOTIVATE

BBC	UK	Nozema	NL
Bosch	D	RAI	I
CCETT	F	Retevision	E
BERKOM*	D	Rohde&Schwarz	D
EBU	CH	TDF	F
IRT	D	Televes	E
ITIS	F	Teracom	S
Mier	E	Thomcast	F
Nokia	SF	* Coordinator	

Mobile channel

The mobile channel is characterised by multipath propagation and Doppler effect. The multipath propagation causes different strong attenuation in the receiving signal depending on elapse time, amplitude and phasing of the echo paths. The Doppler effect causes a frequency shift depending on transmission frequency f and speed of the receiver v. The Doppler frequency is determined by $f_D = v/c \, f \cos \alpha$ (c speed of light, α angle between receiving path and direction of movement).

OFDM is an effective method to combat the distorsions of the transmitting signal caused by the multipath propagation. The received signal can tolerate echoes by insertion of a guard interval if the longest echoes are within this interval. In the case of Doppler frequency an efficient channel estimation can remarkably improve the performance of the receiver.

Mobile lab and field tests of Deutsche Telekom

Deutsche Telekom Berkom carried out extensive measurement series in the laboratory and in the field to investigate the performance of DVB-T receivers in a mobile environment. For all measurements a 2K-FFT signal was used.

We used for laboratory measurements a failure criteria determined by the subjective assessment of picture quality. A sufficient picture quality is achieved if no errors are visible in a picture sequence of 20 seconds. This method is called the subjective failure point (SFP) method.

The artificial two paths model with Doppler shift was generated in a channel simulator for the laboratory measurements. The critical case of 0 dB echo in all measurements was used.

Figure 1 shows the results of laboratory measurements. The C/N behaviour for different DVB-T modulation schemes (QPSK, 16-QAM, 64-QAM with code rate 1/2 and QSPK and 16-QAM with code rate 2/3) versus speed at an echo delay of 20 µs is shown. QPSK (CR=1/2 and 2/3) and 16-QAM (CR =1/2) show no noticeable increase of C/N values at higher speeds. However, the C/N values of 16-QAM with CR=2/3 and 64-QAM with CR=1/2 are increasing from a speed of 100 km/h.

Three suitable modes could be identified for mobile reception of DVB-T, QPSK, 16-QAM and 64-QAM with code rate 1/2 for each.

Thresholds of the minimum receiver input voltage for the AWGN and the mobile channel can be given as a result of the laboratory measurements. These thresholds are contained in Table 1 for the investigated modes QPSK, 16-QAM and 64-QAM with code rate 1/2 each. Levels higher than these thresholds guarantee error free pictures at the receiver.

Threshold	QPSK	16-QAM	64-QAM
AWGN	16 dBµV	22 dBµV	30 dBµV
Mobile	22 dBµV	29 dBµV	38 dBµV

Table 1: AWGN and Mobile Thresholds

Deutsche Telekom Berkom made field trial measurements to study the performance of a DVB-T receiver in real mobile environments in the area of Cologne. The ERP of the transmitter was 1 kW. The transmission of DVB-T signals performed in the UHF channel 40 (626 MHz). The same modes were investigated as in the laboratory tests.

The main objective of the field tests was to check the identified mobile thresholds in Table 1 in a real mobile environment. If the thresholds are correct then a prediction of the expected Video Error Rate for the route can be given on the basis of a field strength prediction.

The field tests have confirmed the results obtained from the laboratory tests of the DVB-T modes with the simple 0 dB artificial echo model. The thresholds for the examined receiver (corresponding to the constellation order) guarantee a faultless mobile video transmission. The identified mobile thresholds correspond to a coverage probability of 99 %. These thresholds can be seen as a first basis for the planning of services. Further investigations are still needed.

"Mobile MOTIVATE DVB-T Lab Tests"

The "Mobile DVB-T lab tests" were organised in November 1998 to compare the behaviour of state-of-the-art receivers and to study the performance in a mobile environment. Three different channel profiles were defined (easy, regular and difficult profile) to perform these tests with a channel simulator.

Nine receivers have been tested which constitute a large panel of equipment for different purposes (professional, consumer and experimental demodulators). The measurement results made clear that mobile DVB-T reception is possible even with currently available receivers. Six suitable modes (three for the 2k mode and three for the 8k mode) could be identified for mobile reception. All of them have the code rate 1/2. Table 2 contains the reachable speed on average of all receivers and the necessary C/N ratio at a speed of 100 km/h of the 2k and 8k mode for the case of easy profile.

Modulation	Data rate [Mbit/s]	Average speed	C/N [dB] at 100 km/h
2k QPSK ½	4.98	400	9
2k 16QAM ½	9.95	250	15
2k 64QAM ½	14.92	190	21
8k QPSK ½	4.98	100	10*
8k 16QAM ½	9.95	70	17*
8k 64QAM ½	14.92	50	-

Table 2: Measurement results of mobile reception in the 2k mode (based on UHF channel 43), (* C/N at 50 km/h)

The speed limit is approximately reduced by the factor of four in the 8k mode case. One receiver was already optimised slightly towards mobile reception and achieved much better results in difficult reception conditions and 8k mode.

Next Generation Mobile Receiver

From this reference MOTIVATE started to optimise the algorithms for mobile reception.

The mobile reception of DVB-T results in two additional components the system has to cope with. On the one hand the Doppler frequency has to be taken into account, on the other hand the channel transfer function is no longer a static channel, but a fast time variant channel. For stationary or even portable reception it is not necessary to provide a channel estimation which is able to follow fast variations of the channel transfer function.

The optimisation of channel estimation using Wiener filter algorithms and FFT leakage equalisation, the optimisation of antenna diversity in a mobile receiver provided first encouraging results.

Further simulation work is needed in 1999 before a specification for the next generation mobile DVB-T receiver could be given and implementations on a hardware platform could be realised. Prototypes receivers will be tested in MFNs and SFNs, in order to evaluate the real gain of the network for coverage in a mobile environment. Hierarchical modulation offers a real possibility to combine the robustness of QPSK modulation for mobile reception and much higher data rates of 64 QAM modulation for stationary reception.

Network structures

The MOTIVATE project investigates coverage aspects for DVB-T services by using simulation and prediction tools and by measuring the performance of DVB-T in both laboratory tests and field trials. The network topology is being optimised by the selection of the antenna polarisation, the combination of MFNs and SFNs, the use of gap-fillers, microcell/macrocell and the choice of suitable DVB-T modes (modulation, code rate, guard interval).

Partners in MOTIVATE adapted existing planning software for DVB-T urban networks and first mobile DVB-T measurements were performed and compared with prediction models. One main outcome of the project will be the implementation guidelines for mobile DVB-T reception to set up transmitter networks. To ensure that these guidelines are soundly based, MOTIVATE carries out laboratory measurements and field trials.

Hierarchical Modulation

Enhanced mobile and portable reception was experienced by applying the hierarchical transmission scheme as specified for DVB-T. One high priority data stream (HP) and one low priority stream (LP) were transmitted independently using a QPSK modulation within a 16- or 64-QAM modulation. This means, two bits of the encoded HP stream are used to select the quadrant of one complex carrier and 2 or 4 bits of the encoded LP stream are used to form the constellation point within the selected quadrant. Therefore, a subset of broadcast services transmitted in one TV channel is routed to the HP stream and the other part of programmes are routed to the LP stream.

With hierarchical modulation different service coverage areas for the HP and the LP data stream will exist. The main questions investigated in MOTIVATE concerning hierarchical modulation were:

- Does hierarchical modulation allow mobile or portable reception of the HP stream even if there is no reception of the LP stream ?

- What is the loss in performance for the reception of the LP stream using hierarchical modulation compared to the reception performance of a conventional, non-hierarchical 16- or 64-QAM ?

- What is the difference in C/N performance and in the size of the service coverage area between mobile or portable reception of the HP stream compared to the stationary reception of the LP stream ?

- What is the difference in C/N performance and in the size of the service coverage area between mobile reception of the HP stream compared to portable reception of the LP stream ?

The results of the field trials performed in MOTIVATE showed that there is a high robustness for mobile or portable reception of the HP stream. Even if the constellation is totally noisy an excellent reception of the audio and video is possible. The loss in performance for the reception of the LP stream using hierarchical modulation compared to the reception performance of a conventional, non-hierarchical modulation in average is 1.4 db for the receiver tested.

Mobile Services

Mobile reception of DVB-T could bring new features to broadcast networks, making applications and services accessible and usable by anyone, anywhere, anytime, for business or individual use. A narrowband return channel could be integrated using GSM. Here are some examples of mobile services, some of them will be demonstrated by the MOTIVATE project at IFA'99 and IBC'99.

Digital television for cars, buses and trains

Digital television in luxury cars, buses and trains could become the first service for mobile users. It would use some of the existing programmes with additional traffic and navigation information. An audio description service would be needed to make programmes safely accessible to drivers and front-seat passengers.

At IFA'99 the MOTIVATE project will develop and implement Mobile Multimedia Services into the car environment taking into account the specific requirements given by the resolution, position and size of the navigation display already implemented in cars, the peripherals such as the in-car network, antenna and other communication systems such as GSM. MOTIVATE will customise mobile services for the driver and co-pilot which are mainly interested in traffic, business, travel and other information. In addition the storage capacity of the receiver would allow to download and update a significant amount of data on-the-move.

Mobile contribution links

RTÉ and Deutsche Telekom Berkom have tested mobile transmission of DVB-T signals for contribution links. A low power transmitter can be installed in a vehicle to transmit MPEG-2 signals from a vehicle – even while in motion– to a studio. Tests have been made at the UHF and in the L-Band. This service might be used at sports events, such as the Tour de France or the London Marathon, for interviews with busy politicians, or for the reporters in the field.

Mobile Internet Broadcast

Today, solutions for Internet Broadcast have been developed for stationary reception, mainly using satellite and cable based services. Internet Broadcast is based on an Integrated Receiver Decoder (IRD) which could combine broadcast and telephony. The return channel and interactivity is limited to the bandwidth of the telephony network. Mobile DVB-T together with GSM would allow users to receive Internet in cars, buses, on 'watchmen', laptops, on-the-move. GSM as a return channel for DVB-T was standardised by the DVB project.

IFA'99

At IFA'99 Deutsche Telekom Berkom will set up the full demonstration chain to present mobile DVB-T programmes and services.
The sponsoring partners BMW and TU-Munich will handle all aspects related to the integration of the mobile receiver into the car environment.

Special requirements from car manufacturers are
- an easy to use enter button,

- the size of the display and with it the size of types and information.

- the integration of the mobile DVB-T receiver into the communication network already available including peripherals such as antennas, position of receiver.

- the PC with DVB-T card will be installed in the back of the car.

First applications will contain traffic, business and travel information to meet the requirements of a busy politician or businessman on the way from the airport to the city centre. The content will be broadcasted within two multiplexes available for IFA. The applications designed for the MOTIVATE demonstration will allow a maximum data rate of 2Mbps.
Further mobile data services will be shown at IFA'99. The MOTIVATE demonstration should promote DVB-T as a mobile system.

CONCLUSIONS

MOTIVATE could have an impact on political and business decisions on a national and European level. The successful implementation of DVB-T for stationary reception in the UK and Sweden will help to accelerate political decisions in other European countries; the successful verification and demonstration of mobile DVB-T could open up new possibilities for digital terrestrial broadcasting, offering value-added services that could make terrestrial broadcasting an attractive proposition even in countries where there is substantial penetration of cable and satellite.

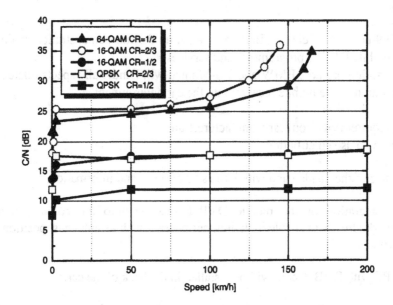

Figure 1: C/N of different DVB-T modes at different speeds (UHF channel 43)

Author Index

Lecture Notes in Computer Science

For information about Vols. 1–1526
please contact your bookseller or Springer-Verlag

Vol. 1563: Ch. Meinel, S. Tison (Eds.), STACS 99. Proceedings, 1999. XIV, 582 pages. 1999.

Vol. 1565: P. P. Chen, J. Akoka, H. Kangassalo, B. Thalheim (Eds.), Conceptual Modeling. XXIV, 303 pages. 1999.

Vol. 1567: P. Antsaklis, W. Kohn, M. Lemmon, A. Nerode, S. Sastry (Eds.), Hybrid Systems V. X, 445 pages. 1999.

Vol. 1568: G. Bertrand, M. Couprie, L. Perroton (Eds.), Discrete Geometry for Computer Imagery. Proceedings, 1999. XI, 459 pages. 1999.

Vol. 1569: F.W. Vaandrager, J.H. van Schuppen (Eds.), Hybrid Systems: Computation and Control. Proceedings, 1999. X, 271 pages. 1999.

Vol. 1570: F. Puppe (Ed.), XPS-99: Knowledge-Based Systems. VIII, 227 pages. 1999. (Subseries LNAI).

Vol. 1571: P. Noriega, C. Sierra (Eds.), Agent Mediated Electronic Commerce. Proceedings, 1998. IX, 207 pages. 1999. (Subseries LNAI).

Vol. 1572: P. Fischer, H.U. Simon (Eds.), Computational Learning Theory. Proceedings, 1999. X, 301 pages. 1999. (Subseries LNAI).

Vol. 1574: N. Zhong, L. Zhou (Eds.), Methodologies for Knowledge Discovery and Data Mining. Proceedings, 1999. XV, 533 pages. 1999. (Subseries LNAI).

Vol. 1575: S. Jähnichen (Ed.), Compiler Construction. Proceedings, 1999. X, 301 pages. 1999.

Vol. 1576: S.D. Swierstra (Ed.), Programming Languages and Systems. Proceedings, 1999. X, 307 pages. 1999.

Vol. 1577: J.-P. Finance (Ed.), Fundamental Approaches to Software Engineering. Proceedings, 1999. X, 245 pages. 1999.

Vol. 1578: W. Thomas (Ed.), Foundations of Software Science and Computation Structures. Proceedings, 1999. X, 323 pages. 1999.

Vol. 1579: W.R. Cleaveland (Ed.), Tools and Algorithms for the Construction and Analysis of Systems. Proceedings, 1999. XI, 445 pages. 1999.

Vol. 1580: A. Včkovski, K.E. Brassel, H.-J. Schek (Eds.), Interoperating Geographic Information Systems. Proceedings, 1999. XI, 329 pages. 1999.

Vol. 1581: J.-Y. Girard (Ed.), Typed Lambda Calculi and Applications. Proceedings, 1999. VIII, 397 pages. 1999.

Vol. 1582: A. Lecomte, F. Lamarche, G. Perrier (Eds.), Logical Aspects of Computational Linguistics. Proceedings, 1997. XI, 251 pages. 1999. (Subseries LNAI).

Vol. 1584: G. Gottlob, E. Grandjean, K. Seyr (Eds.), Computer Science Logic. Proceedings, 1998. X, 431 pages. 1999.

Vol. 1585: B. McKay, X. Yao, C.S. Newton, J.-H. Kim, T. Furuhashi (Eds.), Simulated Evolution and Learning. Proceedings, 1998. XIII, 472 pages. 1999. (Subseries LNAI).

Vol. 1586: J. Rolim et al. (Eds.), Parallel and Distributed Processing. Proceedings, 1999. XVII, 1443 pages. 1999.

Vol. 1587: J. Pieprzyk, R. Safavi-Naini, J. Seberry (Eds.), Information Security and Privacy. Proceedings, 1999. XI, 327 pages. 1999.

Vol. 1590: P. Atzeni, A. Mendelzon, G. Mecca (Eds.), The World Wide Web and Databases. Proceedings, 1998. VIII, 213 pages. 1999.

Vol. 1592: J. Stern (Ed.), Advances in Cryptology – EUROCRYPT '99. Proceedings, 1999. XII, 475 pages. 1999.

Vol. 1593: P. Sloot, M. Bubak, A. Hoekstra, B. Hertzberger (Eds.), High-Performance Computing and Networking. Proceedings, 1999. XXIII, 1318 pages. 1999.

Vol. 1594: P. Ciancarini, A.L. Wolf (Eds.), Coordination Languages and Models. Proceedings, 1999. IX, 420 pages. 1999.

Vol. 1596: R. Poli, H.-M. Voigt, S. Cagnoni, D. Corne, G.D. Smith, T.C. Fogarty (Eds.), Evolutionary Image Analysis, Signal Processing and Telecommunications. Proceedings, 1999. X, 225 pages. 1999.

Vol. 1597: H. Zuidweg, M. Campolargo, J. Delgado, A. Mullery (Eds.), Intelligence in Services and Networks. Proceedings, 1999. XII, 552 pages. 1999.

Vol. 1598: R. Poli, P. Nordin, W.B. Langdon, T.C. Fogarty (Eds.), Genetic Programming. Proceedings, 1999. X, 283 pages. 1999.

Vol. 1599: T. Ishida (Ed.), Multiagent Platforms. Proceedings, 1998. VIII, 187 pages. 1999. (Subseries LNAI).

Vol. 1601: J.-P. Katoen (Ed.), Formal Methods for Real-Time and Probabilistic Systems. Proceedings, 1999. X, 355 pages. 1999.

Vol. 1602: A. Sivasubramaniam, M. Lauria (Eds.), Network-Based Parallel Computing. Proceedings, 1999. VIII, 225 pages. 1999.

Vol. 1605: J. Billington, M. Diaz, G. Rozenberg (Eds.), Application of Petri Nets to Communication Networks. IX, 303 pages. 1999.

Vol. 1606: J. Mira, J.V. Sánchez-Andrés (Eds.), Foundations and Tools for Neural Modeling. Proceedings, Vol. I, 1999. XXIII, 865 pages. 1999.

Vol. 1607: J. Mira, J.V. Sánchez-Andrés (Eds.), Engineering Applications of Bio-Inspired Artificial Neural Networks. Proceedings, Vol. II, 1999. XXIII, 907 pages. 1999.

Vol. 1609: Z. W. Raś, A. Skowron (Eds.), Foundations of Intelligent Systems. Proceedings, 1999. XII, 676 pages. 1999. (Subseries LNAI).

Vol. 1610: G. Cornuéjols, R.E. Burkard, G.J. Woeginger (Eds.), Integer Programming and Combinatorial Optimization. Proceedings, 1999. IX, 453 pages. 1999.

Vol. 1615: C. Polychronopoulos, K. Joe, A. Fukuda, S. Tomita (Eds.), High Performance Computing. Proceedings, 1999. XIV, 408 pages. 1999.

Vol. 1621: D. Fensel, R. Studer (Eds.), Knowledge Acquisition Modeling and Management. Proceedings, 1999. XI, 404 pages. 1999. (Subseries LNAI).

Vol. 1625: B. Reusch (Ed.), Computational Intelligence. Proceedings, 1999. XIV, 710 pages. 1999.

Vol. 1629: H. Leopold, N. García (Eds.), Multimedia Applications, Services and Techniques - ECMAST'99. Proceedings, 1999. XV, 574 pages. 1999.